——

No PEOPLE had sung the praises of peace so ardently, had prayed for the blessings of peace so fervently, as the Jewish people. But apostles of the peace idea as they were and must be, they recognised that there were greater evils even than war. For a nation whose imperial sway was the most beneficent the world had ever seen to be false to its ethical ideals would be a greater calamity for mankind, a greater blow to civilisation, than war itself. Therefore, believers in Messianism though they were, they must recognise that there were times when, in the language of the prophet Joel, God spoke to the nations and bade them, 'Beat your ploughshares into swords, and your pruning hooks into spears; let the weak say, I am strong.'

ISIDORE HARRIS

'Jewish Patriotism', 12 Sept. 1914, West London Synagogue
(*Jewish Chronicle*, 18 Sept. 1914, p. 27)


A RABBI of the older generation said that the war years of '14–'18 were a nightmare for him, when he entered his pulpit week after week, in struggle and torment. As he looks back, he says, he does not know how he stood it.

I heard his words, not altogether understanding them. It is no harder, I said to myself, to stand in a pulpit in wartime than in peacetime. God's laws are eternal and changeless. War or no war, Jews with conviction know where they stand.

And now we are in another war and in an age of frightfulness and destruction when the imagination is beggared and men's spirits are darkened and their hearts ashamed at the spectacle of bestiality and cruelty and murder. God's laws, although they are indeed eternal and changeless, take on another aspect. They do look different in the glow of incendiary bombs and against the growling, angry background of explosion and fire and death.

JACOB PHILIP RUDIN
'God In the Blackout', 2 Oct. 1940, Great Neck, New York

THE LITTMAN LIBRARY OF
JEWISH CIVILIZATION

*Dedicated to the memory of*
LOUIS THOMAS SIDNEY LITTMAN
*who founded the Littman Library for the love of God*
*and as an act of charity in memory of his father*
JOSEPH AARON LITTMAN
יהא זכרם ברוך

*'Get wisdom, get understanding:*
*Forsake her not and she shall preserve thee'*
PROV. 4:5

*The Littman Library of Jewish Civilization is a registered UK charity*
*Registered charity no. 1000784*

# JEWISH PREACHING IN TIMES OF WAR

## 1800–2001

◆

**MARC SAPERSTEIN**

*May 15, 2014*
*For Sue and Jimmy,*
*with gratitude for your*
*wonderful friendship,*
*Marc*

Oxford · Portland, Oregon
**The Littman Library of Jewish Civilization**

*The Littman Library of Jewish Civilization*

*Chief Executive Officer: Ludo Craddock*
*Managing Editor: Connie Webber*

*PO Box 645, Oxford* OX2 OUJ, UK
*www.littman.co.uk*
———
*Published in the United States and Canada by*
*The Littman Library of Jewish Civilization*
*c/o ISBS, 920 NE 58th Avenue, Suite 300*
*Portland, Oregon 97213-3786*

*First published 2008*
*First published in paperback 2012*
*First digital on-demand edition 2012*

*A catalogue record for this book is available from the British Library*

*The Library of Congress catalogued the hardback edition as follows:*

*Jewish preaching in times of war, 1800–2001 / Marc Saperstein*
*p. cm.*
*Includes bibliographical references and index.*
*ISBN 978-1-904113-54-6*
*1. War—Sermons.   2. War—Religious aspects—Judaism.   3. Jewish sermons,*
*English.   4. Jewish preaching—History.   I. Saperstein, Marc.*
*BM538.P3 J49 2007     296.4'7—dc22                    2007021831*
*ISBN 978-1-906764-40-1*

*Publishing co-ordinator: Janet Moth*
*Copy-editing: Gillian Somerscales*
*Index: Marc Saperstein*
*Design: Pete Russell, Faringdon, Oxon.*
*Typeset by Hope Services (Abingdon) Ltd.*
*Printed in Great Britain by Lightning Source UK, Milton Keynes,*
*in the United States by Lightning Source US, La Vergne, Tennessee,*
*and in Australia by Lightning Source Australia, Scoresby, Victoria.*

*This book has been printed digitally and produced in a standard specification*
*in order to ensure its continuing availability.*

FOR TAMAR

*in the hope that this kind of sermon
will no longer be necessary*

# Preface

THE FOURTH OF JULY 1863 was a Saturday, and Sabato Morais, a Sephardi immigrant from Italy serving as religious leader of the Mikveh Israel Congregation in Philadelphia, delivered a sabbath morning sermon as he did each week. This particular sabbath was unusual, for three reasons. In America it was Independence Day, an occasion for celebration of a distinctive national identity. For Jews it was the seventeenth day of Tammuz, a traditional day of mourning and fasting, commemorating the breaching of the walls of Jerusalem, that began a three-week period of solemnity (though when it falls on the sabbath, the actual fast is postponed until the following day). This contrast in moods between the American and the Jewish calendars created a challenge for the preacher, one that could recur periodically, as we shall see. But there was a third component that made the 1863 date unique: it followed immediately upon the conclusion of the Battle of Gettysburg. That Saturday morning, the news of the outcome of the battle was not yet accessible to Morais in Philadelphia—it would be published in special-edition newspapers that afternoon. When he prepared the text of his sermon, and when he delivered the words from the pulpit, it was still unclear to the preacher and his congregants whether the Confederate armies that had penetrated into Pennsylvania would break through the Union lines and threaten Philadelphia, Baltimore, or Washington, DC.

Yet another factor influenced the content of the sermon. The heading over the published text, which appeared in a Jewish weekly six days later, states that it had been delivered on the previous sabbath 'at the request of the Philadelphia Union League'. This patriotic organization was founded in 1862 in strong support of the war effort and the policies of President Lincoln. In the text of the sermon, Morais confirms the heading, saying that he was 'officially asked to recall [the occasion, that is, Independence Day] to your memory', and that 'A stirring oration on political topics may perhaps be anticipated as the most fitting manner of complying with the request.' This suggests that there were Christians in Philadelphia who cared about opinions in the Jewish community and recognized the role of the preacher in influencing their attitudes. It stands to reason that members of Morais's own community would have been aware of this request, and that—as he indicates in his remark about 'a stirring oration'—expectations for the sermon would have been keen.

Yet Morais says that—both because of the date in the Jewish calendar and because of the bleakness of the current military circumstances—he cannot give the upbeat, inspirational, patriotic address that the Union League would have wished, and some in the audience might be expecting. The prevailing mood (which would change so dramatically in just a few hours) is reflected in the preacher's choice of a biblical text, words spoken by King Hezekiah during the Assyrian siege of Jerusalem: 'This is a day of trouble, of rebuke, and derision' (Isa. 37: 3). He continues to present a gloomy picture of contemporary events, alluding in a highly rhetorical passage to the great battle some ninety miles away:

The murky clouds which have long hovered all over the American horizon, gathered at length menacingly nearer to our houses. The thunder was ready to burst upon our heads, and we—in our mad security—neglected to set up the lightning rods, wherewith to blunt its violence. Behold, my hearers! the deplorable consequences and weep. The dust raised by the feet of invasion has tarnished our escutcheon. Havoc and devastation rage in our borders ...

Perhaps the last national public figure in America who spoke this way and was celebrated rather than ridiculed for it was the Reverend Martin Luther King Jr.

Despite the despondency of his biblical text as applied to the contemporary situation, the preacher cannot totally ignore the occasion being commemorated throughout the northern states on that day. And so he says, 'I am not indifferent, my dear friends, to the event, which four score and seven years ago, brought to this new world light and joy.' Three days later, Abraham Lincoln spoke to a small group; according to the transcript printed in the New York *Tribune*, *Herald*, and *Times* on 8 July, he said, 'How long ago is it?—eighty odd years— since on the Fourth of July for the first time in the history of the world a nation by its representatives assembled and declared as a self-evident truth that "all men are created equal."'[1] Morais also could have said 'eighty odd years ago'; instead he used a phrase echoing the King James translation's 'threescore years and ten' (Ps. 90: 10), evoking an unusual event with what was then an unusual phrase. Needless to say, Abraham Lincoln elevated the level of his discourse from 'eighty odd years' to 'four score and seven years' for the dedication of the Gettysburg cemetery some three months later, possibly borrowing from the published text by the Philadelphia Sephardi preacher.[2]

Although this text is not included among the sermons to follow (though two others by the same preacher are), I cite it here in order to illustrate several aspects of the nature and importance of the book's subject matter. First, it exemplifies the often painful dilemmas of the preacher about what to say at critical moments when one's country is at war. Morais clearly had a difficult decision to make

[1] Lincoln, *Collected Works*, vi. 319.
[2] Morais's sermon was published in the *Jewish Messenger* on 10 July, and it is conceivable that Lincoln read it and stored the phrase away for later use. The full text published in the *Jewish Messenger* is available on the website of the University of Pennsylvania Library, <sceti.library.upenn.edu/pages/index.cfm?so_id=1661&PagePosition=40&level=2>.

about the message of his pulpit communication on this day. His choice was signalled with his very first words: a biblical verse that undercut any expectation of a celebratory mood. Morais and the other Jewish preachers had to assess both what they felt impelled to say and what their listeners needed to hear. In times of failure and discouragement and confusion—and many of the sermons in this book reflect such contexts—is it the preacher's role to invoke God's judgement and rebuke the listeners, as part of the broader society, for their shortcomings and sins? Or is it rather to rally the people to what may be a misguided faith in the government's wisdom, the army's proficiency, and God's beneficent favour? Was it appropriate to raise critical questions about the policies of those in power, or was it the preacher's task to inspire the will to sacrifice for the national cause? How should the preacher speak about the enemy? Should he emphasize their otherness, their evil, or the common human bonds they shared with the congregants? Should he articulate the consensus of the listeners, or challenge their complacency? Such questions faced preachers in more normal times as well, but they often took on a terrible urgency in times of war.

Second, the passage extracted from Morais's sermon demonstrates the need for a full knowledge of the specific occasion in order to appreciate the nuances and resonance of the text. In this regard, we might contrast the topical wartime sermon with a different set of sources. The hot topic of historical writing during the past few decades seems to be memory: the ways in which what occurred in the past is constructed, articulated, and transmitted after time has elapsed. A burgeoning scholarly literature written by historians addresses a number of related questions. What are the narratives told in various societies about their origins and formative events, their traumatic trials, their triumphant achievements? How are these narratives incorporated into public observances, secular rituals? How are they displayed in museums? What are the messages communicated by monuments and memorials, whether in a new space that takes on a different significance because it becomes associated with the events of the past or in a space where the event occurred—the *lieu de mémoire*? How do the narratives serve as inspiration for, and how are they transformed by, novelists and poets, artists and musicians? How are claims about the past mobilized and exploited to justify positions taken on contested issues from subsequent eras?

Quite different from the sources for memory are sources more or less contemporary with the events: the newspaper, the diary, the topical sermon. Unlike the historian's monograph, the memoir, or the theological treatise written long after the events, these contemporary sources—often produced in moments when someone pressed by a deadline or other time constraints felt compelled to write or speak, drawing from limited and even erroneous information—take us back to a unique moment in the past with all its ambiguities and uncertainties, when the future was as opaque to everyone as the future is to us today. For Morais the fate of his community, his city, his adopted nation remained precarious as he spoke; had the news of the decisive victory ninety miles away reached him a few hours earlier, he would have spoken quite differently.

Such contemporary sources also situate us in a context in which many of the ideas that have become part of the unchallenged consensus in our collective memory were being fiercely contested. Who questions today the belief that Lincoln was a great leader who represented the highest values of American culture? There were some in Morais's audience who undoubtedly held a very different view. How many challenge the assumption that Germany was the villainous aggressor in the First World War, that Britain should of course join the war effort alongside Russia, that the natural sympathies of Americans had to be with Russia, Britain, and France? Who would argue today against the claim that when Nazi Germany invaded Poland, or when it defeated France and began the bombing of London, America's role was to enter the war against Hitler's forces as soon as it possibly could? Like contemporary newspapers and diaries, clearly dated topical sermons often demonstrate that these pillars in the edifice of the American and British collective memory were once precarious and subject to fierce contention.

Third, this study focuses on major speeches, many of them rather long (though not by the standards of their own time) and crafted in a cultivated rhetorical style—a mode of communication certainly out of favour today. The idea that a large group of people should sit still and attentively listen to one person deliver a speech that might continue uninterrupted for thirty minutes, forty-five minutes, a full hour, raises hackles and suspicions. To many it seems elitist and undemocratic. The more popular model for public communication about controversial issues is the panel discussion, in which a panellist is rarely permitted to put three sentences together without being interrupted and challenged.

Comparing the format of contemporary American presidential debates with the famous Lincoln–Douglas debates of 1858 yields a staggering disparity. In the 2004 debates, each question was allowed a two-minute response, followed by a ninety-second rebuttal, with the possibility of one-minute rejoinders. In their first debate, Douglas's opening statement was almost an hour long (4,215 words), Lincoln's reply was allotted an hour and a half (8,298 words), and Douglas ended with a half-hour response (3,350 words); the same format, with the order reversed, applied in the second debate.

Even special occasions intended to permit a full speech, in which ideas can be developed and arguments supported—the American State of the Union address, the rally speech by a candidate standing for office—rarely allow the speaker to engage the audience in uninterrupted communication. No hostile interjection is tolerated, but such occasions are expected to generate frequent interruptions by applause, ideally with the audience rising to its feet: a pattern that destroys the rhythms of fluent oral communication, breaking up paragraphs into disconnected fragments and placing a premium on effective 'sound bites'. In many circles of the Jewish community, the sermon as reflected in the following texts is clearly out of fashion, replaced by the much more informal *devar torah* intended to initiate a discussion. Perhaps the only arena in which extended, uninterrupted oral presentations are permitted is the university lecture hall; yet even here the hour-long lecture in the traditional format is increasingly being displaced by the Power Point presentation.

The sermon from the nineteenth or early twentieth century differs from most contemporary public speaking not only in its length but also in the rhetorical level of its discourse. With rare exceptions, speakers in public life today tend to avoid elevated language intentionally different from normal conversation: unusual words, artistically crafted phrases, lengthy and complex sentences, rhetorically stylized paragraphs, frequent citation of literary works, emotionally charged (and sometimes melodramatic) delivery. The words 'oratory' and 'oratorical' are not considered compliments today as they once were. The regnant mode of public discourse is the plain style: everyday, down-to-earth language, simple sentences, short paragraphs, delivered in a conversational tone at a volume appropriate for conversation (and therefore dependent on electronic amplification). This is true even for addresses delivered in large convention halls: with the exception of some forms of evangelical Protestant preaching, contemporary speakers rarely raise their voices and hardly ever shout, for the most important audience is understood to be reached by the cold medium of television.

Most of the sermons in this book were written and delivered against the background of a very different aesthetic of discourse, one in which the elevated style of communication, replete with citations of or allusions to the Bible and the great works of English and American literature (especially poetry) and drawing on an array of rhetorical tropes, was expected, appreciated, and consciously cultivated by the significant percentage of the Jewish preachers represented in this book who, like Morais, were born outside the United States and Britain and had to learn English as a second language. The disparity in styles may be exemplified by the contrast between Julia Ward Howe's 'Battle Hymn of the Republic'—'He is trampling out the vintage where the grapes of wrath are stored | He has loosed the fateful lightning of his terrible swift sword'—and Irving Berlin's 'God bless America, land that I love, | Stand beside her and guide her | Through the night with a light from above'; or by the contrast between 'four score and seven years ago' and 'How long ago is it?—eighty odd years'. My hope is to demonstrate that this material, though strange to contemporary sensibilities, retains its power to move and is eminently worth reading and studying.

* * *

Throughout most of my academic career, I never imagined that I would some day publish a book on nineteenth- and twentieth-century material. I trained as a medievalist, and my doctoral dissertation and first book were in the field of Jewish intellectual and cultural history in thirteenth-century southern France. A subsequent focus on the history of Jewish preaching and the sermon as source for Jewish history, literature, and thought led me beyond the Middle Ages into the early modern period. Yet the chronological end point for my *Jewish Preaching 1200–1800* reflects a decision that the nineteenth century opened a new chapter of the subject, one I believed I had neither inclination nor adequate training to investigate. My subsequent books, *'Your Voice Like a Ram's Horn': Themes and Texts in Traditional Jewish Preaching* and *Exile in Amsterdam: Saul Levi Morteira's Sermons to a Congregation of 'New Jews'*, respected the chronological boundary line of their predecessor.

I was first led to violate this boundary by a filing cabinet filled with the type-scripts of sermons delivered by my father, Harold I. Saperstein, a congregational rabbi in Lynbrook, Long Island, from 1933 until his retirement in 1980. In addition to the timeless homilies that could have been delivered a decade earlier or repeated two decades later, many of these sermons were delivered in response to specific historical events, including, in the Jewish context, the Nazi accession to power, the increasingly devastating news about the destruction of European Jewry, the establishment of the State of Israel, and the ordeal of Soviet Jewry; and, in the American context, a lynching in Maryland, the assassinations of President Kennedy and Martin Luther King Jr, the civil rights movement and the Vietnam War. I recognized this to be material of historical significance, documenting how a synagogue rabbi responded, and what he communicated to Jewish congregants, at critical moments in this half-century. My decision to select one sermon per year during this period and to publish them with introductions and full annotation led to the book *Witness from the Pulpit: Topical Sermons, 1933–1980*. The research necessary to explicate the abundant references and allusions in these texts provided a quick education in twentieth-century American Jewish history.

This venture, combined with an invitation by Jacob Neusner to write the article on 'Sermons in Modern Judaism' for the E. J. Brill *Encyclopaedia of Judaism* supplement of 2004, led to wider reading in the sermons of the period. I began to focus on specific questions. *Witness from the Pulpit* contained some very strong sermons on Nazism, the persecution of German Jewry, and the Second World War. Having taught a course on the history of the Holocaust each spring since 1987, I had wondered what rabbis were saying to their congregations in the first years of the war, as the news about European Jewry got worse and worse. This curiosity led to a paper delivered at the 2001 World Congress of Jewish Studies, based on High Holy Day sermons from 1939 to 1943. At one point, I thought of doing a formal sequel to *Jewish Preaching 1200–1800*, including a comprehensive

selection of Jewish sermons from all major centres of Jewish life during the subsequent two centuries. The vast amount of extant material, however, led me to
conclude that I could not hope to cover all countries and all subjects. While the
current book is chronologically and structurally a sequel to the earlier, with a
broad introductory survey followed by a selection of annotated texts, the selection of texts is limited to the United States and the United Kingdom (with one
from Canada), thereby obviating the need for translation. Furthermore, its subject is limited to the presentation of sermon texts revealing what Jewish religious
leaders said to their people when their countries went to war.

Some explanation must be given of the principles according to which sermons were selected for inclusion. First, as just noted, the selection is taken from
sermons delivered in English-speaking lands, primarily the United States and
Britain. Consequently, reference to sermons by German, Austrian, French,
Russian, or Israeli rabbis responding to the wars being fought by their respective
countries is made on occasion for purposes of comparison only. Expanding the
purview to include more countries would have required narrowing the chronological scope of the book. An illuminating collection could be made of Jewish
sermons delivered in various countries in the context of a single war; the
Napoleonic Wars, the Franco-Prussian War, and the First World War seem to
me to be especially promising for this purpose. Obviously, this would require a
significant amount of translation, some of it from languages (Yiddish, Russian)
that I do not command. It would also require detailed investigation of the various national histories of the respective countries and their Jewish populations to
facilitate the kind of annotation I have provided for the selected texts presented
here. I preferred the full sweep of the past two centuries and their most important wars to the deeper probing of a single example.

Not all the sermons were delivered in English. The first two, by British preachers during the Napoleonic Wars, were delivered in Spanish and German, respectively; they were, however, immediately translated and published as pamphlets in
English, so that if the words printed below are not precisely what the congregations heard, they constitute the public record chosen by the preacher to make his
message accessible to a wider audience. The same is true for mid-nineteenth-
century sermons delivered by German-speaking American preachers (Sermon 5,
by Michelbacher; Sermons 8a and 8b, by Einhorn). Sermon 15 by George
Silverstone, dating from the early weeks of the First World War, was delivered
either in English or in Yiddish, but published by the preacher in Hebrew. That is
the only full text that I have translated for the sake of this volume.

A second principle of selection relates to the primary purpose of the book:
to explore the deepening identification of Jews with the governments and the
peoples of the countries in which they were living by examining what Jewish
religious leaders said to their congregations when their own countries went to

war. I have therefore not included sermons by American or British rabbis responding to Israel's wars of 1948, 1956, 1967, 1973, 1982, or 2006. Such sermons could indeed be the basis for another fine book, on preaching by Diaspora rabbis about Zionism and the State of Israel, including its wars. But to include this material here would have diffused attention from the thematic focus.

One divergence from this principle is the inclusion of sermons by one British and two American rabbis on the Franco-Prussian War. The intrinsic interest and rhetorical power of these sermons led me to step beyond my general guideline. Benjamin Artom denounced the failures of British society at a time when British entry into the war was being hotly contested (Sermon 10); Isaac Mayer Wise, a Bohemian Reform rabbi who seems to have avoided any political or military pulpit discussion of the American Civil War, now articulated a strong identification with the values represented by the newly united Germany (Sermon 9); and Sabato Morais, an Italian Sephardi with traditionalist religious and liberal political sentiments, clearly identified with France and expressed the wish that America could intervene militarily to ensure the safety of Paris (Sermon 11). The issues raised by this war for the preachers, especially the challenge to the regnant assumptions about nineteenth-century civilization and progress represented by a conflict between two great European powers, with patriotic Jews in both armies, are extremely relevant to the mood in the summer and autumn of 1914.

Because of my focus on the historical significance of the material, I have included only sermons that are clearly dated, preferably by the preacher himself or by some authoritative external source (for example, a newspaper in which it appears), or at least by an unambiguous internal reference (for example, to an event that had occurred within the previous several days). The significance of a sermon delivered in September 1965 criticizing American policy in Vietnam (Sermon 31a) is quite different from that of a similar sermon delivered five or even two years later. Unfortunately, many collections of sermons published years after their delivery, either by the preachers themselves or by editors, fail to include the date of delivery, and could therefore not be considered for inclusion.

I have used the terms 'Jewish preaching', 'Jewish homiletical art', and 'sermons' broadly. Obviously, a rabbi's address to a congregation during the worship service on the evening or morning of the sabbath, or on the holy days and festivals, fits the category of 'sermon' whether or not traditional Jewish texts are employed for a homiletical purpose. As we shall see, wars provided new occasions for Jewish preaching, including days of national prayer or thanksgiving, on which the liturgy of special prayers would be incidental to a special oration. Nevertheless, such gatherings, attested from the Napoleonic Wars to the First World War, were of a fundamentally religious nature, and the preachers themselves generally characterized their addresses as 'sermons'.

Of more questionable status is the address delivered at the Sunday morning gatherings of Reform congregations in the late nineteenth and early twentieth

centuries. The speakers themselves used a variety of terms to describe their orations on these occasions, including 'addresses' (Stephen S. Wise), 'discourses'
(Joseph Krauskopf), and 'lectures' (J. Leonard Levy). I have included examples
by Krauskopf, Levy, Wise, and Leo Franklin, even though these texts generally
do not begin with a biblical text and are certainly far more deeply rooted in contemporary realities than in traditional sources. Some might be all but indistin-
guishable from the preaching of liberal Christian clergy on the same day. Each
was, however, delivered by a Jewish religious leader to a largely Jewish audience
in the context of a worship service, generally in a synagogue (Wise, whose synagogue building was inadequate to the size of the audience, described his Sunday
morning addresses as delivered 'before the congregation of the Free Synagogue
at Carnegie Hall', and published them in a series called 'Free Synagogue Pulpit').

Ideally, the sermons to be included would have been delivered by well-
known, influential preachers, have significant content of historical importance,
be expressed with obvious rhetorical power, use Jewish sources in an illuminating and original manner, be constructed artistically, and—in short—clearly
demonstrate their value both as historical sources and as models of Jewish
homiletical art. Of course, it is not always possible to find texts that measure up
to all of these standards. In the case of the earlier wars, there is little selection to
be made. The two dating from the Napoleonic Wars (Sermons 1 and 2) appear
to be the only extant British Jewish sermons pertaining to war from the period;
the previously unpublished American sermon from the War of 1812 (Sermon 3)
is the only such text known. There is no known text of an American Jewish sermon devoted to the Indian Wars or the Mexican War; I am aware of no British
Jewish sermon on the 'Indian Mutiny' other than the one I have included
(Sermon 4). It is only from the American Civil War onwards that a selection
becomes possible.

With the abundance of material from the twentieth century, the selection
becomes somewhat subjective. For example, the two sermons included from
Rosh Hashanah 1941 could not be more different. The first, by the Reform rabbi
Maurice N. Eisendrath of Toronto (Sermon 25), is long, sprawling, and disorgan-
ized, but it communicates a prophetic passion in a fierce, detailed denunciation
of contemporary attitudes towards the war; it is of considerable historical importance for assessing the tenor of liberal Canadian Jewry, and much of Canadian
society, at a time when the United States had still not entered the fighting. The
second, by the Conservative rabbi Israel H. Levinthal (Sermon 26), delivered in
Brooklyn the following morning, has far less specific historical significance, yet
it is a gem of Jewish homiletical art, poignantly expounding and applying two
rabbinic statements to dramatize the bleakness of the Nazi domination over
most of the European continent, while also offering at least the possibility of
hope for a better future.

All the texts are extensively annotated. Jewish and non-Jewish texts cited by the preachers are of course identified, but much of the annotation explicates references and allusions to elements of the contemporary context that everyone in the audience would have understood, and so did not need to be made explicit in the oral communication, but that require explanation today. Addressed to a familiar audience at a specific moment, the sermon is by its nature an allusive genre. The preacher can refer to 'the dramatic events of the past few days', to an incident that had become the topic of widespread discussion, or to a name that had briefly become common currency in the newspapers but has since descended into obscurity, confident that the listeners would follow. Except for the sermons following 11 September 2001, readers today will need help in appreciating the meaning, and the power, of such allusions.

At times, allusiveness is used by a preacher for a very different reason: not because events or people are so familiar as to make specificity superfluous, but because the sermon's message is so controversial as to make ambiguity desirable. A parable may be told without explicit unpacking of its meaning; a biblical narrative may be recounted and explored without full application to the present.[3] I suggest that the extended use of a narrative about King David's census by the New York rabbi Samuel Myer Isaacs in the middle of the Civil War (Sermon 7) *may* have been intended as an allusion to President Lincoln's highly controversial policy regarding military conscription, but there is sufficient ambiguity to preserve deniability. In this case, too, annotation is necessary to suggest the meanings that at least some in the audience would have heard.

In order to present the full context at the moment each sermon was delivered, I have made abundant use of contemporary newspapers, with frequent quotation because they are not readily available for readers to consult. I also include in the notes references to similar passages in other Jewish and in Christian sermons delivered contemporaneously, in order to suggest to the reader how representative the specific text was of the pulpit discourse of the time.

Readers may want first to read through the entire text of a sermon without looking at the footnotes, in order to get a sense of what it would be like to hear, albeit without full understanding, and then to consult the notes for a sense of the fuller resonance it would have had to the contemporary listener.

---

[3] I remember hearing a stunning sermon delivered in the winter of 1990 at the Ramot Zion Synagogue in French Hill, Jerusalem, in which the preacher discussed the arguments that might have been made in Pharaoh's court to persuade Pharaoh that he should never meet face to face with Moses—who had Egyptian blood on his hands, wanted to lead a revolutionary liberationist movement, showed little respect for the ancient religious traditions of the host society, did not even have the full support of his own people, and so forth. There was little doubt in the minds of the listeners that the preacher, while claiming to abide by the ground rules of not discussing politics from the pulpit, was weighing in on a burning issue of the day: whether the Israeli government should negotiate with Yasser Arafat.

Where the material becomes abundant, I have tried to represent preachers from various points within the spectrum of the Jewish religious community: Sephardi and Ashkenazi, Orthodox and non-Orthodox. With the exception of Silverstone (see above), I have not included immigrant rabbis who preached in Yiddish and published their sermons in Yiddish or Hebrew. At least in their published material, they seem to show very little interest in matters of war, except in so far as it affects Jews in other lands. Some well-known twentieth-century rabbis in all of the streams of contemporary Judaism are not represented, and more than one reader is likely to miss his or her personal favourite. In some cases the appropriate material may simply not be extant, but there is considerable material from the two world wars that remains untapped. Given the limited space available in an anthology covering two centuries and two countries, choices were inevitable.

I am aware that representation from the American Conservative and the Reconstructionist movements in the second half of the twentieth century is lacking—though there are two sermons by one of the founders of the Jewish Theological Seminary of America (Sabato Morais: Sermons 6 and 11) and two by one of its first and most illustrious graduates (Joseph H. Hertz: Sermons 17 and 28). Efforts to find an appropriate Vietnam-era sermon by a non-Reform rabbi were not successful. Chronological considerations explain the absence of women until the very last section of the book, since the first woman rabbi was ordained in 1972, when the Vietnam War was winding down. I hope that the reader will focus on the extraordinary material that is here, rather than on what is perceived to be missing, which may some day fill additional volumes edited by others inspired to preserve this legacy and investigate it further.

I would emphasize that work to recover the legacy of modern Jewish preaching remains in its infancy. Arguably, the four most accomplished and important American Jewish preachers of the nineteenth century were Isaac Leeser, Isaac Mayer Wise, David Einhorn, and Sabato Morais. Where can one read the sermons of these towering figures? Leeser's sermons were published in ten volumes ending in 1868, and never republished. A small selection of Einhorn's sermons were published in German in 1880 and 1911, but never translated. No volume of sermons by I. M. Wise or Morais has ever been published, despite the fact that both preached regularly over several decades, that many texts of their sermons were published in contemporary newspapers, and that the importance of these figures for the history of Reform and traditionalist Judaism in the United States is beyond dispute. Similarly, while a higher percentage of leading British Jewish preachers of the late nineteenth and early twentieth centuries published collections of their sermons, many important texts remain scattered in issues of Jewish newspapers. Much work is still required simply to make these rich texts accessible in proper, modern editions, so that their riches can be plumbed not only by scholars, but also by new generations of readers analogous to the listeners for whom they were originally intended.

\* \* \*

Most of the research for this book, as well as much of its writing, was undertaken during two one-semester research leaves from The George Washington University. For the autumn of 2002 I was invited to be the Rabbi Hugo Gryn Fellow in Religious Tolerance at the Centre for Jewish–Christian Relations in Cambridge, England, an institution founded by my former student Dr Edward Kessler. During this period, in addition to completing my book *Exile in Amsterdam*, I was able to use the resources of the Cambridge University Library and the British Library for the British material up to the end of the First World War. Especially valuable were the collections of contemporary Christian sermons, the complete collection of the *Jewish Chronicle*, partly on microfilm and partly in the printed issues, and the on-line access to all issues of *The Times* of London, which I used at the Cambridge University Library. (The *Jewish Chronicle* has just recently provided on-line access to back issues of the paper since its establishment in 1841, which will make future research on the history of Jewish preaching in Britain considerably easier.)

The second research leave was as Starr Visiting Fellow at Harvard's Center for Jewish Studies in the spring of 2005. It was at Harvard's Widener and Andover Divinity Libraries that I did the research for the American material up to the end of the First World War. They gave me invaluable access to very many nineteenth-century American Christian sermons, and to newspapers, both general and Jewish, with the technology that enabled a page on a microfilm reader to be scanned on to a CD-ROM that was immediately accessible on a personal computer. The Harvard Library also provided access to the on-line database of the *New York Times*, an extraordinarily helpful resource that I used in particular for annotating material between 1898 and 1945.

Other libraries I have used include the New York Public Library, the British Library's Newspaper Collection at Colindale, the libraries of the Jewish Theological Seminary of America and Yeshiva University, the Klau Library of the Hebrew Union College–Jewish Institute of Religion, the Library of the Center for Jewish Studies at the University of Pennsylvania, the Gelman Library with its I. Edward Kiev Collection at my home institution during this research, The George Washington University, and—in the final stages of preparation— the Library of Leo Baeck College in London.

Archival collections of personal papers have been critical to this project. Especially important have been the American Jewish Archives in Cincinnati, from which I have used material from the papers of James Koppel Gutheim, Maurice N. Eisendrath, Abraham Feinberg, and Ferdinand Isserman, including two previously unpublished sermons printed below. The Israel H. Levinthal Papers at the Joseph and Miriam Ratner Center for the Study of Conservative Judaism Archives of the Jewish Theological Seminary of America provided raw material that supplements the abundant published work of this master preacher. The John Rayner Papers were donated to the library of Leo Baeck College, London, only after the book was all but completed, but within this extraordinarily rich and rigorously organized collection of sermon typescripts from an entire career I have found interesting texts from the 1956 Suez campaign and the 1982 Falklands War to which brief references have been made.

The single most important collection for this work is that comprising the massive ledger and other papers of Sabato Morais at the Library of the University of Pennsylvania. The ledger—running to more than 500 pages—contains Morais's clippings of newspaper transcripts of many of his sermons delivered during a long and distinguished career at the Sephardi Synagogue in Philadelphia; this astonishingly rich resource has been made available on-line by the university library. In addition, the Morais Papers include manuscript texts of many of his sermons. As is evident from the passage cited at the beginning of the Preface, and the sermons below delivered during the Civil War and Franco-Prussian War, Morais was one of the most accomplished Jewish preachers of the nineteenth century. The scholarly work of Arthur Kiron continues to mine this resource in a manner that illuminates many aspects of American Jewish life.

The Archival Collection of the American Jewish History Society has been extremely useful, providing access to important material pertaining to Gershom Mendes Seixas in the papers of the Seixas family and in the Jacques Judah Lyons Collection, including his previously unpublished sermon printed below, as well as other relevant documents in the Myer S. Isaacs Collection.

Many larger synagogues have maintained significant archival collections including the texts of sermons by important rabbis. Most important for this project have been the Leo M. Franklin Archives, Beth-El Congregation, Bloomfield Hills, Michigan; the Joseph Krauskopf Papers, Keneseth Israel Archives, Philadelphia; the archives at Temple Rodef Shalom in Pittsburgh, containing material by J. Leonard Levy and Solomon Freehof; and the Temple Israel of Boston Archives, with material by Roland B. Gittelsohn.

\* \* \*

In the spring of 2004 Alan Dodkowitz, my student at George Washington University, won a George Gamow Fellowship for students aiding faculty research. The task we agreed upon was for him to visit several archival collections of unpublished papers by American rabbis, and to identify significant sermons delivered during times of war. In constant consultation with me, Alan went to libraries in Cincinnati and New York and archives at large synagogues in Detroit and Philadelphia, where he found a significant amount of unpublished material to supplement the published texts I had already reviewed. His photo-offsets of such sermons, and the notes he made about them, provided me with important preliminary material as I began my own intensive study of unpublished American texts.

Jonathan Sarna, this generation's pre-eminent master of American Jewish history, read the entire typescript of this book. His encouragement about the significance of the source material was extremely important to me, and his long list of suggestions—identifying mis-statements of facts, suggesting additional bibliography, recommending expansion of specific points—have helped make this a better final product. Lawrence Hoffman also provided valuable feedback following a reading of the full typescript, as did Todd Endelman and Dane Kennedy, who read early versions of much of the British material.

Rabbinic colleagues Colin Eimer, Barry Freundel, Elias Lieberman, and Alexandra Wright graciously made their unpublished sermons available to me for review and inclusion in the book; I am confident that readers will share my gratitude to them.

My academic colleagues Menachem Blondheim, Kimmy Caplan, David Cassell, Gad Freudenthal, Arthur Kiron, and Richard Menkis have been especially helpful in directing me to material of which I had been unaware, and responding to my questions about it.

The following also have aided my work by responding in person or by correspondence on specific research questions: Charles Berlin, Pierre Birnbaum, Judith Bleich, Naomi W. Cohen, Ed Kessler, John Klier, Olga Litvak, Edward Luft, Ivan Marcus, Michael Meyer, Pamela Nadell, Benjamin Nathans, Yohanan Petrovsky-Stern, Marc Lee Raphael, David Roskies, Marsha Rosenblit, Herman Prinz Salomon, Jeremy Schonfield, Lance Sussman, Arnold Jacob Wolf.

I am greatly indebted to archivists at collections from which I have used sermons for this book. Tireless in their response to my requests and my questions have been Gary Zola and Kevin Profitt of the American Jewish Archives, a uniquely rich repository of relevant sermons. Also helpful have been Martha L. Berg (Rodef Shalom Congregation, Pittsburgh), Meaghan Dwyer (Temple Israel, Boston), Ellen Kastel (Jewish Theological Seminary of America), Julie Koven (American Jewish Historical Society), Holly Teasdle (Beth-El Congregation, Bloomfield Hills, Michigan), Ruth Dancyger (The Temple-Tifereth Israel, Cleveland), and the volunteers at the Keneseth Israel Archives (Philadelphia).

In addition, the following archivists have responded to specific research questions: Pamela Elbe (National Museum of American Jewish Military History), Lois England (Washington Hebrew Congregation archives), Eric Greenberg (Philadelphia Jewish Archives), Leonard Groopman and Paula Simmonds (Shearith Israel 1654 Society Archives), Miriam Rodrigues-Pereira (Spanish and

Portuguese Jews' Congregation), Wendy Turman (Jewish Historical Society of Greater Washington); also Moshe Coriat, Alison Ma'ayan, and Meir Persoff.

I am deeply grateful to David Jacobs, an overflowing wellspring of information about Anglo-Jewish history, for recommending the picture used on the dust-jacket.

Sara Japhet, with whom I shared a research office while we were Visiting Starr Fellows at Harvard's Center for Jewish Studies, was a constant source of companionship and encouragement during long hours in front of computer screens, enriching my insight with probing questions and intriguing suggestions drawn from her enormous knowledge of biblical material.

From my first contact with the Littman Library about possible interest in publishing this book, I have been impressed with the combination of professional efficiency and individual attention demonstrated by its leadership. Connie Webber, Ludo Craddock, and Janet Moth have all been extraordinarily responsive partners in this publishing venture. Gillian Somerscales, my copy-editor, has read my typescript with remarkable attention to minute details as well as larger conceptual matters. She has been responsible for recasting my submission in a form consistent with British usage and Littman practice; her stylistic acumen has saved me from many infelicities of expression and her commitment to completeness has impelled me to hunt down dozens of missing bibliographical data. I am most grateful for her devotion to this material.

The final stages in the preparation of this book for publication, including the compiling of the two comprehensive bibliographies, responding to the substantial number of copy-editor's queries, proof-reading, and compilation of the indices, were carried out in my new position as Principal of the Leo Baeck College in London. I very much appreciate the support for this project I have received from my colleagues at the College and its Board of Governors.

All of the research and writing for this book was done during a new period in my personal life, in which Tamar de Vries Winter, a friend since the spring of 1967, became a life partner. She shared with me both of my research leaves—in Cambridge, England and in Cambridge, Massachusetts—and has enriched my work and as well as my life. This book is lovingly dedicated to her.

# Contents

## PART VI
## WARS OF THE LATER TWENTIETH CENTURY

## PART VII
## RESPONSES TO 9/11

# Note on Editorial Practice

—

*Editorial Intervention*

In order to render these very disparate texts as readily accessible to a modern reader as possible, some minor intervention has been applied to bring punctuation, capitalization, and spelling more closely into harmony with current usage. Where a printed version of a sermon does not convey in its paragraph divisions the natural pauses and changes of direction in the address that would have been apparent to a listening audience, some new paragraph breaks have been introduced. Similarly, errors in texts that exist only in manuscript or typescript form have been silently corrected. The guiding principle has been to make these texts available as the best evidence we have for an event of oral communication between preacher and congregation at a critical moment.

*Biblical Citations*

Citations for quotations from the Bible are given throughout in parentheses, e.g. (Jer. 32: 10), whether they were included in the original text or have been added by the editor. Chapter and verse numbers follow the Masoretic text of the Jewish Bible and may in some cases differ slightly from those in the Christian Bible.

*Footnotes*

Footnotes that appeared in the original texts are reproduced at the foot of the page, cued by the symbol indicators *, †.

Editorial footnotes appear below these original footnotes, cued in the text and at the beginning of each note by arabic numerals in superscript, thus: [1].

*Gendered Language*

In the introductory material and editorial annotation, following references to 'the preacher' I use male pronouns, rather than 'he or she' or 'his or her', because for almost 90 per cent of the period covered by this book women Jewish preachers were extremely rare and anomalous exceptions to the general practice. See my discussion of the new female voice in the past generation in the Introduction (pp. 31–2).

# Note on Transliteration

———

THE transliteration of Hebrew in this book reflects consideration of the type of book it is, in terms of its content, purpose, and readership. The system adopted therefore reflects a broad approach to transcription, rather than the narrower approaches found in the *Encyclopaedia Judaica* or other systems developed for text-based or linguistic studies. The aim has been to reflect the pronunciation prescribed for modern Hebrew, rather than the spelling or Hebrew word structure, and to do so using conventions that are generally familiar to the English-speaking reader.

In accordance with this approach, no attempt is made to indicate the distinctions between *alef* and *ayin*, *tet* and *taf*, *kaf* and *kuf*, *sin* and *samekh*, since these are not relevant to pronunciation; likewise, the *dagesh* is not indicated except where it affects pronunciation. Following the principle of using conventions familiar to the majority of readers, however, transcriptions that are well established have been retained even when they are not fully consistent with the transliteration system adopted. On similar grounds, the *tsadi* is rendered by 'tz' in such familiar words as bar mitzvah, mitzvot, and so on. Likewise, the distinction between *ḥet* and *khaf* has been retained, using *ḥ* for the former and *kh* for the latter; the associated forms are generally familiar to readers, even if the distinction is not actually borne out in pronunciation, and for the same reason the final *heh* is indicated too. As in Hebrew, no capital letters are used, except that an initial capital has been retained in transliterating titles of published works (for example, *Shulḥan arukh*).

Since no distinction is made between *alef* and *ayin*, they are indicated by an apostrophe only in intervocalic positions where a failure to do so could lead an English-speaking reader to pronounce the vowel-cluster as a diphthong—as, for example, in *ha'ir*—or otherwise mispronounce the word.

The *sheva na* is indicated by an *e*—*perikat ol*, *reshut*—except, again, when established convention dictates otherwise.

The *yod* is represented by *i* when it occurs as a vowel (*bereshit*), by *y* when it occurs as a consonant (*yesodot*), and by *yi* when it occurs as both (*yisra'el*).

Names have generally been left in their familiar forms, even when this is inconsistent with the overall system.

# INTRODUCTION

## Modern Jewish Preaching

I T I S U N R E A L I S T I C to attempt in this introduction to survey all of Jewish preaching in the modern period. From the middle of the eighteenth century to the beginning of the twenty-first, there is such a multitude of diverse material that some selectivity is necessary. Limits of space and expertise compel me to exclude in the present context all but passing references to some of the great Jewish preaching traditions of the modern period. These include such celebrated German preachers as Leopold Zunz, Michael Sachs (considered by Stein-schneider to be perhaps the most famous preacher of his time), and Nehemias Nobel (the favourite rabbi of the philosopher Franz Rosenzweig), and Austrians including Isaac Mannheimer, Adolf Jellinek, and Moritz Güdemann. The impressive tradition in France is represented in the late nineteenth and early twentieth centuries by such noted preachers as Zadoc Kahn and Jacques-Henri Dreyfuss, each of whom published many volumes of sermons and eulogies. In eastern Europe, the hasidic movement developed its own tradition of homileti-cal discourse, sermons delivered by the rebbe in Yiddish but usually preserved in Hebrew texts. Non-hasidic preaching in eastern Europe had great exemplars of its own, including the patriotic Polish preachers Izaak Kramsztyk and Marcus Jastrow during the period around the uprising of 1863, Isaac Nissenbaum of Warsaw during the First World War, and Kalonymos Kalman Shapira during the Second. Some of the most celebrated preachers of eastern Europe migrated to Britain or the United States, and delivered their messages in Yiddish under very different circumstances in these countries. Others went to Israel, generating an enthusiastic following in the ultra-Orthodox communities. And throughout this period, rabbis in Middle Eastern countries with Jewish communities— Morocco, Egypt, Yemen, Iraq—preached to their people in Arabic. Though reference will be made to some of these, I will focus here on preaching in Britain and the United States by representatives of the Orthodox, Conservative, and Reform movements (but not by the ultra-Orthodox, whose Yiddish and—in Israel—Hebrew preaching is a very different tradition).

## CHANGES IN THE MODERN SERMON

### *From Exegesis to Exposition*

Perhaps the greatest transformation in the sermon of the modern period is that the exegetical dimension lost its centrality, often becoming peripheral or disappearing entirely. In the Middle Ages and early modern period, the interpretation of biblical verses and rabbinic statements was such an integral component of the sermon that in some cases the boundary line between the genres of sermon and commentary became blurred.[1] Indeed, many medieval sermons contain extensive passages in the 'homily' form, in which the preacher discusses a series of consecutive verses from the biblical lesson or one of the Psalms. One of the favourite rhetorical forms used by preachers and commentators alike was to raise a series of exegetical and conceptual problems in a scriptural passage or rabbinic aggadah, and then to resolve each problem in the course of the ensuing discussion.[2]

In nineteenth-century preaching, whether Sephardi or Ashkenazi, Orthodox or Reform, this exegetical impulse diminished dramatically. It is not that the textually based sermon was completely abandoned (although in some cases, in the late nineteenth and twentieth centuries, it was, as will be noted below). Many nineteenth-century and some twentieth-century sermons begin with a biblical verse, called by the preacher his 'text', though the verse is not necessarily from the Torah lesson of the week. Isaac Mayer Wise, leader of the American Reform movement, counselled, 'Never preach a sermon without a text from the Bible, a text containing the theme which you can elaborate. The text is the best proof in support of your argument. A sermon without a text is an argument without a proof.'[3] The preacher may spend some time discussing the original context of the verse before applying it to the main issue he wants to address (see Sermons 4, 5, and 10 below by David Woolf Marks, Maximilian Michelbacher, and Samuel Myer Isaacs). Occasionally the preacher will use the various parts of the verse, or different interpretations of the verse, as headings that structure the divisions of his sermon (as David Einhorn does in the second example included here, on Amalek). Absent from the mainstream sermons, however, is the preoccupation of medieval and early modern preachers with exegetical problems: identifying the difficulties in the verse, reviewing the attempts by earlier commentators to resolve the problems, then suggesting

---

[1] See M. Saperstein, *Jewish Preaching*, 74 n. 26. Some famous preachers (Moses Alsheikh of Safed (*c*.1580–*c*.1594) is a prime example) published biblical commentaries using material from their sermons reorganized in accordance with the order of biblical verses.

[2] See M. Saperstein, 'The Method of Doubts'.

[3] I. M. Wise in *American Israelite*, 21 Sept. 1899, p. 4, cited in Friedenberg, *'Hear O Israel'*, 71.

the preacher's own solution, proposing various interpretations of the verse, each with its homiletical significance. Where homiletical exegesis had been the centre of gravity for the earlier preachers, now the biblical verse becomes a springboard catapulting the preacher into the central topic of his address.[4]

The detailed exploration and exegesis of rabbinic texts plays even less of a role in the modern sermon. In the classical Sephardi form, a rabbinic dictum was cited at the beginning of the sermon immediately after the 'text' from the scriptural lesson, and the dictum, homiletically interpreted, was eventually incorporated into the sermon.[5] A few of the Sephardi preachers at the Bevis Marks Synagogue in London continued this tradition into the eighteenth and early nineteenth centuries; but by the middle of the latter century this homiletical tradition was largely ignored or forgotten.[6] Where rabbinic statements do appear in the sermons, they are usually cited without rigorous probing or analysis.

This is not to suggest that modern Jewish preaching is devoid of effective homiletical use of aggadic passages. A fine example is the sermon delivered by Abraham Geiger in Frankfurt am Main on 18 October 1863, the fiftieth anniversary of the 'Battle of the Nations' at Leipzig, when a coalition of forces defeated Napoleon's army in a strong blow for German independence.[7] Recalling the 'glorious victory that German strength and German courage won', Geiger insists that the emotions of exaltation aroused at the time are no longer appropriate for the children and grandchildren of those who waged the battle. At this point, he introduces the rabbinic dictum in which God rebuked the ministering angels for singing a song of praise to Him following the deliverance of the Israelites from their Egyptian pursuers: 'My creatures are drowning in the sea, and you are singing a hymn of praise?'[8] The preacher first explains the statement in its original context: ' "That Israel, liberated, should burst into jubilation is understandable, but as for you", said the Lord to His angels, "who look down from the open heavens, should you feel joy at the

---

[4] See on this change the classical study by Altmann, 'The New Style of Preaching', and Blondheim, 'Divine Comedy', 198.

[5] This form may be seen in the 1756 fast-day sermon of Isaac Nieto (Roth, *Magna Bibliotheca Anglo-Judaica*, 323, no. 17), the sermon that Haim Isaac Carigal delivered in Newport on the holiday of Shavuot 1773 (Carigal, 'The Salvation of Israel'), and the fast-day sermon of Moses Cohen d'Azevedo in 1776 (Roth, *Magna Bibliotheca Anglo-Judaica*, 325, no. 26), but not in the Thanksgiving Day sermon of 26 Nov. 1789 by Gershom Mendes Seixas.

[6] David de Sola, delivering a sermon (not listed in Roth) on 24 Mar. 1847 in Bevis Marks on the day of a general fast because of the potato famine, exemplifies the tradition, beginning by citing Isa. 16: 9, followed by BT *Shab.* 55a ('Death is the result of sin'). But the continuation of the sermon had little to do with either of these texts. Abraham P. Mendes of Birmingham, England, began the sermons in his published *Sermons* with a Torah text, but without a rabbinic dictum.

[7] For a contemporary Jewish sermon responding to this victory, see M. Saperstein, '*Your Voice Like a Ram's Horn*', 158–9.

[8] BT *Meg.* 10b, *San.* 39b. On the original context of this dictum, see Heinemann, *Aggadah and its Development*, 175–9.

thought that men rage against men, . . . should you, indeed, exult while corpses are piled high?"' And then he applies the dictum to the present situation:

The nobler spirit of mankind grieves at the sight of men and nations torn by strife and discord; it covers its head in sorrow at the sight of the maimed, of the tears of the families of the fallen, of destruction and of the smoldering habitations where peace and prosperity formerly dwelt. We shed a tear for those who gave their lives for the independence of the nation, and for the fathers and mothers who were robbed of many a precious hope. But at the same time we proclaim: Away with hatred and jealousy! Let us look with human compassion also upon the enemies who fought the battle on those days. Even they, against whom we had to draw the sword of battle, were human beings, imbued with what is noble and divine; let us then shed a tear even for the fallen foe.[9]

It is a moving example of a preacher using the rabbinic literature to challenge the pervasive patriotic mood of the preaching occasion. (For another fine example of the homiletical use of an aggadah, in this case as the structural framework of the sermon, see Israel H. Levinthal's 1941 sermon below.)

### New Occasions

The traditional occasions for a sermon—sabbath, holy days, life-cycle events, dedication of a new synagogue building—remained unchanged in the modern period. But in some environments associated with new movements in Judaism, the context for the major weekly sermon shifted dramatically. In late nineteenth-century America, many large Reform congregations began to hold weekday worship services on Sunday mornings, the only day of the week when all would be free to attend. Since the liturgical component of such gatherings was significantly curtailed in comparison with sabbath worship, the major focus of the gathering was a rather lengthy sermon, lecture, or address delivered by the rabbi.[10] Some of the most celebrated, eloquent, and influential

[9] Weiner, *Abraham Geiger and Liberal Judaism*, 254; original text in Geiger, *Abraham Geigers Nachgelassene Schriften*, i. 400–1. Cf. also the use of this aggadic dictum by Immanuel Jakobovits (Sermon 33 below) and, under considerably more difficult circumstances, by Morris Joseph near the beginning of the Great War ('The War and Our Responsibility', 22), and by the chief rabbi Joseph Hertz on Passover 1941: *Early and Late*, 2. For another stunning application by Geiger, see his sermon 'On the Admission of Jews to Citizenship', 252–3, where he takes the aggadic statement that Moses yearned to enter the Land of Israel so that he could fulfil the additional commandments applicable only in the Land (BT *Sot.* 14a) and applies it to Jews rejoicing in the additional responsibilities of citizenship in Germany!

[10] On the development of the Sunday service with its major address, see Meyer, *Response to Modernity*, 290–2. Kaufmann Kohler introduced a Sunday service in Chicago Sinai Congregation in 1874, while retaining the Saturday service, and this arrangement was continued by his successor, Emil G. Hirsch. When (in 1879) Kohler came to Beth-El Congregation in New York, he succeeded (where Einhorn had failed ten years earlier) in instituting the Sunday service there. See D. E. Hirsch, 'Biography of Rabbi Emil G. Hirsch', 421–2; Olitzky, 'The Sunday-Sabbath

liberal Jewish preachers in the United States, including Joseph Krauskopf in Philadelphia, J. Leonard Levy in Pittsburgh, Leon Harrison in St Louis, Emil G. Hirsch in Chicago, and Stephen S. Wise in New York, drew their largest audiences on Sunday mornings.

By the middle of the twentieth century this practice had all but disappeared, to be replaced by a new focus for American Jewish preaching: the late Friday evening service. Traditionally, the Friday evening service was relatively brief; its timing depended upon the sunset, to be followed by the sabbath evening meal in the home. As the mandated scriptural readings occurred in the morning, sermons were rarely included in the evening service.[11] In the twentieth century, Reform and many Conservative synagogues began to set the Friday evening service at a fixed time, unchanging throughout the year, late enough to follow rather than precede the sabbath evening meal. The idea was that this service would be the central activity for families on Friday nights. Since the liturgy remained fairly brief, there was ample time for a twenty- or twenty-five-minute sermon.[12]

These new contexts affected the substance of the discourse. Most rabbis who gave a major address on Sunday morning or on Friday night also had sabbath services on Saturday morning, when the Torah was read, and when their message was generally connected with the scriptural reading. This liberated the address on Sunday or Friday from the need to be anchored in a fixed scriptural passage, offering the preacher the opportunity to speak on any topic he considered to be of interest and concern to the listeners, including a wide range of political and cultural as well as religious themes. With titles often announced in advance, a controversial topic became a major motivation for attendance at synagogue.

In addition, from the eighteenth century on, we find sermons delivered by Jewish preachers on occasions not of specifically Jewish concern, but rather pertaining to the wider society in which Jews are living. On such occasions both Jews and Christians would be in their respective places of worship listening to the religious messages of their respective leaders; this sense of a shared experience was conducive to a sense of national identity among Jewish communities in their various countries. Through the first third of the nineteenth century, when synagogues in both Britain and the United States had no established tradition of a regular weekly sabbath sermon, the occasional

Movement', 75–88, and 'Sundays at Chicago Sinai Congregation', 356–68; 'Sunday Services for the Hebrews', *New York Times*, 19 May 1879, p. 2.

[11] For unusual evidence of Friday night preaching in certain eighteenth-century European communities, see M. Saperstein, *Jewish Preaching*, 28.

[12] On the late Friday evening service, see the sources listed in Caplan, 'The Life and Sermons of Rabbi Israel Herbert Levinthal', 12 n. 40. In the 1950s and 1960s, the Friday night service attracted 'by far the largest number of worshippers' in South African Orthodox synagogues, according to the chief rabbi; see Rabinowitz, *Light and Salvation*, 11.

sermon on dates established by national or state authorities was one of the most important opportunities for pulpit discourse.

One such occasion was the government-mandated 'day of fast, humiliation, and intercession'. In England, such days were initiated by Parliament and proclaimed by the Crown. One was observed at the approach of the Spanish Armada in 1588 and several during the plague of 1603. During the 1640s the 'fast sermon' delivered before Parliament became a regular event, indeed one of the most important for Puritan preachers.[13] But the day of public fasting and prayer appointed because of a particular threat or catastrophe continued through the eighteenth and nineteenth centuries. We find Jewish preachers delivering sermons on such fast-days proclaimed because of natural events, such as the Lisbon earthquake, a cholera plague, or the potato famine,[14] and, all too commonly, on the outbreak of war, or a defeat of the nation's armies. In Britain, Jewish preachers delivered sermons to their congregants on fast-days proclaimed near the beginning of the Seven Years War, the 'Revolt of the American Colonies', the Napoleonic Wars, the Crimean War, and the 'Indian Mutiny'.[15] (In the exordium for his 1854 sermon following the outbreak of the Crimean War, D. W. Marks reminded the older members of his congregation of no fewer than five such days of humiliation proclaimed by the Crown between 1801 and 1811 in circumstances of military defeat or fear of invasion. The current situation, he noted, was far less dismaying.[16])

[13] See Trevor-Roper, 'The Fast Sermons of the Long Parliament'.

[14] Isaac Nieto preached on Friday, 6 Feb. 1756, a day of general fast proclaimed because of the earthquakes in Portugal and other locations (Roth, *Magna Bibliotheca Anglo-Judaica*, 323, no. 17); the sermon was published both in the original Spanish and in the author's translation into English (copy of English text in Harvard's Houghton Library). David Brandon preached at the Bevis Marks Spanish and Portuguese Jews' Synagogue on Wednesday, 21 Mar. 1832, a day of general fast because of the cholera epidemic: 'the awful visitation of a grievous malady which has recently appeared, and committed serious ravages in this city' (Roth, *Magna Bibliotheca Anglo-Judaica*, 327, no. 40; copy in the British Library); for the context, see Morris, *Cholera 1832*, 129–58. David Aaron de Sola preached at the Bevis Marks Synagogue on Wednesday, 24 Mar. 1847 'on account of the dearth now unhappily prevailing' resulting from the failure of the potato crops. On 17 Oct. 1847, David Woolf Marks emphasized in his sermon the gratitude felt for autumn's unexpectedly rich harvest (*Sermons Preached on Various Occasions*, i, sermon 9).

[15] For Hirschel Levin in the Seven Years War, see M. Saperstein, *Jewish Preaching*, 347–58. On Moses Cohen d'Azevedo's fast-day sermon for 13 Dec. 1776 (I consulted a copy at the Jewish Theological Seminary of America), see Katz, *The Jews in the History of England*, 280. Sermons on the remaining occasions are printed or discussed below.

[16] *Jewish Chronicle*, 12 May 1854, p. 273. This sermon was not included in the second volume of Marks's sermons. The occasions specified were: [13 Feb.] 1801 (a continental war terminated by the 'inglorious peace of Lunéville'; [19 Oct. (Roth, *Magna Bibliotheca Anglo-Judaica*, no. 28)] 1803, when the hopes of peace were shattered; early 1806 (when the 'tide of conquest swept over the whole of continental Europe'); [6 Apr.] 1809 (after the 'disastrous battle of Corunna'); and 1811, when all of Europe was chained to Napoleon, and 'it appeared that England herself . . . must soon yield to the torrent that was gathering around her'.

In America, the tradition of the fast-day sermon, brought over by the Puritans from England, was well established in colonial times; according to Ellis Sandoz, it was proclaimed (or, more precisely, 'recommended') at least sixteen times by the Continental Congress during the Revolutionary War.[17] Our first record of Jewish participation is a sermon preached by Gershom Mendes Seixas at New York's Shearith Israel Synagogue, where he was cantor, on 9 May 1798, a day of fasting and national humiliation proclaimed by President John Adams in the context of an unofficial naval war with France.[18] President Zachary Taylor proclaimed Friday 3 August 1849 a day of national 'fasting, humiliation and prayer'—the first such day since the War of 1812, except for one in 1841 following the death of President Harrison—because of a plague of cholera; having originated in India, the epidemic was currently (in the words of Isaac Leeser, who delivered the sermon at Philadelphia's Mikveh Israel Synagogue) 'spreading its ravages throughout the land'.[19] On a 'national fast day' proclaimed for 4 January 1861, Jewish preachers used the occasion not only to express their hope for the preservation of the Union, but also to stake their positions on the incendiary issue of slavery (see below).

The death of a monarch or member of the royal family was an occasion for shared mourning, articulated through pulpit discourse. One of the most challenging such tasks for the preacher was the death in 1780 of the Austrian empress Maria Theresa, widely known as perhaps the most anti-Jewish monarch of the eighteenth century. Yet at a solemn memorial service in Prague, Rabbi Ezekiel Landau eulogized the empress in flattering terms that appear to express a genuine admiration for qualities appreciated by contemporaries in the larger community.[20] After the death of Kaiser Wilhelm I in 1888 Moritz Levin, the preacher of the Berlin Reform-Gemeinde, delivered a eulogy at the memorial service entitled 'Kaiser Wilhelm: ein Messias unserer Zeit' (Kaiser Wilhelm: a messiah for our time).[21] A few months later, when the new Kaiser Frederick III died, he was eulogized not only by German Jewish preachers but by Sabato Morais in Philadelphia, who called him 'the Prince of

---

[17] See Stout, *The New England Soul*, esp. 27–8; Bosco (ed.), *The Puritan Sermon in America*; Sandoz (ed.), *Political Sermons of the American Founding Era*, i, p. xxi.

[18] See on this Friedenberg, *'Hear O Israel'*, 13–16.

[19] Leeser, 'The Plague'; not surprisingly, Leeser affirms the traditional providential explanation of the plague as a divine chastisement for national sin (p. 197). He noted the end of the plague in a discourse on 27 Nov. 1849 (*Discourses*, viii. 261).

[20] M. Saperstein, *'Your Voice Like a Ram's Horn'*, 445–84.

[21] M. Levin, 'Kaiser Wilhelm: Ein Messias unserer Zeit'. Fifty years later (on 6 Apr. 1934), in a Pesach sermon criticizing the super-patriotism and assimilationist aspirations of German Jewry, the chief rabbi Joseph Hertz exemplified by referring to 'the Rabbi of the Berlin Liberal Synagogue who published a sermon under the title, *Kaiser Wilhelm: ein Messias unserer Zeit*' (J. Hertz, 'A Moral Challenge', 156).

Peace' and said—according to the newspaper report of the sermon—that he 'could never forget the withering rebuke the Crown Prince, the departed, gave anti-Semitism by visiting a synagogue while a court chaplain and professors at royal institutions stirred up the hydra of fanaticism against a loyal people who chose to worship in such a shrine'.[22] A rather bizarre formal expression of grief for a dead head of state was made by Zadoc Kahn, chief rabbi of France, in conducting services of mourning, including a eulogy at the Great Synagogue of Paris, for the Russian tsar Alexander III (d. 1894), despite his anti-Jewish policies. The American rabbi Joseph Krauskopf explained to his congregation that this was a proof of the loyalty of French Jewry: it was 'not because the Chief Rabbi of France, and his Jewish followers, sympathized less with their persecuted brethren, but because they loved France more; Russia was the ally of France, and her friendship for France weighed more in the hearts of the patriotic French Jews than her hatred of her Jews'.[23]

Jewish preachers in Britain eulogized every British monarch, and many of these sermons were published. In some cases, the personal qualities or policies of the deceased are given little emphasis, while a more general ethical message is delivered. For example, at the death of William IV in 1837, although the preacher, D. M. Isaacs, refers to 'many instances of Royal favour experienced by many of our community', he declines to go into detail about them, and soon shifts to from the eulogistic to the homiletical mode: 'Now, at the Bier where Royalty is laid, learn the mutability of all mundane affairs. See him, who yesterday wielded the sceptre of these domains, to-day a tenant of the grave.' The lesson, therefore, is to prepare oneself for death even in the midst of life.[24]

Not surprisingly, special eloquence was inspired by the death of Queen Victoria. Her long reign, earlier commemorated in sermons at her diamond jubilee in 1897, allowed Jewish leaders to review and to celebrate the dramatic improvements in Jewish status over which she had presided. As one preacher put it,

---

[22] *Public Ledger—Philadelphia*, 18 June 1888; clipping in Sabato Morais Ledger, 391. Cf. the eulogy for Frederick by Moses Jacobson of Gnesen, 'Der beste deutsche Mann'.

[23] Krauskopf, 'Condemned Unheard', 3.

[24] D. M. Isaacs, 'Funeral Oration' (Roth, *Magna Bibliotheca Anglo-Judaica*, no. 43), 6, 11–12. That this may have been a commonplace in eulogies for a dead monarch can be seen in the following passage from the sermon delivered by John Donne in the place where the body of King James I was lying in state: 'how poore, how faint, how empty, how frivolous, how Dead things, must you necessarily thinke *Titles*, and *Possessions*, and *Favours*, and all when you see that Hand, which was the *hand of Destinie*, of *Christian Destinie*, of the *Almighty God*, lie dead?' Donne, *Sermons*, 58, and cf. 206. For a fine general survey of contemporary Christian preaching at the death of British national leaders, see Wolffe, 'Responding to National Grief', with brief comments on Jewish preachers at p. 293.

We Jews shall never forget that it was during her reign that we lost the Ghetto bend and learned to stand erect. Sixty-four years ago, the Jew, even in this land of enlightenment, was a barely tolerated alien. He was excluded from the boon of a liberal University education. He was ineligible for State Service. He was debarred from Parliamentary representation. What a marvellous change has taken place in two short generations, thanks largely to the example of good Queen Victoria.[25]

In the United States, we know of at least two Jewish eulogies given at the death of President William Henry Harrison, by Isaac Leeser in Philadelphia and by Jacques Judah Lyons in New York.[26] Probably the most poignant inspiration for preaching in nineteenth-century America, however, was the assassination of Abraham Lincoln. This occurred on Friday night; Leeser, in Philadelphia, learned of the shooting from newspapers the following morning while walking to the synagogue, and the news of Lincoln's death was disclosed during the sabbath morning worship service. Virtually every American rabbi spoke on the following Wednesday, 19 April, a national day of mourning, as Lincoln's body was being taken to its burial place in Illinois.[27] These sermons reveal a sustained effort to articulate the special qualities of Lincoln both as a human being and as a political leader—sometimes using explicitly messianic rhetoric—and later to apply these qualities to the contemporary challenges of the body politic.

Almost a century later, President John F. Kennedy was killed in the middle of the day on Friday, at a time when most rabbis were well along in the process of preparing what they planned to say that evening or the following morning. Suddenly, to preach the planned sermon seemed inconceivable. The challenge was to decide what to say a few hours later, when synagogues throughout the country would be filled to overflowing with Jews who expected and needed to hear some articulation of the meaning of this disaster from the pulpit.[28]

[25] Hyamson (Dayan (rabbinic court judge) of the United Synagogue), 'In Memoriam', 165. See also the eulogy by the chief rabbi, Hermann Adler, 'The Late Queen'.
[26] Leeser, *Discourses*, iv. 30–45 (discourse 3); see Sussman, *Isaac Leeser*, 124; Jacques Judah Lyons Collection, P-16, box 6, folder 341.
[27] Fourteen of these sermons—some in English and some in German, some published immediately as pamphlets, others preserved in different forms—were gathered together with dozens of sermons from the following sabbath and on subsequent anniversaries of Lincoln's birth in a marvellous collection called *Abraham Lincoln: The Tribute of the Synagogue*, edited by Emanuel Hertz. An apparently complete text of the sermon preached by the Brooklyn rabbi Godfrey Taubenhaus on the assassination of President McKinley was given by the *Brooklyn Eagle*, 20 Sept. 1901, p. 14.
[28] For a collection of such eulogies and tributes (including many by military chaplains), see Kellner, *Sunset at Mid-Day*; also Rudin, *Very Truly Yours*, 273–4; Freehof, 'Our Martyred President'; H. Saperstein, 'Martyr for the American Dream'; Rayner, 'John F. Kennedy'; Jakobovits, *Journal of a Rabbi*, 271–5; Brodie, 'Tribute to the Late President'. In an analogous situation in France—after the assassination of the president by an anarchist in 1894—the chief rabbi Zadoc Kahn preached at the memorial service: Marrus, *The Politics of Assimilation*, 145.

Occasionally, sermons were delivered at the death of non-Jewish figures beyond the category of national leadership. A striking example is the tribute by Reform rabbi Abba Hillel Silver to Pope Pius XI on 19 February 1939.[29] Needless to say, the death of a leading rabbi, or of a non-rabbinical Jewish leader, was an occasion for homiletical oratory in observance of a tradition going back centuries.

Other government-mandated occasions for preaching were times for celebration and thanksgiving: military victory, an abundant harvest following a famine, the escape from an epidemic ravaging other areas. The earliest known Jewish sermon delivered in English on the American continent, on 15 August 1763, was occasioned by a day of thanksgiving proclaimed by the civil authorities of New York following the peace treaty that ended the French and Indian War.[30] When the new President George Washington proclaimed a national day of thanksgiving, following the request by both houses of Congress, for Thursday 26 November 1789, Gershom Mendes Seixas was requested by the lay leaders of Shearith Israel to provide an appropriate service of thanksgiving, and the discourse he delivered was printed a few weeks later.[31] Another day of thanksgiving, though in a more sombre mood against the background of the bitter conflict between North and South that would soon erupt into civil war, was designated for Thursday 29 November 1860, and again special discourses were delivered by Jewish preachers, including Isaac Leeser.[32] Until 1863, thanksgiving days in November were ordinarily proclaimed separately by the governors of the individual states; beginning in 1863 a presidential proclamation made this institution a regular national holiday. Services were held and sermons deliv-

[29] Silver, 'Pope Pius XI'. There has been controversy in recent years about the role of this pope with regard to the Jews, but Silver, a strong leader of American Zionism, shows no ambivalence. The deceased was 'not given to adroitness or evasion. He was not a diplomat. He was a man of God.' He denounced 'the false Christianity of the Nazis', 'extreme nationalism', 'anti-Semitism'. He was, in short, one of the 'righteous among the Gentiles'. Of course, the eulogy is a genre not given to a balanced evaluation of strengths and weaknesses of character, but there was no need for Silver to devote his sermon to the late pope at all. Similarly positive attitudes were expressed by Louis I. Newman in 'We Are All Semites Spiritually'. Hermann Gollancz spoke movingly about Archibald Tait as the Archbishop of Canterbury lay on his deathbed in 1882 ('Archbishop Tait'); Hermann Adler eulogized Henry Cardinal Manning in 1892 ('The Death of Cardinal Manning'). Both prelates were praised for their outspoken support of Russian Jews in 1882.

[30] Joseph Jeshurun Pinto at New York's Shearith Israel Congregation; see Friedenberg, 'Hear O Israel', 5–6; H. P. Salomon, 'Joseph Jesurun Pinto'. Three years earlier an order of service, composed by Pinto for the 'Day Appointed by Proclamation for a General Thanksgiving to Almighty God, for the Reducing of Canada to His Majesty's Dominions' (23 Oct. 1760) was printed in New York (Singerman, Judaica Americana, no. 32; H. P. Salomon, 'Joseph Jesurun Pinto', 22, with reproduction on pp. 25–6). No sermon is mentioned in this context, however.

[31] Seixas, 'A Religious Discourse', pp. ix, 12, 13–14. On this sermon see Mahler, 'American Jewry and the Idea of Return to Zion' (Heb.); Friedenberg, 'Hear O Israel', 10–12.

[32] Leeser, 'The Israelites' Thanksgiving'; Gutheim, 'Thanksgiving Day Sermon'.

ered; some of them were reported in the newspapers, others individually published—including that by David Einhorn reproduced below (Sermon 8a).[33]

Additional celebratory preaching occasions included the coronation of a new monarch, the jubilee anniversary of a monarch,[34] the birth of a child in the royal family, and the recovery of a monarch from a serious illness. Moses Jacobson, rabbi of the congregation of Gnesen near Posen, published a collection of his patriotic sermons from the 1890s which included five addresses delivered on 27 January, in 1893, 1894, 1895, 1899, and 1900, as part of the birthday celebrations of Kaiser Wilhelm II, and one on 21 March 1897, the hundredth anniversary of the birth of Kaiser Wilhelm I.[35] This collection also includes two sermons delivered on the occasion of municipal elections, emphasizing the obligation of Jews to participate in the political process.[36]

In the United States, the national holidays became preaching occasions, Christians and Jews alike taking the opportunity offered not only by Thanksgiving but also by Independence Day on 4 July.[37] The anniversary of Lincoln's birthday was marked by sermonic tributes well into the twentieth century. Between the two world wars, Armistice Day on 11 November presented a regular opportunity—either on the day itself or on the sabbath (or Sunday) immediately preceding or following it—for preachers to express attitudes towards war and peace, including increasing disappointment with the results of the Great War and the Paris peace conference.[38]

To a considerable extent, then, the occasions for Jewish preaching were determined by events in the wider environment as well as by the rhythms of the

[33] An interesting sermon by Sabato Morais from 1885 discusses the problems of the Thanksgiving observance: attendance by Jews at services is consistently low; the rabbi must devote 'considerable thought and literary labour' to preparing a sermon that few will hear; efforts by Philadelphia rabbis to organize a 'union service' rotating from synagogue to synagogue were undermined when the lay leaders of the largest congregation refused to allow their synagogue to be closed on Thanksgiving Day. See 'On the Ill Treatment of the Chinese in the Far West', 1–3 (I am grateful to Arthur Kiron for sending me a copy of this manuscript text). A twentieth-century development along similar lines was the 'union service' with Christian congregations.

[34] This practice, exemplified by sermons delivered at the diamond jubilee of Queen Victoria, continued with the jubilee of Queen Elizabeth II in 2002.

[35] Jacobson, *Reden über des Staates Führer, Dinge und Fragen*, 1–50.

[36] Ibid. 95–117 (Nov. 1893 and Oct. 1895). The 'election sermon' in America was a different genre, delivered in the presence of the state governor and legislature after the election of officers: see Stout, *The New England Soul*, 29–30; Bosco (ed.), *The Puritan Sermon in America*, ii–iii.

[37] On 4 July 1864, a Monday, David Einhorn delivered a sermon called 'The Saving Angel in the Midst of Destruction', beginning, 'Wieder feiern wir unter schweren blutigen Kämpfen das Geburtsfest der Republik . . .': K. Kohler (ed.), *David Einhorn Memorial Volume*, 129–39.

[38] For Lincoln's birthday, see the many sermons delivered between 1892 and 1927 dated 12 Feb. in E. Hertz (ed.), *Abraham Lincoln*, beginning p. 191. For Armistice Day addresses, see Franklin, 'The Armistice Anniversary' and 'A War without Armistice'; Enelow, 'Armistice Day'; H. Saperstein, 'Must There Be War?'

Jewish calendar.[39] This was especially true in Britain and the United States in the first half of the nineteenth century, when qualified preachers were scarce and when the institution of a weekly sermon as an integral component of the sabbath service was not yet firmly established. As a result, a substantial percentage of the sermons preserved—and probably of the sermons actually delivered—are occasional addresses, often delivered on weekdays, reacting to the same events (and sometimes in similar ways) as Christian preachers in the vicinity of the synagogues. In the decades after the American Civil War, with the gradual growth of the British and American Jewish populations and the increasing number of qualified immigrant preachers, occasional sermons continued to be delivered, but were more likely to be integrated into the normal pattern of weekly preaching.

There were also occasions of celebration internal to the Jewish community: the installation of a new chief rabbi, the inaugural sermon of a rabbi taking up an important new post, the laying of a cornerstone for a new synagogue building, or the consecration of the synagogue on completion of the building (in Britain, frequently an occasion on which the chief rabbi was invited to preach; in America, one on which a well-known preacher might well be asked to travel some distance to grace the new pulpit). Many such occasions were used to define publicly the principles for which the rabbi or the synagogue stood.[40]

### Different Media for Preservation

A third distinctive feature of the modern Jewish sermon pertains not to the sermon itself but to its influence after it was delivered. The extant texts of premodern sermons are predominantly preachers' collections of their own work, copied by scribes and either safeguarded in libraries (occasionally in private collections) in manuscript form or printed. This format was relatively unusual in the first half of the nineteenth century; it regained popularity in the late nineteenth and twentieth centuries, which produced hundreds of such collec-

---

[39] One traditional preaching occasion that seems to have become more important in the nineteenth century was the Sabbath of Consolation, following the fast-day Tishah Be'av. A significant number of the sermons printed in the *Occident* during the 1840s were delivered on this sabbath.

[40] In the middle of the nineteenth century S. M. Isaacs of New York travelled widely to speak at the dedication of synagogues, as shown by Simon, 'Samuel Myer Isaacs', 65–6. James Koppel Gutheim gave sermons at a cornerstone-laying in New Orleans and at a consecration in St Louis, as well as in his own New York: *The Temple Pulpit*, 37–76). One of the last public appearances of Sabato Morais's life was to preach the dedicatory sermon of the new synagogue building of Shearith Israel (*New York Times*, 13 Nov. 1897, p. 7). For a fine review of thirty-two dedication sermons delivered in nineteenth-century Germany and Austria-Hungary as evidence for changing conceptions of the synagogue, see Meyer, ' "How Awesome Is This Place!" '

tions in many different languages. The first volume of published sermons written and delivered by a Jew in German appeared in 1813;[41] the first collection in English was apparently Isaac Leeser's two-volume *Discourses on the Jewish Religion*, published at Philadelphia in 1837. These were followed by an 1839 translation of sermons delivered by Gotthold Salomon in the Hamburg Temple during the 1820s, and then the 1851 volume by David Woolf Marks of the West London Synagogue of British Jews, containing sermons from the 1840s.[42]

A related type of volume is the compilation of contemporary sermons by several rabbis. A striking nineteenth-century example is *The American Jewish Pulpit: A Collection of Sermons by the Most Eminent American Rabbis*,[43] including examples (some translated from German) by eighteen different preachers representing a spectrum of theological positions. In the twentieth century, similar collections cut across denominational lines.[44] The Reform movement in the United States began to publish an annual 'Set of Holiday Sermons' in pamphlet form, representing the preaching of the Reform rabbinate on the holy days of the Jewish calendar; this was published from 1906 to 1965. The Rabbinical Council of America (Orthodox) began publishing a *Manual of Holiday and Sabbath Sermons* in 1943 and continued to do so virtually every year from 1951 through to its jubilee anthology of 1985.

Beginning in the eighteenth century, options other than books became available for the preservation and dissemination of the sermon text. Especially appropriate for the occasional sermons described above was publication in pamphlet form. We find an increasing number of sermons printed in this way and sold or otherwise distributed soon after the time of delivery. As we shall see, some were translated from the language of delivery into the language of

[41] Sorkin, 'Preacher, Teacher, Publicist', 121, referring to Joseph Wolf's *Sechs deutsche Reden, gehalten in der Synagoge zu Dessau*, published in 1813. The German texts were accompanied by a Hebrew translation. Individual German Jewish sermons were published in pamphlet form during the eighteenth century.

[42] Leeser, *Discourses*, vols i and ii (on the original 1837 publication of these two volumes, see Sussman, *Isaac Leeser*, p. 88); G. Salomon, *Twelve Sermons* (three of Salomon's sermons had been translated and published in Dutch in 1825: Wallet, 'Religious Oratory', 174); Marks, *Sermons Preached on Various Occasions*, vol. i. This last volume is said to have been 'undertaken at the request of the Council of Founders' of the West London Synagogue, considered important because of a 'dearth of Jewish discourses in the English language'. According to Curtis Cassell's unpublished biography of Marks (lent to me by the author's son, David Cassell), the book was extensively reviewed both in the Jewish press and in the *Christian Reformer* and *Kitto's Journal of Sacred Literature* (Cassell, 'David Woolf Marks', 37).

[43] A similar collection of fourteen sermons by thirteen British preachers (Orthodox and Reform) plus the chief rabbi of Paris was published in the *Jewish Chronicle* in 1885–6, collected as *The Jewish Pulpit: Annual Volume* (1886).

[44] e.g. E. Hertz (ed.), *Abraham Lincoln*; Teplitz (ed.), *The Rabbis Speak*; id. (ed.), 'Best Jewish Sermons' series; *Living Words*.

the host country. Publication was often initiated by the lay leaders of the synagogue where the sermon was delivered, reflecting a desire on their part to give wider exposure to the sentiments expressed from their pulpit. In the case of some occasional sermons (for example, that delivered by David Einhorn on Thanksgiving Day 1863, Sermon 8a below), the proceeds of the sales were set aside for a specific charitable cause.

A few of these printed sermons were used for political purposes. The printed text of Seixas's 1798 sermon on a national fast-day was advertised in two Democratic newspapers because of its perceived support of the moderate Jeffersonian position on France.[45] When Morris Raphall of New York delivered his famous (or infamous) 'pro-slavery' sermon on 4 January 1861, arguing that slavery was not considered a sin in the Bible, it was reprinted in pamphlet form and distributed by the Unionist party leaders, according to a contemporary diarist, in 'hundreds of thousands of copies . . . in all the states of the Union', generating an enormous controversy.[46] After the British chief rabbi Hermann Adler's patriotic sermon of 4 November 1899 (Sermon 14 below), following serious military reverses suffered by British troops in South Africa, 600 copies were circulated to the press, and bound copies sent to the queen and leading government ministers.[47] It was reported in early 1915 that 'The patriotic speech delivered by Rabbi Maze [of Moscow] in introducing a Jewish deputation to the Tsar has so impressed His Imperial Majesty that he requested that a copy might be sent to the Court. The Jewish community hopes to obtain permission to distribute a few hundred thousand copies of it in the country.'[48] Clearly, what was said by Jewish preachers in times of war was thought to be of interest beyond the walls of the synagogue.

Printing sermons in pamphlet form continued into the twentieth century. Several rabbis (for example, Joseph Krauskopf in Philadelphia; J. Leonard Levy in Philadelphia as Krauskopf's associate and then in Pittsburgh) had their weekly addresses transcribed and printed (in Krauskopf's case over a period of

[45] Schappes, *A Documentary History*, 90.

[46] The text of sermon is accessible ibid. 405–18, and at <www.jewish-history.com/raphall.html>; see also a diarist on the printing of the sermon: www.jewish-history.com/Salomon/salo14.html> (7 Jan. 1861). Cf. Friedenberg, 'Hear O Israel', 46–52; Bertram Korn states that 'This sermon aroused more comment and attention than any other sermon ever delivered by an American Rabbi': *American Jewry and the Civil War*, 17. Even in England, Gustav Gottheil of Manchester weighed in on the topic, preaching and publishing 'Moses versus Slavery' in 1861.

[47] Alderman, *The Jewish Community in British Politics*, 43–4. The full text, with annotations, is published as Sermon 14 below.

[48] *Jewish Chronicle*, 29 Jan. 1915, p. 20. The reference is to Rabbi Jacob Mazeh of the Choral Synagogue in Moscow, a strong leader and defender of Jewish interests for some thirty years. For his own version of the event, which reports some of the content of his extemporaneous speech but nothing about a request that a text be sent to court, see Mazeh, *Zikhronot*, ii. 31–3.

thirty-six years).[49] Sometimes, the pamphlets from a full year would be gathered and issued in a bound volume, imitating a practice of noted Christian preachers.[50] A different yet related pattern, still current though going back to the nineteenth century, is for a congregation to subsidize the publication of its rabbi's sermons for the High Holy Days, either regularly or in a particular year. Such pamphlets are generally distributed to the membership of the congregation and to rabbinical colleagues.[51]

Jewish periodicals and journals of the nineteenth and early twentieth centuries regularly printed sermons by leading preachers.[52] The general press also showed occasional interest. Raphall's 'pro-slavery' sermon of January 1861 was printed in the New York *Herald*, and various journals carried forceful rebuttals to the thesis of the sermon by other rabbis. Some of the sermons delivered at the time of the assassination of Abraham Lincoln were preserved in newspaper articles.[53] As we shall see, wartime sermons by Jewish preachers were often covered in the general press alongside those of their Christian colleagues, those of Sabato Morais in Philadelphia during the Civil War (of which one is reproduced as Sermon 6 below) being especially impressive examples.[54]

Sermons by the southern rabbis Max Heller of New Orleans and William Fineshriber of Memphis in the first decades of the twentieth century were

[49] According to Israel Levinthal, who as a high-school student reported on Krauskopf's Sunday lectures for a Philadelphia newspaper, the entire text of each lecture was written in advance and memorized by Krauskopf, who spoke pacing from one end of the pulpit to the other (*The Message of Israel*, 145–6). On Levy, see Freehof and Kavaler (eds), *J. Leonard Levy*, pp. xi, 41. In addition to the sixteen cycles of his Pittsburgh sermons, printed from stenographic transcriptions, eight cycles of Philadelphia sermons were published in this form. Needless to say, the historical value of such texts is considerable.

[50] Spurgeon, *The Metropolitan Pulpit*; Savage, *Unity Pulpit* and *The Messiah Pulpit*.

[51] e.g. Moses, 'On the Height'.

[52] Full texts of sermons were printed regularly by e.g. the first Jewish periodical in the German language, *Sulamith*; Isaac Leeser's *Occident*; Samuel Isaacs' *Jewish Messenger*; Isaac Mayer Wise's *Israelite* and its rival *Jewish South*; and London's *Jewish Chronicle*.

[53] A particularly moving example is an article in the *San Francisco Daily* of 16 Apr. 1865, apparently written by a member of Congregation Emanuel, which reports that the rabbi, Elkan Cohn, was handed a note informing him of Lincoln's death as he ascended the pulpit to deliver the sermon he had prepared. Initially overcome with emotion, the rabbi recovered and spoke extemporaneously, the correspondent recording for his article the 'substance' of the words—a version that, he confesses, does not do justice to the eloquence of the moment, yet retains its power in print. See E. Hertz (ed.), *Abraham Lincoln*, 138.

[54] Dozens of Morais's sermons were printed or summarized in the *Philadelphia Inquirer*. Since the handwritten texts of his sermon are extant, they can be compared with what was printed. In the case of his Thanksgiving sermon for 1863, the *Philadelphia Inquirer* published a short summary (apparently written by a reporter and based on the full text), while the *Jewish Messenger* a few weeks later published Morais's text in full. For a discussion of the cultural significance of publishing synopses of sermons in the general press, see Blondheim, 'Cultural Instruments of Communication', 67–8.

summarized and cited, often quite sympathetically, by local newspapers.[55] On 21 December 1925 the *New York Times* reported briefly on a sermon by Rabbi Stephen S. Wise entitled 'Jesus the Jew', which argued that Jesus was a great moral leader, whose faith and life are 'a part of the Jewish possessions and of the very fiber of our Jewish heritage'. In response, the Union of Orthodox Rabbis demanded Wise's resignation as national chairman of the United Palestine Appeal, which Wise indeed tendered, although the resignation was eventually refused by the Zionist Executive.[56] The New York Reform rabbi Louis I. Newman's strong pulpit condemnations of British policy towards Palestine following the 1939 White Paper, extensively reported by the *New York Times*, led to pressure from the board of his synagogue for him to resign from his leadership position in the militant Revisionist Zionist movement.[57]

From the outbreak of war on 1 September 1939, the *New York Times* gave extensive coverage of rabbinical sermons in New York, not only during the High Holy Day season each year, but sometimes week after week. These reports never included lengthy quotations; they are snapshot versions consisting of a few sentences from each of many different texts, aimed at identifying the major themes addressed. The passages quoted may not reflect what the preachers thought was the most important content, or what the congregants were most likely to remember. Nevertheless, these summaries are an extremely important source for Jewish preaching in times of war, and for the public perception of such preaching.[58]

Of course, most surviving sermon texts exist not in print but among the preachers' papers, whether in handwritten or typed format. Important collections of this material are held by the American Jewish Archives in Cincinnati, the Jewish Theological Seminary in New York, and the American Jewish Historical Society and the Leo Baeck Institute (both components of the Center for Jewish History, also in New York). Other significant collections

[55] See the essays by Bobbie Malone and Berkley Kalin in Bauman and Kalin, *The Quiet Voices*, and citations in nn. 187, 188 below.
[56] Voss (ed.), *Stephen S. Wise*, 132–3; Urofsky, *A Voice that Spoke for Justice*, 192–202. The *New York Times* reported only that Wise asserted (on the basis of Joseph Klausner's scholarship) that Jesus actually lived and was not just a myth (21 Dec. 1925, p. 24); reports of the controversy continued in the paper's issues of 24 Dec. (p. 14), 25 Dec. (p. 26), 26 Dec. (p. 3), and virtually every subsequent day through to 4 Jan. On 25 Jan. 1926 another of Wise's Sunday sermons was reported in the *New York Times*, this one criticizing the Coolidge administration for not intervening in the coal strike, which had continued for four months and looked as if it might fail.
[57] Medoff, *Militant Zionism in America*, 65–6; reports of Newman's sermons on this issue are in *New York Times*, 21 May 1939, p. 26, 9 July, p. 24, and 16 July, p. 24.
[58] The rabbis who seem to have been favoured with most consistent quotation were Louis I. Newman (Reform, Rodeph Sholom), Joseph Lookstein (Orthodox, Kehilath Jeshurun), David de Sola Pool (Orthodox, Spanish and Portuguese Jews' Synagogue), Milton Steinberg (Conservative, Park Avenue Synagogue), and Israel Goldstein (Conservative, B'nai Jeshurun).

exist in the archives of individual congregations, in local universities near the preachers' congregations, and in local historical societies.[59]

The final decade of the twentieth century witnessed a new mode of preserving and disseminating sermon texts: placing them on the website of the congregation where they were delivered.[60] Whether this should be classified as an ephemeral or permanent category of sermon preservation remains to be seen.

In some cases, both newspaper accounts and the author's own text of the sermon have survived, and textual divergences reveal some interesting examples of discrepancies between what was said, what immediately became part of the public record, and what was later published. In David Woolf Marks's sermon on the 'Indian Mutiny' (Sermon 4 below), the text printed soon afterwards in the *Examiner* contains the sentences: 'We may rest satisfied, that the nation will not abnegate its right to demand a searching inquiry into the circumstances that have placed in peril an empire, and cause the most precious blood of the land to be poured out like water. But this is not the time to enter on such an inquiry.' This passage does not appear in the published collection of Marks's sermons, probably because an adequate inquiry did not occur. When the *Jewish Messenger* printed a report of Rabbi Morris J. Raphall's fast-day sermon of 30 April 1863, it eliminated a strong passage of general criticism that was included in the report published by the *New York Times*. On the other hand, a specific condemnation of 'the action of Congress, which evaded the payment of a very large sum of money, long and justly due to the heirs of a Jew residing in Philadelphia who in the darkest hours of the war of Independence had devoted his vast wealth to the service of his adopted country', published by the *Jewish Messenger*, was not included in the *New York Times* report.[61]

As we shall see below, Sabato Morais criticized President Chester Alan Arthur by name from the pulpit for signing in 1882 a compromise version of the Chinese Exclusion Act, but this reference was omitted from the newspaper

---

[59] Congregations: Beth-El, Detroit (texts of more than 1,500 sermons by Leo Franklin); Temple Israel, Boston; Keneseth Israel, Philadelphia; Rodef Shalom, Pittsburgh. Universities: Emory (Jacob Rothschild); Case Western Reserve (A. H. Silver); New Jersey Historical Society (Solomon Foster).

[60] For an especially impressive example, see the online Sermon Archive of Baltimore's Congregation Beth Tfiloh (sermons mostly by Rabbi Mitchell Wohlberg): <www.bethtfiloh.com/podium/default.aspx?t=17397>, accessed 12 Dec. 2006.

[61] *New York Times*, 1 May 1863, p. 2; *Jewish Messenger*, 8 May 1863, p. 154. The reference is to the claims made by Haym M. Salomon for the repayment of debts owed to his father, Haym Salomon; repayment was urged by the Senate Committee on Revolutionary Claims in 1860 and 1862, but not passed by Congress. The strong passage of sweeping social criticism included in the *New York Times* is cited in the introduction (n. 3) to Sermon 7 by Isaacs below.

account (below, p. 57).[62] Rabbi Elias Lieberman of the Cape Cod Synagogue, speaking on Friday night, 14 September 2001, about the attacks on the World Trade Center and the Pentagon, said: 'That President Bush has expressed a determination to make the "war against terrorism" the central focus of his presidency says more to me about his inadequacies as a leader than it does about any real potential to end a scourge which is incredibly complex in nature.' This passage was recorded and played on National Public Radio the following morning. When the sermon was placed on the synagogue website, the sentence was changed to read: 'That our country's leaders have expressed a determination to make the "war against terrorism" their central focus for the foreseeable future says more to me about our sense of helplessness than it does about any real potential to end a scourge which is incredibly complex in nature.'[63] In the absence of videotapes—the only truly reliable evidence for a sermon—the texts we depend upon must often be carefully questioned.

## Language

The medieval and early modern tradition was that sermons be delivered in the vernacular language spoken by the Jews of the congregation, even if they were later written, copied, and eventually published in Hebrew. As the liturgy and the mandatory scriptural readings were read entirely in Hebrew, this would have been the only component of the worship service for which the vernacular was used.[64] In the modern period, sermons in the vernacular were taken for granted in Italian congregations, but in Germany and other central European countries the matter was fiercely contested by the Orthodox as a sign of assimilation and encroachment by the Reform movement.[65] At times, the decision of rabbis to preach in a particular vernacular had significant political implications. Reform rabbis in Hungary generally preached in German, but in 1848 a wave of Hungarian patriotism induced Löw Schwab of Pest and Leopold (Lipót) Löw of Pápa to preach in Hungarian.[66] Patriotic Polish preachers

---

[62] The cuttings in Morais's ledger, taken from the Philadelphia newspapers in which many of his sermons were printed, bear frequent authorial corrections in the margin; it is not clear to me whether Morais was indicating thereby that the newspaper accounts misrepresented the original text, or whether he was editing for possible future publication. Morais presents an ideal case for analysis, for he kept these cuttings as well as his own original texts, enabling comparisons between the two to be made.

[63] The original version was confirmed to me by Rabbi Lieberman in an e-mail of 17 Sept. 2001.

[64] On the earlier period see M. Saperstein, *Jewish Preaching*, 39–44.

[65] Guttmann, *The Struggle over Reform*, 9–13, and full texts on pp. 182–3, 252–7, 262–5, 267–8, 291.

[66] Both were subsequently arrested for having hailed the Hungarian declaration of independence in their sermons. See Patai, *The Jews of Hungary*, 245, 283; Baron, 'The Revolution of 1848', 92–100. A family tradition held that a patriotic sermon delivered by Leopold Löw as a field chaplain on the eve of battle was ordered by Louis Kossuth to be 'read to every section of the

Izaak Kramsztyk and Marcus Jastrow switched from German to Polish in the exhilarating period leading up to the abortive Polish uprising of 1863.[67]

During the seventeenth and eighteenth centuries, as Jewish migration increased, a pattern was sometimes established whereby the sermon would be delivered in the language of origin, preserving a linguistic and cultural distance between the Jewish community and its Christian neighbours. Thus in communities of Iberian emigration, such as Amsterdam and London, sermons were delivered in Portuguese (or Spanish) throughout the seventeenth and eighteenth centuries. Sermons 1 and 2 below, delivered in London in 1803 and 1805 during the Napoleonic Wars, were spoken respectively in Spanish at the Sephardi Bevis Marks Synagogue and in German at the Ashkenazi Great Synagogue, though they were quickly published in English. The first English sermons were apparently delivered by Tobias Goodman at Liverpool's Ashkenazi synagogue in 1806; it was not until a generation later, in the early 1830s, that English sermons became standard at the Bevis Marks Synagogue of London with the appointment of David de Sola as cantor and preacher.[68] A few years later, the 'Founders' Declaration' of the West London Synagogue included the principle that sermons, delivered in English, should be 'inspiring and instructive',[69] a goal fulfilled by the appointment as senior minister of David Woolf Marks, one of the giants among nineteenth-century Jewish preachers. Around the same time, it was resolved at the Great Synagogue in London to find a competent preacher who could deliver sermons in English; but the only plausible candidate was not elected, 'and the Great Synagogue remained without religious discourses' until the practice of regular sermons in

patriotic army': 'Miss Rosalia Loew', *American Jewess*, 2/9 (June 1896), 474–5; I have found no confirmation of this in the scholarly literature.

[67] See on this Wodziński, *Haskalah and Hasidism in the Kingdom of Poland*, 160–5, 187, and Finkelstein, 'History of the Rabbinical School of Warsaw', 170–5. Kramsztyk and Jastrow were arrested following their leadership in Jewish patriotic demonstrations in 1861 and exiled (together with the chief rabbi of Warsaw, Baer Meisels) before the beginning of the uprising. Jastrow, though serving at the 'German Synagogue' of Warsaw, later wrote, 'I believe it my duty to address my co-believers, who are considered to be Poles, in the Polish language' (ibid. 164).

[68] De Sola, *Biography of David Aaron de Sola*, 17–20; cf. Hyamson, *The Sephardim of England*, 258, 260: 'Although a stranger to the English language, [David de Sola] soon became a master of it, and it was not long before he was preaching in English with a facility that might well make his hearers believe that it was his native tongue'. In the Netherlands, the first sermons printed in Dutch (though delivered in German or Portuguese) dated from the first decade of the nineteenth century; the first delivered in Dutch were apparently from the 1830s, despite the opposition to Dutch preaching by both chief rabbis in Amsterdam. See Wallett, 'Religious Oratory', 170–6. Note also the 1832 call for sermons to be delivered in proper German in the synagogues of Vienna and Pest as a means of improving the 'degenerate wildness' of the Yiddish language used by contemporary Jews in their synagogues: Gilman, *Jewish Self-Hatred*, 161.

[69] Kershen and Romain, *Tradition and Change*, 21.

English was established in the second half of the century by the chief rabbi appointed in 1845, the German Nathan Adler.[70]

In the United States, Gershom Mendes Seixas wrote out and delivered his occasional sermons in English from the late eighteenth century, as did Isaac Leeser in the next generation. Yet Leeser, writing in October 1844, could enumerate only a handful of 'regular English preachers', plus three who preached in German, in the entire country, at a time when European synagogues were experiencing a renewed 'taste for pulpit eloquence', met by men of 'high attainments, who have taught the people in words of glorious eloquence, such as have seldom been equalled, never surpassed among any of the various classes of Christians'.[71] In 1855, the leaders of New York's Congregation Emanu-El noted that 'there has long been a desire on the part of the members of Emanu-El to have English spoken in the pulpit', yet its minister, Leo Merzbacher, was unable to comply, and it was not until after his death the following year that an 'English lecturer' was hired.[72] On 19 April 1865, the national day of mourning following Abraham Lincoln's assassination, at least five major sermons by American rabbis were delivered in German, four of which were subsequently published in pamphlet form.[73] In 1872 the *New York Herald* reported only eight rabbis in the entire country whose English was good enough for public speaking.[74] David Einhorn, an intellectual spearhead of the Reform movement, tried to make commitment to the German language an ideological principle, on grounds both of accessibility to his largely immigrant audience and of loyalty to the origins of the movement, and continued preaching in German throughout his career; however, despite the hope expressed in his valedictory sermon ('Ich bin ein Hebräer!') that German would continue to be heard in sabbath sermons alongside English, his congregation, Beth-El of New York, abolished German from the pulpit soon after his retirement in 1879.[75] Italian

[70] Picciotto, *Sketches of Anglo-Jewish History* 332–3; Roth, *The Great Synagogue*, ch. 16.

[71] Leeser, 'The Demands of the Times'; compare the similar survey in his 1841 introduction to the third volume of his *Discourses* (p. vi). Cf. Lachoff, 'Rabbi Bernard Illowy', 47.

[72] Jick, *The Americanization of the Synagogue*, 143–4.

[73] See E. Hertz (ed.), *Abraham Lincoln*, title pages on pp. 14 (David Einhorn, Philadelphia), 56 (Henry Hochheimer, Baltimore), 78 (Jonas Bondi, New York), 140 (Liebman Adler, Chicago). In addition to these texts, the German text of the sermon from that date by Bernhard Felsenthal of Chicago is given (ibid. 100–5), as is the German sermon delivered on 1 June 1865 by Benjamin Szold of Baltimore, which was published as a pamphlet (title page, ibid. 40).

[74] *New York Herald*, 22 July 1872, cited in J. R. Blumberg, 'Rabbi Alphabet Browne', 6.

[75] Jick, *The Americanization of the Synagogue*, 144–5. A selection of Einhorn's sermons (including the valedictory) was published in 1880 under the title *Ausgewählte Predigten und Reden*, with a further selection appearing in the 1911 *David Einhorn Memorial Volume*; both collections were edited by Kaufmann Kohler. For overviews, see Kober, 'Jewish Preaching and Preachers', esp. 128–31 on America, and the bibliography of published American German-language sermons, ibid. 131–4; also B. Cohen, 'Early German Preaching in America', which includes a more complete bibliography of sermons (pp. 127–33).

immigrants, such as Sabato Morais in Philadelphia and Benjamin Artom in London, having no constituency that understood their native language, began preaching in English within a very short time of arriving in their adopted lands.

In the 1880s older rabbis in the United States were still preaching in German. At the same time a new generation of immigrant rabbis from eastern Europe—many of whom expressed an opposition in principle to preaching in English as a sign of contamination from the Reform movement—established the Yiddish sermon as a major medium of pulpit discourse.[76] During periods of unusual historical stress, the transition to preaching in a new vernacular might be dramatically accelerated. A striking example from the twentieth century is provided in the sermons delivered by Ignaz Maybaum, himself a recent immigrant, to a congregation of German refugees in London during the Second World War. Until the war began, he preached in German; once England was at war with Germany, various psychological needs made it imperative for both preacher and listeners to abandon the familiar mother-tongue in favour of a new language.[77] Plotting the linguistic lag-time in immigrant communities tracks an interesting cultural marker: how long does it take before a congregation composed entirely of immigrants, including an immigrant rabbi, begins to listen to sermons in the new vernacular?[78]

## *Incorporation of Literary Material*

Yet another distinctive characteristic of modern Jewish preaching is the often profuse employment of quotations from non-Jewish literature, especially poetry. Medieval and early modern Jewish preachers quite frequently resorted to parables or exempla that can be traced to external literary sources,[79] but direct quotations from purely literary works (as opposed to philosophical texts) are extremely rare.[80] By the second half of the nineteenth century, however, the

[76] Caplan, 'The Concerns of an Immigrant Rabbi', 192–215. Opposition to preaching in the 'vernacular' had been voiced by traditionalist rabbis in the early part of the nineteenth century: see Guttmann, *The Struggle over Reform*, 11–12. On immigrant rabbis in England in the 1880s and 1890s preaching in Yiddish on the High Holy Days, see Gartner, *The Jewish Immigrant in England*, 196.

[77] Maybaum, *Man and Catastrophe*, p. viii: 'One cannot, even when most of the listeners are German-speaking, preach in the German language while German bombers, as on the Day of Atonement, 1940, roar overhead during the service.'

[78] Note the following passage in a letter written by M. B. Simmonds to Isaac Leeser, dated 9 July 1841, from St Thomas, Virgin Islands: 'A fellow has been employed by our sapient rulers as Minister, who considers Tephilin [phylacteries] as foolishness. You are therefore able to draw an inference what effect it must have on all parties. For my part I stay at home. He gave them a sermon in Dutch and although not one present understood one single sentence it was lauded to the skies' (private collection). [79] See M. Saperstein, *Jewish Preaching*, 93–100.

[80] Cecil Roth once wrote that any Italian Jew 'with the slightest pretext [*sic*] to education was familiar with Dante and with Petrarch. Rabbis quoted them in their sermons, and exegetes

practice had become standard, and not only among the Reform preachers, as we shall see. It is perhaps not surprising that the giants of English literature—Shakespeare, Milton,[81] Keats, Tennyson—are frequently summoned to the preacher's aid, but we find also quotations from Dryden and Pope, Oliver Goldsmith and Thomas Gray, Blake and Wordsworth, Byron and Browning, Rudyard Kipling and Rupert Brooke. Among the Americans, Longfellow, Emerson, James Russell Lowell, and William Cullen Bryant are popular sources. Sometimes the poets are identified, but often they are cited anonymously, as if it could be assumed that their work would be familiar to the auditors.

Many Orthodox British preachers, such as Simeon Singer of the New West End Synagogue, Aaron Asher Green of the New Synagogue at Hampstead, and Hermann Gollancz of the Bayswater Synagogue (who held a D.Litt. from the University of London), drew profusely from their readings of English literature in their sermons.[82] Sometimes the literary passages are integrated seamlessly with classical Jewish texts; sometimes the poetic passage is cited at the very end of the sermon. I shall illustrate the use of literature with reference to sermons delivered by two British chief rabbis.

Hermann Adler employed literary quotations to considerable effect. In his sermon of November 1899 on the Boer War, he invokes a highly rhetorical passage from Milton's *Areopagitica* to express the patriotic resolve of the British population galvanized after a military reversal:

As we note this wondrous outburst of enthusiasm, the great words of Milton are recalled to us: 'Methinks I see in my mind a noble and puissant nation, rousing herself like a strong man after sleep, and shaking her invincible locks; methinks I see her as an eagle mewing her mighty youth, and kindling her undazzled eyes at the full mid-day beam'. (See below, p. 291)

In the sermon he delivered on Yom Kippur, seven weeks earlier, he had discussed the Dreyfus judgment, expressing the consternation and anger generated

---

mentioned them in their biblical commentaries' (Roth, *The Jews in the Renaissance*, 33). But he provides not a single example, and I know of none.

[81] Perhaps the most surprising use is of Milton's poem 'The Morning of Christ's Nativity' by Morris Joseph (see Sermon 16 below).

[82] See e.g. Singer, *Sermons*, 191 (Tennyson), 196 (Michelangelo), 207 (Oliver Wendell Holmes), 214 (Charles Swain), 216 (W. M. Praed), 221 (Edward Young), 233 and 254 (Shakespeare), *Jewish Chronicle*, 20 Oct. 1899 (Shakespeare), *Jewish Chronicle*, 12 Jan. 1900 (Goldsmith); Green, *Sermons*, 143 (Tennyson), 145 (Keats), 149 (Tagore), 156 (Dekker), 160 (Gray), 211 (Milton), 232 (Browning); Gollancz, *Sermons and Addresses*, i. 12 (Pope), i. 24 and 111 (Tennyson), i. 44 (William Cullen Bryant), i. 124 (Emerson), i. 171 (Wordsworth), i. 240 (Shakespeare), i. 286 (Shirley), i, 461 (Dryden), ii. 53 and 263 (Ruskin), ii. 61 (Horatius Bonar, nineteenth-century hymn writer), ii. 166 (Shakespeare), ii. 230 (Edward Young), iii. 104 (Samuel Johnson), iii. 155 (Bryant), iii. 34 (Euripides), iii. 231 (Shakespeare).

by the new verdict recently announced by the French court (which, though pardoning Dreyfus, reasserted his guilt), but insisting that justice would prevail through an (unidentified) citation from Longfellow's poem 'Retribution':

There is a retribution which sooner or later overtakes every nation that forgets and rejects the eternal distinctions of right and wrong ... God is the Judge, and abaseth the one and exalteth the other. It was so with all the colossal empires of antiquity—with Assyria the strong, with Babylon the proud, with Greece and Rome. It was in our own time so with the kingdom of Spain.

> Tho' the mills of God grind slowly, yet
> They grind exceeding small;
> Tho' with patience He stands waiting
> With exactness grinds He all.[83]

Later in the same sermon, he turns to another American poet to reinforce the same theme:

It is not for the first time in history that we have seen

> Truth on the scaffold, wrong upon the throne.
> But the scaffold sways the future,
> And behind the dim unknown,
> Standeth God within the shadow,
> Keeping watch above His own.

The God of Judgement will not leave the righteous in the hand of the wicked, nor condemn him when he is judged.[84]

Nothing seems inappropriate about the chief rabbi citing a Christian poet in a Yom Kippur sermon at the Great Synagogue, and publishing the text in the most widely read and highly respected Jewish journal in England.

Adler's successor as chief rabbi, Joseph Hertz, was if anything even better versed in English and American literature. Sometimes he will use a poetic passage at the beginning of a sermon, to introduce a central idea, as if it were a classical Jewish text, as in this sermon of 1917 for the holiday of Hanukah:

The poet Longfellow, speaking of the men and women of the olden Jewish Communities, of their courage and constancy says,

> Trampled and beaten were they as the sand,
>     And yet unshaken as the continent.
> For in background figures vague and vast,
>     Of patriarchs and prophets rose sublime,
> And all the great traditions of the past
>     They saw reflected in the coming time.

---

[83] H. Adler, 'The Dreyfus Judgement', 12.
[84] Ibid. 13, citing James Russell Lowell, 'Once to Every Man and Nation'.

> And thus forever with reverted look
> The mystic volume of the world they read,
> Spelling it backward like a Hebrew book . . .

This is a striking thought of great beauty that the true Jew views life in the light of Israel's past.[85]

Another sermon by Hertz, delivered at the Great Synagogue in 1916 on the Day of Intercession, 1 January, incorporates two familiar passages from English poetry. The first, by Rudyard Kipling, had been written shortly before. Reminding his listeners of the widespread dream of universal peace in the first years of the twentieth century, the assumption that human history was a story of 'unbroken triumphal progress', the preacher evokes the devastating impact of the outbreak of war in August 1914:

And then in one day a cataclysm engulfed civilization; and the poet could truthfully exclaim,

> 'Our world has passed away, / In wantonness overthrown;
> There is nothing left to-day, / But steel, and fire, and stone.'

None could have foretold that civilized mankind would rush back to savagery with such dreadful fervour.

The preacher omitted the more familiar opening lines of Kipling's poem—'For all we have and are, | For all our children's fate, | Stand up and meet the war | The Hun is at the gate!'—perhaps as inappropriate to the mood of the occasion. Yet Kipling's theme of rallying to the cause of defending the fatherland is indeed introduced a few moments later in the sermon with an unidentified passage from one of the greatest classics of English literature.

Is there nothing for which to bless God, amid all this disaster? Consider the spirit of stern resolve that has come over the men and the women of the nation, the

> Courage never to submit or yield,
> And what is else not to be overcome—

The readiness for unbounded sacrifice, as soon as it was realized that we were confronted by a powerful foe who desired nothing less than England's annihilation.

One wonders whether Hertz was aware that he was quoting from Book I of *Paradise Lost* the fallen Satan's defiant challenge to God, the refusal of evil to submit to good![86]

---

[85] J. Hertz, 'The Eternal City of the Eternal People', 213, citing Longfellow's 'Jewish Cemetery at Newport'.

[86] J. Hertz, 'Through Darkness and Death unto Light', 27–8; see Sermon 17 below. Hertz repeated this quotation during the Second World War, applying it to the pluck of the British at Dunkirk and during the Battle of London ('Intercession Sermon', 63). He seemed especially to like Rudyard Kipling, quoting passages from his poems in sermons on the silver jubilee and at the death of King George V (*Sermons, Addresses and Studies*, i. 58, 61–2).

As with Adler's citation of Milton during the Boer War, in both of the citations from Hertz's Great War intercession sermon there is total solidarity and identification with the values of the country in which the preacher is speaking. One final example of his use of English literature expresses a somewhat different stance with considerable power. The occasion is 13 December 1942, a day of fasting and prayer for the Jewish victims of Nazi mass murder. While strongly endorsing the war effort, Hertz confessed from the pulpit of the Sephardi Bevis Marks Synagogue—the Ashkenazi Great Synagogue being unusable because of bomb damage—that he was 'dumbfounded by the amazing indifference displayed in high and low places in this country toward the annihilation of millions of defenceless people'.

Will Britain and her Allies encourage and help the few remaining neutral states to receive such refugees? Will at least the children be saved from mass-poisoning in the lethal chambers of Hitler . . .? Shame covers us, as Jews, as Englishmen, as human beings, that even to such questions we are not sure of an affirmative answer . . . Therefore we turn to our beloved England, that has for so many centuries been the conscience of Europe; that has been the leader in so many humanitarian crusades; and we agonizingly exclaim in the words of the poet:

> England, awake! Awake! Awake!
> Jerusalem thy sister calls.
> Why wilt thou sleep the sleep of death
> And close her from thy ancient walls?

The implication is clear: England has betrayed its historic role as 'the conscience of Europe', and the most effective way of awakening the country to its higher calling is by citing its own poet, William Blake. Mobilizing to save actual Jewish victims of a murderous oppression is a purpose that Blake would not have recognized as his original intention, but it is an extremely effective rhetorical use of the poem.[87]

## The Struggle for Freedom of the Pulpit

Freedom of the pulpit—a principle taken for granted by rabbis in Britain and America today—was by no means universal during this period; it eventually prevailed following a prolonged struggle between preachers and the lay leadership of their congregations. During the Middle Ages there were occasional, albeit largely ineffective, efforts to ban certain kinds of content from sermons—especially radical allegorical interpretations of biblical or rabbinic passages by philosophically inclined preachers.[88] But even in a community such as seventeenth-century Amsterdam, where the lay leadership played a dominant

---

[87] J. Hertz, 'England, Awake', 84.     [88] See M. Saperstein, *Jewish Preaching*, 380–3.

role, there is no hint that the *mahamad* (synagogue wardens) ever tried to impose prior censorship by requiring preachers to present their texts for advance approval.[89] In the early nineteenth century, however, a committee of elders of the Spanish and Portuguese Jews' Synagogue of London, recommending that a weekly sermon be delivered in English, proposed that the text of each sermon be submitted to a committee of three elders before delivery to ensure that it contained nothing 'inimical to our religious doctrine or . . . hostile to the established institutions of the country'.[90] Although this recommendation for a weekly sermon in English was not approved, occasional sermons were still submitted for prior approval by the *mahamad*. Up to the middle years of the century, published sermons bore the imprint of approval from the lay leaders; when one preacher published a Passover sermon in 1839 without such approval, he was reprimanded by the *mahamad*.[91]

In 1825, following an open dispute with their spiritual leader or haham Jeosuah Piza, the regents of the oldest Jewish congregation of the New World, in Curaçao, passed the following regulation: 'In his sermons the rabbi was not to speak against the government, nor against the administration of the community by the *parnasim* [the people passing the regulation], *nor against the members for their conduct, whether in religious or civil matters.*'[92] In mid-century Germany, one of the leading Reform preachers, Leopold Stein of Frankfurt am Main, refused to submit to a review of his sermons by the congregation's board of directors; the resulting conflict led to the termination of his appointment as rabbi.[93]

In the United States, Isaac Leeser expressed a desire to preach regularly from the beginning of his tenure as cantor of Philadelphia's Mikveh Israel Synagogue in 1829, but approval for a weekly sabbath sermon in English did not come until 1843. During the intervening years, when he preached sporadically, he was instructed by the *parnas* (synagogue president) that he could preach only if he notified the *parnas* of his intention at least a day in advance. In this

---

[89] Saul Levi Morteira's sermons were written by him in Hebrew each week before he delivered them in Portuguese, but it is doubtful that members of the mahamad could even have read the Hebrew texts, much less review them for problematic content. The only time they appear to have become involved was when Morteira and Manasseh ben Israel apparently used their pulpits to attack each other (M. Saperstein, *'Your Voice Like a Ram's Horn'*, 413, with reference to H. P. Salomon). Quite different was the abortive attempt instigated by a Jesuit professor in Prague to require Jewish preachers to submit the texts of their sermons for review of potentially blasphemous content three days in advance of delivery. See Schweinburg and Eibenschuetz, 'Une confiscation'.

[90] Picciotto, *Sketches of Anglo-Jewish History*, 320; Hyamson, *The Sephardim of England*, 272.

[91] Hyamson, *The Sephardim of England*, 255, 260–1.

[92] Emmanuel, *History of the Jews in Netherlands Antilles*, 613, article 24m, emphasis added; cf. also ibid. 503 on later rabbis' resistance to attempts to control their preaching.

[93] Wiener, *Abraham Geiger and Liberal Judaism*, 56.

case there was no question of censorship of the content; even so, Leeser considered this stipulation a 'degradation of the ministry', although he complied with it.[94] Leeser's successor, Sabato Morais, was less tractable. Beneath the text in his ledger of his Thanksgiving sermon for 24 November 1864, printed in the *Philadelphia Inquirer* the following day, Morais wrote:

I very much regret that this discourse is so badly printed that it is scarcely legible. A history is connected with it. Copperheads became so enraged by reason of it, that I got a hornet's nest around my ears. Men dressed in brief authority would have stopped my speaking altogether, but I appealed to my constituents, and after three months' silence returned my free speech as formerly.

This episode, as documented in the minutes of the Mikveh Israel Adjunta (lay leadership) and Congregation and recounted by Bertram Korn, culminated in the vindication by the congregational membership on 9 April 1865, overriding the Adjunta, of Morais's right to preach 'on moral and religious subjects' whenever he desired, and 'on the subjects of the day . . . whenever the Synagogue may be opened by order of the *Parnas*'.[95] In a later sermon, however, Morais conceded that Rosh Hashanah was not an appropriate time to speak out from the pulpit on political issues such as the Chinese Exclusion Act; a Thanksgiving Day sermon, however, when Jews were gathered on an occasion of national significance, was entirely fitting for a discussion of policies that affected the nation as a whole.[96]

In Cincinnati, the board of Congregation B'nai Jeshurun resolved in April 1860 'to notify the Rev. Dr. [Isaac Mayer] Wise that the Board disapproves of all political allusions in his sermon and to discontinue the same [the political allusions] in the future'—feeling moved to issue this injunction despite the general policy of Wise not to address political matters in his preaching.[97]

Others fought a courageous battle to establish the principle of free speech from the pulpit. In his 1909 memorial oration on the centenary of the birth of David Einhorn, Emil G. Hirsch praised him as a champion of the integrity of the rabbi and preacher against the influence of wealthy laymen:

---

[94] Sussman, *Isaac Leeser*, 61–2, 103–4, 136.

[95] S. Morais, 'Thanksgiving Day Sermon', 1864; Korn, *American Jewry and the Civil War*, 44–6. Korn was unaware that a text of the Thanksgiving 1864 sermon that aroused the controversy was indeed extant, clipped by Morais from the *Philadelphia Inquirer* for his ledger. The phrase 'men dressed in brief authority' is an allusion to Shakespeare's *Measure for Measure*, II. ii ('man | Drest in a little brief authority'); I am grateful to Arthur Kiron for this identification.

[96] S. Morais, 'On the Ill Treatment of the Chinese in the Far West', 3–4. Morais was responding to an actual instance in which congregants complained that their rabbi's sermon addressing the 'Chinese question' was inappropriate for Rosh Hashanah.

[97] Temkin, *Isaac Mayer Wise*, 173, 175–6. For Wise's earlier problems regarding preaching in Albany, see Sarna, *American Judaism*, 93.

We, who believe that the pulpit, if its message is meant to be effective and vital, must be free, owe this great preacher of ours a debt of gratitude beyond compare and computation. No woman ever was more jealous of her virtue and purity than was he of the right of the preacher to be free, to be true to himself, his convictions, his principles, his God . . . He pilloried mercilessly the 'barons by the grace of the Almighty Dollar', who had attempted to inhibit their Rabbi from making allusion to the proceedings of the Philadelphia Conference [of the radical wing of Reform rabbis].[98] He exposed pitilessly their impudence, when they arrogated to themselves influence over decisions concerning questions, for the treating of which the knowledge of the expert in theology was indispensable. Superbly did he disregard the counsel of timid souls to be cautious in the handling from the pulpit of slavery. And in asserting his right, in the name of Judaism, to protest against the iniquitous institution, he, courting the martyr's fate, rendered American Israel a service greater than any other to his credit.[99]

Hirsch uttered these words against the background of the most dramatic episode in the battle for freedom of the pulpit, when Stephen S. Wise, under consideration for appointment as rabbi of New York's influential Congregation Emanu-El, demanded the freedom to preach without prior approval from the board of trustees. When this demand was refused, he established the 'Free Synagogue' of New York, in which freedom of the pulpit was a fundamental principle.[100] (Ironically, in his inaugural sermon as rabbi of Emanu-El, delivered on 21 November 1868, James Koppel Gutheim had said, 'I should deem myself unworthy of my position here, unworthy of your confidence, if I were to permit any of you to dictate what or how I shall preach, while I remain your minister', without apparent objection. The decisive point in the later conflict may have been Wise's style, rather than the substance of the issue.)[101]

Occasionally, various congregations in the United States and Britain attempted to constrain their rabbis from speaking about 'political matters' from the pulpit, especially in tense contexts such as the struggle against segregation in the American South, but with limited success.[102] During the first months

---

[98] See on this Meyer, *Response to Modernity*, 255–8.

[99] Emil G. Hirsch, in K. Kohler (ed.), *David Einhorn Memorial Volume*, 466–7.

[100] For Wise's 'Open Letter to the Members of Temple Emanu-El of New York on the Freedom of the Jewish Pulpit', see his autobiography, *Challenging Years*, 82–94; see also his sermon 'Shall the Pulpit Be Free?'. Sarna, discussing this incident, mentions the 'long-established American practice' of lay control of the pulpit: *American Judaism*, 251.

[101] Gutheim, *The Temple Pulpit*, 33–4. Gutheim, however, did not generally address political topics in his sermons; to his previous congregation in New Orleans, he said, 'I do not conceive it to be the province of the pulpit to discuss the political questions of the day and to point out the course which should be pursued; I believe it to be a perversion of its function' (Gutheim, 'Thanksgiving Day Sermon', 23–4).

[102] For Britain, see Kershen and Romain, *Tradition and Change*, 153, on the case of the West London Synagogue and Rabbi Harold Reinhart in 1934. For the American South, see Bauman and Kalin (eds), *The Quiet Voices*, *passim*.

of the First World War, a reader of the *Jewish Chronicle* was so incensed by a sermon in a West End synagogue in which the preacher maintained that the sufferings of the Belgian people were only the just retribution for the atrocities committed by the nation in former years in the Congo, and by another Jewish preacher who attacked from the pulpit the head of a well-known Jewish catering firm because his company had dismissed German waiters, that he urged individual listeners who felt strong opposition to a sermon to rise and publicly express their disapproval of what the preacher had said. The editor of the *Chronicle* disagreed, writing:

If the minister is to be muzzled, if he is to be dictated to as to how he must think, and what he should say, then, if he is a brave man, he will surrender his post, and if he is not, he will become a hypocrite in canonicals. Besides, if one is to set up a censorship over the minister's opinions, where is the process to begin, and worse still, where is it to end?[103]

This is the position that eventually prevailed.

In some cases, while sermons were not subjected to formal review by a board of laymen, there existed an understanding that the pulpit was not an appropriate venue for the discussion of political, economic, or military matters that clearly lay outside the realm of the rabbi's expertise. In the midst of the US war with Spain at the very end of the nineteenth century, the *Jewish South* wrote editorially, 'A wise act was that of the Presbyterian ministers of Richmond when on Monday last they decided upon resolution to preach in future about religion, not of war.'[104] Some of the leading preachers agreed. Gershom Mendes Seixas, preaching in 1798 on a highly charged national fast-day amid fears of war with France, said, 'I shall not take it upon me to enter into any civil or political discussion upon the subject, but shall confine myself entirely to the nature and consequence of such actions as are consistent with the true spirit and principles of religion.' Isaac Leeser, alluding to the European revolutions of 1830 and 1848, said that 'religion has no part to play in the mighty and terrible dramas which have late been enacted; at least it has no business to interfere actively and visibly in public affairs'. Eulogizing Abraham Lincoln sixteen years later, he noted, 'Respecting Mr. Lincoln's political career and character it does not become me to speak; politics is not the province into which a minister of religion should

---

[103] *Jewish Chronicle*, 6 Nov. 1914, p. 27.

[104] *The Jewish South*, 13 May 1898, p. 6. The rationale was as follows: 'The occupant of the pulpit should remember that in his congregation are many of equal intelligence with himself, who are just as capable as he of forming an opinion on a new book or play or on a public question. When they hear him in his ministerial capacity render decisions which they feel to be faulty, they naturally lose faith in his judgement, and begin to have their doubts as to the soundness of his theological views, thereby greatly impairing his usefulness and influence. But let him stick to his specialty—religion—and any reasonable statement which he may make will be accepted unquestioned, a procedure that will benefit both minister and congregation.'

enter.' Isaac Mayer Wise thought similarly. The texts of his sermons show little explicit reference to specific non-religious controversial issues of the day (though see his address on the Franco-Prussian War, Sermon 9 below); as we have seen, the board of Wise's B'nai Jeshurun synagogue informed him that it 'disapprove[d] of all political allusions' in the rabbi's sermons.[105] Other preachers refused to accept a narrow definition of the religious domain that would exclude many important topics from their sermons. Sabato Morais, speaking about a garment workers' strike in the summer of 1890, declaimed: 'May the day never dawn, when the disciples of prophets and sages, to whose keeping practical religion has been entrusted, shall be muzzled, that they may not denounce social iniquities.'[106] J. Leonard Levy, speaking in Pittsburgh in November 1914, addressed his listeners directly on this issue:

Most earnestly do I plead with you, keen business men as you are, that you do not argue, as I heard some rather foolish person said concerning one of my recent discourses, that I have no business to talk about business in this pulpit, urging that men come here not for business but for religion. Criticisms of that kind grow out of the absurd folly which conceives of business and religion as something apart. Business must be made religious.[107]

In the highly charged environment of apartheid South Africa, Chief Rabbi Louis I. Rabinowitz quoted in a sermon an article he had written on 'The Synagogue and Jewish Ethics', stating, 'I am sure that the reader will be wryly amused, for instance, to hear that a member of my congregation wrote a letter to the Council asking them to forbid me from speaking on the native question, but to confine myself to Jewish ethics!'[108] As we shall see below (Sermons 31a and 31b), Roland B. Gittelsohn of Boston insisted, against strong opposition, that it was indeed a rabbi's prerogative to speak about the US government's policy in the Vietnam War.

---

[105] For Seixas, see the text in Schappes, *A Documentary History*, 90. For Leeser, see 'The Strength of our Religion', 89, and 'Mr Lincoln's Death', 134. For Wise, see Diner, *A Time for Gathering*, 147. Samuel Myer Isaacs, speaking of David Einhorn's need to flee for his safety from Baltimore to Philadelphia, wrote, 'It seems that he has been mistaking his vocation, and making the pulpit the vehicle for political invective . . . A Minister has enough to do, if he devotes himself to the welfare of his flock; he can afford to leave politics to others' (see the introduction to the Sermon 7 below).

[106] S. Morais, manuscript sermon from the summer of 1890, cited in Maxwell Whiteman, 'Western Impact on East European Jews', 127–8 (cf. his letter of 15 Aug. 1890 published in the *Jewish Exponent*, digitized image, Sabato Morais Ledger, 441). Note, however, his qualification, cited above, about discussing political issues on occasions such as Rosh Hashanah.

[107] J. L. Levy, 'The War against War, II', 21.

[108] Rabinowitz, *Sparks from the Anvil*, 198; the undated sermon was delivered c.1953. See also his poignant confession in a later Yom Kippur sermon of having chosen 'expediency over principle' in response to a government request to state the views of Judaism on the 'racial question': id., *Light and Salvation*, 315–17.

## Women in the Pulpit

A final innovation, coming near the end of our period, is the emergence of women's voices in pulpits across the United States and Britain. Records of western Jewish women preaching go back at least to the 1890s, when Ray Frank addressed American congregations, and continue in the twentieth century with Lily Montagu in England, Regina Jonas in Germany, and Helen Hadassah Levinthal in the United States.[109] However, it was not until the last quarter of the twentieth century, following the first formal ordination of a woman rabbi by the Hebrew Union College–Jewish Institute of Religion in 1972, that female voices from the pulpit began to have a significant impact on many aspects of Jewish preaching in Britain and America.

A stunning example of this new strand in the tradition is a sermon for the Kol Nidrei service on Yom Kippur 1990, delivered by the American Margaret Moers Wenig under the title 'God Is a Woman, and She Is Growing Older'. One doubts that any male rabbi would even have conceived of preaching on such a theme. Despite the startlingly radical sound of the title, the substance draws from the traditional imagery of the High Holy Day season: remembrance, the opening of the books, the signature of every living being, God's longing for human beings to return, even the variety of metaphors for God in the liturgical poem 'We Are Your People'. The poignant eloquence and rhetoric of this passage, however, are quite distinctive; one imagines it delivered not in thundering cadences but in a calm, tranquil, almost conversational manner befitting the intimacy of the domestic scene it evokes.

On Rosh Hashanah, the anniversary of the day on which she gave us birth, God sits down at her kitchen table, opens the Book of Memories, and begins turning the pages. And God remembers.

'There is the world when it was new and my children when they were young . . .' As she turns each page she smiles, seeing before her, like so many dolls in a department store window, all the beautiful colors of our skin, all the varied shapes and sizes of our bodies. She marvels at our accomplishments: the music we have written, the gardens we have planted, the skyscrapers we have built, the stories we have told, the ideas we have spun.

'They now can fly faster than the winds I send', she says to herself, 'and they sail across the waters which I gathered into seas. They even visit the moon, which I set in the sky. But they rarely visit me'. Pasted into the pages of her book are all the cards

[109] On Ray (Rachel) Frank, see Litman, *Ray Frank Litman*; Clar and Kramer, 'The Girl Rabbi of the Golden West'. On Lily Montagu, see Umansky, *Lily Montagu*; Montagu, *Sermons, Addresses, Letters, Prayers*. On Regina Jonas, see Kellenbach, '"God Does Not Oppress Any Human Being"'; Sarah, 'Rabbiner Regina Jonas', esp. p. 7 on her preaching. On Helen Hadassah Levinthal, see Nadell, *Women Who Would Be Rabbis*, 80–5.

we have sent to her when we did not bother to visit. She notices our signatures scrawled beneath the printed words someone else has composed.

There are pages she would rather skip. Things she wishes she could forget. But they stare her in the face and she cannot help but remember: her children spoiling the home she created for us, brothers putting each other in chains. She remembers seeing us racing down dangerous roads—herself unable to stop us. She remembers the dreams she had for us—dreams we never fulfilled. And she remembers the names, so many names, inscribed in the book, names of all the children she has lost through war and famine, earthquake and accident, disease and suicide. And God remembers the many times she sat by a bedside weeping that she could not halt the process she herself set into motion.

Tonight, Kol Nidrei night, God lights candles, one for each of her children, millions and millions of candles illuminating the night, making it bright as day. Tonight God will stay awake all night, turning the pages of her book.

God is lonely tonight, longing for her children . . . God would prefer that we come home.[110]

There is not yet enough relevant evidence available to determine whether the voices of women from the pulpit have significantly influenced the rhetoric and the content of sermons addressing the problems of their countries on going to war, although as the twenty-first century moves on the quantity of material is significantly increasing.

## THEMES IN MODERN JEWISH PREACHING

### *Jewish Doctrine in Internal and External Conflicts*

Many sermons delivered in the nineteenth century and the first half of the twentieth were devoted to an exposition of Jewish doctrine. Quite frequently, these discussions have an apologetic or polemical purpose, in relation either to internal Jewish divisions or to the pressure of Christian missionaries.

Eight years after his installation as chief rabbi in 1845, Nathan Adler published a sermon delivered at the Great Synagogue on the sabbath of Hanukah entitled 'Solomon's Judgement: A Picture of Israel'. Noting his general reluctance to print his sermons, 'because the spoken word must always lose much of its original warmth thereby', he explained that he had decided to publish this one because of the crucial importance of its topic: the belief that the oral law, transmitted in rabbinic texts, was as divine in origin as the written law of Scripture. After briefly referring to the 'struggle without', against Christianity and Islam, he focused on the 'struggle within', against those Jews who believe in the divine revelation of Scripture but who 'deny the divinity of the oral law'. His position is relatively moderate in tone: 'not all is divine which is found

[110] Wenig, 'God Is a Woman', 256–7, 261.

in the writings of our sages . . . yet the existence of an oral law cannot be denied'. Those who reject this 'attempt to divide Judaism [and] extinguish its vitality'.[111]

Within a few months the same printer (John Wertheimer) published four lectures delivered by David Woolf Marks at the West London Synagogue on the 'sufficiency of the Law of Moses as the Guide of Israel', described in the first lecture as his response to Adler's sermon. Marks had already argued against the divine character of the oral law in his 1842 consecration sermon; here he seized on Adler's statement that 'not all is divine' in the rabbinic literature and probed the problematics of differentiating between what is and what is not. His most powerful rhetorical argument is that Adler's insistence that the oral law is necessary to understand Scripture is analogous to the Roman Catholic claim that Scripture is impenetrable without the authoritative tradition of the Church. Yet Adler expects Jews to read this 'impenetrable' Scripture every week in the synagogue without the accompanying interpretation of the oral law that he claims is necessary to understand it. This, Marks claims, is less consistent than the Catholic practice, which discourages the ordinary believer from reading and studying Scripture. Thus sermons, in their oral and published forms, became part of a continuing debate between the two streams of nineteenth-century British Judaism, engendering considerable discussion in articles and letters to the Jewish press.[112]

In addition to the oral law, the sabbath became a major issue of contention between the Orthodox and Reform movements. This institution came under great pressure in the nineteenth century as Jewish workers became more integrated into the general economy. British and American preachers across the spectrum of Judaism tried to defend its integrity and railed against its violation. The similarity in their rhetoric of rebuke bespeaks a serious underlying social problem that the pulpit alone was incapable of redressing.

As early as 1841, a sermon delivered in Charleston, South Carolina, where the first Reform synagogue in the United States had been established, railed against the 'new ways, including the violation of the festivals and Sabbaths', by those who 'fear being impoverished by our forsaking our daily toil'.[113] A

---

[111] N. Adler, 'Solomon's Judgment'; I used the copy at the Cambridge University Library.

[112] Marks, *Torah Or, 'The Law Is Light'*, 5, 19, 23, 10. For examples of some withering polemical sermons against Liberal Judaism from the twentieth century, see J. Hertz, 'The "Strange Fire" of Schism', and *The New Paths*.

[113] 'The Dangers of Israel', dated Charleston, 19 Feb. 1841, but not published in the *Occident* until more than two years later: <www.jewish-history.com/Occident/volume1/june1843/danger.html>. The author of the sermon is not identified, but may have been Jacob DeLaMotta, who led the traditionalists at this time. For the conflict that inspired it, see Meyer, *Response to Modernity*, 233–5; Sarna, *American Judaism*, 83–6; Tarshish, 'The Charleston Organ Case', 411–49; Hagy, *This Happy Land*, 240–56.

generation later, in a Rosh Hashanah sermon, Isaac Mayer Wise insisted that
the proper observance of the sabbath was one of the absolute obligations of the
Jew. Other rabbis recognized with empathy the problem of those who cannot
control their hours of work. Therefore the option of shifting the main weekly
worship service to Sunday became a polarizing issue even within the Reform
movement, not to mention between Reform and Orthodox rabbis. In his inaugural sermon at Chicago's Sinai Congregation on Rosh Hashanah 1880, Emil
G. Hirsch explained why he wanted to hold services on Sunday. In 1888
Kaufmann Kohler preached at Temple Beth-El in New York on the topic 'Are
Sunday Lectures Treason to Judaism?', and after Joseph Krauskopf instituted
a Sunday morning service at congregation Keneseth Israel in Philadelphia, his
associate J. Leonard Levy devoted one of his Sunday morning lectures to the
topic 'Which Sabbath Ought We Observe?'[114]

Such tinkering with the rhythms of the Jewish calendar infuriated the
traditionalists. On 15 December 1888 Benjamin Szold of Baltimore preached
in German (perhaps responding to Krauskopf) on the topic 'The Sabbath';
the title of the address, announced in advance, attracted a large audience.
After rehearsing the reasons for the traditional observance of the sabbath,
Szold delivered as the heart of the sermon a polemic against synagogues that
hold 'public divine service' on Sunday, even if they retain the sabbath on its
traditional day. These, he maintains in his rhetorical climax, are like politicians who straddle the fence, bigamists, or 'Jews who, in order to keep on
good terms with both Jews and Christians, wind the *Tephilin* about their left
hand and with the right grasp the rosary'.[115] The text of the sermon was published shortly afterwards. The same year, another pamphlet was published
with the title *Sabbath or Sunday?*, containing three sermons delivered by
David Davidson at a Cincinnati congregation. Although a preceptor at the
Reform movement's Hebrew Union College, Davidson took the same position as Szold, denouncing those rabbis who would abolish the sabbath in
favour of Sunday, but also excoriating the rabbi who preaches on both days as
'the veritable double-faced Janus', guilty of making 'war against Judaism,
principle, self-respect'.[116] Clearly this was a battle being waged from the

---

[114] E. G. Hirsch, 'The Crossing of the Jordan', 152 ('I deny that this step [to provide services on
Sunday morning for those unable to attend on the sabbath] is a surrender of Jewish principles');
K. Kohler, 'Are Sunday Lectures Treason to Judaism?' 19–30; J. L. Levy, 'Which Sabbath Ought
We Observe?' For a review of the debate in the 1870s sparked by Kohler's instituting the Sunday
service in Chicago, see Olitzky, 'Sundays at Chicago Sinai Congregation', 359–61; also 363–3 and
365 on Hirsch.                                          [115] Szold, 'The Sabbath', 6, 12.
[116] D. Davidson, *Sabbath or Sunday?*, preface. Cf. also Hermann Gollancz's 1895 sermons on
'The Sabbath' and 'Which Is the True Sabbath?' and Joseph Hertz's scathing condemnation of
the Sunday service (and especially Emil G. Hirsch) in *The New Paths*, 10–11.

pulpits and the printing presses, and being followed with considerable interest in the community.[117]

Another doctrine that aroused considerable controversy, in the context of both internal Jewish disagreements and the continuing tension with Christian missionaries, was the doctrine of the messiah and the ultimate redemption of the Jewish people. David de Sola, preaching at the Bevis Marks Synagogue on the sabbath following the fast-day of Tishah Be'av (Sabbath 'Nahamu') of 1833, noted that it had been an 'invariable custom' in this congregation and others that sermons on this sabbath be devoted to the subject of the 'future restoration'. He therefore set out to provide 'clear proofs'—from Scripture, plain reasoning, and historical sources— that this restoration was yet to come. The sermon was published in pamphlet form soon after its delivery.[118] A few years later, Isaac Leeser devoted seven discourses over a period of fourteen months to the topic of the messiah in the context of Christian missionary activity in the United States.[119] That the doctrine of the messianic restoration remained a significant point of controversy within Judaism is clear from the statement by Emil G. Hirsch of Chicago near the beginning of the following century: 'Nine hundred and ninety-nine out of every thousand Orthodox Jews who pray regularly to go back to Jerusalem would be stricken with apoplexy if the messiah should suddenly announce that they could go back.'[120]

A sermon for the sabbath following Tishah Be'av delivered in the early 1840s by David Woolf Marks, and published in the American *Occident* of November 1843, reveals the shift of focus in this debate from the internal concerns of Jewish belief to the external context. In some ways it is quite traditional, echoing a famous statement by Moses Mendelssohn that 'the Scriptural view of Israel's restoration does not in the remotest degree affect us in any of the duties we, as good and loyal citizens, owe to our country, nor does it in any way prevent us from rendering ourselves useful in the land of our birth'.[121] But Marks

[117] The sabbath was not the only controversial occasion in the Jewish calendar. The Reform innovation of confirmation on the holiday of Shavuot was also defended from the pulpit, as in the sermon by S. M. Schiller-Szinessy at Manchester on the first day of the holiday (24 May) in 1852, when the first confirmation was held in the Halliwell Street Synagogue: 'Confirmation: a Genuine Jewish Institution'. A strong defence of Reform was given by Schiller-Szinessy in his sermon at the dedication of the congregation's new synagogue on 25 Mar. 1858, as recorded in the *Jewish Chronicle* of 9 Apr. 1858.

[118] Sola, 'Consolation of Jerusalem', 4, 17, 20; I used the copy of this sermon in the British Library.                      [119] Sussman, *Isaac Leeser*, 87; Leeser, *Discourses*, ii. 253–372.

[120] *New York Times*, 15 Nov. 1909, p. 6.

[121] On the sabbath before Passover in 1842 the Revd Abraham Rice of Baltimore delivered a sermon on 'The Messiah' making the same assertion: 'The idea of Messiah has nothing to do with the state; we can and should do nothing to hasten the time of his coming; all we have to do is to observe our laws in such a manner that it may be the pleasure of the Most High, to hasten the approach of this time. But so long as we live among the gentiles, we are commanded to obey

then goes on to mobilize his conclusion—that the redemption will be achieved 'through the immediate and miraculous work of God, and not by the combination of human powers'—in the service of a broader polemic. He refers to 'many hundreds of enthusiasts [in this country], who fancy themselves the immediate agents of God for bringing about the salvation of Israel', in contradiction to 'plain Scriptural doctrine'. Responding to the charge 'that we do not take to heart the consequences of the societies that are forming about us, and that we make no effort to oppose the attempts that are made to convert [us]', he continues,

My friends, we do take these things to heart. We deeply lament that, in days of such universal privation and distress . . . the vast sums which are annually expended upon an attempt which eighteen centuries have proved to be vain and hopeless, are not directed to a quarter where sorrow might be alleviated, where the hungry might be fed, the naked clothed . . . But as regards Judaism itself, we have no fears from such societies . . . [W]e rely principally upon the truth of the word of God, that He will ever be a wall round his people, that He will preserve them in their faith and identity as his great witnesses to the end of time.

Thus, with considerable rhetorical skill, the theological claim that redemption is a supernatural event that cannot be effected by human initiatives is used to undermine the efforts of Christian 'enthusiasts', within a context of concern for victims of socio-economic deprivation, for whom the resources mobilized to convert the Jews could more humanely be directed.[122]

Sometimes rabbis felt compelled to transcend the niceties of allusion and euphemism to address the Christian challenge directly. As already noted, beginning in October 1835 Isaac Leeser devoted a series of seven sermons to the Jewish concept of the messiah, which he published in the second volume of his *Discourses* in 1837. Near the beginning of the first of these addresses he spends more than a page summarizing the 'Nazarene' doctrine of the messiah held by 'our opponents', before outlining the Jewish teaching, which itself is interspersed with a sustained polemic: 'The absurdity of a divided deity is thus made perfectly manifest, it being so completely disconsonant with common

the laws of the respective states. A clear proof of the truth of this position is furnished us by the prophet Jeremiah.' For Mendelssohn's statement about the belief in Jewish redemption and duties as a citizen, see Mendes-Flohr and Reinharz, *The Jew in the Modern World*, 48–9. Unlike Marks, Rice does not include any clear allusion to Christian doctrines or missionary efforts; his argument in this sermon is against Jews who question the need for, or reasonableness of, this belief.

[122] Marks, 'Sermon on the Sabbath Nahamoo'. Cf. sermon 14 in vol. i of Marks's *Sermons Preached on Various Occasions*, dated Sabbath 'Nahamu', 12 Aug. 5603 (1843), which is quite similar in theme, but with a different biblical text and virtually no actual verbal repetition. The sermon published in the Nov. 1843 *Occident* must therefore have been delivered earlier, perhaps in the summer of 1842. For the Christian missionary societies focused on Jews, see Scult, *Millennial Expectations*, ch. 6; Endelman, *Radical Assimilation*, ch. 5.

sense.' The doctrine of the incarnation is 'an invention of heathen poets'. These long discourses repeat arguments made by Jewish authors over many centuries; perhaps the most interesting passage is Leeser's defence in the second of them of his outspoken, even belligerent, pulpit style:

Now, although it is abhorrent to all correct sentiment to attack others, or to wound their feelings in so essential a point as religion, still would that cowardice be much more blameworthy which would prevent Jews from speaking of their own laws in their own assemblies, in a country where equal rights are guaranteed to all the inhabitants by the constitution and the laws of the land . . . Complaisance and forbearance are, truly speaking, great virtues, which ought to be cultivated; but their exercise should never degrade them into the kindred vices of affected politeness and meanness; and better far would it be were our mouths stopped by the violent arm of arbitrary rule, than that we should surrender tamely to worldly expediency what we refused to yield amidst the heavy persecutions we had to encounter—I mean the right of honestly believing the truth and of boldly expressing what we believe.[123]

In England, both Nathan Adler and David Woolf Marks published collections of sermons responding to missionary arguments that they must have felt were taking a toll. Adler's was first, published in 1869. Here he mentions specifically the Societies for Promoting Christianity among Jews, which, he maintains, turn 'bad Jews into worse Christians'.[124] Marks waited until 1884 before publishing nineteen lectures that focus on issues that divide Christians and Jews, one of them a response to the February 1872 issue of the journal *Hebrew Christian Inquiries*, which had criticized him.[125] American rabbis of the next generation also argued openly against Christian doctrines, undoubtedly in response to missionary efforts directed against the wave of east European immigrants. Thus Joseph Krauskopf of Philadelphia devoted major addresses to the topic 'Jesus—Man or God?' both in 1900 and in 1915, and in 1901 gave a series of six lectures (later published as a book) on 'A Rabbi's Impressions of the Oberammergau Passion Play'.[126]

## Jewish Suffering

Jewish preaching was always responsive to suffering within the local community. During or after a period of distress the preacher was expected to articulate

---

[123] Leeser, *Discourses*, ii. 254, 269, 270–1. In 1850 he returned to the apologetic mode, noting that there is occasional need for a 'controversial sermon' in order to prove the superiority of the Jewish religion; much of the discourse is devoted to a rebuttal of the need for vicarious atonement ('God our Atonement', 341–2). [124] N. Adler, *Naftulei Elohim*, 2.

[125] Marks, *Lectures and Sermons Preached on Various Occasions*, 132.

[126] In the foreword to his book on the Passion Play, Krauskopf referred to 'the widespread interest which the treatment of the subject awakened, and the keen desire of large audiences, and of a yet larger reading public—both of Jews and non-Jews—to hear and read more and more' (*A Rabbi's Impressions*, 11).

some interpretation and guidance that would comfort and reassure the listeners, and inspire them to keep the faith.[127] It is not until the seventeenth century, however, that we begin to find responses from the pulpit to hardships suffered by Jewish communities in other countries.[128] In the nineteenth century, improved communications brought distant Jewish communities psychologically closer together; alongside the identification with the national welfare demonstrated in sermons on government-proclaimed occasions (see above), we find increasing evidence of response to the suffering of Jews far away, usually alongside a call to practical measures of assistance. The phenomenon of a new 'antisemitism' itself became an increasingly popular topos for sermons.[129] The celebrated legal cases against Alfred Dreyfus in France (1894–1906),[130] Mendel Beilis in Ukraine (1913),[131] and Leo Frank in Georgia (1913) generated powerful responses from the pulpit.[132]

Not surprisingly, especially strong emotions were aroused by reports of violent attacks against Jews. An early example is provided by the notorious Damascus Affair of 1840. On 24 July (23 Tammuz) 1840, Isaac Leeser delivered in Philadelphia a sermon called 'The Sorrows of Israel'. As appropriate for the weeks leading up to Tishah Be'av, a day of mourning for the destruction of the Temples and other catastrophes, he recounted at great length and with considerable rhetorical power the sufferings of Jewish people through history. Despite the hope that conditions were improving, zealots and fanatics were still attempting to extinguish the lamp of Israel:

---

[127] M. Saperstein, *Jewish Preaching*, 167–79, 286–300.

[128] See e.g. the sermon by Saul Levi Morteira that I have analysed in *Exile in Amsterdam*, 123–40, 393–407.

[129] An early example is Lilienthal, 'The Prejudice against the Jews', 9–10; also E. G. Hirsch, 'The Ancient Anti-Semite and his Modern Successors'; Singer, 'Answer Him Not'; Joseph, *The Message of Judaism*, 80–8.

[130] See esp. Chief Rabbi Hermann Adler's Yom Kippur 1899 sermon at the Great Synagogue in London (cited above to illustrate Adler's use of American poetry: see n. 83). While the second part of the sermon is devoted, appropriately, to the religious failings of British Jewry, the first part is a powerful condemnation of France: the day the decision was rendered was for France 'more disastrous than Waterloo, more humiliating than Sedan'. Cf. *Jewish Chronicle*, 22 Sept. 1899, p. 23, on Haham Gaster's 'impassioned and eloquent language on the Dreyfus Affair' the same day; and, in the United States, Krauskopf, 'Condemned Unheard'.

[131] See the extensive quotations from sermons on the Beilis trial in *Jewish Chronicle*, 17 Oct. 1913, pp. 14–15 (A. A. Green, Joseph Hochman) and 24 Oct. 1913, pp. 27–8 (D. Wasserzug, Joseph H. Hertz).

[132] On the Leo Frank case, see S. S. Wise, 'The Case of Leo Frank': 'What this pulpit speaks today ought to be spoken in ten thousand pulpits of as many Christian churches . . . I remember well that not a few Jews in France maintained in the dark and troublous Dreyfus days that it were better to let one Jew perish than expose all his people to peril. There are times when a life must be defended zealously because it represents a principle that ought to stand' (p. 85). See also Krauskopf, 'To the Front', 7.

The same fables, the falsity of which has been often proved, the absurdity of which is too apparent to deserve a serious refutation, have been again revived, and it has been said that we need the blood of gentile victims to celebrate our sacred festivals. The Mussulman and the Papist have joined hands to fasten this foul charge upon our brothers of the East; and many have been dragged to prison, subjected to torture and every species of cruelty, nay, some are said to have expired under the infliction of their fiendish persecutors. Ay, these victims have cried for help, but none stood forth to aid them!

The sermon continues with a very conventional response to this situation: a tirade of self-criticism, directed against those Jews who have aroused the cupidity of their neighbours by their accumulation of wealth, become indifferent to religion, and forgotten the Jew's obligations to God: 'We ate the food which his law prohibits; we violated the Sabbath of his ordaining; we intermarried with the gentile women . . . we refused to circumcise our male children; we reformed, as we called it, our simple worship.' The suffering of the Jews in Damascus is presented here not as a call to active political or financial support, but as a warning of the divine punishment that may be looming over the Jews of the United States: 'May not the reports we hear be the muttering of the distant thunder, which ere long may burst over our own heads, in all the fierceness of a destroying storm?' This is the traditional pattern of rebuke, reaffirming the ancient model of sin and punishment.[133]

Towards the end of 1859, in the context of an invasion by Spanish forces, Jews in Morocco were subjected to attacks by fanatical local Muslims, and thousands fled across the Straits to seek refuge in Gibraltar. Sermons by London rabbis were reported in issues of the *Jewish Chronicle and Hebrew Observer* from November that year. The correspondent reporting on the sermon given on 19 November by David Woolf Marks writes that the preacher applied the concluding phrase of Deuteronomy 6: 5, 'with all your means', to the situation of the Moroccan Jews: '3000 of your fellow-worshippers, huddled together near the rock of Gibraltar, without the shelter of a roof, and barely supplied with a daily ration of bread, and who . . . have abandoned the land where they were born . . . to become exiles and mendicants'. The preacher praised the compassion of the Governor of Gibraltar, but—again according to the correspondent—

---

[133] Leeser, *Discourses*, iii. 158–9, 164, 168; cf. Sussman, *Isaac Leeser*, 109. A month later, Leeser was the principal speaker at a large Philadelphia protest meeting on behalf of Damascus Jews, stressing a unity of Jews throughout the world that did not conflict with their duties as citizens to the countries in which they lived: *Discourses*, iii. 347–64; Sussman, 111–12. Both sermons evoke what has come to be called the 'lachrymose conception' of Jewish experience in exile, illustrated in the protest address by a citation from Byron's 'Hebrew Melodies' (p. 350). The best current study of the events and their repercussions outside the Middle East is Frankel, *The Damascus Affair*.

drew a contrast between the enlarged views of the Christian philanthropists of
Gibraltar and the narrow and sectarian spirit (as he described it) manifested by the
[Jewish] Board of Deputies, which even on the neutral ground of charity would not so
overcome its sectarian prejudice as to invite the co-operation in the general movement
of the members of the West London Synagogue.

The sermon concluded with a 'stirring appeal to every congregant' for contributions to aid the needy.[134]

The sermon delivered by Hermann Adler on 28 May 1881 in response to the
news of pogroms against the Jews of Russia harks back to the 'internal rebuke'
model of Isaac Leeser. The actual text has apparently not been preserved;
according to the summary in the *Jewish Chronicle*, the preacher

dwelt earnestly on the duty of every Jew to do his part toward silencing the voice of
calumny by showing forth genuine patriotism, shunning every dishonest deed and act,
discarding every dishonourable means of earning a livelihood, refraining from obtru-
siveness, love of display, and extravagant luxury, and by cultivating a dignified self-
respect. He besought his hearers, many of whom were natives of the country in which
such deplorable outrages had recently taken place, to prove their sympathy with their
brethren by contributing to their relief, and to help in the banishing of all racial
antipathies and religious discord.[135]

Greater focus on the actual events is revealed in the sermon delivered by
J. Polack on 19 June at a special Sunday service in Liverpool, reporting that 'ten
thousand Jews in one district of Russia had been rendered homeless in one day,
and the stopping of telegraphic communication, with postal censorship, prevented the full extent of the atrocities from being presented to the people of
this country'.[136]

Among the array of responses elicited by the pogroms of 1881–2 were the
special *seliḥot* prayer services for forgiveness held in communities throughout
the Russian Pale of Settlement, sometimes accompanied by the rabbinical
declaration of a penitential fast. These services often included a sermon by the
communal rabbi or a respected layman, which generally reaffirmed the traditional doctrine of persecution as punishment for Jewish sins, but also incorporated other elements such as calls for charitable contributions to assist the
victims of the attacks, rebuke of the behaviour of wealthy Jews in the commun-

---

[134] *Jewish Chronicle and Hebrew Observer*, 25 Nov. 1859, p. 7. This sermon was not included in
the second volume of Marks's sermons; I was directed to this text by Curtis Cassell's unpublished
biography of Marks. The previous issue of the *Chronicle* (vol. 16, no. 257, 18 Nov. 1858, p. 5) reports
the sermon delivered by the Revd A. L. Green on 12 Nov.
[135] *Jewish Chronicle*, 3 June 1881, p. 11. The summary of the sermon Adler gave five weeks later
at a Manchester rally and appeal for relief funds also includes an element of self-criticism,
describing inappropriate behaviour by Jews in England (*Jewish Chronicle*, 8 July 1881, p. 6).
[136] *Jewish Chronicle*, 24 June 1881, p. 8.

ity, discussion of emigration to the Land of Israel, denunciations of anti-semitism, and implied criticism of the government.[137]

An especially powerful event occurred at a special service on a day of public fasting (observed even by the 'enlightened' Jews) held at St Petersburg on 18 January 1882. The sermon was delivered by the state rabbi, Avraam Drabkin (one of the first rabbis to preach in Russian), who chose as his text from the weekly biblical lesson the obviously resonant verse, 'The foe said, I will pursue, I will overtake, I will divide the spoil' (Exod. 15: 9). The journalist Peretz Smolenskin, describing the occasion, wrote,

My pen trembles in my hand as I recall the impact these words had on those present in the synagogue. It was as if a single sigh burst forth from the hearts of all the lis-teners, quickly transformed into a thunderous sound that made the walls of the syn-agogue rattle . . . Rabbi Drabkin had to desist from his sermon for about ten minutes until those present were able to restrain their weeping. Then he went on to compare the fate of the Jewish people to the fate of the righteous Joseph: 'Like our people in its exile among the nations that make its life bitter, so was Joseph hated by his broth-ers, who could not speak well of him. "Joseph recognized his brothers, but they did not recognize him" (Gen. 42: 8)'.

According to the report of the distinguished Zionist Mordecai ben Hillel Hakohen (less detailed on the content than Smolenskin), 'even the rabbi who was preaching could not restrain himself: he covered his face with his hands, and wept like a small child'.[138]

In 1905 another series of pogroms swept through the Pale of Settlement as the tsarist forces suppressed an abortive revolt. On 11 November Rabbi Hermann Gollancz addressed the Bayswater Synagogue with a strong attack on both the perpetrators and the bystanders. At the very outset, the theolog-ical question is raised: 'Who can read the accounts which have reached us during the past week . . . without asking, "Is there a God in the world? Have judgement and justice ceased to exist?"' Most of the sermon, however, focuses on human behaviour. This was not spontaneous plunder carried out by the lowest class; according to 'unimpeachable authority', it was 'directly engineered and encouraged, ordered and paid for, by men who wear an official uniform'.

[137] I owe this information, based on reports in contemporary periodicals, to Professor John D. Klier of University College London. Prof. Klier is preparing an extended study of the pogroms and the Jewish responses to them.
[138] Dinaburg (Dinur), 'From the Archive of Peretz Smolenskin' (Heb.), 81. Smolenskin went on to report that newspaper correspondents were present, and that they asked for the text of Drabkin's sermon so that they could print it in Russian as an accurate, detailed account of the fast, but that no report was printed, lest sympathy for the Jews be aroused in the hearts of the indif-ferent Russian population (pp. 81–2). See Hakohen, *Olami*, i. 192–4 (I owe this reference to Benjamin Nathans). On the impact of the sermon, see Dubnow, *History of the Jews in Russia and Poland*, ii. 286; cf. Elon, *The Israelis*, 72.

Therefore, it was not enough for Christians to express their sympathy for their Jewish fellow citizens. The civilized world, the representatives of the Christian Church, the British and American governments, must intervene and act to teach Russia 'the lessons which are necessary and which brook no delay, unless the world is prepared to witness the most terrific conflagration, which will involve, if not a larger area, at least the whole continent of Europe'. As for the Jews, the crisis of their brethren in Russia 'is a blow dealt out to *us*'. Practically, 'we Jews, elements of one body, must do our utmost to relieve the present dire distress'.[139]

During the First World War, reports reached the west about the suffering of Jews in eastern Europe, near the front between German and Russian forces. The sermon devoted to this topic by Rabbi George (Gedaliah) Silverstone of Washington, DC in October 1914 is printed below (Sermon 15). A year later, as the Russian armies were driven back, the civilian Jewish populations began again to suffer intense upheaval. The *Jewish Chronicle* of 5 November 1915 carried a headline (albeit on an inside page) proclaiming in large type: 'The Russo-Polish Agony: Horrors of the Russian Holocaust: Eloquent Appeals at Representative Meeting'. A subsection of the article, entitled 'Dr. Gaster's Eloquent Appeal', included a long quotation from an address given by the haham of the Spanish and Portuguese community in London.[140] Hermann Gollancz had already addressed this issue, exhorting his listeners on 23 September 1915:

Let us not forget the claims of our sorely oppressed brethren, especially in the land of Eastern Europe, whose unfortunate lot it has been to reside in those districts which have twice or three times been the camping-grounds or battlefields of the respective fighting sides. The misery of these tens of thousands, hundreds of thousands, it is possible that the number may reach millions, of our own kith and kin—brother Jews and sister Jewesses—is appalling ... Have a care for these, too, as the appeals for help reach your ears. May they reach your hearts![141]

---

[139] Gollancz, 'The Russian Crisis'. Cf. the address delivered by the chief rabbi, Hermann Adler, eight days later, at a special service held at the Great Synagogue 'in memory of the martyrs who perished during the Russian massacres', 'The Russo-Jewish Martyrs'. See also Gollancz's sermons on Kishinev ('The Prayer *Av ha-Rahamim*' and 'Kischineff!!'); E. G. Hirsch, 'The Responsibility for the Russian Massacres'; Freudenthal, 'Predigt bei der Trauerfeier'; and the review of addresses at public rallies in C. Adler, *The Voice of America on Kishineff*, esp. 65–6 (David Philipson) and 169–74 (Krauskopf).

[140] *Jewish Chronicle*, 5 Nov. 1915, pp. 16, 18. Gaster was the haham of the Spanish and Portuguese community, and his 'eloquent appeal' on behalf of the east European Ashkenazi Jews was a strong sign of Jewish solidarity.

[141] Gollancz, 'The War and the Jews of Eastern Europe', 241. Gollancz returned to this theme in Jan. 1917 with a sermon entitled 'Agony Cry of a Brother', a poignant appeal on behalf of the Jews in Russia and Eastern Europe suffering from 'ruin, starvation, death'.

American rabbis, though removed from the actual area of the war, were not insensitive to the suffering of their relatives in eastern Europe, and conveyed the realities with considerable pathos. On the sabbath following Tishah Be'av in 1916, Elihu Wolf Kochin, an Orthodox rabbi in Pittsburgh, evoked suffering of monumental proportions:

In this year—the third in which most of the Jews of Europe are in great distress— many thousands of Jews have fallen on the battlefield, leaving countless widows and orphans, hungry, destitute of everything. The terrible murders occurring in Russia right now are unimaginable, the pen cannot describe the condition of Israel . . . Many thousands of Jews have died or were killed at home because of false libels invented against them. As for the old, the women and children left alive, the Russian military commanders have moved them into the interior of Russia, to an unfamiliar place where no Jew has ever lived because of the evil decree prohibiting Jews from living there. But now, during the war, the decree has been removed, and they have deported the Jews of Lithuania and Poland. But even there they have found no rest; thousands of Jews have died there of hunger, and no native Jews are there to take pity on the refugees. From the time our land was destroyed, no sorrow has befallen Israel like that of these years, and who knows when the end of it will come, when Judah and Israel will be saved? For the new sorrows are such that they make the old ones forgotten.[142]

Following the armistice, the situation of the Jews in Poland continued to deteriorate, and on 26 June 1919 a service of prayer and mourning was held in London at which Chief Rabbi Hertz preached on 'Our Polish Brethren'. Presenting a historical review of east European Jewry before, during and after the war, he described in detail pogroms in Minsk and Vilna, concluding that while the Allies might have no responsibility for the massacres of Jews in Ukraine, they did indeed bear responsibility for the violence in Poland.[143]

These sermons provide a useful background for the homiletical responses to the far greater catastrophes undergone by European Jewry during the Nazi period. Here I must pass over sermons from the pre-war period to focus on what rabbis were saying on the High Holy Days during the war, as the news

[142] Kochin, 'Sermon on Sabbath *Naḥamu*' (Heb.), 8; my translation. See also the powerful evocation of the suffering of east European Jews and the fierce condemnation of American Jews for their indifference in a sermon by Moses Simon Sivitz of Pittsburgh delivered in Feb. 1917: 'Eulogy for Those Who Have Fallen in the War' (Heb.), 244–6 (I am grateful to Kimmy Caplan for directing me to these texts). On the 'wholesale expulsions' of the Jewish population from the war zone beginning in the spring of 1915, see *The Jews in the Eastern War Zone* (New York: American Jewish Committee, 1916), 61–7, 98–9.

[143] J. Hertz, 'Our Polish Brethren'. Morris Joseph also participated in this service of prayer and mourning (Kershen and Romain, *Tradition and Change*, 120); his horror at the suffering of east European Jews and the general state of 'direst poverty, famine, and disease, and despair' following the armistice is expressed in *The Spirit of Judaism*, 220. In the United States, see Krauskopf, 'The Ukrainian Pogroms', concluding, 'We made it our war-cry, "A World Safe for Democracy". Let our peace-cry be: "A World Safe for the Jew".'

from Europe became progressively bleaker. Sermons from 1939, delivered soon after the outbreak of war and the fall of Poland, already reveal a sense of gloom stemming from what was perceived as unprecedented disaster. With a perspicacity perhaps transcending what the empirical evidence justified at that time, the New York Conservative rabbi Jacob Bosniak spoke of the Nazi programme, adopted six years previously, as calling for 'the destruction and annihilation of the Jews all over the world'.

These sermons evince more than just a sense of threatened disaster; they reflect a perception of unprecedented fatefulness. Bosniak continued, 'We live in a moment of historic significance when the fate of our people, nay the fate of the entire world is in the balance.' His fellow Conservative rabbi Israel Levinthal noted, 'We find ourselves today in one of the saddest moments in world history, and certainly in Jewish history', continuing:

The impossible has come to pass ... 'The world is hanging on nothingness' (Job 26: 7) ... It is hanging on a thread; any moment it may fall in ruins. All civilization is threatened with annihilation!

As far as the Jew is concerned, there is no period in his sorrowful past that offers a parallel to the tragedy that has come upon him today ... And the worst of all is our helplessness! It seems that there is no ray of comfort for us ... We stand bewildered. We cannot believe our eyes. After all, this is the twentieth century. How, then, is it possible for the world to become once more an arena of bloodshed? ...

We are baffled and we ask: Wherefore has this destruction come? [144]

During 1940 the situation deteriorated considerably, with the German conquest of western Europe (including the stunning fall of France) and the bombing of London. Without minimizing the suffering endured by other victims of Nazism in Europe, many recognized that the Jewish fate was unique. Here is Reform rabbi Irving Reichert in San Francisco:

But however grimly the world tragedy has affected the mood and temper of the generality of mankind, to us of the House of Israel its results and implications are vastly more appalling. For not only has the Jew participated in the common anguish of his countrymen in lands despoiled by tyranny, but he has been deliberately singled out for added indignities that exhaust the repertory of persecution. Jewish life has been destroyed in a thousand communities where once it flourished brilliantly ... Pauperism and degradation, torture and banishment have been meted out to our people in lands whose glory they established with gifts of genius and generosity. [145]

Against this background, rabbis refer to the toll the events are taking on Jewish morale, with sermons on the motif 'Where is your God?' ('Ayeh eloheikha?': Ps.

[144] Bosniak, 'The Distinction of the Jew', 48–9; Levinthal, 'Wherefore Is the Earth Destroyed?', 40. [145] Reichert, 'How Can We Find Happiness in the New Year?', 225.

42: 4). Jacob Rudin, a disciple of Stephen S. Wise, was only one of many who invoked this theme:

I address myself to the central question that flung itself mockingly upon my mind. The question which has been asked me time and time again, the question which I know is in your minds and upon your hearts.

Where is God in this blackout of humanity? How can he permit this savagery to come to pass? How can He allow the destruction of little children, of cities and of homes, to go on unchecked?[146]

Answers ranged from the assertion that the suffering was divine punishment, for the failure of Western civilization to live by God's moral values, to Rudin's insistence that God was in the bomb shelter with the victims.

The High Holy Days of 1941 were overshadowed by the lightning German invasion into the Soviet heartland and the consignment of almost two million more Jews to Nazi domination. Some preachers emphasized the universal nature of the calamity. Israel Levinthal said that beyond 'the agonizing cry of the millions of souls that have departed on the battle-field or in bomb-stricken lands of Europe . . . It is the Soul of the World that is departing!' (see Sermon 26). Others laid greater stress on the unique Jewish role as victim. In Leeds, Eliezer Berkovits—somewhat ironically, in the light of what was to come—said, 'In the course of the last year the Jewish Tragedy has reached a climax which can hardly be surpassed. The Jewish nation is bleeding from a thousand and more wounds.'[147]

By September 1942 reports of a concerted policy of mass murder of Jews by the Nazis had been publicized in the western media. Rabbis again strained to find words that would express the dimensions of the disaster, now worse than had been imaginable at the time of their earlier sermons. On Rosh Hashanah, Harold Saperstein of Long Island referred back to the previous June, when German forces had executed all the men in the Czech town of Lidice and burned it to the ground in retaliation for the assassination of Reinhard Heydrich.

We Jews, unheralded, have had thousands of Lidices. Community after community has been destroyed; communities [that] now have not a single living Jew. The expressed purpose of the Nazis has been the complete elimination of the Jews from Europe. Fortunately, there are limits to the human imagination. For if we really comprehended what the news items reveal of the unending exile and deportation, the pitiless scourges of famine and disease bound up with ghettoization, the ruthless slaughter, we could no longer eat or sleep. We would not be human if we could ever laugh again. And yet the news reports are understatements of the reality.[148]

---

[146] Rudin, 'God In the Blackout—1940', 235–6 (for the entire text, see Sermon 23 below).
[147] Levinthal, 'Is It Death or Rebirth of the World that We Behold?', 10; Berkovits, 'God's Precious Son', 87.          [148] H. Saperstein, 'The Mount of Sacrifice', 94.

In his 1943 Kol Nidrei sermon, an Orthodox rabbi in the Bronx, Akiba Predmesky, dramatically assumed the role of the messenger of disaster to the high priest, Eli, in 1 Samuel 4. Each component of the heartrending news is presented in its original context, then applied to the present. 'Israel has fled before its enemies and there has been a great slaughter among the people.'

Aye, from the English Channel to the Mediterranean, from the Baltic to the Black Sea, from the marsh-lands of Russia to the yellow earth of China, Israel has been defeated. In the past year, two million Jews have been murdered in cold blood, in Hitler's Europe alone. Five millions more are now imprisoned behind thick Ghetto walls and enslaved in his labour camps, driven out of all phases of normal economic life, forced to wear yellow patches and armbands as a badge of shame. Everywhere millions of Jews have been robbed, despoiled, disfranchised, tortured and degraded.

The second component of the message, the news that Eli's two sons have been killed, personalizes it for the aged high priest; this too Predmesky applies to the congregation: 'How many of us who are here tonight had fathers and mothers in Poland, brothers and sisters in Germany, relatives and friends in Russia, of whom we have not heard since the beginning of the war . . .?' By this time, the congregation knew what was to follow:

But there is still a third and more tragic message that I must bring to you on this holy eve—a message which even the heroic High Priest Eli felt to be the most heart-rending and the most threatening of all: *va-aron he-Elohim nilkahah*, the Ark of G-d has been taken by the enemy! In every land that has been conquered, in every country that has been vanquished, in every city where the hordes of barbarians have passed, our synagogues have been burned to the ground, the Holy Arks desecrated, and the Sifrei Torah, the Scrolls of the Law, trodden and spat upon. Our great schools of learning in Lithuania and Poland are closed; our famous Yeshivoth of Slobodka, Telz, Mir, destroyed; and countless numbers of their scholars, rabbis, and leaders, tortured and executed. It is in this last phase of destruction, in this capture of the Ark of G-d, that our greatest danger lies. A danger that threatens the very survival of our people, a danger that imperils the immortality of Israel.

Stepping back from the tragedy evoked by these words, one may appreciate them as a magnificent moment of homiletical theatre, cogent application of one of the bleakest chapters in the Bible, skilful building to a climactic moment to which the listeners must have responded with intense anguish and sorrow.[149]

---

[149] Predmesky, 'The Ark of G-d Has Been Taken', 55, 57–8. Cf. also J. Hertz, 'The "Battle of Warsaw"', a sermon delivered eight months later, at a special 'service of mourning and prayer for the Martyrs of the Warsaw Ghetto', in which the preacher mourns the murder of 'at least three million' Jews, the 'mass crucifixion of a whole people', warns of the danger awaiting nearly a million more now 'at the brink of annihilation through the nazification of Hungary', and condemns the general silence in the Allied countries and the 'strange reticence and heathen indifference' of the lay leaders of Anglo-Jewry.

The texts of these sermons reveal that large numbers of Jewish listeners in synagogues were exposed to powerful presentations of the incipient disaster, based on the best available information. These texts challenge the claim of a 'deafening silence' over the fate of European Jewry. I doubt that there was any American rabbi in the three major movements (I am not competent to judge about the ultra-Orthodox community) who failed to address the European Jewish tragedy in at least one High Holy Day sermon in each of the years reviewed here. While some preachers tried to reassure their congregations by evoking the survival of the Jewish people despite persecution in previous ages, others intuited and even tried to articulate the insight that this was something fundamentally new.

Yet there was no plausible political response to this disaster. The hortatory element in the sermons is primarily religious: keep the faith, do not despair about being a Jew, shoulder with energy the grave responsibilities of ensuring Jewish survival in the United States, give generously to Jewish welfare institutions that are alleviating the plight of victims in Nazi-occupied Europe, fight the forces of intolerance, oppression, and divisiveness in American society, support the embattled Jewish community of Palestine. At the beginning of the Nazi regime the issues for American Jews, reflected in strong sermons on the High Holy Days of 1933, seem to be more controversial: public anti-Nazi demonstrations, the economic boycott of Nazi Germany. Once the war begins, there is a sense of bewilderment and helplessness, with no course of action available that might actually save the masses of endangered Jews.

In the decades after the Holocaust, anxiety about persecution came to be focused on the fate of Jews in the Soviet Union, a subject that must await treatment in a different context.[150]

## Zionism and Israel

Zionism aroused the eloquence both of opponents and of fervent supporters. Some of the greatest preachers of the late nineteenth and early twentieth centuries were antagonistic to Zionism. Though insisting that America was still 'exile' and a return to the Land of Israel was the ultimate destiny of the Jewish people, many (though certainly not all) of the Orthodox were appalled by a modern political movement seeking to take Jewish destiny into its own hands and working to establish a secular Jewish state in pre-messianic times.[151] At

[150] For a few examples of sermons on Soviet Jewry, see H. Saperstein, 'Jewish Life behind the Iron Curtain' and 'The Ordeal of Soviet Jewry'; Teplitz (ed.), *The Rabbis Speak*, sermons by Klaperman, 66–73 (1964), Jick, 87–91 (1965), Kertzer, 114 (1968), and Maurice Davis, 140–1 (1970).
[151] For a review of the complex attitudes of Orthodox immigrant rabbis as reflected in their sermons, see Caplan, *Orthodoxy in the New World*, 288–302.

the other end of the religious spectrum, most Reform rabbis repudiated the national definition of Jewish identity, insisted on a universalistic religious mission for the Jewish people that could be fulfilled only in the Diaspora, and refused to concede the Zionist premise that Jews would never be accepted as equals in the countries where they lived as minorities.[152]

On 23 December 1898 the *Jewish Exponent* of Philadelphia devoted three long columns to a sermon given by Henry Berkowitz, rabbi of the Reform congregation Rodef Shalom, on 'Why I Am Not a Zionist', a fine articulation of the liberal anti-Zionist position. Though recognizing the emergence of virulent anti-Jewish sentiments, he insists that this is not the way of the future: 'while there is a strong party of Judaphobists in nearly every European country, yet these noisy agitators are held in check by the fair-minded and moral elements of each land . . . The press of all civilized countries is voicing the sentiment of the people with almost perfect accord against the outrageous invasion of human rights in the Dreyfus case.' To highlight the racial (we would say 'ethnic' or 'national') identity of Jews, he argues,

is simply to fall into the trap of those who for political reasons have brought back old race hatreds into the world to set heedless and thoughtless men against their fellow-men. Teutons against Slavs. Huns against Magyars. Aryans against Semites. It is a sad blunder which Zionism here commits to urge upon the Jews to draw apart on racial lines.

For Berkowitz and those who thought like him, the 'solution of the Jewish problem is not the Jewish race or the Jewish state, but the Jewish religion'.[153]

In England, too, there was strong opposition to the new movement. The chief rabbi, Hermann Adler, who had visited Palestine and shown sympathy for the Hovevei Zion movement, which encouraged Jewish agricultural settlement,[154] was firmly opposed to Herzl's political Zionism, though his argument is different from that of Berkowitz. Echoing an assertion about the nature of Jewish messianism that we have seen in David Woolf Marks's sermon on the messiah from the 1840s, but now speaking in the new context of the First Zionist Congress, Adler told his audience at the North London Synagogue in November 1898, 'It is not declared in the prophetic books that our return to Palestine is to be accomplished by our instrumentality and at the period we desire. It is distinctly announced that our redemption is to be effected by

[152] For overviews, see Polish, *Renew our Days*, and Greenstein, *Turning Point*.
[153] H. Berkowitz, 'Why I Am Not a Zionist', 171. Cf. J. L. Levy, cited in Freehof and Kavaler (eds), *J. Leonard Levy*, 56–8. Joseph Krauskopf, somewhat surprisingly, expressed in Jan. 1897 a much more favourable attitude on Palestine as a homeland for Russian Jews following a visit to Russia: see 'The People without a Country'.
[154] See his sermon delivered at the Great Synagogue in June 1885, 'A Pilgrimage to Zion'.

Divine interposition at such time as seemeth good in God's sight.'[155] On this issue, the chief rabbi came down on the same side as the spokesman for the most liberal wing of the British Jewish spectrum, Claude G. Montefiore, though for a different reason. In an 1896 sermon at the West London Synagogue, Montefiore insisted that Jews should 'set against the political idea of Jewish nationalism, the religious idea of Jewish universalism'.[156] Like Adler and many other extremely patriotic British Jews, Montefiore believed that the aggressive assertion of Jewish nationhood was historically anachronistic, and that it would undermine the position of Jews at home and play into the hands of the antisemites.

Other rabbis were more ambivalent. Morris Joseph has been described as 'totally opposed', on the basis of a statement he made in 1898. And indeed, even in 1917, with 'British soldiers fighting their way into the Holy Land', he said from the pulpit that personally he believed that the more political the new Jewish order was, the further it would be from his ideal. But that sermon reveals sympathy for the model of cultural Zionism propounded by Ahad Ha'am (1856–1927), and another sermon, delivered a few weeks after the foundations for the Hebrew University were laid on Mount Scopus (on 24 July 1918), shows considerable enthusiasm for this concept.[157]

On the other hand, Zionism was also passionately expounded from the pulpit. One of the most eloquent and influential preachers of eastern Europe was Isaac Nissenbaum. Although he wrote that his homiletical style was influenced by Jellinek, he developed his own voice in support of the Jewish national return to the Land of Israel, and managed to incorporate this theme in many of his holiday sermons in Warsaw. An integral part of this message was a powerfully bleak evocation of the nightmare of Jewish exile, with its concomitant effect on the psychology of the Jew, dramatized all around him during the years of the First World War and its aftermath, but present in more subtle ways even in the more tolerant countries of western Europe. Preaching on Passover in the first years of the century, Nissenbaum reviews the new Jewish settlements in Palestine with pride.

[155] *Jewish Chronicle*, 25 Nov. 1898, p. 13, with lengthy citations cited in Jakobovits, *The Attitude to Zionism of Britain's Chief Rabbis*, 4–6; cf. Alderman, *Modern British Jewry*, 231. In addition to the religious argument, Adler was concerned about the implications of the Zionist movement for perceptions of Jewish loyalty: Alderman, *Modern British Jewry*, 232.

[156] Montefiore, 'One God, One Worship', cited in S. Cohen, *English Zionists and British Jews*, 166–7; cf. Kershen and Romain, *Tradition and Change*, 116.

[157] Kershen and Romain, *Tradition and Change*, 116, quoting Joseph's statement that he 'abhorred the notion of a militant Jewish state'. For the sermons, see *The Spirit of Judaism*, 58–75. The Revd Dr Wolf of the Manchester Reform congregation asserted unambiguously that it was the 'duty of all true Jews to support the Zionist cause': Kershen and Romain, *Tradition and Change*, 117, citing *Jewish Chronicle*, 9 Oct. 1903, pp. 14–15.

Truly the time has already come when we should clothe our national feelings in deeds.
We say today, 'Next Year in Jerusalem.' Yet many of us have the capacity to be next year
in Jerusalem; why then are we satisfied with just with this proclamation? I am not even
speaking about settling in the Land of Israel, which is an obligation on whoever is able
to live there without depending upon others for sustenance . . . I am speaking about
*visiting* the land of Israel. Every middle-class person can find the money and the time
to visit the Land of Israel at least once in his life . . . From all the nations, thousands visit
our land every year . . . but hardly any of our own brothers go there. That is why our
portion in the land is weak.[158]

In Warsaw, Nissenbaum introduced the practice of preaching once a month in
Hebrew as an integral part of his national sentiments.

Another celebrated Zionist preacher was Zevi Hirsch Masliansky, who emigrated from eastern Europe to New York in 1895. The first president of Israel,
Chaim Weizmann, wrote in his memoir of the impact of hearing as a child the
'moving orations' of this 'famous folk-orator'.[159] Masliansky was apparently the
kind of preacher whose effect was achieved largely through his fiery delivery.[160]
But his published sermons, in Yiddish and English, convey something of his
homiletical style. Speaking about Jacob and Esau, he develops the familiar
typology of the relationship between gentiles and Jews, hands and voice, power
and spirit, in irreconcilable, everlasting conflict. But suddenly, at the end, he
shifts gear:

Sweet is the voice of Jacob and mighty are the hands of Esau. Happy the individual or
the nation that possesses both . . . Just as the 'hands' without the 'voice' are valueless, so,
too, is the 'voice' without the 'hands' of little avail . . . This is the ideal that the children
of Jacob today are seeking to realize even this day: to combine father Jacob's melodious
voice with uncle Esau's practical hands. Herein lies the strong appeal of Zionism.[161]

---

[158] Nissenbaum, *Festive Occasions* (Heb.).

[159] Cited in Fisch, *The Zionist Revolution*, 5. Cf. the description by Zalman Shazar of the
impact made upon him as a child by hearing the Maggid of Minsk (Benjamin Hakohen
Shakovitzki, 1871–1938) deliver a eulogy: *Morning Stars*, 67–8.

[160] For an appreciation, see Jacob Bosniak's tribute on 28 Apr. 1935: 'He never received any
formal training in the art of public speaking, nor had he precedents by which to be guided. He
developed his own technique, methods and forms of delivery and swayed his audience according
to his purpose. He made them convulse with laughter at one moment and shed tears in the next
moment. Even those who could not understand the language he used were moved by his eloquence . . . To hear his incisive and scorching words of sarcasm and irony, of reproach and condemnation, pronounced with the all-consuming fire of his powerful countenance—especially
when he denounced Jewish enemies or ridiculed our false messiahs—was like seeing flames of fire
envelope the speaker as well as the audience' (Bosniak, *Interpreting Jewish Life*, 146, 148). Cf.
Levinthal, *The Message of Israel*, 131–2.

[161] Masliansky, *Sermons*, 103–10. Masliansky generally spoke for one hour (Caplan, *Orthodoxy
in the New World*, 126); the texts in this book would take far less time to deliver, and must have
been highly revised.

Only the gentle reminder, earlier in the sermon, that Esau is 'our uncle' signals the unexpected divergence from the traditional rabbinic valuation of Esau as evil, a figure from whom Jews have nothing to learn.

The dynamics began to shift with the First World War, the Balfour Declaration, the devastating oppression of east European Jewry during and immediately after the war, and the emergence of Nazism. Hermann Adler's successor as chief rabbi in England, Joseph H. Hertz, took a quite different stance towards Zionism. On the sabbath of Hanukah in 1917, he preached on the 'Eternal City', noting that Jerusalem had been 'victoriously entered by His Majesty's Forces' a few days before, and proclaiming: 'What a privilege it is to have lived to see such a world-historic event!' (Presumably the significance was not the potential incorporation of Palestine into the British empire.) Citing one of Judah Halevi's Zion poems, he envisions a new future with undreamt-of possibilities.[162] In his eulogy for Baron Edmond de Rothschild seventeen years later, he emphasized the baron's love for Zion and belief in the sacredness of its soil (inspired, the eulogist claimed, by reading Graetz's *History of the Jews* as a young man), and noted that at the 'outbreak of the Nazi tragedy', Palestine was the only place in the world 'ready at hand to absorb an appreciable number, tens of thousands, of the victims of that revival of barbarism'.[163]

On 7 November 1947, with the United Nations debating the partition plan, the revisionist Zionist rabbi Louis I. Newman of New York preached in full confidence of the outcome: 'it is now only a matter of time before we . . . shall have the . . . privilege . . . the honor . . . and the joy of witnessing the official birth of the Third Hebrew State'. Most of the sermon was devoted to reassuring his apparently nervous congregants that the establishment of a Jewish state would have no effect on their status as American citizens. Then, towards the end, he launched into an almost euphoric peroration:

But we are witnessing the harbinger of the Messianic days in our own time. At last after nearly [nineteen] hundred years, a Jewish State, a free and independent and sovereign State, though small in area, is to be born. Let us shed ourselves of our fears, our prejudices, our misconceptions and our suspicions. Let us rejoice; let us be glad, not only for the people of Israel who are emerging from bondage, but for ourselves, whose lives as Jews will take on new substance, new dignity, new nobility, new serenity. We will cease to be a problem to the world; we will no longer be a disembodied folk. We will be re-born, and the world will be the richer.[164]

Six months later, at the actual establishment of the state, Harold Saperstein of Long Island, after a cautious though optimistic assessment of the military

[162] J. Hertz, 'The Eternal City of the Eternal People', 217–18.
[163] Id., 'Baron Edmond de Rothschild', 129–30, 132.
[164] Newman, 'Our American Citizenship and the New Jewish State', 7.

situation in Palestine, similarly turned to a more lyrical mode: 'We are seeing
the fulfilment of prophecies made thousands of years ago (Amos 9: 11–15). How
can it fail to have an effect upon us? Visiting Israel for Jews will be more than
a visit to the land of our ancestors. It will be a sacred pilgrimage to the centre
of our inspiration.'[165] At this historic juncture, the sermon played a significant
role in mediating between the tradition and a new reality that felt to many like
a dream fulfilled. It served a similar purpose at the time of the Six Day War in
1967, when politics and military strategy seemed—at least temporarily—to
be infused with a transcendent radiance, an experience of searing anguish
followed by deliverance from peril that cried out for articulation in the broad
context of Jewish historical memory.[166]

Immanuel Jakobovits identified himself as a religious Zionist throughout
his career. His 1961 sermon at the Orthodox Fifth Avenue Synagogue in New
York, commemorating the thirteenth anniversary of Israel's establishment,
described the new state's achievements since 1948 as the most outstanding item
on the short credit page of human gains and advances during the past six
decades, 'the most constructive event of the century'. On succeeding Joseph
Hertz as Britain's chief rabbi he became the first holder of that post to speak
of Zionism in his installation sermon, pledging to use his office to help 'in the
upbuilding of the Land of Israel, by encouraging *aliyah* [emigration to Israel]
and by freely aiding the spiritual and material growth of Israel'. Less than two
weeks after his installation, on 5 June 1967, when the very survival of Israel
seemed to hang in the balance, he was speaking at a mass rally at the Royal
Albert Hall, where his predecessor Hertz had spoken to mobilize public opinion on behalf of Jewish victims of Nazism. His pledge harked back to that era:
'We are not going to have another Holocaust in the martyred history of our
people. The hope of two millennia, the toil and sacrifice of two decades, is not
now going to be wiped out in two weeks or two months.' Through the remainder of his tenure as chief rabbi, he remained a passionate spokesman for Israel's
well-being, though occasionally trenchant in voicing sentiments of Jewish self-
criticism (for which he himself was attacked in some circles).[167]

Even for lifelong Zionists, the Israeli incursion into Lebanon over the summer of 1982 provoked deep anguish and ambivalence: discomfort over aspects

[165] H. Saperstein, 'Israel and Us', 144. See also Halpern, 'The Birth of a Nation': 'the greatest
and most heart-warming event that has happened to our people in almost 2,000 years'
(pp. 228–9); Abrahams, 'The Proclamation of the Jewish State', 341: 'the State of Israel, phoenix-
like, rose again from the ashes of its ruins. So have the words of our prophets been fulfilled . . .
The exile is ended. It has lasted 1878 years.'
[166] Levinthal, 'The Miracle and the Message of Israel's Triumph'; H. Saperstein, 'A Great
Miracle Happened There'; Abrahams, 'Israel's Victory'.
[167] Jakobovits, 'Israel's Bar Mitzvah'; id., *The Timely and the Timeless*, 3–16; id., '*If Only My
People . . .*', 18–21.

of Israeli policy and behaviour, yet anger at unbalanced and unfair criticisms launched against Israel. This is one of those situations where the preacher feels the need to walk a tightrope in affirming both the aspirations of Zionism and an understanding of Jewish ethics, justifying the need for military power, yet insisting that Jewish uniqueness requires living by moral standards that may not be applied to other nations. In London, Chief Rabbi Jakobovits sent out a circular letter to rabbinic colleagues before Yom Kippur, containing extracts from his Rosh Hashanah sermon, which included some searing rhetorical questions:

Have we forgotten that the Covenant between God and our people stipulated over and over again that the Land would be ours only on condition that we would observe His laws and be an exemplary people? ... In our tribulations, are we really making an all-out effort to prove ourselves worthy as the generation blessed to witness our Return, resolved to build a model society of righteousness in Israel, and to conduct ourselves as upright, God-fearing Jews wherever we live?[168]

On that same Rosh Hashanah, the Reform rabbi David Polish, one of the pre-eminent younger rabbis among American Zionists during the crucial decade of the 1940s, formulated this problem as the tension between power and the claim to being chosen by God.

Make no mistake: we cannot ever relinquish so much power that the only way open to us is either Masada [mass suicide] or the chimneys. But when power becomes a people's way of life, the claim to chosenness becomes a mockery ... We cannot be both chosen and like all the nations. We cannot be chosen and claim, as some of Israel's Rabbis do, that the war in Lebanon is a holy war. We cannot be chosen and claim, as some Israeli Rabbis do, that the Arabs in the West Bank are descendants of the Biblical Amalekites and therefore (by implication) deserve to be exterminated. We cannot claim chosenness and accept the charge of one Israeli on television that all Palestinians are beasts. Chosenness means that we have not been permitted to live by the rules of the world, and still are not permitted. We have made the most of this, amazing and enraging mankind ...

Israel has been compelled to fight for its existence ... But having demonstrated its strength, all of us are learning that there are limits to the mystique of power. The ancient prophet, Zechariah, was not indulging in mere fantasy when he declared, *Not by military might nor by power, but by God's spirit*. He was making a political statement that in his day (and we can add, even more in ours), military solutions are temporary ... To depend only on the force of arms brings on an alternative which is a grim certainty—continual warfare where the intervals between conflict become narrower.

---

[168] Jakobovits, circular letter and extracts from the chief rabbi's sermon, in *L'Eylah*, 2/5 (Spring 5743 [1983]), 2–6. Attempts to discover a full version of this Rosh Hashanah sermon from the Office of the Chief Rabbi and the family of Rabbi Jakobovits have not yielded an extant text.

Neither Israel, nor the Middle East, nor America, nor the Soviet Union can continue on this path without invoking a terrifying final solution for humanity.[169]

Ironically, the massacre of Palestinians by Christian militias passing through Israeli checkpoints at Sabra and Shatila, which occurred immediately after Rosh Hashanah 1982, would make these issues even more agonizing.

## Social Justice

Traditional Jewish preaching in the medieval and early modern periods showed relatively little concern for what we would call 'social justice'. When preachers employed the rhetoric of rebuke, it was applied to sins internal to Jewish society. From their perspective as minority communities dependent upon the protection of royal power, Jews were extremely apprehensive about any movements of social unrest, peasants' uprisings, and revolutionary challenges to the existing power structure, as they often began or ended with attacks upon Jews perceived as visible, accessible, and vulnerable representatives of the forces of oppression.[170]

This pattern changes in the modern period, for several reasons. First, Jews began to identify more with the states in which they were being granted citizenship and with the societies into which they aspired to integrate. As they gathered together on national days of prayer under conditions of war while their neighbours were similarly assembled in their churches, it seemed natural to appeal for funds that would support the victims of war—the widows and orphans of soldiers who would not return, the wounded and disabled veterans—no matter what their religion. Second, the Reform movement highlighted universalistic elements of Jewish tradition, stressing God's concern for all human beings, and especially for the downtrodden and disenfranchised. This doctrine was associated with the biblical prophets, whose denunciations of those who performed sacrificial rituals while ignoring the injustices permeating the surrounding society were invoked in support of the central Reform principle that ethical behaviour is more important than ceremonial observance.

We find indications of this new consciousness in the first half of the nineteenth century. Gershom Mendes Seixas, preaching in December 1804 on a day

---

[169] Polish, ' "Why Do the Nations Rage?"—"How Can Jacob Stand?" ' For a review of sermons by thirty-six rabbis delivered during the High Holy Days of 1982 relating to the Israeli incursion into Lebanon, see Daniel Jeremy Silver, 'What We Said about Lebanon' (unfortunately, the sources cited in the article are not identified).

[170] See e.g. Ezekiel Landau's horror at the 1785 revolt of the Bohemian serfs in a sermon for the sabbath preceding Passover: M. Saperstein, *'Your Voice Like a Ram's Horn'*, 451. Only occasionally do we find in medieval or early modern Jewish sermons an expression of concern reaching beyond the Jewish community. For an example, see M. Saperstein and Kanarfogel, 'A Byzantine Manuscript of Sermons' (Heb.), 173.

of thanksgiving proclaimed by the government of New York City for being spared an epidemic that ravaged other parts of the country, said that 'Among the various duties we owe to our heavenly Father, there are none perhaps more important than attending to the poor, the widow, and the orphan.' Several of his other sermons are devoted to the theme of charity.[171] In Britain, David Woolf Marks, preaching on the sabbath before the national day of thanksgiving for an abundant harvest in the autumn of 1847, reflected upon the potato famine of the previous year and emphasized the importance of benevolence and philanthropy, especially the obligation of his congregants to give to the poor.[172] Two years later, David de Sola preached in the Bevis Marks Synagogue on another thanksgiving day, this one in response to the ending of the recent cholera epidemic. His sermon underscored the listeners' obligation of gratitude to God, which must be fulfilled through the support of 'sanitary committees' and assistance to the poor that would improve their living conditions and therefore their health.[173]

On Yom Kippur 1894, 10 October, Chief Rabbi Hermann Adler preached in the Great Synagogue of London on 'The Sinners in Zion'. He began by contrasting contemporary preachers, who tend to deal 'too much with generalities', with the prophets of old, who 'spoke with a plain bluntness that could not be mistaken, aye, with a grand passion of scorn and hate for all that was evil and corrupt. It is this plain speaking, this direct practical application, which invests their admonitions with such undying sublimity.' After discussing his text from Isaiah 33: 14–17, he proceeded to the application, which addressed very directly, with a vehemence not generally associated with this diplomatic personality, the prevalent business practices of his time in a passage of considerable rhetorical power:

Can they persuade themselves that they despise the gains of oppression, who try to exact the utmost toil out of their labourers and employees in return for the scantiest wage, the barest pittance that can keep body and soul together—not a *living* but a *dying* wage? Or they who take advantage of the necessities of their workmen and women, compelling them to labour on the Sabbath? Or they who are money-lenders, and who claim usurious rates of interest from the victims whom they have entrapped, who corrupt youths by advancing money and pandering to their vices and follies? Or they who defraud unsuspecting creditors who have trusted to their debtors' honesty? Or they who remove goods before bankruptcy, and thus flagrantly defraud and rob?

'I do know', he went on to say, 'that there are unhappily Jews who are guilty of these practices, which are denounced in the public press and universally

---

[171] Friedenberg, 'Hear O Israel', 13, 17.
[172] Marks, 'On the Day of Thanksgiving for the Abundant Harvest', 124, 130–1.
[173] Sola, 'Sermon Delivered at the Spanish and Portuguese Jews' Synagogue', 4–5, 9.

condemned. I should be shamefully remiss in my duty were I to forbear
from severely castigating such practices . . . If Isaiah were in our midst, how
would he thunder forth his denunciations!'[174] A sermon like this justifies the
association of 'prophetic Judaism' with the establishment centre of British
Jewry.[175]

Nor was Adler an anomaly among British Orthodox preachers. One of the
most popular, highly reputed for his eloquence, was the Reverend Simeon
Singer of the New West End Synagogue. In May 1906, speaking on Leviticus
25: 35 ('If your brother, being in straits, comes under your authority . . .'), he
devoted his sermon to the 'Sweated Industries Exhibition' at Queen's Hall. It
cast, he noted, 'a lurid side-light on modern civilization', challenging the
assumption of inevitable progress, and serving to 'rouse the conscience of the
people of England'. He asserts that recent legislation has improved conditions
for workers in factories, but not for the workers in the 'home industries', who
often work twelve hours a day, under conditions injurious to their health, to
earn nine or ten shillings a week. 'Would that one of the ancient Hebrew
Prophets were alive in our midst!' he proclaimed. 'If the eloquence of the
Prophets was raised specially on the side of the poor and oppressed, it was
because these classes stood most in need of advocates.' Again, this is 'prophetic Judaism' from an unexpected quarter.[176]

A few years before Adler's sermon on economic justice, in the summer of
1890, Sabato Morais of Philadelphia, who had been actively involved with
several other rabbinical colleagues in trying to broker a compromise resolution
of a strike by some 800 immigrant Jews against the Philadelphia Cloak
Manufacturers' Association, decided to devote a sermon to the topic. This
included an outspoken condemnation of the sweat system and the exploitation
of the immigrant labourers by 'rich individuals who still begrudged the scanty
loaf ate by men and women and children herded together' in conditions unfit
for human habitation. Although in the negotiations he had to navigate a mine-
field between radical anarchists, 'scabs', and management, in the sermon his
sympathies with the strikers were apparent. Nor did his involvement end with
the sermon; his efforts to resolve the conflict continued throughout the sum-

[174] H. Adler, 'The Sinners in Zion', 168–76.
[175] This term is generally associated with Reform Judaism: see W. Jacob, ' "Prophetic Judaism" ';
S. S. Wise, 'The Social Message of the Hebrew Prophets'; Levy in Freehof and Kavaler (eds),
*J. Leonard Levy*, 203–5: 'Now these Prophets have been rediscovered during the past half-century.
Until then they were almost neglected by Jew and Non-Jew . . . They insisted that religion had
an economic content . . . Religion meant to them all that the orthodox claim for religion, but it
meant a great deal more: it meant the application of the themes of religion to the social, the economic, the political, the national, the international life.'    [176] Singer, 'Sweated Industries'.

mer, until the strike came to an end—the first strike in the American garment industry in which a rabbi served as an arbitrator.[177]

Another theme of profound concern to Morais was US immigration policy and the treatment of immigrants in the United States. As we shall see in Sermon 6 below, delivered during the Civil War, he conceived of America's role as being 'the pattern of freedom and the haven of the oppressed'. He was accordingly incensed by the Chinese Exclusion Act of 1882, and in a sermon immediately following Thanksgiving Day 1885 he explicitly criticized former President Chester Alan Arthur for signing a compromise bill that forbade all immigration from China for ten years. He also lambasted the 'brutality of a loose population in Washington territory' and the humiliation of Chinese in the west by a 'perjured jury that acquitted an assassin because the victim was only a Chinaman' and 'an iniquitous judge at San Francisco'. Nor did he hesitate to condemn a California rabbi, not mentioned by name, for supporting the restrictive legislation—'an event that dishonoured the title of Rabbi. Let it sink into eternal oblivion.'[178] In 1892, when the law was being extended for another ten years, Morais returned to the subject in his sabbath sermon of 7 May, reviewing the stance he had taken seven years earlier and expressing his consternation at the new bill, 'worthy of the dark ages', which condemned the Chinese to six months of hard labour and then being shipped back to China 'if convicted of the heinous offense of treading the ground on which Washington and Lincoln walked'.[179]

The high point of Jewish social preaching came in the late nineteenth and early twentieth centuries. In America, forceful, eloquent orators—Joseph Krauskopf in Philadelphia, Emil G. Hirsch in Chicago, J. Leonard Levy in Pittsburgh, Leon Harrison in St Louis, Morris Newfield in Birmingham, Alabama, and Stephen S. Wise in New York—most of whom delivered their

---

[177] This account is based on Whiteman, 'Western Impact on East European Jews', 124–33. According to Arthur Kiron, the original text of the sermon does not appear to be in the Sabato Morais Papers in the University of Pennsylvania Library, so I am dependent on Whiteman's citations. Cf. Sabato Morais Ledger, 441, for Morais's letter to the strikers, and ibid. 470 for his condemnation of the sweating system four years later, featured on the first page of the *Jewish Exponent*, 19 Oct. 1894.

[178] S. Morais, 'On the Ill Treatment of the Chinese in the Far West' (my gratitude to Arthur Kiron for providing a copy of this sermon). Cf. Corré, 'Sabato Morais and Social Justice in Philadelphia', 24–5. Corré notes that in Morais's text of the sermon, the former President Arthur is censured by name for giving in to prejudice and political pressure by signing a compromise bill, but that the account in the *Philadelphia Jewish Record* omitted this reference (p. 25). For the anti-Chinese violence in the fall of 1885, see Sandmeyer, *The Anti-Chinese Movement in California*, 97–8.

[179] *Public Ledger—Philadelphia*, 9 May 1892; Sabato Morais Ledger, 447. The extensive references to the sermon of ten years earlier indicate that he had removed it from his file and had it in front of him when he prepared the new one. In this newspaper account, the explicit reference to President Arthur remained (see n. 177 above).

message of social and economic justice at Sunday services, spoke at times to as
many as a thousand worshippers. It has been argued that such preachers, who
had little use for ritual or ceremony, and often dispensed almost entirely with
post-biblical Jewish sources in their preaching, disciplined Jews in their growing affluence, laid the foundations for new institutions of Jewish philanthropy,
and inculcated an awareness that responsibility for the state of the workers, the
poor, the oppressed was an integral part of what it meant to be a Jew. This
often entailed using the pulpit to voice criticism of government policies and
even the practices of wealthy Jewish employers, speaking out in a way that
required considerable courage, provoking as it did not only vigorous controversy but marked antagonism. The 'Social Gospel' ideal of their Protestant colleagues provided a natural context in which these preachers could claim the
mantle of 'prophetic Judaism'.[180]

Thus J. Leonard Levy justified talking about economic issues from the pulpit
as an 'unavoidable duty' by claiming the precedent of Jeremiah's application of
religion to the economic life; so the contemporary synagogue and church must
take on the role of the prophets. He criticized 'the present tariff system', though
conceding that such criticism was 'political heresy'.[181] He also addressed issues
of poverty and socialism, and specific scandals of government corruption.[182]
Leon Harrison, devoting a sermon of March 1914 to Abraham Lincoln and contemporary politics, made Lincoln into a spokesman for the current liberal agenda. He maintained that Lincoln would defend the small trader against the
monopolist, promote reform in the selection of candidates and oppose the influence of the bosses, favour national legislation for the protection of women and
for women's suffrage, oppose child labour in New England and the South,
endorse a law mandating compulsory arbitration of industrial disputes, honour
international treaties, and foster peaceful union with all great powers, including
arbitration of issues not vital to national existence. In short, he concluded,
Lincoln would have a profile very much like President Wilson.[183]

The Great Depression beginning in 1929 understandably brought forth
from the pulpit poignant expressions of empathy for those adversely affected

[180] Freehof and Kavaler, introduction to id. (eds), *J. Leonard Levy*, 25, 31; cf. ibid. 206; also Sarna,
*American Judaism*, 195–7, with bibliography at 401 n. 106. On the 'Social Gospel' preachers, see
Handy (ed.), *The Social Gospel in America*; Bos and Faries, 'The Social Gospel'; Holland (ed.),
*Sermons in American History*, 282–307. The preaching practice of Washington Gladden, the most
famous of the 'Social Gospel' figures, was to give a more traditional sermon on Sunday morning
and to deal with social issues in lectures on Sunday and Wednesday evening (Edwards, *A History
of Preaching*, 650); this is in a way analogous to the practice of those rabbis who delivered Torah-
based homilies on Saturday morning and wider lectures to large audiences on Sunday mornings.
[181] J. L. Levy, 'The Butterfly', 199, 207.
[182] Freehof and Kavaler (eds), *J. Leonard Levy*, 139, 145.
[183] Harrison, 'What Would Lincoln Do in the White House Now?'

and criticism of the social and economic policies that had led to so many heart-breaking reversals of fortune. In Wilmington, North Carolina, Benjamin Kelson devoted his sermon for the seventh day of Passover in 1930 to a jeremiad of social criticism, metaphorically applying to contemporary American society the ten plagues of ancient Egypt. Included were many references to economic life:

We squander our capital in the production of luxuries for the few while the many are undernourished ... We pay able-bodied men and women wages that keep them just above the starvation level, and destroy the efficiency they would undoubtedly have were they decently fed and housed ... Men and women are shot at for asking for higher wages; people protesting against unemployment and innocent bystanders are clubbed in the streets ... Many an employer would give justice to his workers were he not afraid of the condemnation of his fellow-employers.[184]

As a young rabbi at the Holy Blossom Temple of Toronto, Maurice N. Eisendrath, speaking on the first Rosh Hashanah following the stock market crash, acknowledged the devastating reversals that had dislocated many lives:

And how many there are to whom life has denied even these material compensations! How strenuously have they laboured to build their fragile house of cards, only to have them levelled to the ground by the first gust of an ill-blown wind; their petty fortunes, their business, their savings, perchance of a lifetime, swept ruthlessly aside by the irresistible tempest of economic depression, by ravaging wars, by the crushing onslaught of giant combinations—yea, by a conspiracy of forces wholly beyond their individual control.[185]

A few months later, in a Sunday morning address, Gerson B. Levi of Chicago spoke about the impact of the depression on American society. Undercutting a government announcement that the wages of unionized workers had been maintained at their high levels, Levi cited notices in the newspaper in which artisans and craftsmen offered 'Plastering at any price', 'Carpentering at 85 cents an hour'. He deplored the toll taken by modern industrialization, with its assembly-line system of manufacture:

We have taken the worker who had a whole craft in his hands and we have made him a fragment. We have drilled people, men and women, day after day, to do a certain fragment of a job and we say that man is successful the moment his fragment of a job is done in time to fit in with the fragments of others ... Character or no; honesty or no; willingness or no; except as these qualities show themselves on a moving belt.

He laments not only the circumstances that have driven families to destitution, but the policies that then rob those very families of their privacy and humiliate

---

[184] Kelson, 'Ten Plagues of Today', 73, 75.      [185] Eisendrath, 'A New Basis for Religion'.

them in the public domain: newspaper listings of the names and addresses of the neediest families; centralized bread lines and soup lines that 'sacrifice the self-respect of the people whom we help'. The sermon ends with a strong call for public theatres and government unemployment insurance.[186]

Civil rights for African Americans became a defining issue for many twentieth-century American preachers. Rabbis (especially those of northern backgrounds) serving congregations in the South were in an especially challenging position, and the stances they took on civil rights and integration often became a source of considerable tension both within their synagogues and in the larger communities. The sermon was by no means the only, or perhaps even the most important, vehicle for addressing this issue, but some of the Southern rabbis spoke out with impressive courage from their pulpits.

Max Heller, a German-speaking immigrant from Prague, came to Temple Sinai, the largest synagogue of New Orleans, in 1887. Disillusioned by a wave of prejudice and violence in the 1890s that lasted into the new century, he exclaimed in his sermon on Yom Kippur 1909, 'Why today there are people, right around us, who are too stupid or too inhuman to understand that the negro has a soul, with the same rights as our own, to all of God's truth and beauty.' Because the Jew was 'the oldest and most unflinching victim of persecution', it was his obligation to 'frown down every inhuman barrier that separates races, ranks, and creeds'.[187] William Fineshriber brought a commitment to social justice with socialist inclinations to the Memphis congregation he served from 1911 to 1924. The local newspapers frequently reported, summarized, and quoted from his sermons, especially one on the Ku Klux Klan delivered in October 1921, in which he asserted that the 'mob law' of the Klan was 'far more dangerous than Bolshevism'.[188]

The Reform rabbi Jacob M. Rothschild addressed racial segregation directly in his Yom Kippur sermon of 1948, delivered shortly after his arrival at the oldest and most influential synagogue in Atlanta and in the context of the 'Dixiecrat' presidential campaign. Mentioning a series of specific incidents

---

[186] Levi, 'A Challenge to Society of Days of Depression'.

[187] Cited by Bobbie Malone in Bauman and Kalin (eds), *The Quiet Voices*, 34, from *American Israelite*, 16 Sept. 1909. See also the description of Heller's 1898 sermon 'Modern Intolerance', on the Dreyfus trial and racial prejudice, and his memorial sermon following the assassination of President McKinley, decrying—among the other evils he had seen during the previous decade— 'the drunken mob that kindles a pyre around a chained negro' (ibid. 27, from *Times Democrat*, 19 Feb. 1898, and 32, from *Daily Picayune*, 20 Sept. 1901). For the fuller picture, see Malone, *Rabbi Max Heller*, esp. ch. 6.

[188] Cited by Berkley Kalin in Bauman and Kalin (eds), *The Quiet Voices*, 59. By contrast, Morris Newfield, a Reform rabbi in Birmingham from 1895 to 1940, spoke out for many progressive causes including the rights of labour, but did not apparently support from the pulpit civil rights for blacks: see Cowett, 'Rabbi Morris Newfield', and Cowett, *Birmingham's Rabbi*.

as illustrations of 'the growing race hatred that threatens the South', he rebuked both the militant bigots and his own people. It is not that Jews had committed overt offences against the negroes, he said:

I feel certain that we have treated them fairly; certainly we have not used force to frighten them . . . No, our sin has been the deeper one, the evil of what we didn't do . . . Millions of us must know the truth—but we keep silent, even though the word is in our own hearts. The problem is ours to solve, and the time for solution is now . . . There is only one real issue: civil rights.[189]

Ten years later, 'The Temple' of Atlanta would be bombed, partly in anger at the rabbi's leadership.

During the heyday of the civil rights movement between 1954 and 1965, some Southern rabbis opposed militant challenges to the status quo, but others condemned segregation strongly from their pulpits. Perry Nussbaum used his Rosh Hashanah sermon of 1955 to impress on his congregation in Jackson, Mississippi, that '[the Negro] believes what you and I as Jews have hungered for ourselves during 1900 years of history—that every man has a natural right to share in God's gifts: the right to life himself, and to give his children the best possible training; the right to economic security, the right to political equality'.[190] William Silverman, of Nashville, Tennessee, denounced in early 1958 the policy of public silence both as a violation of the moral ideals of 'prophetic Judaism' and as a strategic error:

The Negro is the symbol to galvanize the mobilization of the bigots for warfare against all spiritual values. The ultimate objective is to attack the principles and precepts of the Judeo-Christian way of life. There is a time when silence is cowardly. There is a time when our faith must commit us to moral action. Now is such a time.[191]

This was a new version of an argument used a generation earlier by Jewish leaders warning against Nazism: 'Don't think they are only against Jews; they are opposed to the core values of our civilization.' Here it is the Negro in the American South who is the visible victim of a bigotry that ultimately endangers Jews and others as well.

Parenthetically, almost the same argument was used by Louis I. Rabinowitz, a distinguished scholar who served as chief rabbi of the Transvaal during the tumultuous years from 1945 to 1961. Most South African rabbis refrained from

[189] Rothschild, 'The Greater Sin', 173–4. Rothschild's widow wrote that he 'gradually accustomed his congregation to hearing his opinion on the segregation issue by speaking of it at least once during each High Holy Day season and on two or three other occasions every year': Janice Rothschild Blumberg, quoted in Bauman and Kalin, *The Quiet Voices*, 263–4.
[190] Cited by Gary Zola in Bauman and Kalin (eds), *The Quiet Voices*, 242.
[191] Cited in Staub, *Torn at the Roots*, 58, from *American Judaism*, 7 (Jan. 1958), 11. See also the other examples cited by Staub on that page.

speaking out publicly against the apartheid system, knowing that to do so would attract condemnation from Jews and non-Jews alike. Rabinowitz was a courageous exception. Preaching in the late 1940s on the weekly biblical lesson 'Metsora', he described the natural tendency to turn away from unpleasantness and pretend that such things as filth and evil do not exist, a tendency which ultimately is destructive not only to others but to oneself. He clinched this point by citing at length a newspaper article from the previous Sunday containing a 'vivid and horrifying account of the non-European Hospital here in Johannesburg'. The article 'would in itself call for immediate redress solely in the name of suffering humanity', but it goes on to appeal to the reader's (and thus the listener's) self-interest through the newspaper's emphasis on the danger to the European population of the scandalously inadequate treatment of native Africans suffering from tuberculosis and other infectious diseases. The preacher then concluded:

There you have it—we ignore unpleasantness and filth at our own personal peril. And what applies to physical disease applies with equal force to the diseases of the spirit. Is it not the whole sad history of 1933–1939? The world saw the miasma of evil slowly but inexorably spreading and thought it could ignore it—until it spread over the world. It is good that we turn our minds from time to time to unpleasant things, to the seamy side of life, for we ignore it at our peril.[192]

A few years later, he expressed his often-reiterated Zionist commitments in emphasizing the timidity and fearfulness of Jews in the Diaspora towards their non-Jewish neighbours: 'The Jew, rendered fearful by the sense of insecurity, which comes from being a vulnerable minority in all countries, has been afraid boldly to proclaim that such and such an act is contrary to the ethical principles of his faith.'[193] His record of condemnation not only of government policies but of Jewish involvement in the apartheid system—though not as outspoken as he later said he wanted to be and should have been—is both poignant and inspiring.[194]

In the United States, a high point of the civil rights movement was the 'March on Washington' of 28 August 1963, itself reaching a climax in Martin Luther King's 'I have a dream' speech. Reporting to his congregation the following sabbath, Harold Saperstein cited not only King's famous peroration but also another speech, by a colleague, Joachim Prinz, who had been rabbi of a Berlin congregation during the Hitler regime. Prinz said to the enormous crowd that the most disgraceful problem of the Hitler era was silence. 'America must not be silent', he insisted, but instead must speak up and act—'not for the

[192] Rabinowitz, *Out of the Depths*, 132–3.   [193] Id., *Sparks from the Anvil*, 198.
[194] See the treatment by Mazabow, *To Reach for the Moon*, esp. 145–56.

sake of the Negro, but for the sake of America'.[195] Among many other rabbis, Jacob Rudin made this the theme of his Rosh Hashanah evening sermon a few weeks later, saying, 'This isn't the other fellow's fight. It is our fight—here in Great Neck [an affluent Long Island suburb] . . . Because Jews are Jews, we need to be in this struggle.'[196]

Three years later, civil rights were still a burning issue for many Jewish preachers, although by then the movement had changed. The articulation of a new ideology of 'black power' by Stokely Carmichael and others in the spring of 1966 raised a dilemma: was this a legitimate form of group pride and assertiveness, comparable to the Zionist revolution, or was it a dangerous abandonment of the principle of non-violent resistance that had made the civil rights movement so inspiring? Eugene Lipman, previously director of the Reform movement's Commission on Social Action, addressed 'black power' in his Yom Kippur sermon in 1966, delivered at Temple Sinai, Washington, DC:

Black Power was an inevitable development so long as violent White Power refused to accept any of society's decisions—legislative, judicial, or moral—and continued its naked violence against everyone who does not advocate White supremacy. Black Power was inevitable so long as respectable middle-class White citizens continued to insist on their right to make a mockery of human equality by fleeing from integrated housing, by fleeing from integrated schools, by fleeing from an integrated economy, by indifference or open sabotage . . . Black Power is inevitable when the real situation of Negroes—social, economic, educational—is shown to be worse than in 1954: more unemployment, more segregated housing, more segregated schools. That's where Black Power came from, from our hatred, hypocrisy, and indifference.[197]

His refrain in this passage, 'Black Power was inevitable', is not a ringing endorsement of the new programme. It is, rather, a powerful criticism of forces in American society that naturally led to this development, a condemnation of the failures of Jews to pursue with sufficient energy the goal of social justice— failures that require confession and atonement—and a call to concrete action to promote the cause of equality. The modern Jewish preacher, like his

[195] H. Saperstein, 'The American Dream, in Color', 222–3. For a recent discussion of Prinz's address to the rally (available as text and audio at <www.joachimprinz.com/civilrights.htm>), see Staub, *Torn at the Roots*, 45–8.

[196] Rudin, 'The March on Washington', 258. Cf. his powerful defence of the civil rights movement on Yom Kippur eve three years later: id., *Very Truly Yours*, 259–69.

[197] Lipman, 'Black Power Slogans'. See also his strong sermon from Yom Kippur 1963 entitled 'Racial Justice: A Pledge of Conscience', addressing his congregants about their apparent uneasiness over the March on Washington a few weeks earlier: 'I am ashamed for you, because you have to be pushed and cajoled and begged and occasionally shouted at to accept the smallest, most insignificant kind of responsibility in the most important American movement of the twentieth century, in solving the deepest religious problem we face in our society. I am ashamed for you because you are so determined to do nothing' (pp. 23–4).

predecessors in previous centuries, still felt impelled 'to tell My people its sin' (Isa. 58: 1); now, however, the sins were conceived in a broader context.

## War and Peace

We turn now to the subject of the present anthology. War became an important theme in Jewish preaching in the eighteenth century, when sermons delivered on occasions connected with war reveal Jews' attitudes in the context of the new roles they were expected to play as citizens of the state. I have previously published my translation of a sermon delivered by the British chief rabbi Hirschel Levin (Hart Lyon), shortly after his arrival at the Great Synagogue in London from Germany, on a national day of fasting in response to military reverses and severe economic hardship in the late 1750s, near the beginning of the Seven Years War. A second sermon in his collection of manuscripts was the product of a markedly different mood, delivered on a day of celebration proclaimed by the Crown following a military victory. These sermons reflect a new kind of awareness: rarely before had the battles between non-Jewish kings been a matter of Jewish concern in a context devoid of any messianic speculation.[198] A year or so after these sermons were delivered, an English translation appeared in London of a sermon delivered by Rabbi David Fränckel in Berlin as a sermon of thanksgiving following the victory of Britain's Prussian allies over the Austrian forces at Leuthen. It contains a powerful evocation of the ravages of war, its patriotic fervour tempered by enlightened universalistic sentiments.[199] From this point on, the sermon responding to the circumstances of war would become a significant (though previously uninvestigated) subgenre for Jewish preachers in Europe and the United States.[200]

The content of the sermons presented below will be discussed in relation to the conditions in which they were delivered in the individual introduction

[198] M. Saperstein, *Jewish Preaching*, 347–58; Jewish Theological Seminary of America Library Manuscript Collection, MS R 79 (Adler, 1248), fo. 23b; M. Saperstein, *'Your Voice Like a Ram's Horn'*, 150–2.

[199] *A Thanksgiving Sermon for the Important and Astonishing Victory [of Leuthen]* (Roth, *Magna Bibliotheca Anglo-Judaica*, 324 no. 18). In M. Saperstein, *'Your Voice Like a Ram's Horn'*, 152, I followed Alexander Altmann in attributing the authorship of this sermon to Moses Mendelssohn. Gad Freudenthal has now persuasively argued that the sermon was written not by Mendelssohn but by Fränckel himself: see Freudenthal, 'R. David Fränckel, Moses Mendelssohn, and the Authorship of a Patriotic Sermon (Berlin, 10 December 1848)' (forthcoming; I am grateful to the author for providing me with a draft copy of his article). Freudenthal has also discovered and published the text of a sermon delivered by Fränckel on 28 December 1745 following a victory by the forces of King Frederick the Great over Austria, apparently the earliest known example of this genre of Jewish preaching: Freudenthal, 'Ein symbolischer Anfang'.

[200] See my brief overview of central European sermons for the period ending 1815, 'War and Patriotism in Sermons to Central European Jews: 1756–1815', in *'Your Voice Like a Ram's Horn'*, 147–61.

to each text. Rather than review that material here, I will suggest some general questions that emerge from this category of Jewish homiletical literature. The first relate to the nature of the text itself. What are we reading? A full text written or typed by the preacher before delivery? A stenographic transcription or a tape recording made during delivery? A publication in pamphlet form, translated into English and printed soon after delivery? A version prepared for publication in a collection of the preacher's sermons years later? A transcript published in a Jewish weekly journal? Passages of direct quotation or a reporter's summary in a general daily newspaper? The texts below include examples of all these types (except for the tape recording, which is, of course, the most accurate version of what the preacher actually said). Needless to say, each type presents methodological challenges in evaluating its reliability as a record of verbal delivery.

Other questions pertain to the context. Do we know the precise date on which the sermon was delivered? If so, is it identified by the preacher, or deduced from internal evidence? What was the actual occasion on which the sermon was delivered? Had the preacher simply decided to devote his weekly sermon to the topic of war? Was the decision driven by a dramatic event (the first sabbath following an attack, or following the government's declaration of war)? Was the day one chosen by the government for a special war-related purpose, or an occasion suggested by the Jewish calendar? What happens if a day of national fast declared by the British Crown or American government conflicts with a Jewish holiday that forbids fasting and requires rejoicing—or if a day of national rejoicing is declared on an occasion in the Jewish calendar demanding sombre reflection?[201]

What external events lie in the background of the sermon, and to what extent do they inform the resonance of the preacher's words?[202] How was the

---

[201] See the opening paragraph of Sermon 4 below by David Woolf Marks. This problem was recurrent in America during the Civil War period. A national fast-day on 26 Sept. 1861 occurred on the second day of Sukkot; another fast-day on 22 Apr. 1862 fell on the first day of Passover; 4 July 1863, a day of national rejoicing, fell on the Jewish fast-day of 17 Tammuz; and 1 June 1865, the day of national mourning for the fallen President Lincoln, came on the second day of Shavuot. Such conflicts forced religious leaders to wrestle publicly with issues of identity.

[202] To give one example, here is a passage from a sermon by Emil G. Hirsch entitled 'Men of Light and Leading': 'It seems to me that our country needs today in all its affairs men of genius who will ascend the mountain and commune with our God, and also men of talent who, standing from afar off, behold God and bow to him. Popular passion, the passion of those who eat and drink while they behold God's manifestation, is the unsafest guide of a nation's destiny . . . Let us be calm. Our Moses and our Aarons must ascend the height where God speaks (cf. Exod. 24: 9). The passion of the people who eat and drink (cf. Exod. 24: 11), the voice of the demagogue must not be heeded.' From internal evidence it is clear that the sermon was on the weekly biblical lesson 'Mishpatim', and that the preacher was probably alluding to some actual issue of contention. Knowing that it was delivered on 21 Feb. 1898 (see *Reform Advocate*, 26 Feb. 1898, p. 32), six days

war developing on the ground? Had there been significant battles—victories or defeats—in the recent past? Did the contemporary media suggest that the momentum was on the side of the forces of the preacher's country, or against them? What was the political mood in the country? Were criticisms being levelled against those in government responsible for making decisions about the war, or the commanders in the field responsible for implementing such decisions? Was the very decision to go to war being questioned, or was there a broad consensus about the legitimacy, necessity, morality, even sanctity of the war effort? Were people arguing that their leaders in government had not been truthful in their explanations of the basis for war? Were there pressures for ending the state of belligerence as soon as possible, even if it meant a compromise on the maximalist goals? Was there consensus for pressing on to the enemy's unconditional surrender, despite the cost in additional bloodshed and national treasure?[203]

How is the opposing side portrayed in the sermon? Does the preacher resort to vilification or demonization of the enemy as the absolute Other, either a primitive savage devoid of civilized feelings or an embodiment of evil?[204] Or is there some recognition of and empathy with the enemy soldiers as human beings like those fighting on one's own side, some recognition of heartache in the homes of parents, children, wives in the other country?[205] Are the problems and tensions of the preacher's own environment overlooked or suppressed in sermons addressing the situation of a nation at war? To what extent do we encounter self-criticism, warnings about injustice in the preacher's own society?[206] Is war presented as ennobling for a nation, promoting social cohesion and personal self-sacrifice, or as dehumanizing, cheapening the value of human life, raising dangers to the fundamental liberties and rights of citizens back home?

What values are cited in the preacher's justification of the war? Is it a matter of national self-interest or honour, necessity or revenge? Or are higher

after the explosion of the USS *Maine* in the Havana harbour, and that the clamour for revenge was being fed by the popular press and resisted by President McKinley, lends the words a far more powerful resonance. This question of context is crucial for the interpretation of Sermon 7 below by Samuel Isaacs, as discussed in the introduction to that piece.

[203] See the resistance to a premature peace expressed in Sermons 5, 6, and 21 below by, respectively, Michelbacher, Morais, and Franklin.

[204] See the rather embarrassing rhetoric about the primitive character of the enemy in Sermons 3 and 4 below by Seixas and Marks respectively; also the passage by Isaac Leeser cited in the introduction to Sermon 5.

[205] See the passage by Abraham Geiger cited above (pp. 3–4)—admittedly after the lapse of fifty years. Similar attitudes towards the defeated French enemy are reflected in sermons on the Franco-Prussian War by Leopold Stein and Adolf Jellinek.

[206] This element is pronounced in Sermons 5 and 19 below by Michelbacher and Stephen S. Wise, respectively.

values, more abstract values, invoked (to protect the Union, to liberate the slaves, to free the oppressed Cubans, to make the world safe for democracy, to end all wars)? Is the war presented as a battle on behalf of civilization, or as evidence of the breakdown of civilization?

How do the sermons of the Jewish preachers relate to those of their Christian counterparts delivered on the same occasion? Are Jewish preachers more or less likely to support the war effort than their Christian colleagues? Is there a noticeable difference between the use of Old Testament texts by Christian and by Jewish preachers? Do we find claims that war is by nature a violation of core Jewish values and of God's will, and explicit encouragement of listeners not to participate in the fighting, as voiced by some Christian clergy?

How do Jewish preachers deal with the reality that Jewish soldiers are fighting in the opposing armies, and killing their fellow Jews?[207] Do they take pride in the fact that Jews are fighting loyally and patriotically in the armies of their enemies, or is this a source of consternation and embarrassment? Can one correlate the positions taken regarding war with the identification of the preacher within the spectrum of Jewish religious movements (Reform, Conservative, Orthodox)?[208] Is a rabbi who has emigrated from Germany, preaching to congregants of German background, likely to hold a different position on America's role in the European war between 1914 and 1916 from that taken by a rabbi who has emigrated from England? Is a Sephardi rabbi more or less likely to support the US war against Spain in March and April 1898 than his Ashkenazi colleague? Was memory of the historical experience of the Jews in Spain, or in Russia, likely to influence attitudes about waging war with Spain, or joining an alliance with Russia?[209]

What happens if a rabbi has strongly opposed going to war from the pulpit in the months (Krauskopf in respect of the Spanish–American War) or years (Levy and Stephen S. Wise in respect of the First World War) before the decision is made? Once hostilities have begun, does he continue to hold firmly to his earlier position, or does he rally round the flag? If the latter, how does he explain his shift?[210] Does he concede in his sermons that he—or his congregants—may

[207] This theme is raised by many preachers, especially in the First World War; see especially Sermon 15 below by Silverstone, and the discussion in the introduction to it.

[208] Judith Bleich has shown me the typescript of her forthcoming article entitled 'Military Service: Ambivalence and Contradiction', in which she makes the intriguing point that in the early nineteenth century, liberal European rabbis, who valued integration and acceptance highly, were more likely to be enthusiastic about Jews in military service than their Orthodox counterparts, whereas by the second half of the twentieth century the liberal rabbis were more likely to be strongly critical of their government's militant policies and supportive of young Jews who refused to serve.

[209] For a strong critique of this kind of historical argument by Jewish preachers, see Solis-Cohen, 'An Unholy War', cited in the introduction to Sermon 13 below by Krauskopf.

[210] See also the introduction to Sermon 13 below by Krauskopf.

continue to harbour misgivings?[211] What happens when preachers who have supported the war effort decide that they can no longer do so, that they must speak out in opposition to the government policy (as for example on Vietnam)? How do they explain such a reversal, how defend themselves against the charge of giving aid and comfort to the enemy?

How is God used in the sermons? Are the war in general, and the vicissitudes of the particular campaigns at hand, presented as reflecting a divine providential plan, even if this includes devastating reversals for one's own forces?[212] Is there a claim of divine approval for the war and for one's own side? Or is there an effort to detach God from responsibility for the events?[213] How do preachers deal with their awareness that their colleagues in the enemy nations are also sincerely praying for God's support on the battlefield, for the triumph of their nations' forces; or indeed, that they themselves are praying for the destruction of human lives on the enemy side?[214] Is the war seen as a vindication of God, or as a phenomenon that raises fundamental questions about the efficacy of prayer and the validity of faith?

[211] See the guarded comments by Seixas and Marks in Sermons 3 and 4 below, and the more explicit statement by Max Heller of New Orleans on 6 May 1898, two weeks after the declaration of war on Spain: 'I am aware that among these hearers of mine there are many who disapprove, in all conscience, of this present war; who call it an unrighteous waste, a political pretence . . . I think it is a righteous, a noble, an unselfish war' (Heller, 'The War with Spain', 5).

[212] This assertion of providence characterizes all the American Civil War sermons reproduced in this volume, as well as those by I. M. Wise on the Franco-Prussian War (though he rhetorically asks 'Where, where is God's justice?') (Sermon 9 below), Krauskopf (Sermon 13 below) and Kaufmann Kohler on the Spanish–American War, and even one by Krauskopf from the First World War: 'What is this world war, but *God's Day of Judgement*. What are these corpse-strewn battle-fields, but *God's Place of Visitation*?' ('Ḥad Gadya', 195). In this the Jewish preachers were very much in accord with their Christian colleagues.

[213] See Sermon 18 by Levy below. This became a central issue in the Second World War sermons, when the assertion of divine providence was problematic outside the ultra-Orthodox camp. Virtually everyone preached a sermon on the topic 'Where Is God?'. Examples from 1940 include Sermon 23 below by Rudin and the beginning of Sermon by 29 by Wurzburger; Reichert, 'Where Is thy God?' (Yom Kippur, 1940); Franklin, 'Every Man's Problem' (Rosh Hashanah, 1940), 3: 'Where Now Is thy God?'; Newman, 'Why Hast Thou Forsaken Me?' (Rosh Hashanah, 1940); Abba Hillel Silver, 'Our Responsibility for Evil' (Rosh Hashanah, 1940), 60: '[E]specially during the last few months, I have heard men ask: "Where is God?"'; Jung, 'God in the Crisis' (1940), 25: 'The cry of the moment is, Where is God in the Crisis?' Similarly, from the following year, in a sermon for Kol Nidrei 1941 entitled 'Where Is God?', Levinthal said: 'I am a Rabbi now more than 30 years. I must admit that never in all that time have I been challenged as I have in the last year or two with the questions, ' "Where is God?" '

[214] This issue is raised in the Napoleonic war sermon of Isaac Luria (Sermon 1 below). Cf. Krauskopf's comments in Sermon 13 below on the Spanish invocation of their saints. The position articulated by the Revd W. S. Crowe on 24 Apr. 1898—'That two nations of the same faith should appeal to the same God for vengeance on each other is a theological difficulty, a doctrinal embarrassment, a religious absurdity, which the thinking people of the world cannot much longer abide. The very sentiment of prayer is fatally compromised' ('Prayer and War', 10)—would become almost a standard topos in the preaching of both Christians and Jews during the First World War.

Finally, how are the classical sources of tradition used in the sermons? Is there a tendency to invoke the most bellicose verses of the Bible: 'The Lord is a man of war'(Exod. 15: 3); 'I will gain glory through Pharaoh and all his warriors, his chariots and his horsemen' (Exod 14: 17); 'The Lord's war with Amalek throughout the ages' (Exod. 17: 16); 'Beat your ploughshares into swords, and your pruning hooks into spears' (Joel 4: 10)? Is the nation's military effort described as a 'holy war'?[215] How much emphasis is given to the standard biblical expressions of the value of peace (Isa. 2: 4)? Are the verses used by the preachers simply homiletical window-dressing, or is one convinced that they genuinely derive guidance and insight from the sacred Scripture?

For the preacher making such decisions about both rhetoric and substance, the Jewish preaching tradition provided little guidance. It is not until the middle of the eighteenth century that we begin to have evidence of Jews identifying with the national armies of the states in which they lived, not until a generation later that Jewish soldiers begin to be conscripted into national armies.[216] In the face of the dramatic shift in the experience of modern Jews represented by the national days of fasting and humiliation shared with their Christian neighbours, historical memory could not be of much help. Right up to the end of the nineteenth century, very few of the sermons delivered and published in the context of earlier wars were readily accessible to Jewish preachers even a generation or two later. (In this respect, their situation was markedly different from that of Christian preachers, who had access to many printed sermons by colleagues of previous generations.)

Whether or not Jewish preachers were successful in meeting these challenges will need to be determined by the reader of the texts that follow. One general conclusion emerging from this material concerns the extent to which Jewish preachers supported the positions of their governments. When the United States or Britain remained on the sidelines of a war, the preachers mobilized their resources to lament the evils of war and the glories of peace. When their countries entered a war, the tendency was almost universally to rally round the flag, justify the cause, and demonstrate the loyalty and patriotism of their people. This last goal was accomplished by emphasizing in their sermons the number of Jewish soldiers fighting and dying for their country (as

[215] On the First World War see Silver, 'The Battle Hymn of America', 3, 'for this *is a holy war*' (emphasis in original); Freehof, 'Judaism and the War': 'We do believe that this is God's war . . . for religious people this war must be a holy war'; Hertz, Sermon 28 below on Passover 1942: 'We are thus combatants in the most sacred conflict in human history.'

[216] For Ezekiel Landau's address to the first Jewish conscripts, see M. Saperstein, *'Your Voice Like a Ram's Horn'*, 25. Cf. the similar address delivered a century later by the grand rabbin of Paris, Zadoc Kahn, to the students from the French rabbinical seminary called to military service under the new military law: 'Allocution prononcée à l'occasion du départ des Séminaristes israélites pour l'armée', 19–30 (citing Landau's address at pp. 29–30).

well as for others), and by gaining maximum exposure for the sermon itself by circulating the text to newspapers and publishing it in pamphlet form.

It is not until Roland Gittelsohn's address of Rosh Hashanah 1965 on Vietnam (Sermon 31a) that I have found evidence of a Jewish religious leader explicitly condemning from the pulpit the fundamental wartime policies of the government.[217] In some cases, to be sure, Jewish preachers have drawn upon the resources of the pulpit and their own natural abilities to provide comfort and encouragement and reassurance to their listeners, to instil confidence in the justice of their cause and the ultimate victory of right; one thinks especially of the first years of the Second World War, when this outcome was not at all empirically obvious. In many cases, sermons ended with a humanitarian appeal to contribute to charities established to help widows, orphans, and wounded combatants. In the broader scheme, however, the extent to which sermons have been used to mobilize support for government policies that were not always as noble, disinterested, or wise as they were presented, and the extent to which preachers from Jewish as well as Christian pulpits have served as articulate mouthpieces for nationalistic propaganda and as effective instruments of social control, remains a disturbing phenomenon that requires further scrutiny and analysis.[218]

[217] The sermon is printed below (pp. 492–9). An earlier example is the British Liberal rabbi John Rayner, near the beginning of his career, preaching about the Suez campaign at the Liberal Jewish Synagogue on 11 Nov. 1956, and saying, 'I may be hopelessly misguided and misinformed, but I can see no escape from the conclusion that the British Government has acted wrongly' (Rayner, 'Morality and Expediency in International Conduct', 8). But this guarded statement is far more moderate than Gittelsohn's broadside attack.

[218] On this role of Christian preachers during the First World War, see Ray H. Abrams (a sociologist from the University of Pennsylvania), *Preachers Present Arms*. Abrams reaches the provocative conclusion that, on the whole, the Christian clergy 'took the verdicts of the Administration and proclaimed them as the judgements of Almighty God' (p. 248).

# PART I

# THE WARS
## OF THE
# NAPOLEONIC
# ERA

# CHAPTER ONE

A

# PENITENTIAL SERMON

PREACHED IN THE

SPANISH AND PORTUGUESE

## JEWS' SYNAGOGUE,

IN BEVIS-MARKS,

On 3rd Hesvan, 5564, A.M.

ANSWERING TO THE 19TH OF OCTOBER, 1803
IN CONFORMITY TO

## A ROYAL EDICT,

APPOINTING THAT DAY TO BE OBSERVED AS

## A GENERAL FAST

AND

FOR THE PURPOSE OF INVOKING BY PENITENTIAL PRAYER,

SUCCESS TO HIS MAJESTY'S ARMS, &c.

BY J. LURIA

*LONDON*
PRINTED BY WILLIAM LANE,
AT THE
*Minerva-Press,*
LEADENHALL-STREET
1803

*By the KING*

—

# A PROCLAMATION
## For a General FAST

*GEORGE* R.

WE, taking into Our most serious Consideration the just and necessary War in which We are engaged, and putting Our Trust in Almighty God that He will graciously bless Our Arms, both by Sea and Land, have resolved, and do, by and with the Advice of Our Privy Council, hereby command, That a public Day of Fasting and Humiliation be observed throughout those Parts of Our United Kingdom called *England* and *Ireland*, on *Wednesday* the Nineteenth Day of *October* next, that so both We and Our People may humble Ourselves before Almighty God, in order to obtain Pardon of Our Sins, and in the most devout and solemn Manner send up Our Prayers and Supplications to the Divine Majesty, for averting those heavy Judgments which Our manifold Provocations have most justly deserved; and for imploring His Blessing and Assistance on Our Arms for the Restoration of peace, and Prosperity to Us and Our Dominions: And We do strictly charge and command, that the said Publick Fast be reverently and devoutly observed by all Our loving Subjects in *England* and *Ireland*, as they tender the Favour of Almighty God, and would avoid His Wrath and Indignation; and upon Pain of such Punishment as We may justly inflict on all such as contemn and neglect the Performance of so religious and necessary a Duty: And for the better and more orderly solemnizing the same, We have given Directions to the Most Reverend the Archbishops, and the Right Reverend the Bishops of *England* and *Ireland*, to compose a Form of Prayer suitable to this Occasion, to be used in all Churches, Chapels, and Places of Publick Worship, and to take Care the same be timely dispersed throughout their respective Dioceses.

Given at Our Court at *Saint James's*, the Fourteenth Day of *September* One thousand eight hundred and three, in the Forty-third Year of Our Reign.

GOD SAVE THE KING

NAPOLEON was the kind of immense historical presence whose personality and policies were bound to capture the imagination of Jews, no matter how they were affected by his career. French preachers spoke of him in their sermons with an adulation transcending the conventional compliments paid to monarchs in the modern period. He is 'God's chosen'; some indeed used language of clear messianic resonance.[1] In the United States, when word arrived that Napoleon had ordered the convening in Paris of a 'Great Sanhedrin' of rabbis and other Jewish notables, Gershom Mendes Seixas, the religious leader of New York's Shearith Israel Congregation, spoke of it from the pulpit as if it were the harbinger of the messianic era.[2] As far away as Russia, Napoleon's exploits aroused interest and controversy among Jews whose world-view did not encompass political intrigue or military strategy.[3]

In 1801, as the conflict between the two major powers on opposite sides of the Channel continued, French preparations for an invasion of England began. On 13 February that year a special service was held at the Bevis Marks Synagogue to pray for 'the success of His Majesty's arms, and the spreading of . . . peace over us', and the order of prayer was printed soon afterwards.[4] When a peace agreement was signed in Amiens, there was celebration on both sides.[5] But on 18 May 1803, with the terms of the Treaty of Amiens unfulfilled by either party, Britain again declared war on France. As Napoleon prepared his Grande Armée of 100,000 for the assault, along with special invasion craft, fear of the onslaught ran high in England.[6] Senior government officials determined that if a French army did succeed in landing on British soil, London could not be held, and arrangements were made to move the King and the royal family

[1] 'It is thus beyond doubt that he is God's chosen one, and that God continually protects the actions of the just' ('Il est donc indubitable, que c'est lui qui est l'élu du Seigneur, et que le Seigneur protège sans cesse les actions du juste'): Sinzheim, *Sermon prononcé dans la grande synagogue à Strasbourg*, 4. For the messianic discourse, see the poem published in Mevorakh (ed.), *Napoleon and his Era* (Heb), 59–72, esp. 66; R. Schechter, *Obstinate Hebrews*, 201–3, 228–9.

[2] See the passage from his sermon cited in Mendes-Flohr and Reinharz, *The Jew in the Modern World*, 136; cf. Shulim, 'Napoleon I as the Jewish Messiah', on an anonymous Republican in Virginia who thought of Napoleon as the peacemaker of Europe and potential saviour of humankind, and another anti-Napoleon satirical writer who reports that Jews view Napoleon as their messiah.

[3] See H. Levine, ' "Should Napoleon Be Victorious" '; Mindel, *Rabbi Schneur Zalman*, 261–2; documents in Mevorakh (ed.), *Napoleon and his Era* (Heb.), 182–9, and in Mendes-Flohr and Reinharz, *The Jew in the Modern World*, 137–8.

[4] Szajkowski, 'Judaica-Napoleonica', 999, no. 327; Hyamson, *The Sephardim of England*, 136, in the context of a lengthy review of the special services and sermons held on national occasions (pp. 135–7), which nevertheless fails to mention the sermon reproduced here.

[5] Szajkowski, 'Judaica-Napoleonica', 987, nos 179–81.

[6] For a current semi-popular overview, see Pocock, *The Terror before Trafalgar*, e.g. 90–119; for greater detail, see Wheeler and Broadley, *Napoleon and the Invasion of England*, and, most recently (focusing on public discourse), Semmel, *Napoleon and the British*, 41–63 and 100–1.

to safe refuges further inland.[7] With regulations against foreigners tightened, Nathan Mayer Rothschild was assured by a friendly justice of the peace that he could have leave of residence in Manchester, but requested his London agent to procure a renewal of his passport, just in case.[8] Swept along by a wave of patriotism, many Jews volunteered for military service.

On 15 August 1803 Solomon Hirschel, recently arrived in Britain to assume the position of chief rabbi, is reported to have preached in the Great Synagogue on the duty of taking up arms in defence of the country, though insisting at the same time that the ritual precepts of Judaism (such as the observance of the sabbath) should not be neglected save in emergency.[9] A few months later, according to a contemporary news-sheet, Hirschel addressed a practical clash of loyalties for Jewish volunteers when, on the fast-day proclaimed for 19 October 1803, ten regiments were instructed to parade through the city, attend the worship service in one of the churches, and take their oath of allegiance there. The news-sheet reported:

By an order from their High Priest[10] they were prohibited from attending in our churches during the time of Divine Service. The High Priest, however, expressed his highest concurrence to their taking the oaths of fidelity and allegiance to our king and country. These gentlemen accordingly took the oaths, either upon the drilling-grounds of their respective corps, or in the vestry-room of the churches, as circumstances required. They were sworn upon the Book of Leviticus instead of the New Testament.[11]

The compromise arrangement seems to have been satisfactory.

On the actual morning of the fast-day, the editorial page of *The Times* invoked all the newspaper's considerable prestige on behalf of the event, in what it conceded was an unconventional endorsement:

---

[7] Fremantle, *England in the Nineteenth Century*, i. 385–6.

[8] Davis, *The English Rothschilds*, 22.

[9] Roth, *The Great Synagogue*, 203–4; Roth neglects to provide a source for his statement. The text of this sermon was not published and is apparently not extant; it would be interesting to compare it with the much better-known sermon delivered on 10 May 1789 by the chief rabbi of Prague, Ezekiel Landau, to the first Jewish soldiers conscripted into the Austrian army, and printed in *Hame'asef*. See M. Saperstein, 'Your Voice Like a Ram's Horn', 157.

[10] This was the name given to the chief rabbi in the Christian media (see Picciotto, *Sketches of Anglo-Jewish History*, 309; Barnett, *The Western Synagogue*, 5; Endelman, *The Jews of Georgian England*, 132 bottom). The printed version of Hirschel's sermon following the Battle of Trafalgar (Sermon 2 below) includes on its title page the line 'erroneously styled the High Priest'.

[11] Roth, *The Great Synagogue*, 203; here too he does not give the source for this quotation. *The Times* of 20 Oct. reported that the Seventh Regiment proceeded to Aldgate Church: 'As many Gentlemen belonging to this corps are Jews, when the oath of allegiance was administered to the Corps, they retired to the Vestry to receive it, according to the forms of their religion' (p. 2). For a description of the fast-day and the swearing of the oath of allegiance in the churches on 19 Oct. 1803, including descriptions from the *Gentleman's Magazine*, see Wheeler and Broadley, *Napoleon and the Invasion of England*, ii. 130–1. There is, however, no mention in this passage of Jews. Cf. the similar report cited in Katz, *The Jews in the History of England*, 286.

Perhaps the British nation were never summoned upon a more solemn and more awful occasion than the present, to prostrate themselves before the Divine Being, and solicit His protection, 'in whose hands are the issues of life and death'. We are aware that a periodical Journal, like ours, is not considered as the usual channel for conveying religious instruction; but by whatever means such instruction may be conveyed, it ought to be always welcome; and if any circumstance can justify a departure from established forms, it is the present crisis . . .

We shall, therefore, confidently expect the great satisfaction of seeing an universal reverence testified by all ranks of people for this day of religious humiliation. We allow, that it is a day appointed by human authority only, but all seasons are proper for the great duty of worship, and there is something at least sublime and impressive in the spectacle of a whole people uniting, on the same day, and almost at the same hour, in supplications to their God, and in earnest solicitations for his divine assistance.[12]

The following day, as if to underline this theme of inclusiveness, *The Times* wrote in its review of the various religious services that

The Rev. Solomon Hirschel assembled the Mosaic Congregation together at the Great Synagogue, Duke's Place, and delivered a patriotic Sermon, taking his text from the 10th Chapter of Numbers, Verse 9, and from the 21st Chapter, Verse 1 of Proverbs: And if ye go to war in your land against the enemy that oppreseth you, then ye shall blow an alarm with the trumpets, and yet shall be remembered by the Lord your God, and ye shall be saved from your enemies. After which prayers were read.[13]

At the Bevis Marks Synagogue, the lay leaders asked Isaac Luria to deliver the sermon. Little is known about Luria. His death was announced in the first edition of the new Jewish periodical the *Hebrew Intelligencer* as having occurred on 26 December 1822 at age 76,[14] which means he was born in 1746. Moses Gaster wrote that he was a member of the rabbinical court under Raphael Meldola.[15] Roth lists one earlier publication—a Spanish sermon for the sabbath before the festival of Purim, delivered for the same congregation and printed in 1784. The current sermon was also delivered in Spanish; the introduction (not reproduced here) states that many members of the congregation who had been present in the synagogue on the fast-day had urged him to publish an English translation. The author expresses the hope that the text will enhance sentiments of affection and loyalty towards King George III among the younger generation of Jews, and demonstrate to all who may read it 'the firm bonds that inseparably attached the Jews of these realms to the cause of their King and

---

[12] *The Times*, 19 Oct. 1803, p. 2.

[13] *The Times*, 20 Oct. 1803, p. 3. This sermon was never published, and there is no indication that a text is extant. No mention is made in the *Times* article of the service at Bevis Marks Synagogue.                         [14] Picciotto, *Sketches of Anglo-Jewish History*, 398.

[15] Gaster, *History of the Ancient Synagogue*, 162.

country!'[16] (It is possible that the public notice given by *The Times* to Hirschel's 'patriotic sermon' at the Ashkenazi Great Synagogue without any mention of Bevis Marks was a significant impetus to quick printing of this sermon in English.) The text—like most similar ephemeral publications—is extremely rare; there is apparently just one copy in Britain, in Oxford's Bodleian Library.[17]

A review of some of the other sermons delivered on the same day and subsequently published allows a comparison of the content of Luria's discourse with those of his Christian counterparts. Needless to say, the application of biblical models (especially from the Hebrew Scriptures) to yield insight into contemporary conditions characterizes all the sermons.[18] The most important common theme was the insistence upon a providential order that regulated the events of history in accordance with divine justice, with the corollaries that military defeats or threats represented a chastisement for national sins, and that prayer, fasting, and other means of atonement should be practised in the hope of averting or at least mitigating God's punishment. In addition, both Luria and the Christians maintain that while prayerful repentance is important, it must be undertaken alongside military preparations, not as a substitute for them.[19] As part of these preparations, Jews should be willing 'to administer, with a resolute and persevering courage, our personal services in the defence of this kingdom'. In this Luria differs from Hirschel Levin, who asserted in his Seven Years War sermon that the only contribution to be made by Jews to the war effort was through their prayer.[20]

[16] Luria, 'A Penitential Sermon', p. vi. The claim that the author was urged to publish the text by those who heard it, or by the leaders of the congregation, is a recurrent topos that may go back centuries, reflected in Christian publications as well.

[17] Miriam Rodrigues-Pereira, Honorary Archivist, has informed me that there is no copy in the possession of the Spanish and Portuguese Jews Congregation. No reference to this author (as contrasted with his celebrated sixteenth-century namesake) is listed in the catalogues of the British Library or the University Library in Cambridge, or in the Library of Congress, the New York Public Library, or the Harvard University Library. The Hebrew Union College notes an Isaac Luria with dates 1724–1806, but lists no publications by him. I am grateful to the Jewish Theological Seminary of America for providing access to this text.

[18] One of the Christian sermons mentioned in the *Times* article of the following day used as its text 'And the Lord said unto Moses, wherefore criest thou to me? Speak unto the Children of Israel, that they go forward' (Exod. 14: 15), which bears a somewhat ironic note for a day of fasting and prayer. An obvious choice was Isa. 37: 33–5, promising God's protection of Jerusalem against the threats of the taunting Assyrian invader, used by Charles Wellbeloved, 'A Sermon preached on . . . the day of national humiliation'; ten pages of the sermon are devoted to a detailed narration of the biblical event, before the preacher applies it to the present circumstances. I consulted copies of the Townsend and Wellbeloved texts at the Andover Harvard Theological Library.

[19] Note the formulation by John Townsend: 'Having an army of praying souls before the throne of grace, and an army of loyal citizens ready to march and join the regular force of the country . . . I do think that God will crown your efforts with signal success': 'The Goodness of God to Israel', 40.          [20] See M. Saperstein, *Jewish Preaching*, 352–3.

Yet there are characteristics of Luria's address, beyond the occasional passing reference to rabbinic literature, that differentiate it from the sermons delivered in churches on that day. First, Luria seems unwilling to specify the national sins, while the Christian preachers exemplified the moral decay of British society with condemnations of sexual immorality, profanity, and the slave trade.[21] Second, the often contemptuous disparagement of Napoleon in the Christian sermons is absent from Luria's text, perhaps reflecting an ambivalence stemming from the emperor's benevolent policies towards Jews;[22] we shall note the same phenomenon with regard to Solomon Hirschel's sermon two years later (Sermon 2). An important motif that understandably does not appear in the Christian sermons is Luria's insistence on the loyalty of Jews to their country, not only in England, but wherever Jews live, carrying out the instructions of the prophet Jeremiah to the exiles in Babylonia. This will become a central theme of Jewish discourse at the beginning of the First World War.

Related to this is the theological problem of people in the enemy country praying to God for the success of their armies with the same fervour; this theme, too, will become increasingly pronounced in sermons from later wars. Here it is specifically applied to the French Jews, who—the preacher concedes—are doing the same thing his own people are doing. His strong defence of those French Jews—including the insistence that they could not possibly be praying for the devastation of Britain, and that, if reports to this effect should be confirmed, it could only be the result of compulsion—suggests that he was responding to an accusation made against the loyalty and trustworthiness of British Jews because of the behaviour of their French co-religionists. While emphasizing Jews' loyalty to their own lands, he insists that they are a nation scattered in exile, and could not wish harm to members of their own people.

The structure of the sermon reflects the lingering influence of the traditional Sephardi model,[23] though with indications that it is breaking down. It follows that model in beginning with a biblical text, followed by a rabbinic

[21] See Lovegrove, 'English Dissent and the European Conflict', 272–5. Note Wellbeloved: 'The shores of the Atlantic too . . . resound with the voice of mourning, either in the families whom British merchants have plundered of their kindred and their friends, or in the luxurious plantations, which rise and flourish by the oppressive labours of an unpitied slave' ('A Sermon preached on . . . the day of national humiliation', 25).

[22] For Townsend, Napoleon is 'like another Pharaoh' ('The Goodness of God to Israel', 31). Wellbeloved refers to him as 'the usurper', who 'has shown his utter contempt of all religion and degraded it, by rendering it subservient to the cause of lawless power and cruel tyranny. And now having thus openly despised and ridiculed the God of truth, he dares to call himself His appointed minister' ('A Sermon preached on . . . the day of national humiliation', 16–17).

[23] On this model, see M. Saperstein, *Jewish Preaching*, 66–9; id., *'Your Voice Like a Ram's Horn'*, 111–12.

dictum, and including an invocation of divine aid for the preacher. But the biblical text read at the beginning is taken not from the weekly lesson or the haftarah, its accompanying reading from the prophets, but from a different passage in the early prophets, and the dictum is not actually cited at the beginning but summarized in order to amplify the biblical text. Nor is there any real discussion or exegetical probing of that text; it is mentioned at the outset, then all but put aside. And the invocation of God's aid, which should come at the conclusion of the exordium or introductory section, appears two-thirds of the way through the sermon. Except for a few statements that the preacher is nearing the end, the listeners would have no reliable means of understanding the sermon's structure while they were listening to it. Nevertheless, though this text provides no evidence that its author was a master preacher, it contains passages of considerable force and historical interest.

# SERMON

---

וידעו כל הקהל הזה כי לא בחרב ובחנית יהושיע ה'
כי לה' המלחמה ונתן אתכם בידינו

*And all this assembly shall know that the Lord saveth not with sword and spear,*
*for the battle is the Lord's and he will give you into our hands.*

(1 SAM. 17: 47)

I CANNOT commence the present discourse with a happier illustration of the text I have chosen for this occasion than by prefixing the ideas of our learned Theologists in Yalcut.[24]

It is remarked in their comment on the above recited verse that when David contemplated the gigantic figure of Goliath the Philistine, and perceived him so valiant and well-accoutred, he exclaimed, 'Who will be able to face so formidable a warrior?' But when he reflected on the arrogance and blasphemy of his challenger, his dilemma subsided, and he expressed a willingness to enter the lists with him: because Goliath was not upheld by a reverence of the Deity, because his confidence in victory rested solely upon the valour of his arms, and being elated with pride, he did not attribute the event of battle to the all-powerful hand of Providence. It was then that he publicly held forth, 'All this

---

[24] See *Yalkut shimoni, nevi'im rishonim*, sect. 127.

congregation shall know that the Lord doth not save with sword and spear, for the battle is the Lord's and he will give you into our hands' (1 Sam. 17: 47).[25]

Under circumstances not altogether dissimilar, and influenced by the same pious sentiments which acknowledge the issue of all arduous contests to proceed from a Divine interposition, His august Majesty, King George, has graciously ordered this day to be set apart for a Fast, and solemn intercession with our Creator, in consequence of his being engaged in war with other nations, and the threatening appearance of invasion from the enemy's coasts. He most wisely adjudged these means to be essentially necessary towards conciliating Divine favour; also in imploring protection for his numerous fleets and armies, and for the final attainment of an honourable and permanent peace from all those powers, whose minds are at present obdurately bent on war and devastation. He has devoutly appointed this solemnity, in hopes that we may be enabled to avert the wrath of the Lord, incurred by our manifold transgressions, and to strive to effect our peace with Him by a discontinuance of our evil doings; to the end that we may become deserving objects of His clemency and holy protection.[26]

Now it is apparent how great is the anxiety of each man's mind under apprehensions for the preservation of all the comforts so habitual to our frail nature in our social capacity, and while a daring invader holds forth his hand to wrest them all from us by a sudden blow, be it my task, in this awful juncture, to call forth the devotion of this holy congregation, in hopes to ward off this most grievous of all calamities, pursuing the method which the Sovereign of the land has so worthily and benignly pointed out to all his subjects; and this hath the particular recommendation attached to it, that his own dignified observance of this day (if we suppose it only equal to the general tenor of his exemplary zeal in the cause of religion),[27] affords the best guide and justest criterion to all

[25] The minor stylistic differences between this and the rendering of the verse at the beginning of the sermon may be the result of the translation from the original Spanish.

[26] Luria reports the general sentiments but not the precise wording of the royal proclamation, dated 14 Sept. 1803. See the text preceding the introduction to this sermon.

[27] George III was indeed respected by his subjects as a devout Christian; *The Times*, writing editorially on the links between religion and war, asked rhetorically: 'Do we not ourselves live under the benignant sway of a Sovereign, whose reign has been resplendent with victory, and whose private life has been distinguished by religion and piety?' (20 Oct. 1803, p. 2). A modern historian has written: 'He was popular with a people who beheld in him a shining example of qualities supposed to be distinctively English. Religious, faultless in his family life, a patriot . . . he was at the same time stubborn generally, but particularly so upon questions affecting his religious convictions' (Fremantle, *England in the Nineteenth Century*, i. 117–18).

It seems to have been conventional for religious leaders, in praising their monarch, to emphasize his or her religious piety. We find the same phenomenon, for example, in a French Jewish

descriptions of his subjects, how it ought to be observed. Let us then imitate his illustrious example, and it will be no longer dubious that success will finally crown our fervent supplications.

The royal edict contains various directions. It orders all the subjects of his Majesty's realms to use abstinence and humble prayer—to implore, prostrate before the Divine throne on this day, an acquittal and pardon for all the offences wherewith we have justly provoked the Lord's anger—to beseech with earnestness victory and constant success to his arms both by sea and by land— to invoke the Supreme Being to incline the hearts of our enemies to solicit a glorious, solid, and durable peace—removing from their imaginations that wild and ambitious spirit which actuates their present proceedings, and which seeks its gratification in the subversion of the wise and enviable Constitution of these kingdoms, and the annihilation of the justly acquired fame, glory, and honour which this nation has so distinguishedly attained, and which God in His bounty has so favourably allotted to its portion.

That we ought to make a right use of this penitential day, and that its institution is exactly suited to the end proposed, we have the sanction of the wisest of Kings in the Proverbs, saying, 'When a man's ways please the Lord, he maketh even his enemies to be at peace with him' (Prov. 16: 7).

Having then ascertained the end for which we are assembled in this house of worship, I am confident, my brethren, that we shall not confine ourselves either to a formal or reluctant compliance with the recommendations of the royal edict, for it is natural that we should espouse our country's cause with the most heartfelt enthusiasm, since there is not a single instance on record, in any part of the world, of our nation having shrunk from the most unequivocal testimonies of allegiance towards those States which have granted them favour and protection: so that it is impossible for us to lose the recognised features of true and faithful subjects.[28]

On all occasions our feelings are in unison with the most loyal of our fellow-citizens; but we feel a more powerful stimulus by the grateful sense we entertain

sermon delivered at a ceremony celebrating military victories on 13 May 1809, which lauds Napoleon as 'a perfect model of piety and gratitude toward the supreme Source of all' ('un modèle aussi parfait de piété et de reconnaissance envers le Dispensateur suprème de toutes choses'): Cologna, 'Discours pronouncé . . . à l'occasion des actions de grâces', 7. See also S. Sègre on Napoleon as the 'pious emperor', kneeling in prayer after a victory: Schechter, *Obstinate Hebrews*, 211.

[28] This historical motif of Jews' loyalty to the countries of their residence will be taken up by later preachers, specifically with regard to Jewish military service; see e.g. Michelbacher, Sermon 5 below, n. 24.

in consideration for the different privileges and the security we are partakers of under the mild government of this country. These lead us, at this hour, to implore the forgiveness of our sins as the medium to deserve, in common with others, the blessings of peace and tranquillity, and further induce us to offer up to Omnipotent God an earnest prayer for the preservation of the sacred person of our Gracious Sovereign King George the Third—for the general success and prosperity of his armies and navy—for the subjugation of his enemies—for the tranquillity, peace, and happiness of this kingdom wherein we sojourn.

We do not assume merit to ourselves on account of the deep concern we feel for the safety and prosperity of the British Empire; it is the consequence of a religious injunction handed to us by the prophet Jeremiah, and is only enhanced by the partiality we entertain for this happy land. It says, 'And seek the peace of the city whither I have caused you to be carried away captives, and pray unto the Lord for it; for in the peace thereof shall ye have peace' (Jer. 29: 7).

However the excellence and propriety of the prophet's recommendations are obvious, still I am led to believe that you will not think it superfluous or tedious in me to illustrate it by quoting, on that point, the very judicious and energetic maxim of our learned Rabbins in their incomparable tenets of Abot: 'Constantly pray for the peace and welfare of the kingdom and government, for if there were no subordination, one would swallow each other alive'.[29]

Thus we see the authority of Holy Writ pronounces it an indispensable obligation for all the House of Israel to co-operate in the security and welfare of the land they live in; and in no case can there be a weightier responsibility for our actions having that tendency than on this particular period of danger and anxiety. It behoves us to be liberal in our pecuniary aids, and to administer, with a resolute and persevering courage, our personal services in the defence of this kingdom,[30] in order to baffle the giddy and insidious projects of a powerful, vigilant, and inveterate foe. But as we find in the history of nations that all human prowess has frequently failed—that great strength, and matured council, are often attended with defeat and disappointment, we should look upon the proud array of battle as a mere instrument of Providence, and keep in mind that the important decision of victory ultimately depends upon the Supreme

[29] *Avot* 3: 2; note that there is no exegesis or discussion of the passage, such as an earlier preacher would probably have engaged in; it is simply presented as self-explanatory.

[30] As we shall see in subsequent sermons, virtually every Jewish address delivered on an occasion designated by the government in wartime includes an appeal for support of charities established to aid those suffering from the consequences of conflict, in addition to the 'personal service' that is required.

Arbiter of events, whose will determines the balance of our destinies, and not that little might wherewith we display our boastful vengeance.

We are not to neglect or despise the happy circumstances of our forward preparations, and the formidable front we oppose to our enemies;[31] for the Divine goodness has granted us those advantages, and they were excited by a consciousness of the superior blessings which Providence has apportioned to this land. Thus the noble and unanimous display of this nation's valour, and its determined spirit to resist invasion, imply not only patriotism, but a sense of gratitude to the Author of all good; and this conduct fulfils one of the main objects of religion.[32] It is desirable that we should daily augment our resources for war; but it is even still more desirable that we should continue to entertain a religious sentiment for what we possess, and build our hopes upon the same foundation, to speedily surmount all our difficulties.

Every reflection that beams on our mind shews the urgent necessity to perform this day's duty, which is to meditate, with stedfast thought and susceptible heart, upon the purpose for which we are assembled. To treat this matter with indifference cannot be looked upon in any other light than that of a criminal negligence, for our prayers are as 'the voice of Jacob' (Gen. 27: 22), and we received assurances of old that they were admissible to the Lord of the Universe.[33] May the penitence and affliction of this auditory therefore draw down upon us the compassion of the God of Israel, so that our petition, urged with a sincere and contrite spirit, be granted to this kingdom, from the exalted mansion of the Supreme King of Kings!

How admirably adapted to kindle the warmest emulation in our bosoms, and to ground hopes for the fulfilment of our desires, is that most honourable and glorious distinction which our great legislator Moses declared in our behalf in these words, 'For what nation is there so great, who hath God so nigh unto them, as the Lord our God is in all things that we call upon him for?' (Deut. 4: 7).

It is a self-evident conclusion that the duties I have enlarged upon are enjoined to all our brethren, the children of Israel, wheresoever they dwell, and under whatsoever government they are protected. A non-compliance therein would constitute not only disloyalty to their country, but also a violation of a

[31] That is, although prayer is important, military defences and practical preparations should not be overlooked.

[32] That is, dedication to defence of the country is an expression of gratitude to God for its resources, and such expression is a religious duty.

[33] The reference is probably to BT *Git.* 57*b*; cf. *Genesis Rabbah* 65: 20.

religious precept. It is hence natural to suppose that such of our brethren as reside in countries avowedly hostile to these realms will also offer up prayers to Almighty God for the prosperity and success of the arms of such as are the enemies of this land, in direct opposition to those supplications which we this day, and other days, make choice of.[34] To presume that our petition will be accepted, and theirs rejected, through our superior merit, would argue a self-conceit on our part. But our hopes are derived from a higher source—the peculiar justice of our cause—engaged in self-defence, and in the immediate support of our independence. It is allowable in us to draw an almost positive inference, that the prayers which our brethren say in the land of our enemies are not of a tendency to invoke (God forbid the supposition!) the downfall of these kingdoms, and the subversion of their governments. The Jews, from their situation in the enemy's unsettled land, have a fair claim to general commiseration, instead of being rendered liable to the least severe animadversions on their supposed conduct. How credulous are those who affect to believe that our brethren abroad can have acted in a manner so wild and irreligious![35] Who of us can join in this belief? although the enemy may feel destitute of all other than those forlorn hopes, to inflict on us the least sensible injury.

Let us investigate certain considerations. Are we not a nation split into innumerable divisions, dispersed in all countries over the face of the globe, awaiting the term of our captivity, for the promised restoration of our pristine glory? Is it probable then, nay possible, for brethren in one common state of affliction to court a measure that would pierce their own bowels at every stroke their weapons plunged into the entrails of their same brotherhood?[36] No one can suppose a nation so totally lost to the feelings of humanity as to present a spectacle of a body of men each prowling for a brother's blood, for no other

---

[34] The sermon by David Sinzheim, mentioned in n. 1 above, when published in French had the following statement appended after the closing prayer on behalf of Napoleon and Josephine: 'In all synagogues, prayers and hymns are addressed to God each day, morning and evening, for the preservation of the lives and well-being [*bonheur*] of the Imperial and Royal Majesties, and for the safety and well-being of their armies' (Sinzheim, *Sermon prononcé dans la grande synagogue à Strasbourg*, 7). For a splendid recent review of patriotic public prayers and sermons by French Jews in the Napoleonic era, see Birnbaum, *Prier pour l'État*, 52–65. No prayer is included from 1803, however.

[35] This clearly suggests that the preacher was responding to an accusation circulating about the loyalties and behaviour of French Jews (perhaps with the implication that British Jews might be a fifth column). A few moments later, he refers to 'such rumour'.

[36] On this theme of the pain felt by Jews in one country when Jews in the armies of an enemy country are killed, see the vignette cited by George (Gedaliah) Silverstone, below: Sermon 15, p. 307.

motive than because he is preferably situated on an opposite shore. Our law, the primary source of all morality, will not be suspected of favouring the views of implacable revenge, nor will it admit its sectaries to advance too far into political animosities.

A further corroboration that such rumour is unfounded may be drawn from the consideration that if any disaster was to befall the credit or resources of these kingdoms, our brethren that sojourn in the enemy's land would feel the destruction as well as ourselves. It would be the ruin of thousands, since it is a well-known fact that the capitals and effects of many thousand foreigners are centered here.[37] I would be trespassing on the patience of my hearers to canvass this matter more at large.

If in the general form of prayers adopted by our brethren in France or its dependencies (and which I do not believe to be the case) there be any thing contained bordering upon asperity or fanaticism, it certainly arose from compulsion exercised over them in one way or other, for, as I have before laid down, religion is the harbinger of love to mankind, and not of boundless persecution. Here—God be praised!—we enjoy an unrestrained freedom of worship, and are incapable of misapplying it; our intercessions at the fountain of Mercy are pure, sincere, and undissembled, for on the tranquillity and security of these favoured kingdoms depends not only our preservation, but likewise that of the greater part of our brethren elsewhere.[38]

Our enemies openly and arrogantly boast the multitude of their armies, and other means of force, to enable them to undertake the invasion of this country.[39] But such haughtiness should not dishearten us, which, in the sequel of my discourse, I will prove by various examples; and, lastly, shall conclude with an abridgment of the prayers framed for the august and solemn occasion.[40] But previously I deem it consistent with gratitude to tender my obsequious acknowledgments to the Gentlemen Superintendents of this holy flock,[41] for

---

[37] Luria refers here to the role of England as a commercial centre on which many in other countries depend for their economic security.

[38] This sentence alludes to (and expands) the famous instructions of Jeremiah to the Babylonian exiles to 'seek the welfare of the city to which I have exiled you and pray to the Lord in its behalf; for in its prosperity you shall prosper' (or 'in its tranquillity [*shelomah*] you shall be tranquil') (Jer. 29: 7).

[39] Cf. the sermon by Townsend: 'But now he threatens to fight us, yea, he is represented as being elated with the certainty of conquering us, at our own doors!' ('The Goodness of God to Israel', 31).          [40] An indication to the listeners of what remains for them to hear.

[41] The wardens of the synagogue, listed in the dedication on p. v of the pamphlet: Joseph Saportas, President; Emanuel Israel de Piza; Jacob Mocatta; Jacob Osorio; and Gabriel Israel Brandon, Treasurer.

the distinguished honour they were pleased to confer on me in their request that I should perform this part of the functions of the day. Although I fear that I am not competent to the right discharge thereof, I nevertheless humbly crave the kind attention of this devout auditory, and earnestly implore the Divine aid and power to perform this solemn undertaking using the words of the royal Psalmist, 'Let thine hand help me, for I have chosen thy precepts' (Ps. 119: 173).[42]

Fearful of having dwelt too long on the first part of the sermon, I shall in the subsequent adhere to brevity as much as possible. In specifying those most important fundamental truths of religion and morality, either by argument or exemplification, that have a reference to the purport of our wishes this day, I place a reliance that the superior information and devout inclinations of my audience will greatly contribute to elucidate my imperfect sketches, and ensure that fervour and unanimity of sentiment commensurate to the magnitude of the occasion.

Penitence, and reformation of our evil proceedings, you will all agree, are the surest means of approximation to the Divine presence, to claim his aid and assistance to deliver us from the power of the enemy. Thus we read in the first book of Samuel, in the continuance of the wars which the Philistines carried on against our forefathers in the time of Heli, and nearly throughout the years of Samuel and those of David, that when the children of Israel found themselves oppressed and cast down by the fatal effects of hostility, they are those spoken of by Scripture, 'And all the House of Israel lamented after the Lord' (1 Sam. 7: 2). And on their application to the prophet Samuel, God's minister for relief, he thus replied, 'If ye do return unto the Lord with all your hearts, then put away the strange Gods and Ashtaroth from among you, and prepare your hearts unto the Lord, and serve him only, and he will deliver you out of the hands of the Philistines' (1 Sam. 7: 3). The Holy Scripture proceeds to inform us of their strict compliance and amendment: 'Then the children of Israel did put away the Baalim and Ashtaroth, and served the Lord only' (1 Sam. 7: 4). And having reformed themselves, the following edict of the Prophet ensues: 'And Samuel said, gather all Israel to Mizpeh, and I will pray for you unto the Lord' (1 Sam. 7: 5). Which prayer, according to the description given in the Scripture, was accompanied by drawing of waters, and pouring them out before the Lord, with fasting and a confession of their sins (1 Sam. 7: 6).

---

[42] This expression of gratitude and invocation of divine help for the speaking mission would ordinarily signal the end of the introductory portion of the sermon. The preacher therefore proceeds to state that the rest of the sermon will be relatively brief.

It does not appear in the context what waters these were, but in my humble interpretation, they were showers of tears distilled from their eyes, expressive of the sincere repentance of their crimes, and which they spilt before the Lord.[43] The effects of so singular a contrition and reformation procured the riddance of their enemies, the Philistines, as the Scripture plainly declares: 'So the Philistines were subdued, and they came no more into the coast of Israel; and the hand of the Lord was against the Philistines all the days of Samuel' (1 Sam. 7: 13).

What a powerful lesson this, my beloved brethren, how to prepare your hearts in this hour of anguish, to obtain a like safety for these kingdoms! Your atonement must be equally great, and your inward compunction raise all the latent powers of the soul; and while we pour ourselves forth to that effect, it is permitted that I should remind you a second time, that 'our voice is the voice of the House of Jacob'.

The numerous forces which the arrogant enemy has collected to invade this country ought not to dispirit us for a moment, even were not our opposing force invincible, as the justice of our cause, under God, must dispel all our uneasiness, and inspire a confidence that 'the same providential hand that saves with numbers extends victory to the few'.[44] When Sennacherib, with a strong and matchless army, invaded the territories of Israel, and the capital city of Jerusalem in the fourteenth year of the reign of King Hezekiah, nothing could exceed the insolence of the haughty invader. He insultingly provoked Hezekiah with all kinds of reproachful challenges, and caused him much uneasiness. In this dilemma, our King assembled his forces, and poured forth the anguish of his soul to his Omnipotent Creator.

The Almighty inspired the Prophet Isaiah to promise the Prince a victorious issue, and that neither himself nor his country should be harmed by his pre-sumptuous and tremendous antagonist. The Scripture uses these words: 'Whom hast thou reproached and blasphemed? And against whom hast thou exalted thy voice, and lifted thine eyes on high? Even against the Holy One of Israel' (2 Kgs 19: 22). And the Prince is told to rely that, through the same road by which he came, he should shamefully return, and that he would never have the power of coming to disturb the quietness of that city, because he had placed too much confidence in his presumptuous strength.

[43] The preacher follows here the commentary *Metsudat david*: 'they aroused themselves to draw forth and make flow the water of tears, which they poured out in prayer before God'.
[44] Cf. 1 Sam. 14: 6.

This instance from the sacred pages, descriptive of God's interference to curb a violent spirit of dominion and aggrandizement, is a subject I shall dismiss with reluctance; but I must guard against exceeding the due bounds of a sermon. I shall therefore close by drawing a consequence that, however the Lord permitted Sennacherib to conquer and usurp cities for a while, it was decreed that his attack against Jerusalem should end in his own confusion, and that our city should stand firm as a rock, notwithstanding other Potentates had fallen into his merciless hands.

It cannot escape notice what affinity this history bears to the immediate circumstances of this country at the present day. It may perhaps be the province of the future historian to depict the person of our invader in the identical colouring of Scripture, and when alluding to the virtues and excellence that embellish the character of the British Sovereign, in addition to his paternal affection to all ranks of his subjects, is it not likely that the comparison will be closely drawn with Hezekiah?—a Prince highly meritorious and beloved, and one especially blessed with the Divine regard.

In the instances of David and Goliath, and, lastly, of Sennacherib with Prince Hezekiah, we gather undeniable proofs that not only every exertion of valour and the assemblage of a numerous armed host are requisite to oppose in battle, but that it is equally necessary to implore victory at the feet of the Almighty's throne, and to deserve his protection by an undeviating righteousness.[45] Let us, while our hearts are penetrated by pious meditation, pray that our enemy's intentions may be frustrated, who load us with threats, through envy of our happy situation, and the concord that prevails among us; and who, flushed with the easy conquest, or rather usurpation, they have recently made of other States, flatter themselves with an easy access here. But no—it will not happen; for we trust in Providence that the text will be literally verified and accomplished—

וידעו כל הקהל הזה כי לא בחרב ובחנית יהושיע ה'
כי לה' המלחמה ונתן אתכם בידינו

And all this assembly shall know that the Lord saveth not with sword and spear, for the battle is the Lord's and he will give you into our hands.        (I SAM. 17: 47)

---

[45] The verse may actually be taken to imply that military strength is not necessary in order for those in God's favour to be victorious; the preacher is therefore careful to state that both are required. Solomon Hirschel makes the same point in his sermon of 1805: see Sermon 2 below, p. 98 n. 20.

On the conclusion of this discourse, allow me to present you with the abridgment of a prayer formed for this day's service, which I shall repeat with a sincere devotion, prostrate before the Divine presence, and I am sensible that everyone present will rapturously accompany me, as is becoming in his Majesty's most faithful and loyal subjects.

Omnipotent Creator and most merciful King! We confess before Thee that it is our manifold offences against Thy will which have drawn down upon us this indication of Thy anger, and proved the cause of the present trouble and affliction that overspread this nation, in the menaces of our enemies and persecutors. Deign, O Merciful Father, to receive our contrition, while prostrate we implore, with a humble and penitent mind, that Thou wouldst, through Thy Divine mercy, put Thy wrath away from us, and re-establish us in Thy favour, causing the designs of our enemies to be totally frustrated. May the sacred person of his august Majesty King George the Third, be shielded by Thy bounteous hand! May his days be lengthened into a series of happy years! And may he continue the beloved parent of his duteous subjects throughout a glorious and prosperous reign!

O powerful God! Grant Thy aid to the arms of our illustrious Monarch both by sea and land, that his undertakings be crowned with success, and the enemy be obliged, in compliance with reason and justice, to become suppliants for a restoration of peace, compatible with the glory and honour of his crown.[46] Influence his counsellors and ministers with a right judgment, that they may pursue those steps most conducive to the welfare and tranquillity of these kingdoms. Inspire valour into the hearts of his Generals—steadiness and unanimity into his troops, in order that his enemies, seized with dread and panic, fly before us.

Be Thy mercy also invoked for us, Thy peculiar people,[47] that we may constantly practise, in our dispersion, the observance of Thy Divine law, that we continue to adhere at all times with true faith to our Sovereign, and comply, as faithful subjects, with his royal edicts. Also cause the happy period to draw nigh, O Supreme Lord, when all the nations of the earth shall adore Thy unity, and acknowledge Thee the Supreme and Omnipotent Creator,[48] the Cause of

[46] The crown of King George; Napoleon's coronation as emperor was still more than a year in the future.

[47] *Am segulah*, a phrase that does not appear in the Bible, but is derived from Exod. 19: 5; cf. Rashi on Deut. 26: 17.

[48] Echoing the words and ideas of the 'Aleinu' prayer, which concludes Jewish worship services with this universalistic hope.

all Causes, like Thou promisedst by the hand of Thy prophet Zephaniah, 'For then will I turn to the people a pure language, that they may all call upon the name of the Lord, to serve him with one consent' (Zeph. 3: 9). Amen.

# CHAPTER TWO

A

# SERMON

PREACHED
AT THE

## GREAT SYNAGOGUE, DUKE'S PLACE,

On the 14 Kislev, (A.M.) 5565 [5566]

ANSWERING TO

## THURSDAY, 5TH OF DECEMBER, 1805

BEING THE DAY APPOINTED

FOR A

GENERAL THANKSGIVING FOR THE SUCCESS OF HIS MAJESTY'S
FLEET UNDER LORD NELSON, OFF TRAFALGAR;

BY THE

## REV. SOLOMON HIRSCHEL,

PRESIDING RABBI

(ERRONEOUSLY STYLED THE HIGH PRIEST)

OF THE GERMAN JEWS IN LONDON

*LONDON*: T. MALDEN, 1805

Solomon Hirschel was the youngest son of Hirschel Levin, who served as chief rabbi of the German community in England from 1758 until 1764. Born in 1761, he was the only British chief rabbi before Israel Brodie in the mid-twentieth century to have begun his life in the country. However, his family left England for Halberstadt in 1764, and he was educated in Europe. After serving for nine years as rabbi in the Prussian city of Prenzlau, in 1802 he was invited to take up the chief rabbinate of the German Jewish community of London, a position that had been vacant (with an acting chief rabbi) for ten years following the death of David Tevele Schiff. Although he knew hardly any English, his British birth made him a popular appointment.

Hirschel had an impressive appearance, reflected in several portraits, including one in the pamphlet of his Trafalgar sermon. He reportedly had a ready wit, and a mastery of mathematics as well as of traditional Jewish texts.[1] Although demeaned by opponents as a man of few scholarly accomplishments,[2] he had a significant library of Judaica, including some 120 manuscripts, which went upon his death to the London Beit Hamidrash. He worked together with the Sephardi haham Raphael Meldola in trying to defend the traditions of Jewish life,[3] and supervised the preparation of the Hebrew text for an 1822 edition of a prayer book (with English translation).[4] His term as chief rabbi was marked by frequent conflicts with Jews in the community;[5] towards the end of his life he was embroiled in the controversies surrounding the establishment of a congregation led by David Woolf Marks that insisted on reforms in the ritual. Todd Endelman characterizes his impact on Anglo-Jewish life as 'limited'.[6]

Preaching was not a major interest or preoccupation of Hirschel's—subsequent chief rabbis were quite different in this regard—nor was there much sustained demand for it within the synagogue. Indeed, one of the ordinances passed by the wardens of the Great Synagogue in 1826 required that the rabbi receive prior permission from the wardens if he wanted to deliver a sermon on the sabbath afternoon.[7] This reflected a general situation: at this time, regular preaching was more likely to be heard in smaller confraternities than in the

[1] For the circumstances of Hirschel's election and his character, see Roth, *The Great Synagogue*, 181–5.
[2] One opponent, Levi Alexander, published in 1808 a pamphlet entitled 'The Axe Laid to the Root, or Ignorance and Superstition Evident in the Character of the Rev. Solomon Hirschel . . .'; see Roth, *The Great Synagogue*, 186–9.
[3] Roth, *The Great Synagogue*, 186; Picciotto, *Sketches of Anglo-Jewish History*, ch. 41: 'A Chief Rabbi and a Haham'.       [4] Ruderman, *Jewish Enlightenment in an English Key*, 238–9.
[5] On these quarrels, see Picciotto, *Sketches of Anglo-Jewish History*, 144–9; Roth, *Anglo-Jewish Letters*, 228–36; Katz, *The Jews in the History of England*, 326–9; Ruderman, *Jewish Enlightenment in an English Key*, 246–9.       [6] Endelman, *Jews of Georgian England*, 144.
[7] Ibid. 143, based on the minutes of the vestry meetings entry for 29 Jan. 1826.

major synagogues.[8] Hirschel never mastered English well enough to preach effectively in it. Yet Cecil Roth described him as 'a learned and eloquent preacher' and cited a non-Jewish writer, William Hamilton Reid, as having reported that his sermons frequently addressed the theme of universal tolerance.[9]

Hirschel's sermons were generally given in response to specific events or challenges. After the death of Raphael Meldola in 1828 he delivered, 'in English instead of his Native Yiddish, with which he is more familiar', a eulogy at the graveside; after the death of Nathan Mayer Rothschild in 1836 he delivered the eulogy in English in the presence of dignitaries including the Lord Mayor of London.[10] His 'Address delivered on Laying the Foundationstone of the Intended New Synagogue' was published at London in 1837.[11] In January 1807 he devoted two sermons to the threat posed by Christian missionaries, who planned to open a free school for Jewish children; printed abstracts of the sermons in Hebrew and English were distributed among the Jewish population.[12] More dramatic occasions were provided by the varying fortunes of the nation at war.

We have seen an example of Hirschel's patriotic activity in the introduction to the previous sermon; here we continue the story. On 21 October 1805 the British fleet under Lord Nelson won a stunning victory against the combined naval forces of France and Spain. It was a fateful battle—some have claimed that the very survival of England was at stake—for it ended the immediate danger that French ships could dominate the Channel, allowing the Grande Armée to invade. But when the news arrived in London a few weeks later, it was accompanied by the devastating report that Lord Nelson himself had been fatally wounded in the battle and had succumbed to his injuries a few hours later. Thursday 5 December was designated by the Crown a day of thanksgiving for the victory (it was not yet known on that date in England that three

[8] Endelman, *Jews of Georgian England*, 136–7; Roth, *The Great Synagogue*, 259.

[9] Roth, *The Great Synagogue*, 185–6. Unfortunately, no note is provided for the reference to Reid, who wrote about Jews in the *Gentleman's Magazine* and in other, separate, works such as *The New Sanhedrin* (1807). Hirschel's command of English was defended by Hyman A. Simons in his uncritical and undocumented (and therefore not fully reliable) biography, *Forty Years a Chief Rabbi*, 37.

[10] For the Meldola eulogy, see Simons, *Forty Years a Chief Rabbi*, 37, citing the *Sunday Herald* of 3 June 1828, where the eulogy was (according to the author) published in full. For the Rothschild eulogy ('delivered in impeccable English'), see ibid.; Roth, *The Great Synagogue*, 186.

[11] This was the second building of the 'New Synagogue', on Great St Helen's Street, designed by John Davies and completed in 1838.

[12] Endelman, *Jews of Georgian England*, 241–2; Katz, *The Jews in the History of England*, 370. The school was opened, but did not achieve any significant success in attracting or converting Jews. Picciotto described Hirschel as 'an uncompromising foe to conversionists; but he was mild in manner and desirous of avoiding religious controversies with non-Jews, and especially careful not to give offence to Christians' (*Sketches of Anglo-Jewish History*, 308–9).

days earlier Napoleon had won the greatest victory of his career at Austerlitz against the forces of Austria and Russia). Nelson's state funeral would be held in January.

As on all such occasions, Jews gathered in their synagogues at the same time as their Christian neighbours assembled in their churches; a special liturgy was followed, and the chief rabbi delivered to his congregants a sermon explicating the meaning of the events celebrated. Comparison with reports of other sermons given on this occasion reveals several predictable common themes that will be exemplified in the annotation below: the importance of expressing humble gratitude to God; the role of divine providence, even when administered through apparently natural causes; the mixture of jubilation with intense shock and grief; the appeal for financial support of widows, orphans, and the wounded.[13] Like Luria's sermon from October 1803, discussed above, Hirschel's sermon does not contain the vilification of Napoleon (as the 'Tyrant', the 'Oppressor of Nations', the 'Enemy of God') found in some of the Christian sermons; again, perhaps knowledge of Napoleon's relatively benevolent policy towards Jews produced a measure of ambivalence. On the other hand, Hirschel devotes considerable attention to a theme I have not found documented in the Christian texts: whether it is proper to rejoice at the victory of one's own nation when this victory entails suffering and death among the enemy. It is possible that Hirschel had access to the manuscript of his father's discussion of this theme in a sermon delivered on a similar day of thanksgiving during the Seven Years War.[14]

The following sermon was delivered in German and 'arranged and rendered into English by a friend'.[15] It was apparently the first sermon delivered at the Great Synagogue to be published. Roth reports that, according to a contemporary account in the *Gentleman's Magazine*, the sermon 'breathed a strain of true piety, a great loyalty and universal benevolence'.[16] A century later, the 1908 *Dictionary of National Biography* entry on Hirschel describes this sermon as one that 'attests his simple faith and political loyalty'.

---

[13] See Lovegrove, 'English Dissent and the European Conflict'.          [14] See n. 35 below.

[15] According to Katz, the translation was done by Joshua van Oven, 'one of the leading Jews in London' (*Jews in the History of England*, 286; on van Oven in this period, see Ruderman, *Jewish Enlightenment in an English Key*, 97–8.

[16] Roth, *The Great Synagogue*, 214, provides no reference, and I have not found any reference to Hirschel or his sermon in the *Gentleman's Magazine* of December 1805 or all of 1806, though other sermons from the same date were reviewed, as noted below.

# SERMON

---

*And when he had consulted the people, he appointed singers unto the Lord,*
*and that should praise the beauty of holiness as they went out before the army, to say,*
*Give thanks unto the Lord, for his mercy endureth for ever.*

(2 CHR. 20: 21)*[17]

WHEN the children of Moab and Ammon came in vast numbers against Jehoshaphat, King of Judah, he had recourse to prayer; and when the army 'rose early in the morning to go forth to the wilderness of Tekoa, as they went forth, Jehoshaphat stood, and said, Hear me, O Judah, and ye inhabitants of Jerusalem. Believe in the Lord, your God, so shall ye be established; believe in his Prophets, so shall ye prosper. He then appointed singers to go forth before the army, singing and praising the holiness of God, and to say, give thanks unto the Lord, for his mercy endureth for ever' (2 Chr. 20: 20–1). To order a thanksgiving previous to the accomplishment of the event appears rather premature, but such was Jehoshaphat's confidence in the Almighty, such his belief in his goodness (as predicted by Jahaziel, son of Zachariah, who had said, 'the battle is not yours, but God's' (2 Chr. 20: 15), that he considered it as already gained, and therefore commanded the thanksgiving to form a part of the pious hymn.

Without the assistance of Heaven, Jehoshaphat was indeed convinced he could not withstand the multitude that was pouring down upon him, for in his prayer, he says, 'O God, wilt thou not judge them? For we have no might against this great company that cometh against us, neither know we what to do, but our eyes are upon thee' (2 Chr. 20: 12). Now, 'as they believed in God, they were established'; as they 'believed the Prophets, they prospered' (cf. 2 Chr. 20: 20). Indeed, it is only by such trust in the Almighty, and confidence in his Prophets, that we can hope for success in any of our undertakings through life; and in this view we ought to be particularly happy in being under the government of a wise and pious

---

* This is the proper rendering of the Hebrew, and so it is expressed in several parts of the Psalms, viz. Psalm 105 v. 1, Psalm 106 v. 1, etc. etc., and not *praise the Lord*, as the Bible has this passage.

[17] The King James version renders the Hebrew as 'Praise the Lord, for His mercy endureth forever.' Hirschel apparently used the German 'Bibel' or the English 'Bible' to refer to a vernacular version (as contrasted with the Hebrew *Tanakh*).

King, who, suitably impressed with these holy sentiments, occasionally calls upon his subjects to assist him in imploring the aid of the Supreme Creator for the subjugation of his enemies, in order to effect a lasting peace.[18]

No one at this time doubts the superintendence of a Divine Providence over all sublunary creatures (as the Psalmist says, 'God is good to all, and his mercies are over all his works': Ps. 145: 9) and it is this interference of Heaven in our favor that we so devoutly pray for. The various skeptical and contradictory opinions of the ancient unenlightened philosophers are vanished and buried in oblivion, and even the irreligious of the present day are obliged to acknowledge the existence of God and his providence.[19] Little, very little, is to be feared from the flimsy texture of modern philosophy. The austere and virtuous lives of the ancients, indeed, inspired a certain veneration for their persons, and, of course, for their opinions; but the luxury and sensuality of the moderns, place their principles in so suspicious a point of view that virtue has nothing to apprehend from their influence.[20] It behoves us, therefore, by our conduct through life, by a proper and religious carriage towards the Supreme Being and our fellow-creatures to endeavour to deserve the succouring hand of Providence; to call for it with all due humility and prayer; and gratefully to acknowledge the blessings it bestows on us. Such are the sentiments of the good, and such the sentiments of our virtuous Monarch and his council, who, deeply impressed with gratitude

[18] The endorsement of the occasion as evidence for the wisdom and piety of the monarch who ordained it was almost a commonplace in the fast-day sermons. Cf. the sermon by the preacher's father, Hirschel Levin, in M. Saperstein, *Jewish Preaching*, 350 (and see n. 35 below for another parallel).

[19] This claim for universal acceptance of the belief in divine providence contrasts with the beginning of another published sermon delivered by a Christian preacher, Nicholas Bull, on the same day, which begins with a reference to the 'children of disobedience' who see only chance in nature and 'the effects of human folly or sagacity' in historical events: 'A Thanksgiving Sermon, for the Victory of Trafalgar', 5.

[20] It is striking how little threat Hirschel recognizes in deism or the philosophical challenges to traditional theology by such thinkers as David Hume. A month after this sermon, the *Gentleman's Magazine* published a lengthy review of a book by Henry Kett called *History the Interpreter of Prophecy*, quoting from it the following passage: 'We have seen the progress of infidelity accelerated with a force that is truly astonishing. No people has escaped a taint from its contagious breath. Papists and Mahometans, Jews and Christians, have felt its baneful influence.' Appended to 'Jews' is the following note: 'David Levi laments the extraordinary scepticism which has lately infected the Jewish people, and considers it a sign of the near approach of the time of their restoration to their own land' (*Gentleman's Magazine*, Jan. 1806, p. 45, citing Kett, *History*, 183). In his *Dissertationes on the Prophecies of the Old Testament*, completed between 1793 and 1800, Levi referred to those Jews 'of the nation, that are deists, and who consequently do not believe in revelation, as also those who are so indifferent about the truth of prophecy, and who never care for nor desire a restoration, and in consequence laugh at the idea of a Messiah coming to redeem them': Ruderman, *Jewish Enlightenment in an English Key*, 89. This is a very different picture from the one drawn by Hirschel a few years later.

for the late unparalleled success at sea, off Trafalgar, have appointed this day, a day of praise and thanksgiving before the Lord, without whose aid all mortal endeavours are vain. 'For the King is not saved by the multitude of an host, a mighty man is not delivered by much strength; behold the eye of the Lord is upon them that fear him, upon them that hope for his mercy' (Ps. 33: 16, 18).

But, great as our reliance ought to be on God, and confident as it behoves us to be of his protecting the just and righteous cause, it is nevertheless our duty at present not with folded arms to wait his interference, but to put forth our own exertions and employ all the powers which the Almighty has blessed us with for our own preservation, and hence it is essential to be prepared at all points to defend ourselves in war (or, if necessary for that purpose, to attack our enemies), trusting to the favorable aid of Heaven in a just cause.[21] Heretofore, indeed, when our forefathers (the children of Israel) were true to their God and, to answer an extraordinary purpose, the Almighty was pleased to work *miracles* for their deliverance, all nature underwent a change to fulfil the intentions of the Most High, such as the plagues of Egypt, the destruction of Pharaoh in the Red Sea, the fall of Jericho at the sound of trumpets, etc. etc.; and even afterwards, when we were less deserving of favor, and the exertions of our own powers were called forth, the fortune of war was only determined by the immediate interposition of Divine agents, such as occurred at the fall of Sennacherib, and the circumstances mentioned in our text,[22] etc. But, alas! Our sins have hindered us from the enjoyment of such immediate protection: the period is no more, when it was said, 'The Lord shall fight for you, and you shall hold your peace' (Exod. 14: 14). Since the time of the second Temple, the course of nature has not been disturbed; all events are regulated according to their natural consequences;[23] and our success is not in proportion to our merits, which is only regulated by the mediate operations of Divine Providence,[24] and not by visible

[21] Cf. the similar point made by Isaac Luria in his 1803 sermon (p. 84 above).

[22] On the 'fall of Sennacherib', see 2 Chr. 32; for the 'circumstances mentioned in our text', see 2 Chr. 20: 17–24.

[23] A translation of the Hebrew phrase *olam keminhago noheg* (BT *AZ* 54*b* and elsewhere).

[24] i.e. by intermediate causes of the natural world, as opposed to obvious supernatural interventions in the natural order. Cf. the following passage from a Christian sermon delivered the same day: 'Christian England expects every man will acknowledge this victory to be of God. He held the winds in the "hollow of his hand" till the enemy was vanquished; and then, for ten days after, they incessantly blew' (Thanksgiving Day Sermon by Mr. Watkins at St. Swithins, *Gentleman's Magazine*, Dec. 1805, p. 1109). Similarly, in another sermon from that day the preacher asserted: 'Whereas, the true notion of Providence is that God ordains the means with the end, and the means which He employs are, for the most part, natural causes' (Horsley, 'The Watchers and the Holy Ones', 351).

manifestation of supernatural means. Our chief dependence, therefore, is on the assistance which the Almighty will vouchsafe to our arms. As the wise Solomon said, 'The *horse* is prepared for battle, but *safety* is of the Lord' (Prov. 21: 31); whilst, therefore, we neglect no means of human preparation, we must never omit propitiating the assistance of the Almighty.

Let us, then, by a strict observance of the ordinances of God, hope to find grace in his sight; that his protection may favor our exertions to humble our enemies, the enemies of peace; and may he graciously accept our thanksgivings of this day, for the glorious victory he has permitted us to gain over their combined fleets.[25]

It may, perhaps, not be improper somewhat to investigate the nature of a thanksgiving or rejoicing on such an occasion. It is not to be imagined, that the destruction of our fellow-creatures, who have fallen in battle, or been drowned in the sea, can be a source of gratification to us, or of complacency to a beneficent Deity. No, humanity forbids such a thought; and even our text of this day strongly exemplifies that such a reflection was a drawback on the great rejoicing, since Jehoshaphat does not exactly quote the whole verse of the Psalmist, viz., 'Give thanks unto the Lord for it is good; his mercy endureth for ever' (Ps. 106: 1), but only says, 'Give thanks unto the Lord, for his mercy endureth for ever' (2 Chr. 20: 21).[26] The Talmud notices this omission of 'it is good',[27] and accounts for it by remarking that the destruction of wicked men constituted part of the facts, and as 'God does not desire the death of the wicked, but that he may turn from his ways and live' (Ezek. 33: 11), so the success of the day could not be correctly styled *good*, since peace without bloodshed would have been preferable.

Whatever comes from God is good. Nor are the words *'It is good'* used in Scripture, but when a *complete good* is meant; hence we do not find the expression in the relation of the works of the second day of the creation, although it is used in that of every other day.[28] Now, whatever good may result from a victory, it cannot be said to be a *complete* unalloyed good; and hence Jehoshaphat's omission, since, however necessary it may be for the arrangement of the affairs of this nether world, that the Almighty must occasionally clothe himself with

---

[25] That is, the combined fleets of France and Spain.

[26] Note how the preacher returns to Ps. 106: 1 and this theme at the conclusion of his sermon.

[27] BT *Meg.* 10*a*.

[28] See *Genesis Rabbah* 4: 6 and Rashi's commentary on Gen. 1: 7: the phrase 'God saw that it was good' was not used on the second day because the work of the water was not completed until the third day.

severe justice, yet it were to be wished that peace and harmony reigned on earth, and then the good would really be *complete*. The evil that occurs in this world cometh not from God, but from man himself. Nothing but good emanates from the Divine Essence, and it is the deeds of man which prevent the influence from reaching him. Thus circumstanced, he might as well say the sun does not shine, when he had raised a wall which hides the rays of that luminary from his sight.[29] Thus saith the wise King, 'The foolishness of man perverteth his way, and his heart fretteth against the Lord' (Prov. 19: 3). No, God is all goodness, 'and his mercies are over all his works' (Ps. 145: 9).

As a further exemplification that the destruction of our fellow-creatures ought not to be the final cause of war,[30] I must remind you that, although the Lord had, for their sins, doomed the seven nations of Judea to destruction, and had commanded our forefathers 'Not to leave a soul alive' (Deut. 20: 16), yet we were obliged to offer peace unto them, the acceptance of which would have spared the execution of that dreadful sentence.[31] Nay, according to the precepts of our Rabbis, we are directed in the siege or blockade of a town always to leave a part open for the flight of any of the inhabitants who would save themselves.[32] We also find Isaiah lamenting the evil about to fall upon Moab, when he says, 'My heart crieth out for Moab' (Isa. 15: 5). And Habbakuk, deploring the destruction of the nations, exclaims, 'When I heard, my belly trembled; my lips quivered at the voice; rottenness seized my bones, and I trembled within myself' (Hab. 3: 16).[33] The Prophets of the Lord (Iarchi remarks) are not like

[29] This insistence that human failures, not God's punishment, are the source of evil in the world would become a commonplace in twentieth-century Jewish preaching about war (except among the ultra-Orthodox); Hirschel's analogy suggests the philosopher Martin Buber's metaphor of the 'Eclipse of God'. On the other hand, he insists that the victory of the British forces is indeed a sign of divine providence.

[30] 'Final cause' in the Aristotelian sense of 'ultimate purpose'.

[31] See Maimonides, *Mishneh torah*, 'Hilkhot melakhim' (Laws of Kings), 6: 4. Here is perhaps an apologetic note, responding to the attacks made by Enlightenment thinkers such as Voltaire and Thomas Paine on 'Old Testament' morality, as exemplified by the genocidal massacres of the Canaanites. In *The Age of Reason*, published in 1794 and 1795, Paine wrote that the account of the instructions to massacre a civilian population in Num. 31: 13–18 was 'too horrid for humanity to read or for decency to hear'; the Book of Joshua was a 'military history of rapine and murder . . . savage and brutal' (pp. 119–20, 125). See on this theme E. Davidson and Scheick, *Paine, Scripture, and Authority*.

[32] The marginal note says, 'Maimonides, Lex Regium'. The exact reference is *Mishneh torah*, 'Hilkhot melakhim' (Laws of Kings), 6: 7.

[33] This reading of the reason for Habakkuk's dismay links it with 3: 12 ('You trample nations in fury'). Many commentators read it differently; for example, David Kimhi (*c.*1160–1235) explained the dismay as a response to the report about the future suffering of Israel at the time of the advent of Gog ('a people come to attack us', at the end of the same verse); Abraham ibn Ezra (1092–1167) says simply, 'because of the lack of food'.

the Prophets of the idolaters: Balaam would have cursed and annihilated Israel, but the holy Prophets grieve for the evils which befall the nations.[34] Thus Habbakuk further exclaims, 'How can I rest in the day of trouble, when he cometh up against the people, to cut them off?' (Hab. 3: 16). And, after a long and sublime lamentation throughout the chapter, very emphatically concludes with, 'Although the fig-tree shall not blossom, neither shall fruit be in the vine, the labour of the olive shall fail, and the field shall yield no meant, the flock shall be cut off from the fold, and there shall be no herd in the stalls, yet will I rejoice in the Lord, I will joy in the God of my salvation' (Hab. 3: 17–18). Thus, after having bewailed the evils which he predicted should fall upon the nations, he rejoices, and thanks God for his own salvation, and not in a spirit of triumph over a fallen enemy.

Thus we see that humanity was always a paramount consideration even in wars against Pagans; how much more must we be influenced at present, when all civilized nations unite in the belief of the true God![35] Their destruction then can surely be no source of pleasure or exultation, nor can we have the most distant idea that such could be the ground on which our virtuous and humane King has commanded this a day of thanksgiving. The true ground of thanksgiving to God on such an occasion is not, then, that of exultation over the fall of our fellow-creatures, but the gratitude that we must feel at having ourselves escaped a similar destruction, with which we were threatened, and from which we had no right of preference to expect the peculiar deliverance which God has vouchsafed to grant unto us, seeing that we are sinful creatures in common with

---

[34] Rashi on Isa. 15: 5. (The name 'Iarchi', meaning 'of the moon' or 'from Lunel', was frequently used for Rashi between the sixteenth and nineteenth centuries.)

In the classical rabbinic texts (e.g. *Genesis Rabbah* 52: 5 and parallels), the contrast between gentile and Jewish prophets is usually made on the basis of God's manner of communication, not the content of their message or depth of their empathy. Isa. 15: 5 is not cited in the rabbinic literature.

[35] In this passage, Hirschel seems to be echoing the sermon delivered by his father, Hirschel Levin (Hart Lyon), as rabbi of the Great Synagogue, on a day of thanksgiving following a military victory in the Seven Years War almost fifty years earlier. There too, the preacher raises the problem of rejoicing at the destruction of other human beings: 'If God did not want to destroy those pagan nations that lived in antiquity, that did not believe in God or His salvation at all . . . how much more is this true for the nations among whom we, the people of Israel, find refuge, who treat us with kindness and mercy, who are religious and act in accordance with the values of truth, justice and peace. God forbid that we should rejoice in their downfall!' ('Derashot', Jewish Theological Seminary of America Library Manuscript Collection, MS R79, fo. 23b, cited more fully in M. Saperstein, *Jewish Preaching*, 151). Hirschel may very well have owned the manuscript of his father's London sermons and consulted it for this occasion. Cf. also the use of this theme in the thanksgiving sermon delivered by Rabbi David Fränckel following the Prussian victory at Leuthen in Dec. 1757: M. Saperstein, *'Your Voice Like a Ram's Horn'*, 151–2 with references in n. 15.

the rest of mankind.[36] Although we may lament the necessity of the evil attached to it, yet it is our indispensable duty to thank the Supreme Director of all things for our salvation, and our gratitude should prompt us to amend our ways, and walk uprightly before the Lord. The good and evil in this life are so mingled that neither can ever be said to be unalloyed, yet we are bound to praise God for the good that befalls us on all occasions, and in battle, where the evil must necessarily preponderate on one side or the other, we ought surely to be thankful when the good falls to our share.[37]

Many circumstances in common life evince influences of this commixture of good and evil. A man, for example, who may grieve exceedingly at the death of his father, must yet say the prescribed blessing on the receipt of an inheritance which descends to him in consequence.*[38] A man may be attacked by villains with a design to murder him, whom he fortunately may overcome and destroy; surely such a man must rejoice and thank God for his escape, although he may shudder at the idea of having shed human blood. And Solomon says, 'Rejoice not when thine enemy falleth, and let not thy heart be glad when he stumbleth, lest the Lord see it, and it displease him, and he turn away his wrath from him' (Prov. 24: 17–18). Thus it is evident that in thanksgiving, we are grateful for our escape and future preservation from the machinations of the enemy, but not in the spirit of malicious triumph over the destruction of our fellow-creatures.

Another more important source of rejoicing and thanksgiving may be found in the conviction which this glorious victory must impress on our minds of the justice of our cause and of its rectitude in the sight of God, whence we may form every reasonable hope of ultimate and complete success. For when the various probabilities of success in battle are considered, we shall find them principally to arise either from a superiority in numbers, a greater adroitness in manœuvre, or a miraculous interference of Providence in favor of the most worthy. Now, as

---

* The Jews have set forms of benedictions for most occurrences in life.

[36] The end of the sentence is a rather surprising formulation; although the referents of the 'we' and 'us' are not entirely clear, they apparently refer not to the Jewish people but to the British, including the British Jews. But this assertion that the British are sinful like all others would seem to be in tension with the later claim that 'this glorious victory must impress on our minds . . . the justice of our cause and . . . its rectitude in the sight of God'.

[37] Here the preacher is still speaking of the necessary mixture of good with evil expressed in the destruction of the opposing forces, but the theme prepares the way for the application of this motif to the death of Nelson.

[38] The law is stated in *Shulḥan arukh*, 'Oraḥ ḥayim', 223: 2: 'When one's father dies, he says the blessing [ending] "the judge of truth". If there was money that he inherited, and he has no siblings, he also says the blessing, "who has kept us alive . . .". If he has siblings, instead of that blessing, he says the blessing [ending], "who is good and does good".'

it is well known that in this battle we were much inferior in number,[39] and no very extraordinary stress is laid on the manœuvres we employed;[40] nay, as it even appears that the enemy had address enough to oppose two ships to one of ours (which, however, drove off her opponents, and ultimately took them),[41] it is evident the victory cannot be ascribed to either of these two causes. Now, as we have already remarked that miracles have ceased, since we have ceased to deserve them, there only remains one way probable to account for it, viz. from that increased energy which the consciousness of a right and just cause infuses into man, and which, under God's providence, inspired our seamen with a double portion of courage on this occasion.

Our Rabbins were impressed with a similar sentiment when they directed a dispute about property (between two parties, neither of which could produce evidence to substantiate his claim) to be settled by single combat,[42] from the conviction that a consciousness of truth and right gave additional confidence and strength to its possessor. 'Let the weak say, I am strong.'[43] In this view we may consider the present victory as a proof, and congratulate ourselves on fighting in a true and just cause. But with all these advantages, we must deplore a misfortune with which the Almighty has thought fit to visit us. The fall of Lord Nelson is a severe evil, a loss not easily repaired. His piety made him favored of God, and his courage, his skill, and his activity made him the darling of his country. While his successes have been the pride of his countrymen, his name has been the terror of the enemy. 'Alas! How are the mighty fallen in the

[39] One of the earliest accounts of the battle and of Nelson's death, by William Beatty, the surgeon on Nelson's ship, spoke of the 'inferiority of the British Fleet' in comparison with the combined fleets of France and Spain: Beatty, *The Death of Lord Nelson*, 20. The actual numbers were twenty-eight British ships against thirty-three French and Spanish ships (Bennett, *The Battle of Trafalgar*, 214).

[40] Here the preacher seems to understate the importance of Nelson's tactical innovations, on which see Bennett, *The Battle of Trafalgar*, 214; Howarth, *Trafalgar*, 72–4. The report of the thanksgiving day sermon by a Mr Watkins at St Swithins, published in the *Gentleman's Magazine* of Dec. 1805 (pp. 1108–9), has the preacher stating that God 'gave Lord Nelson that thought, by which he contrived a method of attack unusual in naval engagement', thereby affirming the doctrine of providence while giving the fallen hero his due.

[41] This may refer to the British ship *Temeraire*, which, at one point had French ships lashed on either side of it; see Beatty, *The Death of Lord Nelson*, 35; Bennett, *The Battle of Trafalgar*, 194, 197.

[42] BT *BB* 34*b*–35*a*.

[43] This apparently refers to the principle *kol de'alim gevar*, 'whoever is stronger will prevail', imposed, as the preacher states, when the judge in a contested matter (usually of right to property) has no basis for determining whose claim is right, and there is no possibility that acceptable proof can be produced in the future. Hirschel's rationalization of this principle ('from the conviction that . . .') is not in the classical sources, and it would obviously not work if each claimant sincerely believes that he is in the right.

midst of battle! O, Nelson! Thou wast slain in thine high place' (cf. 2 Sam. 1: 25). Let us then here regard the hand of God, and not be extravagant in our exultation, but still remember that all is in the hands of Him who causeth death and who bringeth again to life. Thus whilst he has permitted us to triumph over our enemies, he has deprived us of our leader, our mighty one! His will be done. 'The Lord has given, the Lord has taken; let the name of the Lord be blessed' (Job 1: 21). We have not only lost a gallant hero, as great in war as any that went before him, but we have lost a good and a pious man. All his hope, all his dependence, was on God, and to God did he, with due humility, ascribe the victory of the Nile.[44] His language was modest, his conduct religious, and his humanity exemplary. Such a man was worthy of the favor of Providence; nor did it ever fail him. May his successors imitate his example, and thus prove deserving of the protection of Heaven, and like him become invincible.

Our commentators explain the verse, 'The Lord repayeth them that hate him to their face, to destroy them' (Deut. 7: 10) by an axiom, that the wicked are suffered to prosper in this world, as a reward for what good they may have done, to their utter destruction in the world to come;[45] and on this ground it is, that those who truly fear God are more happy under the troubles of this life, than if they had enjoyed a measure of unmixed comfort and pleasure; for, impressed with a due sense of the sinful nature of man, prosperity appears to them but an ambiguous blessing, and might prove only the wages of the wicked in this world, but which might be followed by destruction in the next. Thus also sayeth the wise Solomon, 'A sore evil have I seen under the sun, riches kept for the owners therefore for their hurt' (Eccles. 5: 12), and truly such it may prove, since, by puffing up their pride and vanity, it may occasion them to commit excesses, and forget the watchful eye of Providence, by which they lay a sure ground for their ultimate ruin and destruction in the world to come.

But if God, in his mercy, favors mankind with success and blessings, while at the same time he mingles therewith some misfortune, whereby they are

---

[44] See Southey, *The Life of Nelson*, 152; Bennett, *Nelson the Commander*, 138; Walder, *Nelson*, 282. Nelson's dispatch to the First Lord of the Admiralty began: 'Almighty God has blessed His Majesty's arms in the late battle with a great victory.' In his thanksgiving day sermon 'Victory Mourning', William Kingsbury of Southampton said: 'It was a pleasing trait in the character of the lamented Lord Nelson that he acknowledged God as the giver of victories' (*Gentleman's Magazine*, Feb. 1806, p. 151). For Nelson's invocation of God before the beginning of the battle of Trafalgar, see Beatty, *Death of Lord Nelson*, 24 (repeated in all the other accounts); his last words were 'Thank God, I have done my duty' (ibid. 48, 49).

[45] The editor wrote in the margin, 'Yarchi, Abarbanel, etc'. See Rashi ad loc., based on the Aramaic Targum, and cf. *Midrash tanhuma* (Buber), 'Vayigash', 8. Abravanel cites and discusses Rashi's interpretation as one of two plausible readings of the verse.

reminded of his Omnipotence, and their own imbecility, this surely is the greatest manifestation of Divine goodness, since, by this means, they are still awed into a due reverence of the Almighty, and will not easily be deluded into a wicked and presumptuous course of life, but endeavour, by suitable and pious adoration, to deserve his future favor.

We may easily apply this sentiment to the present circumstances, for notwithstanding the great victory which Heaven has been pleased to allow us authorizes very extraordinary rejoicing, yet, to the penetrating eye, much appears necessary to be done. The enemies have yet great power on the continent; there are yet a number of ships in their harbours; and we have lost an Admiral whose very name struck terror into them: thus it is evidence, Heaven has left enough in store to make us sensible how much we are in want of its assistance, and hence we are not likely to run riot from our success, but still bear in mind that 'God has saved us from our enemies and put them to shame that hated us. In God we boast all the day, and praise his name for ever. Selah' (Ps. 44: 8). Under such impressions, therefore, we are to esteem the unfortunate death of Lord Nelson as a salutary memento, the recollection of which should ever so regulate our future conduct, that we may find grace in the eyes of the Lord;[46] and as our text expresses, 'By the belief in the Lord our God, so shall we be established; and the belief in his Prophets, we shall prosper (2 Chr. 20: 20). Then will many future Nelsons arise in our Navy, and all our exertions prove successful, and our wars bring forth peace.

With this train of sentiments, we may also expound the 21st Psalm of David's, 'The King shall surely joy in the strength' of his faith in thee, 'O Lord'; and when through this faith, he, on every occasion, implores 'thy salvation, how greatly will he rejoice' in meeting with it (Ps. 21: 2).[47] For if at all periods he has thy protection when prayed for, then assuredly 'hast thou given him his heart's desire, and hast not withholden the request of his lips' (Ps. 21: 3), for if, not too much elevated by success, he continues gratefully sensible of thy goodness, and in unfeigned humility, prays for its continuance, then also he is convinced that the goodness which he has experienced is not the partial reward allotted to the unworthy in this world, whilst it insures their destruction in the next. Such,

---

[46] Cf. the thanksgiving day sermon of Watkins reported in the *Gentleman's Magazine* (Dec. 1805, p. 1109): 'England expects every man to show forth his gratitude to God by his life and conduct.'

[47] The original text places the words from the psalm in italics and the expository words added by the preacher in roman type. Homily-style expositions of complete psalms in the context of a larger sermon were common in Jewish preaching from the sixteenth century onwards; see e.g. the sermon by Moses Almosnino in M. Saperstein, *Jewish Preaching*, 224 n. 16, 229 n. 37.

however, might not be the case if thou shouldst 'anticipate him with goodly blessings' unasked, and which might prove transitory and unsubstantial, like 'the golden crown thou settest on his head' is a mere ornamental emblem of royalty, which may easily be put away; but 'he has' only 'asked life of thee, and thou gavest him length of days for ever and ever. Thus is his glory great in thy salvation: Honour and majesty hast thou laid upon him, for thou hast made him most blessed for ever' (Ps. 21: 5–7a), and thence, since his favor in thy sight is continual, thou 'hast made him exceeding glad in thy countenance' (Ps. 21: 7b). That is to say, having thy countenance in all the difficulties which he occasionally meets with, but which he does not fear, 'for the King trusteth in the Lord, and through the mercy of the Most High, he shall not be moved. Be thou exalted, O Lord, in thine own strength, so will we sing and praise thy power' (Ps. 21: 8, 14).

I might easily carry on this paraphrase to the completion of the chapter, but I will not trespass on your time; yet I cannot conclude without expressing the great pleasure and satisfaction I feel on account of the active proof which I understand you are this day about to give of your gratitude to Heaven, by charitable donations in aid of the widow and the fatherless. This indeed is a duty we owe to God, and good deeds, conjoined with due adoration, must always insure to us the blessings of Heaven.

On no occasion can charity be so well timed, and on no persons can it be so properly bestowed, as on those in whose behalf it is now to be collected, and so impressed am I with its being an imperious duty incumbent on us that even if the plan had not already been set on foot, and arranged by the public at large, we ought spontaneously to have come forward, and brought our aggregate subscription to that noble institution, the *Patriotic Fund*.[48]

What ought we not to do for those brave men who, disregarding all endearing ties at home, disregarding of all personal danger, boldly advance to chastise the enemy; who, without any sinister motive, and desire of plunder, go forth to battle, prompted by the love and the salvation of their country! It is our indispensable

---

[48] Italics in the original. Lloyd's Patriotic Fund subsidized the presentation of swords to heroes of naval battles, as well as subsidizing a school for orphans of men serving in the navy, called the 'Royal Naval Asylum'. Lord Nelson was a patron of the school, as were the Jewish brothers Abraham and Benjamin Goldsmid (<www.mariners-l.co.uk/GreenwichRoyal.html>). Many of the thanksgiving day sermons published in pamphlet form included on the title page the words 'For the Benefit of the Patriotic Fund', and virtually all preachers concluded with an appeal 'for the relief of those who will have to lament the misfortune of battle as long as they live' (*Gentleman's Magazine*, Dec. 1805, p. 1109). The *Gentleman's Magazine* reported 'immense collections' at the special services (ibid. 1168).

duty to lighten their hearts, and relieve them from the grievous reflection of the forlorn states of their families in case of their fall, a reflection that must deject them in the day of battle. Powerful, therefore, is the claim which the poor widow and the orphan must have on us, who are protected by the valor and loyalty of the fallen husband and father. In our cause, and for our safety, he died; the wife, the child, crieth unto us for bread; shall we dare to withhold it? If, as men, as citizens, we must attend to such solicitations, how much more ought we as Jews, who are cherished and protected in this happy country, even as its own children! Cast out from the land of our forefathers, we find this land congenial to us. Surely then its cause is our cause, and we ought, on every occasion, to evince ourselves grateful for its fostering protection.[49]

Let, then, your liberality shew that you are ready by deeds, as well as words, to propitiate the favor of the Most High; and remember that you 'Serve the Lord with fear, and rejoice with trembling' (Ps. 2: 11). So may you deserve to see the day when 'Nation shall no more draw the sword against nation, nor shall they learn anymore the art of war' (Isa. 2: 4), but 'All flesh shall come up to bow before the Lord' (Isa. 66: 23), and say 'Give thanks unto the Lord *for he is good*, his mercy endureth for ever' (Ps. 106: 1).[50]

[49] Later in the century, preachers would similarly emphasize the special beneficence of Britain towards its Jewish citizens, but substitute the motif of full equality for mere tolerance and protection.

[50] The printed text indicates the emphasis on the words 'for he is good', stressed by the preacher earlier in the sermon as expressing the difference between the divine nature and the imperfect rejoicing of Jehoshaphat and those celebrating on the present occasion, despite the military victory. Note that when the preacher cited the verse earlier (see n. 26 above), he rendered the verse 'for *it* is good', referring to the forthcoming battle. The Hebrew, *ki tov*, is ambiguous and can sustain either interpretation, though the one used here is far more common.

# CHAPTER THREE

## GERSHOM MENDES SEIXAS
# FAST-DAY SERMON
### 2 FEBRUARY 1814

#### CONGREGATION SHEARITH ISRAEL
#### NEW YORK

Gershom Mendes Seixas, born in 1745 or 1746, was the product of what was then considered a 'mixed marriage': his father, Isaac, was born in Lisbon and became a merchant in New York and Newport; his mother, Rachel Levy, was of Ashkenazi background. Though apparently he received little formal education and remained throughout his life essentially an autodidact, he assumed responsibilities as minister at New York's Congregation Shearith Israel in 1768.[1] His formal position as cantor involved responsibility for the worship services and preaching on special occasions.[2] One such occasion was a service held upon the approach of the British fleet in New York Bay in August 1776, following a decision that the synagogue should close rather than continue to function under British rule.[3] An unconfirmed tradition reports that he said this might be the last worship to be conducted in the almost fifty-year-old building on Mill Street, and that this address was delivered with such feeling and eloquence that 'many of his listeners, we are told, were moved to tears by his pathetic words'.[4]

[1] According to some, in 1766. Biographical material is taken from Hühner, 'The Patriot Jewish Minister'; N. T. Phillips, 'Rev. Gershom Mendez Seixas'; Pool, *Portraits Etched in Stone*, 344–75; two full critical studies written concurrently: Kessner, 'Gershom Mendes Seixas', and Marcus, 'The Handsome Young Priest'; also Angel, 'Seixas, Gershom Mendes'.

[2] On the formal responsibilities of the cantor as specified in 1795, see Pool, *Portraits Etched in Stone*, 359; for a more detailed review of the various functions of Seixas, see Marcus, 'Handsome Young Priest', 410–20. For a review of preaching at special patriotic services in this period, see Marcus, *The Colonial American Jew*, 971–4.

[3] On this dramatic and symbolic incident, see recently Sarna, *American Judaism*, 33–4; Diner, *The Jews of the United States*, 47–8. Sarna notes that services were held intermittently at Shearith Israel under the British.

[4] Hühner, 'The Patriot Jewish Minister', 2, providing no source other than 'It is related . . .'. N. T. Phillips, 'Rev. Gershom Mendez Seixas', 42, adds that the sermon was delivered in English, and that 'tears were shed by all present, men and women alike'; it is unclear whether this was

Seixas fled from New York to Stamford, Connecticut, taking with him some of the Torah scrolls and sacred ceremonial objects from the synagogue. Four years later he was invited to Philadelphia, where a new Sephardi congregation, Mikveh Israel, was being established. At the dedication ceremony for the new building on 13 September 1782 he composed a special version of the traditional prayer said by Jews on behalf of the country in which they live. This invokes God's blessing and protection specifically upon

His Excellency the President, and the Honorable Delegates of the United States of America in Congress assembled; His Excellency George Washington, Capt. Genl. and Commander in Chief of the Federal Army of these States; His Excellency the President, the Honorable the Executive Council, and members of the General Assembly of this Commonwealth, and all Kings and Potentates in alliance with North America.

It also asks God's blessings upon those who were fighting in the American armed forces:

The Lord of Hosts be the shield of those who are armed for war by land, and for those who are gone in ships to war on the seas. May the Lord fight for them; may they, their rulers, their leaders, and all their allies joining them in battle equally experience Thy goodness, and may Thy angels have them in charge, and save them from death and all manner of distress.[5]

At the end of the war, Seixas returned to New York and in March 1784 re-assumed his duties at Shearith Israel.

Two of the sermons of this pioneering religious leader were published as pamphlets,[6] but, although there have been two thorough studies of Seixas's thought using the published and unpublished material,[7] there seems never to

simply an expansion of Hühner's statement, or whether both were based on a common source not identified. In reviewing the closing of the synagogue, none of the latest studies of Seixas noted in n. 1 mentions the sermon, indicating perhaps that the authors could find no reliable source for it. Pool writes that Seixas 'gave a solemn farewell address' (*Portraits Etched in Stone*, 350), but adds no details about its content or impact.

[5] A copy of the text is in the Jacques Judah Lyons Collection of the American Jewish Historical Society, box 2, no. 87. For a description of the ceremony, see Wolf and Whiteman, *The History of the Jews of Philadelphia*, 121. In his biographical article on Seixas, Phillips designated this text a 'memorable patriotic address', and erroneously quoted the phrase as 'His Excellency George Washington, Commander-General of these Colonies' ('Rev. Gershom Mendez Seixas', 43). For a fuller discussion in context, see Sarna, 'Jewish Prayers for the US Government', esp. 206.

[6] Seixas, 'A Religious Discourse'; id., 'Discourse Delivered in the Synagogue in New York'. Both have been discussed by Marcus, 'Handsome Young Priest', 424–5, and Friedenberg, *'Hear O Israel'*, 10–16; see also the article by Morris Schappes, 'Anti-Semitism and Reaction', discussed below.

[7] Kessner, 'Gershom Mendes Seixas'; Marcus, 'The Handsome Young Priest'. The unpublished sermons, found in the American Jewish Historical Society Archives, are listed by Marcus on pp. 410–11.

have been any effort to publish an appropriate edition of all the surviving texts. Most of the extant sermons were delivered on thanksgiving days or national days of fasting, humiliation, and prayer. Some of these were associated with war, others with outbreaks of pestilence. One example of the first category was delivered on 9 May 1798, a national fast-day proclaimed by President John Adams to prepare public opinion in support of military measures against France ('the United States of America are at present placed in a hazardous and afflictive situation by the unfriendly disposition, conduct, and demands of a foreign power'). A study of more than a dozen Christian sermons delivered in the charged atmosphere of that day revealed that the great majority were vehemently anti-French and supportive of, if not enthusiastic about, the prospect of war. The sermon by Seixas, by contrast, begins with the text 'Behold how good and how pleasant it is for brethren to dwell together in unity', recalls the aid given by the French during the American Revolution, and urges the listeners to turn away from the 'terrific [i.e. terrifying] ideas' that fill the imagination at present.[8] The second wartime sermon, delivered on 2 February 1814 during the War of 1812, has, so far as I am aware, never before been published.[9]

But for circumstances beyond his control, Seixas might have delivered a similar sermon earlier in the war. Not long after the conflict began, President James Madison declared 20 August a 'national day of public humiliation and prayer', and accordingly a special service was held at Shearith Israel following the regular afternoon service. But Seixas was sick on that day; the sermon was delivered by a layman, Isaac Gomez, and no text of it seems to have been preserved.[10]

By the end of 1813 the course of the war, with its military failures, had provoked considerable popular discontent with the Madison administration. Reports of discussions about seeking an honourable peace were greeted with enthusiasm, and there were even suggestions that individual states might negotiate separate

[8]  Schappes, 'Anti-Semitism and Reaction, 1795–1800', esp. 120–8; id., *A Documentary History*, 89–92. For another example of a preacher invoking France's aid to America during the revolution, see Sermon 11 below by Sabato Morais, delivered during the Franco-Prussian War.

[9]  In the early years of the century Leon Hühner referred to and cited passages from the sermon in 'The Patriot Jewish Minister', 4–5, and, later and more briefly, in 'Jews in the War of 1812', 184–5; see also N. T. Phillips, 'Rev. Gershom Mendez Seixas', 47–8. Neither of them identified the date of the sermon correctly; Hühner placed it in the context of the Hartford Convention, which was held some nine months after its delivery (Nathan Kaganoff followed Hühner, saying that the sermon was delivered while 'the Hartford Convention was in session'—which Hühner did not write: Kaganoff, 'The Traditional Jewish Sermon in the United States', 31). Nevertheless, Hühner's assertion that Seixas's urging his audience to support the government should be understood in the context of strong criticism coming from other circles is correct. No date appears on the manuscript; my dating is based on external evidence about the New York fast-day.

[10]  Pool and Pool, *An Old Faith in the New World*, 131, based on the minutes of the congregation. No sermon is mentioned in conjunction with the following such day, held on 9 Sept. 1813.

peace agreements with Britain. The specific background to the present sermon was the British–Indian campaign of late December 1813 in an area stretching from north-western New York State across the Canadian border, which saw reversals for America beginning with the fall of Fort Niagara on 19 December and culminating with the capture and destruction of Buffalo on 30 December.[11] The mood in some circles is expressed in an editorial by a New York daily newspaper published on 10 January, which describes

our own country, smarting under the wounds that our national character has received from the defeat and disgrace which have terminated the last campaign, and while our administration are at their wits' end how to recruit an army for another; public affairs are in the utmost disorder, with an empty treasury, and an accumulation of debt amounting to nearly or quite 200 millions of dollars without having provided the means of paying it off; while public confidence in our rulers is daily diminishing, and a series of oppressive and unpopular measures threaten we know not what of evil, and fear to conjecture.[12]

Perhaps even more disturbing than the military defeat itself was the campaign's impact on the civilian population. Reports in the New York press included accounts of savage attacks against civilians by Indian tribes, wholesale destruction of residential property, and widespread homelessness in the harsh winter conditions. Here is an example, reproduced in the *Evening Post* of 12 January from the *Ontario Repository* of 4 January:

The enemy followed up their success, and soon after entered the village of Buffalo. Here all was confusion, alarm, distress—the inhabitants who had remained in the village were got off as well as possible, and we have heard of but one outrage on the defenceless . . . The reader must picture to himself, for language cannot describe, the horror which prevailed. The fate of the place was known to be fixed! Buffalo was to be sacrificed to the vengeance of the foe!—AND THE WHOLE OF THIS PLEASANT, FLOURISHING VILLAGE HAS BEEN LAID IN ASHES!!!!

Such is the horrid character which this war has assumed—a war of plunder and of burning![13]

The continuation of the article, modifying the most alarmist reports—'It is not known that any women or children were killed. It is reported that a considerable number are in comfortable quarters near Fort Niagara, with a guard to protect them, and that some have been sent across the river'—may not have

---

[11] For a review of these events, see Babcock, *The War of 1812 on the Niagara Frontier*, 125–38 (he describes the spoliation of the frontier, culminating with the fall of the fully supplied Fort Niagara, as 'the crowning act of imbecility of the entire war', 137); Berton, *Flames across the Border*, 94–99; G. F. G. Stanley, *The War of 1812*, 219–24.

[12] *New York Evening Post*, 10 Jan. 1814, p. 3. The conclusion is one of enthusiastic support for an honourable peace with Britain, then at the peak of its military powers.

[13] *New York Evening Post*, 12 Jan. 1814, p. 3.

made as great an impression as the emotional language and screaming capitals that preceded it.[14]

On 8 January, a committee of citizens from Canandaigua addressed a letter describing the conditions of the surviving civilians to influential figures in Albany; the letter was reported in the *Post* on 20 January, from 'Albany Gazette'. On 24 January, the *Post* printed the text of an identical letter, this one addressed to leading citizens of New York, which had been received the previous day:

Niagara county, and that part of Genesee which lies west of Batavia, are completely depopulated. All the settlements in a section of country forty miles square, and which contained more than twelve thousand souls, are effectually broken up. These facts you are undoubtedly acquainted with, but the distresses they have produced, none but an eye-witness can thoroughly appreciate. Our roads are filled with people many of whom have been reduced from a state of competence and good prospects to the last degree of want and sorrow. So sudden was the blow, by which they have been crushed that no provision could be made either to elude or to meet it. The fugitives from Niagara country especially, were dispersed under circumstances of so much terror that, in some cases, mothers find themselves wandering with strange children ... Afflictions of the mind so deep as have been allotted to these unhappy people, we cannot cure. They can probably be subdued only by His power, who can wipe away all tears. But shall we not endeavor to assuage them? To their bodily wants we can certainly administer.[15]

It was this publicity that led the New York City Common Council, in its meeting of January, to set 2 February as a 'day of fasting, humiliation and prayer, [on which] the people of this City are requested to abstain from all business and labor ... and to assemble in their respective places of worship and devote themselves with humble and contrite hearts to the offices of religion'. At the same meeting, the council appropriated $3,000 from the city treasury for the relief of 'our brethren in the west' of New York State, and 'respectfully recommended to the different religious Congregations of this City to cause collections to be made for the same purpose in their respective Churches on the day above set apart'.[16]

The New York City day of fast and prayer does not appear to have been a resounding success. The total amount of money contributed was considerably

---

[14] The *Post* was certainly not the most sensational of the New York papers. Two days later, it excoriated the *Advocate* of the previous day for its suggestion that the United States employ the 'Western tribes to use the tomahawk and scalping knife against the enemy', stating that the article was 'as usual, filled with blood and massacre, barbarities, rapine and murder, smoking ruins, reeking blood and so on': 14 Jan. 1814, p. 2.

[15] *New York Evening Post*, 20, Jan., p. 3, 24 Jan., p. 3.

[16] *Minutes of the Common Council*, vii. 667. The full text of the Common Council motion was read near the end of the sermon from a separate sheet (not included in the sermon manuscript), and is included below.

less than that gathered from a small group of 'benevolent gentlemen'.[17] Neither the *Spectator* nor the *Evening Post* provided any coverage in the issues following the event. No other sermon from the occasion seems to have been preserved. While the proclamation requested that the people of New York 'abstain from all business and labor on that day', there is no indication in the press that this exhortation was observed widely, or indeed at all. The order of service at Shearith Israel indicates that it was held in the mid-afternoon, immediately before the *minḥah* and *ma'ariv* prayers, and therefore at a time that would not interfere unduly with the work schedule. The 'Bishop and Clergy' of the churches participating in the appeal issued a statement beforehand, begging leave, 'with all possible deference for those who have proposed this plan, to express the hope that it will not be considered as a precedent for calls of a similar kind in future'.[18]

On 2 February, the day set aside for fasting and prayer, the *New York Spectator* reported that, while the House of Representatives of the state legislature had unanimously approved a donation of $50,000 for the relief effort, the Senate voted for an indefinite postponement of the resolution, thereby deciding that 'no legislative relief shall be afforded to those frontier inhabitants, who, by the events of this miserable and wicked war, have been stripped of their all, and cast houseless, and naked, and perishing with hunger, upon the charity of their fellow-citizens'.[19]

Of the funds that were generated, the contribution from the Jewish community formed a significant part. At its meeting of 14 February, twelve days after the fast-day, the Common Council recorded the mayor's report

that he has received the following sums collected in the following Churches in pursuance of their recommendation, to wit,

| From the Episcopal Churches | | | $908.84 |
| " | " Moravian | " | 43.75 |
| " | " German Lutheran | " | 112.35 |
| " | " Congregation Sheareth [*sic*] Israel | | 140.00[20] |

---

[17] These men, probably those named in the original letter from Canandaigua, had contributed $3,023 (*Minutes of the Common Council*, p. 686).

[18] *New York Evening Post*, 27 Jan. 1814, p. 2.    [19] *New York Spectator*, 2 Feb. 1814, xvii, no. 1659.

[20] *Minutes of the Common Council*, vii. 685. In a letter written soon after the event, Seixas actually put the amount collected as $149.25. De Sola Pool noted that the amount was more than one-ninth of the total collected by all New York churches, extraordinary for a Jewish population 'perhaps about 1/300th of the total population of 92,448 at that time': 'Gershom Mendes Seixas' Letters', 202, citing Papers of the Seixas Family, box 2, folder 1, letter 6; cf. Pool, *Portraits Etched in Stone*, 367, where he gives the figure as £140. By contrast, Marcus writes that Seixas was 'troubled over the meager amount. Not many had come to the services and the rich had been anything but generous' ('Handsome Young Priest', 420).

The personal circumstances in which Seixas composed his sermon are described in a letter written to his daughter two days later. He began 'to compose a short address to the congregation' on Monday at noon,[21] two days before the special event, apparently in the synagogue:

I had written one page and in came an impertinent intruder (I believe) with a design to find out if I meant to comply with the recommendation of the common council—but I was mum on the occasion . . . came home and found Simon Judah to spend the snowing day—auntee came in the afternoon, and Mrs. Jacobs chose to stay 3 hours after your aunts left us—so I had to proceed by candle light again, wrote 3 hours more while the gossips were chatting.[22]

This is a rare indication of the challenges of finding quiet space and uninterrupted time for a man living with a large number of children and many visitors in a relatively modest-sized home.[23]

The Torah text is chosen from the end of Deuteronomy—not the scriptural lesson for the week—and not very much is done with it except to establish the fundamental principle of human free agency and responsibility for one's actions. This leads, however, to an important historical passage, indicating the questions and doubts widely discussed in the press about the wisdom of the policies taken by the Madison administration pertaining to the war effort (which the preacher says he will not discuss in detail), especially in the light of the recent defeats in the vicinity of Buffalo and Niagara. By mentioning the failures yet refusing to allocate blame because of a professed ignorance of the causes, the preacher validates the questions in the minds of the listeners while subverting any tendency towards concrete political opposition.[24] What follows is a ringing assertion of the responsibility of citizens in a democracy to support their chosen leaders, even (or perhaps especially) when things are not going well.[25]

After this introductory section, Seixas turns to a different biblical passage to illustrate the evil of war: the preference of David, in the last chapter of 2 Samuel, for his people to be punished directly by God through a plague rather than to suffer military defeat at the hands of other human beings, because of his first-hand knowledge of the horrors of war. This leads to a prayer for providential protection against 'the evils that are now pending over our

---

[21] The brevity of the address is indicated also in the order of prayers written at the conclusion of the sermon text: 'a short address by the Sheliah Tsebur [leader of the congregation] in English'. At 1,700 words, it probably would have taken about fifteen minutes to deliver, extremely short for sermons of that time.

[22] Pool, *Portraits Etched in Stone*, 366–7, citing Papers of the Seixas Family, box 2, folder 1, letter 6.

[23] On the atmosphere in the Seixas home, see Marcus, 'Handsome Young Priest', 435.

[24] For another example of an expression of uncertainty about government policy alongside a repudiation of open dissent and a call for support, see Sermon 4 by Marks below.

[25] On this theme in the context of Seixas's political philosophy, see Kessner, 'Gershom Mendes Seixas', 462–4; Marcus, 'Handsome Young Priest', 426.

heads', followed by a powerful evocation, based on reports in the newspapers and suffused with pathos and horror, of the conditions of 'fellow citizens' in the northern part of the state, resulting from the actions of an 'enraged foe' and the 'savages of the wilderness' whom the enemy incited. A second passage of prayer for deliverance from 'impending evils' leads to the appeal for relief funds, an integral component of the purpose of the day. In this context, Seixas read the full text of the resolution of the city's Common Council declaring the day of 'fasting, humiliation and prayer' as it had been publicized in the media. After announcing that it was now up to the congregants to fulfil their responsibility as they saw fit, he drew his address to a close—echoing the text from Deuteronomy—with a general appeal to his people to fulfil every duty to God and to fellow human beings. The sermon finishes with the concluding words from Ecclesiastes, in Hebrew and in English translation: 'the conclusion of the whole matter: Fear God, and Keep His commandments: for this is the whole duty of man' (Eccles. 12: 13); certainly an unexceptional, even conventional, ending.

The sermon text does not impress as one of the more distinguished examples of Jewish homiletical art. It is difficult to quarrel with the historian Jacob Rader Marcus's rather harsh critique of the corpus of Seixas's extant sermon texts as reflecting 'the confusion of the autodidact':

His sermons are not distinguished for their precision, their clarity, or their proper transitions. There is no real coherence. Many of this phrases are obscure; some sentences are incomprehensible and unintelligible; the punctuation is almost always inadequate. It is clear that this man could not coordinate his thoughts into a logical and consistent whole . . . Judging from his literary relics, he was anything but a great preacher. He was not even a good preacher.[26]

Yet this sermon, as the only known extant Jewish preaching text responding to any American war before 1861, delivered before the flagship Jewish congregation of the nation, expressing the ideals of loyal support for the government despite its failures and empathetic commitment to fellow citizens in their time of need, it is a text of considerable historical significance.

# SERMON

IN THE 30th Chapter of Deuteronomy, in the 15th and 16th verses, you will find these words, 'Behold I set before you this day life and good, death

---

[26] Marcus, 'Handsome Young Priest', 438–9.

and evil, which I command you this day, to love the Lord thy God, to walk in His ways and to observe His commandments, His statutes, and His judgments; that thou mayest live and increase, that the Lord thy God will bless thee in the Land whither thou comest.'[27]

Hence it is evident that good and evil proceedeth according to the disposition of man, whether he chooses to act conformably to the will of God, and to obey His Law, and thereby ensuring to himself the promised blessing; or by refusing to obey the commandments, to involve himself in evil, which will inevitably ensue, in consequence of disobedience and ultimately produce death and destruction.

By the sacred history we are informed of all the perceptive and practical duties necessary to establish the religious and moral Law, to conduct us to virtue and to happiness. And when Moses had brought the children of Israel to the confines of the promised land, he there recapitulated the duties incumbent on them, and on us, their descendants, to perform through every sphere and every situation in life, and leaves *us* to choose between the two extremes of good and evil, with their subsequent rewards or punishments. By these positions we are convinced that man is a free agent, and consequently is responsible for all transgressions, whether of commission or omission.

I mean not to criminate or condemn any individual. I speak in general terms, collectively. Neither shall I say anything relative to political measures pursued by the administrators of our government, nor shall I pretend to attribute for the failure of success causes (only known by the departments of state) and which have produced events that are not so favorable as might have been expected by the citizens at large.[28] It is sufficient for us to know that our rulers are chosen to be the judges on all affairs concerning the welfare of their constituents. They (the ruling powers) have declared war, and it is our bounden duty to act as true and faithful citizens to support and preserve the honor, the dignity, and the independence of the United States of America! that they may bear equal rank among the nations of the earth.

That war is a real evil attending mankind cannot be denied, and King David viewed it as the greatest of all punishments that could possibly be inflicted on

[27] I cannot identify the translation used by Seixas for this extract; it is not the King James version.

[28] On the very day of the religious gatherings in New York, President Madison released a message containing a letter from the Secretary of War, with various documents, in response to a House resolution of 31 December 'requesting such information as may tend to explain the causes of the failure of the arms of the United States on the northern frontier'.

man, for, as you will find in the 2nd Book of Samuel, Cap 24th, Verse 14th, that when the prophet Gad was sent to David to propound three plagues for him to choose of,[29] that he answered, 'And David said unto Gad, I am in a great strait: let us fall now into the hand of the Lord (for his mercies are great) and let me not fall into the hand of man' (2 Sam. 24: 14). David was a warrior. He knew the horrors of war, and deprecated so dismal a calamity, but on consequence of his presumptive sin, his people were visited with pestilence, which continued for three days, and destroyed 70,000 men (2 Sam. 24: 15).

When David saw the destroying Angel of the Lord hovering over Jerusalem and had already seen the havoc that was made in the surrounding cities, he offered himself a willing victim to appease the wrath of God (2 Sam. 24: 17), as he was conscious of having been the sole instrument of bringing so great and dreadful a punishment [an Evil] on the people by his having required them to be numbered, to shew his worldly grandeur and his pomp of power through vainglory and self-sufficiency, without considering the impotence of man when he endeavours to render himself independent of his Creator.

Let us humbly implore the God of Israel to protect us in this direful day of tribulation, to strengthen our faith in His divine providence, to grant us His special grace, to avert the evils that are now pending over our heads and surrounding us with all the apprehensions of horror that can be committed by an enraged foe, who has sanctioned the savages of the wilderness to prosecute the war in the most barbarous and inhuman manner, contrary to the laws of nature and of civilized nations.

Witness the distressed situation of our fellow-citizens on our frontier settlements, in the northern boundaries of our State: driven from their peaceful abodes in this inclement season of the year, their houses sacked and burned, destitute of food, of raiment and of every necessarie of life, often without a place to shelter them from the severities of a winter season and the most piercing cold, which is much more forcibly felt in those parts than we can be properly sensible of with all.[30]

---

[29] The choice was seven years of famine, three months of military defeat leading to flight from his enemies, or three days of pestilence (v. 13). Cf. the use of this passage in a Civil War context by S. M. Isaacs (Sermon 7 below).

[30] This refers to the British and Indian campaign beginning with the attack upon and seizure of Fort Niagara on 19 December and culminating in the destruction of Buffalo on 30 December, including the torching of large areas of civilian housing and the creation of a substantial refugee population in a particularly cold winter.

Consider for a moment the distresses of 12,000 souls, in such a pitiable situation;[31] men, women, and children, widows and orphans, who, after seeing their blood-stained villages, their houses burnt, deprived of parents, husbands, and sons, with many of their nearest and dearest connexions massacred by ferocious savages[32] and the unrelenting mercenaries of an implacable and inhuman enemy, whose thirst for vengeance overrules all bounds of moral and social obligations, prompted to the most atrocious acts of diabolical dispositions, in order to gratify their insatiate fury.[33] Think! oh think! My brethren, what must such a multitude suffer! Deprived of every earthly comfort, where it is not in the power of one to help another, and all equally oppressed both in body and mind, many would despair in such a miserable situation, but it is to be hoped that the kindness of Providence will still strengthen their minds to support the trials they are now laboring under.[34] Who can hear so deplorable a recital without a sense of feeling! Humanity is shocked with the melancholy narrative, and no one can refrain from sympathizing on so woefull a catastrophe.

You are now called upon to exercise yourselves in pious and religious worship, to acknowledge your transgressions, humbly to supplicate the supreme Lord of Heaven and Earth, the Creator of all things, the Lord of Hosts is His

[31] This figure appears to have been taken from the letter from Canandaigua (see the introduction to this sermon), where it is provided as the total number of inhabitants of the region of forty square miles said to have been 'completely depopulated', with all its settlements 'effectually broken up'. The resolution of the Council inspired by this letter says 'thousands of our fellow citizens have been driven from their habitations'.

[32] Neither the letter, nor the Council resolution that followed, say anything about massacres or about 'ferocious savages'. This image is based on British and American reports that, contrary to British policy, Indians (possibly intoxicated) attacking Lewiston on 22 December engaged in indiscriminate slaughter of the inhabitants (see Babcock, *The War of 1812*, 127–9). These reports became generalized to apply to the fate of the entire refugee population.

[33] The reference to a 'thirst for vengeance' and 'insatiate fury' indicates that the listeners would probably have known that the campaign against the American inhabitants of the Niagara region was at least in part a reprisal for American burning of Canadian habitations, especially the town of Niagara (on 10 Dec. 1813) and the village of Newark (on 19 Dec.) by forces under the command of Brigadier-General George McClure. The cycle of events was outlined in the *New York Evening Post* editorial of 12 Jan. (p. 2), which reported that McClure's forces 'set on fire and burnt to the ground about 150 houses, inhabited chiefly by females, who were thus driven abroad in a most inclement night to perish with cold'. See Babcock, *The War of 1812*, 116–20, and his conclusion that Newark's 'wanton destruction under these circumstances and in this season of the year naturally called for stern and immediate measures of retribution' (p. 122); indeed, the 12 Jan. *Post* editorial, reviewing the cycle of events, referred to the British campaign against Fort Niagara and Lewiston as 'a swift and sure vengeance' for the 'base outrageous and inhuman act'—McClure's destruction of Newark.

[34] Perhaps echoing the statement in the letter from Canandaigua: 'Afflictions of the mind so deep as have been allotted to these unhappy people, we cannot cure. They can probably be subdued only by His power, who can wipe away all tears.'

*Name*. Vouchsafe to accept our prayers and penitence, O Lord! Deliver us from our present impending evils, and guard us in future from those who rise up against us; frustrate the designs and machinations of the enemy; restore us to the bosom of peace, that we may enjoy the blessings of life that are attendant on the practice of virtue, that we may manifest our gratitude unto Thee, O Lord, for the many advantages we still possess, through Thy infinite mercies; and let us be always ready and willing to ameliorate the condition of the unhappy, and in the first instance of benevolence enable us to assist our fellow-citizens in the Northwest Territory[35] at this important juncture. It is chiefly for the purpose of collecting some pecuniary aid for the disastrous inhabitants who are now appelled[36] from their former places of residence, that the Corporation of our City has so strongly recommended the observance of this day to every religious society in the city, that each and every individual might have opportunity of contributing his mite[37] towards relieving in some measure the unhappy sufferers, whose claims on our benevolence are justly founded.

For the better information of those assembled, it may not be amiss to read the recommendation of the Common-Council as published in the public prints of the City, which is as follows:[38]

Whereas it appears from a communication addressed to the Mayor of this city, that the most calamitous events have occurred on the Western frontier of the state, whereby an extensive Country has been depopulated and thousands of our fellow citizens have been driven from their habitations destitute of the necessaries of life, and exposed to the rigors of the season, and to all the privations and evils of poverty, and it being incumbent on us at all times to humble ourselves before the Almighty to supplicate His mercy, and more especially at the present time to pray that the calamities

---

[35] The preacher's use of the term 'Northwest Territory', which at the time applied to territory established by the Northwest Ordinance of 1787, eventually divided into the states of Ohio, Indiana, Illinois, Michigan, and Wisconsin, is misleading; Hühner follows him, writing of 'relief of the sufferers of the Northwest Territory' ('Jews in the War of 1812', 174). The phrase used in the City Council's proclamation, reproduced below at the end of this sermon, is 'on the western frontier of this state'; the order of the service appended to the last page of the sermon refers to 'the relief of the inhabitants of the Northwest part of this state'.

[36] 'appelled' appears to be the word Seixas wrote; I take it to be synonymous with 'expelled', although the *OED* does not list such a verb.

[37] The word 'mite' is defined by the *OED* as 'a small contribution of money made to a cause, charity, etc., esp. a sum which is as much as the giver can afford'. Although the needs of the recipients are dramatically evoked, this is certainly not a high-pressure appeal.

[38] The two following paragraphs shown here in extract form are not in the manuscript. I have used the text of the Common Council proclamation from 24 Jan. 1814, recorded in the *New York Evening Post* of Tuesday, 25 Jan. 1814, p. 3, and in *Minutes of the Common Council*, vii. 667. The preacher presumably read either from an official copy of the proclamation distributed through the city or from the newspaper.

which afflict our Country may be removed, and that those which menace us may be averted—

It is, therefore, Resolved, that Wednesday, the second day of February next, be set apart as a day of Fasting, Humiliation and Prayer, and the people of the city are requested to abstain from all business and labor on that day, and to assemble in their respective places of worship and devote themselves with humble and contrite hearts to the offices of religion, and to those devotional exercises which are suitable to an occasion so solemn, and at a crisis so important to the well being of our country.

After having heard the foregoing, wherein everything is truly and pathetically described, it is needless to say any more on the subject; it now rests with you to act as you feel disposed. I humbly pray that the blessing of God may attend you; that you may ever be directed to comply with every duty, both to God and man; that you may always choose the good and reject the evil,[39] that ye may ever incline to pursue the paths of righteousness, to practice the works of piety, benevolence, and charity—to act justly and walk humbly—to divest yourselves of worldly prejudices, to conciliate the affections of your fellow creatures, to cultivate the faculties of the mind, and to act in all things conformably to our holy Law, that ye may enjoy life and good, with all the promised blessings that are set forth by Moses and the Prophets. And know of a surety that to love and fear God, observe His commandments, His statutes, and His judgments, that ye will merit his providential [one faded illegible word] and protection, both now and forevermore, as it is said by the wisest of men, in the last [chapter and verse of] Ecclesiastes:

סוף דבר הכל נשמע את האלהים ירא ואת מצותיו שמור כי זה כל האדם.
*'The conclusion' etc. [of the whole matter: Fear God, and*
*Keep His commandments, for this is the whole duty of man]*
(ECCLES. 12: 13).

[Immediately after the text of the sermon in the manuscript, Seixas wrote an outline for the Order of Service to be held that day, including the opportunity, following his 'short address . . . in English', of 'offerings to be made individually for those who are disposed to contribute towards the relief of the inhabitants of the northwest part *of this State'*.]

---

[39] Echoing the verse from the text in Deuteronomy read at the beginning of the address.

# PART II

# THE WARS
## OF THE
# MID-NINETEENTH
## CENTURY

CHAPTER FOUR

## DAVID WOOLF MARKS
# GOD PROTECTS OUR FATHERLAND

*Preached on the day of*
*Humiliation and Prayer, as appointed by*
*Her Majesty in Council to be held for*
*the troubles in India*

### 7 OCTOBER 1857

**WEST LONDON SYNAGOGUE OF BRITISH JEWS**

A FTER the final defeat of Napoleon and the termination of hostilities with America in the War of 1812, Britain enjoyed close to four decades free of significant military conflict. This hiatus ended with the country's entry into the Crimean War between Russia and Turkey in the spring of 1854. The Crown ordained another day of fast and humiliation on 26 April, and the *Jewish Chronicle* carried reports of the sermons delivered by Jewish preachers for several weeks thereafter. Eager to bolster support for Britain's intervention on the side of Turkey, Jewish spokesmen were able to appeal to an argument with special resonance for their listeners. As one of them put it, 'the Sultan of Turkey had caught the sympathizing spirit of the age, . . . he had bestowed liberty upon our heretofore persecuted brethren'.[1] By contrast, the tsar of Russia (Nicholas I) was known as 'the modern Pharaoh'.[2] Jewish sympathies thus comfortably coincided with British policy. Abraham Pereira Mendes of the Birmingham Hebrew Congregation described the composition of the enemy's military forces as a fulfilment of biblical apocalyptic prophecy. Gog, he asserted, clearly refers to Russia, the *gag*, 'roof', or uppermost part of the then known world. Rosh,

---

[1] The reference is undoubtedly to the reformist Khatt-i Sherif or 'Noble Rescript' of 3 Nov. 1839, bestowing civil equality on non-Muslims ('These Imperial concessions shall extend to all our subjects of whatever Religion or sect they may be: they shall enjoy them without exceptions'). See Vucinich, *The Ottoman Empire*, 160–1.

[2] M. B. Levy, 'Fast-Day Sermon', delivered in the Western Synagogue, St Albans Place.

Meshekh, and Tuval, the other geographical terms in Ezekiel 38 and 39, refer to Russia Proper, Muscovy, and Tobolsky.[3] Thus the prophecy, in mentioning various nations, could only be applied to Russia, 'in whose camp Fins from the frigid north stand ranged by Poles from the genial plains of central Europe, while Sclaves and Cossack hordes from the southern steppes assemble beside Tartar bands from Asia'.[4] The portent of 'a great shaking in the land of Israel' was therefore a matter of deep concern.

Among the Crimean War sermons extensively cited by the *Jewish Chronicle* was one by David Woolf Marks, one of the most impressive leaders of British Jewry in the nineteenth century.[5] Born in 1811, he lived to the age of 98 and was active until the very last years of his life. He served for some sixty years as 'minister' of the West London Synagogue of British Jews,[6] the flagship of Reform Judaism in England, and his personal stature was a significant force in guiding the synagogue and the movement during periods of fierce attack by the Orthodox establishment. Appointed in 1848 to the Goldsmid Chair of Hebrew at University College London, he served in that position for fifty years, though he had no formal academic credentials and was largely self-taught. In May 1874 he was elected vice-dean of University College, and the following May he was elected dean of the Faculty of Arts for the year.[7] Unlike some of the more radical among his German colleagues, he advocated a moderate Reform both in practice and in doctrine, insisting on strict adherence to biblical sources, and repudiating such rabbinic innovations as the second-day holiday observance in the Diaspora.[8]

---

[3] This association of the three major regions of Russia with the three terms was not uncommon in nineteenth-century eschatological speculation: *Rosh* was understood to refer to 'Rus', or 'Russia Proper' (the European part), *Meshekh* to 'Muscovy' (the Eastern part), and *Tuval* to 'Tobolsky' (the northern part). The accepted view was that these three originally independent states united under the common name of Russia. Wilhelm Gesenius identified *Rosh* in Ezekiel 38: 2–3 and 33: 1 with Russia in his *Lexicon*, first published in German in 1810–12 and reproduced in English translation in 1836 and 1850. Christian millennialist thinkers predicted the defeat of Russia in the Crimean War on the basis of this passage in Ezekiel: see Boyer, *When Time Shall Be No More*, 84–6, 154–5, 382 n. 11. Similarly, the controversial Jewish preacher Benjamin Cohen Carillon, who served in various communities of the Caribbean and whom Mendes replaced as minister of Montego Bay, Jamaica, in 1847, asserted: 'Rosh is Russia, Meshech Muscovy, and Tubal Tobolsky' (<users.aol.com/bible2007/gogmagog.htm>); on Carillon in St Thomas, see J. M. Cohen, *Through the Sands of Time*, 66–79.

[4] *Jewish Chronicle*, 5 May 1854, 261–2. Mendes did not include this sermon in his volume of *Sermons* published in London the following year.

[5] *Jewish Chronicle*, 12 May 1854, p. 273; on Marks's review of the fast-days proclaimed during the Napoleonic Wars, see the introduction to this volume, p. 6 above.

[6] Marks had no formal rabbinical training or ordination, and he never used the title 'rabbi', which—for most of the nineteenth century in England—was reserved for the chief rabbi.

[7] *Jewish Week*, 22 May 1874; *Jewish Chronicle* 28 May 1875; both quoted in Berger, *The Jewish Victorian*, 373.

[8] A proper critical biography of Marks is still a desideratum for British Jewish history. I have consulted an unpublished monograph ('David Woolf Marks') by Rabbi Curtis Cassell, who

Marks had a reputation as an immensely talented and effective preacher. On the occasion of his eighty-ninth birthday, the *Jewish Chronicle* estimated that in fifty-eight years at the West London Synagogue he had preached some 2,000 sermons, and 'his voice and delivery are almost as fine to-day as they were in his prime'.[9] An appreciative article published by the *Chronicle* following his death on 3 May 1909 said that 'He set a standard of pulpit eloquence to which synagogues have since endeavoured to attain. It was his very power of preaching which caused other synagogues to introduce sermons as an integral part of their services.' In the same issue, the Reverend Isidore Harris paid tribute to him as 'the Chrysostom of the Jewish pulpit; as an orator at communal gatherings he was probably without an equal. An exquisite charm of literary style combined with a rich and musical voice to invest his stately utterances with a rare eloquence.' In a eulogy delivered as his memorial service, Morris Joseph, his successor at the West London Synagogue, spoke of 'his eloquence, his fervour, his felicitous diction, his oratorical skill, his charm of voice', and in a tribute at the time of his death Hermann Gollancz, his successor as professor of Hebrew at University College London, wrote, 'Personally, I have the liveliest recollections of the power, the fascination, and the earnestness of this eloquent preacher and pastor, and I doubt whether it is possible for any human being to drive his words home as he did, who did not at the same time feel the force of his own views, and speak out of the fullness of his heart.'[10]

The first volume of his *Sermons Preached on Various Occasions* appeared in 1851; containing twenty-four sermons from the first decade of his service at the West London Synagogue, it was one of the first collections of sermons by a British or American Jewish preacher to be published in English. This was followed a decade later by a second volume containing twenty-two sermons delivered between 1854 and 1862, including the one that follows. He also published a volume of sermons responding to Christian conversionary arguments and a pamphlet of sermons (*The Law Is a Light*) defending the principles of Reform in response to a sermon by the chief rabbi, Nathan Adler. Countless others of his sermons were summarized over the years by the *Jewish Chronicle*.

The text reproduced below is unusual among Marks's sermons in being a response to a specific historical event. The background to this address was the outbreak of violence on the Indian subcontinent in May 1857, soon called the 'Indian Mutiny'. The capture of Delhi by insurgents and the evacuation of its Christian inhabitants dramatized the seriousness of the challenge to British

served in the West London Synagogue, made available to me by his son David Cassell, to whom I am deeply grateful.

[9] *Jewish Chronicle*, 17 Nov. 1899, p. 17.
[10] Isidor Harris in *Jewish Chronicle*, 7 May 1909, p. 20; cf. Cassell, 'David Woolf Marks', 126–8; Morris Joseph in *Jewish Chronicle*, 7 May 1909, p. 22; Gollancz, *Fifty Years After*, 257.

control. More alarming still were reports that flowed into England throughout the summer of atrocities committed by the Indian rebels: torture and rape, mutilation of men, women, and children, massacres of Europeans and plundering of their property. In the introduction to his exhaustive treatment of these atrocities, their reporting in England, and the British reprisals, Andrew Ward wrote:

I have tried to depict the massacres at Cawnpore unflinchingly because though they were more terrible than anything I hope you can imagine, they were less atrocious than the British public was encouraged to think, and more complicated than either imperialist or nationalist historians have made them out to be. I have tried not to spare the reader the horrors of British retribution because they were more atrocious than the British public was encouraged to think.[11]

It is impossible to understand the sermon below, delivered before the reprisals but in expectation of them, without knowing of the harrowing reports given mass circulation by the media and the public revulsion and fury they inspired.

On 28 September British newspapers printed Queen Victoria's proclamation of a 'Day of National Humiliation and Prayer' to be held on the following Wednesday, 7 October. This institution had been used quite frequently in the early part of the century, as Marks himself noted (see below, n. 34); more recently, similar days had been proclaimed for the cholera epidemic of 1849 and the Crimean War of 1854–6. On this occasion, services were held and sermons were delivered in all the great churches of Great Britain, and most of the smaller ones. The spectacular Crystal Palace, built for the 1851 Great Exhibition, with a floor area of 19 acres—four times the size of St Peter's in Rome and six times the size of St Paul's—was filled to overflowing with more than 23,000 worshippers who gathered to hear C. H. Spurgeon, one of the most influential British preachers of the century, then still near the beginning of his dazzling career.[12] Newspapers covered the sermons delivered on this day extensively; on 8 October *The Times* devoted four six-column pages of small print to a summary of more than 130 sermons delivered in London pulpits (though none by Jewish preachers), material reviewed in an article by Brian Stanley. In addition, the Cambridge University Library has a volume in which separately published pamphlets of nineteen sermons delivered on this occasion were bound together.[13] Together, these texts provide a context in which to situate and evaluate what Marks chose to emphasize.

[11] Ward, *Our Bodies Are Scattered*, p. xviii. On the British retribution, see nn. 44, 45 below, and the comment by Joseph Hertz on Num. 31: 11 in *Pentateuch and Haftorahs*, 704.

[12] Spurgeon, 'Fast-Day Sermon', 373–88; id., *Autobiography*, 533–4 ('the largest congregation to which I ever preached'); Pike, *The Life and Work of Charles Hadden Spurgeon*, i. 272–80.

[13] B. Stanley, 'Christian Responses to the Indian Mutiny'; Cambridge University Library 6.21.37 (many of these were sermons delivered outside London).

Common to the sermon below and most of those delivered by Christian preachers on the same day were expressions of disbelief and outrage at the ingratitude demonstrated by the rebels towards a benevolent, humane, and enlightened British rule, and of horror at the reports (which turned out to be exaggerated) of atrocities committed against British civilians, the discourse of contempt applied to the primitive savagery of people who could behave in this manner, the need for a decisive military response to defend the British empire, the obligation to support relief efforts on behalf of the casualties of war and their families, and the assertion that God was the source of hope for the vindication of justice, right, and true faith. Missing from Marks's sermon is the theme of self-criticism that pervades much of the Christian preaching (appropriate to the mood of the day): the affirmation that the devastating mutiny was a divine judgement upon Britain for its sins as a nation, and the specification of such sins as British involvement in the opium trade, the toleration of prostitution on the streets, and the failure of British institutions in India (such as the East India Company) to combat adequately the idolatrous and immoral religious beliefs of the natives and adequately to support and promote the Christian faith.[14] There is no recognition in Marks's sermon of sins, failures, or shortcomings on the British side; indeed, in his interpretation of Psalm 3 he specifically repudiates this view. God is the source of hope, not the power providentially responsible for the disaster.

Conversely, Marks emphasizes a theme that is understandably missing from the Christian preachers, who took it for granted: solidarity with Christian neighbours and the patriotism of the Jews of Britain. Phrases such as 'loyal citizen', 'good patriot', 'our duty as good citizens', 'patriotic spirit', 'a citizen amongst citizens', 'the patriotic and self-denying spirit' liberally punctuate the sermon, as if it were necessary to convince either the listeners or a putative audience outside the synagogue. He even finds it necessary to raise the familiar challenge to Jewish patriotism—the traditional Jewish prayer for the messianic restoration in the land of Israel—and he responds in the traditionalist (not the radical Reformist) manner, affirming the belief for the future, but insisting that it has no relevance to contemporary Jews' behaviour as citizens and does not diminish their love for the land of their birth.

The other polemical thrust of the sermon is the reference to 'whatever opinions we may entertain with respect to the causes which have produced this

[14] B. Stanley, 'Christian Responses to the Indian Mutiny', 279–81. Within the Cambridge Library pamphlets, the purported compromise with idolatry and the failure to promote Christianity is emphasized frequently and with considerable force. Only one of the preachers, Edmund Kell, takes what he knows will be the unpopular position that there is 'something cancerous in the nature of our connexion with India, which with a determined hand we should eradicate', and that 'we have no moral right to reign over India, if we can only do so at the expense of her people's blood' ('What Patriotism, Justice, and Christianity Demand for India', 4).

serious rebellion'. There were indeed some Christian (largely nonconformist) preachers on this day of humiliation who condemned the 'inordinate, secular, selfish ambition' that characterized British rule in India.[15] It is difficult to determine how many in Marks's congregation were critical of specific aspects of British imperial policy. But the thrust of his message is clear: this is not the time to indulge in 'harsh and intemperate criticisms'. Nor is it appropriate to 'indulge a maudlin sentimentality' about future British reprisals—which in fact turned out to be more savage than the acts that provoked them. Marks was uncompromising in his support for a brutal repression of the revolt and a vindictive, even indiscriminate, punishment of the population responsible for its excesses.

Throughout the text, there are passages that reveal the rhetorical power for which Marks was known. The care with which he wrote is revealed even in the peroration following his announcement that 'My sermon draws to a close': 'Let us pray that the effects of God's blessing may be made practically evident in the readiness . . .; in the cheerfulness . . .; in the fortitude and patience . . .; in the courage and intrepidity . . .; in the moderation, the mercy, and the humane spirit . . .' This was an age of polished prose, and Marks was a preacher who obviously took pride in the crafting of his message.

The impact of Marks's sermon was felt beyond the circle of those who heard it delivered. Some two weeks after the day of fast and humiliation, the *Jewish Chronicle and Hebrew Observer* of 23 October 1857 cited at length the following article from a general political weekly, the *Examiner*:

When a pretext is wanting for excluding the Jews from the legislature, it is always affirmed that there is something in their faith repugnant and hostile to the institutions of a Christian state. Strange that this hostility should never show itself in times of our public trials and afflictions. On the contrary, however, we always find the religion of the Jews prompting them to share the sorrows, as they do all other burthens, of their Christian fellow-subjects; upon all such occasions as the late day of humiliation they meet in their synagogues in the same spirit that draws the rest of the community to their several places of worship, and lend their voices with sincerity to the universal prayer. They are free from the reproach of the children of the market places. When

---

[15] The quotation is from James Spence, cited in B. Stanley, 'Christian Responses to the Indian Mutiny', 283. Cf. Spurgeon, 'India's Ills and England's Sorrows' delivered at the Surrey Gardens Music Hall two months earlier: 'The government of India has been a cruel government; it has much for which to appear before the bar of God. Its tortures—if the best evidence is to be believed—have been of the most inhuman kind; God forgive the men who have committed such crimes in the British name' (p. 342). Cf. also his fast-day sermon: 'The sins of the government of India have been black and deep. He who has heard the shrieks of tormented natives, who has heard the well-provoked cursing of dethroned princes, might have prophesied that it would not be long before God would unsheath his sword to avenge the oppressed. With regard to India itself, I am no apologist for our dominion there' ('Fast-Day Sermon', 382).

have we mourned to them and they have not lamented. In this point of view the service performed on the Wednesday before last, at the West London Synagogue of British Jews, is worthy of attention and remembrance. We are told that a large congregation was assembled to join in a special form of prayer, and then a sermon by the Rev. Professor Marks, of which the following is the outline which appeared in the 'Globe'.

The *Jewish Chronicle* did not reproduce the text of the sermon, but the *Examiner* (and, apparently, its source in the *Globe*) reported its content quite accurately, with extensive quotations; some of them diverge slightly from the text that Marks later printed, including a significant sentence later omitted, and Marks's concluding prayer, as will be noted below. The *Chronicle* then reported the concluding comment in the *Examiner* article, as follows:

This is requiting evil with good. How long shall we persist in requiting this good with evil? Thus preaching and praying the Jews draw a purer religion from one half of the Bible than those narrow griping Christians who worry them with paltry persecutions extracted from the whole.[16]

This article reveals that what Jewish preachers said on a public occasion such as the day of fast had repercussions in the broader society, and that the Jewish press recognized the importance of the positive public relations effect of a strong statement of support for the nation's war effort. Presumably that was precisely the effect that Marks intended.

# SERMON

ליי הישועה

*With the Lord is help*
(PS. 3: 9)

BRETHREN, the proclamation of our Gracious Sovereign, the Queen, has summoned us to-day, in common with the rest of our countrymen, to the house of God,[17] the appointed place whither mankind have repaired, genera-

[16] *Jewish Chronicle and Hebrew Observer*, 23 Oct. 1857, p. 1189, drawing on *Examiner*, 17 Oct. 1587, pp. 659–60; I consulted microfilms of both in the Cambridge University Library. I was unable to consult the *Globe*, which apparently summarized and quoted the sermon without comment.

[17] Cf. Hirschel Levin's sermon, in M. Saperstein, *Jewish Preaching*, 347–58, esp. the reference to the royal proclamation on p. 350, and Sermon 1 above by Luria. Note the emphasis on solidarity with Christian neighbours in response to the queen's decree.

tion after generation, in times of private grief and of national calamity. We come here to humble ourselves before Almighty God, the Supreme Controller of events, and prayerfully to implore His guidance and His help, under the affliction in which the state is plunged:[18] for rebellion has raised its sanguinary banner in an important part of Her Majesty's dominions, and the wildest passions of savage nature have been let loose, inflicting horrors at the recital of which the heart turns faint, and causing the fate of an empire, as it seemed at one time, to tremble in the balance.[19] As a Jewish congregation we could have wished that the present solemn national gathering had not been fixed for a day that falls within the week of Tabernacles, when the Synagogue Services consist wholly of hymns of festive joy and praise.[20] Still I am not aware that there is any day in the calendar, how sacred soever it be, on which it is not lawful for us, as true Israelites and devoted

---

[18] This echoes in part the formulation of the queen's proclamation: 'so both we and our people may humble ourselves before Almighty God in order to obtain pardon of our sins, and in the most devout and solemn manner send up our prayers and supplications to the Divine Majesty for imploring His blessing and assistance on our arms for the restoration of tranquility': *The Times*, 28 Sept. 1857, p. 4, col. 2, cited in B. Stanley, 'Christian Responses to the Indian Mutiny', 279 n. 16. It is striking that Marks omits the phrase 'to obtain pardon of our sins' and—as noted above—does not include any element of self-criticism in the sermon.

[19] As is common in such sermons, the preacher does not need to explain in detail the actual circumstances, which all in the congregation would have known, referring only in general terms to the outbreak of what was then called the 'Indian Mutiny' or the 'Sepoy Rebellion'. Cf. Spurgeon: 'My brethren, our hearts are sick nigh unto death with the terrible news brought us post after post, telegraph after telegraph; we have read many letters of the *Times*, day after day, until we have folded up that paper, and professed before God that we could read no more. Our spirits have been harrowed by the most fearful and unexpected cruelty' ('India's Ills and England's Sorrows', 342).

[20] The first day of the Sukkot holiday in 1857 was Saturday, 3 October. The mandated 'Day of Humiliation and Prayer' was thus in the middle of the festival (*ḥol hamo'ed sukot*), one of the days that have a status intermediate between holiday and ordinary days in Jewish practice. Sukkot is designated 'the season of our rejoicing' (*zeman simḥatenu*), and the 'Day of Humiliation' thereby created a tension between the Jewish calendar and the secular calendar, which the preacher had to acknowledge. Cf. the report of the sermon delivered by Rabbi Dr Schiller-Szinessy at the Cooper Street Synagogue of Manchester: 'Although this season (the Feast of Tabernacles) was appointed for "rejoicing before the Lord", still, as citizens of Great Britain, it was the duty of Israelites to obey the command of their beloved sovereign, and to join their fellow subjects in proclaiming this a day of profound humiliation before God' ('Fast-Day Sermon'). When a day of national humiliation, prayer and fasting was proclaimed by President Lincoln for 26 Sept. 1861 (falling on the holiday of Shemini Atseret), S. M. Isaacs, preaching in New York, said that 'the moment we are called upon to unite with our fellow citizens in praying to God in humility, unmindful even of the festive symbols around us, our heart and soul co-operate with them, animated by the same feeling of pure patriotism'. However, Morris Raphall, also in New York, said that 'in this collision between Divine and human authority, the One commanding a solemn feast, the other a penitential fast, there can be no question for you, my friends, or for me, as to which we ought to obey . . . I cannot bid you to fast when He bids you to feast. I cannot harrow your feelings with a penitential lecture, when God bids you rejoice' (both cited in *Jewish Messenger*, 4 Oct. 1861, p. 51).

patriots, to unite with our fellow countrymen of all sects and creeds, in sending up a national cry to Heaven for support, when calamity befalls, or danger threatens, our common Fatherland.[21]

The text, from which I preach, comprises two simple Hebrew words; but they embody a truth of the first magnitude: ליי הישועה, 'With the Lord is help' (Ps. 3: 9). The Psalm, in which the text is found, forms part of the present especial service;[22] and a very few moments' reflection will satisfy my hearers, that nothing could be more in keeping with the day on which we are met together, than this prayerful hymn of the Hebrew Monarch.

'With the Lord is help.' A short, but most expressive phrase, in which we recognise the hope and the faith that beat in the heart of a loyal citizen and a good patriot in times of national disaster.[23] The psalm owes its origin to the melancholy period in the reign of David, when a fearful rebellion had broken out and the horrors of civil war were distressing the land. Of the many afflictions to which humanity is exposed, war, under any circumstances, may be considered amongst the most trying and severe.[24] Wheresoever it rages, industry ceases, and the great masses of mankind, whose daily loaf of bread is only to be procured by the labour of their hands, find their expectations cut off. It impoverishes whole communities, reduces to ashes the homesteads of thousands, 'moistens the soil with human gore, makes mothers widows and children orphans, and it rarely opens for the conqueror a path that does not lie over putrefying heaps of mortality, over pillaged cities, ravaged fields and smoking ruins'.*[25] But

* Channing.

[21] Again the theme of Jewish patriotism and solidarity with Christian neighbours is emphasized. The suggestion that there was actual danger threatening the 'common Fatherland' (as opposed to the empire) goes beyond the facts at the time, as Marks notes further in the sermon.

[22] Referring not to the standard liturgy for the Jewish holiday week but to the special liturgy for the 'Day of Humiliation'. Jewish congregations routinely composed a liturgy for such occasions, and many of these were published (sometimes with the sermon) in pamphlet form.

[23] Marks's characterization again emphasizes the patriotism of British Jews.

[24] An evocation of the horrors of war, as seen in the following sentences, appears to be a commonplace in Jewish preaching for such special occasions. Cf. e.g. the passage from Moses Mendelssohn's 'Friedenspredigt' cited in M. Saperstein, 'Your Voice Like a Ram's Horn', 160–1.

[25] The reference is to William Ellery Channing (1780–1842), an extremely prolific Unitarian minister and a fierce critic of war. Cf. his 'Remarks on the Life and Character of Napoleon Bonapart', pt. II, in his Discourses, Reviews, and Miscellanies, 149. Cf. also the following sermon from 1835: 'Let me ask, then, what is the chief business of war? It is to destroy human life; to mangle the limbs; to gash and hew the body; to plunge the sword into the heart of a fellow-creature; to strew the earth with bleeding frames, and to trample them under foot with horses' hoofs. It is to batter down and burn cities; to turn fruitful fields into deserts; to level the cottage of the peasant and the magnificent abode of opulence; to scourge nations with famine; to multiply widows and orphans' (Discourses on War, 50–1). Cf. also Wagenknecht, Ambassadors of Christ, 65–6.

deplorably great as these evils are, they are multiplied tenfold in a case of civil war, like that to which the psalm of the text refers. The unnatural Absalom raises his hand against his father's life and his country's peace.[26] Many of the veterans whom David has so often led to victory, abandon his standard and go over to the usurper; and the aged king who has raised his country to an eminence it never attained before, is compelled to quit his capital and go forth as an exile and a wanderer. Scarcely a post reaches David that does not announce some fresh desertion or gross act of treachery; and, overwhelmed by the magnitude of the rebellion, and chief of all by the painful reflection that his own son is seeking his life, he appeals in his distress to the All-seeing God, and exclaims, יי מה רבו צרי רבים קמים עלי, 'O Lord! how mine enemies do increase; how numerous are they that rise up against me' (Ps. 3: 2).

In the second verse, the Psalmist sketches a picture which is but too familiar to times of civil strife, when those who take no direct part in rebellion, but profess attachment to the government established by law, do nevertheless inflict the most serious mischief on the cause to which they pretend to be true, by speaking the language of despair; and by assuming to interpret the present misfortune as a special visitation of Providence for some undefined sin into which the nation has fallen, or for some imaginary wrong committed by the Government.[27] All this is made as clear, as if pages had been devoted to the description of it, in the few words uttered by the Psalmist, רבים אומרים לנפשי אין ישועתה לו באלהים, 'Many say of me, no help is to be expected for him from God' (Ps. 3: 3). But, plunged as David is, in the deepest distress, he does not despair. He appeals to the Almighty, the great disposer and controller of events, whom he regards as 'his shield and the lifter up of his head' (cf. Ps. 3: 4) and, placing a firm reliance in the 'Rock of Ages', the sorely stricken king declares that 'he can lay him down and sleep', though 'surrounded by enemies who set themselves up against him' (cf. Ps. 3: 6–7). The Psalmist concludes his pathetic hymn with the utterance of the sentiment of the text ליי הישועה, 'With the Lord is help' (Ps. 3: 9), at the same time offering up a devout petition for the prosperity of the commonwealth (על עמך ברכתך) (Ps. 3: 9), as if he had

[26] The title of the Psalm (v. 1) is 'A Psalm of David when he fled from his son Absalom'. For the circumstances of Absalom's rebellion, see 2 Sam. 15–18.

[27] The preacher is alluding to other theologians who have explained the military reversals as God's providential punishment of Britain for its moral or religious failing; see the material cited in nn. 14–15 above. In accordance with his scriptural text, Marks asserts the need for reliance upon God, but rejects the traditional theodicy linking national disaster with punishment for sin.

purposed to bequeath to us the lesson, that it becomes the patriot to lay aside all his private sorrows, when danger threatens the peace and the independence of his country.[28]

Turning aside for a while from the general bearing of the chapter of the psalm, I would nevertheless exhort my hearers to keep the text itself constantly in view, in as much as it embodies the idea that pervades the Scriptures, and which influenced the Hebrew people in all their national misfortunes, as well as in every struggle which they made for upholding their commonwealth in its integrity. 'With the Lord is help', cried Moses (Exod. 14: 13–14), when his people were placed in the most imminent peril on the shores of the Red Sea; and the self-same sentiment is echoed by David at the most critical period of his eventful life. To what part soever of the Bible we turn, we may be sure to light upon this cardinal truth, proclaimed by the Hebrew people in the time of national peril. It falls from the lips of Gideon when the liberties of Palestine are threatened by a ruthless invader, it is uttered by Hezekiah when his capital is besieged by Sennacherib, and also by Mordecai when utter extermination appears to be the impending fate of the Jewish exiles in the dominions of Persia.[29]

To-day the self-same truth is proclaimed aloud in our Synagogues; for, like our ancient fathers, we have no sentiments nearer at heart than those of the love of God and the love of our country. The Lord God of Hosts, in whom our ancestors placed their trust, is also the 'Tower of our strength' (cf. Ps. 61: 4) and the fortress of our hope; and the same patriotic spirit which animated the Hebrews of a by-gone age when they prayed for 'the prosperity of Jerusalem' (Ps. 122: 6), must unquestionably warm the breast of every one of us today whilst we are imploring the Almighty for the welfare of Britain. It is true that we have deep religious associations with the land of the Patriarchs, and that, in conformity with the promises of prophetic Scripture we maintain the belief that Israel will be restored to that land at the period of Messiah's advent, when all, existing political relations will be adapted to the glorious events consequent upon the coming of the regenerator of the human race.[30] But until that period arrives—a period of which no account is taken by Israelites in any of their

[28] Thus the end of the psalm, in which David for the first time moves beyond his personal affliction to invoke blessing upon God's people, provides a model for the patriot at present.
[29] Gideon: Judg. 6: 16–17, 7: 15; Hezekiah: 2 Kgs 19: 15–19; Mordecai: cf. Esther 4: 14 (though, as is well known, there is no explicit mention of God in the Book of Esther).
[30] Though the minister of a Reform congregation, Marks shows here that he did not take the more radical position of many Reform Jews in rejecting the territorial and political dimensions of Jewish messianic belief.

relations as citizens—[31] the political Jerusalem of every Jew is the land of his birth,[32] the land where he is a citizen amongst citizens, in fine, his native land, whose welfare and prosperity are identified with the dearest affections of his soul.[33]

Hence, brethren, we can bring home to ourselves to-day and in the fulness of the old Jewish spirit, the pious ejaculation of the text; and we can proclaim it, as in times past Englishmen were wont to give expression to it, when their country had to put to the hazard of the sword its honor, its glory, its independence, and, at a period no farther distant than the opening of the present century, its very claim to a place on the map of Europe.[34] In this Synagogue to-day there must be present some who remember the implicit faith which the nation placed in the sentiment of the text, and how, relying on the Divine protection, England's sons persevered amidst the neutrality of some states and the bondage of others, until the phantom of a *Western Empire* passed away and the safety and the independence of Britain were secured.[35]

[31] Here Marks echoes the position classically taken by Moses Mendelssohn at a time when the Jewish hope for restoration under the messiah in the land of Israel was invoked by opponents of Jewish emancipation: this hope 'has no influence on our conduct as citizens', and is reserved for synagogue and prayer (see Mendes-Flohr and Reinharz, *The Jew in the Modern World*, 43). Cf. Marks's statement in a sermon for Sabbath 'Nahamu', 12 Aug. 1843: 'On our actual social and political relations, however, the doctrine of our final ingathering does not exercise the slightest possible influence' (*Sermons Preached on Various Occasions*, i. 207).

[32] Cf. the formulation of Gustav Poznanski, cantor of Beth Elohim congregation in Charleston, at the dedication of a new synagogue in 1841: 'this synagogue is our *temple*, this city our *Jerusalem*, this happy land our *Palestine*', in Plaut, *The Growth of Reform Judaism*, 9; also Bernard Illowy's 'Fast-Day Sermon' of 4 Jan. 1861: 'such should be our earnest prayer for the peace and prosperity of our Jerusalem, I say *our* Jerusalem, for until the time that it will be pleasing in the sight of the Lord to protract the fulfilment of his promises, this country will be our Jerusalem' (<www.jewish-history.com/Illoway/sermon.html>).

[33] Compare, with this entire passage, the quotation from an 1845 sermon by Marks printed in the *Jewish Chronicle*, in Plaut, *The Rise of Reform Judaism*, 136–7, including, 'To this land we attach ourselves with a patriotism as glowing, with a devotion as fervent, and with a love as ardent and sincere as any class of our British non-Jewish fellow citizens.'

[34] Reference is to the Napoleonic Wars (see Sermons 1 and 2 above by Isaac Luria and Solomon Hirschel, respectively). In his Crimean War fast-day sermon (see Introduction above, p. 6), Marks reviewed the many such days at the beginning of the century, including the one in 1811 'when all Europe was chained to the car of him that had done battle for universal empire, when every continental port was closed against our commerce, when famine and want were daily consigning to a premature grave hundreds of our countrymen, and when it appeared that England herself, which till then had stood undaunted and unconquered amid the wrecks of nations, must soon yield to the torrent that was gathering around her': *Jewish Chronicle*, 5 May 1854, p. 273.

[35] The idea of a 'Western Empire' followed upon Napoleon's coronation as emperor in Dec. 1804.

Happily, the national disaster which we now deplore in the Temple of God, is not to be compared in magnitude with the danger in which the Jewish state was involved at the epoch marked by the psalm of our text. Thank God we are at peace at home; and so far from there being anything like impatience manifested of the sceptre of the Queen, there is not perhaps to be found in the three kingdoms, a subject in whose affections our Royal mistress does not reign. The scene of violence and strife is India, where British rule has been recognised for more than a century, and where the native populations have almost in every instance been treated with clemency and tender consideration, contrasting strangely with the tyranny that prevailed during the centuries when the country was governed by the Moguls and their Satraps.[36] Against this merciful and humane rule, however, an alarming rebellion has broken out, accompanied by deeds of horror to which it would be difficult to find a parallel in modern times. It might have been hoped that we had survived the age when acts of atrocity like those of which we have recently heard, were capable of being committed. The outrages that have been perpetrated on defenceless women and children make the heart turn sick; and the tortures that have been inflicted in order to gratify the most savage lusts, throw the mind back on what the Bible records of the crimes of the Canaanite nations, and for which a just and retributive Providence decreed their extermination from the earth. There is scarcely a deed of horror familiar to savage life that has not been practised by the rebels in their sanguinary career.[37] They have overthrown the institutions which it cost civilization years and years of toil to build up; they have shaken the Empire to its foundations; and they are now engaged with England in a mortal struggle, the

[36] A characteristic statement of the ideology of empire as benefiting native populations incapable of governing themselves in accordance with enlightened European standards.

[37] Cf. Spurgeon: 'O Earth! Thou hast beheld crimes which antiquity could not parallel; thou hast seen bestial lust gratified upon the purest and the best of mortals' ('India's Ills and England's Sorrows', 342), and 'Not to-day shall I detail their acts of debauchery, bloodshed, and worse than bestiality—this tongue will not venture to utter what they have dared to do' ('Fast-Day Sermon', 380); also the sermon by James Charles of Kirkcowan: 'Ransack all history, whether of civilised or of savage tribes—read through and through the records even of oriental treachery, ferocity, cruelty, and crime—and you will meet with nothing that surpasses, with scarcely anything that parallels the savage, the worse than savage, the hellish atrocities, of which our countrymen and countrywomen have been the victims' ('The Lord's Voice to Britain', 7–8). On the atrocities and their reports in Britain, see Hibbert, *The Great Mutiny*, 212–15 ('most of the appalling crimes rumoured to have happened, and reported as facts in letters to England, bore scant relation to the truth'), and Ward, *Our Bodies Are Scattered*, esp. 510–15. Marks's passage about the Canaanites is revealing, recognizing that the Bible records a divine command for genocide (Deut. 20: 16–17) and justifying this as punishment for allegedly unprecedented and intolerable crimes (the explanation in Deut. 20: 18 mentions abominations of idolatry, but not atrocities analogous to those mentioned by the preacher here).

issues of which not only involve the preservation of India to the British Crown, but also the raising of a barrier against a new irruption of barbarians that threaten to sweep over a territory containing a population of two hundred millions of souls, and to engulph every vestige of the monuments which a century of progress and of humane and enlightened government has raised up.[38]

Whilst this conflict is raging, our beloved Queen, mindful of the great biblical truth set forth in the text, has convoked the nation, to fall prostrate in prayer to day before Almighty God, and to implore His aid on behalf of the expedition which has just left our shores, for the purpose of crushing this wicked rebellion, of staying the hand of the assassin and of the marauder, and of bringing back peace and security to a land, stained with crime and made drunk with blood.[39] We must all admit the reasonableness of the appointment of such a day of humiliation and prayer; and our presence here denotes our sense of the duty incumbent upon us to implore God to listen to the national cry and to 'send help from His Sanctuary' (Ps. 20: 3). But whilst we appeal to the Almighty, without whose blessing no enterprise can have a successful issue, it behoves us to remember that we are all agents of His Providence, and that we are imperatively called upon at a time like this to make ourselves useful according to our several capacities, and to employ all the means at our command in order to strengthen the hands of the executive and to re-establish the authority of the Law where it has been so rudely violated.[40]

Whatever opinions we may entertain with respect to the causes which have produced this serious rebellion,[41] it is our duty as good citizens to practise self-denial, and to refrain from indulging in harsh and intemperate criticisms, so that we may not in any wise paralyse the arm of the government by discussions of a merely speculative character.[42] [We may rest satisfied, that the nation will

---

[38] It would be difficult to imagine a more emphatic definition of what is at stake: a battle between the forces of progress, humanity, enlightenment, and civilization, against the forces of bloodthirsty, primitive savagery. In this, Marks recast the dominant rhetoric of a battle between enlightened, moral *Christianity* and savage heathen idolatry (see Hanha, 'Religion and Nationality', 168).

[39] Another echo of the language of the proclamation (see n. 18 above), with the addition of phrases that give it a far more belligerent tone.

[40] Thus, while prayer is indeed important, it is not a substitute for action to achieve the political and military goal.

[41] The causes included the issuing by the British of cartridges greased with beef and pork fat, offensive to Hindu and Muslim soldiers, the intervention in the domain of Hindu practices, and the activity of Christian missionaries.

[42] This concedes that criticisms were being made of government policy towards India with regard to the causes of the Mutiny. For the debate in Parliament and in the press, see Metcalf, *The Aftermath of Revolt*, 72–5. Metcalf's conclusion is quite consistent with the attitude of the

not abnegate its right to demand a searching inquiry into the circumstances that have placed in peril an empire, and cause the most precious blood of the land to be poured out like water. But this is not the time to enter on such an inquiry.][43] The immediate object of every right-minded man should be, to put an end to anarchy and license, and to uphold the supremacy of the crown at every cost and under every pecuniary sacrifice. Equally incumbent is it on our part to repose full confidence in those who are appointed to the difficult and responsible task of administering affairs in the disturbed provinces of India. Nor must we display a hostile front to the government, if the humane principles applied to legitimate warfare fail to be employed, in every instance, on the present occasion, whilst dealing with miscreants who have cast a reproach on human nature. To be stern in the day of battle and to be moderate and merciful in the hour of victory, is a maxim that every pulpit ought to inculcate, and it would but ill discharge its office, if it did not claim the exercise of clemency towards every foe, in whom the faintest glimmer of principle or of patriotism might be traced.[44] But to indulge a maudlin sentimentality for those, in comparison with whose crimes cannibalism itself almost becomes tolerable, is to betray great folly and unmanly weakness.[45]

preacher: 'With few exceptions the periodical press, reflecting the self-confidence of mid-Victorian England, . . . simply could not conceive of anyone consciously rejecting the benefits of British rule. Indeed they were at a loss to account for the uprising at all except on the ground that the Indian people were ignorant and credulous, like savages or children, "easily persuaded of the most monstrous absurdities"' (p. 75).

[43] The sentences in square brackets appear in the report of the sermon from the *Globe*, summarized by the *Examiner* of 17 Oct. 1587 (see introduction), but were apparently removed by Marks when he published the text in the second volume of his *Sermons*. One might surmise that in the absence of a 'searching inquiry' following the war, he did not wish to call attention to his assurance.

[44] The text of this sentence in the *Examiner* is somewhat different: 'To be vigorous and stern in the day of battle and to be moderate and merciful in the hour of victory is a maxim that commends itself to all who are influenced by the benevolent precepts of the Bible; and that man were indeed unfit to speak from the pulpit who should fail to preach clemency and indulgence towards those who are betrayed into excesses by misguided zeal, or by any motives, however erroneous, in which can be traced the faintest glimmer of patriotism or of a genuine patriotic spirit.' The version published later seems to reflect not substantive change but stylistic polishing.

[45] These two sentences would suggest that the preacher excluded the Indian rebels from the category of human beings towards whom preachers were obliged to endorse policies of moderation, mercy, and clemency. A few preachers did indeed maintain that justice in reprisal must be tempered with mercy (so that the superiority of Christian to heathen ethics might be demonstrated: B. Stanley, 'Christian Responses to the Indian Mutiny', 282), or warned against 'the indulgence of the vindictive passions' (Ward, *Our Bodies Are Scattered*, 514), or proclaimed that 'I am inclined, if I can, to sprinkle some few cooling tears upon the fires of vengeance', insisting instead on a just and proper judicial punishment (Spurgeon, India's Ills and England's Sorrows', 343). Note, however, Marks's concluding prayer, with the phrase 'in every case where it can prudently be shown, in the moderation, the mercy, and the human spirit which they exhibit in the hour of triumph'.

And, whilst we proclaim our dependence on God, who is all-sufficient to crown with success the arms of our country, let us not be unmindful of what we owe to the wives and children of our brave soldiers who may fall in the present war. When Almighty God reveals Himself to us as the husband of the widow and the father of the orphan, it is very plain that He desires to manifest Himself in these merciful relations through the agency of man.[46] Be it, then, our care to prove ourselves on the present occasion the willing agents of the Lord's gracious Providence, and let us give generously, according to the means with which it has pleased God to bless us, towards the fund that is now being raised for the families of those who are sealing their country's cause with their blood.[47] I need scarcely urge upon you, brethren, the conscientious discharge of this obligation. Benevolence is the birth-right of Englishmen; and, happily, this God-like virtue has never failed to constitute a distinguishing feature in the character of the Israelite.

My sermon draws to a close. Having ascribed all power to Him that controls the destiny of kingdoms and before whom the chapter of the future is laid open like a scroll; and having also endeavoured to indicate, from the prescriptive words of the Psalmist, in what our duties as Jews and citizens consist, when a great calamity befalls our country; let us now echo from the recesses of our hearts the same devout petition with which David closes his exquisite hymn, על עמך ברכתך, *May thy benediction be upon thy people* (Ps. 3: 9).[48] Be this the burden of the petition which is poured forth to-day from every church, chapel, and synagogue in the three kingdoms. And whilst we implore this divine blessing, let us also pray God that we may be permitted to witness its accomplishment from day to day, in the wisdom and foresight of those who are called to Her Majesty's councils, in the perfect concord of their views, and in the energy of their purposes, as well as in the patriotic and self-denying spirit, with which all political biases and private and personal interests are immolated at the shrine of the National weal. Let us pray that the effects of God's blessing may be

[46] An apparent allusion to Deut. 10: 17 and, in a broader sense, to the Jewish doctrine of *imitatio dei* through benevolent acts; see the discussion of the relevant texts in S. Schechter, *Some Aspects of Rabbinic Theology*, 201–4.

[47] The *Jewish Chronicle and Hebrew Observer* reported that 'special services were performed and collections made in all synagogues' (9 Oct. 1857, p. 1173). The description of the Hambro Synagogue states explicitly: 'At the conclusion a collection was made for the relief of the sufferers by the mutiny in India' (16 Oct. 1857), p. 1181. Such appeals for contributions were almost always included in similar gatherings; the preachers strongly endorsed generosity, and the amount raised was sometimes noted in reports by *Jewish Chronicle*.

[48] Referring not to the Jewish people, but to the British people.

made practically evident in the readiness with which her vigorous sons respond to her summons 'To arms'; in the cheerfulness with which they rally round her standard; in the fortitude and patience which they manifest under hardships and trials; in the courage and intrepidity which they display on the field of battle, and, in every case where it can prudently be shown, in the moderation, the mercy, and the humane spirit which they exhibit, in the hour of triumph. Finally, let us pray, that, before the present year is spent, peace will have been restored to the Empire, the wonted activity in every branch of its manufactures and in each department of its varied commerce will have returned, and well grounded hopes will have arisen of the approximation of the happy age predicted for humanity by the inspired Seer: ומחה יי אלהים את דמעה מעל כל פנים וחרפת עמו יסיר מעל כל הארץ כי פי יי דבר, 'When the Lord God shall wipe away the tear from every cheek, and cast aside the reproach of His people (the reproach of humanity) from off the whole world; for the mouth of the Lord hath spoken it' (Isa. 25: 8).

## PRAYER[49]

May He who dispenseth salvation unto kings and dominion unto princes; whose kingdom is an everlasting kingdom; who delivered his servant David from the destructive sword; who maketh a way in the sea, and a path through the mighty waters—may he bless, preserve, guard, assist, exalt, and highly aggrandise our Sovereign Lady, Queen Victoria, the Prince Consort, Albert, Prince of Wales, and all the Royal Family. May the supreme King of Kings through His infinite mercy, preserve her and grant to her life, and deliver her from all manner of trouble and danger; make her enemies to fall before her, and cause her to prosper in all her undertakings. May the supreme King of Kings, through His infinite mercy, incline her heart and the hearts of her counsellors and nobles, with benevolence towards us and all Israel. In her days, and in ours, may Judah be saved, and Israel dwell in safety; and may the Redeemer come unto Zion; O that this may be His gracious will! And let us say, A M E N .

[49] The text of the following prayer, adapted from the standard Jewish prayer for the government which does not appear in Marks's published text of the sermon, is taken from the account in the *Examiner*, based on the *Globe*, as noted in the introduction above, introduced with the phrase 'And from the prayer offered upon the occasion let us give a single passage'. The texts of the prayers written for the occasion for the synagogues of the United Congregations and for the Spanish and Portuguese Synagogue appeared in the *Jewish Chronicle and Hebrew Observer*, 16 Oct. 1857, p. 1179.

# CHAPTER FIVE

## M. J. MICHELBACHER
# A SERMON DELIVERED ON THE DAY OF PRAYER

*Recommended by the President of the CSA*

### 27 MARCH 1863

**GERMAN HEBREW SYNAGOGUE, 'BAYTH AHABAH',
RICHMOND, VIRGINIA**

FOLLOWING Seixas's sermon during the War of 1812, I have found no example of American Jewish pulpit discourse in wartime until the Civil War. What we do find is a passage in Isaac Leeser's eulogy for President William Henry Harrison, delivered on 9 April 1841, the fifth day of Passover, reviewing his role as a military leader in the Indian Wars: 'And when the newly-awakened demon of war again roused the savages to strife and slaughter, [Harrison] led the armies of his country to the onset, and overthrew the dangerous foe.' In this context, Leeser evokes the savagery of the Native Americans in melodramatic passages that exceed even the description by Seixas of the massacre near Buffalo. The danger that Harrison faced was not from 'the warlike sons of ancient Britain', nor from 'the children of gallant France', nor from 'foul treason'; rather, 'it was the war-yell of the fierce, untamable sons of the forest, who slaughtered without mercy the armed man and the defenceless woman; who spared not, in their murderous lust, the aged sire and the timid maiden, and who were strangers to mercy, and unmoved by the innocent smiles of helpless infancy'. Some measure of understanding and even a touch of empathy for the plight of the Native Americans can be detected in the following passage, as well as an acknowledgement of the deceit and greed of those who dispossessed them, but on the whole it portrays the enemy as sharing very little in common humanity with the preacher or his audience. America was won

by the prowess of the civilized Caucasian race from the indigenous inhabitants of the land, more savage than the beasts of their forests, and as uncultivated as the soil on which they trod ... Extermination and an utter obliterating almost have been the fate of many tribes of the once powerful owners of this land, for whom we cannot avoid having pity, though they have often been stained with the blood of many innocent victims; knowing, as we do, that their untutored mind was not rarely goaded on to madness by the bad faith and rapacity of their more lettered, but frequently dishonest neighbours, who came at times, first, to seek a refuge and shelter in the to them unhospitable forest, and then aimed ere long to dispossess their kind red friends of the graves of their forefathers. But these yielded not without a terrible resistance, and many a glade was reddened by the blood of mortal foes, of rival races struggling for the supremacy.[1]

The recognition that, in the Indian Wars, the goal of American policy was not the defeat of any army, but the annihilation of a people,[2] evokes no outrage, but a mere expression of pity; and even this is modified by the reminder that 'they [the victims] have often been stained with the blood of many innocent victims'.

As for the Mexican War of 1846–8, powerfully attacked by such celebrated Christian preachers as Henry Ward Beecher and Theodore Parker,[3] there seems to be no reference to it in Leeser's *Discourses*. Preaching on 26 January 1849, not long after its conclusion, Leeser alluded to the European revolutions of 1830 and 1848, insisting to his listeners, as we have seen above, that 'religion has no part to play in the mighty and terrible dramas which have late been enacted; at least it has no business to interfere actively and visibly in public affairs'.[4] This attitude about the limits of appropriate content for pulpit discourse apparently explains his reticence to address the war. Nor is there mention of the war in any of the sermons from the period published in Leeser's monthly journal, the *Occident*, whose only apparent reference to it is in the seventh toast given at the twenty-sixth anniversary of the Hebrew Benevolent Society: 'Our brethren who are now fighting our country's battles in Mexico. May they always remember that they are the descendents of Joshua, David, and the Maccabees.' The response to the toast stated that 'wherever our brethren were called upon to fight our country's battles they invariably manifested the most indomitable courage, and the purest patriotism'. The speaker mentioned the names of several who 'fought and distinguished themselves during the two wars with Great Britain'.[5]

This attitude to war as a political topic not to be addressed from the pulpit changed dramatically in the years leading to the Civil War. James Koppel Gutheim, preaching in New Orleans on a Thanksgiving Day celebrated on

---

[1] Leeser, 'Pres. W. H. Harrison', 34–6. Leeser's New York colleague, Jacques Judah Lyons, also left a eulogy for Harrison, in which the review of the deceased's performance in the Indian Wars and 'the campaigns of '12 and '13' is considerably less sensational: 'Sermon on the . . . Death of President Harrison', 3–4.     [2] See Weigley, *The American Way of War*, 153.

[3] Beecher, 'Against the Mexican War'; Parker, 'A Sermon of War'.

[4] Leeser, 'The Strength of our Religion', 89; see Introduction, p. 29.

[5] *The Occident and American Jewish Advocate*, 5/190, Jan. 1848, <www.jewish-history.com/Occident/volume5/jan1848/hbsny.html>.

29 November 1860, four and a half months before the war began, said prophetically: 'Our hearts are filled with sad forebodings of distress and gloomy anticipations of anxiety and trouble. The political horizon is overcast. A storm, vast and terrible, is impending and here and there its deep and portentous mutterings are heard.'[6] Some six weeks later, a sermon delivered on a national fast-day about the biblical view of slavery would provoke a firestorm of controversy among Jewish leaders. Once the war broke out, there would be many opportunities for discussions of its progress and its meaning, and many willing to take them.

The occasion for the following sermon was one of the many days of fasting and prayer proclaimed by the governments in Richmond and in Washington, DC during the Civil War years. Jefferson Davis proclaimed nine such days during the life of the Confederacy.[7] While it is difficult to know how seriously the fasting component was taken by the population,[8] religious leaders were apparently committed to observing them as occasions for addressing their people in specially prepared sermons, many of which were summarized in local newspapers and subsequently printed in pamphlet form. The themes were generally the acknowledgement of divine providence, the recognition of failures and sins, and the need to pray, in an appropriate posture of humility, for God's favour. The two sermons that follow this one were delivered by Northern preachers—in Philadelphia and New York—on the fast-day proclaimed by Lincoln a month later for 30 April 1863. The fact that such days were observed on both sides within five weeks of each other indicates a relative stalemate in the military situation: the South had won greater victories, but the economic situation in the North was superior.

[6] Gutheim, 'Thanksgiving Day Sermon', 23. In the continuation of the passage (cited above, p. 28 n. 101), he states that he will remain silent on the 'political questions of the day', which he believed should not be discussed from the pulpit. Although many manuscripts of Gutheim's sermons exist in the American Jewish Archives collection, none is known to date from the Civil War period (I am grateful to Kevin Profitt for this information). Note, however, the following statement in the entry for 13 Apr. 1862 in a New Orleans diary: 'I was some time yesterday in deliberating whether or not to attend Synagogue & finally made up my mind to go . . . [Rabbi Gutheim] was unusually eloquent. Probably our recent victory has stirred the water of his soul, & eloquence comes gushing out' (Solomon, *Civil War Diary*, 329).

[7] Lincoln proclaimed only three. For the details, see Stout and Grasso, 'Civil War, Religion, and Communications', 320, 353 n. 27. This illuminating essay shows that the fast-day with its jeremiad sermon was primarily a northern, Puritan institution, expropriated by the South to become a central component of its national-religious identity (ibid. 320–1).

[8] In his diary, Jason Niles wrote for Friday, 27 Mar. 1863, without any apparent awareness of the irony: 'Day appointed for general fast—rose before day—walked out back of Bap. Church before breakfast. *After breakfast* walked out back of, around and beyond Price's to the old Shoat field' (emphasis added): <docsouth.unc.edu/niles/niles.html>. For criticisms in Richmond's secular press of excessive calls for fast-days, resulting in the politicizing of religion, see Stout and Grasso, 'Civil War, Religion, and Communications', 336, 339–40.

Delivering the sermon in the Bayth Ahabah Synagogue for the German Jews of the Confederacy's capital city was the Reverend M. (Maximilian) J. Michelbacher (1811?–79), who had come to the congregation from Philadelphia seventeen years earlier in 1846.[9] Not much is known about his background. During the war he composed a Prayer for Confederate Jewish Soldiers, which— printed and distributed unofficially by the author—presents the Union forces as a sinister, menacing foe intending 'to desecrate our soil, murder our people, and to deprive us of the glorious inheritance which was left to us by the immortal fathers of this once great Republic'.[10] He also wrote several letters to General Robert E. Lee, requesting furlough leave for Jewish soldiers for the festival of Passover and the High Holy Days, to which Lee replied respectfully but deny-ing the request as unfeasible because 'the necessities of war admit of no relax-ation of the efforts requisite for its success'.[11] There is no reason to think that Michelbacher was the outstanding Jewish religious leader of the Confederacy, and it may be simply an accident that his sermon for this particular fast-day received considerable publicity and has been preserved.[12] Like the prayer he composed, it reflects strong sympathies for the Southern cause. Michelbacher continued to serve the Richmond congregation until 1867, when his contract was not renewed, apparently because of his guttural German accent.[13] A successor who began his tenure in 1879, A. Harris, born in Edinburgh and well educated, was described by the historians of Richmond Jewry as 'the first minister who had mastery of the English language', suggesting that Michelbacher may have preached in German and then had the text translated for publication (see the discussion of Einhorn's sermon, p. 197 below).[14]

[9] 'Rev. Maximilian Michelbacher' was listed as Secretary of the '*Chebrah Gemiluth Chasadim oo-Mish'eneth Yatom Ve-Almanah*', a charitable society for the support of widows and orphans founded in Philadelphia in 1844 (H. S. Morais, *The Jews of Philadelphia*, 144); cf. Berman, *Richmond's Jewry*, 5 n. 15. According to Isaac Leeser, he did preach in German in Philadelphia at this time, and was one of three Jewish German-language preachers in the country in 1844: Leeser, 'The Demands of the Times'.

[10] Korn, *American Jewry and the Civil War*, 103–5 (the text is printed from a copy in the Confederate Museum of Richmond); R. N. Rosen, *The Jewish Confederates*, 211–12. Sarna, *American Judaism*, 116–17, describes this as 'the most widely distributed Jewish Civil War prayer'.

[11] See Korn, *American Jewry and the Civil War*, 110–12; more letters are printed in Ezekiel and Lichtenstein, *The History of the Jews of Richmond*, 161–3. See also Berman, *Richmond's Jewry*, 191–3; R. N. Rosen, *Jewish Confederates*, 230–5.

[12] Indeed, he may not have been the most effective English-language preacher in Richmond. Two independent reports from 1864 indicate that the preacher in the Sephardi synagogue of Richmond, George Jacob, delivered an 'excellent' sermon on Yom Kippur: R. N. Rosen, *Jewish Confederates*, 210–11, 228.          [13] R. N. Rosen, *Jewish Confederates*, 363.

[14] Ezekiel and Lichtenstein, *The History of the Jews of Richmond*, 264, 269. Berman describes Michelbacher as 'preacher of sermons in the German language, twice monthly' (*Richmond's Jewry*, 141). There is, however, no indication in the published text of a German original or of a transla-tor. For a striking picture of Michelbacher in full regalia, see R. N. Rosen, *Jewish Confederates*, 232.

The preacher's introduction, addressed to 'Brethren of the House of Israel', responds to calumnies currently made against Jews in the Confederate States of America: specifically, that they avoid military service, and that they are disproportionately guilty of such widely prevalent offences as speculation in commodities and extortion, charging exorbitant prices to exploit the needs of the people in times of dearth. These same two charges had been discussed in a letter dated 22 December 1862, published in the *Richmond Examiner* in late December or early January, and reprinted in the *Charleston Mercury* of 9 January 1863. The author, who identifies himself only as 'Not a Jew', set out to defend the Jews against precisely these two accusations: 'that they have not furnished their quota of men for the public defence' and 'the . . . charge . . . of "infamous distortion"'. The main thrust of the author's defence is to provide explanations for Jewish behaviour (for example: Jews may be under-represented in the military in proportion to their numbers in the population, but that is because their community includes a high percentage of 'unnaturalized Germans' who by law are ineligible to serve) and to insist that, on both counts, Christians are far more guilty of shameful violations. On 10 January the *Charleston Mercury* editorially endorsed some of the author's sentiments—'The defence of a race of people at the South against unjust aspersions and prejudices is eminently proper . . . We believe the Israelites to be brave, intelligent and patriotic as a race'—though it protested vehemently against the attacks levelled at Christians as a means of defending the Jews.[15]

Michelbacher undoubtedly read the letter and may have been waiting for an appropriate occasion to weigh in publicly on his own. In response to these accusations, he claims to have undertaken research regarding the behaviour of Jews in all the states of the South, and to have found no evidence that could support either claim. The function of his introduction is to assure the listeners that—despite the occasion of a day of prayer, which generally inspires the rhetoric of rebuke—those in the audience will not be subjected to a direct attack from the pulpit.

The body of the sermon, addressed to 'Brethren and fellow citizens', applies the historical narrative of the walls of Jerusalem being rebuilt despite the hostility of powerful neighbours to the situation in the South at present.[16] This

---

[15] This letter has not been cited regarding the background for Michelbacher's sermon. I found it in a word search of an on-line edition of the Charleston paper; I could not find the original text in the Richmond paper, as the Widener Library microfilm is incomplete.

[16] Stout and Grasso make the interesting point that the application of biblical narratives to contemporary political issues was an innovation in Southern preaching, introduced with the secession and the war. Earlier, Southern preachers avoided political content and treated Old Testament history as unique to the Israelite theocracy of antiquity ('Civil War, Religion, and Communications', 321). Michelbacher's use of biblical material was thus in conformity with the practices of his Christian colleagues.

exposition has two components. The first deals with the physical defence of the country. Nehemiah's exhortation not to fear but to think of God and to fight for brothers, children, wives, and homes is obviously relevant to a society at war and physically threatened even on the home front. The wall of Jerusalem being built to separate the sacred space from its surroundings and protect it against its enemies represents the wall of separation between the North and the South. The policy of working with one hand while the other carries a sword is a reminder that there must be no relaxing of military vigilance in periods (such as the winter months) without significant combat. Most intriguingly, the message from Sanballat and his allies suggesting the possibility of negotiation towards reconciliation alludes to the various peace proposals supported by political forces opposed to Lincoln in the North, and Nehemiah's unambiguous repudiation of the proposals expresses the preacher's judgement that such hints of peace from the North are disingenuous efforts to subvert the Southerners' will to continue their battle.

If the first component in the application of the Nehemiah model is a call to continue the struggle with the external enemy, the second component introduces the theme of social injustice on the home front. The Jews' complaint to Nehemiah that there was insufficient food to feed their families and that they were being forced to mortgage their fields and their homes in order to survive ushers in a reprise of the accusation of extortion from the sermon's introduction. Nehemiah's angry demand that the wealthy restore the homes and fields they have acquired through their economic oppression of ordinary workers represents the hope that social justice can prevail in the South at present; that there can be a true civil reformation even in the midst of external danger.[17] The sermon builds to a powerful condemnation of profiteers, speculators, and extortionists—a common theme among Southern preachers, especially on days of fasting—but it is made on the explicit premise that the guilty parties are not Jews. As in most such sermons, the preacher concludes with a prayer, expressing the values he shares with the audience.

The major interpretative challenge posed by this text is whether to take at face value the preacher's insistence that Jews are not guilty of these crimes. The fact that this text was printed in pamphlet form immediately after delivery, in addition to being extensively cited in daily newspapers,[18] suggests that a

---

[17] Michelbacher would indeed have been astonished to learn that some forty years later, a black Baptist preacher of a socialist political persuasion named George Washington Woodbey would invoke Nehemiah as a model for righteous indignation at a capitalist system that robbed the poor through usury and mortgages: Callahan, 'Remembering Nehemiah', 161–2.

[18] Korn states that it was reprinted in the *Jewish Record*, 2/13 (5 June 1863), p. 1 (*American Jewry and the Civil War*, 330 n. 153), after being printed by Southern daily papers (ibid. 215, 330 n. 153). (The *Jewish Record* was a short-lived New York periodical committed to Orthodoxy, founded by Abraham S. Cohen in Oct. 1862 and merged with the *Hebrew Leader* less than three years later;

readership broader than the Jewish community was anticipated. Michelbacher's statement near the beginning that he has never been reluctant to criticize Jews from the pulpit for their failings, and that his conclusions follow a systematic investigation, seem intended to convince outside readers as much as the original Jewish audience. And the suggestion near the end that the accusations being circulated are part of a sinister plot to divert the hostility of the population away from the perpetrators of their misery appears to reflect a genuine insight into the dynamics of scapegoating. Having said all this, however, it is not impossible that there is an encoded message between the lines: On this occasion, I am not going to denounce Jews publicly and run the risk of providing ammunition for our enemies who will hurt our people. But you know who the Jews are who are guilty of the behavior I am denouncing. If the shoe fits . . .

When the text of the sermon was published in the North, Rabbi Isaac Mayer Wise responded disdainfully:

the thing published is no sermon; it is a political rigmarole dictated by some partisan stump speaker. And in the second place, 'The Rev. Rabbi Michelbacher' never was and is not now a rabbi, never made any studies to this end, never received any such title of any authorized person or persons, and to the best of our knowledge never claimed any such title . . . Mr. Michelbacher could as easy write a work on astronomy as he writes a sermon. He can do neither. He can sing and chant'.[19]

The reader will have to judge whether the text deserves such contempt; the historians of the Richmond Jewish community wrote in 1917 that 'Rev. M. J. Michelbacher is better remembered as teacher of the congregational school rather than as its pulpit occupant'.[20] Nevertheless, whatever the stature of this sermon as a literary text, there can be little question that as a historical source its value is considerable.[21]

I have not been able to get access to it to check the text published there.) Korn apparently did not know of the separate publication in pamphlet form, as it is not listed in his bibliography. This is the only Southern Civil War Jewish sermon I have been able to find.

[19] *Israelite*, 9/50, 19 June 1863, p. 394, cited in part by Korn, *American Jewry and the Civil War*, 295 n. 75.

[20] Ezekiel and Lichtenstein, *The History of the Jews of Richmond*, 268.

[21] The pamphlet, in the University of North Carolina Library, is accessible at <docsouth. unc.edu/imls/michelbacher/menu.html>.

# SERMON

---

*Nehemiah 3: 33–5: 13 inclusive.*

## [INTRODUCTION]

BRETHREN OF THE HOUSE OF ISRAEL:

IT IS due to you, to whom I always speak of your faults, without fear, favour or affection,[22] to say, I have carefully investigated your conduct from the commencement of this war to the present time, and I am happy in coming to the unbiased conclusion, that you have fulfilled your duties as good citizens and as men, who love their country. It has been charged by both the ignorant and the evil-disposed against the people of our faith, that the Israelite does not fight in the battles of his country![23] All history attests the untruthfulness of this ungracious charge, generated in the cowardly hearts and born between the hypocritical lips of ungenerous and prejudiced foes. The Israelite has never failed to defend the soil of his birth, or the land of his adoption—the Emperors of France and Russia will bear evidence to the verity of this assertion.[24] In respect to those Israelites who are now in the army of the Confederate States, I will merely say, that their patriotism and valor have never been doubted by such men as have the magnanimous souls of Lee, Johnston, Jackson and others of like manhood. The recorded votes and acts of the Israelites of this Confederacy,

[22] An interesting assertion of the preacher's conception that the function of rebuke was an integral component of his role in the pulpit.

[23] Cf. the passage in the letter to the *Richmond Examiner* cited above (p. 146). In the north, the *Newburg Journal* of New York wrote in 1864 that Jews 'never enter our armies but for the purpose of depleting the pockets of the soldiers, and . . . hang around the camps to take every advantage of their necessities' (Korn, *American Jewry and the Civil War*, 189).

[24] Referring to the role of Jews in the Napoleonic armies and—in a quite different context and frequently as the result of oppressive conscription—in the armies of Russia. Cf. Sermon 1 above by Isaac Luria, similarly appealing to the historical record of Jewish loyalty in times of war, and Sermon 8a below by Einhorn. In the Spanish–American War and the First World War this became an important motif for Jewish preachers and other spokesmen. For example, Rudolph Grossman, rabbi of New York's Rodeph Sholom, spoke thus at a patriotic assembly held on the evening of Sunday, 22 May 1898: 'The allegation that the Jew floats like oil on the water and cares for none but his own, and the accumulation of wealth, is false. Notwithstanding the foul accusations against the Jew's patriotism, it is his greatest pride. No other nation is more patriotic than the Jewish. If you doubt this ask Napoleon, ask Wellington, ask Frederick William II. In the army of to-day of Austro-Hungary there are 1,000 Jewish officers. One quarter of the officers of the French Army are Hebrew, while 10,000 Jewish soldiers battled for the Union in our civil war. Judaism has ever taught patriotism' (Grossman, 'Patriotic Address').

amply prove their devotion to the support of its Government. They well understand their duties as citizens and soldiers, and the young men do not require the persuasion of conscription to convert them into soldiers, to defend, as they verily believe, the only free government in North America. Many of our young men have been crippled for life, or slain upon the field of battle, in the service of the Confederate States, and there are several thousands yet coursing the campaigns of war against those enemies of our Confederacy, who are as detestable to them, as were the Philistines to David and his countrymen.[25]

The humanity and providence of the Israelite for the distressed families of the soldiers of our army, have allayed the pangs of poverty and brought comfort to households, wherein before were only seen hopelessness and misery. In this you have performed your duties as Israelites and as citizens—and, for this, may the God of our fathers shower upon you all the blessings which He confers upon His favorite children![26]

There is another cry heard, and it was even repeated in the Halls of Congress, that the Israelite is oppressing the people—that he is engaged in the great sin of speculating and extorting in the bread and meat of the land.[27] To discover the character of this accusation, I have made due inquiry—the information I have acquired upon this head, from sources that extend from the Potomac to the Rio Grande, plainly present the fact, that the Israelites are not speculators nor extortioners. As traders and as merchants, they buy merchandise and sell the same immediately; the merchandise is never put aside, or hoarded to enhance its value, by withdrawing it from the market. Flour, meal,

---

[25] According to a now dated study of Richmond Jewry, the Hebrew Cemetery in Richmond contains a separate plot of ground dedicated to Jewish soldiers, in which thirty Confederate Jewish soldiers are buried; five Jewish soldiers killed in battle were buried elsewhere in the cemetery (Ezekiel and Lichtenstein, *The History of the Jews of Richmond*, 194–5). A detailed list of soldiers from Richmond serving in the Confederate forces is printed ibid. 176–88. According to one estimate in a letter written during the war, between 10,000 and 12,000 Jewish soldiers were in the Confederate army in 1864, making the granting of furloughs for the holidays impracticable (ibid. 164). The consensus of modern scholarship is that this estimate is highly exaggerated.

[26] Michelbacher had organized a Ladies' Hebrew Association ('Ladies' Chebrah') in 1849; during the war its funds were reportedly used exclusively for caring for the sick and wounded soldiers of the Confederate army (Ezekiel and Lichtenstein, *The History of the Jews of Richmond*, 231). Other charitable work of the congregation during the war is noted ibid. 246–7, 263.

[27] The accusation of rampant 'speculation and extortion' (applied not to Jews but to others in the Confederate states) will return in a generalized form later in the sermon. For a review of the accusations made specifically against Jews in the Confederate Congress during the first months of 1863 by Congressmen Foote of Tennessee and Hilton of Florida, see Korn, *American Jewry and the Civil War*, 211–12, with further sources on pp. 212–14. In the North, the *Israelite* of 29 May 1863 printed a long letter by J. Wechsler complaining about the anti-Jewish libels in the 30 Apr. fast-day sermon by a Revd Mr Phillips of Portsmouth, Ohio (p. 373).

wheat, corn, bacon, beef, coal and wood are hardly ever found in the mercantile magazines or storehouses of the Israelite—he buys some of these articles for his own consumption, but he buys none of them to sell again. He does not extort. It is obvious to the most obtuse mind that the high prices of the Israelite would drive all his customers into the stores of his Christian neighbours; but is such the effect of the price of the Israelite's goods?

The peculiar characteristic of the Jewish merchant is seen in his undelayed, rapid and instant sales;[28] his temperament does not allow him, by hoarding his goods, to risk time with his money, which, with him, is as restless as the waves of the sea that bears the ships that convey the manufactured goods of his customers. I thank God, that my investigation has proved to me that the cry against the Jew is a false one. This cry, though cunningly devised after the most approved model of villainy, will not subserve the base and unjust purpose of hindering the virtuous indignation of a suffering people[29] from tracing the true path of the extortioner, and awarding to him who deals in the miseries, life and blood of our fellow-citizens, that punishment, which the traitor to the happiness and liberties of his country deserves to have measured unto him.[30]

That you may never waver in the strict and cheerful performance of your duties as citizens, listen attentively to the words of God, and may you profit and improve by their instruction! Amen.

[BODY OF THE SERMON]

*And I looked, and rose up, and said unto the nobles, and to the rulers,*
*and to the rest of the people, Be not afraid of them:*
*think on the Lord, the great and terrible, and fight for your brethren,*
*your sons, and your daughters, your wives and your houses.*
(NEH. 4: 8)[31]

---

[28] An interesting characterization of Jewish economic activity as driven by a unique temperament that makes it impossible for the Jew to hoard goods in the expectation that the price will rise.

[29] i.e. the people of the South. The claim is that the true extortioners blame the Jews as a smokescreen to divert attention from their own immoral behaviour.

[30] Korn cites and summarizes this passage in *American Jewry and the Civil War*, 215, but he states that it was delivered on 27 *May* 1863 (p. 330 n. 153) in Fredericksburg (p. 215), both details that conflict with the title page of the published pamphlet. For other Southern defenders of Jews against the accusation of speculation and extortion, see Korn, *American Jewry and the Civil War*, 221–2. A passage in the *Richmond Dispatch* editorial of 7 Apr. 1863 entitled 'Speculators and Extortioners' (not cited by Korn) states, 'Much of the outcry against the Jews is a mere device to divert attention from the shark-like appetites of a good many people who call themselves Christians and patriots.'

[31] Michelbacher used Leeser's translation consistently for his biblical passages rendered in English. This verse, invoked several times as a leitmotif during the sermon, certainly fits the

BRETHREN AND FELLOW CITIZENS:

*The duties of the citizen* are so intimately associated with the services he owes to God, his creator and master, that the patriotism which is comprised in the former, must necessarily depend in its expression upon our hearty and faithful obedience to the commands of Him who hath taught us the ways of Righteousness in the paramount institutes of Moses and the prophets—who hath furthermore impressed upon His people, for the conservation of their happiness and prosperity, a constant recollection of the Divine Code with an humble compliance with all its requisitions.[32]

*Patriotism* has in all ages been the chief theme of the historian and the poet, and we need not turn to the partial pages of profane history, nor go beyond the general chronicles of our own people, in the times of their obedience to the voice of God, for noble examples of self-sacrifice and that pious sentiment, with which they were inspired by the Almighty through the Captains of old, who set their squadrons in the field under the light of the Divinity.

The undaunted Nehemiah, in calling upon the Jews, to defend the unstopped breaches of the walls of Jerusalem against Sanballat and Tobiah, and the Arabians and Ammonites and the Ashdodites, said unto the nobles and to the rulers, and to the rest of the people, 'Be not afraid of them: think on the Lord, the great and terrible, and fight for your brethren, your sons, and your daughters, your wives and your houses' (Neh. 4: 8). These are diamond words, brilliant with the love of country, and pointing with heavenly rays of truth to the Great and terrible Lord of the universe as the friend and protector of him who defends, against a public enemy, his home and his family. The inspiriting words, 'Be not afraid of them', gave vigour to every arm and courage to every heart. The admonition, 'think on the Lord, the great and terrible', recalled the ancient faith of Israel, when nature obeyed the voice of Moses, and the sea divided itself to save the retreating multitude and peacefully stood on either side, to give free passage to the chosen people, and came down again with lashing and furious

context in the South, and is especially appropriate in that, while mentioning God, it is one of the very few biblical verses that directly calls upon the Israelites or Judeans to fight as opposed to relying without fear on God's power (cf. Exod. 14: 14; Josh. 3: 10; Isa. 29: 32–34; Ps. 60: 12–14). (I am grateful for this insight to Prof. Sara Japhet.)

[32] The link between patriotism and piety will be reiterated in the closing prayer ('piety cannot subsist apart from patriotism'). Cf. John Paris of North Carolina: 'The true Christian is always a true patriot. Patriotism and Christianity walk hand in hand' (Chesebrough, *'God Ordained this War'*, 271).

waves upon Pharaoh and his hosts as they adventured in, to defile its bed with the feet of the wicked and the enemies of God.[33]

They recollected the ancient faith of the wandering Israel in the desert, when the people were parched by thirst, and 'the Moses [should be: servant?] of the Lord' smote the rock, which sent forth living streams at his command.[34] It was then they remembered the Lord with increased faith, as retrospection brought, in sublime array, the gracious deeds He had executed aforetime, for the salvation of their fathers, and their souls were animated with heroic daring and invincible determination at the eloquent and heart-stirring appeal of Nehemiah to their manhood, as he stood before them, and, pointing to Heaven in the character of the servant of God, the loyal citizen and patriot exclaimed: 'fight for your brethren, your sons, and your daughters, your wives, and your houses!'

It was on this momentous and perilous occasion, he solemnly reminded them of the *first duty of the citizen in connexion with the first duty of man* as the obedient servant of the most High God. The people were not only taught the divine duty of defending their country in battle, with the death-dealing weapons of war,[35] but they were, through Nehemiah, also commanded to set a watch upon the walls of the city, during the day and night, with the implements of *building and fortifying in the one hand, and the instrument of defence in the other*. 'And the builders, had every one his sword fastened around his loins, while they were building. And he that blew the trumpet stood along side of me' (Neh. 4: 12).

While the Judean patriots were thus progressing in strengthening the defences, the insidious Sanballat with Geshem sent four times to Nehemiah to meet him, but unavailing were the invitations; and the fifth time, he sent by his servant an open letter to terrify and to cause him to take counsel with his enemy (Neh. 6: 1–5); yet was Nehemiah stern, resolved and unyielding, and to the contents of the letter, made fearlessly an instant declaration of their falsehood in

---

[33] The preacher presents Nehemiah's instruction as intertextual, calling upon the people to recall (perhaps from the text of the Pentateuch) God's saving power as manifest in the past.

[34] A strange characterization of the passage (Num. 20: 11), which ordinarily is taken to illustrate precisely the *lack* of faith of the Israelites and perhaps even of Moses. I do not know what to make of the phrase 'the Moses of the Lord'—a Google search yielded only this passage as a source.

[35] By implication, defending the new country of the South is also a 'divine duty' or a holy war. Further on, the preacher states that 'every soul should be clad in the panoply of war, to take just vengeance in the name of the Lord, upon His enemies and ours, for the manifold wrongs they commit against His laws, His justice, and His mercy'.

the words: 'There had been done nothing like these reports of which thou speakest; but thou inventest them out of thine own heart' (Neh. 6: 8.). And thus he continued his course in building and repairing, with the assistance of his countrymen, till through his wise administration, clear foresight and courageous conduct, his enemies went from before him, and departed in fear and trembling. In this wise, he and his compatriots faithfully performed the first and transcendent duty of the citizen; and the Lord was with them.

From this brief, but beautiful and instructive scriptural history, may our fellow-citizens and the Government of the Confederate States of America take lessons of profit, and heed the reserved conduct of Nehemiah towards those who were hostile to him, when they sent messengers and an open letter to deceive and betray! Let it not be, that we take counsel with our enemies, or any portion of them, in the critical period of their warfare against us; and, above all, let us keep our watchmen upon the walls during any term of cessation of arms, as well as in active hostilities! Our business and our duty are to deal in the rugged matters and measures of the latter, till the offenders, who desecrate our soil and pollute our atmosphere, depart from our country in fear and trembling—this is all we require as an independent people, and it is what we will accomplish; if so be, we retain the blessing of the Great Creator by our humility and righteousness before Him, with the spear in the one hand, and the implement of industry in the other—*so help us God!!*

Our enemies may have their intestine feuds—civil war may rage among them—and they may fiercely quarrel among themselves, they may lament the loss of their own liberty, sacrificed to fanaticism, cupidity and ambition in the attempt to enslave us,[36] and may point to us as the cause of the maledictions of offended Heaven against them,[37] and they may even seek our aid in the hour of their calamity, which will surely overtake and crush a wicked people; yet, let us not be deceived and entrapped by the specious words, nor the open letters of a people and government of cunning and treachery! They may even throw out

[36] Divisiveness in Northern society was a common motif in the contemporary discourse of the South, as was the theme of the 'loss of liberty, sacrificed to fanaticism'. Note Einhorn's reference to 'the danger of intestine contention produced by the passions of party' in Sermon 8a below. Preaching in Georgia on the same day as Michelbacher, Stephen Elliott suggested that the outbreak of 'a civil war among the remaining States' and an alliance with a great naval power were the only two ways of attaining a peace on terms acceptable to the South: 'Samson's Riddle', 13.
[37] In difficult times, Northern preachers often explained military reversals as God's punishment for having tolerated the sin of slavery. This motif was especially prominent in the fast-day sermons of 30 Apr. 1863: see the sermons by Storrs (who cites 'our treatment of the Indian and the African'), Bellows, Tyng, and Sloane in *New York Times*, 1 May 1863, p. 2; also Stewart, 'Civil War Preaching', 195.

as a bait, the hint of serious divisions in the North and Northwest, to lull our manly fears and to allure us into a policy, dangerous, if not destructive to the liberties and independence of the Confederate States.[38] If there be incidental advantages accruing to us, from pretended differences and divisions in the condition of their political or military affairs, it will be well for us to be lookers-on, with sword in hand (cf. Neh. 4: 11), ready at all times, for every emergency—we can afford to look on with keen watchfulness and unabated activity and vigour; but we shall not, we must not touch the accursed thing arising from the pollution of Northern necessities, nor permit it to be brought into our camp[39]—and, if we must reply, let it be in the words of Nehemiah: 'There had been done nothing like these reports of which thou speakest; but thou inventest them out of thine own heart' (Neh. 6: 8).

We have fought, and are now fighting, by reason of a virtuous resolution to live apart from those, who for many years marred our peace and increased our anxiety for the preservation of our institutions and our safety, and, who down to the moment of our separation, derided our solemn protests against their repeated violations of our sovereign rights, and have converted a Federal government into a central one, for the purpose of founding a despotism, that we may the more speedily receive the lash of a tyrant.[40] Solemnly have we appealed to God to examine our hearts for the honesty of our intentions; hence, it is no light thing with the sole Creator of the Universe and Supreme Director of our destiny, that we halt for one moment in pursuing that course we have chosen before Him, and for which, at sundry times, our people and our President have implored His guidance and blessing—*and may His guidance and blessing lead us unto the desired attainment of liberty, independence, happiness and prosperity!* Surely, it is no light thing, if we now exhibit before God our friend, the want of any trait that belongs to the perfect character of the defender of one's country. The mission of the patriotic citizen is a great one—with a broad patent in legible characters, all may know him to be a servant of the Lord, and a soldier of the people, whether he belongs to the council or the camp.

May we not reverently conceive that the Almighty, in listening to our prayers, has in the High Courts of Heaven graciously ratified our choice? The

[38] The preacher is suggesting that the reports of deep divisions in the North may be disinformation intended to lure the South off guard.

[39] Echoing Josh. 7: 13; note how Sabato Morais of Philadelphia will use this image a month later in referring to greed and materialism in the North (Sermon 6 below).

[40] The language of despotism and tyranny was frequently used in the North by the Democratic opponents of the Lincoln administration; Clement J. Vallandigham referred to the regime as 'a tyranny equal to that of any upon the face of the globe' (*Speeches, Arguments, Addresses*, 489).

wonderful victories of our arms in answer to our petitions, impress us in our faith therein with this belief[41]—and, if this be so, let him beware, who is slow to perform the first duty of the citizen!

Shall we then trifle with the Great God of Israel, and offend His terrible Majesty, by entertaining alien messengers, whatever the import of their character, or receiving open letters, written in deceit and falsehood by a treacherous foe? Shall we be so weak and credulous, as to trust for our salvation in the false reports and varied rumours adapted to peculiar occasions, and invented for the covert purposes of our circumvention and ruin! *Ah, my God, let us not put from us our confidence in Thee, nor forget the wonderful manifestations of Thy power in our behalf within the last twelve months!*[42] *Thou only art our Saviour and Redeemer, and Thou hast graciously assisted us in building the high wall of separation; and, even now, Thou dost call upon the people of the South in the words Thou gavest to Nehemiah: 'Fight for your brethren, your sons, and your daughters, your wives and your houses!' (Neh. 4: 8).*

Who will dare turn a deaf ear to this Heavenly command, to perform the most eminent work pertaining to the duties of the citizen, while every soul should be clad in the panoply of war, to take just vengeance in the name of the Lord, upon His enemies and Ours, for the manifold wrongs they commit against His laws, His justice, and His mercy, in the pretended name of truth, by cruel imprisonments, and unprecedented deeds of rapine, arson and murder![43] These things cry unto Heaven for retribution, and 'vengeance is mine', saith the Lord (Rom. 12: 19, based on Deut. 32: 35; cf. Jer. 51: 6, Ps. 94: 1). *Arise then, all ye people of the South, doubly armed with your trust in God, and the remembrance of your sufferings, and the wrongs done unto you, 'your brethren, your sons and your daughters, your wives and your houses', and let the shout of your confidence in God go forth to the discomfiture of the enemy, while the thunder of your guns, the flash of your*

---

[41] A common motif in Southern preaching during the first years of the war; see Stewart, 'Civil War Preaching', 191, 196–7.

[42] This alludes to Southern victories at Manassas and at Richmond, Kentucky, for which a national day of thanksgiving was proclaimed in Sept. 1862. Cf. Revd Joel W. Tucker of North Carolina on 16 May 1862: 'Who can read the reports of the battles of Bethel, Bull Run, Manassas Plains, Ball's Bluff, Springfield, Shiloh and Williamsburg, without being convinced that God gave us the victory, and that to him we should render thanksgiving for the glorious triumph of our arms' ('God's Providence in War', 8).

[43] Accusations of Northern atrocities were not uncommon in Southern preaching. One 1863 sermon claimed that 'We are fighting against robbery and lust and rapine'; another that 'Nothing on earth can surpass the beastly brutality and wickedness which the enemy has shown us' (both cited in Chesebrough, *'God Ordained this War'*, 222; for Northern claim of Southern atrocities, see ibid. 88).

*swords, and the gleam of your bayonets, shall give the seal of the blood of the invaders, as a witness unto the Lord of hosts, that we, who have trusted in Him, have signalized the vengeance which is His, and performed the first duty of the citizen, in obedience to His mandates through Nehemiah, in calling upon the name of the most High in the spirit of piety, and 'fought for our brethren, our sons, and our daughters, our wives and our houses'.*

But is the physical defence of one's country against invasion the only duty required of the citizen in the period of war? In what terms shall we condemn them, that have taken advantage of the necessities of the times, to reduce the poor to a condition so deep in poverty, that on the coming of every morrow, the gloom of troublous anticipations thickens with the approach of the fearful period when in the words of Jeremiah, it shall be said in bitterness: 'Happier are those slain by the sword, than those slain by hunger; for those poured forth their blood, being pierced through—these perished without the fruits of the field' (Lam. 4: 9). We already hear a great cry of the people and of their wives against their brethren, who have speculated in the blood of the living, and whose song of joy, in the amassment of wealth, is heard above the fury and horrors of war, the groans of the dying, the screams of the wounded in the battle fields, upon which our gallant soldiers are offering their lives in defence of our brethren, our sons, and our daughters, our wives, and our houses![44]

What answer shall we make to the noble defenders of the country, when they, garlanded with the victories of a hundred fields, return and behold the wan features of their brethren, their sons and their daughters, and their wives—and their houses, no longer the abodes of plenty and cheerfulness! Well may they, in surprise at the ingratitude and atrocity of their countrymen, exclaim: 'Happier are those slain by the sword, than those slain by hunger; for those poured forth their blood, being pierced through—these perished without the fruits of the field!'.[45] Will it come to that pass, that they too shall be compelled 'to mortgage their lands, vineyards and houses that they may buy corn' (Neh. 5: 5), and against which the Jews complained in the presence of Nehemiah, as a great evil, inflicted upon them by their brethren? The generous heart and noble spirit of

[44] Echoing the text from Neh. 4: 8, but now in the first person plural. On the same fast-day, Michelbacher's Christian colleague in Richmond, the Revd William Norwood, devoted a large part of his sermon to a condemnation of profiteers, claiming, according to a scholar's summary, that 'widows, orphans, and crippled veterans were being denied food, clothing, and shelter because many southern businesses were interested in gaining wealth from the war' (Stewart, 'Civil War Preaching', 195).

[45] For food shortages in Richmond in March and April 1863, see Stout and Grasso, 'Civil War, Religion, and Communications', 333.

Nehemiah became inflamed with a just anger, when the great cry of the people and of their wives against their brethren, the Jews, came up before him; and he thus describes his feelings and conduct upon that occasion: 'And it displeased me greatly when I heard their complaint in these words. Then I consulted with my heart, and I upbraided the nobles, and the rulers, and said unto them: Ye exact usury, every one of his brother. And I brought together a great assembly against them' (Neh. 5: 6–8).

And in the concluding part of his address, we are affected with admiration at the justice he meted to every man, who had wronged his neighbour and sinned against God. His remarkable words are well adapted to the present times and events—*O may they be borne by some gracious breeze of Heaven to every village, town and city of our Confederacy!*—let it then be known to all the people of the land, that Nehemiah, the servant of God, said in the settlement of this question before him and the great assembly, which he set against them, 'Give back to them, I pray you, even this day, their fields, their vineyards, their olive yards, and their houses, also, the hundredth part of the money, and of the corn, the wine, and the oil, that ye have lent them. Then said they, We will give back and we will require nothing of them; so will we do as thou sayest. Then I called the priests and made them swear, that they should do according to this promise. Also I shook my lap, and said, so may God shake out every man from his house, and of his toil gotten wealth, that performeth not this promise, and so let him remain shaken out, and empty. And all the congregation said, Amen, and praised the Lord. And the people did according to this promise' (Neh. 5: 11–13).

These events occurred when Sanballat and others, enemies of the Jews, conspired to come and to fight against Jerusalem, and to hinder the building of the wall; yet did not Nehemiah neglect the civil affairs of his country in the midst of a war, that threatened the enslavement of his people with the destruction of the capital city of Judea; but with the steady character of a great chief, that trusts in the Lord, he introduced reformations, which at once remedied the defects exhibited in the disposition of the people and restored to them that moral feeling, whose basis is religion. They became regenerated under his potent and pious sway, and the citizen and soldier adorned with their virtues both the camp and the path of civil life. The people repented and made restitution; and the dark cloud that hung with evil portent over Judea's plains, passed away before the sun of righteousness. Usury and practices of a kindred nature fled from the searching eye of Nehemiah. The man who had inspired his people with the heroism, to defend unto death their brethren, their sons, and their daughters, their wives and their houses,[46] could not patiently observe the oppression of the poor, nor the extorted wealth of the rich; and with a strong hand, supported by the people, rescued them and his country from the most corrupting vice, that can deform the moral constitution of a nation. He saw the beginning of that *divided sympathy* among the people, which is the forerunner of national degradation with the loss of liberty; and, in the midst of the Great Assembly, he denounced the usurer and the despoiler of the poor, and sealed his righteous denunciation with a curse: 'Also my lap did I shake out and said, So God shake out every man from his house, and from his toil-gotten wealth that performeth not this promise, and so let him remain shaken out and empty. And all the Assembly said, Amen, and praised the Lord. And the people did according to this promise' (Neh. 5: 13).

The extortions practiced throughout the length and breadth of the Confederate States, and which appear to have superseded honest trade, to ride upon the back of speculation for the purpose of hunting '*the dear life*' wherever an article of food, fuel and raiment may be found, has already given rise to a fearful cry of the people, who are patriotically assisting to build the wall of separation between the South and the treacherous North; they justly consider that these heartless demons, whom we call speculators and extortioners, are giving aid and comfort to the enemy; and, there are not a few who believe, these men would in no wise assist in subduing the conflagration of a city, because, even in such a calamity, they would seek food for speculation in the ruin of its inhabitants, and, at some brief future day, extort from their wants, the wreck of property saved from the flames![47]

Will the speculator and extortioner heed the cry of the people and their wives for bread and other provisions, necessary to the sustenance of life? Will they listen attentively to instruction and humbly receive rebukes before the Great Assembly, and swear to give back ill-gotten gains, as did the Jews under the inspired counsel of Nehemiah? Will they retrace their steps from the road of wickedness towards that path to which Nehemiah directed his countrymen, and in which only can they ever hope to regain the lost character of the virtuous

[46] Once again echoing the text Neh. 4: 8, this time in the third person plural, and connecting it with a broader circle of responsibility for those in need *beyond* members of the immediate family.
[47] 'From the start of the war, attacks on the sin of extortion filled the pages of both the secular and religious presses. Popular literature, sermons, and legislative initiatives joined in the condemnation' (Berends, ' "Wholesome Reading Purifies"', 152, with extensive references at 164 n. 47). One Southern preacher devoted an entire sermon in September 1862 to 'The Guilt and Punishment of Extortion', condemning the hoarding of consumer goods to make profits (Stewart, 'Civil War Preaching', 195).

citizen and patriot—the only path that can direct them aright, because it is the path of righteousness!

Come up to the bar of Justice and of God, ye vile citizens of a country, ye have caused to bleed at every pore—ye, who are ever ready to plunge the traitor's dagger with stealthy hand into the bosom of your mother in the moment of her most critical danger! *Desist from the sins* charged against you this day—desist from the sin of oppression over the people and the sin of disobedience against the terrible God of Israel, and—*repent, and give back, or,* 'ye shall be shaken out, every man from his house, and from his toil-gotten wealth and be empty' (cf. Neh. 5: 13).

It is not true that you have been compelled to oppress the people, by reason of the peculiar difficulties of your own situation, in respect to your families.[48] It is, because you have the power, or are permitted by the silence of the municipal and civil law and the public authorities, to retain, or remit under usurious contracts; and, you, yourselves, have generated the circumstances to bring forth your own extortion—the monstrous and evil thing that draws its nourishment from the heart's blood of men, women and children! And, it is also, because you have strengthened your power, by sweeping the circuit of many districts of our country, and, have thereby come into possession of those things, that God intended for the common benefit. You have seized and engrossed the meat and flour of the poor—and, while these starve, you complacently look forward to the crisis of famine, with your warehouses filled with the life-giving food, which, by right of nature and nature's God, belongs alike to all, under the wise restriction of just compensation! You purchase the rich offerings of the generous Earth—and await famine and high prices! *If this be so, O God, 'let them be shaken out, every man from his house and from his toil-gotten wealth and be empty!'*

I thank God, that this curse comes not within the circle, or reach of my congregation, and, that its members have kept their skirts clean, and have not committed this great crime against man and Heaven.[49] Continue thus, O my brethren, to fulfil your duties, and turn not away in their performance, to stain your hands with that sinful gain that cometh from extortion. It is the duty of the Great Assembly of the people to set their face against this iniquity, and it becomes us on this occasion to pray, that we may not be tempted to commit a sin so heinous before the God of Israel.

---

[48] Apparently a response or rationalization used by the profiteers.

[49] Contrast the stance taken by David Einhorn at the end of his sermon on Amalek from the spring of 1864 (Sermon 8b below), conceding that some Jews did indeed engage in smuggling, and that they brought 'shame and disgrace upon us and our religious faith'.

It is the duty of the people to satisfy the Lord that their hearts are against this sin, that the skirts of the nation may be cleansed from the curse that He will measure unto the unrepentant individually—that punishment justly due to the enemy of God and man—that punishment justly due to those who refuse to perform one of the first duties of the citizen by reformation and restitution, with a solemn promise before God, the author of all good, to do this evil thing no more! *Let the skirts of the people be cleansed by prayer and humiliation, that the Almighty may continue to protect and bless the Confederate States of America, and that He may presently and with great haste drive far away from our land the Northern armies that now disturb its tranquility. Let our land, O Lord, be dedicated to Thee and Thy service only*; and may the holy name of the God of Israel be forever among us! Amen.

## PRAYER

Again, do we approach Thee, O God of Israel—not as a single meeting of a part, but as the whole congregation of all the people of the land, that trust in Thy protection forever, and who do now come before Thee, to seek it in the midst of dangers, yet *more* appalling than those of the past, that Thou didst put aside without harm unto us!

We are Thy people, O God! who, whether in times of want or pestilence, distress or danger, cannot be kept back from coming unto Thee.

Thou only art our father and friend, and we come before Thee in the dutifulness of children, and with abiding faith in Thy love and a constant fear of doing aught to offend Thee.

O God of our fathers! God of Abraham, Isaac and Jacob! hear our prayers, and listen graciously to our supplications, this day, for our salvation as a people, struggling before Thee for our liberties and independence, now threatened with renewed dangers and calamities, from the combining and concentrating powers of our enemies.

Thou hast, O God, in Thy mercy unto us, foiled from good time to good time their efforts, to circumvent and to subdue and to subjugate Thy people, that trust in Thy mercy and omnipotence! Now, O God, we who trust in Thee, beseech Thee to look into our present condition. Then dost see, O Supreme Giver of Good, the red and savage hand of massacre held with the menace of foreboding evil, over the innocent and nursing infants of our people! Thou doest see, O Supreme Giver of Good, that we are threatened with the destruction of our men, women and children by cruel enemies, that laugh and clap their hands at the calamities they desire to bring upon us, whereby they may outrage and scoff at Thy Super-Excellent Majesty, and say within their hearts that vengeance is theirs and not Thine! O God of Israel! hearest Thou this, and art Thou still or silent? No! Thou, God of our fathers, that art a jealous God, Thou art not silent, nor unmindful of our terrible straits, and, neither wilt Thou permit this wicked intent—neither wilt Thou let come to pass this atrocious thing of blood and crime against Thy people, that this day, in the presence of all the nations of the Earth, proclaim Thee as the only true God, and Saviour!

The man-servants and the maid-servants Thou hast given unto us, that we may be merciful to them in righteousness and bear rule over them, the enemy are attempting to seduce, that they too may turn against us, whom Thou hast appointed over them as instructors in Thy wise dispensation![50]

*Because of Thy strength* in aid of us, our enemies have failed against us, in all the modes and means of warfare known and adopted among the men Thou hast civilized—*because of Thy strength* they have failed; and, behold, O God, they incite our man-servants and maid-servants to insurrection, and they place weapons of death and the fire of desolation in their hands, that we may become an easy prey unto them; they beguile them from the path of duty, that they may waylay their masters, to assassinate and to slay the men, women and children of the people, that trust only in Thee.[51] In this wicked thought, let them be frus-

[50] Here the preacher seems to identify completely with the Southern slaveholder, though he uses the biblical terminology 'man-servants and maid-servants' rather than 'slaves'. He does not invoke the claim of a biblical sanction in the form of the curse of Ham (see Einhorn, Sermon 8a below), but rather espouses the argument, made by Southern clergy, that slavery served a providential function by civilizing and Christianizing part of the African population, as proclaimed, for example, by Stephen Elliott of Savannah in Aug. 1863: 'Let their change from the tattooed savage to the well-bred courteous menial bear witness to their culture! . . . Let the numbers who flock to the table of the Lord attest to the nations the missionary work which is going on amongst them' (Chesebrough, *'God Ordained this War'*, 252).

[51] Michelbacher seems genuinely concerned about the efficacy of Northern incitement of Southern slaves. The view that the 'Emancipation Proclamation', which applied to states that had seceded (and therefore would not recognize its validity) but not to slave-holding states in the Union, was a cynical effort to incite insurrection among the Southern slaves was widespread not only in the South (e.g. in the *Richmond Examiner* editorial of 7 Jan. 1863: 'The pretense that slavery is abolished as an act of justice to the negro will provoke a smile if the hypocritical falsehood did not excite disgust . . . To produce . . . servile insurrection is the real, sole purpose of this proclamation'), but also in Europe (e.g. *The Times*, 20 Jan. 1863, p. 12, according to which Lincoln had recognized that victory must be 'by the stab in the back, or, as Mr. Sumner expressed it, by the incendiary fire lighted in the rear. The negro ally of the Federals to be potent and efficient must be insurgent').

On the other hand, in the sermon cited in n. 50 above, Elliott emphasizes the total absence of concern for the danger of insurgency as proof that the Southern slaves are well-treated: 'Who keep the keys of our houses and who nurse and tend upon our children? Who cook the food we

trated, and cause them to fall into the pit of destruction, which in the abomination of their evil intents, they digged for us, our brothers and sisters, our wives and our children.[52]

Our land and our waters are troubled with the presence of the foes of Thy people. Drive them away, O Lord! Let it be, that their boasted ships of terror may come to naught before the breath of our Lord God, as He sendeth it forth upon the waters of the Great Deep.[53]

Bless, O God, the tillage of our fields, that they may bring forth abundantly for the wants of the people! Give unto each one the bread of life, and let the fat of the land be seen in plenty in the home of every family of the Confederate States of America.

O God! We acknowledge our manifold sins, but look to Thee for forgiveness with deep contrition and repentance.

We implore Thee to turn the hearts of the people of the Confederate States of America generously and kindly every one to the other, that, in the midst of common tribulation, they may cheer and sustain each other till they shall have safely passed through the troublous flood of war, to the happiness of a peaceful land, regenerated by Thy favoured presence forever and ever!

O God! we invoke Thy holy name for protection, because we know that, without the aid of our kind Father in Heaven, we of ourselves can do nothing.

We believe, O God, that piety cannot subsist apart from patriotism—we love our country, because Thou hast given it unto us as a blessing and a heritage for our children; and, now, O God, we call upon Thee, to bring salvation to the

eat and ministry to all our necessary wants? These very slaves! And does the head of any one of us rest less easily upon his pillow? Does any one tremble as he sees his little ones, dearer to him than life, nestled in their bosoms and sung to sleep with their lullabys?' (Chesebrough, 'God Ordained this War', 252). Similarly, from a totally different perspective, Henry Ward Beecher viewed the 'quiet patience' of the black population despite its humiliations as providential: 'Never were a people so many and so tempted that behaved so well under the circumstances as the slaves of the South', thereby demonstrating that there is no danger in Emancipation (New York Times, 27 Nov. 1863, p. 2).

[52] The passage is quoted by Korn, American Jewry and the Civil War, 34, noting that the preacher 'was voicing the fears of most Southerners in this prayer, unjustified fears that the Union would inspire the slaves to savage destruction'. For Southern fears of incitement to slave insurrections in a somewhat earlier period (the summer of 1860, before the presidential election), see McPherson, Ordeal by Fire, 133.

[53] Davis's presidential proclamation of the fast-day referred to 'our enemy, with loud boasting of the power of their armed men and mailed ships'. The naval campaign closest in time and geography was probably the Union effort to capture the fortifications in Charleston harbour in March and April 1863 by using ironclads. In the second part of the sentence, Michelbacher echoes biblical language in Exod. 15: 8, 10, and Isa. 10.

Confederate States of America, and to crown independence with lasting honour and prosperity.

O God! Give cheerfulness to the hearts of our people; and, as a sign of our confidence in Thee and Thy especial protection over us, let the play of the children be seen in the streets of our cities, towns and villages and all places of our country. Let no fear come near our maidens, and be Thou unto our young men a tower of strength, that they may stand with undaunted hearts to shield and sustain the matrons and patriarchs of the people! Drive, O God, the fear of black famine far away from our borders, and open the Omnipotent hand of Thy Heavenly bounty upon all these—the people of this Thy land, which we dedicate anew to Thee this day. And, O God, keep in remembrance this day forever!

Be Thou, O God, with our armies, and inspire the leaders thereof with a pious fear of Thee. Endow them with the faculty of anticipating the designs of the enemy, and the wisdom to thwart every movement of hostility!

Inspire our soldiers with that patriotic courage which comes from the thought of duty to Thee and to their country. Give unto them, sleepless vigilance, vigorous and active bodies and hands, to wield in victory the weapons of battle. Give unto them, when in pursuit of the flying foe, the swiftness of the eagle, and in the fight, let them be as fierce lions among the prey![54]

Send, O God, Thy protecting messengers to our ships of war upon the waters of the rivers and of the great deep! Shield our infant navy from all the dangers of storm and battle; and, in all its engagements with the enemy, let the power of the wonderful arm of the God of Israel be its succour, defence and victory! Let the boast of the enemy's naval superiority in numbers over us, be unto Thee, O Lord, their weakness and destruction. And give unto us, Thy people that trust in Thee, O God of Israel, the crown of triumph!

O God! Give counsel and wisdom to Thy servant, Jefferson Davis, President of the Confederate States of America, and grant speedy success to his endeavours to free our country from the presence of its foes.

Be Thou with him and the legislature of the Confederate Government of America, and give unto them Thy care and blessing.

Send us peace, O Lord God, we humbly implore Thee! and let the buds, that spring forth in this present spring of the year, burst out in smiling blossoms over a land of tranquility and prosperity! Amen! Hallooyah!

---

[54] Echoing 2 Sam. 1: 23.

# CHAPTER SIX

## SABATO MORAIS
# A SERMON ON THE NATIONAL FAST-DAY

### 30 APRIL 1863

#### CONGREGATION MIKVEH ISRAEL,
#### PHILADELPHIA

SABATO MORAIS was born in 1823 at Livorno, a port city in the Italian duchy of Tuscany; his father's family had Portuguese converso roots. He received a broad education from tutors in both classical Jewish texts and European literatures, leading to private ordination, though without a formal advanced degree. His parents also instilled in him a commitment to republican ideals and the movement for Italian national unification (sentiments reflected in the sermon reproduced below). He emigrated to London in 1845 and was affiliated with the Bevis Marks Synagogue of the Spanish and Portuguese congregation; during his years in London he established relationships with Sir Moses Montefiore (also born in Livorno) and the Italian expatriate Giuseppe Mazzini. In 1851 he left London for America, where he was elected minister of the Sephardi Mikveh Israel synagogue of Philadelphia, a position he held until his death in 1897; his funeral was the largest such public event held for an American Jewish leader in the nineteenth century.[1]

Liberal in politics, conservative (though by no means fundamentalist) in religious sentiment, Morais represented middle ground between the innovations of the reformers and the narrowness of some of the traditionalists. His ministry reflected a melding of American, Italian, and Jewish identities, a synthesis of Jewish sources, wide cultural reading, and deep social concerns not only for the welfare of fellow Jews but for the oppressed in the broader community in what has been called a 'rabbinic–humanist' outlook.

Preaching was an important component of his ministry. A *New York Times* tribute near the end of his career said, 'In the pulpit he has a singular gift of

---

[1] Kiron, ' "Dust and Ashes" ', which provides extensive biographical material. Other biographical material in this introduction is taken from Nadel, 'Morais, Sabato'.

eloquence, his words flowing sweetly and melodiously, and his arguments being earnestly convincing.'[2] Nor was the impact of his sermons limited to his listeners. Apparently relishing publicity, Morais regularly sent the texts of his sermons to Philadelphia newspapers and to the Jewish press; Bertram W. Korn wrote that 'More of his sermons were printed in the daily press than any other American rabbi's.'[3] An American citizen from 1854, Morais frequently expressed his pro-Union, republican sympathies from the pulpit, especially on the occasions of national fast and prayer or thanksgiving proclaimed by the government. His outspoken views got him into trouble with the lay leadership of the congregation, which in late 1864 passed a resolution that 'henceforth all English lectures or Discourses shall be dispensed with, except by particular request of the Parnas, made in writing'. (As discussed in the Introduction, efforts to regulate or suppress freedom of the pulpit were characteristic of various American congregations in the nineteenth century.) Morais fought back, and a campaign of his supporters led some four months later to a congregational vote authorizing Morais to preach on 'moral and religious subjects' at his own discretion, and 'on the subjects of the day . . . whenever the Synagogue may be opened by order of the Parnas'.[4]

For examples of his political sympathies and his oratorical style, I will cite two passages from sermons that preceded the text reproduced here. The first is from a Thanksgiving Day sermon delivered on 25 November 1852; Morais strikingly refers to 'hundreds of *us*', pertaining to Jews who fought in the Revolutionary War, and alludes to the revolutionary uprisings of 1848 in messianic terms:

It is this love of liberty, engrafted on the religion of our fathers, that aroused the spirit of hundreds of us to unite their fate with that of the American patriots who gallantly fought for their rights. It was the same spirit of liberty that pervades the institutions of Moses that called to arms multitudes of our brethren when the hour of redemption for the enthralled nations of Europe seemed to have struck; and the same spirit will ever incite the descendants of the Maccabees to join hand and heart with those who rise to root out tyranny from the world, in whatever shape, in whatever disguise it may conceal itself.[5]

---

[2] *New York Times*, 8 Mar. 1896, p. 28.

[3] Korn, *American Jewry in the Civil War*, 44; this can be easily demonstrated by the clippings Morais saved in his ledger, available on-line through the University of Pennsylvania Library.

[4] Korn, *American Jewry in the Civil War*, 44–6; cf. the review of this episode in a broader context by Alan D. Corré, 'Sabato Morais and Social Justice in Philadelphia', 23. (Pamela Nadel's statement in 'Morais, Sabato' that a similar effort to muzzle his outspoken support of abolition took place in the 1850s during the Buchanan presidency seems to be a conflation of this and a different incident.) For Isaac Leeser's earlier problems with this same congregation over the right to preach, see Sussman, *Isaac Leeser*, 61–2, 103–4, 136; for Isaac Mayer Wise, see Temkin, *Isaac Mayer Wise*, 173, 175–6.

[5] S. Morais, 'A Sermon delivered on Thanksgiving Day (November 25, 1852)', 4 (Morais undoubtedly exaggerated the number of Jews fighting with the American army in the revolution). It is

The second is taken from a sermon delivered on a fast-day proclaimed for 26 September 1861, with allusions to the attack on Fort Sumter along with the classical images of Lethe as the river of forgetfulness and Leonidas, the Spartan hero of Thermopylae:

But if the patriotic ardor that seemed to burn in every breast when the national escutcheon was first tarnished has been quenched by the Lethean waters of egotism; if the memory of the past achievements and past glory, contrasted with the present humiliation, does not arouse in our midst the Leonidas that will joyously sell their lives for the maintenance of this peerless Union; if the taunts of the ungenerous foreigner and the sardonic smile of the despots are incapable of inspiriting all to energetic actions, the entreaties offered this day will fail to propitiate the assistance of the Most High.[6]

The structure of the present sermon is fairly straightforward. An introductory section focuses on what may appear to be a relatively minor issue but was apparently one that Morais considered to be of symbolic significance: the wording of the presidential proclamation of the national fast-day (made in response to a request by the Senate, possibly in response to the Southern day of prayer on 27 March). Morais contrasts this with the proclamation of the previous November's Thanksgiving Day by Pennsylvania Governor Andrew G. Curtin, which used language that made Jews feel excluded (and is reproduced here at the end of Morais's sermon).[7] Lincoln's proclamation, containing no reference to Jesus or Christians, is couched in terms that no believing Jews would find offensive. Morais highlights this proclamation as the basis for an occasion in which, 'Harmoniously in thoughts and wishes, we join our fellow citizens of every creed and denomination, who, at this hour, beseech the Lord for the irradiation of His countenance.'

The body of the sermon presents two major themes. The first is introduced by the celebrated verses from the fifty-eighth chapter of the Book of Isaiah in which the prophet, speaking in God's behalf, castigates the people for the insincerity of their observance of a day of fasting and prayer. This warning

---

instructive to compare this passage with the allusion to the revolutions of 1830 and 1848 by Isaac Leeser in a sermon delivered on 26 Jan. 1849: 'religion has no part to play in the mighty and terrible dramas which have late been enacted; at least it has no business to interfere actively and visibly in public affairs' ('The Strength of our Religion', 89).

[6] S. Morais, 'Address Delivered . . . on the National "Fast-Day"'.

[7] Previous examples of exclusionary language used by governors in proclaiming Thanksgiving Days, with protests by Jewish leaders, were reviewed by M. J. Kohler, 'Phases in the History of Religious Liberty in America', 19–23, 30–6. The governors concerned include those of South Carolina in 1812 and 1844 (on the latter, see Sarna and Dalin, *Religion and State*, 111–21), of Pennsylvania in 1848, of New York in 1855, and of Ohio in 1856, the last of which drew responses by Rabbis Isaac Mayer Wise and Max Lilienthal (see Temkin, *Isaac Mayer Wise*, 162–3). Kohler makes no reference to the text or incident discussed here.

against insincerity leads him to a quick review of the national sins that have prolonged the present war—a topic addressed by virtually every Christian preacher on this occasion. Presented fairly quickly and in general terms, they illustrate the general theme of self-centred materialism: 'hands polluted with bribe, . . . minds engrossed in the pursuit of ill-gotten wealth'. Only if the prayers are accompanied by 'unwavering efforts' to change the status quo can there be hope that God will bring about an end to the war.

This leads to the second major theme: the repudiation of a dishonourable, ignominious peace that would come at the cost of dissolution of the American body politic. We have already encountered this theme from a different perspective in the sermon by Maximilian Michelbacher delivered in Richmond a month earlier; there, the target of the preacher's scorn was Northern peace proposals that would result in the loss of Southern independence. The vehemence of both denunciations illustrates the attractiveness in wide circles of the population of an alternative policy that would put an end to the appalling bloodshed. Morais—never mentioning slavery in this context—argues against the 'Peace Democrats' on the basis of his dual identity as 'An Israelite by faith, and an Italian by birth'. That he should refer to the historical precedent of the division of the united Israelite kingdom following the death of Solomon is not surprising; the lengthy invocation of the Italian dream of unification as a model is a stunning example of an immigrant speaking proudly of his continued identification with the land of his origins. Yet the passage ends with a ringing affirmation of America's destiny as one that will merit international respect as 'the pattern of freedom and the haven of the oppressed', an end to be achieved with divine help 'according to our sincerity'.

The peroration turns to a concrete exposition of the efforts needed to demonstrate that the observance of this day is not superficial and perfunctory: a concerted programme of support for the 'thousands of our fellow beings' who are 'exposed to danger and privations', whether on the battlefield or in their homes, through material support of the Sanitary Commission. As was common in the nineteenth century, the sermon concludes with a carefully wrought prayer appropriate to the theme and the occasion.

# SERMON

## [INTRODUCTION]

**M**Y FRIENDS! Towards the close of the last autumnal season, his Excellency, the Governor of Pennsylvania, invited his constituents to jointly thank and praise Almighty God for the manifold tokens of His grace to our beloved Commonwealth.[8] While thus conforming with a time-honored practice, he improved the occasion by setting forth the motives which at that period especially claimed our gratitude. And truly every loyal heart must, at their rehearsal, have throbbed with devotional joy, for the impending evil providentially averted from us, would have proved most direful in its effect.[9] The noble State in which hitherto it has been our fortune to dwell securely would, like others, have been rent in twain by contending armies; rude combatants would have ravaged our smiling meadows and verdant fields. But 'The Lord of hosts was with us; the God of Jacob became the tower of our defence' (Ps. 46: 8). At a look of His displeasure, the swelling tide receded from the insulted shores, and we were saved as at this day.

That celestial deliverance, my worthy hearers, together with the inestimable blessings of a plentiful harvest, were equally shared by all the denizens of Pennsylvania, but none among them could have appreciated these boons more than our brethren, the progeny of Israel.[10] Yet, the Chief Magistrate of this enlightened Commonwealth ignored their existence. By the proclamation he issued, they were excluded from attuning their voices to the national chorus that sung the mighty deeds of the Lord. For how could the disciples of Moses and the

[8] There was no presidential proclamation of Thanksgiving in late November 1862; observance of Thanksgiving that year was proclaimed by state governors (see e.g. *Jewish Messenger*, 21 Nov. 1862, p. 157, for the New York proclamation).

[9] Following the disastrous defeat at the second Battle of Bull Run in early September, as Confederate forces advanced through Maryland the danger of an invasion of Pennsylvania seemed imminent enough for Governor Andrew G. Curtin to instruct militia units to prepare themselves. McClellan's success at Antietam on 17 Sept. stopped the Confederate advance: Dusinberre, *Civil War Issues in Philadelphia*, 143–4.

[10] Morais began his Thanksgiving Day sermon of 1852 by stating, 'If in convening at their places of worship, agreeably to the wise counsel of the governor of our State, our Nazarene brethren have been actuated by a feeling of religious gratitude, the incentive which has prompted us Israelites to repair to these holy courts is even stronger' ('A Sermon delivered on Thanksgiving Day (November 25, 1852)', 3).

prophets have consistently joined in the anthem, which, with invidious distinction, the followers of the Man of Nazareth were principally invited to raise?[11] They doubtless did, as they are wont, pour forth their grateful hearts before the living Redeemer during the solemn convocations enjoined by their religion, but they justly deemed it incompatible with their profession, and unbecoming their dignity to hallow the day set apart by a dignitary whose sectarian zeal rendered him oblivious of the principles enunciated in the American Constitution.

But the course adopted in that instance by the Executive of a single State (and I regret it was ours) exhibits its impropriety still more glaringly when contrasted with the demeanor of the Executive of all the United States. The representative of the nation that has branded religious proscription with infamy does not, like his subordinate, violate the trust committed to his hands. He does not truckle with a worldly policy and gratify the majority to the detriment of a minority, but he considers every member of the grand family that constitutes the republic an integral part thereof. Hence did he, on this day of national humiliation, as on that of public rejoicing, summon *all* to the footstool of the Universal Creator—our gracious God—who abundantly pardons.[12]

[11] For the full text of the governor's proclamation, as published in the *Philadelphia Inquirer*, see below following the end of the sermon. On the day after Thanksgiving 1862, the *Inquirer* wrote near the beginning of its front-page article, 'The Hebrew Tabernacles were not open for public worship. This was not owing, of course, to any disinclination to observe the day, although the proclamation of the Governor, calling especially upon "Christian Churches", might be so construed as not to include Israelites' (*Philadelphia Inquirer*, 28 Nov. 1862, p. 1). The New York governor's proclamations of 1861, 1862, and 1863 (recorded in the *Jewish Messenger*) do not use Christian-specific language, but the New Hampshire proclamation of 31 Oct. 1862 refers to 'the convictions of all Christian people', 'that Christian civilization which is our inheritance', 'the patriotism, courage and Christian faith of our fathers' (cited approvingly in McAllister, *The National Reform Movement*, 296–8). Christian-centric formulations continued to be used in Pennsylvania for many years. In his Thanksgiving address of 28 Nov. 1867, Morais complained that the governor's proclamation contained the phrase, 'the richer blessings of our common Christianity'. Marcus Jastrow addressed precisely the same issue in his 1868 'Thanksgiving Day Sermon', delivered at the Rodef Shalom Synagogue in Philadelphia: 'the Governor of this State has ignored the character of his office, and the character of the Constitution of the United States, by making his own particular belief the basis of a proclamation to the commonwealth, thus intimating that he wishes only such to unite with him in thanksgiving for the country's happiness and greatness who may profess certain Dogmas similar to his own' (p. 5); cf. M. J. Kohler, 'Phases in the History of Religious Liberty in America', 23. And on 9 Nov. 1880 Morais wrote a letter, published in Philadelphia's *Evening Telegraph*, protesting at the Christian-specific language at the end of Governor Hoyt's Thanksgiving proclamation of that year, noting with regret that 'former remonstrations on similar occasions have not succeeded yet in making public officials more guarded in their language, so as to avoid giving offense to a religious community of law-abiding citizens' (Sabato Morais Ledger, 235).

[12] There is no reference to Christ or to Christianity in the presidential proclamation. In this omission Lincoln departed from the resolution of the Senate requesting him to proclaim a day 'to seek [God] for succor according to his appointed way, through Jesus Christ' (cited in McAllister,

My friends, in response to that righteous call, we have entered the courts of our sanctuary. Harmoniously in thoughts and wishes, we join our fellow citizens of every creed and denomination, who, at this hour, beseech the Lord for the irradiation of His countenance. Their cause is our cause, for its peaceful issue will restore unto us the halcyon days whose departure we deeply lament. Its final triumphs will raise us anew to the climax of glory we had formerly attained.

### [BODY OF THE SERMON]

Yet, though we fervently pray that this devotional communion may, like Aaron's burning incense, turn away from us the fierce anger of the Lord; though, with child-like faith, we lean for support upon the arm that sustains the world; still, as we approach these holy shrines, our hearts flutter between hope and fear. A voice from the past utters denunciations: 'Is it such a fast as I have chosen? A day for a man to afflict his soul? Is it to bow down his head as a bulrush, and to spread sack-cloth and ashes under him? Wilt thou call this a fast and an acceptable day to the Lord?' (Isa 58: 5).[13]

My brethren, it is an echo of our national misdeeds. We have been insincere in our professions, else the sword which desolates the land might have long since been replaced into the scabbard. We have not raised ourselves above our prejudices. We have not discarded our preconcerted notion for the reassertion of a grand principle. Our energies that should altogether have converged towards one common centre were directed to opposite ends. My friends, we stand self-condemned; for the history of these inauspicious times, while it records the patriotism and abnegation of some noble-minded Americans, daily chronicles the dishonesty of public men.

But the inspired voice, still crying aloud, says, 'Is not this the fast wherein I delight: to loose the bands of wickedness?' (Isa. 58: 6). Dare we, with

The National Reform Movement, 297–8, who did not acknowledge Lincoln's recasting of the words). On 26 Sept. 1861, Raphall had similarly praised Lincoln for addressing his proclamation of the national fast-day not just to Christians but to 'the people at large', unlike the words of 'some high functionaries, whose narrow views debar them from discerning beyond the pale of their religion' ('Fast-Day Sermon', 26 Sept. 1861, 51–2).

[13] The translation is *not* Leeser's—the first Jewish translation of the Bible into English (1853), which Morais never uses in the sermon—but apparently the King James Version. Morris Raphall, preaching at the Green Street Synagogue in New York on this day, also used verses from this same chapter of Isaiah, condemning the hypocrisy of people called upon by the rulers of the nation 'to weary Heaven with fruitless professions of a penitence they did not feel, and of a humility they did not practice' ('Fast-Day Sermon', 30 Apr. 1863).

hands polluted with bribe, with minds engrossed in the pursuit of ill-gotten wealth, with hearts of stone that will sacrifice the dearest interests of mankind, aye, the lives of myriads, too, in order to obtain some ephemeral power; dare we invoke in our favor the assistance of the God of Justice and Truth?[14] No, let me exclaim it in the bitterness of my soul: 'The accursed thing is in the midst of thee, O Israel! Thou canst not stand before thine adversaries' (Josh. 7: 13).

Like the inflexible Joshua, we must destroy the impious Achans with their plunder. We must convey them to the valley of Achor, there to atone for their guilt. Then will the land be cleansed of her impurities and the breath of God reanimate the drooping spirits of her children. Before the tribunal of the Divine Judge, nations, like individuals, are arraigned and sentenced. And as the Holy Scriptures have promised him a lofty seat on the earth, 'who walketh right-eously and speaketh uprightly, who despiseth the gain of oppression and shaketh his hands that they may not hold bribe' (Isa. 33: 15), so likewise will that people stand high, and be immovable as impregnable rocks, who fulfil the laws of the Eternal.

Oh! that we might awake to that sublime truth, for then probity and virtue would be our political code, the defence of human rights our international deal-ings. Intent upon re-establishing the kingdom of peace in these distracted climes,[15] we would labor with singleness of purpose. We would jointly strengthen the hands of the men at the helm of our ship of State, and soon reach, under celestial protection, the haven of our desires.

My beloved hearers, in the volume of inspiration has been written that 'If we commit our way unto the Lord, and trust in Him, He will bring it to pass' (cf. Ps. 37: 5); but therein it is also declared that 'the hand of the diligent shall bear rule, and the slothful shall be under tribute' (Prov. 12: 24). Our wishes, our hopes, our prayers may be for the speedy termination of a fratricidal war, but unless our unwavering efforts are also for the consummation of that most happy event, blood will continue to flow, and hatred grow irreconcilable.

Think not, however, that I intimate aught derogatory to American honor. The desire for an ignominious peace shall never be harbored in my

[14] On this theme of materialism, cf. Raphall: 'Answer, ye peculators and speculators, who fat-ten on the blood of the hard-worked masses, and who dignify roguery by the name of smartness' ('Fast-Day Sermon', 30 Apr. 1863, cited more fully in the introduction to Sermon 7 by Isaacs n. 3). 'Peculators' refers to embezzlers of public funds for personal enrichment.

[15] 'Distracted' in the somewhat archaic meaning of 'torn or disordered by dissension' (*OED*); 'climes' meaning 'regions'.

breast.[16] An Israelite by faith, and an Italian by birth, I would blush to utter in your presence the word 'dissolution'. With the lessons of history stamped on my mind, can I advocate the death of a nation? Say ye, my fellow-believers, which were our palmy days[17] in the land of promise? When was Judea tranquil within and respected without? Was it not when twelve tribes formed a glorious unit, under the sceptre of our sovereign? Again, from what period do the declining of our ancient power and our unheard of disasters date? Is it not from the unpropitious time that Judah and Israel became two separate kingdoms?[18]

And the aspirations of *Dante*, the inspiring songs of *Petrarch*, the longing of every good and true Italian, have they not ever been for the unity of the delightful peninsula, from the Alps to the Adriatic? Why have the dungeon and the gibbet proved fruitless, and the brothers *Bandiera* ran to martyrdom as to a festive board, but because the idea of a united Italy kindled the hearts of her children?[19] And now that, thank God, the regeneration of that classic land is about to be accomplished, shall we prove false to the teachings that have inspired the latest but most noble of her heroes? Shall we, who were bequeathed a country sanctified by the toils, by the tears, by the abnegation of the best of

[16] The phrase 'ignominious peace' (perhaps coined by Gibbon) was popularized by the congressional War Hawks of 1812, led by Henry Clay. On the same fast-day, the Watertown preacher John Weiss warns about the element that 'still dreams and plots an ignominious peace' ('Northern Strengths and Weaknesses', 16). And the New York Baptist I. S. Kalloch said half a year later, 'As death is preferable to life purchased at the price of honor, so is war, in its bloodiest strifes and ghastliest calamities, infinitely preferable to national peace purchased at the price of national degradation' ('Thanksgiving Day Sermon', 2). This sentence and the following paragraph by Morais should be read against the background of the 'peace-through-compromise' platform of the Democratic critics of Lincoln, representing a position that reached its peak of influence during the first six months of 1863 (Klement, *Lincoln's Critics*, 12–13), and was supported by Jewish leaders including Isaac Mayer Wise (see e.g. Heller, *Isaac M. Wise*, 331–9; Temkin, 'Isaac Mayer Wise and the Civil War'). Close to home, on 18 Mar. the New Jersey legislature, controlled by the Democrats, passed resolutions calling for peace and condemning administration policies: M. Wagner et al. (eds.), *Library of Congress Civil War Desk Reference*, 153). For an analogous repudiation by a Virginia Jewish preacher of apparent overtures for peace a month earlier, see Michelbacher, Sermon 5 above, pp. 154–5.

[17] The adjective is a synonym for a triumphant, prosperous period, when a nation flourished like palm trees.

[18] For another example of using the 'secession of the Ten Tribes' as a negative model in an argument for the importance of Union, see Clement L. Vallandigham's speech to Congress of 14 Jan. 1863, in *Speeches, Arguments, Addresses, and Letters*, 432. Arthur Kiron emphasizes the political context of the passage, but also the larger context of Morais's concept of unity as a 'supreme, essential value', applied to God, truth, and humanity as well as to the nation: Kiron, 'Golden Ages, Promised Lands', 221, 216.

[19] In a sermon delivered in late Nov. 1871 (and printed in the *Philadelphia Inquirer*) Morais celebrated the unification of Italy and again referred to the martyrdom of 'the brothers Bandiera, shot at Cosenza' (Sabato Morais Ledger, 67).

men, barter it for some fictitious advantage? Shall we sunder apart the bonds that knit together in one sublime whole this matchless Republic of the North, to voluntarily sink into the condition of the petty republics of the Middle Ages, that continually battled for supremacy?[20]

No, no. May the hand which would tear a brotherly covenant wither like that of the iniquitous Jeroboam.[21] We must have peace, but not at the cost of our national existence. It shall not be a peace at which our rivals beyond the Atlantic would rejoice, but a peace that will render America what its illustrious founders had made it, the pattern of freedom and the haven of the oppressed. It must be a peace by which our banner may flap its gorgeous folds over every sea and land, and command, as heretofore, universal respect.[22] It must be a peace at the declaration of which, from ocean to ocean, the hallelujahs of a grateful people shall reverberate. And for the attainment of such a peace we must bring into one focus all the powers at our disposal; we must exercise all the virtues of the heart: gentleness, forbearance and forgiveness; we must seek the Lord of Sabaoth with all the ardency of devotion. And He who scrutinizes man's inmost thoughts will judge us according to our sincerity. If we are true to our country, solicitous for the happiness of its inhabitants, ready to sacrifice to it all earthly preferments, He will grant us our petitions. For He alone can smooth the troubled water into a purling brook. He can subdue man's ire and his unruly passions, as it is declared in the sacred pages, 'He stilleth the noise of seas, the noise of the waves, and the tumult of people' (Ps. 65: 8).

## [PERORATION]

And now, my beloved hearers, let this day which has been devoted to the service of the Most High be signalized in our community by deeds of goodness and beneficence. While we dwell here securely, in the fruition of God's bounty, thousands of our fellow beings are exposed to danger and privations. They are the defenders of our Union. But, even on the battle-field, where many lie wounded, and on their couch of sickness, charity—the handmaid of religion—can soften their pangs. More I need not say, in order to strike a sympathetic

---

[20] Southern preachers, of course, repudiated the analogy with Italian unification and invoked the analogy with the American Revolution and the struggle for freedom of Spain's South American colonies, Mexico, and Greece. See e.g. Elliott, 'Samson's Riddle', 11–12.

[21] Referring to 1 Kgs 13: 4, and perhaps alluding to Ps. 137: 5.

[22] Cf. Henry Ward Beecher, preaching in New York on the same day: 'If the old Stars and Stripes are borne again in every part of this land, and over all the world in our national ships, and is everywhere the blood-washed ensign of liberty, then the millennial day will dawn' (Beecher, 'Fast-Day Sermon').

chord in Jewish hearts. But as many a generous gift has been wasted, for want of a systematic distribution, I would urge the ladies of my persuasion to join hands with their sisters of a different creed in the discharge of a philanthropic task.[23]

'The women's branch of the Sanitary Commission' appeals to them, through my agency, for countenance and co-operation.[24]

Its avowed object is to secure our soldiers the receipt of their countrymen's free-will offerings, and the Executive Committee of that Association feel confident that it is only in their power to effectually compass that design. Let, then, a communication that promises so favorable a result be opened forthwith, and let us trust that it will be the channel whence will flow health and comfort to the sufferers. 'And may the works of charity be peace, and the effect of charity quietness and surety for ever' (Isa. 32: 17).

## PRAYER

Father of mercy! In the day of our national humiliation, we have come to seek Thy countenance. Hide it not from Thy contrite suppliants, lest the people whom Thou didst cause to walk in light be enshrouded in utter darkness. Heavy is the gloom that surrounds us, but a benignant look from Thee, O Almighty Protector, can restore serenity to our horizon. Remember Thy compassion, O Lord, and thy loving kindness which are everlasting. For surely Thy watchful Providence signally exhibited towards this country has not departed therefrom. Thou hast not rejected the creatures whom thou hast pleased greatly to exalt. Even from our primeval days, Thy invisible hand led us securely in grievous times. When earthly kings had conspired to crush us beneath the weight of their power, Thou didst raise a deliverer, and he brought us out to enlargement. And because he found grace in Thy sight, Thou didst inspire him with superior knowledge to understand Thy will, and with a spirit of beneficence to execute it. Tutored by the counsel of Thy messenger, we rose to eminence, and stood as a beacon light to distant nations; nay, people we know not triumphed at our glory, and rejoiced at our happiness.

[23] Bertram Korn quoted this passage, identifying it as a response to a letter from Mrs Mary Rose Smith asking for involvement by Jewish women in the Philadelphia branch of the Sanitary Commission; as a result, the Ladies Hebrew Association for the Relief of Sick and Wounded Soldiers was organized in Philadelphia on 11 May (Korn, *American Jewry and the Civil War*, 119).

[24] The US Sanitary Commission, established on 9 June 1861 by presidential decree, coordinated local supply efforts and provided relief to soldiers in battle. Women were extremely active in this organization; recent studies on gender dynamics include Giesberg, *Civil War Sisterhood*, and Attie, *Patriotic Toil*. This passage indicates a different dynamic, namely the role of the commission in fostering inter-religious co-operation.

But now, alas! O Omnipotent! Our delight has changed into mourning. Fear and shame have seized our hearts, for that which formed our national pride is waning apace. This home, which our fathers had built for us to dwell in in brotherly love, threatens to fall. To whom shall we flee for help in our affliction? In whose hands shall we commit the preservation of our precious heir-loom? Unto Thee, O Most high! We call, and at Thy altar we offer supplications. Suffer not the recipients of Thy infinite bounty to be now exposed to danger and sorrow. Oh, deign to cast Thy shield around the structure reared by the good and the faithful, that not a single stone thereof may ever decay. For it is our shelter, it is our comfort. It is the laboratory where the hearts of men are fashioned in one mould, that they may beat in unison of feelings and desires.

Return, O Lord, and repent Thee concerning Thy servants; and if the awful calamity which rages in our borders was decreed against us as a requital for our national misdeeds, let the suffering it has occasioned be deemed a sufficient atonement. Remove Thy chastisement from thy hapless children, and grant, O Almighty Sovereign, that it may leave us wiser and purer in Thy sight. Grant that it may imbue us with a higher appreciation of the blessings Thou hast showered down upon this country and its inhabitants. Then shall we have drawn from Thy judgments a lesson of moderation, of forbearance and discretion.

Ruler of the Universe, at this hour, when the tearful eyes of a whole nation are directed to Thy celestial throne, bid thence a spirit of harmony enter their souls, and be reflected in the works of their Senators and Legislators; for then will this land enjoy their Sabbath of rest; neither ruin, nor migration, nor complaint shall be heard of any more in our territories. God of Israel, in whose habitation reigns eternal peace, grant, we most fervently beseech Thee, peace unto us and all mankind, now and evermore. Amen.

[25] *Philadelphia Inquirer*, 22 Oct. 1862, p. 1.

# PROCLAMATION OF THANKSGIVING DAY IN PENNSYLVANIA[25]

HARRISBURG, Oct. 21.—

The Governor has issued the following proclamation.

In the name and by the authority of the Commonwealth of Pennsylvania, ANDREW G. CURTIN, Governor of the said Commonwealth.

A PROCLAMATION.

*Whereas*, It is a good thing to render thanks unto God for all His mercy and loving kindness, therefore, I, ANDREW G. CURTIN, Governor of the Commonwealth of Pennsylvania, do recommend that Thursday, the 27th day of November next, be set apart by the people of this Commonwealth as a day of solemn Prayer and Thanksgiving to the Almighty, giving Him humble thanks that He has been graciously pleased to protect our free institutions and Government, and to keep us from sickness and pestilence and to cause the earth to bring forth her increase, so that our garners are choked with the harvest, and to look so favorably on the toil of His children that industry has thriven among us and labor has its reward; and also, that He has delivered us from the hands of our enemies, and filled our officers and men in the field with a loyal and intrepid spirit, and given them victory; and that He has poured out upon us (albeit unworthy) other great and manifold blessings.

Beseeching Him to help and govern us in His steadfast fear and love, and to put into our minds good desires, so that by His continual help we may have a right judgment in all things; and especially praying Him to give to Christian Churches grace to hate the thing which is evil, and to utter the teachings of truth and righteousness, declaring openly the whole counsel of God; and most heartily entreating Him to bestow upon our civil rulers wisdom and earnestness in council, and upon our military leaders zeal and vigor in action, that the fires of Rebellion may be quenched; that we, being armed with His defence, may be preserved from all perils, and that hereafter our people, living in peace and quietness, may, from generation to generation, reap the abundant fruits of His mercy, and with joy and thankfulness praise and magnify His holy name.

Given under my hand and the great seal of the State, at Harrisburg, this twentieth day of October, in the year of our Lord one thousand eight hundred and sixty-two, and of the Commonwealth the eighty-seventh.

ANDREW G. CURTIN

By the Governor: ELI SLIFER
Secretary of the Commonwealth

# CHAPTER SEVEN

## SAMUEL MYER ISAACS
# FAST-DAY SERMON

### THURSDAY, 30 APRIL 1863
#### WOOSTER STREET SYNAGOGUE, NEW YORK

SAMUEL MYER ISAACS was born in Holland in 1804 but as a child moved with his family to England, where he lived for the next twenty-five years. He had a respectable Jewish and general education, and achieved enough of a reputation in London to be invited to serve as cantor and preacher at the Ashkenazi B'nai Jeshurun Congregation in New York, which was eager to find a preacher with a strong command of the English language. He arrived in New York with his wife in 1839. In 1846 he became the leader of Congregation Shaaray Tefila, which broke away (apparently with some animosity) from B'nai Jeshurun over doctrinal issues.[1] He remained at this congregation until his death in 1878. Isaacs introduced to New York the practice of regular sermons in English; in this he was apparently, among American Jewish leaders, second only to Isaac Leeser in Philadelphia.

In 1857 he founded, together with his three sons (some of whom shared the preaching responsibilities at the synagogue), the *Jewish Messenger* as a periodical that would express the religious and cultural values of a traditionalist Judaism seeking to define a position between that of the most radical reformers and the opposition in principle to any change at all. In addition to the

---

[1] Biographical material is drawn from Sherman, 'Isaacs, Samuel Myer'; Adler, 'Isaacs, Samuel Myer', in the 1904 *Jewish Encyclopedia* (vi. 635); and the 'Guide to Collections in the Myer S. Isaacs Collection' of the American Jewish Historical Society, accessible at <www.cjh.org/academic/findingaids/AJHS/nhprc/MyerIsaacs1b.html>. (For a striking photograph, see E. Hertz (ed.), *Abraham Lincoln*, facing p. 72.) Isaacs's sermon at the laying of the cornerstone for the Wooster Street Synagogue of Shaaray Tefila was published by Isaac Leeser in the *Occident*. In it, he emphasizes the fundamental importance of order and decorum and the English sermon in worship, suggesting that these were issues in the split. He insists that no inroads must be made into the sacred and inviolable ceremonial laws, yet also that not all ceremonies have the same status (<www.jewish-history.com/Occident/volume4/aug1846/cornerstone.html>). Isaacs's successor at B'nai Jeshurun from 1849, Morris J. Raphall, a man with a much more distinguished education in Judaica, would deliver a controversial sermon in early Jan. 1861 (see pp. 192–3 below).

various literary and historical writings by contemporary authors published in its pages, he frequently reproduced the texts of sermons, including his own, especially those he delivered on the Sabbath of Repentance.

Isaacs generally avoided politically charged controversy in the *Messenger*, steering clear of the vituperative controversy over the biblical justification for slavery that erupted at the beginning of 1861, and—like Isaac Mayer Wise—warning against the use of the pulpit to discuss political issues. Speaking of David Einhorn's need to flee for his safety from Baltimore to Philadelphia, he wrote, 'It seems that he has been mistaking his vocation, and making the pulpit the vehicle for political invective . . . A Minister has enough to do, if he devotes himself to the welfare of his flock; he can afford to leave politics to others.'[2] His sermons generally reflect this stance. He took a strong stand on issues directly concerning Jewish life, including attempts by Christian missionaries to convert Jews and expressions of anti-Jewish prejudice in the general press, but—at least in the sermons accessible to me—did not seem eager to address directly either the local or the national political issues of the time. When the *Jewish Messenger* printed a text of Morris J. Raphall's fast-day sermon of 30 April 1863, Isaacs eliminated a strong passage of general criticism that was included in the text published by the *New York Times*.[3]

Nevertheless, when called upon to preach on a day of national fasting or national thanksgiving—as occurred many times during the Civil War—it was difficult for Isaacs to avoid the issues on the minds of so many of his congregants and neighbours. The question of how much of his fast-day sermon on 30 April 1863 was devoted to a burning political issue is central to our understanding of this provocative text.

The sermon's structure is indicated near the beginning in an introductory section. It begins with a series of rhetorical questions about the need for (yet another) day of fasting, prayer, and humiliation. The answer is simple: such days dramatize and emphasize the dependence of human beings upon God and their need for divine help in all of their undertakings. History—both of America and of the Jews—provides many examples of men ignoring God in

---

[2] Korn, *American Jewry and the Civil War*, 28, citing *Jewish Messenger*, 3 May 1861, p. 133.

[3] *New York Times*, 1 May 1863, p. 2: 'Education should be the guardian of freedom and of virtue . . . But what principles did it actually inculcate—what virtues did it really teach? Did it inculcate respect for free institutions? Answer, ye place-hunters, ye ballot-box stuffers, ye shoulder-hitters, who reduce self-government to a disgusting farce. Did it teach patriotism? Answer, ye spoils-men, ye office-seekers and holders, who cement party lines with the cohesive force of public plunder. Did it teach common honesty? Answer, ye peculators and speculators, who fatten on the blood of the hard-worked masses, and who dignify roguery by the name of smartness . . . [W]hile the best men North and South had long been driven aloof from the affairs of the country, demagogues, fanatics and a party Press had so managed matters that they found themselves in the third year of a destructive but needless sectional war.' None of this appears in the text published by Isaacs in *Jewish Messenger*, 8 May 1863, p. 154.

times of prosperity, then turning to God in times of dire need, and the preach-er indicates that both aspects of this message will be explored in the sermon. This he does in separate sections of the body of the address. A second dichot-omy is also indicated, which will be applied to each section: the punishment that follows sin, and the forgiveness that follows contrition.

After the introduction, the body of the sermon begins with a general review of the life of King David and then a detailed recapitulation of the biblical narrative in the final chapter of 2 Samuel regarding David's insistence upon taking a census of his people (despite the warnings of his military leader Joab), followed by the condemnation of David by the prophet Gad, who gives the king a choice of one among three possible punishments for the people. Those who knew the biblical text might have recognized a significant addition in the preacher's provision of a motivation for David: 'seized by a spirit of vain glory', he ordered the census 'that he might know what a powerful monarch he was, to satiate his empty self-glorification'. Not only is this unstated in the text of 2 Samuel, it contradicts the beginning of the chapter, which characterizes the entire episode as an expression of God's anger against Israel, which led to God's incitement of David. The negative characterization of David continues with another insertion into the narrative: 'Infatuated with his greatness, he was determined not to be thwarted.' Despite David's subsequent contrition, he is forced to choose among three punishments: war, famine, or pestilence; when he chooses pestilence, 70,000 Israelites perish before God stays the hand of the angel, so that Jerusalem and the remainder of the people are spared.

As a general rule, when a preacher devotes more than 750 words to retelling a biblical story, the purpose is to apply it to a significant issue in the present. And so, not surprisingly, Isaacs turns now to his listeners' own time and place: 'We place this view before our hearers, so that they may draw their own conclusions on the presumption of King David.' After several phrases of addi-tional recapitulation, he launches into a series of generalized warnings—'woe to that nation or to those individuals . . . Woe to that nation . . . Sad the con-dition of that land . . . Woe to that land . . .'—that lead on to more explicit application to the spiritual history of 'the land we inhabit'.

Here we encounter a significant and challenging interpretive crux. I suggest a possible reading of the sermon that would see it as intended to address spe-cific contemporary matters that are not explicitly stated by the preacher. King David is a figure for President Lincoln, and the census alludes to one of the most controversial innovations of the Lincoln administration: the Conscription Act that Lincoln signed into law on 3 March 1863, which subject-ed all males between the ages of 20 and 45 to the draft. Viewed by many as the culmination of the administration's assault on civil liberties, it was fiercely criti-cized in many areas of the North. The connection between the census and the draft is expressed in the total cited by the preacher: '1,300,000 valiant men that drew the sword' (cf. 2 Sam. 24: 9), as well as in the earlier census commanded in Numbers 26: 2, to count all Israelites able to bear arms.

No Northern general or cabinet member is known to have opposed the Conscription Bill and warned Lincoln against its consequences, so the role of Joab has no clear analogue in the contemporary context.[4] But the role of Gad does. Perhaps the most visible and articulate critic of the Conscription Bill was Clement L. Vallandigham, the Democratic Representative from Ohio. The speech he delivered in the House of Representatives on 23 February 1863 contains a masterfully cogent articulation of the loss of liberties sanctioned by the bill, and refers to Lincoln as 'the servant President, now the master Dictator, of the United States'.[5] After the bill was passed by Congress and signed by the President, Vallandigham spoke at massive rallies in Philadelphia and in the preacher's home city of New York, where his speech of 7 March 1863 was covered in detail by the local newspapers.[6] In his fierce, passionate, and eloquent attacks on what he considered to be the administration's subversion of fundamental rights of Americans guaranteed by the Constitution, he sometimes presented himself in a prophetic role. Near the end of that New York speech of 7 March he appealed to the administration 'with a voice of warning, prophetic it may be—I trust not, because I trust the warning will be heeded'.[7] His opponents referred to him as a 'false prophet'. In hearing about the role of the prophet Gad, who admonished David for his sin, the figure of Vallandigham might well have occurred to many of the listeners.

Is it conceivable that Isaacs could have intended this strong message, including the criticism of Lincoln, to be communicated by his sermon? Looking back through the prism of the assassination and the profusion of elegiac sermons that followed celebrating Lincoln and idealizing him even in messianic terms,[8] it may seem difficult to imagine a New York Jewish leader aligned with the

[4] A leading historian on conscription in the nineteenth century reports that 'no records were kept of the numerous conferences between Army and Administration leaders' prior to the introduction of the bill into the Congress, and the bill did not originate with the administration (Leach, *Conscription in the United States*, 162–3). This makes the parallel with the biblical account imperfect.

[5] Vallandigham, *Speeches, Arguments, Addresses, and Letters*, 454–78, quotation on 459.

[6] Ibid. 479–502, with the speaker's letter correcting the coverage in the *New York Times* on 502. Catholic papers in New York were vehemently opposed to conscription, with one editor, on 14 Mar., encouraging armed resistance to its enforcement: Man, 'The Church and the New York Draft Riots', 41.

[7] Vallandigham, *Speeches, Arguments, Addresses, and Letters*, 501; cf. Klement, *The Limits of Dissent*, 70: 'Taney's decision must have bolstered V's belief in his ability as a prophet'.

[8] For Lincoln as messiah, see E. Hertz (ed.), *Abraham Lincoln*, 95 (I. M. Wise), 242–4 (Joseph Krauskopf), 291 (J. Leonard Levy). Isaacs represented Jews at the New York city funeral pageant for Lincoln (Sarna, *American Judaism*, 122), but his attitude may have changed in the intervening period, as did that of many of his former opponents.

Copperhead 'traitors' who despised what Lincoln stood for. There are, however, arguments to support the possibility, even the likelihood that this was just
what Isaacs was indeed aiming at. Lincoln is being compared not to one of the
biblical villains but to David, whose overall image remains of course quite positive. Isaac Mayer Wise, though perhaps the best known, was not the only
example of a Jewish leader who strongly supported Vallandigham and the
'peace' policy of the Copperheads.[9] Some Republican newspapers accused all
Northern Jews of being secessionists, Copperheads, disloyal.[10] The antipathy
towards the Conscription Bill in New York would erupt into draft riots some
two months after the sermon was delivered.[11] In the second part of the sermon, addressing his audience as Jews, Isaacs says, 'Do not despair, seeing that
your dearest rights are jeopardized'—a clear allusion to the discourse of the day
about rights understood to be guaranteed by the Constitution.[12] And by citing
the verse 'The heart of kings is in the hand of God' (Prov. 21: 1) and concluding that 'All we can do is to support the government', the preacher shields himself from the possibility of an accusation of sedition.[13] If opposition to
Lincoln's bill was indeed his message, it was presented in a relatively moderate
form.

When Isaacs comes to make the application, however, the reference to
the President and to conscription is well concealed. After an encomium to the
flourishing and prosperity of the United States as a potential 'Eden on earth'
and a unique venue of equality for the Jews, the preacher continues: 'But alas!
for human frailty, the governing classes commenced to number the people,
inaugurated a policy of majority and minority, dissention between the South

---

[9] On Wise's 'Peace Democrat' sympathies during the war (based almost entirely on *The
Israelite*, not on sermons), see Heller, *Isaac M. Wise*, 331–9; Korn, 'Isaac Mayer Wise on the Civil
War'; id., *American Jewry and the Civil War*, 4–48 and *passim*; Temkin, 'Isaac Mayer Wise and the
Civil War'. For another example, see the eulogy for Lincoln by Alfred T. Jones of Philadelphia,
who described himself as 'one who has warmly and earnestly opposed the policy and measures of
Abraham Lincoln', won over only shortly before Lincoln's death: E. Hertz (ed.), *Abraham Lincoln*,
151–2.                                            [10] Korn, *American Jewry and the Civil War*, 189–90.
[11] See the reference and annotation in Einhorn's 1863 Thanksgiving address, Sermon 8a below.
[12] In his journal, the *Jewish Messenger*, on 6 Mar. 1863 Isaacs published an unsigned article
called 'Patriotism' under the rubric 'This, That, and The Other'. The author wrote: 'We hear a
great outcry about the imbecility of the administration, daily our ears are filled with bitter denunciations of President and Cabinet for unconstitutional measures and violations of the rights of
citizens. All this may be founded on a reasonable basis, the officers chosen to administer the
national affairs may be incapable, may have been derelict in duty, may be open to all the charges
brought against them. But what sense is there in indulging incessantly in these violent diatribes
against the Executive?' (p. 80).
[13] This would not have been a paranoid fear. On 2 Sept. 1862, Judson D. Benedict, a minister
from Aurora, New York, was arrested upon orders from a US deputy marshal of Erie County following a sermon delivered two days earlier that presented a New Testament-based justification
for non-resistance (Curran, *Soldiers of Peace*, 69).

and the North; instituted a system destructive to every well-constituted government, "to the victor belong the spoils".' No hint of Lincoln and conscription here, simply vague references to the divisiveness of pragmatic politics. And
an allusion to Vallandigham as prophet appears to be explicitly rejected: *'there
exists no God* to deliver the Divine message to those in authority, to tell them
to choose one of these evils: famine, sword or pestilence. They have already
selected the sword.' The preacher concedes that the parallel has broken down,
leaving open the possibility that the fate of the nation at present will be even
worse than the suffering of the Israelites following from the rash decision of
King David.

I see no way of definitively determining what was the preacher's intention
in this sermon, or how the congregants understood his message.[14] Suffice it to
say that the reading that accords the specific application to Lincoln and conscription primary significance and identifies the vague, general criticisms as
essential obfuscation of secondary importance yields a much stronger sermon.

In its report about the national thanksgiving Day celebrated on 6 August
1863, the *New York Times* editorialized, after reviewing the texts of sermons
delivered that day (including one by 'Rabbi Isaacs'), that 'Treason and
Copperheadism seem to have no voice in the New York pulpit.'[15]

# S E R M O N

*And David said unto God, I am in a great strait.*
*Let us fall, then, into the hands of the Lord; for His mercies are great,*
*but let me not fall into the hand of man.*
(2 SAM. 24: 14)[16]

[INTRODUCTION]

WHY THIS FAST? This humiliation? This national call on the All-
powerful to look upon us with mercy, to help us out of our troubles,
and to re-establish us as a nation of men, submissive to His will and

---

[14] I have not found in the other Civil War period sermons by Isaacs, or in the editorial
statements of the *Jewish Messenger*, indication of a strong stand one way or another on Lincoln,
conscription, or the general policies of the administration, but this reticence would have been
consistent with his general policy (see above). The position taken at the beginning of the war was
'Stand By the Flag!' (*Jewish Messenger*, 28 Apr. 1861, p. 124).

[15] *New York Times*, 7 Aug. 1863, p. 4.

[16] Isaacs uses Leeser's translation consistently throughout the sermon. In the *Jewish Messenger*,
the reference appears incorrectly as 1 Sam. 24: 14).

subordinate to His desires? Why this proclamation from the executive of the United States, calling upon all men to make an appearance before the Being enshrined in holiness, asking Him, in piteous strains, to forgive the sins we have committed, nationally and individually, and again to take us into His favor? Why is the whole of this day devoted to prayer and instruction, to an analyzation of the heart, and a search of the human mind? Because the governing and the governed are fully impressed with the conviction 'That we cannot depend on any thing for help, excepting our Father in Heaven.'[17]

This clear and legible declaration, however humiliating it may be to our overweening self-conceit, is too well established to admit of any refutation. From the dawning of our history to the present period, we have invariably called on Him in our distress, although ignoring His very existence when it has been well with us. Taking a comprehensive view of the subject as Americans, we have every reason to verify that humiliating idea; and narrowing down our remarks as Israelites, we have additional reasons for confirming the words uttered by David,[18] when he was 'delivered from the hands of all his enemies and from Saul ... When in my distress I called upon the Lord, and to my God I cried' (cf. 2 Sam. 22: 1, 7; Ps. 18: 1, 7), and immediate relief was the result. This, alas! has been too often our condition. From Egypt until now, we have ever run to the Divine rock for shelter when threatened by the storms of life, but in the radiance of the sun we have been unmindful of the Creator, 'who formeth light and createth darkness' (Isa. 45: 7 and liturgy).

Let, then, these lessons thus taught give a better tone to our feelings. Let us reflect that however great we may be in our own estimation, we sink into utter insignificance when we reflect how helpless we are without His guidance; and let us be admonished that national calamities and individual misfortunes can only be mitigated by the help of that good Being, whose ears are ever open, even to listen to the words of the humblest suppliant. Let the transgression be great, if contrition be sincere, justice is superseded by mercy, peace succeeds war. The text we have selected affords the most substantial evidence that violating the ordinances of Heaven is sure to be followed by punishment, and at the same time instructs us that forgiveness succeeds the sentence, if in humility we

[17] Cf. Mishnah *Sot.* 9: 15, BT *Sot.* 49a–b; the rabbinic statement is presented as identical with the spirit of the presidential proclamation of the fast-day.

[18] This statement, with the phrases 'as Americans' and 'as Israelites' suitably emphasized in the delivery (though not in the printing), provides a clue to the listeners of the structure of the presentation: the central theme is our turning to God in times of tribulation after ignoring God in times of prosperity, and this will be applied to the listeners in two parts. The first part will be addressed to them in their role as Americans.

acknowledge the power of the Supreme, the righteousness of His judgments and our own unworthiness.[19]

## [BODY OF SERMON]

[1.] On unclasping the volume of the past[20] and meditating on the signal life of David, noticing the many hair breadth escapes he had, from his battles with the giant to his constant warfare against the evil spirit of Saul, from the time he wielded a shepherd's crook to the period when chosen as Israel's monarch; observing his many vicissitudes and ultimately finding him composing an anthem to the glory of the Supreme, who had 'delivered him from the hands of all his enemies, and from Saul' (2 Sam. 22: 1); reviewing his whole life and taking into consideration the many compositions emanating from his Divinely inspired pen, all ascribing glory to the One ever existing God, should we not thence conclude that a man thus constituted, thus exalted, thus miraculously preserved, would become so spiritualized as to have no motives for here below, but that all his thoughts and aspirations would soar beyond this sphere to that good Being who had so signally favored him? So should we argue, were we not to remember that man is mortal, that the best of us, boasting of virtue, are not free from vice. Thus it has ever been, and King David lived but to illustrate the idea that very often after the most grateful emotions have emanated from the heart, self-glorification had entered that seat of vitality and counteracted all the good effected by previous adorations of the Godhead.

He had but just recounted the many beneficent acts of God, just detailed the many battles he had fought, the victories he had achieved,[21] when, seized by a spirit of vain glory, he called upon Joab, the captain of the army, to traverse from Dan even to Beersheba to number the people, that he might know what a powerful monarch he was, to satiate his empty self-glorification.[22] Joab, conscious of the sin the king was about committing, knowing that it was opposed to the Divine will that the Israelites should be numbered, entreated the monarch to revoked his mandate. To use his own words, 'May the Lord thy God add unto

---

[19] Another indication to the listeners of the sermon's structure: two component lessons of the biblical text (punishment for sin, then forgiveness upon contrition) will be applied to each of the roles designated.

[20] A metaphorical expression based on the metal mechanism that fastened the covers of large books.                                    [21] In 2 Sam. 22: 33–49.

[22] This motivation is not attributed to David in the biblical text, which indeed is introduced by the statement that God 'incited David against' the people of Israel (2 Sam. 24: 1). The phrase 'seized by a spirit of vain glory' may reflect a reading of the opening verse in the parallel account in 1 Chr. 21: 1, where it is 'Satan' who 'incited David'.

the people, how many soever they be, a hundred fold more, and may the eyes of my lord the King see it, but why doth my lord the King find delight in this thing?' (2 Sam. 24: 3). But the words fell listless on the royal ear. Infatuated with his greatness, he was determined not to be thwarted. His wish was gratified; he was informed that there were even 'one million three hundred thousand valiant men that drew the sword' (cf. 2 Sam. 24: 9).

The moment the report reached him what a tremendous army he had, 'David's heart smote him that he had numbered the people' (2 Sam. 24: 10), and feeling within himself that he had grievously erred, in contrition of heart he besought God to forgive his iniquity, seeing he had acted foolishly in sinning against the Lord. He was quickly admonished that public sin required public example, and the Prophet Gad was instructed to inform the king that three evils were offered him from which he would be permitted to select one: either a seven years' famine, a three months' destructive warfare, or a three days' pestilence in the land (cf. 2 Sam. 24: 13). David reflected on the matter, and as the various evils passed in review before him, he contended that should he select famine, his subjects would murmur and say that he selected famine, seeing that his wealth would obtain him food from other lands, whilst they would lack sustenance; should he choose war, they would condemn his course from the circumstance that he would place them in front of battle whilst he would protect himself.[23] He therefore thought the best course to pursue would be to select that evil which would fall with the same force on king and subject. Therefore, in the words of the text, he said to Gad, 'I am in a great strait. Let us fall, then, into the hands of the Lord; for His mercies are great, but let me not fall into the hand of man' (2 Sam. 24: 14). The result we know, that seventy thousand fell by pestilence, when the hand of the destroying angel was stayed, consequent on the true penitence of David, the Supreme saying, 'It is enough' (2 Sam. 24: 15). He had vindicated His authority, and the humiliation of the king arrested further calamity. The threshing floor of Aravneh the Jebusite was made an altar on which to pour forth his offerings and his heart's best emotions, and the Lord was entreated for the land, and the plague was stayed (2 Sam. 24: 25).

We place this view before our hearers, so that they may draw their own conclusions on the presumption of King David, who, although publicly warned by Joab of the consequence of his sin, yet, defiantly acting on the impulse of his

---

[23] This psychological–political interpretation of David's choice is taken from *Midrash shemuel*, beginning of ch. 31; it is cited by Isaac Abravanel (1437–1508) in his commentary *Perush al nevi'im rishonim*, 418a.

own erring heart, infatuated with the feeling of self-glorification, had no idea that the God who had so remarkably favored him and his people, so that Israel became the admiration and the envy of the world, that the same Being would take notice of so trifling a departure from the landmarks by which he was bound, and be angry, because he gave vent to his national pride; but he soon found out his error, and perceived that God will not permit His law to be held in abeyance, even to please a king, that from the monarch on his throne to the humblest cottager, all have duties delegated to them, which they cannot disregard without offending the Majesty of Heaven. He will be acknowledged as the Author of all good, and woe to that nation or to those individuals who defiantly trample on His laws, substituting their crude ideas for the laws of perfection emanating from the God-head! Woe to that nation which, disregarding that all good emanates from above, sets up its own authority, and claims all perfection to come from within itself! Sad the condition of that land, which enjoying the best gifts of Heaven, lightly esteems those benefits, and with an avaricious grasp seizes that with violence which confers a curse but not a blessing! Woe to that land, which with boasting and self-aggrandizement diminishes the goodness of Heaven, and arrogates all the virtue, the greatness and the power as belonging to its own exertions! The very eagle perched aloft mourns when she hears this human boast, as if God did not exist; and prophetic spirits pierce the future that such greatness is sure to be weakened by the Power which has been designedly disregarded.[24]

The land we inhabit has, for a series of years, been blessed by the Supreme, as no other country in the globe has been favored. Its history is unparalleled by the chroniclers of the world; from a semi-barbarous nation, it has become a land of civilization and intellect; year by year, it increased in moral as well as in numerical strength. It required no military force to protect its borders, it feared no enemy from without, and never expected foes from within. The idea was that the numerous school houses which studded every portion of the land would create a moral force, sufficient in itself to protect the country against every invidious foe. Its wealth, instead of becoming exhausted by constant immigration, was continually augmented through the instrumentality of that good Being, who appeared to favor this western hemisphere, as if to found an empire where man should find an Eden on earth, where industry should prosper, art

---

[24] Up to this point, the criticism is so general that it is unclear whether it is intended to apply to the Union or the Confederacy or to both. The following paragraph evokes the wonderful flourishing of the country in the past, drawing an analogy with David's unimagined successes.

and science flourish, and where every man should worship his God in accordance with the dictates of his conscience; where we, as Israelites especially, should be enabled to say, here at least [last] we have found a home, here a land overflowing with milk and honey; here the portals of education are as open to us as to others, here there exists nothing to clog our laudable ambition. Here the prerogative we have derived from God Himself can be freely exercised, and no one will deprive us of those rights guaranteed by the constitution. Here, then, we can invite our fellow worshippers from benighted portions of Europe to come and dwell with us, and participate in those benefits of which we so sumptuously partake. Such has been the land of our adoption, and such would still be its condition if we had but reflected that, in the words of the Psalmist, 'However wonderful in our sight, all this greatness emanates from God' (cf. Ps. 118: 23).

But, alas! for human frailty, the governing classes commenced to number the people, inaugurated a policy of majority and minority, dissention between the South and the North; instituted a system destructive to every well-constituted government, 'to the victor belong the spoils',[25] and the small cloud seen in the distance hovers over this once happy land, tending to destroy the best government in the world.[26] What then shall we do, to prevent the overthrow of our blessed union? We know full well that the sword is unsheathed, and that the dark stained fields give indubitable evidence of the blood that has been shed for the hallowed cause, but should we not invoke God that He may commission the destroying angel to stay his hand,[27] and that by His Omnipotent power, He may be pleased to reconstruct this land as it was!

Alas! We fear our words are too weak to convey our heart's emotions. The spirit of prophecy is held in abeyance, there exists no *Gad* to deliver the Divine message to those in authority, to tell them to choose one of these evils: famine, sword or pestilence. They have already selected the sword. Let us then, in humility, pray to the Almighty, that success may crown the efforts of those who wish to preserve the Union, and that the sword may soon be sheathed, so that like of old the people may pour forth their gratitude to Heaven, for the preser-

---

[25] The American phrase was applied to the system of patronage whereby the winner of an election was entitled to give desirable jobs to supporters of his party and campaign. The *OED* cites J. S. Johnson in a congressional debate of 1830: 'The country is treated as a conquered province, and the offices distributed among the victors, as the spoils of the war.' The actual phrase may first be attributed to New York senator William Marcy the following year, <www.britannica.com/ebi/article?tocId=9273688&query=civil%20religion>. Cf. the far stronger attack on the political system by Isaacs's New York Orthodox colleague Morris Raphall, cited above, n. 3.

[26] The allusion is to the Elijah story (1 Kgs 18: 44), although there the small cloud is an encouraging sign of the end of the drought.        [27] Echoing 2 Sam. 24: 16.

vation of these states, where the pilgrim of hope has ever found a realization of his most ardent wishes.

[2.] And now, fellow Israelites, a few words to you. Fortunately for us, no eloquence is required to attune your hearts to prayer, or to stimulate your souls to humility. Opening the chequered leaves of your history will accomplish that object.[28] Reflect how multitudinous have been the proofs of Divine interposition in our behalf—from that period when, like Noah's Dove, we could find no rest for the soles of our feet, when we were compelled to traverse the mazes of existence in search of an olive leaf, but without success. The waters of Meribah constantly overflowed the banks of happiness. There was no friendly eye to sympathize with our condition, but the whole world, a sterile waste and barren land, with scarce an ark in which we could deposit our heirloom, the law of God.[29]

Take this to heart, and then reflect on the blessings you have hitherto enjoyed in this once happy land. Can you do otherwise than in humility to pray to the Supreme to spare this republic, so that again it may be the 'home of the free'? Can you do otherwise than feel within yourselves the benefit it has conferred on you and yours? Believe us, that your hope must rest in God. Why, we would ask, shall you be estranged from religion? In waywardness, you seek instruction where it cannot be found. Disconsolate, you grieve; you fear there will be no peace, you form your own prognostications, that the country is lost. What do we know? 'The heart of kings is in the hand of God' (cf. Prov. 21: 1). 'God will fight for you, do you hold your peace' (Exod. 14: 14). All we can do is to support the government, and to hasten to those fonts of consolation which are open for us.[30]

God will protect us, and amidst the tide of ruin He is with us, in waters which know no ripple. He who did so much for our fathers will not forget His children. Let us not despond, even if some reverses occur. Let us take a retrospective glance, and ponder on nations and empires now crumbled into dust, which were wont to defy the power of Heaven and deify themselves; and then contemplate this glorious land, and we shall feel that Heaven will defend the right, for although we are now straitened, the end will be glorious. Let us do our

[28] This appeal to the vicissitudes of Jewish history parallels the introductory phrase to the first part of the body of the sermon, addressed to the audience as American citizens: 'On unclasping the volume of the past . . .'

[29] A characteristic expression of what S. W. Baron called the 'lachrymose conception' of Jewish life in exile as characterized by continuous instability and persecution.

[30] This does not seem to be a ringing affirmation of commitment to the Lincoln administration; it may be what the preacher felt needed to be said to cover himself from attack, or even from charges of sedition.

duty becoming responsible men, owing allegiance to God; let us, in humility, acknowledge our errors, and solicit forgiveness, and the Divine voice will utter the soul composing words: 'I have pardoned' (Num. 14: 20).

Since, then, we have endeavored to show that it is the pinnacle of knowledge and the climax of wisdom to hold on those principles which preserve a due equilibrium of mind, and counterpoise to all warping influences, you are most earnestly entreated 'to trust in the Lord, and to do good' (Ps. 37: 3). Do not despair, seeing that your dearest rights are jeopardized, be not discouraged because you imagine you perceive a fissure in our national structure.[31] God will be our friend if we will but serve Him in humility, stripped of that religious pride which militates against our belief. Review the wretchedness and misery, the vice and ignorance, the tyranny and oppression, which marked the course of past ages, when poor philosophy buffeted on a raging main, without mast or rudder, concertedly exploring an unknown ocean. Then let your hearts swell with gratitude for the superior light benignly conferred on us to be a lamp to our feet [32] to give knowledge to the soul, rest to the mind, comfort in distress, hope for the future, a stay and refuge in the worst troubles. You will, by contemplation, observe how in every age our God has dealt with his people that their graces might be exercised and improved, 'that it might be well with them in their latter end' (cf. Jer. 32: 39). The direst trials, like implements in the hand of the husbandman, should break up the fallow ground (in the heart) to produce that plenteous harvest, whence accrues glory to God and everlasting comfort to the soul.

There are, as we readily confess, unfathomable depths in the providence of Heaven, and heights of wisdom inscrutable to moral gaze. These are themes we cannot define; but is it, we would ask, because every thing cannot be seen or known, that all must be doubted? No, my hearers, we humbly submit we have shown quite sufficient for every situation, to cause you to pour forth your soul in prayer, and in humility beseech Him to spare our land, so that it may again carry out its destined purpose to spread forth its wings and receive within its heart the wayfaring mariner, tossed about the wide world in search of a haven. May our 'United States' still be enabled to put forth its beacon light, guiding the poor and the friendless, the unfortunate and the refugee to its once happy shores.[33]

---

[31] This is the clearest apparent reference to the debates of the day concerning the loss of rights understood to be guaranteed by the Constitution.    [32] Echoing Ps. 119: 105.

[33] A strong expression of the vision of America as haven, later expressed in Emma Lazarus's poem 'The New Colossus', though it goes back at least to Benjamin Franklin's 1777 letter to his nephew from Paris speaking of his hope to see the United Colonies 'the Asylum of all the Oppress'd'.

[PERORATION]

In conclusion, let the dread ordeal through which we are passing leave its due impression. Let it teach us not to trust to material power. Look at our galaxy of stars, how dim they have become from the scenes of carnage and bloodshed which are depopulating our finest cities;[34] and God only knows when this cruel war will cease! Let the lessons be instilled in our hearts, that we may devote more time to the contemplations of eternity than to the evanescent present. Let us, in humility, implore our God to have mercy upon this country, so that once again united, we may avoid those errors which have nearly destroyed our fondest hopes, injured the bright prospects looming up in the future. Oh may we all be duly impressed by the sad picture we behold, and entreat our Heavenly Father to restore it to its wonted splendor, and let us say, Amen.

[34] This reference to the dimming of the stars may refer figuratively to the lustre of great Americans or to the stars on the American flag (this latter suggestion made to me by Jonathan Sarna).

# CHAPTER EIGHT

## DAVID EINHORN
# TWO CIVIL WAR SERMONS

D AVID EINHORN, one of the most influential spokesmen in American
Reform Judaism during the third quarter of the nineteenth century, emigrated to the United States in 1855 in the wake of a controversial career in central
Europe.[1] Born in Dispeck, Bavaria, in 1808 or 1809, he studied philosophy at the
universities of Würzburg and Munich following his rabbinical ordination in
Fürth. He played an important role in the German rabbinical conferences of the
1840s on questions relating to reform in Judaism. While opposing some of
the more radical reforming tendencies, he championed such innovations as a
vernacular liturgy and eliminating prayers for the restoration of the Jewish state
and the Temple. The liberal positions he adopted led to friction with state
authorities, and following the Austrian government's closure of the Pest synagogue where he served, Einhorn left Europe to accept a position at the Har Sinai
Congregation of Baltimore. Soon after his arrival he launched a German-
language monthly magazine called *Sinai*, and in 1858 he published a new prayer
book, *Olat tamid*, which contained the most radical innovations of any published
in America.

In a sermon delivered on 4 January 1861, a day of national fast and humiliation proclaimed by President Buchanan, Morris J. Raphall of New York
addressed 'The Bible View of Slavery', challenging Christian preachers who
condemned slaveholding as a sin, asserting that the biblical 'doom of Ham's
descendants, the African race', remained 'in full force to this day', and insisting
that slavery is never condemned as sinful in sacred Scripture. The text of the
sermon was published in the *New York Herald*, and subsequently circulated
widely in pro-slavery circles. Einhorn wrote a fierce rebuttal in a series of arti-

---

[1] The following biographical material is based on *Jewish Encyclopedia*, v. 78–9; Korn, *American
Jewry in the Civil War*, 24–7; Meyer, *Response to Modernity*, 244–50; Michael Warner (ed.),
*American Sermons*, 911. On the question of whether Einhorn earned a German doctoral degree in
his post-rabbinical studies, see P. Cohen, 'The Problem of Paganism', 311–12.

cles published in German in *Sinai*. He excoriated Raphall's position with savage sarcasm: 'is Slavery a moral evil or not? It took Dr. Raphall, a Jewish preacher, to concoct the deplorable farce in the name of divine authority, to proclaim the justification, the moral blamelessness of servitude, and to lay down the law to the Christian preachers of opposite convictions.'[2]

When, after the outbreak of the Civil War, Baltimore became the scene of violent confrontations between Unionists and Confederate sympathizers, and Einhorn's name appeared on a list of abolitionists to be targeted by the secessionists—at least in part because of the anti-slavery views he expressed in his sermons—he was persuaded to flee northwards for his safety. The board of trustees of his congregation wrote to him on 13 May 1861, stating that at such time as conditions might make it possible for him to return, 'it would be very desirable—for your own safety, as well as out of consideration for the members of your congregation—if in the future there would be no comment in the pulpit on the excitable issues of the time'.[3] Unwilling to be bound by any such restriction, Einhorn accepted an invitation from Philadelphia's Keneseth Israel Congregation, with a promise of full freedom of the pulpit. He remained in this position until 1866, when he moved to a New York congregation.

It was undoubtedly this experience in Baltimore that prompted Emil G. Hirsch to praise his father-in-law as a champion for the integrity of the rabbi and preacher, when delivering his 1909 memorial oration on the centenary of David Einhorn's birth:

We, who believe that the pulpit, if its message is meant to be effective and vital, must be free, owe this great preacher of ours a debt of gratitude beyond compare and computation . . . Superbly did he disregard the counsel of timid souls to be cautious in the handling from the pulpit of slavery. And in asserting his right, in the name of Judaism,

---

[2] Raphall's sermon was published together with Christian sermons delivered on the same date in *Fast-Day Sermons, or The Pulpit on the State of the Country*. The relevant texts were republished in Ella Mielziner's *Moses Mielziner*, 212–50, quotation on 235 (Einhorn's German rebuttal was translated for this publication by his daughter Johanna, the widow of Kaufmann Kohler). Raphall's text and a rebuttal by Michael Heilprin are also accessible in Schappes, *A Documentary History*, 405–28, and these two with Einhorn are accessible on-line at <www.jewish-history.com/civilwar/raphall.html>. These have been widely discussed: see Korn, *American Jewry and the Civil War*, 20–6 (and p. xvi on the circumstances of Raphall's sermon and its wide publication); Fine, 'Baltimore Jews during the Civil War', 76–8; Friedenberg, *'Hear O Israel'*, 42–58; Jayme A. Sokolow, 'Revolution and Reform', 34–5.

[3] Cited in Korn, *American Jewry and the Civil War*, 26; see Einhorn's account in Schappes, *A Documentary History*, 445–9 (with a different translation of the cited passage on 448). The sermons from this early period dealing with slavery and the Negro have not been preserved, but it stands to reason that they would have contained content similar to that published by Einhorn in *Sinai*; see e.g. the powerful passages cited in Fine, 'Baltimore Jews during the Civil War', 77.

to protest against the iniquitous institution, he, courting the martyr's fate, rendered American Israel a service greater than any other, to his credit.[4]

The first sermon below was delivered on Thanksgiving Day 1863. There had been many presidential proclamations of days to be devoted to national thanksgiving, and a tradition for governors to proclaim a thanksgiving day at the end of November was already established, but this was the first occasion proclaimed by the President as an annual national holiday set for the fourth Thursday in November. The rather upbeat mood of the northern sermons for this day is dramatized by a comparison with the *Philadelphia Inquirer* editorial on the previous year's Thanksgiving:

Thank God? For what? For the rupture of our dear country? For the blood of fifty thousand patriots shed in its cause? For the wounds and pains of a hundred thousand in its hospitals? For the toils and perils of a million in arms, battling for its honor and integrity? For the outpouring of one or two millions of dollars a day of its vital means? For the desolation of unnumbered houses, the anguish of unnumbered hearts? For the orphan's cry and widow's wail? For the black pall of civil war over the whole nation? Shall we thank God for all this, and hallow the day with a religious jubilee, with social feasting and family merry-makings? Even so. Even for all this suffering, which comes, as we trust, like the mother's travail, to bring forth the joy and the worth of a new life, may we still honor the custom of Thanksgiving Day.[5]

Central to the subject of Einhorn's sermon is the theme of divine providence. This was indeed, a characteristic motif shared by preachers in the North and the South, Christians and Jews. The generalization of a leading expert on Christian preaching during the war, that 'Civil War preaching, northern and southern, was based on the fundamental religious premise generally accepted in pre-Darwinian America that God controlled the universe and every thing and action in it',[6] applies to Jews as well. There is no trace here of the questioning of God's relationship to horrific events that will begin to emerge as an explicit problem addressed by many Jewish preachers half a century later, in the First World War: 'How can God allow such things to happen? Where is God now?' The underlying assumption is that the all but unimaginably terrible

---

[4] E. G. Hirsch, in K. Kohler (ed.), *David Einhorn Memorial Volume*, 466–7. See the full discussion by Hirsch of Einhorn as preacher, beginning, 'For him the preparing and the preaching of his sermons was consecrated service at the altar of the God of truth' (ibid. 463–8), and Kaufmann Kohler's briefer characterization, ibid., pp. iv–v.    [5] *Philadelphia Inquirer*, 27 Nov. 1862, p. 4.

[6] Stewart, 'Civil War Preaching', 204; see also 184, 187, 194, 196, 202. The title of the book by David Chesebrough devoted to Civil War Christian sermons—'*God Ordained this War*'—reflects this consensus, as does the title of one of the sermons included, 'God's Providence in War' (pp. 229–37); see the editor's discussion on pp. 5–9. The idea is omnipresent. Perhaps the need to reassert it indicates a response to doubt, to questions that the preacher does not articulate, but it may also simply be a conventional topos expected by the audience.

events of the present reflected the divine plan, whether in vindication, chastisement, or punishment.

In the first paragraph following his biblical text, Einhorn asserts that despite
the continuance of the conflict, with no sign of opportunities for possible
peace, looking at the larger picture of the war's trajectory 'we are made to feel
the presence of an overruling providence, marvelous to behold'. This providential plan is exemplified in several areas of the Northern experience during the
years of the war. First is the prevailing economic prosperity, despite the fears of
an economic collapse, proving that 'God is king, and not cotton'. 'Who has so
ordained it, whilst the South was suffering during all that time of even the necessaries of life? . . . No—the hand of man could not accomplish all this! God
has directed it,[7] God who loves liberty and who hates slavery.' The same pattern is then shown in the other blessings that have sustained the North: the
abating of internal dissensions, the victories in battle, the prevailing consensus
on the evils of slavery. All of this leads to the conclusion that 'God never subjects the world to travail without a purpose', that something noble and uplift-
ing will indeed emerge from the carnage and devastation. 'The divine spirit
that rules the events of the world' has ordained a glorious future for liberty in
a new world.

The tapestry of the sermon is woven out of a group of verses from the biblical lesson of the week, 'Vayishlaḥ', describing the encounter after many years
of separation between Jacob and Esau. These two figures have deep resonance
in Jewish consciousness, as Esau had long been typologically transformed into
a figure for the enemy of Israel: Edom, Rome, Christianity.[8] The typological
use of this motif by a Northern Jewish preacher could be rather heavy-
handed. Yet Einhorn does not fall back on a simplistic 'Esau' as the evil South,
'Jacob' as the divinely chosen North. The verses are used with a subtle fluidity
that confounds the expectations of the listener.

In the introduction, the awareness of divine providence is said to lead us to
proclaim, with Jacob, even before having reached the ultimate goal, 'I am not
worthy of the least of all the mercies and of all the truth, which thou hast spared
to thy servant.' Esau is then presented as a formidable enemy and an obstacle to
progress, threatening 'to smite . . . the mother with the children', a motif that fits
well with the subsequent evocation of the fears aroused by General Lee's incursion into Pennsylvania five months earlier and the threat to the civilian population of Philadelphia. The next motif from the biblical narrative is generalized

---

[7] Cf. the continuation of the presidential proclamation: 'No human counsel hath devised nor
hath any mortal hand worked out these great things. They are the gracious gifts of the Most High
God, who, while dealing with us in anger for our sins, hath nevertheless remembered mercy.'

[8] For the earlier period, see the classic study by G. Cohen, 'Esau as Symbol in Early Medieval
Thought'.

beyond sectionalism: the God of Israel has 'proclaimed to the American people, struggling for their birthright, the promise made to Jacob, *shuv le'artsekha*, "Return to thy heritage and I will deal well with thee"'. The translation spiritualizes the geographical destination of Jacob: it is a return to the American heritage of liberty that will fulfil the promise of a flourishing future.

The danger of 'intestine contention' within the North evokes another phrase from the scriptural passage: politicians have 'with their factious cries and rallying words . . . divided the North "into two camps"'—not as a tactic for the pursuit of safety, as in the source, but as an expression of weakness and peril. Then the motif of smiting the mother with the children recurs, in the fiercest denunciation of the sermon: 'Like fiends from the lowest pools of hell they rushed through the streets, plundering and murdering, and in their Satanic phrenzy sparing neither age nor sex, *smiting the mother with the children*, whose only crime was their dark complexion.' This is no longer a feared future, but a reality of the recent past, and the smiters are not the rebels from the South but an 'infuriated mob' in a 'neighbouring city'—alluding to the riots of the previous July in New York City. Esau is not only across the border; he can appear, without warning, less than 100 miles away.

We have seen the theme of peace appear in sermons by Maximilian Michelbacher of Richmond and Sabato Morais of Philadelphia from the spring of this same year—both preachers repudiating ostensible offers of peace based on compromise and perceived dishonour. Einhorn is not quite as vigorous in his repudiation of such offers, but he is unambiguous in his assertion that the time for peace has not yet come. Here too he resorts to the model of Jacob:

Jacob also wished to make peace with his brother Esau, and to that end offered him droves of sheep and cattle for a present, but not his birth-right, which had caused the quarrel, for that would have relinquished the high mission to which God had appointed him and his offspring. And neither will the American people sacrifice in this struggle their birth-right, the exalted mission of proclaiming freedom to all the world, though many a precious sacrifice it has already cost to bring this war to a happy issue in the interest and for the sake of the nation's divine mission.

Generosity and charitableness are acceptable; compromise on the fundamental issue of slavery is not.

Finally, near the end of the sermon, Einhorn resorts to perhaps the best-known motif of Jacob's story: Jacob wrestling with the 'angel', interpreted by the rabbis as the 'dark spirit of Esau'. But the application has little to do with the South. The message is the conflict between the old order—in Europe, with its tottering thrones of monarchy—and the new: 'And we, the inhabitants of this new world, shall we be afraid or think it even possible that Esau in his robe of purple approaches to smite the mother, our republic, with the children?

Never!' In the final sentences, Liberty, an 'emanation' of the divine spirit, speaks in the voice of Jacob about the *translatio imperii* to the western hemisphere, and exclaims: '*With my* pilgrim *staff* have I crossed the sea to seek a place of refuge here, and *now I have become two bands*, bearing here and there the staff of rule and sway.'

Einhorn usually preached in German, and a German text of this sermon, published in pamphlet form simultaneously with the English version not long after its delivery, was later included in a collection of his sermons selected and edited by his son-in-law Kaufmann Kohler, issued soon after his death and reprinted in the memorial volume of 1911.[9] Kohler does not mention that the text of the sermon was also published in English in pamphlet form, with proceeds from sales earmarked for the Sanitary Commission.[10] The relationship between the English and the German texts is not entirely clear to me. The German text lacks the translation of the biblical verses from Genesis (32: 6–12) that appear as the 'text' at the beginning of the pamphlet, as well as most of the Hebrew of the biblical verses cited in the body of the sermon; also, it contains an interesting characterization of Abraham Lincoln near the end that is absent from the English version. The German as published could have been the original text delivered by Einhorn in German, the translation being made by someone else, although no reference to translation or translator appears in the pamphlet. It is also possible, however, that Einhorn wrote the text in German, arranged for a translation to be made, and—because of the special occasion of a national holiday—delivered the sermon in English. The two texts are generally quite close; occasional disparities between the German and the English text will be noted as they occur.

The structure of the second sermon is simple and evident. The occasion for the sermon was the sabbath before the festival of Purim, when Jewish practice requires, in addition to the standard reading from the Pentateuch, a short supplement: Deuteronomy 25: 17–19, commanding the Israelites to 'Remember what Amalek did to you on your journey, after you left Egypt' and to 'blot out the memory of Amalek from under heaven'—relevant because the villain of the Purim story, Haman, is identified as a descendant of Agag (Esther 3: 1), the king of Amalek. Einhorn chooses for his text a verse not from this Deuteronomy passage but from Exodus, where the war crime of the Amalekites is first recorded. It is one of the most powerful verses a preacher can use in a wartime context, evoking an unprovoked attack against a defenceless civilian population

[9] Singerman, *Judaica Americana*, i. 325, nos 1768–9; Einhorn, *Ausgewählte Predigten und Reden*; K. Kohler (ed.), *David Einhorn Memorial Volume*, 121–8.
[10] I used the pamphlet in the Andover Harvard Theological Library, donated to the library on 22 July 1864 by the celebrated abolitionist senator from Massachusetts; the pamphlet was identified as 'Gift of Hon. Chas. Sumner, Class of 1830'.

by the arch-enemy of the Jewish people, and a divine sanction for a war of annihilation. Any preacher using this verse will need to decide whether he will identify Amalek with the contemporary enemy. If he does, that rhetorical decision
removes the enemy from the category of ordinary human being living under a
different government and transforms him into an aggregate mythic figure as
close to the demonic as most Jewish discourse will allow. It also removes the
conflict from its political and military dimensions and transforms it into a holy
war, validated by divine command.[11]

Although the title—'War with Amalek!'—might lead the listener or reader to
expect the preacher to do just this, it is precisely this decision that Einhorn is
unwilling to take. It is not the soldiers of the Confederate army who are defined
as the contemporary incarnation of Amalek, but a more abstract principle:
'wherever, especially, rude violence with cheaply bought courage makes war upon
defenceless innocence, and wherever a majority in the service of falsehood
directs its blows with ruthless fist against the very face of a weak minority'. Thus
the contemporary war against Amalek occurs not exclusively, or even primarily,
on the battlefield; it is, rather, a war that can be waged on the home front, by
those who are not in uniform. This message is applied to three phenomena that
must be opposed in a holy war. First is the most predictable, 'enslavement of
race'—here is the abolitionist's imperative, never to compromise with the goal of
the eradication of slavery from America; and here the enemy is predominantly
in the South. The second is 'enslavement of the conscience' through religious
intolerance, expressed in the movement to declare the United States a Christian
nation and to change the preamble to the American Constitution to include a
reference to Jesus Christ as Lord, and in the emergence of what appears to be a
new form of anti-Jewish sentiment. Here the enemy is found in elements of the
Christian population in the North. The third is 'enslavement of the spirit'
through worldliness and religious indifference. Here the enemy is within the
American Jewish community—indeed, within the congregation present to hear
the preacher's words. Especially pointed is his denunciation of Jewish smugglers
who—though only a small minority of Jews and of the smugglers in general—
'bring shame and disgrace upon us and our religious faith'. This structure follows
the rhetorical model in the first chapters of Amos, in which the prophet begins
by condemning enemies across the borders, and ends with a fierce denunciation
of social and religious failings at home.

In the biographical essay written for the Einhorn memorial volume,
Kaufmann Kohler wrote:

His sermons delivered on the great national festivals and fast-days, betray an ardent
love for the land of his adoption, such as only a lofty idealist could cherish for the

---

[11] For examples of this use of the enemy as Amalek from opposing sides in the First World
War, see Herzog, 'Das Gelöbnis der Treue', 15–16, and Freehof, 'Judaism and the War'.

Republic; yet in the same measure as he strikes the highest note of jubilant joy when enlarging on the great destiny of the nation, he also holds a mirror up to the people to fill them with shame at their great backsliding and sins which threaten to lead them to woe and ruin.[12]

The following sermons exemplify this pronouncement.

## 8 A

# SERMON DELIVERED ON THANKSGIVING DAY

### 26 NOVEMBER 1863

#### CONGREGATION KENESETH ISRAEL, PHILADELPHIA

#### THE PROCEEDS ARE FOR THE SANITARY COMMISSION[13]

——

*And the Messengers returned to Jacob saying, we came to thy brother Esau, and also he cometh to meet thee and four hundred men with him. Then Jacob was greatly afraid and distressed; and he divided the people that was with him and the flocks and herds and the camels into two bands, and said, If Esau come to the one company and smite it, then the other company which is left shall escape. And Jacob said, O God of my father Abraham, and God of my father Isaac, the Lord which saidst unto me, return unto thy country and to thy kindred and I will deal well with thee. I am not worthy of the least of all the mercies and of all the truth which thou hast spared to thy servant, for with my staff I passed over the Jordan and now I am become two bands. Deliver me I pray thee from the hand of my brother, from the hand of Esau; for I fear him, lest he will come and smite me and the mother with the children. And thou saidst I will surely do thee good and make thy seed as the sand of the sea, which cannot be numbered for multitude.*

(GEN. 32: 7–13)[14]

THIS DAY has been appointed by the President of the United States as a day of Thanksgiving to be observed by the loyal portion of the land, for the manifold blessings that God has bestowed upon us during this terrible

[12] K. Kohler (ed.), *David Einhorn Memorial Volume*, 446.

[13] On the Sanitary Commission, see Sermon 6 above by Morais, n. 24.

[14] It is unclear to me which English version of the Bible Einhorn used for his citations, but it was not Leeser's translation. The German text of the sermon does not contain the verses at the beginning.

crisis of a civil war. And truly there are numerous reasons why every devout mind should join in this public acknowledgment of God's mercies. Although the sad spectacle of fratricidal strife has not yet ceased, nor the time arrived, when we may joyfully wave the olive branch of peace, yet if we duly consider all the surrounding circumstances, the dread and apprehension which filled every heart at the commencement of this horrible conflict, we are made to feel the presence of an overruling providence, marvelous to behold, and which should cause every inhabitant of the North to exclaim in the language of Jacob, קטנתי מכל החסדים ומכל האמת אשר עשית את עבדך, 'I am not worthy of the least of all the mercies and of all the truth, which thou hast showed to thy servant' (Gen. 32: 11).

When the Patriarch spoke these words he had likewise not yet reached the desired goal. At the threshold of his cherished home the picture of his brother Esau arose before his imagination, on whose account, not unlike so many of the loyal sons of our land at the present moment, he had torn himself from the parental embraces, to confront him now as a formidable enemy that desired to check the progress of his journey, 'to smite the mother with the children' (Gen. 32: 12), and everything he held of value. He nevertheless recalled to his remembrance the great things that God had done for him, and drew from this reflection renewed courage, hope and resolution.

And has not God done great things for us also? He has blessed us with a surplus where want was impending, that might have produced the most dangerous consequences. He has maintained peace and order in our midst during the most violent agitations of party strife, and finally he has granted glorious victories to our armies over a potent enemy. Have we not all yet a vivid recollection of the dread and anguish that overtook us when nearly three years ago the Rebels directed their first murderous thrust against the hearts of their brethren; when for the first time the starry banner, the emblem of a world's liberation, was desecrated?[15] Were not the most opulent troubled by the fancied sight of the ghastly spectre of universal impoverishment? Was not bankruptcy, followed by utter stagnation of the channels of trade, the order of the day; and was not nearly every one inclined to practice the most stringent economy, for nobody could tell

---

[15]  The 'desecration' of the American flag at Fort Sumter on 13 Apr. 1861 had a powerful impact in the North. Preaching on the first anniversary of the event, Henry Ward Beecher said: 'That flag had been the honored ensign of our people in their memorable struggle for independence . . . It had been honored in every land . . . Nor was there a port upon the globe where men chose or dared to insult that national emblem. That inglorious wickedness was reserved to our own people! It was by American hands that it was dishonored, slit with balls, and trailed in the dust!' ('The Success of American Democracy', 343). The desecration of the flag does not seem to be a significant motif in the initial reports of the fort's fall.

what the morrow might bring forth, or whether the usual sources of income might not dry up the next moment? Who can deny the prevalence of the delusion at that time, that the North was depending on the South for a living; that cotton, the king which had raised the slaves, and was raised by them, would at one stroke demolish those that dared to dispute his say;[16] that the effects of the war would beggar the merchant and the mechanic, involving the principal cities in one common ruin, that the grass would grow in their streets?

But in the meantime this delusion has been completely cured, for the very opposite of all this has happened—because God is king and not cotton; He makes rich and He makes poor,[17] and not human forethought and cunning. At no former period was the general prosperity among all classes of the community more marked than at present; commerce flourishes as never before; the workingman has a superabundance of employment, and an unexampled degree of luxury and display meets the eye every where. Instead of the grass, we see rows of magnificent palaces in our cities, that seem to have grown up over night. Instead of lamentations over the decay of trade, and the rush of the bustle of traffic, we hear people complain that they are nearly out of breath for the press of business. In place that the war has turned the rich man into a beggar, it has furnished beggars with untold wealth, and the apparition of general destitution has vanished, to be succeeded by the richest flow of blessings.[18]

[16] Einhorn is alluding here to a famous speech before the US Senate by James Henry Hammond on 4 Mar. 1858, in which he said, 'What would happen if no cotton was furnished for three years? I will not stop to depict what every one can imagine, but this is certain: England would topple headlong and carry the whole civilized world with her, save the South. No, you dare not make war on cotton. No power on earth dares to make war upon it. Cotton is king.' Cf. the use of this motif in a Southern sermon from 1861 in Chesebrough, *'God Ordained this War'*, 224.

[17] Echoing 1 Sam. 2: 7. The German text attributes the proclamation directly to God himself: 'Ich bin König und nicht der Baumwollpflanzer! Ich mache arm und reich . . .!' In his sermon of 26 Nov. 1863, delivered in New York, William Roberts gave this idea a more secular form: 'King Corn triumphed over King Cotton' (Roberts, 'Thanksgiving Day Sermon', 2). But Einhorn's source for this proclamation may well have been Morris Raphall, in his famous fast-day sermon of 4 Jan. 1861: 'No, my friends, "Cotton" is not King, and "Human Thought" is not King. *Hashem melech!* Hashem alone is King!' (Mielziner, *Moses Mielziner*, 213, Schappes, *A Documentary History*, 408).

[18] The theme of prosperity in the North was common in the Thanksgiving Day sermons for this day, as e.g. in that by the Revd A. Gorky (German Reformed Protestant Dutch Church): 'He had at the same time not withholden His blessings, had granted us perhaps greater prosperity than at any time before' (*New York Times*, 27 Nov. 1863, p. 3).

In his sermon on Thanksgiving Day 1861, Henry Ward Beecher spoke of the commercial crisis of 1857 as a providential warning to 'put your ship in order', and concluded that, as a result of this being heeded, 'although individual men are failing, yet never was the North so rich, and so competent to carry on this conflict as now' ('Modes and Duties of Emancipation', 340). The following Thanksgiving, he again underlined the economic prosperity (though without Einhorn's hyperbole): 'there never before came to us an autumn when so much labor was so well paid. And,

The past harvest to which the Proclamation of the President especially alludes has been most plentiful,[19] the Iron, Coal and Gold mines having yielded their rich treasures in abundance. Population has increased even whilst a terrible civil war is raging, that has already sacrificed its hundred thousands of victims, thus withdrawing an equal number of persons from their usual pursuits and daily absorbing its millions of treasure.[20]

Who has so ordained it, whilst the South was suffering during all that time of even the necessaries of life? Who has so ordained it that if the opposite had taken place, if the condition of things had been shaped differently and the hideous phantom conjured up by fear had assumed reality, our streets would have been deluged with blood, the struggle for freedom would have changed into a war of all against all, that horrid spectre which threatens to dissolve every social tie? No—the hand of man could not accomplish all this! God has directed it,[21] God who loves liberty and who hates slavery—who declared to you O Israel at your national birth, 'I am the Lord thy God, which has brought thee out of the land of Egypt, out of the house of bondage' (Exod. 20: 2), and who has also proclaimed to the American people, struggling for their birthright, the promise made to Jacob, שוב לארצך, 'Return to thy heritage and I will deal well with thee' (Gen. 32: 10).

on the whole, the poor are going into the winter on a footing much beyond the common average in the preparation made for their comfort and support' ('Our Good Progress and Prospects', 375). The same note was sounded, briefly, in 1863: 'We have had unwonted prosperity' (*New York Times*, 27 Nov. 1863, p. 2). Nevertheless, there were areas of economic depression, especially in the upper Midwest, in 1861–2, where 'war prosperity' began to raise the standard of living only in 1863: Klement, *Lincoln's Critics*, 13, 40–52. And in fast-day sermons, there was of course a tendency to emphasize the other side of prosperity: materialism and greed (see Sermon 6 above by Morais).

[19] Lincoln's proclamation of 3 October, urging the whole American people to observe 26 November as a day of thanksgiving and prayer, began with the sentence, 'The year that is drawing towards its close, has been filled with the blessings of fruitful fields and healthful skies.' Cf. Beecher's Thanksgiving sermon of 27 Nov. 1862: 'Through this year of health, God has made such harvests as seldom have waved across the earth' ('Our Good Progress and Prospects', 374); and that of 26 Nov. 1863: 'There has been a marvelous continuance of good harvests, and God, who has rained manna upon the chosen people in the wilderness, has seemed to give his command to nature that, while we pass over the desert to the promised land, we shall not fail' (*New York Times*, 27 Nov. 1863, p. 2).

[20] Here Einhorn seems to be echoing more language from the presidential proclamation: 'Needful diversions of wealth and of strength from the fields of peaceful industry to the national defence, have not arrested the plough, the shuttle or the ship; the axe has enlarged the borders of our settlements, and the mines, as well of iron and coal as of the precious metals, have yielded even more abundantly than heretofore. Population has steadily increased, notwithstanding the waste that has been made in the camp, the siege and the battle-field; and the country, rejoicing in the consciousness of augmented strength and vigor, is permitted to expect continuance of years with large increase of freedom.'

[21] Cf. the continuation of the presidential proclamation, cited in n. 7 above.

Another imminent danger has God averted from us, the danger of intestine contention produced by the passions of party. When the South initiated the war by the dastardly act of firing on a boat engaged on the friendly errand of provisioning the gallant garrison in Sumter, a simultaneous cry of execration arose from the whole North, and all as one man seemed to stand up for the good cause. But very soon a set of politicians made their appearance on the arena with their factious cries and rallying words and divided the North 'into two camps'[22] in spite of the exhortations of patriots, that the preservation of the national existence requires the subsidence of every partisan strife, and that those who are bound to ward off fatal blows from without, commit self-destruction if they foment contention within. There were even demagogues of such detestable principles in the free states, who openly defended the Rebellion, and tried their utmost to paralyze the efforts of the government.[23] Whilst the ship of state was tossed about in a perilous sea, they tried to bind the hands and feet of the steersman and perhaps designed to throw him overboard in order to get possession of a rich prize.[24]

How readily it might proceed from words to blows if the instigations of party malice would continue unchecked, has been demonstrated by the recent occurrence in a neighbouring city,[25] where in contempt of the majesty of the people an infuriated mob gained the upper hand for a few days. Like fiends from the lowest pools of hell they rushed through the streets, plundering and murdering, and in their Satanic phrenzy sparing neither age nor sex, 'smiting the mother with the children' (Gen. 32: 12), whose only crime was their dark complexion— exhibiting lifted on poles the inanimate bodies of their victims as trophies of

[22] Echoing Gen. 32: 8 from the text. On political divisiveness in the North, see the discussion of the 'Copperheads' in the introduction and annotation to Sermon 7 by Isaacs, and the reference by Michelbacher in Sermon 5 above, pp. 154–5.

[23] In this paragraph, Einhorn is expressing the common Republican perception (which became a dominant historiographical tradition) of the Democrat critics of Lincoln; concentrated in the upper Midwest but influential elsewhere (including in New York and Pennsylvania), these critics, commonly called 'Copperheads', were accused by their contemporary opponents of having sympathy for the rebel South, supporting slavery and anti-negro policies, being members of subversive secret organizations, and participating in dangerous anti-administration conspiracies. The influence of this movement reached a high point in the first half of 1863. The legitimacy of the criticisms of Lincoln remains a matter contention among historians (for a somewhat partisan review of the controversy, see Klement, *Lincoln's Critics*, 1–23 and 64–92, with a less engaged overview on pp. xi–xxxvii). For the peak of Democratic influence in Philadelphia, see Dusinberre, *Civil War Issues in Philadelphia*, 127–60.

[24] This sentence expresses possible acceptance of the accusation of a conspiracy to overthrow the government and depose the President. For an example of an oath reputedly taken by members of the Golden Circle that 'I will not rest or sleep until Abraham, Lincoln, now president, shall be removed out of the President's chair', see Klement, *Lincoln's Critics*, 153.

[25] New York.

their unchecked license and finally completing their orgies by making a bon-fire of a Negro Orphan Asylum.[26] And all this was done as a matter of course, in the name of peace and for the sake of slavery which the 'false Prophets', both Jew and Christian had announced as a divine institution.[27]

If these deeds of horror had spread, and infected other localities, we should surely have witnessed in our country a repetition of the French reign of terror, when the angel of death, in the shape of a scaffold, fled from house to house, to slaughter the adherents of one party today, and their opponents on to-morrow.[28] But God be praised, who has not given us a prey to the ravages of mob-rule. Those spirits of evil shrunk back to their caverns—rest and quiet bless again their wonted places.

Even the recent elections, whose great importance were calculated to pro-duce the most intense excitement, have passed off without any disturbance.[29]

[26] These events occurred on 13–17 July 1863. A *New York Times* article on 16 July (p. 1) carried a subtitle, 'More Negroes Hung'. In his sermon on this same Thanksgiving Day, Einhorn's Philadelphia colleague Sabato Morais alluded to the New York riots in similar terms: 'When I reveal to mind the scenes of blood enacted in a neighboring State, the loose passions that found vent in the slaughtering of a hapless and inoffensive caste of men, the combining of all sinister devices to oppose the application of the law, I believe I utter but the truth when I say that our State is not alone the keystone of the Union but the brightest gem of its crown ... Pennsylvania will never swerve from the path of national rectitude she has voluntarily chosen' (*Jewish Messenger*, 15 Jan. 1864, p. 10); compare the lengthy report in the *Philadelphia Inquirer*, 27 Nov. 1863, p. 8). Henry Ward Beecher, preaching in New York on that day, also alluded briefly to the civil unrest: 'The riots were a lesson and taught us that all who favored Slavery carried death in their garments' (*New York Times*, 27 Nov. 1863, p. 2). For a narrative overview of the events (though not from the perspective of the black victims), see Bernstein, *The New York City Draft Riots*, 18–42, esp. 28–31.

[27] Undoubtedly referring to the widely publicized sermon 'The Bible View of Slavery' deliv-ered by Rabbi Morris J. Raphall of Congregation B'nai Jeshurun on the presidentially proclaimed fast-day of 4 Jan. 1861. Einhorn, as well as other Jewish abolitionists, wrote a strong response to this sermon. See below, n. 61. That these biblical arguments were still hotly contested in Philadelphia during the months leading up to the election of 1863 is shown by Dusinberre, *Civil War Issues in Philadelphia*, 171–2.

[28] A merging of imagery of the biblical tenth plague with the aftermath of the French Revolution. This imagery was also used by Copperhead opponents of Lincoln in a very different context. C. L. Vallandigham said in the House of Representatives (23 Feb. 1863), that those who sought to enforce the conscription bill would, 'like the destroying angel in Egypt, enter every house for the first-born sons of the people', and that, with the suspension of *habeas corpus*, 'the guillotine follows next'; in his New York speech a few days later he claimed that the 'men who are in power at Washington . . . [are] threatening to reinaugurate a reign of terror' (*Speeches, Arguments, Addresses*, 461, 477, 479).

[29] While these were not national elections, much was at stake: the Democrats believed that if they could take control of legislatures in Ohio and Pennsylvania and elect Democratic governors in those states, they could make it extremely difficult for Lincoln to prosecute the war and hon-our his Emancipation Proclamation. Lincoln succeeded in forging an alliance between pro-Union Democrats and Republicans in a National Union Party (a strategy that angered some Republicans on the left). Partly because of the improved military situation, the Democrats running for gover-nor on a 'peace through compromise' platform in Ohio and Pennsylvania (in some cases, a

The verdict of the majority has been respected, as it ought to be in a popular form of government. The nation stood up in the fullness of majesty, and said, לא אמות כי אחיה ואספר מעשי יה, 'I shall not die, but I shall live, and proclaim the works of the Lord' (Ps. 118: 17). And to me is also the promise. היטב איטיב עמך ושמתי את זרעך כחול הים אשר לא יספר מרב, 'I will surely do thee good, and make thy seed as the sands of the sea, which cannot be numbered for multitude' (Gen. 32: 13).

Our emotions of praise and thankfulness to the God of Battles[30] are further elicited by the glorious victories he has granted to us, and the reception of to-day's news of another brilliant achievement of our arms must heighten our manifestations of gratitude.[31] Many are disposed to entertain a low estimation of the advantages which our country has already gained because the desired object in view has not been fully reached. This lessening of the nation's efforts, if it be not affected, betrays a puerile impatience, or a want of discernment which ignores the difficulties that prolong the struggle. The fact is overlooked, although it becomes daily more apparent, that the rebellion had been in secret preparation for a number of years. The Southern aristocracy, conjointly with their Northern allies, had long ago formed a *Golden Circle*, in which they forged, under cover of the night, the iron chains for the perpetuation and extension of slavery.[32] It is forgotten that the present administration found the

platform of 'No Abolitionism, No Emancipation, No Negro Equality'), were defeated. See Dusinberre, *Civil War Issues in Philadelphia*, 171–2: Klement, *Lincoln's Critics*, 13; McPherson, *Ordeal by Fire*, 390–1.

[30] I have not found a Jewish source for this phrase (which does not appear in the German text). It is not used as an English rendering of the biblical *adonai tsevaot* (usually, 'Lord of hosts'; literally, 'Lord of armies'). Some Jewish writers do, however, use the phrase as if it were traditional: e.g. Sabato Morais on the fast-day of 26 Sept. 1861: 'The God of battles will lead to victory', *Jewish Messenger*, 4 Oct. 1861, p. 53; M. J. Michelbacher, 'O Lord of Battles', cited in Korn, *American Jewry and the Civil War*, 105. Could it have been taken from Shakespeare's *Henry V*, IV. i ('O God of battles, steal my soldiers' hearts')? The phrase was also used by Christian preachers (see e.g. Chesebrough, *'God Ordained this War'*, 230).

[31] A dispatch to the Associate Press from Chattanooga, dated Wednesday, 25 Nov., and featured in newspapers the following day (Thanksgiving), describes a major victory of Union forces under the command of General Grant on Tuesday, taking control of Lookout Mountain and capturing thousands of Confederate prisoners along with forty pieces of artillery: *New York Times*, 26 Nov. 1863, p. 1.

[32] The 'Knights of the Golden Circle' were understood in pro-Union circles to be a secret society committed to the fostering of slavery in the South and beyond and plotting revolt against the Lincoln administration. Some historians have maintained that the 'Golden Circle' in the North was largely a 'figment of Republican imagination . . . a bogeyman devised for political gain' (Klement, *Lincoln's Critics*, 18). Einhorn's language here is largely metaphorical regarding the actual policy of the secret alliance. But the widespread consciousness that the secession was the result of a long-standing conspiracy was invoked by Edward Everett in his Gettysburg Address,

treasury and the arsenals emptied of their contents by the same thievish hands which previously helped to guide the helm of state, and which afterwards were lifted with deadly aim against the Union.[33] It is further to be remembered that no former rebellion commanded such a vast extent of territory for its theatre of operations. European monarchs and their abettors offered every facility for the disruption of this republic, and longed with an anxiety engendered by the most intense hatred for the hour when the proud eagle that spread its wings across the ocean should sink exhausted at their feet and reach them the festive bowl filled with its own heart's blood.

Were not grand and extraordinary results attained under all these untoward circumstances? Was it an easy matter to replenish empty coffers and depleted arsenals—to re-capture and to re-occupy numerous fortifications—to block- ade harbours—to penetrate the very centre of the rebellious states—to prevent foreign interference—to defeat repeated attempts of transferring the battle field to Northern soil—and to organize an army and navy under the most adverse circumstances, but which are of such power and magnitude that tyrants pause and tremble at their sight?

Have not we, the people of Pennsylvania, especial cause to be thankful to the Almighty for the signal favors he has shown us a few months ago,[34] when, if the enemy had succeeded of overrunning our State with war, this 'land flowing with milk and honey'[35] would have become a prey to devastation—the Union deprived of its most ample resources—the main artery of its support cut—this beautiful city plundered and levied upon, where the eagle, the ensign of the Republic, first fledged its wings, was in danger of being encircled by a venomous reptile, where the sages of the revolution first gave utterance to the words that

in which he referred to 'this stupendous rebellion, planned, as its originators boast, more than thirty years, ago, matured and prepared for during an entire generation' (*Address of the Hon. Edward Everett*, 36). See also Ayer, *The Great Northwestern Conspiracy*, beginning of ch. 3: 'Upon discovery by Southern leaders that their cause must fail unless "fire in the rear" was at once insti- gated in the North, the Order of the Knights of the Golden Circle, an old Southern institution, was infused with life, and began its pilgrimage Northward.'

[33] On the seizure by Confederate forces of Union forts and arsenals before the actual outbreak of war and even before the inauguration of President Lincoln, see Nevins, *The War for the Union*, i. 18. A year before this sermon, newspapers reported an elaborate 'Conspiracy to Defraud the Government', although this pertained to embezzlement in the New York Custom House; accord- ing to the report, the 'system of trickery and cheating has been carried on for several years' (*Philadelphia Inquirer*, 15 Nov. 1862, p. 1, based on *New York Evening Post*, 14 Nov.).

[34] The reference, of course, is to the victory at Gettysburg in the battle of 1–3 July 1863, with specu- lation about the consequences of a defeat on that battlefield, less than 150 miles from Philadelphia.

[35] The well-known biblical phrase (Exod. 3: 8) applied not to the Land of Israel but to Pennsylvania.

declared a world's liberation. Washington, the Jerusalem of America, would then have fallen, its sanctuary desecrated by an idol,[36] and its lamp of freedom, the delight of nations, extinguished.[37]

And is it of smaller importance that the sentiments of the American people have within the last few years experienced a great change? Is it less a glorious victory because achieved without bloodshed? Exists there in the wide domain of the United States an intelligent patriot who has not arrived at the irresistible conviction that slavery has been the primary cause of the nation's precarious condition, and that only in the ruins of this institution, the Republic will be enabled to rise to unprecedented splendor and excellence? Has not this remarkable, sudden change of opinion already produced the effect that most of the Border States are now engaged in devising means how to shake off this institution, which like a viper fastens on the heels of liberty?[38] Who is now shocked at the sight of a negro regiment?[39] And who ought to rejoice more at this state of things than we, the

[36] Metaphorically invoking the memory of the Jerusalem Temple desecrated by an idol during the Maccabean period.

[37] This motif, on a broader geographical canvas, was used by Edward Everett in his *Address . . . at the Consecration of the National Cemetery at Gettysburg* on 19 Nov., the week before Thanksgiving Day: 'What, in that sad event [i.e. defeat of the Union Army], would not have been the fate of the Monumental City [Baltimore], of Harrisburg, of Philadelphia, of Washington, the Capital of the Union, each and every one of which would have lain at the mercy of the enemy . . .?' (pp. 33–4). On the deep concern about the possible Confederate conquest of Philadelphia as Lee's army moved into Pennsylvania, see Calderhead, 'Philadelphia in Crisis'; Gallman, *Mastering Wartime*; Seitter, 'Union City' (including the sombre mood in the celebration of the Fourth of July, until the news of the victory was published in special editions during the afternoon: p. 13). That sombre mood is reflected in Sabato Morais's 'Independence Day Sermon' delivered on that day (see Preface).

[38] On the fast-day of 30 Apr. 1863 a Boston minister highlighted the dramatic change in policies of the border states during the previous two years. At the beginning of the war, not one 'would send a man to cover Washington', and the Union's best hope was for their neutrality; now Tennessee, Kentucky, Missouri, Maryland, West Virginia, are all, practically speaking, in the Union camp (Weiss, 'Northern Strength and Weakness', 5, 8, 10).

[39] For the changing attitudes towards black soldiers in Philadelphia beginning in the summer of 1863, with black recruits marching through the streets of Philadelphia at the end of June as part of the muster to challenge the invasion of Lee's army, generating sentiments of relief and respect, see Dusinberre, *Civil War Issues in Philadelphia*, 161–70. When Governor John Andrews of Massachusetts received authorization from the federal government in Jan. 1863, to raise a regiment of black soldiers, many in the North were highly critical of the policy. The ill-fated attack on Fort Wagner at Charleston, South Carolina, in July 1863 established the reputation of the 54th Massachusetts Regiment for loyalty and bravery, with the following statement from the commanding General Strong reported on the first page of the *New York Times* on 31 July 1863: 'The Fifty-fourth did well and nobly; only the fall of Col. Shaw prevented them from entering the fort. They moved up as gallantly as any troops could and with their enthusiasm they deserved a better fate.' In his sermon on the same Thanksgiving Day, Henry Ward Beecher discussed the phenomenon at length, beginning, 'The black soldiers that have been regimented and taken to the field, by their courage, by their docility and good conduct under the most fiery trials, have shown that they were men' (*New York Times*, 27 Nov. 1863, p. 2).

descendants of Abraham, of whom forty thousand were carried away into slavery by Titus; who during the dark ages were bartered like chattels, and whom the German emperors used to designate their body-servants?[40]

There are some people who cannot be moved if even the heavens fall, that cannot be made to yield any of their inveterate notions. Persons of this stamp may yet dream of the possibility of a rotten peace, which can only perpetuate the bloody conflict. But God never subjects the world to travail without a purpose. In sorrow and in anguish she brings forth[41] new and shining lights of truth, new and nobler sentiments; washes and cleanses them of old decaying prejudices, wipes away the flood of tears, and dries up the streams of blood that often took their rise in ancient days in order that the earth may be renovated and made joyful. Peace! And who would not desire peace? But we ask for a real, permanent peace, a peace of God in truth and in justice.[42]

Jacob also wished to make peace with his brother Esau, and to that end offered him droves of sheep and cattle for a present, but not his birth-right, which had caused the quarrel,[43] for that would have relinquished the high mission to which God had appointed him and his offspring. And neither will the American people sacrifice in this struggle their birth-right, the exalted mission of proclaiming freedom to all the world, though many a precious sacrifice it has already cost to bring this war to a happy issue in the interest and for the sake of the nation's divine mission.

[40] Josephus states that 97,000 prisoners were taken, but that the price dropped so low that Titus *released* 40,000. Jews were *not* legally chattels (in the German text: *Waare*) under medieval Jewish Christianity or Islam. The German text uses the technical term for the status of Jews according to the German emperors, *Kammerknechte*, for which 'body-servants' is a strange translation, as it renders the Latin *servi camerae*, 'servants of the [imperial] chamber', a status which promised them protection by the highest political authority. Arthur Kiron notes Einhorn's failure to cite the archetypal instance of Israelite enslavement by the Egyptians in this context, explaining that 'For Einhorn, the rationalist, the historicity of the miraculous Exodus model was doubtful even though he viewed its spiritual message as eternal' ('Golden Ages, Promised Lands', 222). Yet Einhorn cites instances of Jewish enslavement, not liberation, as the basis for empathy with the contemporary slaves, so that the miracle at the Red Sea is not directly relevant, and the failure to cite the enslavement in Egypt remains puzzling.

[41] That the 'she' refers back to 'the world' is clear from the German version: 'aber Gott lässt die Welt niemals umsonst kreisen; sie gebärt dann immer unter Wehen und Schmerzen'. This apparently unidiomatic use of female language for 'the world' indicates that the English text was translated from the German. The birth metaphor resonates with the image of the 'birth pangs of the messiah'.

[42] The 'peace' parties were the enemy for the abolitionists, fierce critics of Lincoln's policy. Cf. Sermon 6 by Morais, preaching seven months previously. Supporters of the administration had to assert that they too of course wanted peace, but not at present, and not under conditions of compromise over slavery. For a similar dynamic of attack against those pushing for peace too early as compromising with evil, see Sermon 21 below by Leo Franklin, delivered in Oct. 1918.

[43] Comparing Gen. 32: 14–22 with Gen. 25: 27–34.

A gloomy and anxious night is impending over the nation. Like the one in which Jacob wrestled with the angel, when he contended, as explained by the Midrash, with the שר של עשו dark spirit of Esau. But on the night follows a glorious morning, the spirit of darkness bows himself before the spirit of light, and the vanquished brother, invoking a blessing, lays his hand upon the head of the victor, and says, 'Thou hast prevailed' (Gen. 32: 29).[44] It requires no gift of prophecy to predict a bright future for this country. Look at the old world. Do you not observe how the ancient throne of monarchs totters, how the nations rise against centuries of oppression? Behold the gleaming countenance of young awakened liberty, at whose refulgence the trembling potentates cover themselves again with their purple and lawn,[45] and herd together to take counsel of each other and to dazzle the multitude by their false glare, but at which the nations mock and cry out, 'Not your paint and tinsel we have come to see, but the glorious dawn of liberty, whose lovely rays come dancing toward us from the new world.'[46] And we, the inhabitants of this new world, shall we be afraid or think it even possible, that Esau in his robe of purple approaches to 'smite the mother'—our republic—'with the children'?[47] Never! The divine spirit that rules the events of the world has ordered it otherwise. Liberty, an emanation of this spirit, is designed to be purged and purified of the dark spot that still mars her heavenly countenance, that her light may shine brighter and fuller, and gladden the whole earth with her lustre. A brilliant throne shall be erected for her in the new and in the old world, that when the storms and violent commotions shall have ceased, she may exclaim, 'With my pilgrim staff have I crossed the sea to seek a place of refuge here, and "now I have become two bands", bearing here and there the staff of rule and sway.'[48]

## PRAYER

Bless, O Lord, our country, protect and guard it against enemies from within and without, and grant that it may emerge from this bloody conflict regenerated

---

[44] The German text contains the full verse: 'Du hast mit dem Schicksale und mit Menschen gerungen und bist ihnen beigekommen.'

[45] Lawn was a kind of elegant, fine linen worn by the wealthy. The German text says simply 'ihren Purpur'.

[46] In the German edition, an untranslatable pun: 'Nicht euer Roth ist es, was wir wollen, sondern das Morgenroth der Freiheit.' 'Paint and tinsel' was a popular nineteenth-century idiom for gaudy and pompous external decoration. For Einhorn's conception of the unique providential-historical role of America as destined to proclaim liberty to the entire world, see Greenberg, 'The Significance of America', esp. 181–4.          [47] Again echoing, for the third time, Gen. 32: 12.

[48] Merging Gen. 32: 11 with Gen. 49: 10, but speaking of liberty's future rule and sway both in the New World, to which she had emigrated in search of refuge, and in the Old, as a consequence of her flourishing abroad.

and purified. Invest our people with strength and fortitude, and open Thou the eyes of its wayward children, who have banished themselves from a flourishing Eden, that they may return. Grant us soon the longed for peace, a peace worthy of the precious blood that has already flown, worthy of the broken hearts of thousands of fathers and mothers, worthy of the hot tears shed by many a widow and orphan. Pour Thou, O Lord, a healing balm into the deep wounds of the bereaved families of our heroes slain in battle, and comfort them with the consoling thought that the heavy sacrifices they have offered on the altar of their country are also offered on the common altar of all mankind.

Bless the President and his counsellors. Endow them with strength and with wisdom that they may accomplish the great work Thou hast given them to do.[49]

Bless Israel, imbue it with a spirit of devotion and thankfulness towards this land, the first that broke the chains its children wore for centuries, where they can say, 'With my staff I have passed over the sea, and now I have become two bands' (Gen. 32: 11). Bless this congregation, bless all mankind, with the three-fold benediction: 'The Lord bless thee,' etc. etc. (Num. 6: 24–6).

# 8 B

# WAR WITH AMALEK!

## SABBATH P[ARASHAT] ZACHOR, 5624
## (19 MARCH 1864)

### TEMPLE OF THE CONGREGATION KENESETH ISRAEL,
### PHILADELPHIA[50]

———

*God's is the war with Amalek from generation to generation!*
(EXOD. 17: 16)

AMALEK is represented in the Bible as the arch foe of Israel, for he inflicted upon them the most unheard of cruelties without having been in the least offended by the party attacked; he assaulted the champions of God when

[49] The English text omits the second half of this sentence about Lincoln: 'damit ihn die amerikanische Nation noch in der späteren Zeit mit Jubel nenne: Abraham, den Vater ihrer Völkerheere!'.

[50] The sermon was also published in a German pamphlet, listed in the bibliography of B. Cohen, 'Early German Preaching in America', 128, as 'Predigt, am 19ten März 1864, als am Sabbath P. Sachor, im Tempel der Knesseth Israel Gemeinde dahier gehalten'; several copies are in the Klau Library of the Hebrew Union College in Cincinnati.

they were in a defenceless condition, in a state of utter exhaustion. To carry on a war against such a relentless foe is an act of self-defence, not of vengeance. Hence the war-cry: 'War for God with Amalek from generation to generation!' (Exod. 17: 5). It was a war for the existence of God's people, and hence a war for God Himself. In consequence of this arch-enmity against God and His people, Amalek has assumed the type of the evil principle among Israel. It is Amalek's seed, wherever the evil and wicked rule; wherever, especially, rude violence with cheaply bought courage makes war upon defenceless innocence, and wherever a majority in the service of falsehood directs its blows with ruthless fist against the very face of a weak minority. And thus even today the war cry is heard: 'God's is the war with Amalek from generation to generation!' Let us then consider how this war should be carried on in our own country and under existing circumstances.

## [1]

First,—the necessity is presented to us of a war against the *Enslavement of Race*, which has brought the Republic to the verge of destruction, against an Amalek-seed which is turned into a blood-drenched dragon-seed. Or is it anything else but a deed of Amalek, rebellion against God, to enslave beings created in His image, and to degrade them to a state of beasts having no will of their own? Is it anything else but an act of ruthless and wicked violence, to reduce defenceless human beings to a condition of merchandise, and relentlessly to tear them away from the hearts of husbands, wives, parents, and children? We are told, that this crime rests upon a historical right![51] But, pray, can ancient custom indeed convert an atrocious wrong into right? Does a disease, perchance, cease to be an evil on account of its long duration? Is not the assertion that whatever our ancestors regarded as good, true and admissible, must be so also for us, however much reason and conscience may militate against it—is not that assertion an insult to all mental and moral progress of humanity?[52] If such principles were true, could it ever have been possible to

[51] The argument asserts a historical right, inherent in a widely accepted institution of long standing, as contrasted with a natural right, or a divine right rooted in the Bible, such as the preacher will go on to discuss. An interesting example of an appeal to history appears in a sermon by Stephen Elliott of Savannah on 21 Aug. 1863: the slaves were brought to the South by merchants from the north, 'imposed upon us just so long as it was profitable for those hypocrites to bring them here. And now when they have become interwoven with our whole social life, forming a part of our representation, of our prosperity, of our habits, of our manners, of our affections, all these ties are to be rudely broken asunder' (Chesebrough, *'God Ordained this War'*, 251–2).

[52] The appeal to 'human progress' was an important component of abolitionist argument, countering the conservative claims of a long-standing, entrenched institution. See Ericson, *The Debate over Slavery*, 29–30 and *passim*.

cease burning heretics and witches, aye! even to sacrifice the blood of one's own children? Does not the very establishment of our Republic rest upon the most emphatic protest against so-called Historic Right?[53] Was not the enslavement of Israel in Egypt equally a historic right for Pharaoh and his mercenaries, and did God's judgment not burst upon Israel's oppressors just at the time when this reputed right had been transmitted through centuries? No! justice and truth may be perverted for a long space of time, but not forever. It is positive powers which sooner or later must triumph over ancient prejudices, over usurped titles and privileges, over hallowed atrocities. History is God's tribunal for the nations, and teaches us—often in the most awful manner—the ultimate fate of such usurped rights, a fate which Holy Writ proclaims even to infant mankind in the words: 'God visiteth the transgressions of the fathers upon the children unto the third and fourth generation' (Exod. 20: 5), meaning, as our Rabbins add by way of illustration, אוחזין במעשי אבותיהם, when the children cling to the fatal inheritance.[54]

But it is still further asserted: slavery is an institution sanctioned by the Bible, hence war against it is a war against, and not for, God!

It has ever been a strategy of the advocate of a bad cause to take refuge from the spirit of the Bible to its letter,[55] as criminals among the ancient heathen nations would seek protection near the altars of their gods. Can *that* Book hallow the enslavement of any race, which sets out with the principles, that Adam was created in the image of God (Gen. 1: 27), and that all men have descended from *one* human pair? Can *that* Book mean to raise the whip and forge chains, which proclaims, with flaming words, in the name of God: 'break the bonds of oppression, let the oppressed go free, and tear every yoke!' (Isa. 58: 6). Can *that* Book justify the violent separation of a child from its human mother, which, when speaking of birds' nests, with admirable humanity commands charitable regard for the feelings even of an animal mother (Deut. 22: 6–7)? It is true, the

[53] Note the appeal to the precedent in American collective memory as well as the biblical model that follows. Of course, Southern preachers used the American Revolution as model and precedent to justify their own secession; see Chesebrough, 'God Ordained this War', 218.

[54] Literally, cling to the deeds of the ancestors; see Rashi on Exod. 20: 5, based on the addition of this phrase in the Targum, the ancient Aramaic translation of the Pentateuch. Einhorn uses this principle as the climax of his argument against the claim of right by tradition: simply continuing to do what one's ancestors have done is no defence against divine punishment.

[55] For the use of the letter vs spirit contrast by Christians opposed to slavery, see Noll, 'The Bible and Slavery', 44–6, 51. This argument created more of a problem for the Christians, who were theologically committed to biblical authority based on a 'commonsense literalism' as the supreme guide to life, while Einhorn was not.

institution of slavery was introduced, as legally existing, into the Mosaic Code; but only for this reason, because the deeply rooted evil could not be at once eradicated, and only with the intent to surround the detestable institution with ordinances mitigating the evil; as for instance, the provision according to which a slave should be free when his master had smitten out his tooth; and another, prohibiting the delivery of a fugitive slave to his master.[56]

If it should be asserted that the Bible approves and sanctions everything it allows and tolerates, we would be compelled to the further assertion, that it approves, nay, hallows also polygamy, blood revenge, and even royalty, which it emphatically repudiates; and thus irreconcilable contradictions would arise between its principles and practical provisions.[57] There is an ancient maxim in Judaism: לא נתנה תורה למלאכי השרת, 'The law was not given for Angels;'[58] the law of God was intended for human beings, and is, therefore, a law of education, affording to the human mind the most powerful impulse for development, and, in this spirit, expanding itself more widely and beautifully from its very innermost nature. It is only the slaves of the letter that deny this capability of development—it is only they that convert the letter of the Bible into a slave-whip.[59]

And what shall we say of that perversion which represents negro-slavery as sanctioned by the curse of Noah against a son of Ham?[60] That the negroes are

---

[56] Exod. 21: 26–7; Deut. 23: 16–17. In this passage, Einhorn applies Maimonides' analysis of the purpose of the sacrificial cult (*Guide of the Perplexed*, iii. 32) to the institution of slavery: in both cases, the laws regulating the institution are a concession to human nature, recognizing the impossibility of suddenly abandoning deeply rooted practices (sacrifices, slavery), but not implying that the institutions are desirable.

[57] Einhorn used the argument about polygamy and blood-revenge in his original rebuttal of Raphall (Mielziner, *Moses Mielziner*, 242).					[58] BT *Ber.* 25b and parallels.

[59] This sentence contains some rather elegant rhetorical wordplay. In branding his opponents 'slaves of the letter' (cf. n. 55 above), Einhorn employs a traditional Christian characterization of Jews to suggest that those who would justify contemporary slavery by recourse to the Bible are themselves slaves, but then he immediately transforms its meaning once again to make them taskmasters, perhaps playing on Paul's phrase in 2 Cor. 3: 6, 'the letter kills'. In addition, the original German text of this phrase, 'sie sind es, welche den biblischen Buchstaben in eine Sclavenknute vermandeln', plays on *Buchstabe* ('letter') and *Stab* ('rod' used for beating, as in the Luther translation of Exod. 21: 20: 'Wer seinen Knecht . . . schlägt mit einem Stabe', transformed into a *Knute*, 'whip'). See Einhorn, 'Predigt, am 19ten März, 1864', 6.

[60] See Gen. 9: 22–5. This was discussed at some length by Raphall in his Jan. 1861 fast-day sermon, 'The Bible View of Slavery' (he refers to it as a prophecy rather than as a curse; Einhorn's phrase 'or even a prophecy' at the end of the first sentence of the following paragraph undoubtedly alludes to this). The curse of Ham's son Canaan (often invoked erroneously as the 'curse on Ham') was a staple of biblical defences of black slavery; see Chesebrough, '*God Ordained this War*', 147, 199, 204.

descendants of Ham is purely a fiction;[61] and, besides, that curse is limited only upon Canaan, the progenitor of the Canaanites and Phenicians.

And even aside from all this—how can any command, or even only a moral justification be derived from a curse or even a prophecy? Was the enslavement of Israel in Egypt less criminal, because God in a vision revealed to Abraham this bitter lot of his children? and did not God at the same time when He made this revelation, proclaim also the heavy punishment which was to be inflicted upon their oppressors?[62] No! God commands no war against the black color, but against the dark deeds of Amalek.

## [2]

But, alas! we have, in our own days, to struggle against Amalek also in another respect, namely: against the attempt at the *Enslavement of the Conscience*, against religious hatred and religious violence. Yes, my friends! however startling it may appear in this Republic, it is nevertheless true: a number of ministers of a Christian sect—the majority of Christian Ministers in this country no doubt condemn such attempt as much as we do—design nothing less than to convert our Constitution, the palladium of liberty of conscience, into a prison-fortress of religious tyranny. They desire, as they tell us, to improve the Constitution,[63] but in reality to destroy its very inmost spirit, by an amendment recognizing the American nation as a Christian nation, the founder of the Christian Religion as the ruler of all, and his will as the highest law of the land; and that this principle should be the test for oaths of office and in all other matters![64] Would not the

---

[61] In his reply to Raphall's sermon, Einhorn challenged the assumption that black Africans were the descendants of Ham, citing 'Bunsen in his famous work on the Bible in connection with this passage' (<www.jewish-history.com/civilwar/einhorn.html>). (The reference is apparently to the German scholar Christian Carl Josias Bunsen, whose four-volume work *Die Bibel, oder, die Schriften des Alten und Neuen Bundes* was published in Leipzig between 1858 and 1868). For a current discussion of the influence of the biblical passage, see Braude, 'Three Sons of Noah'; Goldenberg, *The Curse of Ham*, 168–77; Schorsch, *Jews and Blacks in the Early Modern World*, 135–65.

[62] Gen. 15: 13–14. Jewish thinkers laboured to explain how it was just for God to punish the Egyptians for fulfilling a decree that God had made; see, e.g. Nahmanides' comment on Gen. 15: 14, including his discussion of Maimonides' solution in *Mishneh torah*, 'Hilkhot teshuvah' (Laws of Repentance), 6: 5.

[63] Many Christian ministers condemned the absence of any reference to God in the American Constitution as a national sin, for which the North was being punished in the war: see e.g. the fast-day sermon (30 Apr. 1863) of J. R. W. Sloane in New York (*New York Times*, 1 May 1863, p. 2); Chesebrough, '*God Ordained this War*', 104, 121, 207–8.

[64] The text of the amended preamble, ratified by the National Reform Association, with representatives of eleven Protestant denominations from seven Northern states, at its meeting on 3 Feb. 1863, and proposed to Congress on 27 Jan. 1864, is: 'We, the people of the United States,

fathers of the Republic, if they could rise from their graves, utter a threefold woe! over such a devise; would they not call unto the originators of such a detestable scheme with indignation and in a voice of thunder: 'We have nourished and brought up children, and they have rebelled against us!'[65]? If such a device should meet with success, the result would be, that not alone we, the professors of the One in Unity, but also the thousands, aye! the hundreds of thousands who, though bearing the name of Christians, yet cannot recognize the divine authority of the founder of Christianity,[66] would become utterly disabled to take the oath on the Constitution and, consequently, to become citizens; America would become not merely a Christian State, but a real Church State, and Washington, a second Rome;—the President of the United States would be converted into a Pope, and the Congress into an Ecclesiastical Tribunal! Aye! whenever such a theory shall have once been adopted, an irrepressible conflict to the death would, sooner or later, arise even between the different Christian sects. In that case also the majority would design to enslave the minority, considering that the public offices would be regarded as clerical prebends, and the most faithful believers— and as such those stronger in number always represent themselves—would claim for themselves the fattest benefices; and this country, hitherto the pride and glory of the world, would, sooner or later, behold a civil war, the horrors of which would compare with those of the present war as raging hurricanes with the soft whisper of a rustling leaf. Then the citizens would appear at the ballot-box with a Bible in one hand and a revolver in the other, and the blood-stained victors celebrate their triumphs by the bonfires of burning churches. And yet, those men have the effrontery to demand their so-called amendment of the Constitution with

humbly acknowledging Almighty God as the source of all authority and power in civil government, the Lord Jesus Christ as the Ruler among the nations, His revealed will as the supreme law of the land, in order to constitute a Christian government, and in order to form a more perfect union, establish justice, insure domestic tranquillity, provide for the common defense, promote the general welfare, and secure the blessings of life, liberty, and the pursuit of happiness to ourselves, our posterity, and all the people, do ordain and establish this Constitution for the United States of America' (Jim Allison, 'In God We Trust'). A strong rebuttal of this movement, published by a Pittsburgh Methodist journal in May 1863, was printed by Isaac M. Wise in the *Israelite* of 5 June 1863, p. 380. For a full treatment of the NRA, see Allison, 'The NRA . . . and the Christian Amendment'; McAllister, *The National Reform Movement*, 15–16 (the movement's constitution) and 24–5 (birth of the movement and text of the proposed change to the preamble). Cf. N. Cohen, *Jews in Christian America*, 66; Frederickson, 'The Coming of the Lord', 122; Sarna and Dalin, *Religion and State*, 134–7, 168–70.

[65] Echoing Isa. 1: 2.

[66] Referring to the Unitarians, who produced some of the most impressive religious leaders in the North. Cf. Isaac Mayer Wise's alliance with Unitarians against the 'Christian Amendment' movement: Kraut, 'Judaism Triumphant', 190–1.

the view of securing peace, tranquility, justice, and the welfare of the United States! As though the present bloody conflict and the ruling corruption owed their origin to a want of Christian belief—as though the ministers of the South, in their sermons in defence of Slavery, did not refer to the authority of Christianity, just as the ministers of the North do in theirs against that institution; as though religion could at all gain in ennobling power, by presenting to those called upon to drink her heavenly dew, the fatness of the earth as an alluring bait—by degrading it to a milk-yielding cow, to a net for office-fishing; in fine, to an article of trade, in order to open wide the gate for smuggling even in the most sacred domain!

And what age is selected for such revolutionary schemes? The same age in which one state after another of Europe casts off the rusty chains of religious violence:—the very moment in which America arms herself to burst the ancient negro-fetters! While the dead rise again, the living are to be buried; the place of the so-called sons of Ham is to be assigned to the sons of Abraham, the sons of Shem, in whose tents Japhet dwells![67] Yea, it is but of recent date that the Haman cry was heard, that we had our peculiar customs, and hence, were a peculiar nation![68] It is true, we are a peculiar race, and indeed! we need not be ashamed of this peculiarity; for our race is the ancient depositary and mediator of civilization for the nations; our race has given to the world its most precious spiritual treasures; and from our race have sprung the religions of all the civilized nations of the earth. But ever since the destruction of the Temple and our dispersion all over the globe, we have not been, nor do we desire to be, a peculiar nation; we do not desire to return to Palestine, but, as proclaimed by the prophet, be among the nations as the dew from God, as the showers upon the grass, that all of them may be blessed through the descendants of Abraham with the highest salvation.[69] It is exclusively the bond of Religion that still

[67]  Echoing Gen. 9: 27.

[68]  Echoing Esther 3: 8, together with Deut. 14: 2, 26: 8, and elsewhere: *am segulah*, translated in the King James Version 'a peculiar people' ('peculiar' in the sense of 'special'). Like others of the time, Einhorn uses 'race', 'nation', and 'people' interchangeably. I am not certain to which specific event or accusation Einhorn is referring, but the Civil War has been described by a recent historian as 'the worst period of antisemitism in the United States to that date' (Dinnerstein, *Antisemitism in America*, 30; cf. also Jaher, *A Scapegoat in the New Wilderness*, 184–226, and Korn's classic, *American Jewry and the Civil War*, ch. 7 on 'American Judaeophobia'.

[69]  In this repudiation of the hope for return to the Land of Israel and the proclamation of a mission for the Jewish people in the Diaspora to bring blessing to all the nations of the earth, Einhorn shows his break from Orthodox doctrine and his association with the messianic eschatology of the Reform movement. The sentence echoes Deut. 32: 2 (in a totally new context) and Gen. 28: 14. The distinction between religion and nationality and the insistence that Jewish identity at present is exclusively a matter of the former was commonly maintained by liberal Jews as a way of asserting their absolute loyalty to the country in which they lived.

holds our members entwined and it is but natural that, in consequence, we should have also peculiar customs; but these customs have as little in common with a peculiar nationality as the common customs of the Christians of all countries. If to-day a war were to break out between America and England the American Jew would as readily fight against his English fellow believer, as in our day the Prussian Jew fights against his Danish coreligionist.[70]

You are all—thus the Haman cry further maintains—*traders*, and this fact also testifies your peculiar nationality![71] Indeed! we do not know at which to be more astonished, at the narrow-mindedness or the ignorance with which that assertion passes such a condemnatory judgment over a whole religious community. To designate a race which is the guardian of the highest idea of mankind, which has a thousand times sacrificed life and fortune for that idea, and erected spiritual monuments which the world admires and worships; to designate a race that calls heroes of the spirit its own who reach far beyond centuries and thousands of years:—contemptuously to designate that race as a nation of traders is, to use a soft expression, an unmeasured absurdity.[72] Moses, the greatest lawgiver of the world; David, the great king and bard, whose hymns even to this day resound in all Synagogues, Churches and Mosques;[73] the Prophets, whose flaming speeches even to this day bear numberless hearts and souls up to heaven; the Maccabees, the most glorious heroes of the world in the struggle for truth and liberty; the Rabbi of Nazareth, who gave the moral laws of the Jews to numberless heathens, and is worshiped by millions of non Israelites as their Savior; Jehuda Hallevi, Ibn Ezra, and Maimonides, in whom all the knowledge of their time was centred and who were regarded as ornaments of their age;

[70] Referring to the 'Danish' or 'Schleswig-Holstein' War, which began on 1 Feb. 1864 with the Austro-Prussian invasion of Schleswig; see Lindner, *Patriotismus deutscher Juden*, 307–10. It is striking that Einhorn did not refer to Union Jews fighting against their Confederate co-religionists, an example much closer to home. Cf. Sermon 5 by Michelbacher, above, n. 25.

[71] Again, this seems to refer to a specific attack in the recent past. In the background may be a notorious footnote in which Kant refers to the Jews as 'a nation of traders, most of whom—tied by an ancient superstition—seek no civil honor from the state where they live, but rather to restore their loss at the expense of those who grant them protection' (*Anthropology*, pub. 1798, cited in Rose, *German Question, Jewish Question*, 94). But Einhorn seems to be responding to something more immediate. In 1863, a Detroit newspaper referred to Jews as 'the tribe of gold speculators' (Dinnerstein, *Antisemitism in America*, 31, citing Rockaway, *The Jews of Detroit*, 26).

[72] It is the contemptuous context and the gross generalization (as in the passage by Kant cited in n. 70 above) that seems to upset Einhorn, as the phrase 'nation of traders' has frequently been used to characterized the Phoenicians, the Canadians, the British, the Dutch, and others in a complimentary manner.

[73] The inclusion of 'Mosques' does not reflect well on the preacher's knowledge of Islamic liturgy, which is entirely Qur'anic.

Baruch Spinoza, the founder of modern Philosophy, and Moses Mendelssohn, the German Socrates—are they all traders?

And are, peradventure, all the modern Jews traders? There is hardly one branch in science and art, in the cultivation of which Jews have not distinguished themselves with honor; there is hardly one University in civilized Europe, in which Jews do not labor as respected teachers; there is hardly one political office—let me refer only to England, France and Holland—which Jews have not occupied, or do still occupy. In Europe the charge is raised against us, that Jewish minds rule the press and exercise their destructive influence upon art, literature and political life;[74] and in this country we are called a nation of traders! Aye! the contemptuous charge is flung into our very faces, that even the founder of the Christian Religion, despite his omniscience, could not help receiving a Jewish thief and devil among his disciples![75] Why, should that race to which the honor is paid that it had given to the world a Divine Being, be contemptible, because it possessed also a thief and a devil? Do not many nations number among them thieves, and devils, and murderers, and yet, are not entitled to that honor? Should the Jewish race, with its great multitude of divine heroes, not be permitted to possess also moral caricatures without being visited therefore with a wholesale condemnation?

Well then, let us make war upon this Amalek; let us meet this newly-budding religious animosity with all honorable weapons at our command! Let us seek to crush, at its very birth, the many-headed serpent which designs to clutch the Eagle in its coils and to kill him in the very hour of a hot and exhausting struggle, as Amalek attacked weary and exhausted Israel after his departure from Egypt![76] Let us not be lulled into inactivity by a foolish and pernicious feeling

---

[74] Such charges began to appear in German in the middle of the nineteenth century with the increased participation of Jews in various aspects of German culture and society. Especially important is Wagner's essay 'Judaism in Music' (1850), which complains about the 'be-Jewing' or 'Jewification' (*Verjüdung*) of modern art, transforming the great achievements of German creative spirits into an 'art-bazaar': R. Wagner, *Judaism in Music and Other Essays*, 82. Also, Wilhelm Marr's first antisemitic statement, the 'Bremen Letter' published in 1862, stated, 'don't look at this question from the religious side; examine it from the aspect of cultural history, and you will discover a tribe of mongrels whose vital principle, from the time of the patriarchs who traded away their wives, to this day is: selling to the highest bidder'. Marr's treatise *Der Judenspiegel*, published in Hamburg in 1862, spoke of 'the Jewish takeover of the press in Germany'. See Zimmerman, *Wilhelm Marr*, 117, 48.

[75] Again the indication is that Einhorn is responding to a specific text. The terms apply to Judas: 'thief' in John 12: 6, 'devil' in John 6: 70. But the text apparently implies that only Judas was a Jew, whereas Jesus and the other apostles were not.

[76] The many-headed serpent is Hydra, threatening the American Eagle; Einhorn links the mythological creature back with the biblical motif.

of security! Even Moses would not suffer his hands to rest until Amalek was conquered![77]

## [3]

But in order to triumph in this struggle, we must not, above all, forget to make war upon the Amalek in our own midst, upon the *Enslavement of the Spirit*. Let us openly confess it, upon American Israel also the words of condemnation may in many regards be pronounced: 'Jeshurun waxed fat and forsook the Rock of his salvation!' (see Deut. 32: 15).[78] Crude worldliness has become so predominant among us that one must often feel tempted to ask: are these members of that race, which once sacrificed everything for its spiritual treasures? There is indeed no want of Synagogues and Congregations; but many believe to have fulfilled all their obligations towards their congregation when they have paid in cash their dues, and take no further interest in its institutions. How many among us have become utterly indifferent to Israel's sublime mission, to carry the divine truths into all parts of the earth, and to glorify the name of God in the eyes of all nations![79] How many among us, driven on by a restless lust of earthly gain, have lost all sense for man's higher destination, all desire for spiritual elevation! Even young children are often violently torn from their schools to be tied to the yoke of business life, because they cannot too soon learn to worship the almighty dollar![80] The Sabbath, which again and again quickened ancient Israel with the spirit of God, which again and again protected our forefathers against fatigue and exhaustion, and girded them with strength and courage to break through the hosts of Amalek—the Sabbath has been banished from among us, and now bestows its blessings only upon other denominations, that have inherited it from us, and justly ask us: 'Where is your God?'[81] The staff of God has fallen from our hands, and, despite all pomp and

---

[77] See Exod. 17: 11–13.

[78] This is a staple in the rhetoric of rebuke, linking material prosperity with a decline in religious devotion and moral standards. After criticizing outsiders, the preacher now moves on the criticism of his own people.

[79] A clear formulation of the universalistic doctrine of a Jewish mission in the Diaspora, associated with liberal Jewish movements in the nineteenth century. Einhorn has mentioned this theme earlier (n. 69 above), and will return to it in his peroration.

[80] I am unaware of other evidence that child labour was an issue for the Jewish community at this time. Sabato Morais condemned child labour in a Yom Kippur sermon delivered a generation later; see Corré, 'Sabato Morais and Social Justice in Philadelphia', 28.

[81] The question placed in the mouths of the gentiles echoes Ps. 42: 4, usually cited as a response to Jewish suffering, not to Jewish religious laxity in the midst of prosperity. Complaints about laxity in sabbath observance were almost a commonplace in American Jewish preaching of the mid-nineteenth century. To take just one example of many, see H. A. Henry's Shavuot 1862

glitter, we creep weary and exhausted, sighing and panting, through a vast desert affording no oasis, no refreshing well for us and our wives and children, to become a prey for Amalek.

Can it under such circumstances be wondered at, that even domestic fervor, that ancient virtue of Israel, the self-sacrificing conjugal love, the careful attention to the moral and mental culture of those dear to our hearts, the profound reverence for parents, threatens to vanish from our homes? Must not every blossom of the heart and soul droop in such a drought, under such a parching glow? Can it then be wondered at, that the fear of חלול השם, 'of the profanation of the name of God'—a fear which once served the few for a mighty bulwark against the most alluring temptations to bring dishonor upon the name of Israel—is so often crushed by the wild boar of the lust of gain? If that fear still existed among us in its ancient power, Jewish smugglers—to adduce but one illustration—would indeed! belong to the greatest curiosities among the present, sad experiences in our country.[82] I do not mean to say, that such great offences are not committed also by members of other denominations as often as, and perhaps oftener than by our own co-religionists; or that the old saying: 'Little rogues are brought to punishment whereas big ones are allowed to escape,'[83] is not exemplified also in our country; but the crime is far greater when committed by a Jew, because he must know, that the whole Jewish community is made accountable for his offence, that his act inflicts shame, disgrace and misfortune upon his fellow believers.

sermon, 'The Perpetuity of the Law', 257: 'Shall we speak of the Sabbath? Our heart sickens and faints! . . . You know that the Sabbath is the best day for business. "We cannot support our establishments if we close our stores on the Sabbath". Such is the reply to our supplications. The laws of God now-a-days have to succumb to support the luxuries of the mansion.' For the rhetorical device of identifying the religious competitor as superior to one's own community, see M. Saperstein, 'Your Voice Like a Ram's Horn', 45–54. Of course, part of the reason for its use in the present context was the legislation which prohibited labor and other inappropriate activities on Sunday.

[82] Here the preacher is conceding that the phenomenon of Jewish smugglers is not nearly as rare as it should be. This was a hot issue because of its role in the notorious General Order Number Eleven issued by Ulysses S. Grant, expelling Jews from the Department of Tennessee in Dec. 1862, which stated that 'The Jews, as a class violating every regulation of trade established by the Treasury Department . . . are hereby expelled.' A newspaper article asserted that 'the people whose ancestors smuggled for eighteen centuries smuggle yet'; a letter to a Cincinnati newspaper affirmed 'the fact that nineteen out of every twenty cases brought to light, of all this smuggling, turns out to be the work of certain *circumcised Hebrew*'. See Korn, *American Jewry and the Civil War*, 145, 193, 199. In the Southern context, the accusation was more frequently levelled at Jewish 'speculators and extortionists': see Sermon 5 by Michelbacher above.

[83] It has been described as a commonplace message of picaresque literature that great villains go unpunished for the same offences for which 'little rogues' are routinely hanged. For a British example, see the quotation by Fielding in Gatrell, *City of Laughter*, 142.

Let us then make war also upon the Amalek in our own midst! Let us meet them that bring shame and disgrace upon us and our religious faith, with the fullness of our moral indignation![84] Let us display, in this hard struggle for our national existence, sentiments of brilliant patriotism, in every respect, and let us never be found wanting whenever patriotism is appealed to for its gifts and for sacrifices. And above all, let us all rise again from the mire of worldliness unto the consciousness of our sublime world-historic mission, to glorify the One in Unity before the eyes of all the world! Then we shall be able to disperse now as in times of yore, with the war cry: ה' נסי, 'God is my banner!' (Exod. 17: 16), the enemies of our race and our God, and unweary advance towards the exalted goal, to blot out the remembrance of Amalek, the reign of falsehood and darkness, from under heaven.[85] Amen.

[84] This and the previous sentence were quoted by Korn, *American Jewry and the Civil War*, 180, in the context of his discussion of the Grant's General Order and Jewish recognition that some Jews were guilty as charged.

[85] Echoing Exod. 17: 14. In this peroration, Einhorn alludes to the earlier battles and the importance of displaying Jewish patriotism in the context of the Civil War, but gives most emphasis to the last theme: the struggle within the Jewish people to maintain the purity of its religious standards.

# CHAPTER NINE

# ISAAC MAYER WISE
# THE FALL OF THE
# SECOND FRENCH EMPIRE

## FRIDAY EVENING, 9 SEPTEMBER 1870[1]

### TEMPLE B'NAI JESHURUN, CINCINNATI

T HE CIRCUMSTANCES of this sermon were intensely dramatic. Once
again, as in the Napoleonic era, Europe had been plunged into war, with
the outbreak of hostilities between France and Prussia commencing in late July
1870. A string of German victories reached its climax, after a fierce battle, with
the fall of the French fortress of Sedan on 2 September. For France, this was
one of the most humiliating disasters in its history: the Emperor Napoleon III
surrendered to the Prussian King William I, with the loss of forty generals and
almost 100,000 French soldiers. Two days later, the Third French Republic was
declared in Paris. The German army continued its onslaught deep into French
territory.

Needless to say, the citizens of the two principal combatant nations—Jews
and non-Jews alike—perceived these events in dramatically different ways.
From France, we have reports such as the following, published in the London
*Jewish Chronicle* of 19 August 1870 (p. 10): 'a special religious service was held
on the 7th of August . . . at the Consistorial Temple, Paris, when prayers were
offered up for the French army. After an animated allocution of the Grand
Rabbi, Zadoc Kahn, a collection was made for the wounded'; and, from the
French periodical *Archives Israélites* of 1 October (p. 603): 'Sermons suffused
with a great love for our dear fatherland were delivered by the Rabbis during
the two days of Rosh Hashanah . . . [who] knew, through their animated tone,

---

[1] *The Israelite* of 16 Sept. 1870, where this sermon is published (p. 8), provides a header identifying it as having been delivered on 'Friday evening, September 10, 1870', although that day was
a Saturday. As Wise, the editor of *The Israelite*, was more likely to err on the date than on the day,
and as he introduced the late Friday evening service with a lecture into his congregation
(Philipson, *The Reform Movement in Judaism*, 373; Meyer, *Response to Modernity*, 291), I have corrected the date to 9 Sept.

how to inspire the courage of those who would take part in the defense of the capital, and to calm the fears of their families with reassuring words.' Unfortunately, texts of such French sermons from the actual period of the war do not appear to be extant.[2] What we do have is sermons of great pathos and patriotism delivered in the 'Temple of Sedan' on the anniversaries of the fateful battle, examples of memorialization at the *lieu de mémoire*.[3]

The German legacy is richer. Sermons delivered by Rabbis Salomon Ohlenburg and Moritz Rahmer (who edited a homiletical periodical) on 27 July 1870, the national day of prayer proclaimed at the beginning of the war, were published soon afterwards.[4] Most striking is a sermon for the evening of Rosh Hashanah (25 September) 1870 by Leopold Stein of Frankfurt am Main, described as 'one of the best of the contemporary preachers'.[5] Totally devoid of patriotic enthusiasm or celebration of the stunning German victories, the preacher laments the bloodbath of the battlefields and its implications for the idea of human progress:

O height of human misery: who can fathom you? And there is no end in sight that will terminate all these horrors. perhaps they will be surpassed by even greater atrocities.

Unfortunate century, which—according to the general reckoning of time that we follow in our civic relationships—has reached its seventieth year, what must you still experience in your old age? You believed yourself to be a century of Progress? Your stride forward is a murderous stride [*Dein Fortschritt ist ein Mordschritt*], with which on one day you pulverize many thousands of fine human lives into dust. You believed it to be a century of rapprochement and increasing solidarity among the nations? Your celebrated rapprochement takes place on the accursed battlefields, where the satanic forces of enmity between peoples and of artificially contrived hatred between nations derisively sever their rampantly growing blossoms. Alas! Alas! And we are human beings?! Children of God?! Images of the Most High?!\[6]

This vehement dissent from the prevailing mood within the North German Confederation may reflect lingering resentment towards the Prussian leadership

---

[2] Julien Weill, the biographer of Zadoc Kahn, wrote, 'I have in front of me many of these sermons from the *année terrible*. Perhaps a sense of shame, or modesty, prevented him from giving a place in his collections [of printed sermons] to some of these beautiful pages': Weill, *Zadoc Kahn*, 61. These manuscripts may be preserved somewhere in France. Zadoc Kahn did publish two memorial sermons delivered a year or more later for French Jewish officers killed in battle: *Sermons et allocutions*, 243–67.

[3] Dreyfuss, *Sermons de guerre*, 1–30; the first three sermons were delivered on 1 Sept. of the years 1872, 1873, and 1874.

[4] These texts are listed in the catalogue of the Leo Baeck Institute in New York; for a general survey of German Jewish preaching during and immediately after this war, see Lindner, *Patriotismus deutscher Juden*, 327–9.        [5] Philippson, *Die Rhetorik und jüdische Homiletik*, 82.

[6] Stein, 'Der Kampf des Lebens', 4. Cf. also the similar sentiments in Adolf Jellinek's Rosh Hashanah sermon for this year, '5631!: Neujahr 1870', 38–40.

following the Prussian occupation, financial punishment, and annexation of Frankfurt in the summer of 1866. One wonders to what extent these words reflected the sentiments of the congregants, and whether they could have been spoken on the same occasion at a synagogue in Berlin.

Even from the sidelines, in Britain and in the United States, the military and political upheavals aroused powerful emotions. On the day the following sermon was delivered in Cincinnati, the *Jewish Chronicle*, indulging perhaps in a modicum of hyperbole, wrote in its lead editorial:

> In all the record of humanity there is no page more varied, no page, alas! more bloody, than that whose lines are being traced day by day by the men of the present era. The great event which in the last few days has astounded Europe is the fall of the most cele-brated personage of the age—the Emperor of the French.[7]

The meaning of these events was bound to occupy the minds of religious thinkers. As we have seen above in connection with the American Civil War sermons, there was a widespread consensus among Christians and Jews alike at this period that historical and current events—staggering and unexpected as they may appear—reflect the providential control of an all-powerful sovereign ruler of the universe in accordance with the principles of divine justice. German Christian preachers were eager to claim that the stunning German victory was God's punishment for the sinful failings of French national char-acter (sensuality, hedonism, irreligiosity), and of French political philosophy (liberalism and atheistic 'licence').[8] This providential explanation of the war is a central theme of the sermon reproduced below.[9] Isaac Mayer Wise, one of the most influential American Jewish leaders of the nineteenth century, had honoured a pledge to remain silent on political and military issues during the Civil War;[10] now he strongly endorsed from his pulpit the view that the French debacle was part of God's plan.

Wise, born in Bohemia in 1819, studied in a variety of secular and Jewish contexts, although he apparently did not receive a formal degree, and even his rabbinic ordination remains a matter of dispute.[11] The knowledge he acquired of traditional Jewish texts was sufficient to enable him to serve as a schoolmas-ter, with occasional preaching responsibilities, in Radnitz, Bohemia. In 1846 he

---

[7] *Jewish Chronicle*, 9 Sept. 1870, p. 6.

[8] Hoover, *The Gospel of Nationalism*, 37–44, esp. p. 40; Piechowski, *Die Kriegspredigt von 1870/71*, 78–85; F. Stern, *Gold and Iron*, 131.

[9] As indeed it is in the sermon by Jacob Mayer of Cleveland entitled 'The Discipline of Nations under the Government of Supreme Wisdom'.

[10] Heller, *Isaac M. Wise*, 335–6, 362. In this respect he was closer to his position on the Crimean War, when he exulted in the defeat of Russia (ibid. 329).

[11] On Wise's peripatetic education, see Heller, *Isaac M. Wise*, 59–77, 81–2; Temkin, *Isaac Mayer Wise*, 18–24. On the question of his ordination, see Heller, *Isaac M. Wise*, 79, 702.

emigrated to America (he would describe himself as having been 'forced out of my native land by unjust and oppressive laws'—see below—but he was never in trouble with the Austrian authorities). Arriving in New York City, he soon moved on to serve a congregation in Albany. The liturgical reforms he introduced there led to considerable controversy, turbulence, and even violence, before a breakaway group established a new congregation with Wise as their rabbi. In 1854 he was invited to the B'nai Jeshurun Congregation in Cincinnati, which soon grew to become the second largest Jewish congregation in the United States. Not long after his arrival, he established a weekly Jewish newspaper in English called the *Israelite* (and, not much later, a second journal published in German). He energetically pursued his vision of a union for all American Jewish congregations.

In addition to the enormous energy he invested in his periodical publishing responsibilities, Wise was apparently an extremely effective preacher.[12] After his first years he generally did not use a manuscript in the pulpit, preferring the freedom and directness of a more spontaneous delivery, but the written versions prepared for publication in the *Israelite* and elsewhere reveal considerable rhetorical power that must have been even more pronounced in the pulpit at the time of delivery.[13] His pattern was to begin with a biblical text, usually not from the prescribed weekly scriptural extract but from Psalms, and to develop a theme or thesis from it. In the sermon below, the verses from Psalms introduce the theme of divine justice worked out in the events of the world, even though its operation may not always be apparent to those of weak vision. This theme is stated and explicated in the introductory section; the body of the sermon then applies the theme to the career of Napoleon III, an exercise that requires a historical review of the previous twenty years of French history. The review is not intended to be balanced or dispassionate, but rather to fit the providential pattern derived from the text. The conclusion, drawn in the paragraph beginning 'Therefore, brethren', explains with a series of balanced antitheses—'Her Emperor . . . and the world'—why world opinion has turned away from France. As we shall see, this snapshot characterization, which certainly expressed the opinion of Wise's Bavarian congregants, would be challenged in the two somewhat later sermons: Artom (Sermon 10) is essentially neutral, and Morais (Sermon 11) is deeply sympathetic towards the French.

After the vigorous condemnation of France and 'her Emperor', the preacher turns to 'our Germany'. 'Where is God's justice' in the loss of German lives required to impose a providential punishment on France? Here the preacher directs his rebuke to Germany itself as an explanation for its suffering even in

---

[12] On Wise as a preacher, see Heller, *Isaac M. Wise*, 115–16, 260, 484–5; Friedenberg, '*Hear O Israel*', 72–5.

[13] In addition to the sermon below, see the text of his 'Funeral Address' for Abraham Lincoln.

victory, reminding his listeners that the country has 'oppressed all nations around her', and 'driven away, and maltreated her best sons'. The peroration then picks up the questioning mode in an anguished outcry about the 'rivers of blood' that seem necessary to punish 'human crimes and follies'. By the time the preacher concludes, the confident assertion of providential justice applied to France has become deeply problematic; nevertheless, he sets aside uncertainty with an appeal to the traditional messianic hope, identifying this with the inevitable progress of history, in which the world 'improves with every passing decade' and will eventually, inevitably, reach the day when 'national crimes will exist no more, and the national sins be atoned'.

# SERMON

---

*Behold he who conceiveth iniquity will be pregnant with mischief and bring forth falsehood. He who hath hollowed out a pit and dug it will fall into the ditch which he hath wrought. His mischief will return upon his own head, and upon his own skull will his violence come down. I will thank the Lord according to His righteousness, and I will sing praises to the name of the Lord the Most High.*
(PS. 7: 14–17)

## [INTRODUCTION]

IN THESE WORDS, brethren, the sacred bard announces the great doctrine of divine justice; that universal, unlimited and mysterious justice, which no individual, no nation, no generation can escape; that invisible and unfailing distribution of recompense and retribution, by which the equilibrium in the human family is preserved, and its steady progress to the undisturbed enjoyment of happiness is secured. This corner-stone of our faith, brethren, is based upon the entire experience of mankind, and is the only safe foundation of human government. It is also the unfailing oracle to announce the future fate of nations and individuals. Whatever is conceived in iniquity, whatever is begotten in mischief, must result in falsehood and misery. There is no exception to this rule. Lasting success depends on justice.

The sacred bard, furthermore, announces a peculiarity in God's execution of justice, viz: that the punishment which overcomes the wicked is his own work, the result of his own schemes. He falls into the pit which he dug for others. Therefore Jethro, the father-in-law of Moses, acknowledged the divine justice revealed in the events accompanying the Exode, saying: 'Now I know that the Lord is great above all gods, for by the very thing wherein they (the Egyptians) sinned presumptuously punishment was brought upon them' (Exod. 18: 11). Our ancient sages maintained, 'By the same gauge which a man employs to mete out his doings, God uses to mete out the recompense.'[14] This is the most wonderful and most demonstrative in the great plan of Providence: that the crime and its punishment are nearly identical in their natures. Whoever digs a pit for his neighbor to fall into it will be the first to be injured therein.[15] The snare catches the wicked fowler. The stumbling-block placed in the way of the blind becomes an insurmountable obstacle to the wicked perpetrator. This is the surest and clearest demonstration of divine justice.

It is certain that every person observing clearly his or her career of life, scanning and analyzing the doings, omissions, incidents and accidents, would discover precisely the same revelation of divine justice in the individual as in the nation, as in all nations of all ages, for God is revealed in the most minute parts of His creation as distinctly as in the grand unit of the universe. Unhappily, however, [only] a few men possess the moral courage and impartiality to do justice to themselves, and none can penetrate with certainty the moral motives of his neighbor. Thus in numerous instances, we fail to discover God's justice in the fate of the individual. It is in the moral as in the physical realm. God's wisdom and power are no less clearly revealed in the most minute crystal, the flower, the drop of water, the infusorium,[16] as in the system of celestial bodies composing the universe. Our eyes are too weak to see the greatest in the smallest compass, although it is there. We must survey a large field to behold the Lord of Glory revealed in His work. Even so we must review carefully the history of nations, to discover that immutable justice which is clearly manifested in the life of every humble person.[17]

[BODY OF THE SERMON: A]

From this stand point, brethren, let us review the great events of the year 1870. The French Empire, after twenty years of its existence, was overthrown by the

---

[14] *Mekhilta*, 'Shirah' 4 on *Markevot paroh veḥeilo* (near end), providing two examples; cf. also *Numbers Rabbah* 13: 14 (Judah, Joseph, and Tamar).

[15] Slightly expanding the verse in the text (Ps. 7: 16).

[16] In the original, 'infusiorium'; a one-celled protozoan organism.

[17] The introductory section ends with the parallel between God's wisdom in the realm of nature (from the smallest individual beings to the heavenly bodies) and God's justice in human affairs (from the individual to the history of great nations).

German armies, almost as fast as a woodman fells a tree. It is scarcely two months that the warlike intentions of Napoleon upon Germany had become known, and now he is a prisoner in the hands of the King of Prussia.[18] A few months ago the empire was still covered with military glory, and Caesarism was declared to be the choice of the French people;[19] and now the Napoleon dynasty is completely overthrown, without the slightest hope of recovery, the grand army is annihilated, the republic is proclaimed, and the German armies conscious of irresistible power, stand before Paris, threatening to dismember and humble that powerful France, which but a few years ago chastized and humbled Russia and Austria.[20]

'How should one chase a thousand, and put ten thousand to flight, unless their Rock had sold them, and the Lord had delivered them up?' (Deut 32: 30). It sounds almost like a myth of old, like a fairy tale. Disunited and distracted Germany, with her dozens of princes and kings, overthrows the power of solidly united France, and does the marvelous work in one brief month.[21] The world so long used to look to France for the dawn of liberty and the progress of civilization, all at once, as by magic, turns away from France, and sympathizes with Germany. Whence these wonderful phenomena?

It is the arm of the Almighty, the outstretched arm of eternal justice, which has wrought those miraculous changes. Napoleon declared the war, began the war, and he is a prisoner.[22] Whoever shall rely upon the sword, he shall fall by

---

[18] War was declared on 19 July 1870; Napoleon surrendered at Sedan on 4 Sept., five days before the sermon was delivered.

[19] 'Caesarism' (*Césarisme, Cäsarismus, Cesarismo*) was (according to the *OED*) an English neologism of the 1850s, referring to absolutist monarchy in the style of the ancient Caesars, as currently embodied in the rule of Napoleon III.

[20] Russia with the fall of Sebastopol, the home port of the tsar's Black Sea fleet, to French and other Crimean War allied forces (France lost 100,000 men in this war) on 8 Sept. 1855, a goal that was a major preoccupation of Napoleon (see Echard, *Napoleon III and the Concert of Europe*, 45–9'; Austria with the French victory in the Franco-Austrian War of 1859, nominally on behalf of Italy, resulting in the ceding of Nice and Savoy and a return to the frontiers of 1813 in the Alps (see A. Blumberg, *A Carefully Planned Accident*).

[21] For German Christian preachers on the providential unification of the divided German states, see Hoover, *The Gospel of Nationalism*, 37–44. While Wise sees divine punishment for the arrogance of Napoleon, German preachers, as noted above, emphasized sins in the French national character (sensuality, hedonism, irreligiosity) and in French political philosophy (liberalism, atheistic 'licence'): ibid. 40. A more detailed analysis is in Piechowski, *Die Kriegspredigt von 1870/71*, e.g. pp. 78–80: 'Krieg als Offernbarung der Herrlichkeit und Gerechtigkeit Gottes'.

[22] The responsibility for the outbreak of war is, of course, more complicated than this. Technically, the war was declared by France's chief minister Émile Ollivier in the French legislature, four days after Napoleon ordered the army to call up its reserves. Some historians maintain that he was not eager for it, but was provoked by Prussian machinations and pressured by French public opinion into a conflict for which he believed French forces might not be adequately

the sword.[23] God is just. Napoleon appealed to arms, not for the benefit of humanity, not in defense of a sacred cause, also not in the interest of his people; the war was sought simply to secure the throne of France to his son, to his dynasty,[24] and behold that self same dynasty helplessly and hopelessly overthrown. God is just. Napoleon relied upon his army; his faith was not in God, it was in his artillery, and the army is slain and the artillery captured to demonstrate that God is King, and Napoleon is a weak mortal.[25]

Napoleon, contrary to the will of the Italian people, and the vast majority of all civilized men, stole an Italian province; therefore the German provinces of France are now in the hands of her enemies.[26] Napoleon, contrary to the moral sentiment of the majority of mankind, protected the temporal power of the Pope, afforded him the might to oppress his subjects,[27] to impose the canon law on society, and declare it superior to the inalienable rights of man, by the kidnapped

prepared. See Baguley, *Napoleon III and his Regime*, 374–76. Others suggest that, at least earlier in 1870, he viewed war with Prussia as a way out of domestic political embarrassments following disappointing results in a plebiscite on his 'Liberal Empire' policies: Wawro, *The Franco-Prussian War*, 28–9.

[23] Cf. Matt. 26: 52: 'Those who live by the sword shall die by the sword.'

[24] This was a contemporary view among opponents to Napoleon; the British *Spectator*, on 16 July, three days before the declaration, worried that 'Europe must pass through a year, perhaps years of misery, in order that one single man may secure the career and position of one single child' (cited in Raymond, *British Policy and Opinion*, 74; cf. Milwaukee's *Sentinel* on 26 July 26: 'Never was a war waged by a despot for more purely selfish and personal ends than this' (cited in Gazley, *American Opinion of German Unification*, 325). While placing the empire on a firm footing for his son Louis was certainly important to Napoleon (Wawro, *The Franco-Prussian War*, 28), most historians do not recognize this as a significant reason for Napoleon's support of the war.

[25] Napoleon himself may have recognized this hierarchy in an 1869 conversation with his son, in which he is reported to have said, 'You see, Louis, you think that I am the master of the world, but I am nothing but the plaything of destiny. God can strike me down or send me back into exile' (Baguley, *Napoleon III and his Regime*, 376); in the absence of reliable dating for the source of this conversation, one must suspect it to be a 'prophecy after the fact'.

[26] At the conclusion of the Franco-Austrian War, Austria ceded Lombardy to France (which transferred it to Sardinia); Napoleon III also demanded that King Victor Emmanuel II cede Nice and Savoy (which had been restored to Sardinia by the Congress of Vienna) to France in return for French aid in the war. The 'German provinces of France' now under German control are, of course, Alsace and Lorraine.

[27] In 1849, Napoleon launched an expedition to Rome to discourage Austrian advances and protect the Pope, who had fled to Naples, against the Roman republic; when the French took control, the Pope returned, maintained by some 12,000 French garrison troops (Echard, *Napoleon III and the Concert of Europe*, 152), who remained in Rome until the beginning of the Franco-Prussian War. Another military intervention followed in 1858–9; see ibid. 9–19, 141–60, 259–75. Compare the even more extreme anti-Catholic formulation in a sermon on a similar theme delivered by a Cleveland colleague and published by Wise three weeks later: 'under the guard of this [French] army, [the Pope] excommunicates nations, curses humanity, condemns civilization, persecutes liberalism outrages the Jews, and kidnaps the children' (Mayer, 'The Discipline of Nations', 9).

boy Mortara and the publication of the Syllabus;[28] to impose upon the world unreasonable and unjust dogmas, by the instrumentality of the Ecumenical Council,[29] because Napoleon trusted not in God, but next to his armies, he put his confidence in the host of the priests and the credulity of his people. Therefore in the hour of trial the Pope denounced him, the priests deserted him, and the credulity of his people could not protect him against the strong arm of justice.[30]

Napoleon sent his armies and an emperor to Mexico, to sacrifice a republic to his vain ambition, hoping that the American republic would be divided, and one-half thereof be allied to his new empire.[31] That Marshall Bazain, who slaughtered so many Mexicans, is a prisoner at Metz, and that Emperor who devised the death of the American republics, is now a harmless, outworn and broken captive,[32] while the American republics stand proudly and firmly,

[28] On the Mortara affair of 1858, in which a Jewish child in Bologna, said to have been baptized by a Catholic servant woman, was seized from his family by papal order and raised as a Catholic, see Kertzer, *The Kidnapping of Edgardo Mortara*. The 'Syllabus of Errors', was part of a papal encyclical issued by Pius IX in 1864. (The French government actually attempted to suppress circulation of the encyclical within its borders.) Both of these are taken by Wise as examples of the papacy's efforts to impose canon law as superior to individual human rights. Wise may not have mentioned the doctrine of papal infallibility, accepted by the Council on 18 July 1870, because he knew that neither Napoleon III nor the French public approved of the doctrine; the Emperor warned that he would pull the French garrison out of Rome in response to French public opinion if it were to be accepted by the Council. See Kertzer, *Prisoner of the Vatican*, 28.

[29] The First Vatican Council, begun in Dec. 1869, was nearing its end by the time of Wise's sermon. For a view of the Council similar to Wise's held by German Protestant preachers, see Hoover, *The Gospel of Nationalism*, 41. A very different assessment of the relationship between the two events, contrasting them as the way of war and the way of peace, is expressed in a sermon by P. N. Lynch, bishop of Charleston, 'The Vatican Council'.

[30] At the beginning of the war there were reports from Rome that the Pope—perhaps angry with Napoleon III for removing the French garrison from Rome—favoured the Prussian side (*New York Times*, 21 July 1870, p. 1). On 12 Aug. a correspondent from Italy wrote, 'Now that the French troops have left the Pontifical territory, and there is no more present hope of their aid, the ecclesiastics rejoice at the calamity which has overtaken France, and pronounce it the judgment of God' (*New York Times*, 2 Sept. 1870, p. 2). Three days before the sermon, a newspaper account stated, 'The Archbishop of Paris has been requested by the Papal Nuncio to have a contradiction given in all the churches of his diocese to the report of a letter from the Pope to congratulate the King of Prussia on his victories' (*New York Times*, 6 Sept. 1870, p. 2).

[31] At Napoleon III's orders, a French army took Mexico City and in 1864 installed Archduke Maximilian of Austria, a French client, as emperor of Mexico. Following the mounting cost of countering an insurgency led by Benito Juarez, the French legislature demanded that Napoleon III abandon his 'Mexican Adventure', and French troops were ordered to return home at the end of 1866. See Cunningham, *Mexico and the Foreign Policy of Napoleon III*.

[32] On Marshal Achille Bazaine's role in Mexico, see ibid. *passim*; on his role in Metz, see Wawro, *The Franco-Prussian War*, 186–8, 192–204, 240–4. Although the *New York Times* on 3 Sept. headlined 'Surrender of Generals McMahon [at Sedan] and Bazaine', Bazaine's capitulation turned out to be an unfounded rumour; at the time of the sermon he was *not* a 'prisoner at Metz', but his army remained there surrounded by German forces and incapable of effective action, until his capitulation, with 173,000 men, on 17 Oct. (For his fate as a scapegoat after the war, see

and the empire is no more, and France is a republic. God is just. Napoleon mounted the throne of France by fraud, falsehood, perjury and bloodshed.[33] 'Behold he who conceiveth iniquity will be pregnant with mischief and bring forth falsehood' (Ps. 7: 14). He dug the pit that the republic fall, and he fell into the self-same ditch. His mischief has come down upon his own head, his violence has crushed his own skull. God is just.

Therefore, brethren, the sympathy of the world all at once turned from France. Her Emperor was a despot, and the world hates despotism. Her Emperor was the enemy of freedom, and the world loves liberty. Her Emperor was the protector of priestly oppression and ecclesiastical arrogance, and the world demands liberty of conscience. Her Emperor undertook the violent task to stem the current of progress, and the world obeys the divine law of Providence, which is eternal advance and no retrogression.[34] As long as progress was the inscription on the empire's mighty banner, as in the wars with Russia and Austria, and in the liberation of Italy, the world's sympathies were with France. As soon as the empire became the banner-bearer of despotism, retrogression and ecclesiastical obscurantism, the world's sympathies were turned from France.

Yes, brethren, France pays a national debt now. The nation which first on the European continent broke asunder the tyrant's chains, and crushed the skull of despotism; the nation which proclaimed the first great republic of Europe, the majesty of justice and equality of all men; the nation which revolted against one king, because he violated the freedom of the press, and against another because he set aside the right of free assemblage; [35] that self-same glorious and free nation, scared by the spectres of socialism and communism, submitted shamefully, submitted twenty years long to despotic Caesarism. France fed hosts of

Schivelbusch, *The Culture of Defeat*, 118–19.) On Napoleon's poor physical condition before the war began, see Baguley, *Napoleon III and his Regime*, 377–8, 380; on his surrender to King William of Prussia, ibid. 382–3, 387–8.

[33] By means of a *coup d'état* on 2–4 Dec. 1851, ending the Second French Republic: an event famously described (in works that Wise may have known) by Victor Hugo, *Napoléon le Petit* (1852), Pierre-Joseph Proudhon, *La Révolution sociale démontrée par le coup d'état du 2 décembre* (1852), and Karl Marx, *The Eighteenth Brumaire of Louis Bonaparte* (1852; repr. in German 1869). Wise's characterization is closest to Hugo's personal diatribe against Louis Napoleon. For a current review of the historiography, see Baguley, *Napoleon III and his Regime*, 12–68.

[34] Cf. Sermon 10 below by Artom, who sees the war as a severe challenge to this assumption.

[35] The two revolts were in 1789 against Louis XIV and in 1848 against Louis Philippe, the 'Citizen King'. When Louis Philippe's chief minister Guizot placed a ban on political meetings rioting broke out in the streets, leading eventually to the proclamation of the Second Republic with the election of Louis Napoleon as president.

soldiers and priests and neglected her people, the vast majority of which is unable to write or read, because there are no free schools in France.

France is dazzled by the vain show, luxury and trumpery[36] of her nobility, monied aristocracy, soldiery and comedians, and one-third of her people walks the soil of France bare-footed, poor and ignorant. Twenty years long France was systematically degenerated, that the empire could stand; therefore the empire fell. France is weak, her armies slain, her power broken. France pays a national debt just now. No nation can sin thus violently without calling down upon herself the retribution of eternal justice. Let us hope, brethren, let us pray that the republic of France, which God may bless and protect, will make speedy atonement for all those national sins, and restore France to the glorious position among the nations which she so richly deserves, which her past history so eminently gained and maintained until she fell into the hands of Napoleon. May the lesson of the last twenty years convince her of the truth, 'He who hath hollowed out a pit and dug it, will fall into the ditch which he had wrought' (Ps. 7:15).

[BODY OF THE SERMON: B]

And our Germany? Why must the blood of Germany be shed to punish the sins of France? Why must our German sisters, mothers, brides, wives, fathers and brothers mourn over the graves of her slain sons, to punish the crimes of Napoleon? My heart aches with the myriads of my former countrymen, whose fire-sides are deserted and cheerless, whose widows and orphans have so suddenly and largely increased, whose tears are so hot and bitter. Poor fatherland, why must thou be the rod of retribution in the hands of Providence? Military glory only strengthens the hands of kings, and weakens freedom's chances. The acquirement of territory enriches potentates and empoverishes nations. Why must Caesarism and glory be thine, that France be freed of her tyrant and restored to liberty?[37] Where, where is God's justice?

Silent, rebellious heart. God is just. Germany also pays her national debts. Since the days of Charlesmagne, Germany has oppressed all nations around her. Italy, Hungary, Poland, all the Sclavonic nations groan for long and bitter centuries under German oppression, German despots, and German armies.

[36] In the original, 'trumpary'; 'trumpery' is defined by the *OED* as 'showy but unsubstantial apparel, worthless finery'.
[37] The first part of the paragraph focuses on the human losses on the German side as the cost of the providential punishment of France. But now, in a sudden shift, Wise turns to the cost to the victorious nation (in human liberty) of a glorious military victory and territorial acquisition.

The Moravian Christian, the Protestant in Austria, the Catholic in Prussia, and the Jew everywhere up to the year 1848 was an outlaw, a tolerated beast of burden without any rights.[38] Two-thirds of all her peasants were the play-balls in the hands of a petulant nobility, and this very day equality of rights does not exist anywhere in Germany. Poor benighted fatherland, that hath driven away, and maltreated her best sons[39]: thou also payest thy national debt. Thy sons die for the wickedness of their fathers.

## [PERORATION]

Where, O Lord! where and when shall this end? Will mankind always be punished for its crimes, will the sins never be atoned, will always human gore extinguish human crimes and follies? Can mankind not be governed without the execution of thousands of Polish patriots, and the death of ten thousands in the Siberian wilds?[40] Can the human family not be made happy without the constant slaughter in Spain and in Cuba, without the horrors of the Russian Government and the barbarism of Roumania?[41] Must armies constantly kill, destroy and devastate to keep the human family in order?

O God, where and when shall this end? These rivers of blood, this current of tears, these groans, these sighs, these lamentations of the bereft, where and when shall this end? In the dominion of reason and justice, this is the reply to the melancholy question: there, there this shall end.[42] 'I will thank the Lord according to His righteousness' (Ps. 7: 17), for he who punishes justly, rewards righteously. If wickedness ends in retribution, righteousness must lead to happiness. The world, thank God, retrogrades not, it does not vex more wicked; on the contrary, it improves with every passing decade. It advances toward the point, it must finally reach it. The day will come when the nations will acknowledge the majesty

---

[38] A formulation that is clearly exaggerated, but expresses Wise's commitment to the principle of religious freedom for other religious minorities as well as for Jews.

[39] Including the preacher; see his personal statement published three weeks later, reproduced here following the end of the sermon.

[40] Wise alludes, of course, to the Polish rebellion against Russia of 1863–4. No foreign government declared support for the uprising. The revolt was crushed in September 1864 with the execution of members of the Polish provisional government; the number of Polish victims is estimated at 25,000. On Siberia as a place of exile for political dissidents in the second half of the nineteenth century, see Kennan, *Siberia and the Exile System*; Wood, 'Russia's "Wild East"'; Diment and Slezkine, *Between Heaven and Hell*, esp. 67–111. See also Sermon 10 by Artom below.

[41] A Cuban uprising against Spain in Oct. 1868 initiated an unsuccessful ten-year war. New outbreaks of anti-Jewish persecution were reported from Romania beginning in early 1870; the *New York Times* wrote about 'New Persecution of Jews' on 5 June 1870, p. 4.

[42] i.e. 'in the dominion of reason and justice', which is Wise's characterization of the messianic age.

of justice, the dominion of freedom, and the sovereignty of the One and Eternal God, when every man will be his own priest, prince and prophet; then national crimes will exist no more, and the national sins be atoned.

May God grant that the sins of France be atoned with the present republic; that again as in days of yore freedom have its home in France, and that country of revolutions finally exclaim with our sacred bard, 'I will thank the Lord according to His righteousness, and I will sing praises to the name of the Lord, the Most High' (Ps. 7: 18).

Three weeks later, the *Israelite* of 7 October 1870 (p. 9) carried the following personal statement by Wise:

As a man and a citizen, I am a Democrat. Therefore I sympathize with the French republic as I did with Mexico in her struggle against France and Austria. As a Jew I certainly sympathize with the French people which has disenthralled the Hebrew people of Germany, Austria and Italy, where the nobility, priests and soldiers were the lords, and everybody else was a slave. As a German, with thousands of others, I was forced out of my native land by unjust and oppressive laws, and have taken a solemn oath to support no foreign government, hence also not the king of Prussia. As a German I hate Germany's rulers and oppressors.

# CHAPTER TEN

## BENJAMIN ARTOM
# THE WAR

### 17 SEPTEMBER 1870
### BEVIS-MARKS SYNAGOGUE, LONDON

BENJAMIN ARTOM was born at Asti, Piedmont, in 1835. Educated by Italian rabbis, he served a congregation in Naples. At the young age of 31, he received a call to become haham of the Spanish and Portuguese congregations in London, filling this position after a vacancy of thirty-eight years, and to preach in the flagship Bevis Marks synagogue. At his installation service on 16 December 1866 he was identified as 'Professor B. Artom'; his installation sermon, 'The Jewish Pastor in the Present Age', was delivered in French, then translated and printed. Within a year, however, according to one account, 'he mastered the vernacular and then poured forth that impassioned eloquence which kindled every feature of the preacher's splendid physique'.[1]

In 1875 he married Henrietta Habab David, a wealthy widow and sister-in-law of Reuben Sassoon, a member of the family of international merchants. The wedding ceremony was performed by the Ashkenazi chief rabbi Nathan Adler, at Artom's invitation, signifying an effort to transcend division within the Jewish community.[2]

Artom published one volume of sermons in 1873; the second edition of 1876 bore the phrase 'First Series', indicating that further publications were anticipated, but he died suddenly in 1879 and no other work appeared. The volume was reviewed favourably in both the Jewish and the general press, including the *English Independent* and the *Spectator*. As is characteristic of nineteenth-century collections, many of the sermons it contains relate to the themes of the holy days, Jewish belief, and Jewish identity. There is also a sermon on the occasion of 'The Illness of the Prince of Wales', delivered on 23 December 1871, when prayers and sermons in congregations throughout the country were

---

[1] H. S. Morais, *Eminent Israelites of the Nineteenth Century*, 15–17.
[2] The information in this paragraph is taken from Berger, *The Jewish Victorian*, 26, based on obituary notices in the *Jewish Chronicle* and *Jewish World* of 10 Jan. 1879.

devoted to the hope for his recovery. Israel Abrahams, who heard Artom preach on several occasions, described him forty years later as unquestionably 'a great preacher' (though not quite of the rank of Jellinek or Simeon Singer), and spoke of 'His commanding presence, his beautiful voice, his dramatic gestures, his extempore delivery of carefully prepared impromptus'.[3]

The sermon reproduced below is the only one in the book apart from that on the prince's illness that responds to a historical event. Jewish preachers in Britain, like those in America, were of course on the sidelines of this conflict. This is not to say that Britain had no interest in what was happening in Europe. It had pledged in the 1838 Treaty of London to defend the neutrality of Belgium, which had been violated by German forces on their way into French territory, and although the policy of the Gladstone government was neutrality, the question of intervention was heatedly discussed.[4] Yet, because their country's soldiers were not engaged in combat, British Jewish preachers could focus on a condemnation of war in general. The first such sermon reported by the *Jewish Chronicle* was delivered on 23 July, four days after the declaration of war, by A. L. Green at the Central Synagogue, Portland Street. 'The preacher denounced the wickedness of aggressive and ambitious war. The king who initiated an unjust and unnecessary war was a murderer.'[5] The following week's issue contained a report of 'Another Protest from the Pulpit Against the Continental War', a sermon by A. Löwy, who was reported to have said, 'A dismal curtain of uncertainty now enshrouds the coming events of a terrible European tragedy, and to be the author of such a tragedy is to be the perpetrator of a crime without an end!'[6] Then, on 26 August, the *Chronicle* presented a lengthy account of the 'excellent and pathetic sermon' given by the chief rabbi, Nathan Adler, at the Great Synagogue.[7]

Artom's sermon, delivered on 17 September, ten days before Rosh Hashanah, was somewhat late to address the issue. Yet while it repeats some of the motifs from earlier sermons, it has a specificity and power at its core that the others seem to lack. And there is a dramatic difference in stance between this sermon and those delivered earlier by Marks during the Indian Mutiny

[3] Abrahams, 'Artom's Sermons'.

[4] See e.g. Raymond, *British Policy and Opinion*, 167–71, 191–3; Taylor, *The Trouble Makers*, 72–4; Laity, *The British Peace Movement*, 39–43.

[5] *Jewish Chronicle*, 29 July 1870, p. 8; on Green, see A. M. Jacob, 'Aaron Levy Green'.

[6] *Jewish Chronicle*, 5 Aug. 1870, p. 2.

[7] *Jewish Chronicle*, 26 Aug. 1870, p. 8. The most interesting part is a refutation of the claim that the messiah has already come by appeal to the realities of the present: 'Slaughter, havoc, desolation lay waste two of the fairest countries in the world! . . . When we daily hear of such things, can it then be said with assurance that the Messiah has come?' Yet this is not, at least not explicitly, a response to Christian claims, but rather to the liberal claim that 'civilization is the messianic period'.

(Sermon 4 above) and later by Adler during the Boer War (Sermon 14 below). Here we will not find any profession of patriotism, any focus on Britain and its interests, any discussion of the propriety of British intervention as opposed to the risks of isolationism. In striking contrast to the sermon by Isaac Mayer Wise reproduced above, there is no reference here to the defeat of the French or the fall of Emperor Napoleon III, or to the declaration of the French Republic two weeks before the sermon was delivered;[8] or to the fact that, to an extent greater than ever before, Jews in the respective armies of the two belligerents were fighting each other.[9] The treatment of the two combatants is relatively even-handed ('the evils which now afflict two generous nations').

What distinguishes the sermon is the expression of deep discouragement at the very fact of war. It is not a challenge to belief in God, such as we will see in the wars of the following century. Rather, the devastation wrought by the opposing armies, with their technologically sophisticated new armaments, represents a challenge to accepted beliefs about civilization and progress. To understand the context of Artom's message, some background is necessary.

Twenty years earlier the Great Exhibition had opened in the magnificent new Crystal Palace at Hyde Park, an embodiment of the triumph of progress. A recent historian of the exhibition has written: 'Progress was everywhere as the machinery [in the exhibition] promised new forms, new designs, new mechanisms, new results. The machines were, in the words of one commentator, "the epitome of man's industrial progress—of his untiring efforts to release himself from his material bondage." '[10] But the vision of the organizers encompassed more than just material progress: their hope and conviction was that advances in civilization would lead inexorably to peace. Prince Albert asserted in an address to the planning commission that

[w]e are living at a period of most wonderful transition, which tends rapidly to accomplish that great end—to which all history points—the realization of the unity of

---

[8]  An editorial in the *Jewish Chronicle*, 9 Sept. 1870 (p. 7) on 'The Emperor Napoleon', stated: 'The great event which in the last few days has astounded Europe is the fall of the most celebrated personage of the age—the Emperor of the French . . . But we need, as Jews, [to] consider with deep regret that a Sovereign who throughout his reign has, with one exception [his failure to intervene with the Pope in the Mortara case], proved himself not only impartially favourable, but heartily friendly, towards the Jews, has fallen from his high estate.'

[9]  David Einhorn referred to Prussian Jews fighting against Danish Jews in the war that began in Feb. 1864 (see Sermon 8b above); and of course, as Einhorn spoke, Union Jews were fighting Confederate Jews in the American Civil War. In July 1866 Prussian Jews had fought Austrian Jews in the decisive battle of Königgrätz. The *Jewish Chronicle* of 9 Sept. 1870 reported that 'There are no less than thirty thousand Jews in the North German Army. There are great numbers of Jews in the French Army.' An earlier issue (29 July 1870) reported that 'There is a Jewish family at Strasburg, of which two first cousins serve—the one in the French, the other in the Prussian army' (p. 10). Virtually every issue included reports of heroic acts performed by Jewish soldiers, especially on the German side.        [10]  Jeffrey A. Auerbach, *The Great Exhibition*, 106.

mankind . . . The distances which separated the different nations and parts of the globe are rapidly vanishing before the achievements of modern invention . . . Gentlemen, the Exhibition of 1851 is to give us a true test of the point of development at which the whole of mankind has arrived in this great task, and a new starting point from which all nations will be able to direct their further exertions.[11]

Even ten years later, at the International Exhibition of 1862, the pacifist internationalism of the Great Exhibition seemed woefully misguided in the light of the Crimean War, the Indian Mutiny, the American Civil War, and the Wars of Italian Unification.[12] But these wars were far away, or within a single south European country. The outbreak of the Franco-Prussian War, between two nations that symbolized some of the greatest advances of European civilization, was perceived by many as a shattering blow to Prince Albert's messianic assumption that 'all history points [to] the realization of the unity of mankind'. Two weeks before Artom delivered his sermon, the *Jewish Chronicle* printed a synopsis of an article published in Hebrew by the progressive Haskalah periodical *Hamagid* the previous week:

The writer of the article, while asking in how far civilization has contributed by its great inventions and application of the telegraph and other important discoveries, to render man less barbarous and more humane, by a singular coincidence comes to conclusions almost identical with those enunciated in last week's leading article in the Jewish Chronicle, headed 'Judaism and Industry'. The Maggid asks: 'Where is knowledge, wisdom, and understanding? What has not happened in recent years? The Crimean war, the Italian, Danish, American Civil War, Abyssinian, Mexican, Schleswig-Holstein, Spanish Revolution, Austria, and this present awful struggle! How many hecatombs of slain! Such frightful destruction of human beings; tracts of country desolated, and all for what?'[13]

This is a theme that Artom would pick up and develop with considerable power. The critique of the cult of progress had been launched in cultural circles through the idealization of a traditional past associated with the Oxford Movement, Young England, the Pre-Raphaelite Brotherhood, and the Gothic Revival.[14] But there was also a religious critique, and Artom's sermon is a fine articulation of its principles.

In this context the preacher's role becomes not the stirring of patriotic identification with one side, but rather the probing of self-criticism. The British

---

[11] Jeffrey A. Auerbach, *The Great Exhibition*, 60; Hermione Hobhouse, *The Crystal Palace and the Great Exhibition*, 27. This conviction was rooted in the liberalism of Adam Smith, as articulated in mid-century by Richard Cobden and John Bright, and was given concrete expression in the Paris Peace Congress of Aug. 1849 and the Frankfurt Congress of 1850; see Cooper, *Patriotic Pacifism*, 23–9.    [12] See Auerbach, *The Great Exhibition*, 217.
[13] *Jewish Chronicle*, 2 Sept. 1870, p. 9.    [14] See Auerbach, *The Great Exhibition*, 172.

avoidance of combat is not an occasion for complacency. Through the rabbinic dictum cited at the beginning of the sermon and invoked in the middle, he shifts to a discussion of the moral causes of war, and these turn out to be phenomena identified not in France or Germany, but at home in England: the failures of justice, the deterioration of social morality, the decline in the standards of religious instruction. These themes may seem conventional topoi to be found in the rhetoric of rebuke of almost every generation. But Artom gives concrete form to his generalizations in a way that makes the sermon especially vivid—and appropriate for the penitential mood of the period leading up to the High Holy Days.

# S E R M O N

——

*Give us help from trouble, for vain is the help of man.*
*Through God we shall do valiantly; for He it is that shall tread down our enemies.*

(PS. 108: 12–13)

*War is sent to desolate the earth when iniquity prevails, when justice is not done,*
*when the law is erroneously explained.*

(MISHNAH AVOT 5: 11)[15]

MY DEAR BRETHREN,—Everything decays, passes away, vanishes, and falls to pieces before our eyes; a new world insensibly arises in the place of that which we saw in our childhood: the scene is quite changed, new personages appear on the stage of life;—everything departs from us, and plunges into that abyss which is called nothingness; and in the midst of these eternal revolutions, God alone stands for ever and appears majestic in His omnipotence; God alone, while He changes the face of the universe, remains what He was, what He is, and what He will be.

'Athenian sage,' said Crœsus to Solon who, while travelling in order to study the laws and customs of foreign nations, had visited the court of Lydia, and to whom the king had shown with a proud complacency the unrivalled splendour

---

[15] In the classical Sephardi style, Artom begins his sermon with both a verse from the Bible and a rabbinic dictum. See on this form M. Saperstein, *Jewish Preaching*, 67. The preacher will turn to this statement, along with a parallel statement from the Talmud in Tractate Shabbat, in the middle of the sermon.

of his wealth, 'Athenian sage, who can be more fortunate and happy than myself? What can be wanting to my perfect joy? Is not my position, both as a man and as a king, the most enviable upon the earth?' 'O Crœsus,' answered Solon, simply and tranquilly, 'wait, wait until the last day of thy life';[16] אל תאמין בעצמך עד יום מותך, 'Rely not upon thyself till the day of thy death'.[17] Solon's words were prophetic, and Crœsus lost his wealth and his glory, his kingdom and his liberty, and to the mercy of his enemy he was indebted for the preservation of his life.

Nearly at the same time, another king was almost insane through his haughtiness and pride, and thought himself invulnerable, unassailable in his greatness. He was walking on a beautiful terrace at the top of his splendid palace, and looking around him at the city which stood at his feet. 'Is not this', he said in his unconquerable vanity, 'great Babylon, that I have built for the house of the kingdom, by the might of my power, and for the honour of my majesty?' הלא דא היא בבל רבתא די אנא בניתה לבית מלכו בתקף חסני וליקר הדרי (Dan. 4: 27). But in that moment, a tremendous voice was heard from heaven, saying: 'O King Nebuchadnezzar, to thee it is spoken, thy kingdom is departed from thee ... that thou mayest know that the Most High ruleth in the kingdom of men, and gives it to whomsoever He chooses' (Dan. 4: 29). And the Lord's will was instantly carried out. Nebuchadnezzar lost more than his kingdom: he was deprived of his reason; he fled to the woods; he lived for seven years amidst the brutes, the grass was his food, the open sky his roof.[18]

O kings, O princes, do not rely too much upon your thrones, they are vacillating; seek not security in your stately palaces, their basis is weak and fragile; a certain wind blows, they fall to the ground, they are dust, they are no more, even their traces disappear. The events of ancient times are now repeated. Every day we see monarchs deprived of their thrones; we see them take up the staff of a pilgrim and quit their country, not as kings, but as exiles, as fugitives, seldom accompanied by the pity of their subjects, but often followed by hatred and execration.

Is not the greatness of nations as transitory as that of their monarchs? And are the empires more secure than their rulers? Oh, my brethren, were it so, we should not see so many vicissitudes. Look at that country which a narrow

[16] The well-known story of the encounter between the wise Solon and the wealthy Croesus is recounted in Herodotus, Plutarch, and Xenophon (for specific sources, see Aristotle's *Nicomachean Ethics*, beginning of 1, 10). Like his fellow Italian Sephardi Sabato Morais, Artom seemed to enjoy references to classical literature.

[17] *Avot* 2: 5.

[18] Summarizing Dan. 4: 30.

channel divides from us; half a century ago it suffered from great disasters, but it recovered. The country, the towns offered the aspect of prosperity. Its population was increasing, its commerce was flourishing. Oh, it is so pleasing, so refreshing to see the blessed effects of industry and activity! to see the people enjoy the produce of their work and be delighted and happy, 'practise the great law of labor, and enjoy its reward' (Ps. 128: 2). It is refreshing to see in the towns, all busy in the exercise of their arts and professions; the fathers carefully bring up their children to their hereditary industry, and prepare the future welfare of their family; to see wealth acquired by means of honest transactions. It is consoling to see in the country the wonders that human exertions create, to see the invaluable treasures that the hand of man obliges nature to bring forth out of her bosom; to see the labourer together with his family well rewarded for his hard work, happily seated, according to the biblical expression, איש תחת גפנו ותחת תאנתו, 'under his vine or under his fig tree' (1 Kgs 5: 5); to see the joy of the peasant when he reaps his harvest, or when he is gathering in the grapes! That was a happy state of things, but it was not to last.

Suddenly the cursed cry of war is heard, and all that welfare, and all those blessings are gradually blighted. The inhabitants are frightened. All repair with confusion into the fortified towns. The songs of the labourer have ceased, the roads are deserted and silent. No, they are not silent; frightful sounds echo everywhere in the plains, on the hills, and among the mountains. The sound of drums and of trumpets, of guns and of cannons, the engines of death and destruction. The roads are no longer solitary; masses of men approach, but they are soldiers, animated with fury, ready for a deadly struggle, prepared to kill or to be killed. 'The snorting of his horses,' says Jeremiah, almost describing modern events, 'is heard from Dan; the whole land trembled at the noise of the neighing of his strong ones, for they have come and have devoured the land and all that is in it; the cities, and those that dwell therein,' מדן נשמע נחרת סוסיו מקול מצהלות אביריו רעשה כל הארץ ויבאו ויאכלו ארץ ומלואה תבל [וכך, וצ"ל עיר] ויושבי בה (Jer. 8: 16).

Terrible battles are fought, whole ranks, whole battalions, whole regiments fall to the ground, and vanish for ever from the stage of life. A thick smoke envelops the scene of disorder and horror, but out of it mingled cries arise: they are the cries of the wounded and of the dying; the touching lament of the fallen that ask for mercy; the brutal voice of the conqueror that answers: 'No quarter.' They form the chorus of war, which is the curse of mankind. After the ranged battles on the field, there are desperate fights around the fortified towns, and sieges and bombardments, the destruction of the best monuments of art, and the slaughter of peaceful and unarmed citizens, of women and of children, the ruin of whole cities.[19] And can the conqueror derive joy from his victory? Has he not lost the best of his soldiers, the promising youths of the fatherland? Oh, in both countries, among the victors and the vanquished, only mourning and desolation are seen, there is not one family that has not lost one of its dearest members; 'there is not a house where there is not one dead', אין בית אשר אין שם מת (Exod. 11: 30). Yes, Jeremiah spoke truly when he said, 'A cry of distress is heard upon the hills, lamentations and bitter weeping: there are the mothers who weep for their children, who refuse to be comforted for their children who are no more,' קול ברמה נשמע נהי בכי תמרורים רחל מבכה על בניה מאנה להנחם על בניה כי איננו (Jer. 31: 15).

Even when successful, war is a fearful calamity. It creates ruin and misery, and leaves behind a track of blood and of tears. It extinguishes the living forces of nations. It destroys all the treasures that peace had carefully and slowly accumulated for their welfare. It destroys the work of many generations. It precipitates a people from the height of power and prosperity to the depths of humiliation, weakness and distress; it wrests from their hand the sceptre of influence which had formerly been their pride.[20]

This description of the evils which now afflict two generous nations is far from exaggerated, and hour after hour the telegraph brings us gloomier and gloomier tidings with heart-rending details.[21] Our first movement is to address ourselves to the Almighty for commiseration; but we immediately after ask ourselves: do we deserve the mercy of the Lord? Is the present state of society so good that its terrible sufferings should surprise us? When we look at war in a religious point of view, the words of complaint about to be uttered die on our lips, for we see that men have given cause for it. What is the opinion of our sages, who had so high a sense of the duties of man? בעון עינוי הדין ועוות הדין וקלקול הדין חרב וביזה רבה ודבר ובצורת בא לעולם ובני אדם אוכלין ואינן שבעין ואוכלין לחמם במשקל 'Through the sin of neglect of justice, of violation of each other's rights, through neglect of religious instruction and misrepresentation of the Law, war, and plunder, and slaughter, and famine come upon the earth; men eat but are not satisfied, their bread is insufficient'.[22]

[19] The main army of France had surrendered to the Germans, together with Napoleon III, two weeks before the sermon was delivered. The siege of Paris would begin on 19 September, two days after the sermon.
[20] On this topos of the devastating results of war, see Sermon 4 above by Marks, p. 133, including the passage from Moses Mendelssohn.
[21] The improvement of communications technology made the ravages of war more immediately apparent to those at a distance from the battlefield.
[22] BT *Shab.* 33a. Cf. dictum cited at beginning from *Avot.*

And does justice prevail among men? Why the numerous array of legions that each state musters, by which the youths, the vigorous part of the nation, are withdrawn from the fields, from useful professions, from the seats of learning, by which heavy sacrifices out of proportion to his power are imposed upon the citizen? Why? It is because there is general mistrust between nation and nation, because each knows that the sacred voice of justice would not be listened to. Great empires will be ready, at the first opportunity, to extend their limits at the expense of a weak neighbour, and small states which know that the fable of the wolf and the lamb may at any moment become at their cost an historical fact,[23] strive to erect a feeble dyke which may stay for a time the fury of the flood. Treaties are signed with solemn promises and oaths, but they have no greater strength than the parchment on which they are drawn. Instead of justice, brutal force prevails.

Nor are the claims of justice better regarded within each state. Wherever despotism rules, everything depends upon the will of one man, the whole machinery of government is put into motion by one lever, the master—just as a watch is wound up by one key. And whenever the interest, or even the caprice of the master is at stake, then the people demand their due in vain, the balance trembles in the hand of the magistrate, and inclines on the side which the sovereign finger points out. Ask Siberia, and Siberia will speak; question the tears of the wretched exiles, and they will answer.[24] Between man and man the strict rules of justice are equally disregarded; otherwise would the places of punishment be so crowded? Would the criminal courts be, horrible to say, every day engaged in judging acts of dishonesty and deceit, fraud or burglary, rape or homicide? Should we hear so often of crimes against the honour, the property, the life of our fellow creatures?

And yet this is a time when excellent institutions are founded; when the convention of Geneva for the assistance of the wounded, the league of peace, and an association for the suppression of vice are established.[25] It is true that the human mind during these few centuries has achieved wonders; civilisation has

[23] The fable, in Aesop and La Fontaine, tells of a wolf providing one reason after another to justify attacking the lamb; when all of the reasons are shown by the lamb to be false, he eats it anyway, because that is what he wanted to do. (This fable was cited in the context of the debate over the American and British attack on Iraq in the spring of 2003.)

[24] On Siberia, see the reference in Sermon 9 above by Isaac Mayer Wise, p. 233.

[25] The reference is to the Red Cross Convention of 22 Aug. 1864, providing for the neutrality of ambulances and military hospitals. The 'League of Peace' was a pacifist organization founded in Switzerland in 1867. On the 'Society for the Suppression of Vice', see n. 29 below.

put itself at the head of mankind: yet what does all that progress regard?[26] It regards the increase of wealth, it regards the creation of new comforts, it regards a larger and more refined enjoyment of life. But have the advocates of progress done anything for the morality, the education, the edification of the people? Have they tried to improve the heart, in the same measure as they have tried to develop the mind? No, they have not, and it may be truly said that as long as civilisation does not go hand in hand with morality, its effects are not only not good, but hurtful, poisonous and fatal.

Tell me the discoveries that have recently been made in order to root in the human heart love for our neighbours, in order to inspire a deeper fondness for labour and economy, in order to prevent poverty? Instead of that, you will have to announce that fearful implements of death have been invented; the mitrailleuse, which spreads destruction by manifold mouths at the same moment; the chassepots which throw bullets that tear the poor flesh into which they penetrate; the needle and rifle guns which fire with astounding rapidity and kill without a moment of respite:[27] these are some of the results of civilisation when it is not prompted by morality.[28] And is it for such inventions that God has bestowed upon men an immortal soul and a creative intellect? There is a society for the suppression of vice; but what are they doing? Do they strive to prevent vice? Do they study the means of teaching the people of the lowest classes how to like and appreciate sobriety, to shun intemperance and vice, and consequently how to avert misery and misfortune, disease and untimely death? Oh no, they are content with punishing those that have fallen low into the depth of vice. They are not the protectors of Society; they are only its avengers.[29]

[26] On the theme of progress in nineteenth-century England, see Bury, *The Idea of Progress*, 217–37; Radoslav Tsanoff, *Civilization and Progress*, 124–7, 138–46.

[27] The *mitrailleuse* was an embryonic machine-gun, operated by a crank-handle, capable of firing 150 rounds a minute with a range of up to 2,000 yards. The *chassepot* was a high-quality, small-calibre, breech-loaded rifle with a range of up to 1,600 yards. These French innovations were superior to the German 'needle-gun', though the Germans outstripped the French in manpower and morale. See on this Wawro, *The Franco-Prussian War*, 52–4, and, in a more general context, O'Connell, *Of Arms and Men*, 192 (on the Prussian needle-gun) and 208–9 (on the *chassepot* and *mitrailleuse*).

[28] Cf. the sermon delivered by the chief rabbi, Nathan Adler, at the Great Synagogue several weeks before Artom's sermon, contesting the claim that the messiah has already come because 'Civilization is the Messianic period': 'Civilization has done much, very much, for the advancement of the human race. But if it has exercised the ingenuity of man in making great discoveries for his intellectual and material benefit, it has also invented deadly weapons to shorten his existence and hasten his departure from this world' (N. Adler, 'Sermon on the Franco-Prussian War').

[29] An interesting critique, by a religious conservative, of the British Society for the Suppression of Vice, established in 1802. A report from 1872 states that, during the past two years, 'it has been the means of bringing to punishment, by imprisonment, hard labour, and fines, upwards of forty

But the neglect of religious instruction and the misrepresentation of the Law are also assigned as the causes of war: המורים בתורה שלא כהלכה.[30] Society is like a great school with an immense number of children. The multitude consists indeed of a great many childish beings. But just as it happens that if unsound instruction is given, the children will soon grow up into vicious voting men, so if the literature of a country is immoral and even if, though condemning vice, it describes its excess with glowing colours, so as to make it almost alluring, the people will be corrupted—they will say: 'The cup of pleasure is enervating, yet it is so sweet that we cannot help approaching our lips thereto, were it only for one moment.'[31] If the people are not taught the sound principles of religion and morality which is its result, then sensuality, self-interest and ambition will be their sole advisers; and are not these defects the indirect sources of war?

But besides that, there are those who expound the Law erroneously, who, instead of ministering to the people the spiritual food of the divine precepts,

---

of the most notorious dealers [in pornographic and blasphemous literature], and within a few years has seized and destroyed the following enormous mass of corrupting matters: 140,213 obscene prints, pictures, and photographs, 217,772 books and pamphlets' (*The Leisure Hour*, 13 Jan. 1872, at <www.victorianlondon.org/crime/suppression.htm>. For a broader discussion of pornography in Victorian Britain and the efforts to suppress it, see Sigel, *Governing Pleasures*.

[30] *Avot* 5: 11, the dictum cited at the beginning of the sermon.

[31] It is difficult to ascertain how specifically Artom was responding to contentious issues in contemporary English literature. A year after the sermon was delivered, hostile criticism of the poetry of Swinburne and Rossetti came to a climax with a fierce attack by the critic Robert Buchanan entitled 'The Fleshly School of Poetry'. This was the climax of criticisms published since the publication in 1866 of Swinburne's *Poems and Ballads*—a volume that, according to a recent study, was 'attacked with a bitterness rarely equaled in the annals of literary history. Charges of sensuality and immorality, sometimes of paganism and blasphemy, heavily outweighed objections on aesthetic grounds': Clyde Kenneth Hyder (ed.) *Swinburne Replies*, 1. A biographer notes that from 1866 'references to Swinburne as the archetype of the unbeliever become frequent in sermons': Georges Lafourcade, *Swinburne*, 138. Artom's statement seems perhaps more appropriate for Rossetti, whose volume of *Poems* was published in 1870 and reviewed (in many cases quite favourably) in journals during the months before the sermon. Compare with Artom's statement the following formulation, from a largely negative review: 'The author has managed with consummate skill to avoid the intrinsic indelicacy of his subject [in 'Jenny'] but all writers who practise this sort of morbid anatomy do something towards debauching the minds of a certain number of their readers. Such things tend to confound the distinction between morality and immorality': S. N. Ghose, *Dante Gabriel Rossetti and Contemporary Criticism*, 136–7. In 1873 Joseph Lightfoot, preaching in St Paul's, spoke with dismay of an unnamed poet who had a 'divine gift of imagination' but who 'uses the ascendancy which he has gained to corrupt the wells of his country's literature with the poison of sensuality': 'Balaam and Balak', p. 8. However, the reference here, and in Artom, may be to Byron. Compare the statement in a sermon by C. H. Spurgeon delivered on 23 Oct. 1870: 'our life gradually takes the tinge and hue of the thoughts to which we most accustom ourselves . . . Men who have been deeply read in French novels, Byronic poetry, and German metaphysics, have become dissolute and sceptical, and none could wonder. You cannot send the mind up the chimney, and expect it to come down white': 'Think Well and Do Well', 584.

employ their ingenuity and their learning in throwing doubt upon that which is divine; in teaching men not to believe; in emptying the human heart of all religious feelings.[32] When these are totally banished, will not immoral tendencies, by a natural consequence, take their place? We ought not to be surprised if, when society has descended to that degree of corruption, the Lord inflicts upon it severe sufferings, as he said through the Prophet: הנני צורפם ובחנתים 'I will melt them and try them' (Jer. 9: 6). And these incisive and threatening words of the prophet can only mean war, because the heart of man is not easily moved; if a warning is to affect it, it must be a warning of death, an awful crisis, a catastrophe like that which just now fills us with horror. The just hand of God who punishes the wickedness of men by the means of the folly and ambition of men is clearly discernible.[33]

And yet this great event, the war, in spite of its mournful effects, which many amongst us, though not engaged in it, feel so deeply, will not be for us without utility if only we are disposed to learn the lessons that it conveys to men. It teaches us that ambition and an immoderate desire of acquiring, of conquering, and of extending our dominion at the expense of our neighbours are always fatal, but that its final victims will be the ambitious themselves.

It teaches us that the real welfare of nations does not depend upon military glory, the basis of which is a sea of blood and heaps of human corpses, but upon peace, labour, industry, and commerce; upon the development of the natural resources of the country; upon sound instruction, by which the people may learn and practise what they owe to God, to society, and to themselves; I mean their rights and their duties.

It teaches us the necessity of concord, which is as valuable among nations as among individuals; it teaches us that each nation has received its lot from the Lord, in accordance with the words of Moses: בהנחל עליון גויים בהפרידו בני אדם יצב גבולות עמים (Deut. 32: 8) [When the Most High gave nations their homes, and set the divisions of man, He fixed the boundaries of peoples] and it is such a lot as can satisfy its wants; cursed is the nation that attempts to usurp the lot of a sister nation, as it is written in Deuteronomy (27: 17), ארור מסיג גבול רעהו, 'Cursed be he that removes his neighbour's landmark',

---

[32] It is unclear to me whether Artom is speaking about an internal Jewish issue—the influence of religious leaders in the Reform movement—or the broader issue of religious liberalism in British society.

[33] This sentence, asserting the traditional providential justice of God in history, is quite similar to Wise's argument, except that Artom applies it not to a specific political leader but to the failings of modern society in general.

but cursed is also the nation that from cowardice or exhaustion, lets its inheritance be stolen away.[34]

It teaches us that kings are not the despotic masters of the lives of their subjects. They are raised to the throne, in order that they may work for the happiness of the millions of human beings placed under their sway, not in order that when it suits their caprice or their selfishness, they may drag whole hosts to a struggle of destruction, thus exposing their country to devastation and ruin.[35]

It teaches us that human life is short enough, that consequently we ought not to make it shorter, but that we ought to employ it in deserving the protection of the Almighty, an invaluable protection, which will cover us upon the earth and still shelter us after death, and which we shall be able to obtain, if we act righteously, if we do justice and charity, the real foundation of all religions. In accordance with the words of Isaiah (56: 1), שמרו משפט ועשו צדק כי קרובה ישועתי לבא וצדקתי להגלות '[Thus saith the Lord,] keep ye judgment, and do justice; for my salvation is near to come, and my righteousness to be revealed.'

But there is another lesson therein which we ought to take to heart. At the sight of the indescribable miseries to which men are subjected, at the sight of the rapidity with which human life passes away, ought not our heart to be softened and moved by generous emotions? Ought we not to feel our love for our fellow creatures increased, our eagerness to lend them assistance made greater and greater. Oh, my dear brethren, there has never been a time more adapted than this to works of charity, whether it assumes the aspect of liberal contributions, of kind offices, or of prayer. When we represent to ourselves that many more than a hundred thousand human creatures lie down cruelly wounded and are in need of untiring assistance, is it not a duty for us to offer what it is in our power to give, in order that we may have the consolation of knowing that we have at least contributed to the comfort, perhaps to the recovery of one sick man?[36] When we see around us so many wretched strangers who have fled from the advancing legions, from the bearers of fresh devastation and bloodshed, ought we not to feel eager to lend our service by advice or by consolation to these foreigners, to whom Moses recommends us to show kindness, because we

[34] The first curse applies to Germany, where the strong public sentiment for the annexation of Alsace and Lorraine was manifest (and noted in London) by the middle of Aug. 1870; the second curse suggests that the French are to blame for their military disaster and loss of territory.

[35] Apparently a reference to Napoleon III, emperor of the French, who had been deposed on 4 Sept., following his capture by the Germans two days earlier. This, and not the success of the Prussian king, William I, would have provided the 'lesson' mentioned by the preacher.

[36] Cf. Sermon 4 above by Marks, with its appeal for donations to a relief fund.

have in our wanderings acquired the experience of that which strangers must have to suffer? Is it not written, ואוהב גר לתת לו לחם ושמלה, The Lord 'loveth the stranger in giving him food and raiment' (Deut. 10: 18)? And when we see that the plague of war has not yet quenched its fury, that the struggling parties are prepared for fresh fights, ought we not to raise our supplications to the Father of all creatures, that He may in His mercy stop the fiery and bloody quarrel, that He may inspire the warriors and their leaders with more humane feelings, that He may prevent this year from closing amidst blood, and the new year from opening amidst slaughter?

Are these lessons to be useless to us? Ah no! I hope not. The heart of an Israelite is naturally prone to mercy. Yes, the children of Israel who during the past have suffered so much, have learnt how to pity and assist the sufferers, and through their inexhaustible charity are deservedly called the descendants of Abraham, המרחם על הבריות בידוע שהוא מזרעו של אברהם אבינו.[37] I am sure, therefore, that I shall not have spoken in vain; I am sure that some assistance will be given, some kindness shown; that every heart will now pray with me for the restoration of peace unto Him who, as the Talmud says, אפילו בשעת כעסו הקב"ה זוכר את הרחמים, 'even in the moment of His wrath remembers mercy'.[38] I am sure that every soul will raise itself with mine unto Him who never rejects a prayer prompted by charity and uttered with sincerity, and Who formally promised unto Moses, ונתתי שלום בארץ, 'And I will give peace in the land' (Lev. 26: 6).

## PRAYER*[39]

Almighty God! Omnipotent and Invisible King of all created things, before whom the greatness of those who dwell in a house of clay is as nothing, their strength and valour are as vanity; we fall upon our face with emotion and fear, because a sad intelligence has reached us that has made both our ears tingle. Two noble and powerful nations have mustered their numerous legions, and have begun a deadly conflict with each other, armed with fearful implements of death for their mutual destruction; their land is desolate, terror prevails all

---

* This prayer, of which the original Hebrew follows, was recited for many weeks during the Franco-Prussian war, in the Synagogues under the supervision of the author.

[37] BT *Bets.* 32b.                                   [38] BT *Pes.* 87b.
[39] The *Jewish Chronicle* report of the sermon introduces the prayer as follows: 'The spiritual chief of the Sephardim [sic] congregation concluded with the following soul-thrilling and pathetic prayer for Peace, recited first in the vernacular and afterwards in Hebrew. It had a great effect on the very large congregation assembled': *Jewish Chronicle*, 23 Sept. 1870, p. 7.

around; they have already cast down thousands of wounded; yea, a multitude of strong men have already been slain.

O Eternal, Thou art the God of armies,[40] but Thou art also the Father of mercy and the Master of peace. Oh, listen to our supplication, say unto the war: Spread no further, here shall thy proud waves be stayed. Prevent war from entering our land, prevent sword and shield from being seen in our cities, for much dearer unto us are the results of peace than all the glory and laurels of warriors. Inspire the two nations, their armies and their leaders with love of peace, with mercy and humanity, so that they may cease their work of destruction; stay the shedding of blood, and spare the unarmed and the innocent, old men, women and children, so that they may be convinced that upon their union depends their prosperity; that their struggle is for both of them a curse and a crime. Remove hatred from their hearts, and make them remember that all men are brethren, and Thou art their Father, loving and merciful; then they 'will not lift up sword against each other, neither learn war any more' (Isa. 2: 4)!

Oh, our Lord, who art in heaven, look mercifully at the present crisis! Our Lord, who art in heaven, oh, send peace upon the earth, send peace upon this kingdom! Let it be Thy will that we may live and see days of calm and concord, of quiet and security; the day when Thou, O Lord, wilt ordain peace for us, and bless Thy people with peace, Amen!

---

[40] A literal translation of the Hebrew phrase *elohei tsevaot*, which occurs a dozen times in the Bible, always following the Tetragrammaton.

# CHAPTER ELEVEN

## SABATO MORAIS

# THANKSGIVING DAY SERMON

### 24 NOVEMBER 1870

#### CONGREGATION MIKVEH ISRAEL,
#### PHILADELPHIA

ON 5 SEPTEMBER 1870, following the French debacle at Sedan and the capture of Napoleon III, but before the declaration of the French Republic, the *Philadelphia Inquirer* wrote on its editorial page:

It is not unfair to say that the sympathies of the people of this country are almost entirely with the Prussians, and that they are so arises in a great measure from the regard which the people have for our German citizens. It is true that the intelligent mind of America saw that this present war was forced upon Prussia, that she would have avoided it if avoidance had been possible, and that all the suffering, pain and death which are to be its fruits are traceable to the overweening ambition of the adventurer Napoleon.

Our sympathy for Prussia is only another evidence of the hatred of tyranny and injustice which fills the American mind. We had no quarrel with France any more than we had with Prussia, but our regard for the Germanic element here led us to esteem it there at home, and our natural love of liberty made us rejoice in the defeat of the man who had ruled France with despotic wrong.[1]

This statement reflects a community with a large population of German immigrants (both Jewish and Christian). The editorial projects positive attitudes towards the 'intelligence, thrift, industry' of the German Americans—'Honest, educated, energetic and genial, they made good citizens, and their advent was helpful to the Republic'—back on the Fatherland, and Prussia is identified with the 'hatred of tyranny and injustice' that characterizes the American sensibility.[2] France is identified almost entirely with the capricious

---

[1] *Philadelphia Inquirer*, 5 Sept. 1870, p. 4.
[2] Ibid. For other examples of praising the admirable traits of German national character, see Gazley, *American Opinion of German Unification*, 495–6, 348–9.

rule of Napoleon III. This represents the dominant trend of American public opinion even in areas without a significant German American population: decidedly pro-Prussian, for various reasons.[3]

Speaking on Thanksgiving Day two and a half months later, Morais takes a very different tack.[4] Prussia is now presented as an awesome military power that has not only humiliated its opponent but threatens to destroy its capital city. Like Isaac Mayer Wise and the editorialist cited above, he evinces disdain for Napoleon III; however, he identifies France not with the Emperor but with Paris, the centre of science and the arts, a place of magnificence and beauty, the very survival of which is in peril. And—in a historical argument that plays a central rhetorical role—he associates France with Lafayette, bound up with the founding of the American Republic and specifically with Philadelphia's Independence Hall, a few blocks from where Morais was speaking. The preacher expresses pride in America's quick recognition of the new French Republic, and a wistful desire that America could now intervene militarily to ensure the safety of Paris.

In this, Morais reflects the shift of American public opinion to greater sympathy for France after Sedan, a shift prompted by the removal of Napoleon III and the proclamation of the Republic, empathy with the humiliated and suffering underdog, reports of German brutality and atrocities, the German seizure and commitment to annexation of Alsace and Lorraine, and—in some circles—a grudging admiration for the desire of the French to continue fighting.[5]

It is difficult know to what extent Morais's position represents his own liberal Italian background and values, as opposed to the general movement in American opinion as Paris became more imperilled. For the change in public opinion did not apply to the German American community, which on the whole remained fiercely attached to the German cause right up to the end of the war. There was a huge 'triumphant procession' of German Americans in Philadelphia on 5 September 1870, and another massive celebration on 14 May 1871. On that Sunday morning, Samuel Hirsch of Philadelphia's Keneseth Israel Congregation preached to a large gathering on the theme of gratitude to God 'as men, as Jews, as Germans'. He maintained that the French had initiated the war on 'a flimsy pretext, an imagined outrage upon the dignity of the French ambassador', and exalted the German idea of liberty which, like the

---

[3] Gazley, *American Opinion of German Unification*, 322–58.

[4] None of the other twelve Thanksgiving sermons published by the *Philadelphia Inquirer* the following day devotes more than a sentence or two to the war in Europe (usually contrasting it with the tranquillity in the United States). (For a fine example of a Christian sermon on the war, see Hepworth, 'War and Civilization', delivered on 25 Sept. at the Church of the Messiah in New York.) It may be that Morais thought of Thanksgiving as an especially appropriate time for discussing political matters (see his sermon 'On the Ill Treatment of the Chinese in the Far West', discussed in the Introduction to this volume, p. 27 above).

[5] Gazley, *American Opinion of German Unification*, 386–92, 395–401.

Jewish idea, encompassed responsibility and duty. 'Yes, it was this feeling of duty, of being able to die for one's duty, that chained victory to the German banners. Thank the Lord for His manifest direction.'[6]

Did Morais's sentiments—supporting in theory the idea of American military intervention and calling for a strong American statement on behalf of embattled Paris—represent the views of his congregants? Was there tension between the Sephardi and German Jewish communities during this period? In Los Angeles, the hostility between German Jews and the small group of French Jews following the outbreak of the war led to the dissolution of the local branch of the Alliance Israélite Universelle, and on 26 August 1870 two leading Jews of the city actually came to blows in a local saloon over the divergent opinions about the war.[7]

Unlike Artom, Morais does not present the war as a shattering challenge to prevalent ideas about progress and civilization. The challenge for civilization in Morais's eyes is not the war itself but the threat of destruction to the city of Paris. Nor does he use it as an opportunity to rebuke trends in his own society. The dominant mood of the sermon is celebratory, as appropriate for the Thanksgiving occasion: an affirmation of America's unique, providential role as a model of freedom and democracy, and a call for strong American leadership, if not with force at least with moral clarity, on behalf of the republican values and cultural achievement threatened by the spectre of 'the burning of Paris'.

# SERMON

———

THE QUEEN of Sheba—supposed to have ruled in Arabia Felix[8]— heard of the renown of King Solomon. Anxious to make the personal acquaintance of a monarch signally gifted, she betook herself to the metropolis of his dominions. The admirable order pervading every department in the royal government, the vastness of its resources, the brilliancy of its surround-

---

[6] S. Hirsch, 'Peace Sermon'; cf. Gazley, *American Opinion of German Unification*, 489, 495, who does not identify the rabbi. On the same occasion a Lutheran pastor said, 'That is the great secret in this war, that the Lord rent the clouds, and put forth his hand. A victory as won by the Germans can only be won through Him' (Gazley, *American Opinion of German Unification*, 496). In his sabbath sermon on the previous day, Marcus Jastrow of Rodef Shalom added, 'We do not, however, rejoice over this disgrace of our enemy. Our heart grieves to see this former friend of humanity defeated—defeated, because he did not hear the voice of Heaven and misunderstood his mission' (Jastrow, 'Peace Sermon').

[7] N. B. Stern, 'When the Franco-Prussian War Came to Los Angeles'.

[8] The ancient term for the southern end of the Arabian peninsula, later 'Yemen'.

ings, and that unsurpassing knowledge which added lustre and majesty to the occupant of the throne, held the distinguished visitor in ecstasy. In a burst of enthusiasm she thus gave expression to her feelings: 'King of Israel! Thy tidings that reached my land concerning thy acts and thy wisdom were true. Yet I believed not, until I came and saw all with my own eyes. Verily, the half hath not been told me. Thy wisdom and thy prosperity excel the report I heard. Happy are thy subjects; happy are these thy officers, who stand continually before thee to do thy wise sayings' (1 Kgs 1: 6–8).

Foreign Potentates! Assemble together in this country, purchased anew by the blood of a people for the good of all people.[9] Ye autocrats, and ye, also, sovereigns of constitutional governments, come to this empire of freedom. Your amazement will greatly exceed that by which an Eastern queen was seized at the capital of Israel's ancient realms. For here will be seen a phenomenon in the history of the human race—a scene which fame can never fittingly portray. Domains, not of a limited but of boundless extent, inhabited by scores of millions of intelligent beings, whose industry enriches the soil, and whose inventive genius widens the commercial world. Here will you behold a nation conscious of its inherent strength, climbing the highest ascents of civilization; a nation asserting its rights, and offering all privileges which are peculiarly its own; a nation whose crown is equity, and upon whose diadem liberty shines in full splendor, not in a spirit of boasting and vanity, but in token of deep gratitude to the Almighty deliverer.[10] You must show those who lord over your fellow creatures the effects of self-government founded upon principles of wisdom and righteousness.

They should be warned. For the hand of time that presses hard on royal pretensions is raising aloft the standard of human rights. A kind Providence has chosen your national home as the ground wherein to set up that glorious ensign. To you has its guardianship been assigned. Vigilantly have you kept watch that none should, with impunity, level against it traitorous arms. This day proves your fidelity. For the many who in the hour of peril rallied to its defense, you did commensurately reward. Men whom injustice repulsed now approach with firm steps the national altar.[11] See, they also lay upon it offerings

---

[9] Referring of course to the Civil War, which had ended less than six years previously.

[10] Until this point in the paragraph, the 'you' addressed are the 'foreign potentates'. The 'you' in the following sentence is ambiguous, but the next paragraph, and indeed the rest of the discourse, form an apostrophe to 'you' the American people, represented by the preacher's listeners.

[11] This and the following seven sentences celebrate the emancipation of the slaves and their inclusion as free human beings in the national Thanksgiving Day.

of thanksgiving. Their hearts swell with joyous emotions as they join in the anthems which resound from the Atlantic to the Pacific ocean. They were degraded. You breathed into them a spirit of manhood. You dignified their existence. You bade them be free. Labor unshackled for the pursuit of happiness. Praised be the Lord! The eternal truths emblazoned upon your escutcheon stand vindicated. Why should you not then openly glory in this country of your possession? Is it not the richest gift of a beneficent God? Has it not yielded untold blessings to mankind? Rome in her palmiest days, treading on the necks of subjugated nations, was a curse. Classic Greece, slaughtering in cold blood her enslaved Helots, was a fiend.

The Republics of medieval ages, reddening the Adriatic Sea and the Arno with fraternal blood; those of modern times torn by internal dissensions, or hired to uphold despotism, are but a misnomer.[12] America is true to her trust. America is the generous hostess, inviting the weary and the faint to the sumptuous board she has spread out. 'Come,' she cries, 'Eat of my bread and drink of the wine I have mingled.' Why should you not glory in this heritage of your fathers? 'Beautiful for situation, the joy of the whole earth.' Varied in climates: holding out the delicious fruits which a tropical sun ripens, and presenting the multifarious products that temperate regions yield. Its mountain peaks and its level plains offer you tributes. What unspeakable delights you enjoy which the dwellers of other lands know not of! How innumerable the comforts which the appliances of art—wherein your country excels—bring within reach of the humblest denizens! And those prerogatives, at the side of which the gold mines of your California and Arizona lost their value: the right to worship God, untrammeled by the dictation of human laws; the right and the facility to attain the highest position in life.

Why should you not glory in this country, which you can call your own? Freedom sings this day her praise. For America did prove herself faithful, when her swift message spoke encouraging words to a brave, though ill-fated people. Pusillanimous Europe held aloof. Cruel Europe heard the rushing of a mighty

---

[12] Morais may well have been thinking of the classic study by J.-C.-L. Simonde de Sismondi, *The History of the Italian Republics*, first published in English in 1832 but republished in 1864; the topic was obviously close to the preacher's heart. As for the modern 'republics', many Americans considered the newly established French Republic to be a misnomer (as newspapers wrote: 'As yet there *is* no French Republic, even in form', some styling it 'the so-called republic', or 'a Republic only in name'); see Gazley, *American Opinion of German Unification*, 394–5. It is unclear whether Morais would have agreed.

host, falling with crushing force upon an enfeebled nation and continued unmoved.[13] America appreciated the struggles of sorely beset France. America commended her aspirations by acknowledging her self-government.[14] Would she could also cast her aegis round the majestic city, the once joyous, but now joyless Paris. Would she could, consistently with honor and the interests of her poor children, enter the lists in defense of a nation to which she is bound in gratitude.[15] But, will not the country for whose independence France bled and poured forth treasure, raise her voice against the perpetration of a deed at which civilization recoils?[16] Can you, O Americans, keep silent when the cradle of military genius, the historic city, is to be laid in ashes? Shall science be left homeless, the arts be driven from their sanctuary, and you heed not their lament? The burning of Paris! What a conflagration! The charred bones of heroes mingling with the dust of falling pyramids. The burning of Paris! What a conflagration! Beauty and magnificence burying their votaries between their own ruins.[17]

[13] Although aid was provided by some outsiders (some Irish volunteers went to France, some serving as medics and others as soldiers; and on Garibaldi, see n. 23 below), most European powers remained neutral, though sympathetic to France and concerned about the German victories—despite a French diplomatic offensive that mobilized such literary figures as Victor Hugo to inform 'humanity and the civilized states' of their duty to save the French republic (Wawro, *The Franco-Prussian War*, 187–8, 238–9). In Britain, for example, although many called for greater British initiative, no serious consideration had been given to military intervention at the time of the sermon: see Raymond, *British Policy and Opinion*, 167–71, 191–3, 239–41.

[14] The reference is to a letter from Elihu Washburne, American ambassador to France, to Jules Favre, stating that he was authorized to recognize the French Republic proclaimed without bloodshed following the capture of the Emperor Napoleon III at Sedan, and to extend the congratulations of the American government and people (see Gazley, *American Opinion of German Unification*, 385). French newspapers on 8 September praised the United States for this quick recognition of the Republic; for example, the *Journal de Paris* asserted that 'America had merited well of the civilized world for addressing [to] France in the hour of peril and misfortune words of consolation and hope. By recognizing the French Republic, America opens the way of peace. It must be that the peoples of the Continent will follow her example' (cited in *New York Times*, 9 Sept. 1870, p. 1, col. 2).

[15] Here the possibility of American intervention on behalf of France is raised; however, although Morais endorses the idea, he indicates his awareness that such military intervention is in reality not feasible.

[16] For the use in pro-French circles of the historical argument about the role of France in support of the United States during the Revolution, see Gazley, *American Opinion of German Unification*, 361–3. He cites the *New York Times*, explaining the attitude of many Americans: 'The France that aided us in the Revolution is stricken down and bleeding, and the foot of the conqueror is on her breast. Should not we all . . . remonstrate against her further punishment and degradation?' (p. 362).

[17] At this time, with Paris besieged and threatened by German bombardment (which would indeed begin, without warning, in early January 1871), the total destruction of Paris was considered to be a real—and, for Morais, a devastating—possibility.

Free Americans! Let your powerful voice be heard. Say that Paris should not be tied to the triumphal car of her insatiably ambitious, though valiant, foe.[18] Remember, it is no more the royal seat of an usurper, but the city of the people. The man who summoned the furies to scourge his noble land, the executioner of France, shall never again pollute her ground.[19] Him you must despise, who, Amalek-like, when he saw you faint and weary, devised your destruction. Mexico revealed his perfidy[20] as Rome showed him false.[21] But France is liberal. The bayonets of the Empire which sustained the mitred King on his rickety throne have ceased to stand as a menace to Italy. Sensible of that redeeming fact the illustrious patriot, the Cajus Fabricius of our age,[22] has made common cause with the defenders of Paris. The arms of Garibaldi and of his gallant legions have already won victories; but what his prowess may fail to achieve, your high standing among the family of nations might accomplish.[23]

Prussia has too fearfully evinced her superiority. The humiliation of her opponent should suffice a power that aspires to lead the van of progress.[24] Surely vain would be popular knowledge if the heart keeps shut against the softening influences of education, if raging passions remain uncurbed, if national pride adds ferocity to combatants. Your kindly representations will be listened to with deference, the good among all the children of men will bid God-speed to efforts so mercifully directed. If even unsuccessful, you will have raised for yourselves a name for honor and for glory. America should not enter into 'entangling alliances'.[25] The welfare of mankind is too greatly involved in her

[18] In the absence of military intervention, the preacher calls for a strong American statement that Paris should not be subjected to German bombardment.

[19] And indeed, Napoleon III, released from German captivity in March 1871, went into exile in England with members of his immediate family; where he would die in 1873.

[20] See Sermon 9 above by Isaac Mayer Wise, n. 31. On the powerful image of Amalek, which Morais invokes here with regard to French policy, see Sermon 8b above by David Einhorn.

[21] See Sermon 9 above, n. 30. Morais had no more sympathy with this aspect of Napoleon's politics than Wise did.

[22] A Roman general and statesman of the third century BCE, known for his integrity. The reference to classical history is characteristic of the broad culture drawn upon by the Italian-born Morais.

[23] Garibaldi pledged his aid to the newly proclaimed French Republic on 7 September and arrived in Tours from Italy during the second week of October, at a time when the French were being defeated by the Germans at Orléans. His forces had some success in guerrilla-type attacks against the Germans in early November, although his military efforts were not significantly successful: Viotti, *Garibaldi*, 172–9; Wawro, *The Franco-Prussian War*, 262–3.

[24] Here is an appeal to one aspect of the German self-conception—leading the van of human progress—which is in tension with other nationalistic and militaristic components. Morais proceeds to suggest that Prussia might well respond to a strong American appeal to save Paris.

[25] The phrase is generally associated with the advice in George Washington's farewell address of 27 Sept. 1796, although the precise phrase does not appear there.

happiness. Too dear are her political interests, that they should at all be placed in jeopardy. But she should ever be the beneficent mediator, the friend of humanity, striving to mitigate the horrors of war, to reconcile difficulties, that peace may be ushered in, thus exemplifying the great principles enunciated by her founders, showing that where liberty is enthroned the religion of love is predominant.[26]

Beloved hearers, I hold in my hand the first Thanksgiving proclamation of the father of your Republic. After acknowledging the manifold favors signally bestowed upon the country by Almighty God, the stupendous deliverance which His hands wrought, and through which the colonists established an independent and stable government; and after recommending that a certain day be set apart to jointly praise the Dweller in the Heavens, he continues so: 'Let us unite in most humbly offering our prayers and supplications to the great Lord . . . to protect and guide all sovereigns and nations, especially such as have shown kindness to us, and bless them with good government, peace and concord.'[27]

Among those who suffered for your cause, among the generous who enlisted in your ranks to secure for you the precious inheritance now enjoyed, the people of France stand pre-eminently. The name of the most illustrious is inscribed on your roll of honor. The imposing likeness in the Hall of Independence attests a nation's gratitude.[28] Could that immortal son of France but speak, could America, he so fondly loved, learn his wish from his sainted lips, she would join this day with her ardent prayers a sisterly interposition for the safety of the

[26] An interesting formulation of the preacher's vision of America's role in the world, seeming to reconcile a politics of non-intervention with active moral involvement in international affairs.

[27] This was the proclamation made by George Washington on 3 Oct. 1789, following a request by Congress, recommending and assigning Thursday, 26 Nov. 1789 as a day of 'public Thanksgiving and Prayer': <earlyamerica.com/earlyamerica/firsts/thanksgiving/thankstext.html>. Morais cites this text, relevant to the day of the sermon, in order to emphasize the responsibility towards nations that 'have shown kindness to us' in the past. Note that in speaking about the Revolutionary War period, he rhetorically distances himself as a recent immigrant by speaking of 'your Republic', 'your cause', and 'your roll of honor'.

[28] Referring to the Marquis de Lafayette, as he goes on to specify. Recruited by the Philadelphian Benjamin Franklin, Lafayette arrived in Philadelphia on 27 July 1777, and four days later became the youngest general in American history. When President James Monroe invited him for a state visit in 1824, he electrified crowds in Philadelphia between 28 September and 4 October. He was ceremoniously welcomed in the Assembly Hall of the State House, where he delivered a speech that led to its being renamed the 'Hall of Independence'. See Idzerda, *Lafayette*, pl. 5 following p. 134 for the full-length portrait made for Independence Hall by Thomas Scully, Philadelphia's leading portrait painter, and p. 135 for Max Rosenthal's 'Interior View of Independence Hall, Philadelphia, 1856', showing the portrait of Lafayette prominently displayed.

country of Lafayette.[29] Our Thanksgiving would then be a practical demonstration of our religious professions, a fulfilling of that universal creed that teaches the brotherhood of nations. And God, who delights in mercy more than in sacrifices, would look down approvingly, and crown us with His choicest blessings.

Lord of all flesh! Infuse within us sentiments of commiseration for suffering humanity; for, verily, the practice of beneficence is the highest worship the creatures can offer their creator. By it our nature becomes spiritualized even while we tread the earth, for that genial virtue is the reflection of Thy Divine self in the soul of man. It does behoove the people Thou hast bountifully cared for to sing Thy praises in unison of hearts and show forth Thy loving kindness. It is meet that the children of the land Thou hast enlarged and strengthened, and enriched and exalted, should acknowledge that from Thy hand all this hath come. It is proper that they should recognize as Thy highest favor the rising of deliverers in the time of their danger, and the great salvation their eyes beheld; that they should glory in the wisdom Thou didst impart to their ancestors; in the might wherewith Thou didst gird their defenders; in the exhaustless treasures Thou didst place within their reach for the weal of generations yet unborn.

But Thy inspired servant of old hath taught that he who glorieth should glory mainly in this: That he understandeth and knoweth that Thou art the Lord, doing mercy, justice and charity upon earth, and that in those things Thou delighteth.[30] We therefore beseech Thee, O Source of all good, to purify our lives that we may copy Thy heavenly attributes, and spread broadcast the seeds of happiness. Let nations rejoice that righteousness hath a sanctuary in America, and at its shrine her children bend. Grant, O Most High God, that from this country of our inheritance, peace go forth, shadowing beneath its pavilion all the inhabitants of the globe. For then will Thy kingdom be established, and the Messianic era we long to hail gloriously dawn.[31] So may it be. Amen.

---

[29] Here the preacher—having begun by raising the possibility of American military intervention, and then calling for at least a formal diplomatic statement—limits himself to Thanksgiving Day prayers for the safety of France.                                    [30] Echoing Jer. 9: 23.

[31] Note the central role to be played by America in the messianic scenario of world peace.

# PART III

# THE WARS
## OF THE
## LATE
## NINETEENTH
## CENTURY

# CHAPTER TWELVE

## H. PEREIRA MENDES
# THE PLAGUE OF INCONSISTENCY

### 23 APRIL 1898

#### SHEARITH ISRAEL, NEW YORK

Henry Pereira Mendes, born in Birmingham, England, in 1852, counted among his lineage three branches of leaders of the British Sephardi community. His father, Abraham Pereira Mendes, minister of the Birmingham Hebrew Congregation, published in 1855 one of the earlier collections of English-language sermons,[1] succeeded Benjamin Artom as haham of the London community, and in 1883 moved to the Touro Synagogue in Newport, Rhode Island. His mother, Eliza, was the daughter of David Aaron de Sola, haham of the Bevis Marks congregation in London and sister of Abraham de Sola, who took up a rabbinic position in Montreal.[2] Eliza's mother was the daughter of Raphael Meldola, haham of the London Sephardim in the first half of the nineteenth century. Here, then, was someone who grew up exposed to fine models of the homiletical art.

H. P. Mendes received a fine general education in addition to his training in Jewish texts, studying at Northwick College (a Jewish boarding school established by his father) and University College London. Later, he earned an MD degree from New York University. After serving for several years as minister of the Sephardi congregation in Manchester, he was chosen in 1877 as cantor and

---

[1] Mendes, *Sermons*. Most of these sermons begin with a text from the weekly pericope (though without a rabbinic dictum in the classical Sephardi style); an introductory section is generally followed by an outline of three related topics that leads into a three-part sermon, concluding with a prayer. Note his sermon on the Crimean War, cited in the introduction to Sermon 4 above. Biographical material on H. P. Mendes is taken from Angel, 'Mendes, Henry Pereira'; Pool and Pool, *An Old Faith in the New World*, 192–202; Markovitz, 'Henry Pereira Mendes: Builder'.

[2] See references to sermons by David de Sola in the Introduction, above. The preaching of Abraham, who wrote a biography of his father, has been studied recently in several articles by Evelyn Miller and Richard Menkis.

preacher of Shearith Israel in New York, the flagship congregation of American Sephardim, succeeding J. J. Lyons. He remained with that congregation for the rest of his active career. Like his elder colleague Morais in Philadelphia, he combined a staunch commitment to tradition with an openness to non-Jewish culture, a willingness to work with non-Orthodox rabbis on Jewish and humanitarian causes, and an engagement with broad social and political issues. He was instrumental in establishing the New York Board of Jewish Ministers, the Union of Orthodox Rabbis, and the Jewish Theological Seminary of America.

Between seventy-five and a hundred sermons, some in the preacher's own manuscript and others in the form of clippings from newspaper accounts, have been preserved in the Piza Mendes Collection of Shearith Israel. Rabbi David de Sola Pool, who heard Mendes preach many times, wrote that he was 'gifted with a clear, ringing voice of unusually sympathetic quality, precision of diction, and a rich and poetic vocabulary. His emotional and hortatory messages lifted him to a spiritual and tender kind of oratory. The Bible was the constant source of his inspiration.'[3] Towards the end of his career, he taught homiletics at Yeshiva University's Isaac Elhanan Seminary.[4] Mendes preached on a wide array of topics, including antisemitism, the persecution of Russian Jews, Zionism, defense of Orthodoxy and condemnation of Reform (especially the Sunday service), and the role of Jews on of issues of general public concern; he also delivered a eulogy for President McKinley.[5] Given his committed opposition to armed conflict between nations, his preaching during times of war must have been especially passionate.

On 3 March 1898 the *New York Times* published a letter written two days earlier by Mendes, urging that the United States submit its claims against Spain, following the sinking of the USS *Maine* in the harbour of Havana on 15 February, to a court of arbitration to be composed of professors of international law in distinguished universities of various countries.[6] Six weeks later, on the sabbath, when the war officially began, as patriotic fervour began to sweep along even strong opponents of American intervention (see Sermon 13 by Krauskopf below), Mendes reiterated his call for arbitration in a sermon

[3] Pool and Pool, *An Old Faith in the New World*, p. 195.    [4] Ibid.
[5] Markovitz, 'Henry Pereira Mendes: Builder', 173–83, 67–72. Mendes gave an address on the rights of children before the Society for the Prevention of Cruelty to Children in 1878 (Pool and Pool, *An Old Faith in the New World*, 197). The governing board of Shearith Israel fixed the length of the sermon at thirty minutes when Mendes assumed his position (ibid. 19).
[6] New York Times, 3 Mar. 1898, p. 6. Mendes went on to propose that the great nations purchase Palestine and set up a neutral rehabilitated Jewish nation there that would function as arbitrator of international disputes. The *American Israelite* of 10 Mar. 1898, ignored the idea of an international court of arbitration and lambasted Mendes as one of 'a few wrongheaded zealots . . . who live in bygone centuries' (p. 4).

called 'The Plague of Inconsistency'. The following day, the sermon was featured in an article published in the *New York Herald*. Five days later, the *American Hebrew*, which did not bother publishing the text of the sermon, ran a full-page rebuttal by L. N. Hirschfield, which stated, 'The worthy Doctor's abhorrence of war in general is evidently so deep that it has prevented his grasping the salient facts of the present situation.' The author was especially incensed at Mendes' claim that the persecuted Jews of Russia deserved at least as much attention as the persecuted Cubans.

Does not such a statement place American Jews in a prejudicial light before the country? Does it not convey the impression that we are unable to view a large question of state except through the spectacles of a racial grievance against a land some four thousand miles distant from us? To my mind such a standpoint warps and distorts that whole-souled patriotism which we owe to the United States.[7]

I have found no record of what Mendes said following the American entry into the war, although the synagogue raised an American flag to be hung every day 'until the arms of the United States shall prevail over Spain', and its Sisterhood joined in collecting funds for the War Relief Fund. On behalf of the newly formed Union of Orthodox Congregations, Mendes petitioned the military authorities to grant Jewish servicemen furlough for the observance of Jewish holidays. Unlike Maximilian Michelbacher's similar application to Robert E. Lee during the Civil War, which was politely denied, Mendes' request was approved by the War Department.[8]

Morais would remain staunchly committed to the principle of arbitration rather than war as a way of solving conflicts between nations. He attended the World Parliament of Religions in 1893, and some four months after the beginning of the First World War addressed an audience of largely Christian clergy (the text was published a few months later in the *Christian Conservator*, a newspaper of the Church of the United Brethren in Christ, as an article entitled 'The Clergy and the War'). 'My brothers', he said,

it is for us of all men to proclaim the horrors of this war, its crime, cost, and curse, to condemn the wastage of human life, the immolation of manhood, the desolation of women's hearts. But let us also use our pulpit to suggest remedy . . . It is time that war was declared an anachronism, except when one's country is actually invaded.

He went on to call for an international court of arbitration and a world university, leading to a 'United States of Europe'.[9] One can only imagine his dismay

---

[7] *American Hebrew*, 29 Apr. 1898, p. 769.

[8] Pool and Pool, *An Old Faith in the New World*, 335; cf. Markovitz, 'Henry Pereira Mendes: Architect', 376.

[9] *Christian Conservator*, 14 Apr. 1915, p. 11. The dating of the text in Dec. 1914 is apparent from internal references to the imminent beginning of Hanukah and Christmas.

when, once again, despite his misgivings, the United States itself went to war.[10] The following text is taken from the article in the *New York Herald*, apparently based on a transcript, but with subheadings added as reproduced here.[11]

# S E R M O N

WE FIND this country going to war with another which has been guilty of cruelty and injustice. It is a grand thing to be the champion of 300,000 ill-treated and starving people in Cuba. Perhaps it would be a grander thing to be the champion of 3,000,000 of ill-treated people, many of whom are starving and who are concentrated in certain districts. I refer to the oppressed Hebrew in Russia.

It surely cannot make any difference to this great country that Spain is weak and Russia is strong. But 'circumstances alter cases', you might say. Ah, yes! But it seems to me there is a plague in the house, the plague of inconsistency.

This nation is interfering either from disinterested or from interested motives. If it is disinterested motives which appeal to this country, then the same disinterested motives should appeal to all the other great nations. They should, therefore, unite with America in expelling the Spanish. But America will not have them. That is to say, that although America would take action with the great nations on behalf of suffering Armenians,[12] yet the great Powers may not co-operate with America on behalf of suffering Cubans.

---

[10] With America's entry into the war, the Shearith Israel Sisterhood once again mobilized on behalf of the War Relief Fund (Pool and Pool, *An Old Faith in the New World*, 335–6). A year and a half later, the Board of Shearith Israel asked Mendes to preach an appropriately patriotic sermon on the sabbath of 12 Oct. 1918, in connection with a new campaign for the Fourth Liberty Loan (Markovitz, 'Henry Pereira Mendes: Builder', 72). Unfortunately, the text of that sermon is apparently not extant.

[11] Efforts over more than a year to determine whether the preacher's full text of this sermon has been preserved in the Piza Mendes Papers of Shearith Israel have not yielded a positive result, as the archives of the congregation are being relocated and are currently inaccessible. If the full text should be discovered, it would of course be instructive to compare it with the truncated newspaper version.

[12] Following massacres in 1895 and 1896, public opinion in Britain, France, Russia, and the United States, inspired by William Gladstone's passionate denunciations, pushed leaders to consider intervention against the Ottomans. A few months after the sermon was delivered, this international pressure was undermined by the visit to Constantinople of Kaiser Wilhelm II, who treated the sultan with great courtesy and respect.

## CALLS WAR A CRIME

You do not need me to remind you that it is our duty to support this government, right or wrong; to give our lives, and to spend of our means wholeheartedly for any war which the government of this country undertakes. But while we render loyal obedience to the temporal needs of the country of our adoption, we cannot forget the Bible. This being so, it becomes us to say that all war is a crime, except in self defence.

Let me now place before you the teaching as regards the destruction of the war ship in peace times.[13] Here again we plead for arbitration. But we go further than the Americans, because we say that if Spain was responsible her crime is less a crime against America than it is a crime against civilization. It becomes an international, not an America affair.

## SHOULD BE PUNISHED BY POWERS

If Spain is, by the great Powers, judged guilty of the crime of Amalek,[14] her name should be stricken off the roll of nations, her country and possessions disposed of as the Powers decide, and her people merged with other peoples.[15] A terrible punishment, you will say. Yes, but the blowing up of the ship was a terrible crime.

It was a grand opportunity for America to advance the grand Anglo-Saxon mission of elevating the doctrine of 'peace and good will to all men' far above the doctrine of tooth, nail and claw.[16] For the one speaks the man. For the other snarls the brute.

For the sake of humanity, civilization, righteousness and international honor, we say that Spain should be made to suffer whatever penalty should be imposed on it by the arbitration of all the nations—arbitration which should first be invoked before the cannon thunder.

---

[13] Referring to the destruction of the *Maine* in the harbour of Havana.

[14] The crime of Amalek was to attack the weak stragglers at the rear of the Israelite lines (Deut. 25: 19). It seems rather strange to liken this to an attack upon a warship, even if it was in harbour.

[15] While the method of adjudication is progressive, the punishment proposed—the elimination of Spain as a country and the forced assimilation of the Spanish people—seems brutally disproportionate to the crime. Perhaps it served a rhetorical purpose, appealing to the desire for revenge, but contingent on a mechanism of international consensus that could not possibly have been implemented.

[16] Juxtaposing the New Testament proclamation (Luke 2: 14) with an allusion to Tennyson's famous formulation, 'Nature, red in tooth and claw' ('In Memoriam A.H.H'.), crystallized in the expression 'fight tooth, nail and claw'.

# CHAPTER THIRTEEN

## JOSEPH KRAUSKOPF
# A TIME OF WAR, AND
# A TIME OF PEACE
### *A Sunday Lecture*

## 1 MAY 1898

### REFORM CONGREGATION KENESETH ISRAEL,
### PHILADELPHIA

JOSEPH KRAUSKOPF, born in Ostrowo, Prussia, in 1858, emigrated to America as a teenager. A member of the first class of the newly established Hebrew Union College in Cincinnati, he was ordained in 1883. After four years in Kansas City, Missouri, he assumed responsibilities as rabbi of Keneseth Israel Congregation in Philadelphia in October 1887.[1] He immediately established the practice of a regular Sunday morning service with a major address; the sermon reproduced below indicates that 1 May 1898 marked the conclusion of the eleventh year of these services. The Sunday morning discourses addressed a variety of subjects, including but not limited to specifically Jewish concerns. Indeed, in many of them the use of Jewish source material was extremely limited. The texts of these addresses were printed in pamphlet form and distributed to those who attended the following Sunday.

Krauskopf was known as a spellbinding orator. Israel Levinthal, son of a Philadelphia Orthodox rabbi and himself one of the most distinguished preachers in the Conservative movement, described how, as a young reporter in 1904 on Jewish matters for Philadelphia's *North American*, he was impressed by Krauskopf's sermons:

He was a gifted orator who would discuss timely themes with eloquence, and he attracted overflowing congregations every Sunday . . . Dr. Krauskopf used a flowery

---

[1] For biographical material on Krauskopf, see A. J. Feldman, 'Rabbi Joseph Krauskopf'; Beifeld, 'The Americanization of Reform Judaism'; and the uncritical biography by Blood, *Apostle of Reason*.

language and a most effective delivery. The Temple had a wide pulpit, almost like a stage, and Dr. Krauskopf would walk from one end to the other, pouring forth his thoughts. The strange thing about his speaking is that he memorized every Sunday lecture. At the Saturday morning service, when he delivered a brief sermon, he spoke extemporaneously; but the Sunday sermon was memorized ... [Often I would marvel] at the remarkable gift that was his to memorize the sermon and yet be able to deliver it in so eloquent and effective a fashion that no one suspected that the flow of his speech was not spontaneous. I was a devout admirer of his oratory, and I would observe most attentively every nuance of his voice, his every gesture, every expression on his face.[2]

During the months leading up to the Spanish and American declarations of war, and especially after the explosion in Havana harbour that sank the *Maine*, as anti-Spanish emotions were fanned by the 'yellow journalism' spearheaded by Randolph Hearst, many religious leaders urged from their pulpits that peace be given a chance. Condemning the 'wild clamors for blood, blood, blood', many Christian clergy pleaded for diplomacy and reasonable compromise as an alternative to war, and many rabbis joined them.[3] On 21 February 1898, the first Sunday after the *Maine* disaster, the Chicago Reform rabbi Emil G. Hirsch concluded his sermon with an application to the current circumstances of an enigmatic verse from the week's scriptural lesson:

The demagogue is pernicious, the politician who plays the part of the statesman will, like Aaron, erect an idol which the people may worship but to their harm. War or peace is the great solicitude of the nation. War is the last resort. It is an awful responsibility, and only that nation has the right to face it that has exhausted every other means and has been scrupulous in its regard for justice. Two hundred and fifty brave American sailors have met a noble death at their post of duty ... Shall death reap a still richer harvest? Let us be calm. Our Moses and our Aarons must ascend the height where God speaks (cf. Exod. 24: 9). The passion of the people who eat and drink (cf. Exod. 24: 11), the voice of the demagogue must not be heeded.[4]

---

[2] Levinthal, *The Message of Israel*, 145–6. Cf. the description of John Angell James, one of the most popular British pulpit orators of the nineteenth century: for an important sermon, he wrote out a full text and then memorized it; his brother sat with the text in hand to prompt if necessary, but reported that James hardly ever forgot a single word (Pike, *The Life and Work of Charles Hadden Spurgeon*, i. 105). Similarly, it was generally believed that Michael Sachs, rabbi in Berlin, preached extemporaneously (usually for an hour), and there was considerable surprise at the appearance after his death of a two-volume edition of his *Predigten. Aus dessen schriftlichem Nachlass herausgegeben*. It turned out that he devoted considerable time and effort to memorizing what he had written. See Phillipson, *Die Rhetorik und jüdische Homiletik*, 30 (editorial note by M. Kayserling); cf. ibid. 81–2 and H. Saperstein, *Witness from the Pulpit*, 5.

[3] May, *Imperial Democracy*, 140–1. Unfortunately, May provides no documentation for the Jewish clergy he cites or summarizes, and misidentifies Joseph Stolz as an 'orthodox Rabbi'.

[4] E. G. Hirsch, 'Men of Light and Leading'. Two weeks later, the *Advocate* published a full text of the sermon, in which Hirsch wrote: 'The passions of the people are appealed to by the demagogues—the little clowns who by some political tidal wave ... have been swept into the senate chamber or the house of congress. They are playing for the galleries—they spout and shout

In Boston on Sunday 13 March Rabbi Charles Fleischer of Temple Adath Israel delivered a sermon entitled 'War', first to a Cambridge church and then to his own congregation, stating, 'These days one could almost wish to take to the woods, in order to escape the constant cannonade of war-like words which fill the air. However, we must not flee, but stay and fight against war as becomes soldiers of peace.'[5] Even stronger in his opposition was Godfrey Taubenhaus of Brooklyn, preaching on 27 March on the text 'Nation shall not lift up sword against nation' (Isa. 2: 4), citing with approval a hypothetical prophet who says, 'War is a curse under all circumstances. Let no man venture it. No man has the right to purchase the gratification of his vanity at the cost of so much misery and devastation . . . I pray that our country should be saved from the disgrace and affliction of bloodshed.'[6] As we have seen above, the *New York Herald* of Sunday 24 April reported the previous day's sermon by H. P. Mendes in which he characterized American interventionist policy towards Cuba as suffering from a 'plague of inconsistency'.

Once war was declared, however—first by Spain, and then by the United States—most Jewish (and indeed Christian) preachers used their pulpits not just to affirm the duty to support the government in the war effort, but to offer a ringing endorsement of the justice of the American cause.[7] It was the rare exception to find a public statement by a Jewish leader such as the letter of 29 April to the *American Hebrew* by the Philadelphia physician, scholar, and community leader Solomon Solis-Cohen:

abhorrent as it is to hear the war cry of the savage echoed in the pulpits of Christianity, it is still more painful and a thousand times more abhorrent . . . to hear Jewish preachers re-echoing the savage and brutal teachings of the Christian clergy . . . History condemns the Mexican war, it will condemn the Cuban war. But whether or not we hold

---

"War" . . . They will do the shouting—the shooting and the dying will be left to others' (p. 65). Hirsch's editorial following the declaration of war struck a much more guarded note about the forces that drove American policy than we will find in Krauskopf's message (*Advocate*, 30 Apr. 1898, p. 176).

[5] Fleischer, 'War'. Fleischer went on to condemn the 'peculiar "patriotism"' that 'gives our whole nation the ridiculous aspect of Shakespeare's soldier—"jealous of honor, sudden and quick in quarrel, seeking the bubble reputation even in the cannon's mouth"', and predicted that 'except through haste and mismanagement, we shall not take up arms against Spain or any other set of fellow-beings'.          [6] Taubenhaus, 'Nation Shall Not Lift Up Sword'.

[7] The *New York Sunday Herald* reported a stunningly bellicose, jingoistic, almost racist sermon by Kaufmann Kohler called 'God's Ultimatum to Spain' ('Spain, the land of bull fights, brutality and ignorance! Spain the land that expelled Jew and Moslem and set foot on American soil to ravage the land and exterminate the inhabitants . . . has no claim to be regarded as a civilized nation'). The full text, published in the *American Hebrew*, adds the sentence, 'The Latin race has no share in the building up of the new manhood expected to grow upon this God-kissed soil of liberty'; the same issue announced sermon titles for the following weekend including 'My Country, Right or Wrong', by J. Silverman of Temple Emanu-El (see nn. 16, 21, 36, 43 below).

this view, let us not drag our religion into disgrace by allusions to Spain's conduct toward the Jews as justifying the present war.[8]

Krauskopf first addressed the issue of war with Spain in his Sunday lecture of 20 March 1898, entitled 'Beating Plowshares into Swords'. While he did not take the pacifist position that war is the greatest of all evils and can never be justified, his lecture is an expression of dismay over the prevalence of warfare among the nations in the last decade of the nineteenth century; a fierce condemnation of the 'yellow journalism' luridly appealing to base emotions in the call for war (with ironic jabs at the Christian preachers who seem to have totally forgotten many famous teachings of the gospels); an appeal to the unique destiny and mission of the American nation for the propagation of peace in the world; and a paean of praise for the wisdom and policies of President McKinley in striving to find a peaceful solution to the quarrels with Spain.[9]

The discourse reproduced here is the first delivered by Krauskopf after the formal declaration of war by the US Congress.[10] Following the introduction, which deals with the country's new situation, the first substantive part is intended to explain the preacher's dramatic change of attitude during the previous six weeks. Echoing the earlier lecture in many points, he reviews his prior position. Then he asserts his current view: not that McKinley had been wrong and the warmongers right, but that the declaration of war despite all the efforts to reach a diplomatic solution convinced him that the war had been declared in God's heavenly council.

The theological underpinning of the sermon is a reassertion of a traditional providential view of God in control of history, patient with Spain despite its many sins (going back at least four centuries), yet certain to punish the unrepentant sinning nation to reassert justice in the world. We have seen this providential approach to war in sermons at the beginning and the middle of the nineteenth century, and here now at its end. Sixteen years later, with the outbreak of the First World War, this position will become far more problematic, at least among liberal thinkers.

---

[8] Solis-Cohen, 'An Unholy War'; on the letter's author, see P. Rosen, 'Dr. Solomon Solis-Cohen'.

[9] Krauskopf, 'Beating Plowshares into Swords'. See specific references and citations in nn. 19, 21, 23 below. Of course, not all clergy had been pushing for war; see e.g. the article 'Should We Go to War?', in the Church of God paper *The Gospel Trumpet*, 14 Apr. 1898, p. 4: 'There is no place in the New Testament wherein Christ gave instruction to his followers to take the life of a fellow-man . . . "If thine enemy hunger, feed him, if he thirst, give him drink"—not shoot him' (quoted by Strege, 'An Uncertain Voice for Peace', 115).

[10] The Archives of Congregation Keneseth Israel have graciously furnished me with a copy of Krauskopf's manuscript of the sermon; written in a flowing hand it has been edited by the author, with words and phrases blotted out and occasional insertions, all of which are reflected in the printed edition. It is impossible to determine whether the corrections were made before or after delivery.

The use of history is a central part of Krauskopf's presentation. He outlines the history of Spanish mistreatment of the Cuban people, culminating in the atrocities committed under the rule of Captain General Valeriano Weyler y Nicolau; he draws an analogy with the considerably lesser grievances of the American people outlined in the Declaration of Independence; and he sets the Spanish Cuban policy in a broader context of atrocities against the Jews and Moors, beginning in 1492, and against the Protestant inhabitants of the Netherlands in the second half of the sixteenth century. The historical record is an integral part of the claim of providential sanction for the campaign against Spain.

Two powerful rhetorical passages build to the climax of the sermon. The first is based on a pronounced use of anaphora and parallelism, repeating the frightening word 'Doomed' in what must have built up a powerful crescendo: 'Lo, the End of once proud and mighty Hispaniola! Doomed, because she has tyrannized, where she ought to have ruled! Doomed, because she has hated, where she ought to have loved!'—and six additional such phrases. The second was apparently triggered by the media. On 24 April a *New York Times* article stated that women of the Spanish aristocracy were 'organizing religious associations, under the auspices of the Bishops, for the purpose of holding, day and night, special services of prayer for the success of the Spanish arms'. The following day, a brief article reported the diocesan letter issued on the previous day by the Archbishop of Madrid: 'The Archbishop makes the war appear a question of good and evil, with Spain all white and the United States all black. He appeals to all the saints to protect the Spaniards, almost promising invulnerability against American bullets.'[11] Krauskopf incorporated the motif of Spaniards appealing to the saints for protection into the rhetorical climax of the sermon. Rather than contesting the Catholic belief in the intercessory power of the saints, he accepts it as a premise, but then juxtaposes the souls of the martyrs of Spanish persecution through the ages appearing in an intercessory role against Spain, and overpowering the moral force of the Spanish-sympathizing saints. While Jews and Moors, as well as contemporary Cubans, are cited, the greatest emphasis is given to the persecution of Protestants in the Netherlands under the Duke of Alva.

During the summer of 1898, Krauskopf was appointed a special field commissioner of the National Relief Commission, and in that capacity travelled to inspect and help equip field hospitals in Florida and Cuba. A report published in Emil G. Hirsch's *Reform Advocate* emphasizes his meeting with Jewish soldiers in Cuba.[12] Krauskopf referred back to this experience in several later

[11] *New York Times*, 24 Apr. 1898, p. 7; 25 Apr. 1898, p. 7.

[12] *Reform Advocate*, 16/1, 20 Aug. 1898, pp. 1–3; see on Krauskopf's mission Korn, 'Jewish Welfare Activities', 221–3.

sermons, especially during the First World War.[13] His associate J. Leonard Levy described himself as 'the first man in our country to offer my services as a volunteer in 1898 in the American–Spanish war', adding that, since that war ended, 'I have been an unfailing advocate of what is known as the pacifist policy. I am a converted man.'[14] For Levy's modification of that pacifist position as America entered the Great War, see his Sermon 18 below, delivered on 8 April 1917.

# S E R M O N

—

*To everything there is a season, and a time to every purpose under the heaven . . .*
*A time of war, and a time of peace.*

(ECCLES. 3: 1, 8)

*The Lord is merciful and gracious, long-suffering and abundant in goodness and in*
*truth. He shows kindness unto the thousandth's generation, forgives sin,*
*but He will surely not clear the guilty.*

(EXOD. 36: 6–7)

THIS IS THE LAST of another season, the eleventh, of our Sunday Services,[15] and, according to our custom, this should have been the day for casting a glance backward, to review the season's work, and to note the advance, if any has been made. That backward glance, however, will not be made to-day; not, indeed, for fear that its revelations will not compare favorably with preceding ones, but because we need our eyes elsewhere; to-day, we need them for a close inspection of the present, and for a diligent inquiry into the immediate future. A crisis has arisen, of an importance immeasurably surpassing the most momentous of congregational perplexities, a national crisis, at the side of which congregational interests, and be they the highest, utterly fade into insignificance. Our nation is at war, not in the interest of conquest, not for the sake of national aggrandizement, not for a display of military skill,

---

[13] e.g. Krauskopf, 'To the Front', 1; id., 'To Prepare or Not to Prepare?', 51; id., 'Hands that Toil and Hearts that Feel', 85; he undoubtedly spoke of this experience in the autumn of 1898, but I have not had access to those addresses.      [14] J. L. Levy, 'The War against War', 4.

[15] Thirty-six volumes of Krauskopf's Sunday addresses were published, beginning in 1888 and ending with the year 1922/3.

not for a test of the destructive power of modern armaments, but wholly for the sake of peace among nations, for the sake of good-will among men.[16]

And noble as these motives are, they are not of our own choosing. It is God's will, not ours, that our army is mobilized and that our navy stands ready to belch forth death and destruction upon Havana and its people. It was in the Council Chamber on High, that war was declared; it was from the Judgment Seat of the Almighty Arbiter, that the *fiat* went forth: 'Let there be War!' And there is war. It is God, who has willed this armed conflict, it is He, who engages in it; we are but the weapons in his employ, are but carrying out the will of the Commander of all Commanders, of the Ruler of all Rulers, of the King of Kings.[17]

I have been very slow in arriving at this conclusion. I believed that the difficulty between the United States and Spain was of man's creation, and, therefore, of man's solution, and I was greatly strengthened in my belief seeing that both Ex-President Cleveland and President McKinley, both wise men, both men schooled in the affairs of nations, were actuated by the same conviction.[18]

Conscious of the hellishness of war, and of the brutality of man, once he had entered upon bloodshed and devastation, I deemed it our most sacred duty to steer clear of passion and revenge, to maintain a dignified calmness, and

[16] This was a common theme in justification of the war by those who despised the jingoists. Krauskopf's associate J. Leonard Levy had said from the same pulpit the previous Sunday: 'This war is not for self; it is for others. If we desired Cuba, if behind this crisis, there were, on the part of our government, a movement for annexation, if it were a war of aggression and for aggrandizement, then it were a dreadful thing, and our flag would be nothing but a debasing idol' ('The Altar at the Hearth', 7). Cf. Joseph Silverman of New York's Temple Emanu-El, preaching on 1 May: 'It is the most unselfish, the most righteous war waged in this age. It is not a war for gain, nor for territory, nor for glory. All that we shall gain from it will be debts, and sorrow, perhaps, in thousands of homes. It has already demonstrated to the world that America is the champion of liberty, equality, and justice' ('My Country Right or Wrong'); also Revd Washington Gladden: 'not for territory or empire or national honor, but for the redress of wrongs not our own, for the establishment of peace and justice in the earth' (cited in Trask, *The War with Spain*, 58).

[17] Note the far more cautious formulation by Isaac Mayer Wise in the *American Israelite* following the declaration of war: the war is here, 'whether by the will of God or the decree of the Congress of the United States, will become manifest by its ultimate result . . . It may be the will of Providence, that we should bring all those sacrifices which war demands . . . It may be the will of Providence that this chosen people of free men drive out the Canaanites and the Philistines from the promised land' (*American Israelite*, 28 Apr. 1898, p. 4); see the overview by J. Abrams, 'Remembering the *Maine*', with quotation on p. 443.

[18] Cf. his address of a month earlier: 'The firm hand of an experienced pilot is at the helm of our nation, and he is endeavoring his utmost to steer us clear of the shoals and rocks, that are now threatening us . . . He has given us ample proof that we can safely trust him' ('Beating Plowshares into Swords', 6). For the desire of Cleveland and McKinley to avoid war with Spain over Cuba, see May, *Imperial Democracy*, 112–30, 148–59; Smith, *The Spanish–American War*, 30–43; Corry, *1898*, 22–3, 82–100.

to leave no recourse untried toward an honorable and amicable settlement of the grievous complication.[19]

Conversant with the gradual growth of the humaner impulses within the hearts of men, and of the gradual spread of fraternal sentiments among the peoples of the earth, I believed that the time had come for nations to adjust their difficulties with the weapons of reason and by means of peaceful arbitration, instead of bloody battles.[20]

Interpreting our Nation's different origin from that of other nations: its having been founded in peace and for peace, and not in or for bloodshed, its having been established by and for lawful possession instead of by and for rapacious and cruel conquest, I believed it Divinely commissioned to serve in the Temple of Humanity as the High-Priestess of Peace, as the preacher and teacher of it unto the nations of the earth, and that it would be a violation of the decree of destiny to stain our hands with the gore of war,[21] to saturate our or the enemy's

[19] This statement characterizes Krauskopf's position following the sinking of the *Maine* on the night of 15 Feb.: one similar to that of President McKinley, who ordered an investigation of the cause of the deadly explosion and attempted to involve various international diplomats as mediators and to restrain the pro-war sentiments of Congress, until, on 20 April, he signed a congressional joint resolution giving Spain three days to meet American demands that it relinquish its authority and government in Cuba. On 20 March Krauskopf had said: 'If there is to be war, let us quietly and patiently await the command from him, whom we have chosen for our Commander-in-Chief. And we may rest assured that such a command will never be given, till every avenue for an honorable settlement of our difficulty with Spain had been hopelessly barred, and every effort at arbitration had been exhausted' ('Beating Plowshares into Swords', 6–7).

[20] Cf. Ingersoll, 'Spain and the Spaniard': 'I am in favor of an international court ... and before fore this court I think all questions between nations should be decided, and the only army and the only navy should be under its direction, and used only for the purpose of enforcing its decrees ... Until there is such a court, there is no need of talking about the world being civilized.' Yet on 1 May, in a major lecture, he described the war against Spain as 'the holiest of all wars' (*Chicago Tribune*, 2 May 1898, p. 2).

[21] Here Krauskopf echoes the peroration of his 20 Mar. address: 'Our nation [i.e. the United States] has a destiny, our people [the American people] a mission. Not like other nations has ours been founded ... Others started in bloodshed, and established themselves by and for conquest. We started in peace, and for peace, and peace must continue to be our nation's destiny, our people's mission' ('Beating Plowshares into Swords', 7). Note the conception of a providential role for America expressed in terms reminiscent of ideas about a Jewish 'mission' to the nations of the world. Cf. the comments of Joseph Silverman (Temple Emanu-El of New York) at the opening session of the Central Conference of American Rabbis' convocation in Atlantic City on 5 July 1898: 'in this glorious, triumphal hour when America is marching with her hosts to carry her doctrines, if not her flag, into every land of the world—we see at home a realization of some of Israel's prophecies, dreams and mission. Not for conquest does America fight, but for the highest ideals of humanity, which Israel has carried from Sinai to America' (*CCAR Yearbook, 1898–99 (5659)*, 7).

land with the hearts' blood of our or our enemy's flowering youth and manhood, to orphan and widow thousands and tens of thousands of happy homes, to end or blight countless of successful or promising careers.

Firm in my faith that the nineteenth century had witnessed a change in the definition of patriotism, that while in former times it was believed to manifest itself in a readiness to slay and pillage, to devastate and destroy, in our day it shows itself rather in saving life, in preserving property, in safe-guarding honor, in fostering good-will, I believed that the true patriotism would bring about the desired peace, without a sacrifice of honor, or the loss of life.[22]

Fully relying on the statesmanship of our Chief Executive, and observing the strenuous efforts made by him for averting the threatening calamity, and conscious of the calmness and quiet required by him, during such trying times, I strongly condemned that brutal clamor for immediate revenge, that so boisterously and so sensationally and even so insolently resounded in press and on platform, and that heated the passions of the people, and goaded on their representatives in the national Capitol,[23] and which, but for the skillful leadership in both Houses of Congress, might have precipitated the Nation into the conflict, before it was yet prepared for attack or defense, and before its cause was yet fully justified before the tribunal of the nations.

And, finally, assured of the weakness of Spain: of her internal dissensions, her exhausted treasury, her impaired credit, her enfeebled army, her great distance from us, and convinced of our many advantages: our ample means, our

[22] Echoing his statement on 20 Mar., 'The true patriotism, that in former times displayed itself in a readiness to slay and pillage, to devastate and destroy, shows itself in our day in saving life, in preserving property, in safeguarding honor, in fostering peace and good-will' ('Beating Plowshares into Swords', 5).

[23] In his earlier speech Krauskopf had vehemently attacked 'this mendacious, war-mongering press, this panderer to man's basest passions . . . this raging, foaming, loud-mouthed sensational press' ('Beating Plowshares into Swords', 5), as well as the preachers who 'all over the land, vied with the daily sensation-mongers in clamoring for war' (ibid. 6). Cf. also the sermon by Leo Franklin on 11 Feb. 1899: ' "Blood for blood, life for life" was the cry that rang and resounded for weeks and months before the outbreak of our war throughout this Christian country' ('The Law of Retaliation', p. 9). Some Christian preachers similarly denounced the 'clamor for immediate revenge'. For example, W. H. P. Faunce, preaching at the Fifth Avenue Baptist Church in New York the previous Sunday, asserted, 'Any man to-day who tries to foment the passions of revenge by the cry of "Remember the Maine" is reverting to the brutal instinct of the savage ages' ('God in the Nation's Life'). And William S. Rainsford of St George's Episcopal Church, on the day of Krauskopf's sermon, took a similar line: 'Let us attack all this talk of revenge . . . Let us deny and denounce all this talk about "Remember the Maine". Who shall speak of vengeance in this holy cause for which this war is being waged? Let us, like a great Nation, be tolerant' ('Who Is My Neighbor?'). For anti-Spanish public opinion generated by Hearst papers, see Corry, *1898*, 82–5; Edgerton, *'Remember the Maine'*, 47–9; Procter, *William Randolph Hearst*, 95–119.

well-nigh unlimited credit, our natural resources, our nearness to the scene of action, and above all, the justice of our cause, I felt that, if wise statesmanship be but displayed, if due time be but given Spain, if due leniency be but displayed toward her natural sensitiveness and traditional pride, she would at length come to her senses, recognize the weakness of her cause, and the folly of engaging us in war, yield to our just demands—not for power or territory for ourselves,[24] but simply for peace and justice for her own Cuban subjects.

But the stern fact that we are at war to-day with Spain, despite our long-tried patience and forbearance, despite our President's noble and pains-taking efforts for an amicable adjustment of our difficulty, has convinced me that it is the will of God and not our own free choice, that we are standing to-day arrayed against each other with drawn swords and murderous guns, that cruel war has at length been determined upon by Providence, as a final and effective measure for the suppression of Spanish atrocity, and for the ending of her dominion, at least in the Western Hemisphere.

Of a truth, God had been merciful and gracious and long-suffering with Spain. He had borne long and patiently with her many and cruel transgressions. Again and again had He given evidence of His wrath against her sins. He had humbled her to the dust, from one of the loftiest positions in all the world. He had stripped her of her power, that once was the greatest of all the nations of the earth. He had taken her treasures from her, that once were the richest of all the lands.[25] But he had not crushed her altogether. She had rendered some service to the cause of humanity; she had made some contributions to the progress of man which merited some consideration for her, at the tribunal of God. That consideration lay in the opportunity given her to atone for her past brutalities, and to obtain the favor of God and man, by dealing justly and loving mercy and walking humbly before God. He had left her a pittance of her former vast empire in the New World, as a witness of the depth into which she had sunk, and as a silent appeal to her to do away with the evil, that had brought her downfall upon her, and that was still clinging to her.

But, she would neither be admonished by witness, nor would she give ear to appeal. Neither would she profit by the examples of the fates that had befallen

[24] A repetition of the motif of national selflessness stated at the end of the first paragraph, and restated yet again at the end.
[25] Cf. Ingersoll, 'Spain and the Spaniard', drawing the same contrast but in a totally secular manner: 'At one time Spain was the greatest of powers, owner of half the world, and now she has only a few islands, the small change of her great fortune . . . souvenirs of departed wealth, of vanished greatness.'

ancient brutal and blood-thirsty and God-defying nations. She continued her outrages upon Cuba, trampled upon justice, throttled every liberty, sneered at the world's appeal for mercy, laughed the threat of divine vengeance to scorn; made of bloodshed a pastime, and of starvation a sport. It was the old story of her brutality, in former centuries, against the Jew and the Moor, against the Peruvian and Mexican, against the Protestants of the Netherlands.[26] And God's deep measure of patience and forbearance was full to the brim at last. And He decreed that there shall be an end to Spanish atrocity in Cuba and has appointed us, the people of the United States, to drive her, and for ever, from off our hemisphere, and to restore peace and prosperity to the devasted [sic] and famine-stricken island of Cuba, and secure liberty for its long and brutally tyrannized people.

Verily, the fate of the Cubans has, with the exception of the Jews of Russia, been the most cruel of modern times. Had their island been a province of a different nation and tongue and people and creed, acquired by bloody conquest, and continuing, relentlessly hostile, it could not have been more atrociously treated than it has been at the hand of its mother country. That a state of insurrection exists there now, and has existed there for some years, is not surprising The surprise is that a Cuban still exists there to rebel, or that Spanish tyranny could still run riot there, and force rebellion. For what could have been done to hasten the utter extermination of the Cuban that Spain has left undone? What could have been done to arouse the Cuban, man, woman, and child, to rise in righteous wrath against the heartless tyrant, and never lay down their weapons, until either death—more merciful than their brutal oppressor—has put an end to their sufferings, or they had expelled the fiendish monster from their once beauteous but now devasted [sic] island, what could have been done to accomplish this that Spain has left undone?

I cannot but believe that if the inhabitants of that island had been of Anglo-Saxon stock, there would either have been no Cuban alive today, or no Spanish flag would to-day have floated over that Island. How our hearts burn with indignation at the mere reading of the oppressive measure of George III against the American colonies, and how our souls are thrilled with patriotism at the accounts of the valorous uprising of the young and feeble colonies against their powerful mother-country, of their heroic struggles and undaunted perseverance, though many times excelled in number and skill, though a score of

---

[26] These victims of Spanish brutality in the past, mentioned in passing here, will be invoked later with great rhetorical force at a climactic moment near the end of the sermon.

times defeated and crushed, ever rising anew with ever rejuvenated strength, ever fighting on with ever increasing hope, until at last they swept the tyrant from off the land and shore, and kept him at a safe and respectful distance ever after.

And yet, what were the tyrannies the colonies suffered, compared with those with which Spain has cursed Cuba and the Cubans, now nigh unto four hundred years?[27] From the very first, Spain considered Cuba as created and existing solely for the purpose of furnishing an abundance of revenue for her insatiable greed. The first report given of it by Columbus, as being 'the most beautiful and most fertile island that eyes have ever beheld',[28] has been its first misfortune. Its beauty proved its fatality; its fertility its curse. It has been used as a miserably kept milch-cow, ever since. It has had its choicest and richest substance drawn from it, for the tyrant's enjoyment, within the island or at home. But once did it enjoy a brief respite from Spanish atrocity, that was a little over a century ago, when England had possession of it. Unfortunately for the Cuban, however, that respite lasted but ten months.[29] Spain resumed her former hold, and with a cruelty more devilish than before. No burden was so heavy that Spain would not lay upon the Cuban; no tax so great that she would not levy upon him; no official so cruel whom she would not set in absolute authority over the unfortunate. With the honorable exceptions of Generals Campos and Blanco, no Governor and no official ever went to Cuba for any other purpose than that of enriching himself, of impoverishing the land, of outraging the people's sense of right and justice.[30] 'The Cubans', says Mr. Murat Halstead, 'became the victims of

[27] This rhetorical comparison of the Cuban grievances against Spain as significantly greater than those of the Americans against Britain as recited in the Declaration of Independence may have been taken by the preacher from Murat Halstead (quoted a few lines further on; see n. 28 below), who himself quotes a manifesto written by Señor Estrada Palma, beginning: 'We Cubans have a thousandfold more reason in our endeavor to free ourselves from the Spanish yoke than the people of the thirteen colonies when, in 1775, they rose in arms against the British government' (Halsted, *The Story of Cuba*, 405).

[28] I have not found this precise quotation attributed to Columbus. Cf. the text of Columbus's report in Halstead, *The Story of Cuba*, 535–8, and Edgerton, *'Remember the Maine'*, 181–2.

[29] On the period of English control in 1762, see Halstead, *The Story of Cuba*, 33–4, 215–52.

[30] Cf. ibid. 395: 'There is a gallery of portraits in the palace at Havana of the Spanish generals for nearly two hundred years, a superb array of uniforms and striking Spanish faces, and they were all stern rulers, and with few exceptions they used their great office oppressively for the benefit of the official class, regardless of the interests or the susceptibilities of the people.' Captain-General Arsenio Martínez Campos succeeded in ending the Ten Years War of 1868–78 with the 'Treaty of Zanjon' and was known as the 'Pacificator' (ibid. 88; cf. Smith, *The Spanish–American War*, 4, 10). Captain-General Ramón Blanco y Erenas, who had previously served as Captain-General of the Philippines, replaced Weyler in October 1897 as a more conciliatory figure (Smith, *The Spanish–American War*, 24).

endless rapacity; each swarm of flies when gorged, giving way to another, each equal to its predecessors in greedy appetites and profligacy, at the expense of the people, who, as a last resort, rebel and lay waste with fire and sword the island they love.'[31] Oh, if all the innocent blood that Spain has shed and all the tears that she has cruelly caused to fall, were gathered together they would form a sea, wide and deep enough even to float the formidable battleships, which she is now arraying against us, and if all the sighs and moans and cries, which she has pressed out of the hearts and souls of agonized peoples, could be gathered together, their united sound would outroar the thunder, that shook the city of Havana, when Spanish treachery sent the noble *Maine* and her gallant crew to their watery graves.

Bad as had been the state of affairs in Cuba for centuries, the worst had not been reached until Weyler came, that third in the world's triumvirate of monsters, that fit associate of Torquemada of his own country,[32] and of Ivan, the Terrible, of Russia, that Weyler, who immediately after his arrival entered upon his hellish work of extermination, established his bloody *trochas*,[33] tore more than 200,000 peaceful and hard-working peasants from their fields and labor, and concentrated them in the cities, and literally starved, in enforced idleness, nearly one-seventh of the island's population.[34]

But, there is a limit even to Spanish atrocity. Weyler's brutality aroused the indignation of the whole civilized world, and his victims' cries of despair and

[31] I have not found this quotation in Halstead's *The Story of Cuba* or his *Our Country in War* (both published in 1898); it may be taken from some speech or article that came to the preacher's attention. For a description of the destruction of property by Cuban insurgents as well as Spaniards, see Halstead, *The Story of Cuba*, 356–76 (esp. 365–6), and 418.

[32] The link between Torquemada and General Weyler was not uncommon in the rhetoric of the time; Ingersoll, in 'Spain and the Spaniard', asserted that 'There has been no break between Torquemada and Weyler, between the Inquisition and the infamies committed in Cuba.' It is somewhat surprising that Krauskopf brings in Ivan the Terrible here; given the horrific passage to come, the Duke of Alva would have been more relevant as the third person in the triumvirate of evil-doers.

[33] Defensive line ditches, some 200 yards wide, filled with various obstacles, and guarded by towers and blockhouses (Smith, *The Spanish–American War*, 11).

[34] On Weyler and his policies, especially the concentration of civilian populations, see Smith, *The Spanish–American War*, 18–24. Hearst wrote in his *Journal* on 23 Feb. 1896: 'Weyler the brute, the devastator of haciendas, the destroyer of families, and outrager of women ... Pitiless, cold, an exterminator of men ... There is nothing to prevent his carnal, animal brain from running riot with itself in inventing tortures and infamies of bloody debauchery' (quoted in Jones, *Crucible of Power*, 247–8). The House resolution passed on 13 Apr. 1898 stated that Spanish policy in Cuba was responsible for 'causing the death, by starvation, of more than two hundred thousand non-combatants, the victims being, for the most part, helpless women and children' (Halstead, *Our Country in War*, 497). Thomas Dixon, Jr, preaching at the New York Opera House on 1 May, upped the ante, stating that the Spanish 'have actually starved to death three hundred thousand women and children, besides the hosts shot and cut to pieces' ('The Battle Cry of Freedom', 2).

shrieks of agony, stirred at last, and to the core, the active sympathy of the people of the United States. Our repeated cry of 'Halt!' 'Enough!' that has rung throughout the world, and that has awakened reverberating echoes everywhere, rebounded, however, unheard from the Spaniard's ears. And so has he compelled us to see whether his ears can be reached, and his deafness cured, by means of American batteries and cannonades.

And should even this method fail, then perhaps his eyes will teach him what his ears have refused to learn. Then perhaps he will read on the flag of *The Republic of Cuba*, floating proudly and majestically on the heights of Morro Castle,[35] or, he will read on the disasters and strifes and havocs and ruins, at home, the fatal words, written in the hand-writing of Nemesis:[36] Lo, the Doom of Spain! Lo, the End of once proud and mighty Hispaniola! Doomed, because she has tyrannized, where she ought to have ruled! Doomed, because she has hated, where she ought to have loved! Doomed, because she has cursed, where she ought to have blessed! Doomed, because she has impoverished where she ought to have enriched! Doomed, because she has outraged, where she ought to have protected! Doomed, because she has violated, where she should have held sacred! Doomed, because she has wounded, where she should have healed! Doomed, because she has murdered, where she should have kept alive! Doomed, because she has proven herself a vulture, a hyena, a harpy, a vampyre, a devil, where she should have been a mother, a protectoress, a guide, a Guardian Angel.

From the Courts on High the decree has gone forth, that Spain shall furnish another powerful illustration of the oft-taught and oft-experienced truth, that there is no concealing from the all-penetrating eyes of Nemesis, no outrunning the swiftness of its feet, no passing beyond the reach of its arms, no reliance in a trust in its forgetfulness. Punishment may be slow in coming, but come it will. God is merciful and patient and long-suffering but He never clears the guilty, and the punishment is often all the severer for His longer patience.

[35] Italics in the original: an envisioned symbol of Cuban independence, Morro Castle dominates the approach to Havana harbour.

[36] In Greek mythology, the goddess of inexorable retributive justice. Krauskopf was apparently fond of this rhetorical device, which he had used in an address ten weeks earlier: 'Nemesis still rules, and she neither sleeps nor slumbers. She may tarry long, but she comes; and when she comes there is no mistaking her; and when she leaves there is no distrusting any longer in a God or Justice' ('The Martyr-Race', 5). Here he seems to merge this figure with the biblical motif of divine justice and the 'hand-writing on the wall' from Daniel. Cf. Joseph Silverman (n. 21 above): 'By the lurid illumination of the war's conflagration we can read the doom of Spain—"*Mene, mene, tekel upharsin*"—You have been weighed in the balance and been found wanting' (*CCAR Yearbook, 1898–99 (5659)*, 8).

The avenging hand that is slowest to rise often deals, when raised at last, the quickest and most telling blow. To the long unpunished miscreant the eye of God may seem shut, and His hand and feet may seem shackled, but when with amazing suddenness the search-light of outraged Right and Truth and Justice is turned full upon him, and an iron grasp clutches him, and blow upon blow is dealt him, he no longer doubts the judgment of God, nor forgets it either.[37]

Poor deluded Spaniards! In vain is your prostrating yourselves now, as the newspapers report, before your Blessed Saints, and your beseeching them for success in your armed conflict with the United States.[38] It is not we who wage cruel war against you. It is God, it is outraged Justice, it is trampled-down Liberty, it is despoiled Virtue, it is violated Honor that are arrayed against you, and against such formidable hosts all your prayers and all your prostrations will avail naught. Had you prostrated yourself before your God with a clean conscience, before you prostrated the Cuban, had you asked the blessings of God, before you earned the curses of the Cuban, there would have been no need of your present prayers to the Blessed Saints for your success in war against the most peace-loving of all nations, the United States.

Deluded Spaniards, put no trust in your prayers to the Blessed Saints for success in the war, which a long-patient, and a long-suffering God has decreed upon you. Even if they wanted to aid you, their hands would be stayed. From the North and from the South, from the East and from the West a well-nigh interminable army of martyr-spirits would rush in, with the speed and fury of the tornado, and sweep their proffered aid into nothingness.

From the land of Mexico and Peru there would hurry on the protesting spirits of the hundreds of thousands of Cholulans and Montezumans and Incans, who, entirely innocent and wholly inoffending, had been foully massacred by the perfidious Cortez and the treacherous Pizarro.[39] From half of Europe there would sweep in the souls of more than a quarter of a million of Jews and Moors and other so-called heretics who were secretly tortured and publicly executed, amidst unspeakable cruelties, by means of the Devil's own

[37] Cf. the similar sentiments in the sermon by Kaufmann Kohler delivered the previous week: 'God's hand had written the Ultimatum, the *Mene Tekel* of Spanish misrule on this hemisphere . . . God's mills grind slowly but surely. God avengeth the wrong and brings upon tyranny its merited doom, yet He is long-suffering and slow in punishing . . . Is this not a day of divine judgment? *Die Weltgeschichte ist das Weltgericht.* "The world's history is one great judgment day of God"' ('God's Ultimatum to Spain').

[38] *New York Times*, 24 Apr. 1898, p. 7; 25 Apr. 1898, p. 7 (see the introduction to this sermon).

[39] An interesting allusion to the conquistadors not as heroic explorers and pioneers but as mass murderers.

invention, the Spanish Inquisition, and under order of the bloodiest of all the world's executioners, Torquemada, and his no less fiendish successors.[40]

From out of the Netherlands, there would rush in, and with burning and uncontrollable rage, a vast army, counting by the hundred of thousands, of the spirits of those who, for the crime of believing in, and adhering to, Protestantism, were burned, strangled, garroted, beheaded, buried alive, suffocated, starved, maimed, crippled, outraged, by order of that fiend incarnate, the Duke of Alva, he, to whom shedding of blood, and gloating over torture, and planning massacres, and scheming assassinations, and perpetrating perfidies and treacheries, were the only exhilarating pastime of life, he, who enjoys the infamous distinction of having issued the bloodiest sentence of death, that has ever emanated from mind or court of man or devil, the edict of February 16th, 1568, on which he condemned to death, as heretics, all the inhabitants of the Netherlands, an edict, of which the historian of the Dutch Republic, J. L. Motley, says:

This is probably the most concise death-warrant that was ever framed. Three millions of people, men, women, and children, were sentenced to the scaffold in three lines; and as it was well known that these were not harmless thunders, like some bulls of the Vatican, but serious and practical measures, which it was intended should be enforced, the horror which they produced may be easily imagined . . . Men in the highest and humblest positions were daily and hourly dragged to the stake . . . Many a citizen saw himself suddenly tied to a horse's tail, with his hands fastened behind him, and so dragged to the gallows . . . To avoid the disturbances created in the streets by the frequent harangues or exhortations addressed to the bystanders by the victims on their way to the scaffold, a new gag was invented. The tongue of each prisoner was screwed into an iron ring and then seared with a hot iron. The swelling and inflammation, which were the immediate results, prevented the tongue from slipping through the ring, and, of course, effectually precluded all possibility of speech.[41]

[40] Cf. Sabato Morais, speaking in an 1868 Thanksgiving sermon about Spain's past: 'The shades of millions consigned to the rack by *autos da fe* flit before my vision. I see that hideous monster, brought from the Vatican, to devour Andalusia; that accursed Inquisition which turned a lovely spot on earth into a charnel house. Every stone therefore is reddened with the blood of the martyrs of the Jewish faith'; yet, referring to the newly installed revolutionary government, he insists that 'I will not judge Spain by her past' (cited in Kiron, 'Livornese Traces in American Jewish History', 63). Cf. also Moses Simon Sivitz who, four weeks before Krauskopf's sermon, spoke in Pittsburgh of 'Our enemies the cursed Spanish, red from the blood of our ancestors', mentioning 'the cursed Inquisition which sentenced to death myriads [*alfei revavot*] of parents and children of our people' ('Sermon for *Shabbat Hagadol* [the sabbath before Passover]', 108; I am grateful to Menachem Blondheim for directing me to this text).

[41] Motley, *The Rise of the Dutch Republic*; the quotations are all taken from ii. 158–9. The preacher errs in stating that the Duke of Alva issued the edict of 16 Feb. 1568; issued by the Holy Office (the Inquisition), and confirmed by King Philip ten days later, it provided the authority for the execution of virtually any inhabitant of the Netherlands. Motley reported that 18,600 inhabitants were executed under the Duke of Alva's regime.

And from our own country there would rush in the spirits of the two hundred and fifty martyr-sailors of the good ship *Maine*, which Spanish treachery has sunk to the bottom, And these would be followed by the spirits of the hundreds of thousands of massacred and slaughtered and starved Cubans, with that of Maceo in the lead,[42] and against such mighty hosts of martyr-spirits not a thousand Blessed Saints could prevail![43]

On the night of February 15th, immediately after the martyrdom of the men of the *Maine*, the Court on high published its decree in letters of dazzling fire, and high athwart the heavens, that *Cuba shall be Free*.[44] And free Cuba shall be, as long as there shall be a Government at Washington, as long as a man or woman of a brave and loyal heart shall remain in the United States to assure that freedom. We have patiently borne in mind Polonius' advice of 'Beware of entrance to a quarrel', and now we shall also heed his other advice: 'But being in, bear't that the opposed may beware of thee.'[45] She persisted in her cruelty, when we entreated for mercy. She continued in her brutality, when we besought her for pity. She thirsted for war, when we hungered for peace. And she shall now have what she thirsted for, and shall have it until she in her turn, shall cry for the mercy and pity and peace, which she denied to Cuba, and refused to us.

And she shall have it, when she shall ask it, and she shall have at once, and in great abundance. Then, perhaps, will she learn to distinguish between her and our mode of warfare. She will then find that not for aggressiveness nor for aggrandizement, not for conquest nor for revenge, not to add another star of white to the field of blue in our unsullied 'Old Glory' have we entered upon this

---

[42] General Antonio Maceo, a charismatic mulatto leader of the insurgents, ambushed and killed by Spanish forces on 6 Dec. 1896 (Smith, *The Spanish–American War*, 16–21; Edgerton, *'Remember the Maine'*, 41–4). Cf. Dixon's sermon at the New York Opera House on the same day: 'What a host of murdered dead at last hovered over that fatal harbor [of Havana]! With the pale figures of the ill-fated expedition of 1852 crowded the slain men of the *Virginius*, the ghosts of Maceo and [José] Marti and [Joaquin] Ruiz, with the hundreds of thousands of starved women and children, till the pale faces of the martyred dead seemed a host that melted into the clouds and that no man could number!' ('Battle Cry of Freedom', 3).

[43] Cf., also on 1 May, the dramatic yet somewhat tamer statement by Joseph Silverman of Temple Emanu-El in New York on the same morning (echoing Gen. 4: 10: 'The blood of thousands of men, women, and children has cried to heaven, and this war is God's answer to it' ('My Country Right or Wrong').

[44] Cf. Dixon's sermon delivered that day: 'God used Spanish means to work their own death . . . the explosion of a Spanish mine beneath our ship was God Almighty's answer to these descendants of Cain. The roar of that explosion was God's summons to this nation to its solemn duty' ('Battle Cry of Freedom', 2).    [45] *Hamlet*, I. iii.

warfare,[46] that our only motive was to cry a final Halt! to her cruelty and carnage in Cuba, to end the strife and bloodshed between brother and brother, to
plant firmly, and forever, the Dominion of Peace on American Soil.

[46] Recapitulating the thought and the rhetoric at the end of the first paragraph of address.

# CHAPTER FOURTEEN

# HERMANN ADLER
# JUDAISM AND WAR

### 4 NOVEMBER 1899

**NORTH LONDON SYNAGOGUE**

HERMANN ADLER was born in Hanover in 1839 of a distinguished rabbinic family. His grandfather, Marcus Baer Adler, was chief rabbi of Hanover. His father, Nathan Marcus Adler, succeeded Marcus Adler to this post, and then, in 1845, was elected chief rabbi in London, a position in which he served until his death in 1890. His mother was the niece of Nathan Mayer Rothschild. (His elder brother, Marcus, and his younger brother, Elkan, also had illustrious careers in public life.)

Hermann was educated at University College London, where he received a prize and a First Certificate in English Language and Literature, studied Talmud in a renowned yeshiva at Prague (where he worked with the eminent scholar Michael Sachs, and was granted rabbinical ordination), and received a Ph.D. at Leipzig with a thesis on Druidism.[1] Returning to England, he became temporary principal of Jews' College, the seminary established by his father to train modern Orthodox clergymen. In 1864 he began to serve as preacher of the newly established Bayswater Synagogue. He became deputy to his father ('delegate chief rabbi') in 1879, and was elected to succeed him in 1891.

As chief rabbi, Hermann Adler espoused a policy of moderate innovation for mainstream Orthodox congregations, which he believed a necessary accommodation to modernity and citizenship. East European immigrants, who were more traditionalist and less open to change in religious doctrine and practice, became deeply suspicious of his role as chief rabbi, sometimes referring to him as 'the chief Reformer', and establishing a separatist community with rival institutions challenging his jurisdiction.[2]

---

[1] On Adler's education, see Schischa, 'Hermann Adler'; his record at UCL is on p. 258.
[2] See Endelman, *The Jews of Britain*, 167–8, 176, 179; Alderman, *Modern British Jewry*, 146–8. A picture (or caricature) of Adler 'in full ecclesiastical costume' is in Endelman, *The Jews of Britain*, 126. For a fuller treatment of Adler, see Finestein, *Anglo-Jewry in Changing Times*, 168–95.

Adler's first published book of sermons, appearing in 1869, was entitled
*Naftulei Elohim: A Course of Sermons on the Biblical Passages Adduced by Christian
Theologians in Support of the Dogmas of their Faith.* This was an apologetical and
polemical defence of Judaism against the attacks of Christian conversionary
organizations.[3] The second volume (1909), in which the sermon reproduced
below appeared, contains twenty-two sermons Adler delivered as congregational rabbi and as chief rabbi, including a response to the pogroms in Russia in 1881-
2 and in 1905, tributes to Queen Victoria on her diamond jubilee and at her
death, and eulogies for various Jewish dignitaries, including his own father. This
is, however, only a tiny sample of the sermons he gave. On 13 November 1898, in
an address to the Jewish Historical Society, he estimated that he had preached
more than 2,000 sermons since his first in 1859—'not necessarily a good thing';
by the end of his career in 1911, the number was estimated at 'considerably over
2500'.[4] In a long memorial article following his death, the *Jewish Chronicle* wrote:

Possessed of an excellently modulated and sonorous voice, a rich vocabulary, a close
acquaintance with the beauties of many literatures, especially Hebrew and English, a
happy power of illustration, and a delicate sense of humour, Dr. Adler was always worth
listening to, and always 'drew' a large congregation. His dignified bearing in the pulpit,
added to his elocutionary gifts, invested his utterances with a peculiar impressiveness.[5]

His Yom Kippur 1899 sermon in the Great Synagogue, delivered just two
months before the sermon below, was a powerful response to the new conviction
of Dreyfus issued during the previous week, describing it as 'the bitterest day in

[3] The sermons were delivered at the Bayswater Synagogue. In one, he described Societies for
Promoting Christianity among Jews turning 'bad Jews into worse Christians' (*Naftulei Elohim*, 2;
sermon delivered 25 Apr. 1868). Sixteen years later, David Woolf Marks published a volume of
*Lectures and Sermons*, which similarly focused on exegetical and theological issues of dispute
between Christians and Jews. The need to respond to the challenge of Christian missionaries was
thus one of the issues on which the Orthodox and the Reform leaders agreed (although, as Todd
Endelman has noted, those who did convert to Christianity were primarily impoverished Jews
who converted out of material or emotional need, not out of intellectual conviction).
[4] *Jewish Chronicle*, 18 Nov. 1898, p. 23 (this was a parenthetical remark in a lecture on Manasseh
ben Israel); *Jewish Chronicle*, 21 July 1911, p. 22. For a full bibliography of Adler's published work,
including many sermons printed in full or in summary in the Anglo-Jewish press but not included in his published volumes, see Goldschmidt-Lehmann, 'Hermann Adler: A Bibliography'.
Noteworthy among these are 'The Persecution of the Jews in Russia', delivered 28 Jan. 1882; 'The
Nation's Lament', at the memorial service for Prince Albert Victor (the grandson of Queen
Victoria and heir apparent to the throne), 20 Jan. 1892; 'Religious *versus* Political Zionism', delivered 12 Nov. 1898; 'The Dreyfus Judgment', delivered Yom Kippur, 14 Sept. 1899 (see n. 6 below).
[5] *Jewish Chronicle*, 21 July 1911, p. 22. In the same issue, Morris Joseph, minister of the West
London Synagogue (one of whose First World War sermons we will encounter below: Sermon
16) paid tribute to Adler as his teacher at Jews' College: 'What we learnt most from him was how
to preach. Nearly all the instruction I received in homiletics came from him, and my debt to him
in that respect is incalculable. He not only gave us a knowledge of the subject, but imparted some
of that earnestness that always characterized his own preaching.'

modern France, more disastrous than Waterloo, more humiliating than Sedan', and expressing the conviction that 'the terrible miscarriage of justice will convince the world of the folly and the savagery of anti-Jewish hatred, that [such] a vile unreasonable sentiment as this cannot but lead to cruelty and wrong, that anti-Semitism is but another name for the defiance of law and order, and the violation of truth and honour'.[6]

Unlike the sermons by Marks above (Sermon 4) and by Hertz below (Sermon 17), the one that follows here was not the product of a special occasion on which the preacher had to address the topic of war.[7] The Boer War began on 11 October 1899; in the following weeks, the *Jewish Chronicle* reported at length sermons on the war by Simeon Singer at the New West End Synagogue, by Francis L. Cohen, visiting preacher at the Bayswater Synagogue, and by Morris Joseph at the West London Synagogue.[8] Three and a half weeks after the outbreak of hostilities, Adler chose to address the subject in a visit to the North London Synagogue in Islington. Assuming that the congregation had already been addressed by their own minister on the subject of the war, he nevertheless decided that it was necessary to make this the focus of his guest sermon, citing as a reason the military reversals of the previous Monday, which came to be known as 'Mournful Monday'.[9]

Particularly striking to the modern reader is the preacher's total identification not only with the policies of the government but with the cause of empire.

---

[6] *Jewish Chronicle*, 22 Sept. 1899; this sermon was not included in his published volume, though it deserves to be. Endelman, in *The Jews of Britain*, 162 (based on Shane, 'The Dreyfus Affair', 143), cites one sentence from this sermon, ending that 'it behooves us to be more cautious and circumspect than ever before', as suggesting a policy of self-effacement for British Jewry. In the context of the sermon that is not what the preacher is advocating; the phrase introduces the second half of the sermon, devoted to rebuke in the spirit of Yom Kippur, and speaking of failures in British Jewry regarding religious education, worship, and observance of the sabbath and dietary laws, with two sentences on usury. A policy of Jewish self-effacement in public is indeed urged in another Yom Kippur sermon published in the same issue of *Jewish Chronicle*, by Simeon Singer ('Answer Him Not').

[7] No such 'day of humiliation, fasting, and prayer' was proclaimed during the Boer War, although there was considerable discussion as to whether one should be, especially after the serious military reversals of December 1899; see H. Adler, 'The Queen and the War', and Singer, 'The War', both delivered 6 Jan. 1900.

[8] Singer, 'Sermon on Genesis 14: 14'; F. Cohen, 'Our Duty at this Crisis'; Joseph, 'War'. The sermon by Singer is quite similar in sentiment to that of Adler. The sermon by Joseph, in contrast, is a strong anti-war statement in which the preacher refuses to pronounce any opinion on the merits of the present quarrel or which side is in the right. Haham Gaster's sermon on the war ('A Sound of Battle') expresses a position close to Adler's: 'we must say that even the loftiest conceptions of morality are satisfied when we join in fervent prayer for the victory of our arms. England is fighting now the battle for justice, equality, peace, and righteousness'. For a full review of Anglo-Jewish preaching in this war period, against the background of public questioning of Jewish patriotism and accusations of Jewish culpability for the outbreak of war, see Schnitzer, ' "No Conflict of Principle" '.                                                    [9] See n. 15 below.

In this sense it is quite similar to Marks's sermon on the Indian Mutiny
(Sermon 4 above)—though Adler goes beyond Marks in invoking not only
passages of English literature but also the glories of British military history in
the recent past.

Apparently Adler was not content to limit these sentiments to those who
had heard the sermon delivered. It was quickly published, and 600 copies were
circulated to the press, with special bound copies sent to the queen and leading government ministers.[10] Historian Geoffrey Alderman describes Adler as
'a pillar of the establishment and a staunch Conservative', whose defence of the
Salisbury government's policy in this sermon meant taking a strong stand on a
highly political issue.[11] This position was quite similar to that adopted by
the Church of England and most other churches in Britain.[12] Yet ten years
later, in an otherwise glowing review of Adler's jubilee volume *Anglo-Jewish
Memories*, the reviewer suggests that the present sermon 'is perhaps unwisely
admitted into the volume ... Who, looking calmly back now on the Boer War,
will maintain that the pulpits of England honoured themselves by justifying
that struggle?'[13]

# SERMON

## A PRAYER FOR HER MAJESTY'S FORCES IN SOUTH AFRICA

LORD GOD of Hosts! Thou art our refuge and strength, a very present
help in trouble. We draw nigh unto Thee this day to supplicate Thee on
behalf of the brave men, who pass through seas, armed for war in a far-off
land, in obedience to the command of our beloved and venerated Queen and
the bidding of her counsellors. Unto Thee, O Lord, we give thanks, for already
hath Thy right hand helped our troops. Even as Thou hast been with them
hitherto so be with them still: do not leave them nor forsake them. Shield

[10] This was announced at the end of the text of the sermon published in the edition of the
*Jewish Chronicle* appearing immediately after the sermon was delivered (10 Nov. 1899, p. 13).
[11] Alderman, *The Jewish Community in British Politics*, 43–4. On Adler's conception of Jewish
patriotism, see also D. Feldman, *Englishmen and Jews*, 122–3.
[12] For a review of the positions taken by leading clergy, see Davey, *The British Pro-Boers*, 146–53.
'The Church of England would largely support the government through thick and thin' (p. 146);
'except for the Quakers and a rebellious section of Congregationalists in 1901, the churches as
organized bodies did not protest' (p. 152). [13] *Jewish Chronicle*, 11 June 1909.

them in the day of battle. May their lives be precious in Thy sight. Gird them with victory, so that the war be speedily ended. And may the effect of peace be quietness and confidence for ever.

Merciful Father! Bless those that are good and upright in their hearts, who deal kindly and tenderly with the wounded, the faint, and the perishing on the battlefield. Cheer with gladsome tidings the hearts of those who tremble for the welfare of their absent kinsfolk. May Thy comforts soothe the souls of those who weep for the loss of a life dear unto them. Pour forth a spirit of warm compassion upon all the indwellers of this Empire, so that they may hasten to the help of the homeless and of all who suffer from the miseries of war.

Speed the days, we beseech Thee, when nation will no more lift up a sword against nation, when they will not hurt nor destroy, when they will all work together for righteousness and justice, for mercy and peace upon earth. A M E N .

Your minister has no doubt already discoursed to you upon the war in which our country is at present engaged.[14] And when I recur to this theme to-day it is because our hearts have been deeply stirred by the reverse which our troops have unhappily sustained during this week.[15] Our minds are absorbed, even as it becomes loyal Englishmen and Englishwomen, by the critical position of a portion of her Majesty's forces, on whose behalf our prayers have just ascended to our Heavenly Father. We are eagerly awaiting tidings of reassuring significance to be flashed along the electric wire. For even now the far-off veldt may be enveloped in smoke, and there may be thundering the roar of artillery and the shock of battle. At such a time it behoves us to turn to the Divine fount of wisdom, so as to draw from thence spiritual comfort and sustenance. With this view, I will read to you the 46th Psalm.

God is our refuge and strength, a very present help in trouble. Therefore will not we fear, though the earth be removed, and though the mountains be carried into the midst of the sea: though the waters thereof roar and be troubled, though the mountains shake with the swelling thereof. Selah. There is a river, the streams whereof shall make glad the city of God, the holy place of the tabernacles of the Most High. God is in the midst of her; she shall not be moved: God shall help her, and that right early. The heathen raged, the kingdoms were moved: he uttered his voice, the earth melted.

---

[14] Adler, visiting this synagogue as chief rabbi, explains why he is addressing a topic the listeners have undoubtedly heard discussed from the pulpit by their regular preacher.

[15] The reference is to the previous Monday, 30 October, later called 'Mournful Monday', when the British suffered severe setbacks at the Battles of Lombard's Kop and Nicholson's Nek, culminating in the loss by death, injury, or surrender of close to a thousand soldiers. See Maurice, *History of the War in South Africa*, i. 172–95.

The Lord of hosts is with us; the God of Jacob is our refuge. Selah. Come, behold the works of the Lord, what desolations he hath made in the earth. He maketh wars to cease unto the end of the earth; he breaketh the bow, and cutteth the spear in sunder; he burneth the chariot in the fire. Be still, and know that I am God: I will be exalted among the heathen, I will be exalted in the earth. The Lord of hosts is with us, the God of Jacob is our refuge. Selah. (Ps. 46: 1–11)

It is generally accepted, that this Psalm was sung by the sons of Korah at a season of great national peril, when the proud hosts of the Assyrian king had swept through the land. City after city had fallen into the power of the conqueror, and the victorious army stood under the very walls of Jerusalem.[16] The strife and commotion of the political world are described by images borrowed from nature—the earthquake which makes the mountains to tremble, and the billows which threaten to overwhelm the frail bark.[17] But while all is uproar and confusion without, peace and tranquillity prevail in the holy city. 'God is in the midst of her; she shall not be moved. He is our refuge and strength, a very present help in trouble. The Lord of hosts is with us; the God of Jacob is our refuge' (Ps. 46: 5, 1, 11). You will recognize the force of the lesson which this Psalm teaches us, though for the arrow we should substitute the magazine rifle, the machine gun for the bow, the bayonet for the spear, and the armoured train for the chariot. For the kernel of this hymn applies to all times and to all ages. God is the sure defence of those who uphold the cause of justice and righteousness. If we place our trust in Him and walk in His ways, we shall not be moved, whatever be the perils that threaten us.

What should be our attitude as Jews in respect to the war? With the exception of the belief in the Unity of God, there is probably no sentiment which entered more thoroughly and persistently into the Jewish national life of old than the aspiration for peace. 'And I will give peace unto the land' (Lev. 26: 6) was declared by Divine beneficence to be the climax of earthly prosperity, whilst war was held to be the greatest national chastisement. The most significant sign of the advent of the golden age of the Messiah will be the fact, that 'nations will beat their swords into ploughshares and their spears into pruning-hooks', that 'nation shall not lift up sword against nation, neither shall they learn war any more' (Isa. 2: 4; Mic. 4: 3). King David proposed to crown the achievements of his career by

[16] The dominant traditional Jewish interpretation of this psalm is eschatological, applying it to the wars of Gog and Magog. Ibn Ezra cites unnamed commentators who apply it to the retreat of Sennacherib in the time of Hezekiah.

[17] For the interpretation of v. 3. as a metaphor for political-military upheaval, see the commentaries of Menahem Me'iri (1249–1306) and *Metsudat david*.

building a temple to the glory of the Most High. For this pious design he had reserved the rich spoils acquired in his various campaigns. But the word of the Lord came to him, saying, 'Thou hast shed blood abundantly and hast made great wars. Thou shalt not build a house unto my name: Solomon shall build it, for I will give peace and quietness unto Israel in his days' (1 Chr. 22: 8, 9).

Yet at the same time it was fully recognized that certain wars were absolutely inevitable—wars to extirpate idol worship and to destroy moral corruption, wars undertaken in self-defence, and to repel invasion. Hence it is that the clang of the sword and shield resound in some books of the Bible, and that there are entire chapters in which is depicted the battle of the warrior, with its confused noise and garments rolled in blood (Isa. 9: 5). But before entering on any campaign the ancient Hebrews sought for the Divine sanction by consulting a recognized prophet. They took the Ark of the Covenant with them into the field, and either the commander-in-chief or a priest appointed for that purpose delivered an inspiriting address bidding the people be of good cheer, 'for the Lord your God is He that goeth with you to fight for you against your enemies to save you' (Deut. 20: 4).

Sentiments such as these, reliance upon Divine help, and the conviction that we have 'our quarrel just', animate the great bulk of the British nation at the present time.[18] It is universally acknowledged that the highest of British interests is peace. The policy of England is a policy of conciliation and forbearance. We acknowledge with gratitude that a potent spirit of peace holds sway upon the throne of England. I may aver, without fear of contradiction, that there is no word in the vocabulary more distasteful to our august sovereign than the word *enemy*. Penetrated by this knowledge, our statesmen have anxiously striven for the maintenance of peace. But they also recognized the fact, that of all policies none is more dangerous, none more calculated to sap a nation's greatness, than the advocacy of peace at any price. There are dangers even worse than war with all its horrors.[19] If we would permit the Continental powers to entertain the idea, that England only

[18] Adler's conviction that it was a 'just' war parallels that of the established Church of England, as well as most Catholic and Methodist clergy. The bishop of Chichester stated that 'the war in South Africa was distinctly a war of defence against aggression, a war of resistance to injustice and cruelty, not for conquest and dominion' (quoted in Davey, *The British Pro-Boers*, 146–7). For the minority of Anglican and other Christian clergy who condemned the war, see ibid. 147–53.

[19] Cf. the sermon delivered on 14 Oct. by Simeon Singer at the New West End Synagogue: 'In the life of a nation, by disposition, by circumstances, and by a regard to its own interests naturally inclined to a policy of peace, there was no moment so solemn and so big with fate as when that policy was set aside and resort was had to the fierce arbitrament of war . . . But there were alternatives more to be dreaded than war' ('Sermon on Genesis 14: 14').

cares for the counter and the till; that, absorbed in her race for wealth and lapped in smooth prosperity, she is indifferent to the interests of her sons in distant lands, and that she could accept insults with equanimity, then the end of her greatness would be in sight. Hence it was that the Government of our Queen had no alternative but to resort to the fierce arbitrament of war, with the view of restoring just and righteous government to the Transvaal, and to vindicate the honour of England.[20]

And the entire nation has been stirred to a grand passion, not of hatred, not of lust of conquest, but of warm, wholehearted patriotism and loyalty—a patriotism as firm and unshaken as are the rocks and cliffs which gird this narrow island in the northern sea, and a loyalty which has knitted together all parties and sections in the fixed determination to uphold our country's fame and honour. And the temporary check which our arms have unhappily sustained[21] has only served to stir still more deeply the hearts of the population of the United Kingdom, and the hearts of our fellow-subjects across the seas, to enkindle their devotion, and to strengthen their resolve. As we note this wondrous outburst of enthusiasm, the great words of Milton are recalled to us:

Methinks I see in my mind a noble and puissant nation, rousing herself like a strong man after sleep, and shaking her invincible locks; methinks I see her as an eagle mewing her mighty youth, and kindling her undazzled eyes at the full mid-day beam; purging and unsealing her long-abused sight at the fountain itself of heavenly radiance, while the whole noise of timorous and flocking birds, with those also that love the twilight, flutter about amazed at what she means.*[22]

Now what is our duty at the present crisis?[23] It behoves us to demonstrate our belief in the righteousness of our cause and our reliance on Divine help by

* *Areopagitica.*

[20] Here the argument is somewhat different: justification by the interests of Britain and its image in the sight of 'the Continental powers'. For examples of this argument of *raison d'état*, see Le May, *British Supremacy in South Africa*, 29–31, including the statement made in the House of Commons shortly before the sermon was delivered: 'The Cape is the very keystone of the British Empire. If we acknowledge, as I think we must, that the Boers had it in their power to engage in war at the moment which suited them, then the British Empire would exist only at the grace of President Kruger' (p. 31).

[21] A reference to the events of Monday, 30 Oct. 1899, later known as 'Mournful Monday' and described as one of the most humiliating days in British military history (see n. 15 above; also Pakenham, *The Boer War*, 156–9).

[22] One of the great purple passages of English prose.

[23] As in most of the sermons delivered on occasions of difficult circumstances in wartime, the preacher turns to the practical question of what Jews in the congregation are expected to do; this includes, but is not limited to, prayer.

offering up our prayers for the brave men who are in peril, for the sick and wounded in the hospitals, both friend and foe, and for all who suffer from the miseries of war. And our fervent supplication must go up to the throne of mercy, that wisdom and insight be vouchsafed to the leaders of the hosts of our Queen, that our arms may be crowned with success, that a speedy and decisive victory be granted, and an honourable peace be established. I am well aware that there are individuals who are inclined to view such prayers as superfluous, and who would criticize such utterances with the cynical sneer, 'Providence is ever on the side of the biggest battalions.'[24] I do not hesitate to stigmatize such an assertion as false, for it has been proved to be false on a hundred battlefields. Was God on the side of the biggest battalions on the day that Judas the Maccabee defeated the drilled legionaries of Antiochus, when, in the words of our liturgy, 'He delivered the strong into the hands of the weak, and the many into the hands of the few'?[25] God on the side of the biggest battalions! When the Spartans repulsed the Persian hosts at Thermopylae, or, coming down to English history, on the days when Scarlett's Dragoons rode through the Russians at Balaklava, and a handful of Havelock's heroes saved our Indian Empire?[26] Our troops and their commanders have already shown by their splendid courage that they worthily uphold the traditions of British valour and British chivalry. And our hearts must

[24] Note the need, encountered for the first time in our sermons, to defend the practice of public prayer in the context of war through a reaassertion of God's providential help for the forces of right. The statement cited, usually with 'God' instead of 'Providence', is generally attributed to Napoleon, though Voltaire cites it as a common witticism ('on dit que [it is said that] Dieu est toujours pour les gros bataillons': 'Letter to François Louis Henri Leriche', 6 Feb. 1770, in *Correspondence*, lxxiv. 80. This need to reply to the cynical dismissal of prayer and of divine power seems to strike a new note, which will become more pronounced in sermons of the First World War.

[25] From the 'Al hanisim' Hanukah insertion into the Amidah prayer, the core of the Jewish worship service: J. Hertz (ed.), *Authorised Daily Prayer Book*, 152.

[26] There is an element of hyperbole in each of these characterizations. At the Battle of Thermopylae in 480 BCE the Persian forces under Xerxes were only temporarily held back by a coalition of Greeks. The heroic death of Leonidas, king of Sparta, resisting the Persians, became an emblem in western memory of bravery in the face of overwhelming odds, but certainly not, as the preacher seems to imply, of divine help for the outnumbered.

The Balaklava battle occurred on 25 Oct. 1854 in the Crimean War; George Lucan, 3rd earl of Scarlett, was one of the commanders. This incident was the inspiration for Tennyson's 'The Charge of the Light Brigade'. It was a disastrous military blunder, leading to the loss of almost 500 of the 700 horsemen involved in the attack. See Woodham Smith, *The Reason Why*, esp. 242–59. (Lord Lucan became popular among British Jews for his role in gaining acceptance for the 1858 bill that enabled Jews to take a parliamentary oath: ibid. 280.)

Sir Henry Havelock and the troops he commanded played an important role in the suppression of the Indian Mutiny during the summer and autumn of 1857 (see Sermon 4 by Marks, above), by fighting to relieve the besieged garrison at Lucknow (for another, earlier, reference to this garrison by H. Adler, see *Anglo-Jewish Memories*, 6). On the posthumous development of the public image of Havelock as a Christian hero and icon, see Hendrickson, *Making Saints*, 94–121.

be filled with mingled sadness and satisfaction, knowing, as we do, that, among the brave men who have fought gallantly, and among those who have fallen in the battle, dying a soldier's honourable death, there have been a goodly number of our brethren in faith who have cheerfully sacrificed their lives in the service of their Queen and of their flag, feeling that it is sweet and glorious to die for one's country. 'Dulce et decorum est pro patria mori.'[27]

A further duty of supreme moment is imposed upon us by this war. Alas! a campaign cannot be entered upon without inflicting grievous physical and mental pain. But this suffering should be assuaged as far as lies in the power of poor mortal hands. An instructive lesson on this head is taught in the second Book of Chronicles, where it is narrated that, when the children of Israel had taken captive those whom we should call non-combatants, the prophet of the Lord indignantly rebuked them. And in deference to his injunctions delegates were appointed to succour the captives. 'And the men who were expressed by name rose up, and took the captives, and with the spoil clothed all those that were naked among them, and arrayed them, and shod them, and gave them to eat and drink, and anointed them and carried all the feeble of them upon asses, and brought them to their brethren' (2 Chr. 28: 15). Unwearied efforts have been made, and are being made by those in authority, to mitigate the horrors of war.

---

[27] The Latin words from Horace, *Odes*, III. 2 (which Wilfred Owen would later brand as 'the old Lie' in his 1917 poem using the first four Latin words as his title) appear in the *Jewish Chronicle* text of the sermon but not in the text later published in *Anglo-Jewish Memories*. Cf. Isidore Harris, preaching at the West London Synagogue on 12 Sept. 1914: 'If, as the poets of all nationalities had sung, "it is sweet and glorious to die for one's country", of no country could this sentiment be more true than our own' (I. Harris, 'Jewish Patriotism').

The emphasis on Jewish soldiers serving and dying in the armed forces of the nation, traceable back more than a century (see the examples in Sarna, *American Judaism*, 37 (from 1787) and in Mendes-Flohr and Reinharz, *The Jew in the Modern World*, 119–20 (from 1791) ), was becoming an increasingly important theme in the sermons of Jewish preachers on various sides in European wars of the late nineteenth and early twentieth centuries (see Sermon 17 by Hertz, below). In a sermon delivered near the outbreak of the Boer War, Francis L. Cohen noted that, unlike the Continental powers' conscript armies, the volunteer British forces contained a relatively small percentage of Jews (F. Cohen, 'Our Duty at this Crisis', 12). The *Jewish Chronicle* listed each week the names of Jewish soldiers serving in action, with a cumulative number of Jewish casualties. Adler returned to this point in his sermon on 6 Jan. 1900: 'I am glad to know that a goodly number of our brethren in faith are among these volunteers. For it would redound to our eternal shame if our young men were not ready, as indeed they are, to endure the sorest hardships, and to shed their life blood like water—prepared to die for their Queen and their country' ('The Queen and the War'). Later, on 19 Mar. 1905, he spoke movingly at the unveiling of the memorial to the Jewish soldiers who fell in the Boer War. On this occasion, he gauged their number as 114—some killed in battle, others dying of disease—and noted that no fewer than 2,000 Jews served at the front ('Address at the Unveiling of the Memorial', 141–2). After the war, however, the number of Jewish soldiers in the British army between 1903 and 1913 dropped to approximately 200, or 0.1% of the total (Hanha, 'Religion and Nationality', 181).

Words fail us adequately to voice our admiration for the tender women who go forth to South Africa as nursing mothers and nursing sisters. This loving provision for the sick and wounded, I may say in passing, is not of such recent origin as is generally believed.[28] We read in the Mishnah, that at periods of grave national emergency in Israel, when war had been declared—'All had to go forth, even the bridegroom *and his bride*, from beneath the nuptial canopy'[29] and the latter surely for no other purpose than to tend and to soothe.

We have all to go forth[30] on such mission of compassion and succour. The war has already been the harbinger of much woe. There are tens of thousands who have been forced to flee from the Transvaal and who have been left homeless and destitute.[31] There are the sick and the wounded—both British and Boer. There are the soldiers who may be permanently disabled. There are the widows and orphans of those who are shedding their blood for their country. There are the wives and children who have been severed by the call of duty from their husbands and fathers. It behoves us to care for all these with loving pity and unwearying generosity. I know full well that a great number of our brethren have already contributed to these various objects with characteristic benevolence. But not merely the rich are called upon to send their gifts to the various funds that have been organized at the Mansion House. All of you are summoned to testify your sympathy practically and without delay in this hour of need.[32]

[28] The beginning of modern military nursing is associated with Florence Nightingale and the Crimean War. (The somewhat forced effort to show a biblical basis or precedent for the practice seems to reveal an apologetical impulse familiar from many books on the Jewish contribution to Western civilization.) An account of the evolution of military nursing published in 1914 states that 'South Africa saw, in fact, the passing of the old and the coming of the new into military nursing', including the formation of a reserve of army nurses and the first use of hospital ships: Billington, *The Red Cross in War*, 19.

[29] Mishnah *Sot.* 8: 7. The words 'and his bride' were italicized in the text, in order to emphasize the basis for the preacher's historical claim.

[30] Echoing the words of the Mishnah and applying them to the contemporary situation.

[31] This refers to British and other foreign 'Outlanders' who fled from homes in the Transvaal in circumstances of uncertainty, fear, and harassment from the Boers. A reported 131,000 crossed the borders of the Transvaal in trains between 1 Sept. and 19 Oct. 1899. On the refugees, see Spies, *Methods of Barbarism?*, 18–19; Farwell, *The Great Boer War*, 56–7 (citing Winston Churchill, who, as a young correspondent, wrote on 5 November, the day after this sermon was delivered, that he 'heard the first confirmation of the horrible barbarities perpetrated by the Boers on the trainloads of refugees'); Pakenham, *The Boer War*, 98, 116–17. The issue of the *Jewish Chronicle* in which the text of Adler's sermon appeared contained, on the facing page, a report about 'the critical times in the Transvaal and the great influx of refugees, viz., men, women and children from Johannesburg to [Cape Town], in order to escape the disastrous consequences of war, and especially the threatened ill-treatment at the hands of the Boers' (10 Nov. 1899, p. 12).

[32] Again, as in the earlier sermons, the preacher appeals for contributions to fund humanitarian relief. Mansion House, the official residence of the Lord Mayor of London, was the address

But the present struggle is also of serious spiritual import to us all. The battles that have to be fought in life are not merely between armed men, nor is it only in warfare that true heroism can be manifested. A great struggle is continually proceeding in the heart of man—aye, and in the world outside—the battle of truth against falsehood, of right against wrong, of vice against virtue, of profanity against reverence; and this conflict is and must be perpetual.[33]

'Man must for ever cause his good inclination to wrestle with the evil passion within.'[34] And how much valour and strength of purpose are needed in this conflict! To you, my younger friends, I would repeat the exhortation, התחזקו והיו לאנשים, 'Be strong and quit yourselves like men' (I Sam. 4: 9). The story is told of Nelson that, when he was quite a child, he had strayed from home, and was at length discovered a long way off quite alone. And when he had returned, his parents said to him, 'I wonder that fear did not drive you home.' 'Fear,' he replied, 'I never saw fear. What is it?'[35] Yes, be fearless in the fight against sin and wickedness. The only fear you should know is the fear of God, the fear to offend and dishonour Him, and you will know no other fear. May our Heavenly Father strengthen you in such resolve, so that you may grow up honourable and pure, truthful and diligent, worthy citizens of England and true sons of Israel. 'And God Almighty bless you and give you the blessing of Abraham.[36] The Lord bless you and keep you. May the Lord cause His face to shine upon you, and be gracious unto you. May the Lord turn His face unto you and give you peace' (Num. 6: 24–6). Amen.

for special disaster funds; a fund for the relief of the refugees had been established by the Lord Mayor a few weeks before the sermon was delivered (Pakenham, *The Boer War*, 117–18). Each week, beginning on 20 Oct., the *Jewish Chronicle* listed contributions to the Refugees Fund, the first two of which amounted to £5,000 each.

[33] Here, perhaps unawares, the preacher is echoing a well-known hadith in which the Prophet Muhammad, returning from battle, tells his followers that having completed the 'lesser *jihad*' of actual war, they must now engage on the 'greater *jihad*' of inner spiritual struggle. This was cited, without attribution, by Bahya ibn Pakuda (eleventh century) in his *Book of the Duties of the Heart* (treatise 5 on 'Wholehearted Devotion' (*Yiḥud hama'aseh*), ch. 5), and thence became a staple of Jewish ethical literature. The *Jewish Chronicle* text of the sermon ends here, although the following paragraph was very likely the conclusion of what Adler actually said; it may have been omitted for reasons of space, as the ending in the *Chronicle* version does not seem appropriately final.

[34] BT *Ber.* 5a.

[35] This story appears (with the young Nelson addressing the remark to his grandmother) near the beginning of Robert Southey's *A Life of Nelson*.

[36] What follows is not, of course, the 'blessing of Abraham', but the priestly blessing. It is not clear to me whether this was a printing error.

# PART IV

# THE FIRST
# WORLD WAR

# CHAPTER FIFTEEN

## GEORGE (GEDALIAH) SILVERSTONE
# ON THE TERRIBLE WAR OF 5675
### *Community Rally for Relief of Jewish Victims*

### 25 OCTOBER 1914

**EIGHTH STREET TEMPLE,
WASHINGTON HEBREW CONGREGATION,
WASHINGTON, DC**

A T the outbreak of what would be known as 'the Great War' and then 'the First World War', British and American Jewish preachers sounded a note quite different from that of patriotic fervour we have seen in the sermons from the Spanish–American and Boer wars. Instead, the dominant motif—undoubtedly influenced by the German origins of many in the congregations of both countries—is one of dismay, discouragement, confusion: a sense of devastating failure that undermines cherished beliefs in progress, even possibly in divine providence. This is in striking contrast with the nationalistic elan evident in the sermons by French, German, and Austrian rabbis at the beginning of the war.[1] Thus the report by the *Jewish Chronicle* on 21 August 1914:

Devoting his sermon to the subject of the War, the Rev. Morris Joseph preached as follows from his pulpit at the Berkeley Street Synagogue last Saturday [15 August]: We resume our Sabbath Services this week in circumstances all but unparalleled in the history of mankind . . . The lust to destroy and slay has taken possession of minds hitherto chiefly concerned to heal the hurt of the world, and to set the feet of mankind more firmly on the high-way of progress. It is a terrifying paradox, a cruel blow to our

---

[1] French preaching, suffused with patriotism, is exemplified in the Rosh Hashanah 1914 sermon by J. H. Dreyfuss, 'Patrie': 'Quel autre objet pouvons-nous proposer à nos prières que le salut de la Patrie?' (pp. 34–5). For German Jewish preaching, see Elon, *The Pity of It All*, 305; Mendes-Flohr, 'The *Kriegserlebnis*', e.g. pp. 227–8 on Leo Baeck's sermon delivered on the day of prayer proclaimed by the Kaiser for 5 Aug. 1914, on which all Berlin's synagogues were filled to capacity. For an especially strong example, see Herzog, 'Das Gelöbnis der Treue'.

optimism and our most cherished ideals. It makes us doubt the value, the reality of our civilization, the stability of righteousness, the fixity of purpose of God himself.

Not unexpectedly, Joseph insists that our first duty is to 'brush such doubts aside', to keep one's faith in God, and to 'rally to the help of our beloved country in her hour of need',[2] but the psychological anguish inflicted by the fighting—even at this early stage—seems genuinely acute.

In the United States, the official policy of the government was neutrality. Yet with the approach of the High Holy Days of 1914, many rabbis felt that the war in Europe had to be addressed. In Philadelphia, the German-born Reform rabbi Joseph Krauskopf, who sixteen years earlier had so enthusiastically endorsed the American war effort against Spain, spoke on the evening of Rosh Hashanah in highly rhetorical terms:

Not in the darkest ages of the past has the world been so full of violence, so crimsoned with blood, so smitten with savagery and outrage, as at this present hour, in this much-bragged-of Twentieth Century. Our eyes roam over scores of battlefields, our feet stumble against the bodies of thousands of human beings slain, of tens of thousands mangled—slain and mangled by fellow human beings who had never known each other, who had never entertained the slightest ill-feeling against each other ... We follow the train loads of wounded and shudder at the sound of their groaning, at the thought of the hundreds of them who will pass from hospital to grave, of the hundreds of others who will re-enter life unfit to resume careers they once followed with distinction and success ... We look upon tens of thousands of human beings entitled to their liberty, needed in their respective homes as bread-winners for their families, yet held as prisoners, huddled together like unto wild animals—ill-clad, ill-sheltered, ill-fed, ill-regarded by those who hold them imprisoned. We enter homes from which went forth in the prime of youth and manhood, and in response to the fatherland's call, husbands and fathers, brothers and sons, who will never, never return, who moulder in some unknown grave or ditch, who have paid with their heart's blood some diplomat's blunder, some monarch's land greed or lust of power.[3]

[2] *Jewish Chronicle*, 21 Aug. 1914, pp. 11–12. This address was not included by Joseph in the last volume of his sermons, but he did include several others on the war (including the one printed as Sermon 16 below); in another, delivered after the armistice, he proclaimed that only Jews and Quakers 'dared to preach peace during the past period of strife when most other men were for war', and that his pulpit was consecrated to preaching peace throughout the five years of awful conflict: 'Peace and Good Will', 224.

[3] *Jewish Exponent*, 25 Sept. 1914, p. 3, 'Dr. Krauskopf on the Failure of our Civilization'. Cf. Krauskopf's colleague Henry Berkowitz, also in Philadelphia on the same day: 'We are startled to find that we have been victims of a great delusion. We had deluded ourselves into believing that what is called "Civilization" is a reality. We find that it is a sham ... The modern giant militarism, like Samson of old, is hurling the full weight of his strength against the pillars of the mighty structure of a false civilization and is doomed to perish in the desolation' ('Dr. Berkowitz on "The Great Delusion"', ibid.).

In New York, Rabbi Maurice H. Harris of the largely German Temple Israel of Harlem lamented the barbarity of war ('How stirred was the civilized world when 1500 persons lost their lives on the *Titanic*—and now such a loss of life is a daily incident') and then proceeded to call for civil disobedience among the peoples of the belligerent nations:

Even where monarchs, bureaucracies, and Governments, trained in the militant school, may be hesitant in relegating war to the past, the masses of the people must decide for peace. If they decide, with an insistent note, 'We will not fight', where is the power of Government to promulgate a war? The old standard set in the Crimean war, 'Theirs not to reason why, theirs but to do and die,' must be rejected by the people. They are not pawns, but living beings. Theirs is to reason why. They must ask what right has a Government to plunge the land into war.[4]

As we shall see, few asked this question from the pulpit when the United States entered the war.

The rabbis cited above were from the Reform movement. There is far less evidence that Orthodox rabbis, who preached in Yiddish and whose sermons were rarely covered in the English-language press, were as concerned with the implications of the war for the general values of culture and civilization. They tended to focus more on the toll taken by the war on the masses of Jewish civilians living on the contested territories of the Eastern Front. An early example is the sermon by Rabbi George (Gedaliah) Silverstone (1871–1944) of Washington, DC which appears below (in my own translation of the published Hebrew text).

Silverstone was a graduate of the yeshiva of Telz (Telsai) in Lithuania. Emigrating soon after completing his studies, he held his first rabbinical position in Belfast, Ireland. In 1904 he came to Washington, where for some decades he served several small congregations. During this period he made several journeys to Palestine, apparently intending to settle there, but each time returning to America after a relatively brief stay. Preaching seemed to come naturally to him, and he published a large number of books based on his sermons; he considered these volumes to be an important resource for his colleagues and took pride in their popularity. While he generally preached in Yiddish, his works were published in Hebrew. Silverstone favoured the shorter sermon, and criticized the practice of those of his colleagues ('rabbis who forget to end their sermons . . . until finally they are forced to end because their legs become weak') who delivered discourses lasting between an hour and an

[4] *New York Times*, 22 Sept. 1914, p. 5; the quotation is from Tennyson's 'The Charge of the Light Brigade'. Harris, a progressive (as well as an author of several books on Jewish history and literature), was a member of the American Committee for Armenian and Syrian Relief during the war.

hour and a half on the sabbath afternoon.[5] The text below reveals that a brief presentation could wield considerable power.

No date is provided for the sermon in the published Hebrew text; the year 5675 given in the title extended from 21 September 1914 to 9 September 1915. My dating is based upon an article in the *Washington Post* of 26 October 1914, describing a community rally on behalf of Jewish victims of the war held the previous evening at the 'Eighth Street Temple', the place of worship of the United Hebrew Congregation. Silverstone was listed as one of the four speakers.[6]

This appears to have been one of the earliest examples of Jewish community mobilization on behalf of east European Jews in the war zone. In Britain at this time the humanitarian concerns of the Jewish community were largely focused on the refugees from Belgium.[7] The first real coverage of the east European problem in the British Jewish press came in the 28 October issue of *Jewish World* ('The Sorrows of Poland') and the 30 October issue of the *Jewish Chronicle* ('Jews of Poland: Terrible Suffering Through the War'), both based on a report from a special correspondent of the London *Standard* at Wilna, who had dated his piece 15 October.[8] The American Jewish Press became aware of the situation slightly earlier. The Yiddish *Vorwerts* of 19 October ran an article headlined 'Half a Million Jews Starving in Galicia', and its lead editorial on 23 October was entitled 'The Current Destruction (*Der Heintiger Khurbn*) Upon our Brothers'. On the same day the weekly *American Hebrew* included a piece called 'Jews Beggared in Galicia', describing the 'terrible devastation and suffering inflicted during the Russian Invasion'. Such reports must have goaded the Washington Jewish community to prompt action.

The content of Silverstone's sermon is certainly appropriate for this occasion. Furthermore, a crucial internal element can be reconciled with my dating,

---

[5] Caplan, *Orthodoxy in the New World*, 120–1; cf. 126, 159. Other biographical material is taken from this book: Telz Yeshiva, 71; Belfast position, 76; visits to Palestine, 82, 297; tenure in Washington, DC, 108, 200; preaching and publication, 137–40, 150, 157–8, 317–19. I am grateful to Dr Caplan for calling my attention to this sermon.

[6] Like virtually all of his Orthodox immigrant colleagues, Silverstone expressed in his sermons and the publications based on them an extremely negative attitude towards Reform and Conservative rabbis: see Caplan, *Orthodoxy in the New World*, 227–8, 277 (where he refers to Reform rabbis as 'total idolaters'), and 281–2; and note his condemnation of the late Friday evening services at the Conservative synagogue Adas Israel, to which men and women came together in their automobiles: 'Sermon against Reform', 5–7. Nevertheless, for this cause, he appeared in a Reform synagogue and shared the platform with a Reform rabbi. For other examples of co-operation in public causes, see Caplan, *Orthodoxy in the New World*, 264.

[7] The *Jewish Chronicle* (together with the *Jewish World*) mounted a campaign, beginning on 16 Oct. with a two-page spread (pp. 5–6) entitled 'Belgium's Agony', to raise funds for Jewish refugees; this was repeated for at least four successive weeks.

[8] *Jewish World*, 28 Oct. 1914, pp. 5, 18–19; *Jewish Chronicle*, 30 Oct. 1914, pp. 12–13; this theme was taken up further in the *Chronicle* issues of 20 Nov. (pp. 6, 8) and 27 Nov. (based on an article in *The Times* of 21 Nov.).

making it all but certain that this is in fact when it was delivered. This is the dramatic story about the Russian Jewish soldier. As indicated in the notes below, this account was widely circulated in eastern Europe; the influential Russian writer S. An-Sky reports having heard it from many different sources on his journey through the Pale of Settlement where most Jews were still required to live, and records a version quite close to that in the sermon.[9] An-Sky's journey began in the spring of 1915, but there is independent evidence that the story was already circulating in the west in October 1914.

The western Jewish press was full of reports about Russian Jewish soldiers in September and October 1914. But these articles had a thrust quite different from that of the story recounted here: they reported with pride the huge number of Jewish soldiers in the tsar's armies—estimated variously at between 250,000 and 350,000—and the wave of patriotic enthusiasm that had spread throughout the Jewish population of the Russian empire. As early as late August Philadelphia's *Jewish Exponent*, in an article called 'The Patriotism of Russian Jews', wrote:

The loyalty now displayed by the Jews of Russia has attracted widespread attention. Even the 'Novoe Vremya', the organ of the anti-Semites, and Mr. Purishkewitch, the leader of the Black Hundreds, find nothing but praise for the Jews of the Empire. Jewish young men in many cities volunteered services in the army. After a patriotic service in the largest synagogue in St. Petersburg, the rabbi, holding a scroll of the law, marched at the head of 5000 Jews in the streets of the capital, displaying the Russian flag and delivered patriotic speeches in the streets.

Similar demonstrations were made in many provincial towns and many Christians who have hitherto been enemies of the Jew now publicly recanted and expressed their regrets for their past actions.[10]

Beyond this general praise, there were frequent reports of the acts of heroism of individual soldiers, behaviour recognized and rewarded by the Russian military commanders and by government officials at the highest level, including the tsar. A typical example is a report from the *Jewish Chronicle*'s correspondent in Petrograd: 'The noted witness in the Beilis trial, Faivel Shneyerson (who was a non-commissioned officer), was killed in the battle of Lemberg after having bayonetted eleven Austrians. His bayonet broke during the charge.'[11] Broader

---

[9] See n. 19 below.

[10] *Jewish Exponent*, 28 Aug. 1914, p. 7. Five weeks later, the same paper cited a private letter from Warsaw: 'I remember the Turkish and the Japanese wars, but I have never seen anything like the general enthusiasm now prevailing. In synagogues I have seen our people weeping as they chanted prayers for victory and the speedy restoration of peace abroad and at home' (2 Oct. 1914, p. 7).

[11] *Jewish Chronicle*, 25 Sept. 1914, p. 15 (this incident was reported in the *American Hebrew* on 9 Oct., p. 669). On the same page the *Jewish Chronicle* reported that crowds of Jews gathered at the Wilna synagogue and 'prayed for the recovery of the hero, Leon Osnas, a native of the city, and a former student of the Paris university', whose heroism in 'saving the colours of his regiment'

points emphasized were the irony that these soldiers were willing to give their lives for a country that had persecuted their own people, and the hope that the strong impression made by Jewish patriotism upon the Russian leadership would lead to a change in the discriminatory policy regarding the Pale of Settlement— a hope that was especially important in justifying support for the alliance between Britain and Russia.

The story told by Silverstone has a very different function: its purpose is not to underline the patriotism of Jews towards all the countries where they lived, but rather to emphasize the underlying unity of the Jewish people, and the sometimes painful tension between that unity and such patriotism. The preacher introduces it by speaking of the reaction of his listeners to the story they have read 'in the newspapers', apparently within the past few days. Confirmation for this story can be found in its appearance in the *American Hebrew* of 30 October 1914, the first issue published after the Washington rally (described on a different page of that issue as 'a monster meeting under the auspices of twenty-seven societies of the District of Columbia').[12]

The fullest version I have found, however, is in the London weekly *Jewish World* of 4 November, which is worth citing at length for comparative purposes:

Here is a story, sent by one of the correspondents at the seat of war, which could well have been foreseen and which illustrates the cruel sacrifice this titanic struggle places upon the Jewish soldiers. The correspondent says:

'A gruesome example of what a Jewish soldier has to contend with when fighting with those who are really his brethren, the Jewish soldiers in the Austrian ranks, and of whom there are thousands in Galicia, occurred in one of the battles near Lemberg, now called Lvoff.[13]

'In one of the hospitals in Petrograd I have seen a Jewish soldier who is raving mad. [At this point, the *American Hebrew* story begins, virtually identical.] His insanity resulted from the following occurrence.

'An Austrian machine gun battery was occupying a dominant position and causing havoc among the ranks of a Russian battalion, which was only lightly intrenched.

led to his being awarded the Military Cross of St George: see on Osnas *Jewish Chronicle*, 11 Sept. 1914, p. 10; 18 Sept. 1914, p. 26; 2 Oct. 1914, p. 18; also 9 Oct. 1914, p. 15, reporting an article from *The Times* (5 Oct. 1914, p. 9) about 'Jewish Private's Heroism', instrumental in the Russian capture of a line of forts at Jaroslav, and one from the *New York Times* (11 Oct., II, 3), 'Jewish Officer Recommended for Order of St. George'.

[12] *American Hebrew*, 30 Oct. 1914, p. 17; the story is found on p. 5 under 'War News', under the heading, 'Whoever Wins, We Lose'.

[13] The Battle of Lemberg, the capital of eastern Galicia, took place between 26 Aug. and 11 Sept. 1914, resulting in the collapse of the Austro-Hungarian front, the loss of 300,000 Austro-Hungarian casualties and 130,000 prisoners, and the establishment of Russian control over the Lemberg region. The city was recaptured by the Austrians the following June.

The battalion was ordered to charge a detachment of infantry covering the machine gun battery and some six hundred paces away from the Russian lines.

'Among those in the first line was this Jewish soldier. He reached the ranks of the Austrians and in a man-to-man bayonet fight he drove his bayonet through the chest of his opponent. As the Austrian fell wounded to death he gasped the Hebrew death prayer which begins 'Hear, O Israel'. The Russian Jewish soldier fell in a faint. When he was found he was a raving lunatic.'[14]

The *American Hebrew* account appears in a column opposite a story about an Austrian Jewish soldier in Galicia, shot in the chest and saved by the Hebrew and Hungarian prayer book he carried in his chest pocket: 'A photograph of the prayerbook, with its pages shot through, appeared in a Prague newspaper and was reproduced in one of the Jewish dailies in this country.' I assume that our story also first appeared in one of the American Jewish dailies, and that Silverstone found it there.

In addition to this narrative from the contemporary newspapers, there are two other major components of the sermon's message, drawn from traditional Jewish literature. The first is an aggadic tale taken from the Talmud about the massacre of Jews by the Romans at Tur Malka. Silverstone uses this to demonstrate the capacity of Jews in antiquity to go about their normal business without any indication of concern for the devastation of their brothers, as if they did not know about it. This is applied directly to the situation of American Jews with regard to the Jews of eastern Europe; the indifference to the civilian victims of the war stands in marked contrast with the vignette he has earlier recounted, producing the message that American Jews appear to care less for their fellow Jews in eastern Europe than a Russian Jewish soldier cared for his enemy. In the context of the occasion, however, the desired conclusion is that American Jews must repudiate this model by generously supporting the collection of funds for humanitarian relief.

The second major narrative element comes from a source in the Zohar, retold and expanded by the preacher. The commandment in Deuteronomy that one who is taking fledglings from a nest must first make sure that the mother bird has flown away produces an empathetic vision of the mother bird, after returning to the nest and finding her fledglings gone, bewailing her loss until

[14] *Jewish World*, 4 Nov. 1914, p. 7. In the *Jewish Chronicle* of 30 Oct. 1914 the commentator whose essays appeared under the pseudonym 'Mentor' (Leopold Jacob Greenberg) wrote: 'From us Jews the field of battle is taking a heavy, heavy toll. The lowest computation gives close on half a million of our people fighting in one army or another, sometimes compelled Jew to fight Jew. Now and again the horror of this situation is presented in all its grimness before our eyes, as when the bayonet thrust of a sturdy Jewish soldier draws with the life-blood of a Jewish soldier of the enemy, the Shemang [*sic*] Yisroel on his stiffening lips.' Though this is recounted with fewer details than Silverstone's rendering of the story, both versions imply that the story is familiar to their respective audiences.

the 'angel appointed over the birds' takes up her cause before God who gave this commandment. The empathy for the mother bird generated from the imaginative exploration of the arcane Torah law is applied homiletically not to the listeners but to the Jews of eastern Europe—mothers returning to their homes from the synagogues to find their children gone, the victims of the war. The source provides hope for a providential, redemptive dénouement to the bloodshed, in the traditional homiletical style.

# SERMON

—

*'When in grief I would seek comfort; my heart is sick within me.'*
(JER. 8: 18)

*'They shall make this declaration:*
*"Our hands did not shed this blood, nor did our eyes see it done"'*
(DEUT. 21: 7)

*Rashi: Could it occur to anyone that the elders of the court are killers?*
*Rather, they say, 'We have not seen anyone whom we sent away without*
*food and without accompanying them.'*

MY BROTHERS and sisters, at this moment there are many corpses on the battlefields belonging to our Jewish brethren. They have left behind widows and orphans without any means of support. If the elders and judges go out to measure the communities surrounding these corpses, they will discover that our brethren in America are closer to the corpses than the Jews in any other country. For only the United States stands outside the war ('neutral'). Whoever fails to provide food for the widows and the orphans may not say, 'Our hands did not shed this blood,' for 'the voice of our brothers' blood cries out to us from the ground'.[15]

Our brothers who took their lives in their hands and fought with astounding bravery on the killing fields, as well as those who live in the vicinity of the battle-fields, they have been the scapegoat for the entire Jewish people.[16] For *we* are not fighting for our country, as is the Russian army, which is fighting for Russia,

[15] Echoing Gen. 4: 10.
[16] Cf. Lev. 16: 10. This does not imply that they were blamed, in the sociological sense of 'scape-goat'; instead it indicates the hope that, through their deaths, they might make atonement for the entire Jewish people.

and the British army for their country, England, and the German army for Germany, and similarly the French and the Turks. Not us. We Jews are compelled to fight for all of these, not for ourselves.[17] If our situation in some countries where we are denied the rights of citizens improves, then our exile becomes bearable. But it is still exile, unless God pours out a wind from on high (cf. Isa. 32: 15). But for our blood that is spilled like water we gain nothing. That is the greatest source of pain.

Whose heart did not throb with agony, whose eyes did not fill with tears, whose blood did not turn cold in his veins upon reading in the newspapers about a Jewish soldier in the Russian army who stabbed with his bayonet a soldier from the Austrian army. The mortally wounded man cried out with his last breath, 'Shma Yisra'el Adonai Eloheinu Adonai Ehad', and with the word *ehad*, his soul departed.[18] When the Russian soldier realized that he had killed one of his brothers, that he had thrust his bayonet into a fellow Jew, he went out of his mind with grief. Alas, alas! that things like this happen in our time.[19]

Of the righteous Joseph, we find in the parashah Va-Yiggash that when there was famine in the land of Canaan, he said to his brothers, 'I am your brother

---

[17] Cf. the address of Samuel Daiches of England in Liverpool on 3 Aug. 1914: 'On this very day nearly half a million of our brethren in the various armies of Europe are ready to fight against and kill one another . . . For what? Not for Palestine. Not for Jerusalem. Not for national independence. Not for Jewish supremacy, and not for the good of humanity; but in order to help the European nations to call down a curse on their own heads and to make Europe into a heap of ashes (applause). This illustrates the depth of a tragedy in the life of the Jewish nation' (*Jewish Chronicle*, 7 Aug. 1914, p. 13). Cf. also the address of the Zionist orator Shemaryahu Levin, cited in the Jewish press the previous month: 'The Russian Jews now fighting in the War of Nations are more numerous than all the English soldiers that have been sent to aid France and Belgium. But other peoples go to war when they want to fight; we Jews must fight whether we want to or not. But still our brothers have shown their courage and their bravery, even though they are fighting for a government that oppresses them and persecutes them' ('Dr. Levin Speaks in Yiddish', *Jewish Exponent*, 18 Sept. 1914, p. 11).

[18] The last phrase, echoing the account of the martyrdom of R. Akiva, BT *Ber.* 61b, is apparently the preacher's addition to the report by the correspondent cited in the introduction to this sermon.

[19] See the introduction to this sermon. This common story was reported by S. An-Sky in his visit to Galicia in the spring of 1915, following reports of atrocities committed against local Jews by Russian soldiers, especially Cossacks: 'Jews on both sides fought each other, brother against brother. From the start, the Jews were gripped by this horror, and represented it in a legend of two soldiers meeting in battle. One soldier bayoneted the other and then heard him shout as he lay dying, "Hear, O Israel, the Lord our God, the Lord is one". I'm not exaggerating when I say that I heard all versions of this story in nine or ten different places . . . In St. Petersburg I was told about a Jewish patient in a military hospital. During an attack, he had bayoneted an Austrian soldier, and the victim had cried out, "Hear, O Israel . . . !" The patient had instantly lost his mind': S. An-Sky, *The Enemy at his Pleasure*, 23. Compare other versions of this story on the same page, and a different vignette on the same theme, ibid. 79. See also Gorky and Sologub (eds), *The Shield*, 193–209.

Joseph, whom you sold into Egypt. Now, do not be distressed or reproach yourselves because you sold me hither; it was to save life that God sent me ahead of you' (Gen. 45: 4–5). Joseph was the most beloved of his father's sons. Yet when he was 17 years old, his brothers took him and placed him into a pit with serpents and scorpions; then they sold him as a slave in Egypt, and because of them he ended up in prison. Yet despite all this, at a time of affliction, when he saw his brothers hungry, he forgot all they had done to him, and he said, 'I am your brother Joseph,' and I will provide you with sustenance. How much the more are we obligated to do everything within our power to help our wretched brothers who are—disgracefully—suffering from hunger in this time of affliction, unprecedented in world history.

Now King Solomon's statement, 'Charity saves from death' (Prov. 10: 2), applies not just to those who give charity; it applies also to those to whom the charity is given. It saves them from death, from the agony of hunger.

R. Assi said, 'Three hundred thousand men with drawn swords went in to Tur Malka, and slaughtered for three days and three nights, while on the other side dancing and feasting was going on, and these people did not know about the others'.[20] I have never understood the meaning of this. How could it be that in one part of the city such a massacre could occur, while in the other part of the city there was dancing and feasting, as if they did not even know about the first part. If—God forbid—ten soldiers [anshei ḥayil: possibly 'ruffians'?] should come into the great city of New York and kill a single person on the street, the entire populace would soon know about this act of murder.

I suggest, rather, that in the time of the destruction of the Temple, there was groundless hatred,[21] and everyone looked out only for themselves, and did not care at all about their neighbours. This is what R. Assi tells us, 'on the other side dancing and feasting was going on, and these people did not know about the others', meaning that they did not *want* to know about the others. For what did they care that their brothers were being killed and slaughtered, so long as it did not affect them, and they could continue their dancing and feasting?

Yes, ladies and gentlemen, we should apply this dictum to ourselves. Our brothers in Russia are being killed and slaughtered in a terrifying manner, they are drowning in their own blood, while we in America are engaged in dancing, and feasting, and going to the theatres, and we don't know about the others.[22]

[20] BT *Git.* 57a.
[21] See BT *Yoma* 9b, where this is presented as the cause for the destruction of the Second Temple.
[22] For the importance of rebuke in Silverstone's preaching, see Caplan, *Orthodoxy in the New World*, 317–19.

The Zohar says, on the verse 'Let the mother go, and take only the young [in order that you might fare well and have a long life]' (Deut 22: 7):

When the mother bird does not find its fledglings in the nest, it bewails them over the mountains and the forests, and the sound is heard in the heights of heaven. Then the angel appointed over the birds goes to the Holy One, Blessed be He, with a complaint: 'Why did you give a commandment like this in the Torah? For the mother bird bewails her fledglings, and her anguish is very great, but You are merciful and compassionate over all your creatures.' Then God says to the angel, 'For this bird there is a spokesman to beseech mercy on her behalf. For my children, who are killed and slaughtered and strangled all the time, in every place, there is no one to act as a spokesman for them and to beseech mercy on their behalf! Therefore, "Behold I will send you Elijah the prophet before the coming of the great and awesome day of the Lord, and he will turn the hearts of parents to their children, and the hearts of children to their parents"' (Mal. 3: 23).[23]

At this moment in Russia, mothers are returning home from their synagogues, where their tears flow like water beseeching mercy before the holy ark from the One who dwells on high, and they do not find their children in their nest, for their children have gone into captivity, to be slaughtered in this terrible war. The sound of the mothers' weeping is heard by our Heavenly Father, for the gates of tears are never locked.[24] He will fulfil His promise to send us 'Elijah the Prophet, who will turn the hearts of parents to their children and the hearts of children to their parents' (Mal. 3: 23), that there may be peace upon Israel. Amen.

---

[23] Cf. *Zohar ḥadash* 87*b* (*Midrash rut*), and later versions in Bahya ben Asher's Torah commentary on Deut. 22: 7; Menahem Recanati, *Ta'amei mitsvot hashalem* [The Complete Reasons for the Commandments] (London, 1963), 75*a–b*; *Perush al hatorah* [Commentary on the Torah], ed. Amnon Gross (Tel Aviv: Aaron Barzan, 2003), Deuteronomy, 80–1; Abraham, Saba, *Tseror hamor* [A Bundle of Myrrh] (Tel Aviv: Offset Brody-Katz, 1975), Deuteronomy, p. 34*b*, beginning *Uvazohar*. None of these sources contains all the elements in Silverstone's elegant retelling.

[24] BT *Ber.* 32*b*.

# CHAPTER SIXTEEN

## MORRIS JOSEPH
# CHRISTMAS AND WAR

### SATURDAY, 25 DECEMBER 1915

#### WEST LONDON SYNAGOGUE OF BRITISH JEWS

MORRIS JOSEPH (1848–1930), a graduate of Jews' College, served as minister in the North London Synagogue before his election as preacher to the Liverpool Old Hebrew Congregation in 1874. His first volume of sermons, published in 1893, contained selections from his preaching at the sabbath afternoon service at the Hampstead Synagogue between 1890 and 1892. One of these sermons, on 'The Sacrificial Rite', repudiates the hope for the restoration of the sacrificial cult, and this liberal stance led to his veto by the chief rabbi, Hermann Adler, when the synagogue elected him as their minister (despite this, he maintained a relationship of respect and friendship with Adler, to whom he paid a moving tribute at Adler's death). A second volume was published in 1907, and a third, containing the present sermon, was published in 1930. This contains sermons 'preached chiefly at the West London Synagogue', in which he succeeded David Woolf Marks as minister. Four of these sermons deal with the First World War as its devastation was unfolding.[1]

A sermon delivered by Joseph in the early days of the Boer War (28 October 1899) was—unlike the patriotic endorsement of British imperial policy and military heroism by the chief rabbi (Sermon 14 above)—a sober reflection on the various costs of war:

We see that War means something more than a picturesque movement of troops, more than the thrilling gallantry of heroes, more than victory and the increase of national glory. It means the sacrifice of many a precious life; it means mourning and pain and misery for the victors, and for the vanquished this and humiliation too; it means the awakening of brutal passions, the resuscitation of 'the ape and tiger', that we would all willingly let die; it means the stirring of inter-racial hatred that may leave a legacy of

---

[1] No date for the sermon reproduced here is provided in the text. The statement further in the sermon, 'This day last year a truce in the gigantic fight was called', refers to the first Christmas of the war, 25 Dec. 1914. In 1915, 25 December fell on a Saturday.

enmity and strife to embitter the coming years. Nay, it means a serious arrest of the world in its march of progress. It means a sudden breaking with all mankind's best traditions, a sudden defeat of all its noblest ideals. It means that the precious foothold won so hardly has been lost, and that, Sisyphus-like, civilisation must begin its painful task over again.

Indeed, he suggested that war shows that we have not advanced much over the Canaanites who immolated their children to propitiate their deities: 'What is War but human sacrifice on a gigantic scale—human sacrifice offered in the name of civilisation, nay, often in the name of God Himself? . . . Are we not doing the same [as the Canaanites] at this very moment, sending forth our sons to death, hurling death upon the foe, in an almost superstitious worship of the demon, War?' Only a firm faith in the world's moral progress can sustain the conviction that some day the horrors of war will so burn themselves into the consciousness of the combatants and the onlooking world that possibility of future conflicts becomes remote. 'In fighting each other, the Boer and the Briton are fighting even more effectively against War.'[2]

A few years later, in *Judaism as Creed and Life*, he wrote,

There are, doubtless, occasions when war is defensible as a less evil than a disastrous and dishonourable peace. But they are less numerous than is usually supposed . . . War is so terrible a calamity, so dark a blot upon our civilization, that the greatest sacrifices should be made to avert it. There are worse things, it is true, than war; but the worst of them is the belief that war is indispensable . . . Such a belief is fatal to the ultimate establishment of universal peace. Nor should such an idea as glory be any longer associated with war. Only that nation should be deemed glorious which has made the greatest efforts, and submitted to the heaviest sacrifices, in order to preserve peace.[3]

He was one of the founders of the Jewish Peace Society, established in early 1914, and served as its chairman for many years.[4]

One can imagine the psychological toll exacted on a man of such convictions by the outbreak of another, greater war, some fifteen years after that sermon was delivered. According to the report in the *Jewish Chronicle*, this was his first response from the pulpit, on 15 August 1914:

We resume our Sabbath Services this week in circumstances all but unparalleled in the history of mankind . . . The lust to destroy and slay has taken possession of minds hitherto chiefly concerned to heal the hurt of the world, and to set the feet of mankind

---

[2] Joseph, 'War', 22; 'the ape and tiger' alludes to Tennyson's 'In Memoriam A.H.H.', end of section 118.

[3] Joseph, *Judaism as Creed and Life*, 456. Chief Rabbi Joseph Hertz incorporated part of this passage in his commentary on Num. 6: 26 in *Pentateuch and Haftorahs*, 595.

[4] See tribute by the Revd John S. Harris at the time of Joseph's death, in *Jewish Chronicle*, 25 Apr. 1930, p. 12 (a letter printed in the 2 May issue, p. 11, asserted that the actual founder was Ethel Behrens, but Joseph gave the Society every support).

more firmly on the high-way of progress. It is a terrifying paradox, a cruel blow to our optimism and our most cherished ideals. It makes us doubt the value, the reality of our civilization, the stability of righteousness, the fixity of purpose of God himself.[5]

He did not question the decision by the British government to enter the war— 'To have remained passive would have been a crime', both against national honour and against the principles of justice and freedom—or the need for British Jews to 'rally to the help of our beloved country in her hour of need'. But one senses in these words feelings not of exhilaration but of profound distress.

# SERMON

I HAVE read that Anton Lang, the impersonator of the Christian Saviour in the Oberammergau Passion Play, was killed in battle a few weeks ago.[6] The event was symbolic. According to the old Apostolic idea the recreant Christian, who has 'tasted the good word', and 'fallen away', crucifies his Lord afresh, and 'puts Him to open shame'.[7] And what faithlessness to the 'Prince of Peace' can be more flagrant than that which has plunged twentieth-century Christendom into the worst horrors of war? Among the many wounds inflicted upon the Master by his followers none has been more cruel or more deadly. The Gospel of Peace and Goodwill, which he claimed to have been divinely chosen to preach, has been flouted, derided, falsified by its plighted adherents. Verily Christ has been slain in this war.[8]

---

[5] *Jewish Chronicle*, 21 Aug. 1914, p. 11 ('A Sermon for the Week: The Rev. Morris Joseph and the War').

[6] This report turned out to be incorrect. Lang, who played Christ in the passion plays of 1900 and 1910, also played him in 1922 and lived until 1938. The *New York Times* of 24 Oct. 1915 carried a short article entitled 'Anton Lang Not Killed: Letter to Relative Here Shows That He is Not Even Fighting'. There had been a previous announcement of his death, based on a letter to a different relative, and the article continued, 'It is believed that a mistake has been made by confusing the identity of the Oberammergau player with that of a relative of the same name.' Whether or not Joseph knew of the correction, the homiletical point apparently seemed irresistible. On Lang, see Krauskopf, *A Rabbi's Impressions*, 46–7.          [7] See Heb. 6: 5–6.

[8] Cf. William Temple (later Archbishop of York and of Canterbury), in a 1914 paper entitled 'Christianity and War': 'Members of the body of Christ are tearing one another, and His body is bleeding as it once bled on Calvary, but this time the wounds are dealt by His friends. It is as though Peter were driving home the nails and John were piercing the side' (cited in Hoover, *God, Germany, and Britain*, 6).

To-day is His birthday. In thousands of churches they are rehearsing the story of the Nativity, with its account of the angelic choir who sing their promise of a glorious era about to dawn on a sorrowing world.

> Yea, Truth and Justice then
> Will down return to men,
> Orb'd in a rainbow; and, like glories wearing,
> Mercy will sit between,
> Thron'd in celestial sheen,
> With radiant feet the tissued clouds down steering:
> And heav'n, as at some festival,
> Will open wide the gates of her high palace hall.[9]

But that Golden Age did not come then, nor has it ever come. On the contrary, the lapse of nineteen centuries finds mankind not at peace, but at war; not the gospel of love, but the gospel of hate dominates the world. Christmas Day, which should be the festival of peace and goodwill, falls in a time of general carnage and rapine; the birthday of the Master becomes a day of mourning at his murder.

The thought will find utterance in many a Christian pulpit this morning. For to no one is the painful disparity between the doctrine and practice of his communion more evident than to the devout Christian himself. The seeming failure of Christ!—a thousand preachers will discuss the theme. As for us, let us be just. 'Christianity is bankrupt,' men cry, and point, as evidence, to the present state of the world. Shall we not rather say that Christendom is bankrupt? What is good, and true, and mighty in the Christian religion is good, and true, and mighty still. It will bear fruit in God's good time. Why should we not acknowledge it, as great Jews, like Maimonides and Jehudah Halevi, acknowledged it?[10] When the simple teaching of the Gospels, as distinguished from St. Paul's pagan travesty of it,[11] triumphs, when men turn to God, the Father, and serve

---

[9] Milton, 'On the Morning of Christ's Nativity'.

[10] This apparently refers to the passage in Judah Halevi's *Sefer hakuzari*, 4, 22–3, where the Khazar king speaks with admiration of the devotion and faith of the early Christian martyrs, and the passage near the end of Maimonides' *Code of Jewish Law* (*Mishneh torah*, 'Hilkhot melakhim' (Laws of Kings), end of ch. 11) in which he affirms that by bringing the knowledge of God and Scripture to many pagans who had no knowledge of them, Christianity served God's purpose and prepared the way for the eventual messianic age. I know of no passage in which Maimonides, who considered Christianity to be a form of idolatry, acknowledged a truth in the Christian religion that is different from the truth of Judaism.

[11] This claim—that Paul perverted the pure (Jewish) teachings of Jesus—was common in Jewish apologetic literature. Joseph will pick up this distinction again in the continuation of his message. Cf. his earlier sermon, 'Judaism and Christianity': 'Christianity won the adhesion of a pagan world two thousand years ago by swamping its Jewish elements with heathen mysticism. It purchased its popularity by debasing the doctrines of its Founder' (pp. 37–8).

Him with one consent, when they practise righteousness and love towards each other all the world over, then Israel's hope, cherished through the ages with pathetic persistence, will be fulfilled. The Gentiles will have been led along the way of their own religions to the one Religion which Judaism enshrines. No; it is not Christianity—true Christianity—that has failed, but its self-styled adherents. The call to God, to rectitude, to peace and brotherliness, has come to them, but they have been heedless of it. Theirs is the defeat.

But, you will say, is this not an admission of Christianity's failure? The very fact that it has pleaded with men in vain proves its impotence. It should have been strong enough to break down their stubbornness, to capture their souls by the sheer beauty of its doctrine. But see where the argument leads us! God himself has been pleading with men for much more than nineteen centuries, and too often pleading in vain. Sin still holds sway; one of the deadliest wars in history is raging. But dare we say on that account that God has failed, that His hand has waxed short? Nay, let us look at home. We Jews, by the theory of our religion, are 'a kingdom of priests and a holy nation' (Exod. 19: 6), bound to be the world's exemplars in rectitude and sanctity of life. Is not the title a mockery, the bond a dead letter? But shall we say on that account that Judaism is bankrupt? When Israel has gotten him 'a new heart and a new spirit' (Ezek. 11: 19), a soul sensitive to the appeal of his God, alive to the splendour of his mission, then the vitality and the power of his religion will be revealed to himself and to mankind.

No, Christianity, in its essence, is still a living religion. In its essence, I say, because, as I have already suggested, we must discriminate. The old theistic and ethical ideas of its Founder are indestructible. We Jews must necessarily believe it because those ideas were derived from the Judaism in which he who taught them was born and nourished. The pagan teachings grafted upon them will perish. And it is to these later accretions that we must look for the causes of the failure of which Christianity seemingly stands convicted. Why is the message of peace and goodwill set at naught by the nations to-day? Why is brotherhood fled from the earth, and war still the favoured arbiter of international disputes? Why is the Master wounded, slain, in the house of his friends? Let a Christian minister answer the question. 'Christianity,' he declares, 'has never dared to call any war wrong.'[12] By Christianity he clearly means the Church; and the

---

[12] I cannot identify the precise quotation, but it is close to the statement in a published sermon delivered on 6 Jan. 1915 by the celebrated American 'Social Gospel' preacher Washington Gladden: 'But it remains a shameful fact . . . that organized Christianity has never in any consistent and concerted way arrayed itself against war' (Gladden, 'The Church and Peace', 50).

accusation is true. Not content with tolerating war, the Church has blessed it. Nay, it has made itself a secular power even more than a religious one. 'Do you submit to the Church Militant?' said the ecclesiastics to Joan of Arc when they held her life in their grasp. 'I submit,' she replied, 'only to the Church triumphant above.'[13] The Church Militant, not the humble, peaceful Church of the Founder, with a kingdom not of this world—there is the origin of half the wars that have devastated the earth.[14] The Church has strained after earthly power and dominion even more eagerly than after spiritual supremacy. It has emphasized the religious differences of men instead of reconciling them, seeking its victories not by conciliation, but by persecution, as we Jews know to our cost, triumphing not by love, but by destruction and death. In one hand it has held the crucifix, in the other the sword. Can we wonder that the world, morally speaking, stands where it does, that the earth is being drenched with blood in this year of grace?

But again let us be just. This conception of the character and mission of the church is old and well nigh outworn; it is fading away before the uprising of a nobler vision. In all the civilized world Religion is being regenerated by the infusion of humanitarian ideas. The signs of it are unmistakable.[15] War is far—very far—from obsolete, but it has lost much of its ancient glamour and glory. It is something of which to be ashamed, something to be apologized for. Even our chief enemy in this present conflict, while extolling war as the maker and preserver of a people's vigour,[16] inconsistently excuses this particular war as one of self-defence. And we, his antagonists, though believing and declaring that our cause is just, confess in our inmost hearts that the means we have chosen to vindicate it are at best a necessary evil, a huge blot on our civilisation. On both sides the confession is translated into action. This day last year a truce in the gigantic fight was called, out of respect for the day's sacred associations.[17] It was a

[13] This distinction between the Church Militant (composed of living Christians and the ecclesiastical institutions) and the Church Triumphant (composed of those in heaven) actually appears in the transcripts of the trials of Joan of Arc for Saturday, 17 Mar. 1431. Joseph may have taken this question and response from Mark Twain, *Personal Recollections of Joan of Arc*, bk 2, ch. 12.

[14] A strong condemnation, continued in the following sentences, of Christian leaders and institutions as responsible for immense human suffering.

[15] The transition to a more positive theme of hope for the future.

[16] See Sermon 17 by Hertz, n. 18, on 'religion of valour'.

[17] It was reported that a Christmas Day truce was proposed by American religious leaders in October 1914: 'the idea originated with Rabbi Pereira Mendes, and has been submitted to Cardinal Farley, Bishop David A. Greer, and Nicholas Murray Butler, President of the Columbia University' (*Jewish Chronicle*, 23 Oct. 1914, p. 21, based on the New York correspondent of the *Daily Mail*). This idea was never officially endorsed by the belligerents; on the spontaneous event, never repeated during the war, see Brown, *The Christmas Truce*.

striking self-contradiction. For if warfare is a glaring anomaly on any one day, it is that always. Is not God ever near us, His word for ever calling to our hearts? Ought not every day, every hour, to be consecrated to Him? Nay, are not men always brothers? Is the duty of forgiveness and compassion subject even to a moment's moratorium? No; for the Christian to think of honouring his Master by a Christmas truce is in effect to dishonour him, to accentuate the sin against love which all war involves. He sees the better way, but deliberately chooses the worse. And yet all such inconsistencies have their good side, for they betray a conscience disquieted, the first stage on the road to repentance. They contain the promise and potency of recovered sanity for mankind. They foreshadow the time when the veil that is spread over all nations, hiding from them the higher truth, shall be rent, when the clash of arms shall cease not for a day, or for a century, but for ever. Let us join our supplications to those of our brothers of all creeds and all nationalities for the speeding of that time. With the English poet let us pray:—

> Oh! let Thy Word prevail, to take away
> The sting of human nature. Spread the law,
> As it is written in Thy holy book,
> Throughout all lands; let every nation hear
> The high behest, and every heart obey,
> Both for the love of purity and hope
> Which it affords to such as do Thy will
> And persevere in good, that they shall rise
> And have a nearer view of Thee in heaven.
> Father of good! this prayer in bounty grant,
> In mercy grant it, to Thy wretched sons.
> Then, not till then, shall persecution cease,
> And cruel wars expire.
>                    Shall enmity and strife,
> Falsehood and guile, be left to sow their seed
> And the kind never perish? Is the hope
> Fallacious, or shall righteousness obtain
> A peaceable dominion, wide as earth
> And ne'er to fail?
>                    The law of faith,
> Working through love, such conquest shall it gain,
> Such triumph over sin and guilt achieve?
> Almighty Lord, Thy further grace impart![18]

To this lovely petition let us cry, with all hearts, Amen! Amen!

[18] William Wordsworth, *The Excursion*, IX. 638–50, 661–6, 672–5.

# CHAPTER SEVENTEEN

## JOSEPH H. HERTZ
# THROUGH DARKNESS AND DEATH UNTO LIGHT

*Intercession Sermon*

### 1 JANUARY 1916

**GREAT SYNAGOGUE, LONDON**

BORN in Slovakia in 1872, Hertz emigrated with his family to the United States when he was 12 years old. He received a BA from the College of the City of New York and in 1894 became the first graduate from the Jewish Theological Seminary, where he studied with Sabato Morais, Alexander Kohut, Marcus Jastrow, and Benjamin Szold. In his graduation address of 14 June 1894 he cited Goethe, Coleridge, and Garibaldi.[1] His first congregation was in Syracuse, New York. After two years here he accepted the offer of a rabbinical position in Johannesburg, South Africa, where he remained—except for a two-year period of deportation during the Boer War (about which he expressed strong reservations)—until 1911. During this time he was vice-president of the South African Zionist Federation, and in 1904 he attended the Fourth Zionist Congress in London. In January 1912 he was installed as rabbi of Orach Chayyim Congregation in New York, and less than fourteen months later he cabled his acceptance of the position of British chief rabbi, succeeding Hermann Adler.

Today Hertz is best known for his editions, with learned commentaries, of foundational works of Jewish religious practice: *The Pentateuch and Haftorahs* (Oxford University Press, 1929) and the *Authorised Daily Prayer Book* (published posthumously in 1948). In addition, his *Book of Jewish Thoughts* was extremely popular. During his lifetime, however, he was known as a forceful and eloquent speaker from both pulpit and public platform, with a fine

---

[1] J. Hertz, *Early and Late*, 122–5.

homiletical sense.[2] He published three volumes of his *Sermons, Essays and Studies* in 1938, and another volume, *Early and Late*, in 1943. These volumes contain abundant evidence of his speaking in response to many events of ceremonial and historical—and, in most cases, tragic—significance, spanning two world wars and the persecution of Jews in eastern Europe both in the wake of the first war and under Nazism.

In his installation sermon as chief rabbi, delivered on 14 April 1913, Hertz said:

Ours is an age of doubt and disillusionment. Times are out of joint. Theological foundations are rocking. Dreams of humanity, that but yesterday seemed within grasp of realization, are dissolving into thin air in face of the malicious race-hatred that is being fanatically preached, and the purposeless human slaughter cynically practised, in the opening decades of the twentieth century.[3]

Sixteen months later, an episode of 'purposeless human slaughter' would begin that made all that preceded it seem almost benign.

Near the beginning of what was then called the 'Great War' the British Crown restored a venerable practice that had been in abeyance since the Indian Mutiny, albeit with a different name: a day of 'intercession service' rather than the traditional 'day of fast and humiliation'. This was set for Saturday, 2 January 1915; both Hertz and his Sephardi colleague, Haham Moses Gaster, composed special prayers for the occasion.[4] A year later, another Intercession Service was designated for Saturday, 1 January. It was on this occasion that Hertz delivered the sermon reproduced below. It is relatively brief, but characteristic of Hertz. He honestly confesses the devastating effect on morale of the events he describes as 'a human tragedy unapproached in civilized history', the difficulty many have in reconciling the nightmare of their time with belief in the providence of a loving God. He incorporates quotations from literature—Kipling and Milton—and refers to Aristotle's theory of the cathartic effect of tragedy. And he applies a stunning rabbinic legend of Adam's despair at the darkness of the first night and God's reassurance that this darkness was not the final

[2] An article of tribute in the *Jewish Chronicle* on his sixty-ninth birthday cited the *Evening Standard* report of a speech by Hertz at a meeting for the 'Palestine Victory Campaign' during the Second World War: 'Dr. Hertz is sixty-nine years old, but there is no weakening in his compact frame and voice of thunder. He denounced the persecution of his people in language which Edmund Burke would have approved, but there was no hint of despair nor any appeal for sympathy in his words. It was a violent, fighting speech' (*Jewish Chronicle*, 26 Sept. 1941, p. 19). See also the posthumous characterization of Hertz as preacher in E. Levine, 'Memoir', 25–6.

[3] J. Hertz, 'Installation Sermon', p. 5.

[4] Hertz's prayer (*Sermons, Addresses and Studies*, i. 354–7) was first published in the *Jewish Chronicle* on 18 Dec. 1914, p. 11; Haham Gaster's prayer appeared two weeks later. Gaster's prayer asks God to 'fight our battles' and 'confound the enemy'; Hertz's asks not for victory, but for protection of British and Allied soldiers, comfort and healing to the bereaved of 'all who weep for the loss of those dear to them', and a speedy end to the war.

reality, together with the verse from the week's Torah lesson evoking both the discouragement of Moses and the promise of a new manifestation of the divine, as a source of hope.

# SERMON

*And God spake unto Moses, and said unto him, I am the LORD; and I appeared unto Abraham, unto Isaac, and unto Jacob, as God Almighty; but by My name Adonay— Eternal—was I not known to them.*

(EXOD. 6: 2–3)

TO MOSES had come the dread realization that, instead of bringing redemption to his suffering people, he had thus far only intensified the misery of his brethren. He is crushed at the seeming failure of his mission. In his anguish, he turns in prayer to the God of his fathers. A new revelation of the Divine nature is then vouchsafed unto him. Formerly men knew God only as *Shaddai*—Almighty; henceforth He would be known unto them also as *Adonay*—the constant and everlasting Friend, abounding in loving kindness and truth, Who redeemeth and delivereth, rescueth and saveth.

After seventeen months of colossal conflict, we of to-day can well understand this uncertainty and disappointment of Moses our Teacher. Ours are times when we too are perplexed by the tardiness of victory for the forces of liberty and civil-ization in their warfare against the new Egypt of brutal and irresponsible power.[5] And for the second time since the opening of this Conflict, the Religious Bodies have arranged that Intercession Prayers be offered up to God, the Shaper of the destinies of nations, for the safety of our cause.[6] If we truly answer this call to prayer and re-consecration to the service of King and Right, nothing less than a new God-like conception, like that revealed unto Moses, will become ours.

Now to attune our hearts to the message of this day, a retrospect upon our spiritual experiences since the Declaration of War is necessary. And I can best condense what our souls have passed through, by recalling to you the following

---

[5] This association of Germany with Egypt and of both with the apotheosis of power will be reiterated near the conclusion of the sermon.

[6] The previous year, the chief rabbi had announced that an intercession service would be held on Saturday, 2 Jan. 1915. (Haham Gaster of the Spanish and Portuguese community had set the date for Sunday, 3 Jan.) See *Jewish Chronicle*, 18 Dec. 1914, p. 11. All synagogues observed the inter-cession service on 1 Jan. 1916.

legend of the Rabbis. When Adam saw the sun go down for the first time and an
ever deeper gloom enfold creation, his mind was filled with terror. God then
took pity on him, and endowed him with the intuition to take two stones—the
name of one was Darkness and the name of the other Shadow of Death—and
rub them against each other, and so discover fire. Adam—the legend continues—thereupon uttered the grateful benediction: ברוך בורא מאורי האש,
'Blessed be the Creator of light'.[7]

This beautiful phantasy is symbolical of the strange mutations of feeling that
have dominated the children of Adam since those unforgettable August days of
1914 which signalized Britain's entrance into the World War. The alarm that
then filled men's minds when they suddenly saw the sun go down, as it were, in
noonday, had in it something of the physical terror that possesses sentient
beings during every total eclipse of the sun. Fundamental facts were shaken for
us, and our ideas became as disturbed as the world's economic and political conditions about us. We, children of the age of science, cherishing the dream of
universal peace, had come to think of the future story of humanity as one
of unbroken triumphal progress.[8] The 'catastrophic view' of history, preached
by ancient prophet and apocalyptic seer—the view that mankind's greatest
spiritual advance takes place through sudden dramatic crises, involving unutterable woe and tribulation upon an entire age—had totally disappeared from
our modern consciousness. And then in one day a cataclysm engulfed civilization; and the poet could truthfully exclaim:

> Our world has passed away,
> In wantonness overthrown;
> There is nothing left to-day,
> But steel, and fire, and stone.[9]

None could have foretold that civilized mankind would rush back to savagery
with such dreadful fervour. No wonder, that for some this world-calamity has

---

[7] Cf. *Genesis Rabbah* 11: 2, BT *Pes.* 54a. I have not found in any of the rabbinic sources the names
of the two stones, apparently taken from Job 12: 22 ('He draws mysteries out of Darkness, He
brings to light the Shadow of Death'), but it is certainly an appropriate linking of the verse with
the rabbinic legend. It may be the preacher's own homiletical innovation; note his use of this
motif later in the sermon.

[8] On the power of this optimistic outlook on history as the ineluctable march of progress, see
the sources noted in Sermon 10 above by Artom, n. 26. The impact of the outbreak of war is
confirmed by the report of a sermon delivered by Morris Joseph on 15 Aug. 1914: 'It is a terrifying
paradox, a cruel blow to our optimism and our most cherished ideals. It makes us doubt the value,
the reality, of our civilization' (*Jewish Chronicle*, 21 Aug. 1914, p. 11).

[9] This is a poem by Rudyard Kipling, beginning, 'For all we have and are, | For all our children's
fate, | Stand up and meet the war | The Hun is at the gate!' This is followed by the lines cited.

put out in their firmament the stars of hope and faith for ever; that they find insuperable difficulty in fitting these things into our sense of the overruling Providence of God.[10]

We are thus witnesses of a human tragedy unapproached in civilized history, a veritable Tragedy of the Nations. Unless, however, we wish to lose our moral bearings altogether, we must stop for a moment and consider the crucial question, What is tragedy? Tragedy has been defined as a confusion in the moral world resulting in calamity. Yet tragedy, the ancients truly held, purifies and purges us, as nothing else can, from the petty and self-centred.[11] It opens the eyes of the spirit, and fills the heart with pity for our common human nature. Take any tragedy, whether in literature or in history—*King Lear*, or the persecutions of the Maccabean martyrs[12]—and from the very furnace of affliction the conviction is borne upon us that somehow all this vast suffering counts as nothing against the spiritual steadfastness and love which it has called forth. The agony passes away, but the types of heroism and devotion it has created remain, an everlasting possession and inspiration of the race. We see this illustrated in our own days. The men who fought and died in Gallipoli[13] have not fought and died in vain. They have created new standards of human courage. Their dead lie on the abandoned cliffs, but the memory of all they did and tried to do will never fade.

And this brings us once more to the paradox of religion. Man, it proclaims, has been endowed by his Creator with the Divine intuition to derive light from darkness and the shadow of death.[14] From deepest woe and vastest sorrow, man can ever reap a harvest of such spiritual power and transcendent worth that, like Adam in the Talmudic legend, he will utter grateful benediction to God for the new light with which his path is henceforth sown!

And indeed has not this tragedy brought consolations as well in its trail? Is there nothing for which to bless God, amid all this disaster? Consider the spirit of stern resolve that has come over the men and the women of the nation, the

[10] An honest and non-judgemental acknowledgement of the toll taken by the war on traditional religious faith.

[11] The purifying, purging, cathartic effect of tragedy ('arousing pity and fear, wherewith to accomplish its catharsis of such emotions') was classically stated by Aristotle in his *Poetics*, ch. 6 (1449b).

[12] As recounted in 2 Macc. ch. 7. It is difficult to see how this account fits the Aristotelian definition or is comparable to the story of King Lear.

[13] Scene of an unsuccessful Allied campaign, planned by Winston Churchill, beginning in April 1915. The last Allied troops were being withdrawn at the time of this service, and the disaster was very much in the consciousness of the British public.

[14] Echoing Job 12: 22 (where it is God, not man, who is the subject), and the *midrash* on Adam cited above (n. 7).

> Courage never to submit or yield,
> And what is else not to be overcome—[15]

the readiness for unbounded sacrifice, as soon as it was realized that we were confronted by a powerful foe who desired nothing less than England's annihilation. Nobly have also the sons of Anglo-Jewry rallied round England in the hour of her need. And our Honour Record will be rendered longer and more luminous now that the large number of our brethren who are naturalized British subjects, or the children of such naturalized subjects, have been admitted to the glorious privilege of fighting for their country.[16] Verily, the horizons of life have been widened both for the nation and its citizens. Millions have been made to feel what mankind steadily refuses to see in times of peace, that there are certain absolute values for the vindication of which no sacrifice, not even the life of our nearest and dearest, is too great.

And as to the feeling that because of this stupendous convulsion religion has failed, let me repeat the question asked by the great scholar whom Jewry recently lost (Dr. Schechter): 'Have we been living in a really religious age when this calamity overwhelmed us?'[17] Surely we cannot speak of anything having failed, when it has not even been tried. Can anyone honestly say that Prussian

[15] A citation from bk I of Milton's *Paradise Lost*, actually part of a famous speech by the fallen Satan after his abortive challenge to God. It is possible that Hertz took the quotation not directly from its source, but from Matthew Arnold's 'On Poetry', where the two lines out of context are cited as one of his 'touchstones': M. H. Abrams (ed.), *The Norton Anthology of English Literature*, ii. 954.

[16] On pride in Jewish soldiers, see Sermon 14 above by Adler, n. 27. The point about Jewish immigrants and the children of immigrants in military service was particularly sensitive following the anti-German and anti-Austrian riots in England in the wake of the sinking of the *Lusitania* in May 1915. Todd Endelman writes that the issue was becoming explosive: 'While well-established, anglicized families sent their sons to war with enthusiasm, immigrant families did not. In the Jewish East End and its provincial counterparts, few were eager to sacrifice themselves or their children in a war in which, in their view, Jews had no stake, a war, moreover, in support of the hated tsarist regime many of them had fled. During the period of voluntary enlistment, few immigrants joined up'. Conscription began only in January 1916, after the sermon was delivered. See Endelman, *The Jews of Britain*, 185. This may explain Hertz's statement that English Jews 'have rallied around', while the immigrants and their children 'have been admitted to the glorious privilege of fighting'.

[17] Solomon Schechter, a distinguished scholar of rabbinic and medieval Judaism, associated primarily with facilitating the transfer of the largest collection of documents from the Cairo Genizah to the University of Cambridge, became in 1902 president of the Jewish Theological Seminary of America, from which Hertz was an early graduate. Hertz delivered a memorial address at Jews' College on 19 Dec. 1915, less than two weeks before the sermon (J. Hertz, *Sermons, Addresses and Studies*, i. 84–9). The sentence cited is from Schechter's address at the commencement exercises of the seminary on 6 June 1915. See S. Schechter, *Seminary Addresses*, 247. Hertz will echo other lines from this address in his final paragraph.

militarism, or the snarling of the nations at one another during the last decade, was religion?

With the victory of Great Britain, the old Egyptian idols and heathen ideals—the worship of brute force and 'the religion of valour'[18]—will be shattered. It will be a chastened humanity that will emerge from the ruins that this War will leave behind it.[19] Let us prayerfully resolve that the new order be a better order, rooted in righteousness, broad-based on the liberty of and reverence for each and every nationality, and culminating in a harmony of peoples. Amen.

[18] A phrase used in Britain after the outbreak of the war to characterize the Germanic ideology of 'might makes right', glorifying power as a transcendent ideal. This ideology was provocatively expressed in a book by Friedrich von Bernhardi called *Germany and the Next War*, published in English in 1911 and again in 1914, which was widely discussed in Britain (see e.g. Joseph, 'The War and the Future', 208–9). Hertz's peroration picks up the motif from the beginning of the sermon: Germany as 'the new Egypt of brutal and irresponsible power'.

[19] Echoing Schechter's June 1915 commencement address: 'What shape this regeneration [of humanity] will take is difficult to say; but if all signs are not deceiving . . . it will not be in the direction of the religion of valor . . . My friends, it will be a chastened humanity which will emerge from a destroyed world, strewn with the *debris* of broken idols and shattered ideals' (S. Schechter, *Seminary Addresses*, 247).

CHAPTER EIGHTEEN

J. LEONARD LEVY

# A TIME FOR WAR, AND
# A TIME FOR PEACE

### SUNDAY, 8 APRIL 1917

#### RODEF SHALOM TEMPLE, PITTSBURGH

*Stenographically reported by Caroline Loewenthal*

J. LEONARD LEVY was born in London on 24 November 1865. He received his Jewish education at Jews' College and his general education at University College, from which he received a BA in 1884. After four years at the Bristol Hebrew Congregation, he decided to emigrate to the United States. Serving first in Sacramento, California, in 1893 he came to the distinguished congregation Keneseth Israel of Philadelphia as the associate rabbi to Joseph Krauskopf. Despite the difference in their countries of origin the two seem to have worked closely together, sharing preaching responsibilities by delivering the Sunday discourse on alternate weeks. All these addresses were published in pamphlet form week by week and bound together in annual volumes. In 1901 Levy left Philadelphia for the much smaller Reform Congregation Rodef Shalom in Pittsburgh, where he remained until his death in 1917. There he continued the practice of the weekly Sunday morning discourse, transcribed, printed, and distributed the following Sunday, under the title 'The Reform Pulpit'.[1]

While still in Philadelphia, Levy voiced an enthusiastic defence of American policy on the Sunday immediately following the formal declaration of war with Spain (one week before Krauskopf's address reproduced as Sermon 13 above). Soon after that he volunteered for service, becoming a chaplain with

---

[1] Even the format of the pamphlets shows the influence of Krauskopf's Keneseth Israel publications, with brief phrases summarizing the content in the margins of each page. The major difference is that Krauskopf's publications were based on a complete text that he had written and memorized for delivery, whereas Levy's were stenographically transcribed from the actual delivery. It is not clear to me what kind of text, if any, Levy used for his delivery. Cf. Freehof and Kavaler (eds), *J. Leonard Levy*, 18.

a volunteer brigade. That experience apparently changed him profoundly: in 1904 he was elected vice-president of the International Peace Union, and not long thereafter organized an international conference for peace held with considerable fanfare at his temple in Pittsburgh. In the autumn of 1914, speaking on 'The War against War', he said that since the Spanish–American War had ended he had been 'an unfailing advocate of what is known as the pacifist policy. I am a converted man.'[2] The following week he spelled out the implications of this position:

if the United States government had the right to draft me today into an army, I would refuse to serve. If the punishment for refusal would be imprisonment, I would go to prison gladly. If the punishment would be that I would be shot to death, I would gladly prefer that I be shot than that the government should direct me to join in wholesale murder—for that is what I believe war to be.[3]

And two weeks later, still on the same theme, he asserted: 'I believe that there is more heroism in destroying germs than in killing Germans, and more bravery in conquering parasites than in capturing Paris.'[4]

Levy's British origins led him to proclaim his natural sympathy for his mother country and his tendency to find 'reasons favorable to the English government' which would support his belief that England would never go to war 'unless behind her act was the overwhelming feeling expressive of the righteous sentiment of the English people'.[5] Yet he recognized that others (such as his former mentor, Krauskopf, and many in his congregation) who loved Germany felt the same about Germany. Indeed, a further two weeks on he returned to this theme, stating that, despite his love of England, 'I would be an enemy to German civilization were I ever to forget what German art, and German culture, and German research, and German science, have done for the world', and an enemy of all civilization 'were I ever to utter a word against the distinguished services of the great German people'.[6] A year later, he protested against the efforts to 'arouse the ire of this nation against all things German', reminding his listeners of the valuable lessons that Germany could teach America through its social programmes and care for the poor.[7] The sermon below, delivered immediately following America's entry into the war, begins with an even more resounding paean to the achievements of German science, culture, and society.

[2] 'The War against War', 4; on his volunteering, see also 'The War against War III', 10.
[3] 'The War against War, II', 7–8.
[4] 'The War against War, III', 8. If this is an original formulation—and my searches have not yet produced a parallel—it is a rather catchy slogan that must have been delivered with considerable passion.                              [5] 'When Dreams Come True', 9.
[6] 'The War against War', 3; this theme recurs in 'The Fruits of War', 15, where he describes his congregation as one whose membership is composed largely of 'men and women who were born in Germany, or their children and children's children'.         [7] 'The Fruits of the War', 23–5.

Despite his sympathies, he supported Wilson's call for American neutrality as one that 'reveals his wisdom and splendid statesmanship'.[8]

The somewhat optimistic tone of 'When Dreams Come True', a sermon delivered on 1 November 1914 expressing the belief that this war would indeed demonstrate that all war is inexcusable, was replaced a year later in December 1915 by a sense of discouragement:

Whatever our opinions and sympathies, we Americans cannot but be filled with horror that, in this enlightened era of human progress, we are forced to hear or read of the shocking details of the world war. We hear of the loss of the young, the crippling of the strong, the destruction of property acquired with years of patient effort, the overthrow of moral standards, the subversion of all the finer and nobler things for which mankind has striven through long eras of self-sacrifice. Surely all this outpouring of human sacrifice, this apparently exhaustless offering on the altar of Mars, ought to mean something to us, ought to speak to us as no human voice can, as no human tongue is capable of doing.[9]

In this address he expressed opposition to the controversial policy of 'preparedness', entailing a major commitment of American resources to armaments. He did not oppose the exportation of arms to Europe (as did his mentor, Joseph Krauskopf), but he wanted the arms to be produced by the American government, not by private companies.[10] A year later, in an address given during the festival of Hanukah, he expressed greater consternation over the manufacture on a massive scale of weapons of destruction:

No greater evidence of the failure of religion to influence its adherents can be adduced than the patent fact that the whole civilized world has been converted into a vast munitions factory . . . Neutrals and belligerents alike are in the throes of a horrid fever whose ravages will be felt for generations to come . . . The Eternal God of Righteousness has been pushed, as it were, from His high and exalted throne, and thereon, in this age of madness, has been placed in the case of each nation, a national deity, in whose nostrils the smoke from the chimneys of the munitions factories must form a sweet savor indeed.[11]

Yet when the United States declared war against the Central Powers, Levy followed the pattern of anti-militarists (and even many pacifists) among the clergy in expressing his apparently unreserved support for the policy of the Wilson administration, in a long, somewhat sprawling, Sunday discourse delivered the following weekend.[12] An introductory section pays tribute to

---

[8] 'The War against War', 1–2.    [9] 'The Fruits of War', 17.
[10] Ibid. 18–21.    [11] 'The Making of Munitions', 8, 11.
[12] Note the generalization by the author of a comprehensive study of European pacifism: 'In 1914, rare was the pacifist in a belligerent nation who did not rally round the flag' (Cooper, *Patriotic Pacifism*, 140).

Germany's achievements, as manifest in admirable progressive social programmes, and laments the setbacks to this progress, from which we may not
recover 'for ages to come'. This is followed by the call to stand by the President
and to give full, loyal support to the nation in repayment of a debt of gratitude
for the sheltering home with which America has provided Jews during the past
few generations. Despite the difficulty for those whose families may still
live under the enemy flag, 'In all matters', he insists, 'we must be Americans
first.'

In the middle of the discourse, and quite without preparation, comes a section beginning: 'Before I proceed further I desire to emphasize one important
thought: please do not blame God for this war!' Levy reports the kinds of question he has been asked since the summer of 1914—'How is it possible that a
good God can tolerate such things to exist?'—and legitimates them by saying
that they arise out of human anguish and do credit to human nature.[13] But, he
insists, 'It is not God who desires war, but man. The European war was not
made in heaven, but on earth; not by God, but by those who, infringing His
divine laws, forced war on others.' This question, and the answer given to it,
are extremely common in the sermons of the First World War, and the same
topos will appear in sermons of the Second as well. They appear to represent a
fundamental break from the nineteenth-century material. In sermons from the
Civil War, Jewish as well as Christian, the assumption of divine providential
control over the events of history, and the corollary that the vicissitudes of the
war experience reflect God's judgement on the participants, seem to be universally accepted in the pulpit. Even in 1898, the invocation of God by Joseph
Krauskopf in a dramatic sermon at which J. Leonard Levy, as associate rabbi,
was present—'It is God's will, not ours, that our army is mobilized . . . It
was in the Council Chamber on High that war was declared'—reveals a theological mindset worlds apart from Levy's, perhaps because the dimensions of
the destruction in the later war were of such greater magnitude. Now, the universal liberal response will be: Don't blame God, blame human beings. The
capacity of people to do evil, to cause unimagined suffering, is the price we pray
for the freedom of the will that makes us human. God is present not as the

---

[13] Cf. the British chief rabbi Joseph Hertz, speaking on 1 Jan. 1916 (Sermon 17 above): 'None
could have foretold that civilized mankind would rush back to savagery with such dreadful fervour. No wonder, that for some this world-calamity has put out in their firmament the stars of
hope and faith for ever; that they find insuperable difficulty in fitting these things into our sense
of the overruling Providence of God. We are thus witnesses of a human tragedy unapproached
in civilized history'; and the British Jewish preacher Morris Joseph, late in 1917: 'We begin
to question our most fundamental convictions. We ask ourselves, "Where is God in all this
terrifying upheaval? Where is His goodness, His omnipotence?"' ('The War and Religion',
199).

manipulator of events, but as the force that inspires human beings to sacrifice themselves for a noble purpose.[14]

The third component of the sermon deals with standards of morality, leading to a reaffirmation of Levy's belief in peace exemplified in the vision of Isaiah, yet poignantly confessing a recognition that he had been wrong: that the world is not yet organized for peace, that the time for international, universal peace—which seemed so accessible just three years earlier—is not at hand. This leads to a surprisingly detailed discussion of the legal issues involved in the violation of Belgian neutrality (one might have expected more of an emphasis on the atrocities attributed to the Germans within Belgium; his appeal at this point is intellectual rather than emotional). Then he turns to the differences between American values as expressed by Wilson and the militaristic values of several leading German intellectuals. This section culminates in an endorsement of universal military service and of an appropriate tax on war profits.

The shift to an upbeat conclusion comes with the introduction of the Passover holiday (the sermon was delivered on the morning of the second day of Passover), with its theme of liberation dramatically exemplified in the fall of the tsarist government and the hope for the liberation of the Russian people. This concatenation of events—American entry into the war, the downfall of the tsar, and Passover—was used by virtually every American Jewish preacher in one way or another over that weekend in April. The sermon ends with the two themes of the biblical text (Eccles. 3: 8) in counterpoint: 'The time for peace will come . . . The time for war is here.'

In his Sunday sermon delivered two weeks later, Levy said, 'I tell you today, were it my last word I would utter to you . . . wake up and realize that before you is the greatest opportunity in all history to become the espousers of the international movement that shall place the nations of the earth under the sway of the one and only God, on the basis of international brotherhood.'[15] He died four days later.

---

[14] Krauskopf addressed the issue in a Yom Kippur 1917 sermon entitled 'Has God Forsaken Man?' It is largely devoted to a discussion of H. G. Wells's book *Mr Britling Sees It Through*, as revealing an example of 'God being held responsible for the misdeeds of men', but it deals only in passing with the impact of the war. On Wells's book cf. also Joseph, 'The War and Religion', 202–3, and Silver, 'Is God In This War?' For this response among Christian preachers, see Hoover, *God, Germany, and Britain*, 7–8.          [15] Freehof and Kavaler (eds), *J. Leonard Levy*, 149.

# SERMON

---

*A time for war and a time for peace.*
(ECCLES. 3: 8)

SINCE WE gathered in this sanctuary last Sunday morning, the nation of which we are a part has crossed the Rubicon in matters international. We are in a state of war. Facts, which history will correctly record, will assign the reasons for our rupture with a people which, until recently, the world regarded as one of the highest of civilized nations.

If we could calmly transfer ourselves back to the early summer of 1914, all of us would realize that we then had the deepest respect for all that Germany was doing for humanity, and the highest praise for the remarkable accomplishments of the German people. At that time the world was going to Germany to learn of industrial efficiency. The nations of the earth were sending their sons and daughters to study in German universities. The healing art, with its indescribable blessings to the sick among mankind, had received some of its finest contributions from among German men of science, and medical diagnosis was an art almost 'made in Germany'. Investigators, at that time, were visiting Germany from the four corners of the earth, to learn of new developments in industrial chemistry, in bio-chemistry, and in allied branches of science which mean so much for human health and happiness. The eyes of the world were gratefully and reverently turned toward Germany in 1914 for the success she had achieved in municipal government, while the great reforms suggested in her social programme—Old Age Pensions, Health Insurance, Industrial Insurance, Child Labor Laws, and kindred progressive legislation—were an inspiration to the advanced thinkers of every civilized nation.[16] These and like accomplishments evoked the world's praise and respect, and, if we can still remember the early part of the year 1914, we shall recall that here, in Pittsburgh, as elsewhere throughout our loved land, the example of Germany was invoked as an inspiring and helpful influence.

---

[16] Praise of German contributions to Western culture and society was a topos of British preaching at the beginning of the war; see Hoover, *God, Germany, and Britain*, 19–20. For a contemporary study of German social legislation, see Dawson, *Social Insurance in Germany*; the author confesses his 'high opinion of the benefits of obligatory insurance, as practiced in Germany now for nearly a generation'. Cf. Stephen S. Wise (Sermon 19 below) on the absence of such safeguards in the American depression of early 1915.

The greatest offence of which the German government is guilty is that the legitimate and peaceful conquest, which was then gratefully being performed, is now stayed; that the forward-looking labors of men and women, bound together for the uplift of the human race, have received a severe setback from which they will not recover for years to come. The constructive programmes on which nations had bent so much energy, and to which so many lives and so much treasure had been dedicated, are now impaired. The advance toward the land of promise has been seriously checked. Moral values have been disturbed. Faith has been rudely shocked. The almost unbelievable situation of international warfare, involving this liberty-loving and devoted land, has arisen. America and Germany are at war.

The die is cast. A hundred million free people have taken up the gage of war. Whether we desire it or not, whether we seek it or not, whether we believe in war as the means of settling international difficulties or not, we are all equally involved in the action of the President of the United States and the national Congress, and all of us must be prepared to bear our proportional share of the national obligation and responsibility. Whether we love peace and believe in unarmed peace, or whether we regard war as an anachronism or an inevitable necessity in such an age, every man who loves America, and every man who believes in the destiny of our country, and every man, woman and child living under the aegis of the starry banner of the land, will, now that the hour calls for service, place at the disposal of our nation, if the heart beats patriotically, their life, their sacred liberties, their possessions, to the end that success may crown the issue which has been raised by recent events.

We may well say with President Wilson that the United States did not seek this war. If any other nation but ours had received one hundredth part of the provocation to which the President has referred, or had suffered one tithe of the affront to international obligations, or had unwillingly been made a party to the brutal disregard for sacredly ratified treaties, war would long since have been declared and entered on in a spirit of outraged self-respect. The psychic trauma caused by the flagrant disregard of national and international rights has been patiently borne, and the best element in America hopes that no permanent harm has been done to the national and international consciousness by the failure of the foe to respect those conventions to which it had sacredly pledged its national honor.

In this hour of grave crisis our hearts go out in sympathetic respect to the great representative of our nation in the White House whose whole course, since the world-war began, has been marked by a desire to keep this nation free from foreign entanglements and to avoid the appeal to the sword. If ever a man deserved the whole-hearted gratitude and support of a whole nation for his untiring effort to keep us far from war's wild and wide desolation, that man is President Wilson. To a man the citizens of this land cannot but feel that he has employed every expedient, as well as every principle of national honor, to help this nation evade the awful last resort of force. Had he listened to the advice of bellicose counsellors, had he been guided by those less patient than himself, less given to self-control, less informed on the international situation, we might have been plunged into war long since, and the dignity, the honor, the democracy, of our land might have been impaired beyond repair. Loyally attached to this our country we cannot withhold—nay, we do not desire to withhold—our earnest need of gratitude to our President; and speaking for myself—for as a citizen I can only speak for myself—I am prepared to serve the cause of the United States to the limit of my humble ability in any way consonant with my position.[17] The cause is equally dear to you, I am convinced, my congregants, and every family in this congregation should be prepared to make the offer of the last measure of devotion to America, now that war has been declared. In complete loyalty we shall stand by the President.

We owe so much to this nation of which we are a part that now there should be no hesitation—even though we had hoped and prayed that war might be avoided—to place at the nation's disposal all we have and are. Look back a generation or two, and who were we, and what were we then? For the most part refugees from lands of oppression, lands where liberty was denied us, lands where opportunity was offered but sparingly to parents and their children! But a little time ago most of our co-religionists who are now in America—thrice-blessed land!—were living under the thraldom of Czar or Emperor who 'could do no wrong', or under the despotism of a state institutionalism which regarded us as inferiors. But few of us were fortunate enough to be born in lands of equal rights and liberties with the rest of our fellow citizens.

Now we and our forebears who live in America, and the children here born of our love, enjoy the full rights and privileges, as well as responsibilities, of

---

[17] Compare the ringing assertion on 22 Nov. 1914 of his unwillingness to serve in the military, even at the cost of imprisonment or death (cited in the introduction to this sermon, above). At this point, it was clear that Levy would not be asked to serve in the army in any capacity, and his formulation 'in any way consonant with my position' retains an ambiguity (his ideological position on war? his position as a rabbi?) that might have enabled him to explain that there had been no fundamental change in his position.

American citizenship. For the most part our immediate ancestry were living in enforced Ghettoes, in circumstances bordering on penury, reduced practically to beggary by the operation of harsh and proscriptive laws or shameful social restrictions. The government of the United States has removed from its statutes every distinction produced by birth, blood or creed. Everything which the government—national, State and civic—can do to establish equality before God and the law has been done. The Jew, like members of all creeds, is in America a citizen, endowed with all the rights of citizenship, and I am firmly convinced that, in the present emergency, my brethren in faith, without regard to the place of their origin, or ancestry, or previous national allegiance, will, to a man, display equal loyalty to the cause of America with the members of other religious denominations.

In all matters we must be Americans first.[18] If we were born under a foreign flag and have become American citizens, we must remember that the oath of loyalty to America expressly involved the renunciation of allegiance to any foreign potentate, king, queen, monarch, emperor, prince or ruler. It is hard for men whose families are still in the warring lands, whose tender recollections [are?] of happy childhood, whose parents still live under the enemy flag, whose dear ones lie buried beneath enemy soil—all of which appeal to their most humane sentiments—to realize the awful wrong that has been done to them by the foe. It is difficult for such men and women to cast out of their hearts all fondness for the land which gave them birth. I sympathize with them in the trial through which they are passing, for being a man of British birth I know how I would feel if, God forbid, the Allies and not the Teutons were the enemy. But we of foreign birth have sworn allegiance to America. We have raised our hands to God to witness our promise of loyalty to the United States—a land that deserves so much gratitude as well as fidelity at our hands—and now, as ever, we shall prove ourselves whole-hearted and devoted sons and daughters of America, prepared to answer the call to serve her cause to bring to complete success the undertaking on which she has entered. We shall serve in the capacity for which each is fitted, proud indeed if we can thus in part pay the debt of eternal gratitude each of us owes to America for all she has been to us and done for us.

Before I proceed further I desire to emphasize one important thought: please do not blame God for this war! I desire most earnestly to relieve Him of

---

[18] As is clear from the continuation, the issue here is not American identity before Jewish identity, but rather American identity before the German identity derived from the early years of immigrants from Germany.

the criticism to which thoughtless persons have subjected His holy name. Many persons have asked me, as a teacher of religion, since the war began in 1914—their tender hearts severely shocked by the awful suffering caused by the world disaster—'How is it possible that a good God can tolerate such things to exist? If He is omnipotent, why does He not interfere and stop the war?' It is a question which arises out of human anguish in the presence of apparently irremediable suffering. The question does credit to human nature. But we err when we imagine that God wants war. It is my unalterable conviction that God does not wish war. We learn in Scripture, 'He maketh wars to cease' (Ps. 46: 10). It is true that there are passages in Holy Scripture which refer to God as a God of war,[19] but the highest flights of the ethical writers of Holy Scripture refer to an era of world peace, and indicate that the 'fruit of righteousness shall be peace' (Isa. 34: 17; cf. Jas. 3: 18). With international righteousness will come international peace. Until then 'the wrath of man shall praise Him' (cf. Ps. 76: 10). For God is Righteousness, and when righteousness is triumphant on earth wars will cease; that is the process by which God maketh wars to cease.

It is not God who desires war, but man. The European war was not made in heaven, but on earth; not by God, but by those who, infringing His divine laws, forced war on others. It was manufactured by politicians, not by the Deity. It was produced by sinful man, though tolerated by an all-just God. It was made because men have not yet caught the glimpse of international brotherhood. It was caused because men are not yet conscious of their social inter-relations, of their independence yet interdependence. It came because mankind had not organized for peace as they have organized for war. It was made because some said, like the ancient Babylonians, 'I will ascend into heaven, above the stars of God will I exalt my throne; and I will sit upon the mount of meeting, in the uttermost parts of the north; I will ascend above the heights of the clouds; I will be like the Most High' (Isa. 14: 13–14).

Man is endowed with will and is thereby enabled to fulfill the purposes of his heart. Out of the exercise of his will has arisen this war, as did other wars in times past. The aggressor might have been met by non-resistance to his evil. The assaulted nation or nations might have turned the other cheek. They might have said to our nation's foe, 'Strike, we shall not raise hand in defence!' But while the ethics of the dominant religion may teach men to turn the other cheek, to resist no evil, to bless those who curse them, to pray for those who

---

[19] e.g. Exod. 15: 3, etc.; cf. the last section of Sermon 21 below by Leo Franklin, from October 1918.

evilly despite them, society has never accepted such a code of ethics, and as long as society endures it never will; for society is rooted in justice, and not in non-resistance.[20] Some few individuals may believe in, and live by, the rules of non-resistant ethics. Some monastics, some hermits, may be willing to obliterate the sense of justice which is essential to the social pact; but a living society must be ruled by the principles of justice, not the other-worldly conception of non-resistance. The boast of America is that it is a government by law. Our law-courts are the foundation on which we have erected the fabric of the State. Law means resistance to evil, opposition to wrong—personal, national, international. The ethics of non-resistance are adapted to a society which believes that the world is momentarily about to come to an end; such principles are not adapted to a society which regards its future as enduring.

In the spirit of justice, therefore, men defend the principles of justice when they are invaded by the foe just as much as they defend their beloved land when that visible domain is attacked. Because men have disregarded the principles of righteousness and have paid no heed to God, we have war, and not because God is not righteous. God can stop wars if He desires, but in doing so He must rob His children of the will with which He has endowed them. If, within certain limits, man is not granted free-will then is he only the highest beast. Without such free-will man's boasted eminence over the beast is naught. Endowed by God with free-will we are at liberty to fulfil our purposes. God wills good, man wills good and evil. Evil results from man's ignorance or unwillingness to obey the divine law. We can do right or wrong as we wish. If we do as God wills we shall do what is right. If we do as God does not will we shall do wrong. Out of the exercise of this power of choice has arisen the war. Please, then, do not continue to hold God responsible for it except as we are His creatures and He did not make us mere automata.

The necessity was, therefore, never more pressing than now that we should seek to interpret the will of God along the path of righteousness. As we begin to investigate we immediately discover that there are two standards of morality. There is an eternal, unchanging standard, and there is a conventional standard

---

[20] Most Christian preachers in the belligerent countries also accepted this principle that the Sermon on the Mount does not apply to international relations. Joseph Dawson, for example, argued that 'Because you can bless Jones or Robinson when he curses you, and offer him the second cheek on his smiting the first, does not make it either feasible or desirable for your country to . . . forgive the injuries inflicted by Germany.' Henry Holland took a similar line: The British people could not say to Belgium, 'We are very sorry, but we have been reading again the Sermon on the Mount, and we cannot therefore keep our word. We must advise you to take it lying down' (cited in Hoover, *God, Germany, and Britain*, 108).

which is ever changing. The unchanging standard is the will of God. The changing standard is the customs and habits of man. The divine standard of righteousness and justice and equity is eternally the same. The human standard of righteousness and justice and equity is constantly changing. God never errs. He alone can do no wrong. But man is not God. Our opinions of right and wrong are progressive. The few have climbed a few steps of the pyramid of progressive ideals, and they see still further steps to be taken. Their outlook is wider and finer than that of those who remain below. Those who have reached the heights have disclosed to those below the beauties and glories of the higher standards. Hence it follows that we have a progressing standard of ethics, a conventional form of ethics, alongside the absolute standard. Nor will we find the triumph of the highest and best among men complete until the mass has been helped forward and upward.[21] Our ways are not God's ways, nor are our thoughts His thoughts.[22]

Hence the two standards, the absolute and the conventional. The best men and women are ever striving to raise the conventional standard toward the absolute standard, and all history is the record of the effort which has been slowly crowned with more and more success. Only, however, as we shall introduce more of God into human life shall we succeed in establishing higher standards. Only when we understand more and more of God's righteousness will our righteousness be more efficient. Only when human standards are so lofty that national deities are forever overthrown and the one, international God established in the hearts of men, only when damnatory creeds are forever obliterated from the text-books of religion and all men alike are recognized as the children of the only God, shall we find the conventional standards of ethics so improved that a crisis like the present will never again return to disturb the normal life of the nations of the earth or overturn the peace and prosperity of the human race.

When that day arrives, and it is coming quickly, individuals and society alike will be bound by the same standards. Today individuals are far better than the mass. See if you can catch the implications of that phrase! Individuals have reached far greater heights than has society as a whole. There are men and women in Pittsburgh, for instance, who could not be gotten to forswear themselves, who would swear to their own hurt and change not.[23] Individuals act

[21] Perhaps intended as a repudiation of the Nietzschean ethic with its concern only for the achievements of the elite.
[22] Echoing Isa. 55: 8.                                    [23] Echoing Ps. 15: 4.

that way. But when they meet in mass formation their acts are motivated by a different method. What one man would scorn to do, whole groups of men do not hesitate to do. Individuals would not dream of killing, of stealing, of perjuring themselves; nations are not always actuated by such a high ethical standard. Until the few individuals who feel themselves bound by the highest standard can obtain the assent and obedience thereto of the mass, we shall still find crises, like unto the one which now confronts us, forced upon us. Society as a whole can move no more rapidly toward the ideal of moral action than the units which comprise society will permit, and because society does not move forward as rapidly as certain individuals are capable of doing, we still have such horrible survivals as war, and slavery, and economic inequity, clinging like barnacles to the ship of state and hampering the progress of the nation, and the nations.

I believe in peace. I regard wars as one of the survivals of the ages when men had not emerged from the brute stage. I pray with all my heart and soul and mind that the day may not be far distant when men will be wise enough to organize for international peace on the basis of justice, as in times past and in the present they have organized for war. I believe that as a man. I believe that as a citizen of this great Republic. I believe that as a Jew, a humble follower of the great prophet Isaiah whose eyes pierced the uncertain darkness of the frontiers of the morrow and drew the outlines of the universal state of world peace. I prefer to follow this first World Peace Advocate rather than any other human teacher. His ideals spell the ultima Thule of human good. For man was created for peace and not for war, for constructive labor and not for destruction and desolation.[24]

Isaiah was wiser than those who ignore him. When the civilized world takes his words and places them in a position of honor on the altar dedicated to a God of righteousness, I a Jew, need do at least no less. Now Isaiah was either ignorant, crazy or sane. Was he ignorant? Well, in all, modesty let me say it, I am a University man, and, thank God, I have had abundant opportunity for quiet reading, and as the world counts knowledge I am supposed to have been able to drink a little of the waters of the Pierian spring.[25] I humbly wish that I possessed a tithe of the knowledge Isaiah possessed. I will place Isaiah at the side of the average professor in psychology, economics, religion, and I am convinced that I shall have no reason to blush for the genius of the Prophet. Isaiah was, then, not

---

[24] Echoing Isa. 45: 18.
[25] Echoing (modestly but somewhat ironically) Pope's famous couplet, 'A little learning is a dangerous thing; | Drink deep or taste not the Pierian spring.'

ignorant. Neither was he crazy. A certain man in Pittsburgh has been making propaganda for the idea that religious persons are neurasthenics. He is one of the worst types of neurasthenics I have ever met, but he is devoid of the religious sentiment.[26] The man who taught 'Justice only justice shalt thou, pursue!' (cf. Deut. 16: 20), the prophet who exclaimed, 'Let justice flow like a river and equity like a mighty stream!' (Amos 5: 24), the genius who said, 'Thus saith the Lord, Do ye justice and execute ye righteousness that My salvation may be nigh to come!' (Isa. 56: 1) were not neurasthenics, nor were they crazy. They were the sane men in an insane world. Their utterances, their principles, their concepts, lie at the very foundations of social life. We are sane in proportion as we follow them; we are insane in proportion as we refuse to gauge our actions by their principles. I rather think that Isaiah was altogether sane when he expressed his ideal of World Peace. He said that it would come 'In the fullness of time' (Isa. 2: 2). He did not say that it was imminent in his day. He knew, as we now know, that only when the mass of men is elevated will his dream come true. Until then it cannot be.

I believe in the world dream of international peace just as much today as ever before. Perhaps the one feature of the war already gained—the founding of the Russian commonwealth—is a step in that direction.[27] Perhaps that fruit of the War already achieved may lead toward a League of Peace among the nations which shall remove the scourge of war from among men. I see no reason to withdraw a single utterance I have made on the subject of International Peace. I withdraw nothing that I have previously said on the subject of international war. I believe that war is hell, as [William Tecumseh] Sherman put it. I believe that war lets loose all the pent-up hates and passions of men. I believe that war is a temporary reversion to what long since might have been an extinct barbarism, and that during war all that we have striven for during the ages that represents the flowering of the spiritual elements in man cannot but be, temporarily at least, lost. I conceive that peace and justice go hand in hand, and that being so I find myself unable to modify in any way what, for years, I have conceived it to be my call and privilege to teach as human duty.

But one thing this dreadful era of world war has taught me: that the world is not yet organized for peace, that the few have not yet succeeded in converting

---

[26] This is the kind of allusion that many in the congregation would undoubtedly have understood, but is extremely difficult to identify today. On the term and the concept of 'neurasthenics' at the time, see Gosling, *Before Freud*; there is no evidence of a connection with religion in this book's material, so my suspicion is that the person in question was not a physician.

[27] Levy will return to this theme, in connection with the Passover holiday, at the end of the discourse.

the many to see through the eyes of Isaiah. I now see that the world is not prepared for peace, that the alignment of free, and independent, and interdepend-
ent, nations is not complete, that much labor is still necessary to prepare the
world to accept Isaiah's ideals, that much effort must still be exerted before the
democracies of the world will be in a position to establish a universal League
which shall find its mission in the maintenance of peace between the nations.
For peace, not war, is the normal state of the peoples of the earth. We are made
for brotherhood, not for international slaughter. We have all of us one Father.[28]
The day of the national deities must be made to pass, and the enthronement in
the hearts of men of the sole God must be complete before we shall forever be
relieved of the dread scourge of war. Until 1914 I thought that time was at hand.
Since 1914 I see that I was mistaken.

On July 22nd, 1914, I was at Mackinac participating in a Peace Conference
held in honor of a century of peace between the English-speaking peoples. The
hundredth anniversary of the Treaty of Ghent[29] was to be fittingly celebrated
throughout this and the mother lands, and we had resolved to erect a bridge
between America and Canada as a physical emblem of the cherished century of
peace.[30] Justice Day, of the Supreme Court of the United States, and Judge
Alton B. Parker, a former candidate for the Presidency of the United States,
participated in the proceedings.[31] Men and women who were usually well-
informed on international affairs joined me in my panegyric on world peace.
We were congratulating ourselves that the millennium was at hand, that
mankind had learned a more excellent way to solve their international troubles
than to add to them by troublesome war. Little did we believe that, within a
week, under circumstances that were absolutely indefensible, the world would
be plunged into a war which has at length embroiled this nation.

[28] Echoing Mal. 2: 10.
[29] The treaty between Great Britain and the United States ending hostilities in the War of 1812
was concluded at Ghent on Christmas Eve 1814, ratified by the Senate on 14 Feb. 1815 and formally proclaimed three days later.
[30] A large committee of American dignitaries, chaired by Andrew Carnegie and appointed in
1910 to plan the events (New York Times, 7 July 1910, p. 3), was called the 'National Committee for
the Celebration of the One-Hundredth Anniversary of Peace Among the English-Speaking
Peoples'. Worldwide celebrations were to begin on Christmas Eve 1914. The idea for a 'Peace
Bridge' across the Niagara River (New York Times, 31 Dec. 1911, Sunday Magazine, p. 9), was put
on ice until after the war, when a new drive to build it was launched in 1919. The bridge was completed and opened to the public in 1927 (<www.niagarafrontier.com/bridges.html#b17>).
[31] William R. Day of Ohio served on the US Supreme Court from 1902 until 1922. Alton B.
Parker, a New York judge, was defeated by Theodore Roosevelt in the presidential election of
1904. Both were active members of the American Peace Centenary Committee.

My reasons for believing up till 1914 that peace was assured were based on my faith in the integrity of civilized nations as maintainers of their treaty relations. On July 22nd, 1914, no living man could have convinced me that a civilized nation would, on the paltry excuse of necessity (*Nothwehr*),[32] have made truck and rubbish of the nation's word of honor, or seek by the meanest, and basest of subterfuges, by alteration of documents, by the suppression of facts, by the exclusion from quoted portions of treaties of the most valid and important phrases, to justify its nefarious acts. No one could have made me believe that the agreements adopted by the Hague Conference in 1907, duly ratified by the governments of Germany and America and others, would have been scrapped on the first occasion possible.

The first article of the fifth section of the conventions adopted at the Hague in 1907 reads, 'The territory of neutral Powers is inviolable.' (See page 122 of Document 1151, issued by the House of Representatives during the second session of the 63rd Congress, and published by the Government Printing Office, Washington, D.C.) That statement was ratified by Germany, whose name stands first among the list of nations signing the convention, for the nations sign in alphabetical order according to their names in French. Germany's name (Allemagne), appears first, and America's follows. I believe, that that signature meant more than a mere drop of ink. I know that I have on several occasions received flattering financial offers to leave this congregation, and only recently I repeated what I had often before said in different words, 'I cannot make a scrap of paper of a contract.' I believed in 1914 that Germany's government was as honorable as an average man. I now see that I was mistaken.

Efforts have been made to cloud the issue. The invasion of Belgium has both been justified and acknowledged as a wrong, by Germany's representatives. Dr. Dernburg, by suppressing an important portion of Article 3 of the Treaty of 1870, seeks to justify Germany. (See 'Obstacles to Peace', by S. S. McClure, page 241.)[33] The Imperial German Chancellor, von Bethman-Hollweg, admits that

[32] This is the term used by the German imperial chancellor, Bethmann-Hollweg, in his speech of 4 Aug. 1914 before the German Reichstag justifying the invasion of Luxembourg and Belgium: 'Gentlemen, we are now in a state of necessity [*Notwehr*], and necessity [*Not*] knows no law'. See *Collected Diplomatic Documents*, 438.

[33] Bibliographical reference in the text. The full text of article 3, as cited by McClure, is: 'This treaty shall be binding on the High Contracting Parties during the continuance of the present war between the German Confederation and France, and for 12 months after the ratification of any treaty of peace concluded between those parties; and on the expiration of that time the independence and neutrality of Belgium will, as far as the High Contracting Parties are respectively concerned, continue to rest as heretofore on the first article of the Quintuple Treaty of the 10th of April, 1839.' Dr Bernhard Dernburg, a German financier, head of the German Red Cross, in

it was wrong. (See 'The German White Book', on page 438 of the 'Collected Diplomatic Documents, Relating to the Outbreak of the European War').[34] We have read of the alleged action of French troops, of the military aviators who, it was said, flew over Belgium into Germany, and of various 'affairs' of which Germany accused France before war was declared.[35] But we have also read the official and apparently trustworthy denials made by the authorized representatives of the French Republic. It would appear that Bismarck's acts at Ems in 1870 were to be duplicated by his peers and successors in 1914.[36] Thus the first of August became to me a veritable *Tisha' B'abh*, a ninth day of Abh (a day of national mourning),[37] for I saw my dream-castles dissipating into space, I saw more than fourteen years of my work disappearing before the coming holocaust that was to be offered to the brutal god of war. When I read the words of the German Chancellor cited above, when I heard men and women justify that act and even undertake to defend it, then I saw that the time of peace was not yet, that 'the fullness of time' had not yet come. The sacred rights and obligations of humanity have been invaded. Hence we have war on earth and

charge of the German Press Bureau and Information Service, and former Colonial Secretary, came to the United States in early September 1914 to counter negative publicity following the German invasion of Belgium. In a *Saturday Evening Post* article cited by McClure, he stated that the treaty between Belgium and the North German Federation expired in May 1872, thereby 'suppressing' the part of the article following the semi-colon. Needless to say, this sentence would have been unintelligible to almost all of the listeners.

[34] Again, the bibliographical reference is in the text; it is unclear to me whether Levy said this or added it in the printed version. Levy refers to the speech before the Reichstag of 4 Aug. 1914, in which Chancellor Bethmann-Hollweg said: 'Our troops have occupied Luxemburg and perhaps have already entered Belgian territory. Gentlemen, that is a breach of international law . . . Thus we were forced to ignore the rightful protests of the Governments of Luxemburg and Belgium. The wrong—I speak openly—the wrong we thereby commit we will try to make good as soon as our military aims have been attained' (*Collected Diplomatic Documents*, 438).

[35] See the letter handed by the German ambassador to the French minister for foreign affairs on 3 Aug. 1914, alleging 'a certain number of flagrantly hostile acts committed on German territory by French military aviators. Several of these have openly violated the neutrality of Belgium by flying over the territory of that country': *Collected Diplomatic Documents*, 240–1. In his speech to the Reichstag the following day, the German chancellor said, 'Aviators dropped bombs, and cavalry patrols and French infantry detachments appeared on the territory of the Empire! Although war had not been declared, France thus broke the peace and actually attacked us' (ibid. 438).

[36] For Bismarck's own account of how he released for publication an edited version of a telegram by order of the Prussian king at Ems concerning negotiations with the French ambassador that 'made this announcement seem decisive, while [the original] version would only have been regarded as a fragment of a negotiation still pending', intending it to 'have the effect of a red rag upon the Gallic bull', thereby leading to the outbreak of war, see McClure, *Obstacles to Peace*, 67–71.

[37] The first day of August 1914, when Germany declared war on Russia, actually coincided with the full-day fast on the ninth day of the Hebrew month of Av, mourning the destructions of the First and Second Temple and other Jewish historical tragedies.

ill-will among men, whereas we might have had peace on earth and good-will among men.

America's hands are clean as she enters to overcome the foe and render war's existence less possible in the years to come. President Wilson's address to Congress on April 2nd—one of the noblest utterances ever made by any statesman—indicates the American point of view of the duty of this nation toward humanity and of the function of the State in general. Compare his words with those of the men whose names have become household words throughout the world in connection with the theories which have made this war possible!

'Not only must the State be obeyed, it must be venerated as a God.' 'Success insured by might is the measure of right.' Who said that? President Wilson? No, indeed! but Hegel, the German philosopher. Treitschke teaches, 'Weak nations have no right to existence; and must be absorbed by powerful nations ... The essence of a State is power. Nothing exists or can exist which is superior to the State.'[38] Von Bernhardi has been teaching, ' "Love God above all things and thy neighbor as thyself." This law can claim no significance for the relations of one country to another ... There never have been and never will be universal rights of men.'[39] Nietzsche says, 'Morality is a symptom of decadence ... War is as necessary to the State as slavery is to society ... Might is the source of right ... There is no right other than theft, usurpation, and violence.' (These citations are quoted from a manuscript just received from an international authority.[40])

In opposition to such doctrines the words of our President appear like the utterance of one of God's chosen Prophets. Certainly not all Germans are willing to acknowledge the authors whose words have been cited above;[41] but all true Americans are prepared to subscribe to these words of our Chief Magistrate:

[38] The first statement by von Treitschke (though in a different translation), and a similar one by Bernhardi, are cited in Bang, *Hurrah and Halleluyah*, 224. For the second ('der Staat ist Macht', from Treitschke's *Politics* (New York: Macmillan, 1916)), see Barker et al., *Why We Are at War*, 179, and Sarolea, *German Problems and Personalities*, 120; also ibid. 127–8 on von Treitschke's doctrine of the weak state (*Kleinstaaterei*).
[39] The quotations are from Bernhardi, *Germany and the Next War*, 29 (love of God and neighbour irrelevant to relations between states), 32 (never universal rights of men); cf. 46 (nothing higher than the state).
[40] Reference is apparently to David Lubin's article that would appear in the *Menorah Journal*, 3 (June 1917), 123–36 (quotations on p. 127). (On the 'unholy trinity' of Bernhardi, Nietzsche, and Treitschke in the British consciousness, see Hoover, *God, Germany, and Britain*, 76–7; also 21–4, 37–40, and notes on 47.)
[41] Actually, the sermons of the German clergy and many other German intellectuals revealed an almost antithetical approach to the war, insisting not on the 'might makes right' doctrine but that Germany's position revealed a far higher moral sensitivity than that of the Allies (see Hoover, *God, Germany and Britain*, 67–84).

We are now about to accept the gage of battle with this natural foe to liberty, and shall, if necessary, spend the whole force of the nation to check and nullify its pretensions and its power. We are glad, now that we see the facts with no veil of false pretense about them, to fight thus for the ultimate peace of the world and for the liberation of its peoples, the German people included; for the rights of nations great and small and the privilege of men everywhere to choose their way of life and obedience. The world must be made safe for democracy. Its peace must be planted upon the trusted foundations of political liberty.

We have no selfish ends to serve. We desire no conquest, no dominion. We seek no indemnities for ourselves, no material compensation for the sacrifices we shall freely make. We are but one of the champions of the rights of mankind. We shall be satisfied when those rights have been as secure as the faith and the freedom of the nations can make them.[42]

This is a noble utterance, one to make us proud that we are Americans. We desire no spot of German soil, no jot or tittle of Germany's possessions. We desire that she permit the world, without *Schrecklichkeit*, horribleness, to proceed along the paths of democracy, of liberty, and moral right. Less than this we have no right to leave as the inheritance of our children. If for this our country needs us, let every loyal American do his duty! If we are too old to serve we must encourage our children to rise in the place of their fathers. We must make every sacrifice for the nation which is our own country, which we rule through the expression of the will of a free people. The world must enjoy peace as its normal and natural state, and the time will soon come—alas, it is not yet here, but it is coming fast—when the people themselves by a plebiscite will determine whether war shall be conducted or not. No nation by itself can act thus without laying itself open as a prey to the foe which refuses such action. Hence the need of internationalism now as never before. The world is to be made safe for democracy, and it will be only by the building of an international code that this will be possible. Perhaps this war was necessary to stir the sluggish minds and hearts of men to understand this.

This is a time of war because we are not organized for peace. A time of peace will come when we learn the important lesson that, as we have been told in times of peace to prepare for war, so in times of war we should organize for peace, an enduring peace, a durable peace, an international peace. The scourge will pass away. The lurid flames of war will be quenched. The red rivers of gore will evaporate. The curtain of fire will be extinguished. The roar of shot

[42] The quotation was introduced a few moments earlier, before the quotations from the German thinkers, as taken from Woodrow Wilson's address to Congress on 2 April.

and shell will be silenced. Around the council chamber will gather those who will decide what they think will be best for us. Against that time we must prepare. The nation's representatives must act in behalf of the people, but the people must first let them know what they expect; and who now does not expect that, to the limit of human possibilities, these international representatives must act as the trustees of humanity to 'make the world safe for democracy and its peace secured on the foundations of political liberty'?[43]

The sacrifices which war will entail are such as we are all called to make sooner or later. All must die. All must suffer. All must sacrifice. All must endure pain at some time or other. These phases of the horrors of war affright only the weak. But the aftermath will, perhaps, induce us the more readily to lend our influence to the formation of an international body whose functions will render peace more certain and war less possible. Voices of men have been raised for such an end, but the world went its careless way and refused to heed. Like voices in the wilderness were the utterances of the few who toiled for peace, and because we were not prepared to maintain peace we are now at war. Once at war the nation has a right to the services of the citizen, and I hope that the Congress will press into the service of the nation those who are most able to render the most efficient service in the present crisis. A few years back it would have been impossible for me to speak as I do at this moment. But men and women would not organize for peace; now they must organize and fight in war—to the end that peace may again spread its wings of benediction over the earth.

I favor the movement now that shall take from every home those who can serve the nation.[44] A volunteer force will take all but the slackers, and in a democracy there should be no reason or room for slackers. I know that it will not be popular to draft the nation to service, but the nation might have employed its years for organization for peace and did not; now the nation can realize what it was that we sought and failed to achieve in the years that are past. Every available person, within certain ages and under certain conditions of domestic needs, should serve the cause which America represents at this time. Nor should the profits of military industry remain the prize for which so many wars have hitherto been conducted in the various lands. The nation makes the sacrifice, the nation should benefit by the profits if there are any. Nothing will so assure the American people that this war is not a capitalistic invention, as the taxation which will be placed on the industries which will profit most by the war.

[43] Repeating perhaps the most famous line in Wilson's 2 April speech to Congress, just cited.

[44] A clear statement on conscription, currently under debate in Congress. See the annotation to Sermon 19 below by S. S. Wise.

The terrible conflict, which has engaged the world in battle for the past two years and more, means more for humanity than the exchange of shot and shell, of high explosive and shrapnel. On the battle-fields of Europe and Asia men are deciding problems which might have been solved in courts of law, had we been organized for peace as we are organized for war. Temporarily the Hague Tribunal is closed and the doves of peace have flown away. But the smoke and the din of the fray will cease, and reason will prevail where hate now directs.

## [PERORATION]

The problem to be solved is one to which we are specially pledged as Americans of Jewish faith. About four thousand years ago, on this Feast of the Passover,[45] our master Moses bade the tyrant, 'Send away the people that they may serve God!'[46] On the banks of the Nile Israel was liberated in the name of the Author of Liberty. On the banks of the Neva within the past week the tyrant has again been overthrown, and Russia is now free.[47] *Sic semper tyrannis*, 'Thus will it ever be with tyranny,' and the annual return of our Festival of Liberty assures us of the success that must come to the American undertaking, assumed as it is for the greater liberty of the peoples and for the wider spread of democracy on the sure foundation of political freedom.

It is hardly to be expected that, over night, the people of Russia will obtain the full measure of liberty which has come to us in America, but the despot is gone, the forces of freedom are triumphant, Siberia has been opened, political prisoners are released, civil and religious restrictions are removed. For all of these blessings may the great name of the God of Liberty, in whose name Israel was in ancient days emancipated from Egyptian bondage, be extolled and glorified! As it was then, so is it now, and it shall ever be. This festival sacredly observed by Israel throughout the world signifies to us not the recurrence of an ancient national Palestinian feast. Were it only that I should advocate its abolition. It is because Passover means to us the Feast of Liberty that it holds a

[45] The Sunday on which the address was delivered was the second day of Passover.
[46] Cf. Exod. 8: 1 and parallels.
[47] The connection between Passover and the overthrow of the Russian tsar was a theme in many (probably most) Jewish sermons delivered on this weekend. On the same day as Levy delivered this sermon, Leo Franklin referred to 'that mighty uprising of the populace in Russia against the wrongs of centuries' which was a source of 'the joy that overwhelms our spirits' ('The Free Man's Burden', 1); Stephen S. Wise noted that 'We are celebrating a gladsome Passover festival, a festival of unwonted, unimagined deliverance, for we have lived to see the day of Russian freedom and it is good . . . Half the Jews of earth that have long walked in the darkness of Eastern Europe have seen a great light' ('The World-War for Humanity', 101–2).

cherished place in the festivals of this congregation. On that foundation of a far-off event has been built the enduring fabric of a universal ideal.

The Rabbis taught that the Passover of Egypt prefigured the *Pesah L'athid*, 'The Passover that is to Be', that the downfall of the one Pharaoh was a forecast of the final overthrow of every Pharaoh, that the emancipation of a handful of slaves on the banks of the Nile was a sign and token of the ultimate emancipation of the human race, that the beginnings of liberty made in Egypt would find their fulfilment in the liberation of mankind in the time when every man shall sit under his own vine and under his own fig-tree, 'and there shall be none to make him afraid' (Mic. 4: 4). That age will yet dawn; the day of emancipation will come; small nations and large nations alike will enjoy the blessings of liberty, democracy, and fraternity; and peace will crown the earth with joy, as a result of a struggle which now engages the representatives of the world's democracies.

When peace shall again be restored and the nations of the earth are once again moving along the highways of peace, we shall readily see that Isaiah was not so crazy as some believe. The ideal of world peace lures us on. Like a sign post with index finger extended we stand indicating the path mankind must pursue: 'They shall no more lift up sword nation against nation, neither shall they learn war any more' (Isa. 2: 4). We shall pursue the business in hand until we have brought the American undertaking to a successful issue; and then we shall look forward to better days and brighter hours for mankind as a result of America's entrance into a contest she long sought to avoid, but in which she now engages, prepared to offer all for mankind's sake and to ask naught for herself except that the world be made safe for democracy.[48] To that end we pledge our lives, our hopes, our nearest, our dearest. All we have and all we are will be offered to America—the knight-errant on the field of chivalry, the champion of universal democracy. The time for peace will come; let us prepare against its coming! The time for war is here; let us serve our nation in the spirit of the great leader whose words have moved us to action!

[48] Again echoing Wilson's 'war message'.

## CHAPTER NINETEEN

## STEPHEN S. WISE

# CAN WE WIN THE WAR WITHOUT LOSING AMERICA?

### 20 MAY 1917

#### THE FREE SYNAGOGUE CONGREGATION
#### AT CARNEGIE HALL, NEW YORK

ORN in Budapest in 1874, Stephen Samuel Wise came with his family to the United States as a small child. His father, Rabbi Aaron Wise, served at Rodeph Sholom Congregation in New York; the son studied Jewish texts with his father and other New York rabbis. After attending City College of New York and Columbia, from which he graduated before his nineteenth birthday, he travelled to Europe to study with the celebrated Viennese scholar and preacher Rabbi Adolf Jellinek, who granted him an individual ordination. Returning to New York in the spring of 1893, he was chosen to be the assistant rabbi at New York's Congregation B'nai Jeshurun under Henry F. Jacobs. Soon after this, he succeeded to the position of senior rabbi following Jacobs's sudden death.

Very little has been written about Wise's tenure at B'nai Jeshurun, perhaps because of the absence of documentary material and Wise's own reticence about these years.[1] The best-known aspect of his career during this period was his embrace of Zionism, including the part he played in establishing the

---

[1] See Urofsky, *A Voice that Spoke for Justice*, 10–12; Shapiro, *A Reform Rabbi in the Progressive Era*, 24–6. Wise himself said hardly anything about these early years of his rabbinate in his memoir, *Challenging Years*, except for a brief report of a sermon on behalf of striking street-car workers in Brooklyn given in 1895 (p. 56). In his history of the B'nai Jeshurun Congregation, Israel Goldstein says nothing about the content of Wise's preaching during his seven-year rabbinate there, characterizing it as 'a period of intensive organization, in the direction of education and philanthropy': *A Century of Judaism*, 210–16.

Federation of American Zionists and his participation in the Second Zionist Congress in 1898.[2] At the same time he also pursued graduate work at Columbia, being awarded a doctorate after writing a dissertation on a medieval Jewish ethical text originally composed in Arabic.

For our purposes, the key issue would have been his position regarding the Spanish–American War. As we have seen above, on the weekend following the formal declaration of war with Spain Jewish preachers throughout New York, indeed throughout the nation, were mustering their rhetorical talents in claiming an exalted justification for the American war effort. Rudolph Grossman at Rodeph Sholom, speaking on 'Patriotism and the Jew', said— according to the *New York Times* report—that 'if ever a war was waged for a holy cause it was this one'. The previous week, Kaufmann Kohler, speaking on 'God's Ultimatum to Spain', pronounced the solemn question in this momentous hour to be 'whether we are indeed worthy to be soldiers in God's army of battlers for men's liberty and sovereignty'. On sabbath morning, 30 April 1898, Wise—24 years old—delivered a sermon at the B'nai Jeshurun Synagogue on Madison Avenue entitled 'The Message of Religion in Times of War'. The text of this sermon has apparently not been preserved. Had it been, we would have had examples of Wise's preaching in three different wars: the Spanish–American War and the two world wars of the twentieth century. It would have been enormously instructive to see whether in 1898, in his first pulpit response to war, he charted his own course.[3]

In 1900 Wise accepted an appointment to be rabbi of Temple Beth Israel of Portland, Oregon, where he remained until 1906. There he established a reputation as a powerful speaker on Zionist issues and on causes relating to domestic progressive reform and social justice. Profoundly influenced by Adolf Jellinek in both the scope and the style of his preaching, Wise achieved a reputation as one of the great orators of his time. His friend and colleague, the New York Unitarian minister John Haynes Holmes, said of Wise that he had 'heard great orators—Robert G. Ingersoll, William Jennings Bryan, Lloyd George, Winston Churchill—but none of them touched Wise for sheer magnificence and plenitude of utterance'.[4] This talent brought him back to New York, and a semi-official offer of the pulpit at Temple Emanu-El, which—as is well known—Wise refused because of the leadership's insistence that 'the pulpit of Emanu-El has always been and is subject to and under the control of the board of trustees'. His public response, and his subsequent founding of the

[2] On his early Zionist activities, see Shapiro, *A Reform Rabbi in the Progressive Era*, 30–4, 41–9.
[3] Wise's sermon topic is given in the *American Hebrew*, 29 Apr. 1898, p. 772. Kohler's sermon was printed in the same issue (pp. 770–1); Grossman's sermon was reported in the *New York Times*, 30 Apr. 1898, p. 3. I have not seen any treatment of Wise's position on the Spanish–American War.
[4] Cited in Shapiro, *A Reform Rabbi in the Progressive Era*, 24.

Free Synagogue in New York, is one of the great chapters in the story of the struggle for a pulpit free from the control of congregational leaders, in which the rabbi could address not only 'religious' questions but a wide array of social, economic, even political issues in accordance with the mandates of his conscience.[5]

By the beginning of the First World War, Wise had already established himself as a leading spokesman both for Jewish causes and for progressive social attitudes. His Sunday morning services, established in 1907 and held at Carnegie Hall from autumn 1910, frequently attracted between 1,500 and 2,000 participants, many of them drawn primarily by the opportunity of hearing Wise preach. Wise also joined with two Christian colleagues in holding 'union services', featuring distinguished speakers on religion and social problems, and drawing mass audiences on Sunday evenings.[6]

When war broke out in Europe in the summer of 1914, Wise frequently addressed pertinent issues from his influential pulpit. The most controversial was the issue of 'preparedness': whether America should prepare itself for the possibility of war by building up its own military forces and armaments. While not an absolute pacifist like his friend John Haynes Holmes,[7] Wise was strongly opposed to militarism, identified with pacifist-oriented organizations, and—like his rabbinic colleagues Joseph Krauskopf and J. Leonard Levy—articulated a strong stand against the policy of preparedness and the underlying rationale that such preparedness increases the chances of being able to live in peace. In December 1914 his position was consistent with that articulated by President Wilson in his message to Congress, and Wise, insisting that it would be 'the folly of follies for our nation to plunge into a militaristic program at this time of all times', urged standing firm against the 'war hysteria that is sweeping over the land', clamouring for military build-up.[8] A year later, Wilson had endorsed the preparedness policy, and Wise went into a loyal opposition.[9] Yet by early 1917, Wise recognized that America might well need to enter the war. In a dramatic meeting of the American Union Against Militarism, in which he had

---

[5] On the conflict with Louis Marshall and the trustees of Temple Emanu-El, see Voss, *Rabbi and Minister*, 53–60; Urofsky, *A Voice that Spoke for Justice*, 50–6; Shapiro, *A Reform Rabbi in the Progressive Era*, 121–36.

[6] See Voss, *Rabbi and Minister*, 105–11; Urofsky, *A Voice that Spoke for Justice*, 65–7.

[7] Voss, *Rabbi and Minister*, 141; Wilcock, *Pacifism and the Jews*, 23.

[8] S. S. Wise, 'Must We Have a Larger Army and Navy?', 3–4; though no date is given in the publication, the date of 13 Dec. 1914 is provided by *Jewish Advocate*, 48/19 (19 Dec. 1914), p. 587.

[9] This can be seen in his address 'Peace-Preparedness versus War-Preparedness', 176–80. He went on a national speaking tour articulating the case against 'preparedness'; see the review of Wise's public and private statements by Shapiro, *A Reform Rabbi in the Progressive Era*, 332–9, and cf. S. S. Wise, *Challenging Years*, 175–6; R. H. Abrams, *Preachers Present Arms*, 37–8.

played a major role, he explained his rethinking of the pacifist position to some of his closest political allies.[10]

The sermon below was not the first delivered by Wise following the formal declaration of war. That address, entitled 'The World-War for Humanity', was given at Carnegie Hall on 8 April. On that occasion—coinciding (as we have seen in Sermon 18) with the second day of Passover—Wise described a mixture of emotions: sorrow, 'deep, abysmal, heart-breaking', in the consciousness that 'the last great war-free realm of earth is to be added to the lands scarred and seared by pitiless war', blended with the joy of a festival whose message has been dramatically fulfilled in the liberation not only of the Jews of Russia but also of the more than one hundred million non-Jewish Russians who have 'bloodlessly wrested their liberties from the hands of tyranny'. Reviewing some of his positions of the past—his sympathies with the Allies, expressed in his Rosh Hashanah sermon of September 1914, his uncompromising conviction of the evil of militarism, his defence of the courageous, principled pacifism of his Unitarian colleague and friend John Haynes Holmes, his repudiation of hatred towards the German people—he adumbrates the message of his later text in the hope that the war can be waged democratically, without turning America into another Prussia, and with the inevitable sacrifices distributed equally. This includes 'the immediate enfranchisement of the women of the nation. We have no right to purport to battle for democracy as long as millions of American citizens are arbitrarily and reasonlessly disfranchised.'[11] Wise makes it clear that he has been prepared to rethink his anti-war convictions, but not to compromise on the fundamental principles of American democracy and social justice.

This theme is expanded with specific current examples in the address reproduced here, delivered a month and a half later against the background of various legislative battles pertaining to the domestic implications of the war effort. Like most of his Sunday addresses, there is no biblical text: that role is played by the sermon's title, which is analysed at the beginning of the sermon. The central thesis is made clear in an introductory section: the reason we have gone to war is to protect the rights of self-determination for each nation in accordance with its own capacity for self-realization, to 'shield the souls of nations from destruction by a brutalizing sovereignty'. The challenge—phrased in an allusion to a familiar passage from the New Testament—is to achieve this

[10] Voss, *Rabbi and Minister*, 142–3; Urofsky, *A Voice that Spoke for Justice*, 138–9; Shapiro, *A Reform Rabbi in the Progressive Era*, 341; Wilcock, *Pacifism and the Jews*, 23–4; R. H. Abrams, *Preachers Present Arms*, 54–5. Wise discussed 'the secret of the transformation of us who have been life-long anti-militarists into unequivocal supporters of the government and its war-policies' and his current view of pacifist ideologies, especially as proclaimed by the 'People's Council', in his 'What Are We Fighting For?', esp. 154–63 (undated, but probably late May or early June 1917).

[11] *Free Synagogue Pulpit*, iv (1916–17) (New York: Bloch Publishing, 1917), 101–20. See the review of this sermon by Shapiro, *A Reform Rabbi in the Progressive Era*, 342–4.

goal without, in the process, losing 'our own soul', the essence of American democracy. Spiritual destruction—'Louvains and Rheims of the spirit'—is as great a danger for America as physical destruction.[12]

This challenge is given concrete form by reference to a number of current issues about which Wise articulates his own position. He was opposed to conscription, but now that it has been passed into law, he wants to be sure that it will end with the end of the war. He urges government support for those who lose their jobs in economic downturns; he vehemently opposes compromise on the industrial safety standards and the rules against child labour. He strongly defends the constitutional freedoms of expression and assembly against the potential incursions of the Censorship Bill. And he calls for a principled repudiation of discrimination against black Americans: 'If, as has been said before in this pulpit, we are to go into the war with clean hands, our hands must be undefiled by wrong done at home to the unoffending.' The address ends with a peroration playing with the 'Wake Up America!' slogan used to generate public support for the war effort, but here applied to the dual challenge of winning the war and keeping holy America's soul.

To be sure, this address is not one of the great exemplars of Jewish homiletical art. It is totally devoid of any distinctively Jewish source material, and consequently the application of ancient texts to current problems, which we have seen to be characteristic of the Civil War sermons, is absent. Indeed, its inclusion in an anthology of 'Jewish sermons' stretches the boundaries of the genre beyond what some might recognize. It is difficult to detect rhetorical purple passages of the kind we found in Krauskopf's Spanish–American War discourse (Sermon 13), or even the stirring moments of inspirational uplift for which Wise was noted. Its purpose was neither to lament the decision to go to war nor to stimulate further the patriotic fervour of the moment. Rather, it was to construct a warning about the potentially negative consequences of the commitment to war for the values America claimed to be defending.[13]

---

[12] This theme was articulated by Christian preachers at the time of the Spanish–American War; an example is Charles H. Eaton of New York's Church of the Divine Paternity on 1 May 1898, in a passage that characterizes much of Wise's message here: 'Temporary emergencies of war should not decide National policies as to money and banking. Stay-at-home patriots should also see that civic problems are not neglected. The war will be an excuse to postpone new municipal improvements. There are the poor and the oppressed in our midst . . . While brave patriots fight for liberty and honor at the front, let the equally brave patriots fight the evils at home' (*New York Times*, 2 May 1898, p. 12).

[13] For a strong statement, from the period before America's entry, of the position that war inevitably dulls the social consciousness, see Leon Harrison of St Louis: 'In the face of these unspeakable miseries, why should we concern ourselves about the atrocities of child-labor or the industrial exploitation of women, though the betterment of these conditions has taxed the energies of our finest and our noblest souls for generations? Why should we fight against the inhumanity of excessive hours for labor? Why should we be stirred to deepest indignation by the wretchedness of the slum-dwellers, of those who live in cellars and dark attics? The danger to be

# SERMON

## [INTRODUCTION]

'CAN WE WIN the war without losing America?' may sound like a strange question, but it expresses a deep and anxious self-searching of our souls.[14] It assumes the truth that to win the war and to keep the soul of America are parallel, yea, identical, aims.

We have gone into the war not because of the *Lusitania* nor yet because of the *Sussex*,[15] nor in truth because of any single ferocity of under-sea warfare, but because these and similar things represent a type of national mind or rather of governmental theory which will either subdue and conquer the world or be overcome by it. To the task of repressing and of combating this world-menace that nations may again dwell amid security and all peoples emerge from under the shadow of the destroying sword—chiefly destructive of the soul of the nation that wields it—we have resolved to dedicate our lives, our fortunes and our sacred honor [Declaration of Independence].

In a sense, it is true that we fare forth into the world of war on behalf of the American ideal. But we war not in order to impose the American ideal—for that were after the *more Germanico*[16]—but to save the peoples of earth from the abhorrent necessity of yielding to the attempt of a masterful sovereignty to impose its will and even its way upon their national existence. Not that the question is as between the Prussianization or the Americanization of the world—the super-imposition of the one were as evil as the other—for we hold that no people, great or small, shall be forced to abate one jot or tittle of its national and spiritual sovereignty by the will or the power of any other sovereignty.[17] In a word, we have

feared is that men should say to themselves, why should a little more or less suffering in the world matter, seeing that we are multiplying it a thousand fold by our own deliberate act and deed' ('The Glory of War—and the Hideous Reality', in *The Religion of a Modern Liberal*, 45–6).

[14] Wise broached a similar question in his sermon of 8 April: 'Must we, as has been urged, lose the best of our own possessions, democracy and individual liberty?' And: 'The question is not whether we shall successfully wage war upon the German government, but whether we shall be equal to the infinitely more difficult task of gaining the victory without losing our own souls' (*Free Synagogue Pulpit*, iv (1916–17), 108, 119).

[15] Both ships were sunk by German U-boats, the *Lusitania* on 7 May 1915, the *Sussex* on 24 Mar. 1916.     [16] 'The Germanic manner or custom.'

[17] Note the striking assertion that the 'Americanization' of the world would be as evil as its 'Prussianization', because the ideal is political and cultural self-determination for each national entity.

gone—not merely been driven—into the war in order to re-affirm and to re-establish, it may be for all time, the truth that every people shall be free to be itself, that its will to live as it will (under obvious limitations) is incontestible, that the soul of every nation, which implies its will and capacity for self-realization, must be inviolate and unassailable if a just international order is in truth to be achieved.

May we not put the matter in the simplest terms? We fare forth to shield the souls of nations from destruction by a brutalizing sovereignty. Shall we in the process submit not to the destruction of our sovereignty from without but through self-surrender to the impairment and undermining of our spiritual sovereignty from within? Happily for the fortunes of the American Republic, the question is not one of gaining the whole world or of losing our own soul,[18] for we have no world nor any part thereof that we will to conquer—but of helping the world to regain the mastery over itself and yet in the process of losing not our own soul.

Can we win the war without losing America? The answer is: nothing that is hurtful to America can be helpful to the cause of victory. The term 'hurtful to America' suggests itself because of the oft-quoted word of a member of the English Parliament, 'A large portion of our elementary school system is in ruins. I will not say as desolate as the ruins of Louvain, but there is to some extent a likeness.'[19] There are Louvains and Rheims of the spirit possible in our own land.[20] The destruction of the Capitol at Washington, perhaps our chiefest architectural glory, would be less hurtful by far than the breaking down of such laws as safeguard women and men in industry and little children from industry.[21]

Be it made very clear that the destruction of the Capitol by shot and shell of invading foe were not as grave as the conscious, willing surrender of the capital, keystone principles of our democracy.[22] Once these have been suffered to sur-

[18] Echoing Mark 8: 36, Matt. 16: 26.

[19] The reference is to Sir James Yoxall. The 'ruins of Louvain', following the German burning of much of that city with its medieval treasures, captured in descriptions (e.g. 'Germans Burn and Sack Louvain', 'Magnificent Gothic Buildings Ruined', New York Times, 29 Aug. 1914, p. 3) and photographic images widely published in the western media, became an icon for German atrocities in Belgium at the beginning of the war. See Hoover, God, Germany, and Britain, 22.

[20] Taking the iconic images of the ruins of Louvain and great Rheims cathedral (bombarded by the Germans on 19–20 Sept. 1914), and transforming them into metaphors for possible spiritual destruction in the United States, the preacher then proceeds to give this idea concrete form in an American context by his reference to the Capitol in Washington.

[21] Wise will return to this theme of the importance of upholding laws that protect workers' safety and prohibit child labour later in the address.

[22] A play on words clearer in print than in sound; the distinction between the two words must have been emphasized in the delivery.

render, the Capitol at Washington would remain nothing more than a sculptured memorial.

### [BODY OF THE SERMON]

Let us frankly deal this morning with some of the tendencies and influences which we hold to be seriously menacing to American life, with those things that we cannot afford to do even in order to win the war. To do them is to lose the war; to have done them will have been to have lost the war, whatever be the outcome of the world's battle with the German Empire, whatever be the issue of the struggle of our gallant Allies on the Western and Eastern fronts with the arms of German militarism. Had this address been made a fortnight ago as had been planned, this pulpit would have lifted up its voice against what it conceived and continues to believe to be the unwisdom of conscription by any name until after a fair and ample trial had been given to the cause of voluntaryism.[23] Had the President with his matchless power of appealing to the soul of the youth of America summoned our sons to volunteer for war service at home and abroad, I believe there would have been such an overwhelming response as would have been the final proof that the vast majority of the American people are unreservedly at one in the support of the President in his determination to check the forces of autocracy wheresoever they menacingly lift up their heads.[24]

Though as loyal American citizens we bow to the will of the Congress of the United States insomuch as for a time in any event it is representative of the will of the American people, let us not be unmindful of the incalculably important distinction between emergency war-policies and permanent peace-principles. Let those who rejoice over the acceptance of the principle of war-conscription by the Republic understand that conscription is for the period of the war and

[23]  Cf. the sermon of 8 Apr. (*Free Synagogue Pulpit*, iv (1916–17), 112–13), and J. Leonard Levy's remarks on 8 Apr. in Sermon 18 above (p. 343). This sentence, in the context of the passage that follows, allows us to date the present sermon, which is undated in its published form. The 'selective conscription' bill was passed by the Senate (after having been passed by the House) on Thursday, 17 May 1917, and enacted as law by President Wilson on the following day. This suggests a date for the address of Sunday, 20 May. Two weeks previously, on 6 May, the majority in both Houses of Congress had already swung to support of the draft system, rejecting the alternative of trying out a volunteer recruitment system, which had been supported by a majority in the House Military Committee in early April (*New York Times*, 10 Apr. 1917, p. 1). For an overview, see Kennedy, *Over Here*, 144–50. It is unclear why the Sunday address on this topic, originally scheduled for 6 May, was postponed for two weeks.

[24]  Cf. the statement of Knute Nelson, a Republican senator from Minnesota (who served in the Wisconsin Volunteer Infantry during the Civil War): 'I venture to say that if the President calls for a volunteer army of 500,000 men, and says it is going to Europe [to] fight, there would be no trouble at all' (*New York Times*, 10 Apr. 1917, p. 2).

that those of us who are most in earnest in believing that our war is a war for democracy are of the conviction that after the war, and as a result of a just and democratically ordered peace, there will be no need for conscription either at home or abroad, that the day of vast standing armies shall have passed forever.[25] But whether or not militarism is to cease, whether or not the shadow of militarism is to continue to enshroud the world, there are some of us who mean earnestly to lift up our voices and put forth every atom of such strength as may be given us to the end that involuntary or conscript military service shall not become a part of the American program and of the American ideal.

Let us dwell particularly this day not so much upon the things that have been done that some day are to be undone, with temporary or emergency war measures that are certain to be repealed when once the crisis of the war has been safely passed, but with obvious tendencies in American life today which must not be suffered to engraft themselves deeply upon our national polity. Sedulously must we distinguish between those acts which are tolerable, perhaps even inevitable, as war measures, and those which are not even debatable in times of peace. Certain tendencies do in time of war gain a hearing and demand the enactment of measures which cannot be suffered even for a moment. There are elementary and inviolable sanctities of a democratic order, which to waive for a moment is to destroy them forever, such sanctities as politically the right of public assembly, never to be relinquished or abated even for one moment,[26] and industrially the right of little children to remain unimpressed and unconscripted by industry.

[25] The issue of a termination date for the conscription bill was fiercely debated even on the day when the Senate passed it, and a clause limiting conscription to the present war was dropped in conference. William Stone, a Democrat senator from Missouri, said in debate, 'I oppose the elimination of the clause that provided for conscription ending with the end of this war. What right have we to force conscription on the country for an indefinite time?' (*New York Times*, 18 May 1917, p. 1). The following day, the Senate attached an amendment to the Army and Navy Deficiency Bill limiting the period of conscription to four months after the end of the war (*New York Times*, 19 May 1917, p. 2); thus it was still an open issue when the sermon was delivered.

[26] On the evening of 18 May, the day the conscription bill was enacted into law, a mass meeting in Harlem of socialists and anarchists, addressed by Emma Goldman and others, protested against the draft. The *New York Times* reported the following day that two police stenographers were in the balcony taking down 'every word that was said', to be reviewed by the authorities for possible future action (*New York Times*, 19 May 1917, p. 11). A little more than a week after the sermon, the mayor of Elizabeth, New Jersey, refused to permit the 'Young People's Socialist League' to hold an open-air meeting of protest against the draft (*New York Times*, 31 May 1917, p. 3). (The text of Goldman's speech—in which she said that 'the war which is now declared by America in the last six weeks is not a war of democracy . . . It is a war for the purpose of trampling under foot every vestige of liberty that you people have worked for, for the last forty or thirty or twenty-five years and, therefore, we refuse to support such a war'—is accessible at <sunsite.berkeley.edu/ Goldman/Writings/Speeches/170518.html>).

However, it is not enough to urge that the temporary or provisional disarrangements shall not be made permanent. Certain things are happening today which would be fraught with deepest menace to the nation if these were to become embodied in the permanent program of our national life. On the other hand, the government and the people of the United States are taking forward steps which can nevermore be retraced. We are thinking and acting solely in the terms of national well-being, and in so doing we are committing ourselves beyond the hope of repeal to new ways of national living, to new methods of serving the commonwealth.

To name but one item in a program of farthest-reaching consequence, the government is prepared not only to conscript arms-bearing warriors but tool-wielding toilers. If it should prove to be necessary, the government will hold itself free to draft mechanics in one State and artisans in another, and transport them to the States on the Coasts or of the lake regions where they may be required to build the ships of which we and our Allies are increasingly in need. So be it, and so ought it to be![27] If, however, our government may employ and even over-employ men now, who will say that the government will ever again suffer such a crisis of unemployment as obtained two years ago? Then men and women and children, through no fault of their own and altogether because of the industrial dislocations incident to the outbreak of the war, suffered, even starved. Our government lifted not a finger in their behalf, and a winter of misery was endured by millions with little or no relief save such as came through the accident of re-employment in war's and related industries.[28] If men should and must toil at the government's command now, then should and must the government employ the involuntary unemployed in justice to the workers who are now being conscripted. If the government may conscript the worker in time of war, the worker may conscript the government in time of peace—as a measure urgent and extraordinary of public safety, of national self-protection and self-conservation when widespread unemployment, ever the result of the want of prevision and statesmanship in industry, and consequent poverty wreak irreparable hurt upon the life and morale of the workers and their families.

[27] Note the support in principle by Wise, a strong ally of labour, for the conscription of industrial workers as part of the war effort.

[28] For a contemporary account of the unemployment and hunger suffered during the winter of 1914/15, see the pioneering social worker Mary E. Richmond, 'To the Volunteers of 1915', 369–71 (part of this passage was cited by Gerson B. Levi in a sermon of 7 Dec. 1930 entitled 'A Challenge to Society in Days of Depression'). On the absence of unemployment insurance at this time, and efforts to redress the problem, see Nelson, *Unemployment Insurance*.

If we are to win the war without losing America, we dare not commit the grievous blunder of sacrificing in the fancied interest of war those industrial standards which have been built up in order to safeguard democracy. In urging as does this pulpit in common with many men and women who are deeply concerned that 'the conservation of our human resources is a prime essential of national effectiveness', it is well to recall the report of a woman physician, who, after an intensive study of the labor problems in munition factories in ten States, declared 'Everything that was needed for rapid production was pushed, and everything that was needed for the protection of the workers was postponed.' The wisest and the sanest among us are urging in the terms of the American Association of Labor Legislation that this is the time

when we can best conserve our industrial army by maintaining the essential minimum requirements for the protection of the workers, when we should avoid the recognized mistakes made by European belligerents in breaking down hard-won standards in the early stress of the war, when our own standards in the interest of national effectiveness should be strengthened with regard to sanitation, safety, hours of labor, wages, child labor, women's work, social insurance, the labor market and administration of labor laws.

Above all, let us not sacrifice the children of the nation in order to win the war. Let us not war upon our children in order to destroy Prussian militarism and imperialism. Every other method and measure should be tried before suspending the restrictions which are imposed upon the employment of the children. Let us be warned by what have rightly been called the disastrous results in foreign countries among which we are told have been the increase of juvenile delinquency, the employment of greatly increased numbers of children under the most adverse conditions, and the necessity of enacting special measures to protect the health of mothers and babes. Child labor must remain the last and not become the first recourse of America. Our children must not be permitted to pay the ruinous cost of war. Children must not be clothed in the backbreaking armor of war. The danger of lightly surrendering standards is shown forth by the circumstance that, while the Council of National Defense urged upon the Legislatures of the States the duty of rigorously maintaining standards as to the health and welfare of workers and that no departure from existing standards should be taken without the request of the Council of National Defense that such departure is essential for the effective pursuit of the national defense,[29] the

[29] The policy of the Council of National Defense, announced in April, followed commitments by both the American Federation of Labor and the National Association of Manufacturers to maintain existing standards, including existing safeguards for the health and welfare of workers.

Legislatures in some States in advance of every suggestion or request are preparing indiscriminately to waive and to surrender all safeguards. These do not seem to understand what Owen R. Lovejoy of the National Child Labor Committee has clearly pointed out, that the policy of recruiting agricultural and factory workers from the school children, eleven to thirteen years old, adopted in Great Britain at the beginning of the war, already stands revealed as shortsighted, and standards too recklessly set aside are now being restored. Let us not outrun every need of national defense by offending against the workers—least of all the women and children of the nation.[30]

Who are they that favor letting down the bars or lowering the standards of safety and protection for the workers? For one thing, they who under war's stern compulsion are prepared to make every concession and surrender to imaginary need; next the never-thinking whom war least of all provokes to serious thought touching industrial safeguards; and above all those whose peace program uniformly makes for the minimizing of industrial safeguards, who are ready to use the war as an excuse for repealing those measures of industrial protection which they have long abhorred. Let us be mindful of the lamentable truth that some of the battle against the conservation of measures for the safety of the worker will be nothing more than the mean device of mean little souls prepared basely to use the war as an excuse for warring upon the life of men and women and children toilers.

As grave, perhaps graver than all these, is the question that is before the American people at this hour under the terms of the Censorship Bill.[31] A people does not rule if it cannot express itself with freedom. A people which is not free to express itself has ceased to be free to rule itself. Infinitely better some blundering by the press than the stifling of public opinion. Apart

[30] A letter from the National Consumers' League highlighted the experience of England in suspending laws limiting the hours of work even for women in war supplies factories; the subsequent impairment of productivity led to an official investigation and a decision to limit drastically the emergency measures that compromised working conditions (*New York Times*, 15 Apr. 1917, p. 3). The programme for farm workers proposed in the United States applied to boys from 15 to 19 years old (*New York Times*, 24 Apr. 1917, p. 5).

[31] The House passed the administration's Espionage Bill with a somewhat modified provision for censorship on 4 May; the Senate considered a softened version on 10 May, struck out all reference to censorship on 12 May and passed the Espionage Bill without the controversial measure on 14 May (*New York Times*, 15 May 1917, p. 1). However, the bill went into conference, with House members continuing to insist on censorship of the press, on 21 May (*New York Times*, 22 May 1917, p. 3); in this sense the issue was still 'before the American people' at the time of the sermon. The Espionage Act was not finally passed—without the provision for censorship of the press—until 15 June. For an overview, see Kennedy, *Over Here*, 25–6; Stone, *Perilous Times*, 146–53 (<www.firstworldwar.com/source/espionageact.htm>, checked 16 July 2006).

from what some of us believe to be the fundamental violation of the First Amendment of the Constitution of these United States in the attempted abridgment of the freedom of the press and of public assembly, one sorrows to record that the censorship measure has the support and sanction of the President and the Administration.[32] Are we to win the war upon Prussianism by adopting the Prussian method of that curtailment of liberty which is the end of liberty? The press does well to serve the nation by protesting against any infringement of its liberties in the guise of an intolerable censorship.[33] But on the other hand, it is almost well that this invasion of the liberty of the press be threatened in order that the press of the nation be aroused to a sense of the danger of limiting the freedom of the people of the United States, not only the liberty of the press but the liberty of expression of every kind and character whatsoever.

It has been grievous indeed to note during the last weeks and months that the press throughout the land has for the most part been indifferent to vulgar and tyrannical attempts to suppress the inalienable liberty of expression of opinion by the people. Imperilling to the inmost well-being of the American Republic as were any measure looking to the censorship of the press, it were no more hurtful to gag and choke the press than to estop the least of American citizens from speaking his mind, from uttering his opinions so long, of course, as his word be not seditious and treasonable. This pulpit would have the American press not only triumphant in beating back and down this threatened impairment of its liberty, but it would solemnly adjure the press of America not only to safeguard its own liberty but every item and atom of the liberties of the people. The limitation of freedom, save under the obvious limitations of the common welfare, is its destruction. Let the press of America understand that there ought to be no censorship *of* the press, and that there ought to be no censorship *by* the press; that censorship by the press is just as deadly to freedom and democracy as censorship of the press. Each is fatal to the freedom of freemen. Then let the press of America not only remain free but keep free and unimpeded every channel of public expression and national communication, written or oral.

[32] While the bill was in conference, and President Wilson continued to demand that the censorship provision be included (*New York Times*, 23 May 1917, p. 1, and 24 May, p. 1).

[33] The American Newspaper Publishers Association had on 25 April unanimously resolved to urge the elimination of the censorship provision from the Administration's Espionage Bill being debated in Congress (*New York Times*, 26 Apr. 1917, p. 4), stating that 'the proposed legislation strikes at the fundamental rights of the people, not only assailing their freedom of speech, but also seeking to deprive them of the means of forming intelligent opinions'.

Much of what I urge rests upon the elementary principle, moral as well as political, first laid down by Edmund Burke, that in all barter there must be some proportion or parity between the price paid and the value of the thing gotten.[34] We have already paid the price, a heavy and a terrible price in that we have gone to war, and that we have taken our part in the great strife. Because we desire neither profit nor conquest, are we not the more justified in insisting that the price to be paid for victory be not too heavy, too terrible, too crushing, the more seeing that we war not for victory but for things infinitely more precious. On every side, we hear voices nobly protesting against the surrender of democracy, our democracy, the voice of them that cry that we are setting out not just to win a war but to win a war for justice, and that therefore there must be no weakening of adherence to fundamental American principles of liberty. A member of the Cabinet has put it well—that ours is a democracy: it would not be worth our while going into the conflict if, when we come out of it, we do not still have a democracy. A group of friends, speaking in the name of the American Union Against Militarism, have said with insight and penetration: 'This war has been declared in the name of liberty and democracy. Let us not undermine our own liberty and democracy.'[35]

A consideration of the highest importance must be borne in mind, if we are fitly to answer the question, can we win the war without losing America?—the number of those whose motives are not altogether unmixed, who will seek to win the war not for the sake of liberty and democracy but for some ulterior purpose not unrelated to personal gain or private advantage. While some of us consider the necessity for war, for any and every war, a thing infinitely regrettable,[36] there are on the other hand those who welcome this war because they hope that

[34] Perhaps referring to a frequently quoted adage from Burke, 'All government—indeed, every human benefit and enjoyment, every virtue and every prudent act—is founded on compromise and barter': *Burke's Speech on Conciliation with America*, ed. Hammond Lamont (Boston: Ginn, 1897), 62.

[35] The American Union Against Militarism was founded in 1915 by Wise, John Haynes Holmes, and other New York pacifists (and near-pacifists) as the 'Anti-Militarism Committee'; it underwent several name changes in the following years (<www.swarthmore.edu/Library/peace/DG001-025/DG004AUAM.html>, checked 3 June 2007); Kennedy, *Over Here*, 33–6. Its Civil Liberties Bureau eventually became the American Civil Liberties Union. Wise broke from the Union with his support of the American war effort, though he remained friendly with many of its members. The statement alludes to a famous passage from Wilson's 'war message' of 2 April (see nn. 37, 46 below): 'The world must be made safe for democracy. Its peace must be planted upon the tested foundations of political liberty.' For the relative absence of opposition to the Espionage Act from American religious circles, see R. H. Abrams, *Preachers Present Arms*, 128–30.

[36] Alluding to his anti-militarist position, recently modified in support of the war effort (see the introduction to this sermon).

some of the things of militarism will not be shaken off for generations. We have not gone into the war in order to obtain new markets, but there are some men of affairs, who after the close of the war will clamor very strenuously that the mighty navy that has been built up should be used for the furtherance of market opportunities abroad. It is only one step from market-hunting abroad with governmental co-operation to debt-collecting by the navy under governmental orders.

We must be on our guard lest our purposes become clouded and our aims confused by reason of the rougher contacts of war. It is safe to prophesy that long before the close of the war men will arise and insist that we cannot forever be bound by the terms of President Wilson's message to the world, and that we have the right to seek some reimbursement of our outlays in the war.[37] These will parallel and duplicate the lamentations of them who deplored the enactment of that covenant by the Senate of the United States which assured the uninvaded liberties of the Republic of Cuba, who sought to neutralize the effect of that statute which brought infinitely more honor to the American people than any martial triumph.[38] It was a great thing for the President to have spoken and for the nation to have heeded his epoch-making message of April 2nd; the real test of the Republic will be at hand when we as a people are faced by the necessity of reaching the decision whether or not as a nation we are to be governed by the terms of President Wilson's Magna Charta in the day of peace.[39]

This is the time for heart-searching, for testing the sincerity of the soul of our nation as we go forth to battle. Unconsciously, the most perfect measure of national preparedness was taken during the years in which amid almost intolerably provocative circumstances we scorned to be a Germany to our own Mexican Belgium. It was the attitude of the President of the United States toward Mexico that won for him and for us the right to utter a new Charter of

[37] Referring to the statement in Wilson's 'war message' to the Senate of 2 April: 'We seek no indemnities for ourselves, no material compensation for the sacrifices we shall freely make.'

[38] Wise appears to be referring back to the congressional recognition of Cuba's independence proclaimed on 20 Apr. 1898, and the subsequent modifications of this principle formalized in the 'Platt Amendment', used to justify American interventions in Cuban affairs in 1906 and 1913. At the time of the sermon, pressures were mounting for a new American military intervention to suppress an insurgency that endangered the sugar crop, and indeed American marines arrived in Cuba in August 1917. See Pérez, *Intervention, Revolution, and Politics in Cuba*, 80–91 and (on the influence of the sugar industry) 129–37.

[39] Echoing his exuberant formulation in the sermon of 8 Apr.: 'The new world-epoch will date from the utterance of the world's Magna Charta spoken for peoples of every race and faith and tongue by the President of these United States' ('The World-War for Humanity', 103).

Freedom for the race.[40] Would not this be the hour for generous and satisfying reparation to the little Republic of Colombia which we once grievously wronged?[41]

We need not leave our own land in order to do the things that shall prove beyond peradventure that it is true that we mean to be just within and without our national borders. We have been startled by the rumors of negro disaffection and revolt, rumors cruelly unjust to the negro race. The negro race is as loyal to the Republic as to [is?] the white race.[42] Would not this be the happiest of hours, not merely for a gesture of generosity to the negro, but for such revision of our attitude toward him as shall make it possible for him to bear his part of the burdens of war with eagerness and even with rejoicing. Time and occasion are alike favoring. Dare we as a nation be greatly just, and in our passion for the nobleness of justice rather than the beauty of generousness, deal wisely and healingly with a great wrong in our American life? This plea is made not at the dictate of expediency,[43] but under the impulse of a deep and solemn consciousness of wrong, under the impact of the will to fit ourselves for the work of securing justice from the mighty of [the] earth and of meting out nothing less than justice to the weak, yea the weakest.[44] If, as has been said before in this pulpit, we are to go into the war with clean hands, our hands must be undefiled by wrong done at home to the unoffending.

[40] For the fear of war with Mexico in the spring of 1914 and Wilson's acceptance of the offer by three Latin American countries to mediate, leading to Wise's praise of Wilson and his exclamation to his congregation that because of the 'promise of peace . . . my cup of joy is overflowing', see Urofsky, *A Voice that Spoke for Justice*, 134–5; 'Peace Leaders Hail Mexican Mediation', *New York Times*, 28 May 1914, p. 2. Cf. the sermon of 8 Apr. 1917 : 'We have gained the confidence of the world in our plea for democracy because we have dealt with Mexico in the spirit of generosity and magnanimity' ('The World-War for Humanity', 116).

[41] Referring to American policy following Colombia's refusal to ratify a lease of the Isthmus of Panama in 1903. The United States supported an uprising against Colombia in Panama and recognized the new Republic of Panama. Construction of the canal was begun in 1906 and completed in 1914; in 1921 (consistent with the sentiments of the preacher), the United States paid Colombia $25 million in return for the loss of Panama.

[42] On the rumors of negro disaffection and disloyalty in the South, purportedly stirred up by German agents, first published by the *New York Tribune* on 4 Apr. 1917, see Ellis, *Race, War and Surveillance*, 5–10. Responses by black spokesmen to these rumours were reported by the *New York Times* on 6 Apr. 1917, p. 11, and 9 Apr. 1917, p. 2.

[43] The argument from expediency being that in order to motivate the American negro 'to bear his part of the burdens of war', it is necessary to offer some inducement of improved status.

[44] A powerful statement of principle and national self-rebuke. Cf. his 1913 statement that in 'denying justice to the Negro . . . in the end the white race will suffer most. No race can violate the moral law with impunity; no race can for years and generations pursue courses that are unjust without mutilating its own moral nature' (cited in Urofsky, *A Voice that Spoke for Justice*, 100).

I think of the great ends which we have set out honestly to attain, and recall that other nations, too, have set out before us upon high and honoring quests. And the manner of the quest became ignoble and the goal defiled, so that moral disaster was doomed to discrown all. I remember a high and great quest of centuries ago when the world willed highly that which, having not holily, it should have desisted to pursue. The holy quest for the recovery of the birthplace and tomb of the founder of Christianity degenerated into a crusade of blood and vengeance against the people made up of his brothers, and it resolved itself for the most part into a bloody and bestial debauch.[45]

There are those who openly mock or grimly smile at our national program, maintaining that the end of this war is bound to be evil, not only because war ever brings curses in its train, but because we are certain to surrender some of the most precious gains of the democratic life howbeit we have set forth to overwhelm them that are democracy's foes. I do not so believe, for my own is too great a trust in the power of my countrymen to achieve their purpose. We have set out upon a high and holy quest. We will not basely stoop in our pursuit thereof. We who enter the war without intent to do evil but rather to release them that are in bondage shall not so falter as to enthrall ourselves. If we can war without hatred of the enemy,[46] can we not triumph without hurt to ourselves? We will no more than to serve the world and not to disserve ourselves through deserting the ideals which are the soul of America.

Yet another reason there is for resolving that we shall not lose America as we strive to win the war. The war must and will be won by them who are ready to lay down their life to the end that victory may crown our arms. Whilst these set forth to win the war, dare we do less than determine that the aims of America on behalf of which they wage war, on behalf of which they are ready to dare and to die, shall not be defeated at home whilst through their service and sacrifice its arms triumph abroad? Whilst these sacrifice themselves for America, we must not sacrifice America on any ground whatsoever. We ask the young men of America to win the war. Let it not become needful for them to demand of us that we, who are to live amid security because of their service and their sacrifice, shall not lose their and our America.

[45] Referring, of course, to the First Crusade and the massacres of Jews in the Rhineland communities at its outset—a warning about the possible perversion of apparently noble sentiments.

[46] Alluding perhaps yet again to Wilson's 'war message': 'We have no quarrel with the German people. We have no feeling toward them but one of sympathy and friendship'. In his sermon of 8 April, he said, 'If this is truly to be a democratic war for a people and against its government, we can prove it in no better way than by refusing to suffer hatred to creep into our hearts' ('The World-War for Humanity', 115).

[PERORATION]

Not very long ago, I was asked to have part in a 'Wake Up America' demonstration[47] from which I absented myself because tawdryness and vulgarity have no part in our international strife. The methods of the circus ring ought not to be associated even remotely with the most sombre event in human history. Wake Up America!—not only to the need of hard fighting which is inevitable, but the duty of preserving inviolate the high aims of this war. Wake Up America!—and wage a war without hatred, without bitterness, without vindictiveness, a war without indemnity exacted from others outwardly or from ourselves inwardly. Wake Up America to the nobleness of our part in the strife not for profit to ourselves nor yet for punishment of others, but for the liberation of all peoples, including above all the peoples of the German Empire, from Caesarism.

Wake Up America to the greatness and the nobleness of our quest, the making secure forever of the sanctity of international covenant and the rights of smaller nations, of democracy for all the world.

> The wind that fills my sails propels
> But I am a helmsman still.[48]

The winds that fill the sails of the American Ship of State are blown from the fields of bloody battle. Yet must the soul of America still be helmsman. Wake Up America and win the war for the world, but hold and keep holy America's soul.

[47] A national campaign by the New York Committee on National Defense to make 19 April (the anniversary of the Battle of Lexington) into a day of patriotic parades and mass recruitment. For the posters by James M. Flagg used in this campaign, see Rawls, *Wake Up America*.

[48] George Meredith, 'Modern Love', stanza 20. The lines are applied to the central message of the sermon.

# CHAPTER TWENTY

# HERMANN GOLLANCZ
# NATIONALISM WITHIN BOUNDS

*A Protest against Extreme Nationalism*

### 7 SEPTEMBER 1918
#### (ROSH HASHANAH)

**BAYSWATER SYNAGOGUE, LONDON**

HERMANN GOLLANCZ (1852–1930) was the son of Samuel Marcus Gollancz, minister of the Hambro Synagogue in London from 1854 to 1899. Born in Bremen, he was educated at Jews' College and University College London; later he received rabbinical ordination from three Galician rabbis, becoming one of the few Jewish clergy in Britain who actually used the title 'rabbi'. In 1880 he was installed as preacher to the New Synagogue in London; subsequently he succeeded the new chief rabbi Hermann Adler as rabbi of the Bayswater Synagogue, which he led for thirty years.[1] The first Jew to receive a D.Litt. degree from the University of London (in 1900), he held the Goldsmid Chair in Hebrew at University College London, previously held by David Woolf Marks and Solomon Schechter, from 1902 to 1924. On 11 February 1922 he preached 'on the completion of 50 years' Service in the Anglo-Jewish Ministry', recalling his first sermon, in the Hambro Synagogue as assistant to his father, at a thanksgiving service in 1872 for the recovery from life-threatening illness of the Prince of Wales, later King Edward VII.[2] In 1923 he became the first English rabbi to be knighted.

---

[1] For a brief overview, see Roth, *Bayswater Synagogue*, and O. S. Phillips and Simons, *The History of the Bayswater Synagogue*, 29–36. Chief Rabbi Hermann Adler's unwillingness to allow Gollancz to use the title 'rabbi', holding that the title should be reserved to the chief rabbi, was a source of tension between them.

[2] Further on the circumstances of this sermon, see Gollancz's *Sermons and Addresses* (1909), p. xii; the sermon is not included in any of his three volumes.

Gollancz published three volumes of his sermons. The first, which appeared in 1909, contains sermons delivered at the Bayswater and other synagogues between 1882 and 1908. In addition to sermons on various aspects of Jewish belief and practice (including the sabbath, the dietary laws, and mixed marriages), many deal with more topical issues such as the themes of Jewish patriotism and antisemitism. Several, delivered in 1890, 1903, and 1905, were written in response to the persecution of Russian Jews.

A number of Gollancz's sermons responding to the First World War were included in his second and third published volumes: in the second, 'At War' (5 September 1914), 'War and the Belgian Refugees' (24 October 1914), 'Remember: a Word on Behalf of the Polish and Palestinian Jewish Exiles' (27 February 1915), 'A Year of War' (sabbath before Rosh Hashanah 1915), 'Darwinism and the War' (Yom Kippur 1915), 'The War and the Jews of Eastern Europe' (Sukkot, 23 September 1915); in the third, ' "Noblesse Oblige": The Motto for Nations as Well as for Individuals' (9 September 1916), 'The World's Guilt in the War' (December 1916), and 'On the Armistice' (November 1918).

The sermon below, delivered on Rosh Hashanah 1918, responds not to the external threat but to an internal issue: the treatment of German-born aliens. There were two main periods of xenophobic activism in Britain during the war. The first followed the sinking of the *Lusitania* on 7 May 1915 with the loss of over 1,000 lives. Passions were stoked by an inflammatory press and anti-'alien' riots broke out in Liverpool the following day, spreading to Manchester and several days later to London. Demonstrations demanded the internment of Germans residing in Britain, and especially in London, for the duration of the war. On 13 May the government proposed a new policy mandating the internment of those non-naturalized adult male aliens of 'hostile origin' who were not already in detention camps.[3]

The second such period was the summer of 1918, immediately preceding Gollancz's Rosh Hashanah sermon. In response to public opinion, agitated by the press and speakers at rallies, and widespread discontent with the practice of making decisions case by case, the government once again considered introducing a stricter internment and repatriation policy. On 24 August a massive rally organized by the National Party in Hyde Park produced a petition calling for the internment of every 'enemy alien' without distinction, eventually receiving well over one million signatures. Throughout the summer, anti-alien sentiment was fostered by articles in newspapers and periodicals. There was a movement in local councils to remove even naturalized Germans from the register of voters.[4]

---

[3] Panayi, *The Enemy in our Midst*, 76–8, 229–34; Cesarani, 'An Alien Concept?', 35–6; Bendlebury, *Portraying 'The Jew'*, 64–6.
[4] Bendlebury, *Portraying 'The Jew'*, 92–5, 213–19.

Against this background, there is some evidence of Jewish preachers joining the voices of those who opposed the waves of xenophobia. Noteworthy is a report of a sermon delivered by the Reverend D. Wasserzug in the Orthodox Dalston Synagogue on the festival of Shavuot (19 May) 1915, less than two weeks after the sinking of the *Lusitania*: 'In our battles with wrongdoing and injustice, we can win only by love, never by hate. To oppose crime by crime, to loot the shops of the alien enemy as a reprisal for the unspeakable crime—the destruction of the "Lusitania"—is, alas! Worse than useless. We only add to the crime.'[5] The protests against the expressions of hostility towards aliens in the summer of 1918 were somewhat more numerous and stronger.[6]

This is the context in which Gollancz decided to devote his Rosh Hashanah sermon, two weeks after the anti-alien rally in Hyde Park, to 'A Protest against Extreme Nationalism'. It always requires a degree of courage for a preacher to criticize his own society during wartime. Generally, a preacher doing this feels compelled to proclaim his own patriotic credentials, as Gollancz does here at two points in the sermon. To be sure, there was a certain degree of Jewish self-interest here, as the anti-alien discourse was by no means free of antisemitism.[7] It is therefore difficult to assess the degree to which the congregation in the Bayswater Synagogue on that Rosh Hashanah would have endorsed the preacher's sentiments, fearing that friends, relatives, even themselves might be victims of the right-wing agenda if it were implemented, or whether they thought that discretion advised a lower public profile. What is clear is that Gollancz enunciates a powerful and principled attack on nationalistic extremism and an endorsement of the fundamental value of inclusiveness, buttressed both by the religious theme of universal divine sovereignty and by an appeal to venerable British traditions.

---

[5] Wasserzug, 'Sermon for the First Day of Shavu'ot', 16. For other statements condemning the anti-alien riots in May 1915, see Panayi, *The Enemy in our Midst*, 276–7.

[6] Panayi, *The Enemy in our Midst*, 277–9.

[7] See e.g. on Leo Maxse, Panayi, *The Enemy in our Midst*, 163–4, 175–7. As Alderman has written, 'the ultra-patriotism and violent anti-German hysteria that swept the nation did not bother to differentiate much between Germans and Jews and, inevitably, soon gave way to a general xenophobic atmosphere from which Jews suffered disproportionately, whether or not they were indeed of German origin' (*Modern British Jewry*, 235, and the continuation of his discussion on 235–9).

# SERMON

---

*For all the earth is Mine.*
(EXOD. 19: 5)
*The earth is the Lord's, and the fullness thereof.*
(PS. 24: 1)

O LORD GOD, King of the Universe!
Before we address our Congregation to-day, let us at the close of the year offer our humble sacrifice of thanksgiving unto Thee for having watched over us during the past year, and spared us amid the dangers and disasters of war. We in this district especially, in the immediate vicinity of a stricken area,[8] have double cause to-day to render heartfelt thanks unto Thee for having saved us and our children as fire-brands plucked out of the fire.[9] Be Thou with us in the future as Thou hast been with us in the past; and renew unto us in the coming year the loving-kindness and tender mercy which until this Thou hast bestowed upon us and our dear ones.

Help Thou the feeble efforts of man to put an end to strife in the world. May the din of war and the clash of arms soon give way to the diviner sound of peace, speedily in our days. AMEN!

No Jew need be told, in so many words, the reason why he is present in this House to-day. It is our New Year's Day. But other creeds also have their New Year's Day. Yet what a difference in the value of the celebration! Unless the ordinary duties of life be invested with the sense of responsibility; unless the regularly recurring seasons of the year speak their message to the heart and soul of man; more than half the value of the duties, more than half the value of our celebrations, is lost. Merriment and tokens of joy are all very well in their way; but the solemn message, the soul-uplifting characteristics, associated with the return of the Sabbath, with the return of the seasons, if they are allowed to

---

[8] The 'stricken area' apparently alludes to the outbreak of the 'Spanish influenza' which had already afflicted the populations of Manchester and London during the summer, and was increasing in the autumn. The 'double cause' for gratitude is therefore having survived, as of Rosh Hashanah, the disasters of war and the dangers of the epidemic. [9] Echoing Zech. 3: 2.

make their appeal to the average man and woman of the world, are of infinitely more value to the individual and the world at large than the clang of joy-bells and the din of noisy celebration.[10]

We Jews have thrown a sacred halo about our New Year, at least those of us who are Jews, and yet people of the world. Better fare and better dress, a New Year's card and a more hearty handshake, do not mark the end-all of what our First Day of the Year was intended to be. If our *Rosh Hashana* had not a *religious* significance, there would be no reason for our observing it at all. And this year, especially, the thought occurs to my mind—on this day in the fifth year of the monstrous world-war[11]—that, as much as any other reflection brought home to us in our liturgy is the idea of *God's sovereignty in the world* from the beginning even unto the end of time.[12]

Had this reflection penetrated sufficiently deep into the minds and souls of men, I venture to think that so infamous a war could not have been set on foot, implying as it does—in addition to all the attendant sorrows and miseries of mankind—an open act of rebellion, on the part of those who set it in motion, against the sovereignty and supremacy of Heaven. If the crowned heads, or the rulers of the various countries of the world, were true to themselves and true to the people they govern, they would understand that there is a Power in the world to whom they owe their throne, or under whom they rule, and that in the sight of that Power, the meanest creature on earth has as much right to live, and to reign in the humble kingdom of his lowly home, as the mightiest potentate that ever reigned from India to Ethiopia.[13]

If, again, the peoples of the earth themselves had been imbued with the true sense of their duties as human beings, with their mission as parts of the world's moving power, with their privileges, and with their responsibilities to the brotherhood of man, they would not have allowed themselves to be cabined,[14] confined, and crippled by the dictates of tyrannical order; but knit together by the international bond of humanity, they would have seen to it that the present dreadful conflict—hell let loose upon earth—would have been averted.

[10] The contrast between the mood of introspection and repentance that characterizes the liturgy of Rosh Hashanah, the Jewish New Year, and the secular New Year's celebration has been a commonplace of Jewish homiletics on this occasion.

[11] As the war started in August 1914, this was indeed the fifth Rosh Hashanah during wartime.

[12] This is indeed a central theme in the liturgy of Rosh Hashanah; see the end of the sermon.                [13] Echoing Esther 1: 1 about Ahasuerus.

[14] i.e. restricted in action and thought, as if in a narrow cabin. The phrase as a whole alludes (probably by memory) to *Macbeth*, III. iv: 'I am cabin'd, cribb'd, confined, bound in | To saucy doubts and fears'.

When in the dawn of Hebrew nationality the Israelites stood at the foot of Mt. Sinai, they heard a voice which addressed them and said: 'And ye shall be unto Me a peculiar treasure above all the peoples; for all the earth is Mine' (Exod. 19: 5).

And so does the psalmist sing: 'The earth is the Lord's, and the fullness thereof; the world and all that dwell therein' (Ps. 24: 1).

Yes, dear brothers and sisters, on the day of reckoning—the ultimate Day of Judgment, of which this is but a type; on the final Day of Memorial, of which this is one;[15] there will be no distinction between prince and peasant, between high and low, between rich and poor; what a man is, not what a man has,[16] will be the thing that counts when the decree goes forth, when the verdict is given. If kings will and princes plan, there is yet a Power above that wills and plans too. If monarchs rule, claiming the submission of men, there is a Power that over-rules the ruler, and claims the submission of the tyrant.

'The earth is the Lord's, and the fullness thereof.' 'For all the earth is Mine,' says God.

And yet, in spite of God's word and will, we see the vicious nature of man, who at times becomes the man-eater; we see his unholy ambitions, peeping thro' the purple robe of sovereignty to claim that which is not his, to seize like a bird of prey upon unhallowed spoils, to plunge the world into an ocean of blood, in order to gratify his insatiable lust for power and dominion; trampling under-foot, in the attempt, millions of his fellow-creatures, millions of his own loyal subjects, in defiance of all that is natural and humane.[17]

What right, I would ask, have kings and rulers to come forth from the limits of their original possessions, and rob neighbouring States of the territory which these have held from their ancestors?

Let this rule of action guide the rulers of the world, and there would be no more wars.

And in view of the insane lengths to which even peoples themselves can pro-ceed, I would go a step further, and ask: 'Is there real justification for the

---

[15] The preacher uses two phrases, 'Day of Judgment' and 'Day of Memorial' (or Remembrance: *yom hazikaron*), that characterize Rosh Hashanah in traditional Jewish discourse, emphasizing that it is a kind of annual rehearsal for the ultimate, eschatological Day of Judgement.

[16] This phrase (with the two components usually in reverse order) is a commonplace of moral-istic literature, attested in the writings of many eighteenth- and nineteenth-century authors. For example, 'capital is not what a man *has* but what a man *is*' (attributed to John Wolcot).

[17] This language evoking the potentially vicious character of human nature when insensitive to the sovereignty of God perhaps reflects the influence of the popular image of a Darwinian 'nature, red in tooth and claw' (Tennyson, 'In Memoriam A.H.H.').

extreme cry of Nationality, which at the present hour is running amuck in the
social and political life of this country?'[18]

I yield to no one in my allegiance and whole-hearted devotion to the Throne
and the ruling Power of this blessed realm;[19] but it is just because I pray from
the depth of my heart and with my entire being that it may remain blessed, that
I note with dismay the jarring tones that meet the ear (one of the symptoms of
war panic) anent the alien enemy, or even the alien.[20]

To my mind, the agitation brought about and kept alive mainly by a few
howling dervishes and members of the shrieking sisterhood[21] is quite unnecessary. Their motive is not quite clear; for if there be suspicion attaching to any
one in our midst, whether he or she be alien or native, open foe or supposed
friend, there need be no difficulty in dealing with such cases; and the loyal
citizen will be only too ready to aid in the task of ridding ourselves of such un-
desirables.

But, alas, the hounds of war once let loose[22] bear in their trail a thousand
wrongs. And one of these, not the least dangerous, is mob-rule; the attempt of
the people to govern the governing powers; the spectacle (to use a commonplace simile) of the tail wagging the dog, when, from one cause or another, irresponsible units in a state set about being more despotic than the vilest despot.[23]

Heaven shield this country from the theories and practices of such pseudo-
loyalists, such extreme nationalists, who would deny to such as are not British-

---

[18] Up until this point in the sermon, the listeners might well have thought that the preacher
was speaking of Germany, with its autocratic ruler, fierce nationalism, and territorial expansion-
ist policies. Following the rhetorical model of Amos 1 and 2, after gaining assent through his
criticism of the enemy, he now turns his criticism to the same phenomenon at home.

[19] The establishment of one's patriotic credentials is a rhetorical necessity when criticizing one's
own country; the preacher will return to this motif later in the sermon.

[20] For the context, see the introduction to this sermon above.

[21] This was a phrase used in the 1890s and 1900s to characterize women agitating for 'women's
rights', especially the right to vote. The Women's Social and Political Union, according to one
scholar, 'exploited a national racial hysteria to further their political ends', and organized a massive parade on 22 July 1916 in support of (among other 'patriotic' goals) the revocation of natural-
ization certificates and the internment of all enemy aliens: Gullace, 'The Blood of our Sons', 132–3
(I am grateful to Dane Kennedy for this reference). I am not certain as to Gollancz's own views
on women's suffrage (note that Stephen S. Wise insisted that the American entrance into the war
heightened the need to provide full suffrage for women: see Sermon 19 above). Before the war,
confrontational behaviour by Anglo-Jewish suffragists created a backlash in some traditionalist
circles, expressed in letters to the *Jewish Chronicle*; see Kuzmack, *Woman's Cause*, 140–1.

[22] Echoing Shakespeare's 'Cry, Havoc! and let slip the dogs of war' (*Julius Caesar*, III. i);
Gollancz uses the same phrase in *Fifty Years After*, 97.

[23] This seems to be a clear allusion to the massive anti-alien rally in Hyde Park a few weeks
before the sermon was delivered (see introduction to this sermon).

born the right to dwell in this country as peaceable and law-abiding citizens! I repeat in effect, that, to my mind this right, this attitude of Great Britain in the past, has been the secret of its place in the world—the mainspring of its blessedness—the explanation of its greatness.[24] Take away the right of asylum for political and religious refugees in this country; introduce restrictive legislation against the foreigner or alien; be vindictive in the application of old rules, or in the framing of new laws, respecting those domiciled here for years; and you pull down the fabric upon which the constitution of this country rests, with a result which its friends and well-wishers would scarcely wish to contemplate.[25] Let it beware, too, lest, at the bidding of some none too disinterested or of some revengeful spirits, it incur the reproachful 'Tu quoque!' when, without sufficient rhyme or reason, it tears up 'the scrap of paper', which at one time, after the strictest scrutiny and upon the recommendation of a number of honourable men and true, it granted to some worthy indweller of this country, who, in turn, pledged by oath his loyalty to the State which received him.[26] If I could speak to that portion of the British people that has yet maintained its sanity of reason amid the perplexities of war, I would say to them:

'You will win this war (I have had that feeling from the start), but you will have difficulties and obstacles, even an occasional set-back; this is for your sins against your fellow-man. Not only our enemies, but, in a different way, you

---

[24] The argument that immigration and the assimilation of foreign populations served as a significant source of the nation's strength was, of course, made even more vigorously in the context of similar debates in the United States. Two classical expressions of different aspects of this idea were Emma Lazarus's Statue of Liberty poem, 'The New Colossus', and Israel Zangwill's play, *The Melting Pot*. For opposition to immigration in the pre-war period, see Gainer, *The Alien Invasion*, and Garrard, *The English and Immigration*; cf. the overview in Endelman, *The Jews of Britain*, 156–62.

[25] This ringing affirmation of the right of asylum reflects a consensus in British politics through most of the period between 1826 and 1905, when no statutes prevented aliens from coming to and staying in Britain as they liked. *The Times* articulated this commitment in Feb. 1853: 'Every civilised people on the face of the earth must be fully aware that this country is the asylum of nations, and that it will defend the asylum to the last ounce of its treasure, and the last drop of its blood. There is no point whatever on which we are prouder and more resolute' (quoted in Potter, *The Refugee Question in Mid-Victorian Politics*, 7; cf. the summary discussion, 1–11, and 112).

[26] Some listeners may have found it difficult to follow this rather dense, allusive, and somewhat convoluted sentence. The reference to tearing up a 'scrap of paper' evokes the beginning of the war, when on 4 Aug. 1914, the German chancellor, Bethmann-Hollweg, reproached the British ambassador, Sir Edward Goschen, for Britain's willingness to go to war over a 'scrap of paper', namely, the Treaty of London of 1839, which bound Britain to defend Belgium's neutrality. But it is used here in a different context, referring to a document of alien status, issued in accordance with proper procedure, that anti-alien forces are now pressing to tear up metaphorically, leading to internment or deportation. The message is apparently that if native-born Jews support this policy, the anti-alien forces may some day turn against them as well and say *tu quoque* (you too).

yourselves are sinning against the laws of humanity.'[27] 'You will win,' I say; 'and therefore all the more reason why you can afford to be, if not generous, yet humane.' But are you?

War itself is cruel enough. Must you render the conditions still more cruel? War accentuates with sufficient bitterness the divisions existing between man and man. Why, then, in time of war, aggravate these dangers, and in one and the same country set class against class, race against race, and sex against sex?

Yet that is what is being done in this very land of freedom, perhaps more than in any other; I should say, this is what is being allowed to be done; for I cannot believe that the English people as a whole, left to itself, and not goaded on and terrorised by the misrepresentations and exaggerations of mischievous agents to see in every one not born on British soil a rebel or a spy, would approve of the extreme measures advocated by some few who are not the friends they pretend to be, but the real enemies and betrayers of this country.[28]

Why persecute and oppress those whose sole crime is that they had the accident to be born in a foreign land, even in an enemy country? Could they control such an occurrence?

Do the English forget that they are a composite race?[29] Does not history speak of the early settlers in this country, the Romans, the Saxons, the Danes, and the Normans?

---

[27] The idea of 'the laws of humanity' gained legal significance in the nineteenth century through international efforts to prohibit certain practices in war, such as the use of specific weapons or armaments (as in e.g. the St Petersburg Declaration of 1868: 'the employment of such arms would, therefore, be contrary to the laws of humanity'). After the conclusion of the war, an Allied commission found that Turkish officials were guilty of 'crimes against the laws of humanity'. Gollancz uses the phrase in a sense broader than its technical legal meaning.

[28] A common rhetorical tactic when responding to mass rallies is to claim that they cannot reflect the will of the majority of the people, who are basically decent, but that they show the effects of agitation by 'mischievous agents', who prey on the people's fears. Cf. the *New Statesman* editorial of 22 May 1915: 'Last week's anti-alien riots made it only too clear that there are journalists of a Prussian ferocity in this country who exercise an evil influence over the mob far beyond what is justified by anything but their shouting' (cited in Panayi, *The Enemy in our Midst*, 230; cf. 215–19 for the summer of 1918). For the 'extreme measures' urged by the National Party in August 1918, see ibid. 94.

[29] This phrase was used by some writers in a positive sense to describe the Irish and the Americans as well as the British. In nineteenth-century racist thinking, racial purity rather than mixture was generally considered desirable. This was challenged by some anthropologists who argued that 'mixed races' were superior to 'pure races', and the principle was conceded even by the influential British racial theorist Robert Knox, who maintained that the mixture of the noble Saxon race and the Slavonic races with their capacity for abstract reasoning produced the racial perfection of the Greeks. See Mosse, *Toward the Final Solution*, 67–76. While this debate lies in the background of Gollancz's use of the phrase, his specific context is historical and leads to the practical conclusion that immigration provides a national asset.

Some say (as if in apology for their own vindictiveness): 'Internment is not a punishment; we do not desire to be vindictive; it is resorted to as a measure of self-preservation.' Others go further, and playing the hypocrite, add: 'It is for the safety of the enemy aliens themselves!'[30] What cant! See the methods of some of these *agents provocateurs*! How could they trust the 'stranger', if they do not trust the Government which they themselves have put into power, and which have given an earnest of their willingness to deal fairly with the whole problem? The legislation proposed is sufficiently drastic to deal with all suspicious cases; and I say, let it be enforced in the most thoroughgoing manner in all cases where there is a scintilla of honest suspicion of disloyalty.[31]

But it has always been the pride of English law in the past that a man is innocent until he be proved guilty. Then in the name of common sense and honesty, in the name of Heaven's law of humanity, I say, leave the guiltless alone and undisturbed. Let not people say (as I have heard it said): 'England is no longer a free country.'[32]

Is it not, alas, one of the signs of a degraded society, when encouragement is given to the 'espionage' of one's own neighbour, and when one sees displayed in an open thoroughfare the invitation to 'inform against local Huns'?

Let there be no mistake as to my personal attitude in this whole matter. I am in favour not only of our defeating Germany, but I firmly believe that Justice demands that she should be punished as well as defeated for her initial infamy, and her monstrous methods in the conduct of war.[33] Though an earnest public

[30] Gollancz was echoing here rationales used even by the government, as in Prime Minister Asquith's announcement of a new internment policy in May 1915: 'We propose that . . . all adult males of this class [i.e. non-naturalized persons of 'hostile origin' residing in Britain] should, for their own safety, and that of the community, be segregated and interned, or, if over military age, repatriated' (Panayi, *The Enemy in our Midst*, 78).

[31] The Hyde Park petition of 24 Aug. 1918 called for internment of every enemy alien without distinction, while the policies proposed by the government applied to male aliens over age 18, with exemptions for 'national' or medical reasons (Panayi, *The Enemy in our Midst*, 93–4). Gollancz seems to endorse internment only where there is a prima facie cause to suspect disloyalty, in accordance with the principle he proceeds to articulate.

[32] For other expressions of concern in the summer of 1918 about the damage to the reputation of Britain caused by the anti-alien agitation, see Panayi, *The Enemy in our Midst*, 278–9.

[33] A return to the establishing of patriotic credentials; cf. n. 19 above. By 'monstrous conduct', Gollancz is undoubtedly referring to the introduction of gas weapons. In a sermon delivered on 9 Sept. 1916, he said, 'Great Britain can, I think, take the boast to herself that she has departed from, and not touched unclean methods in the course of this dreadful world-war; that in spite of great provocation, she has kept her hands clean from adding to the atrocities and brutalities' (Gollancz, ' "Noblesse Oblige" ', 89). Yet he continued to deny the notion that Britain and the Allies were 'sinless' in the war.

advocate in the past of 'Arbitration versus War';*[34] though the father of a son who has now been on active service for four years, and for these two reasons alone would joyously and gratefully welcome the sound of peace; I yet hold that, once in the war, we have for the sake of the world to draw the fangs of the tiger, militarism, so as to render such a war, or any war, impossible in the future.

This theme upon which I have touched might, I think, be treated at great length from an academic standpoint, I mean the Nationalistic view—the idea as to how far each country has the right of self-determination in the matter of admitting, or suffering to dwell within its borders, those not born in the land. Time will not permit me to deal exhaustively with the subject. I dwelt upon some aspects of it in May last when addressing the Congregation of Reading. But I would repeat the significant words to which I have already alluded to-day: 'The earth is the *Lord's*, and the fullness thereof; the world and all that dwell in it' (Ps. 24: 1). 'All the earth is *Mine*' (Exod. 19: 5), says God. Not man, but God gives the right of possession; not man, but God has the right to dispossess. 'Hear, O ye kings; give ear, O ye princes' (Judg. 5: 3).

And on this day above all others, the truth is brought home to us Jews the more vividly, for it is the day of the year on which we in our orisons dwell specially, and at great length, upon the Sovereignty of the Being, who is the Maker of heaven and earth, the Creator of all humankind.

It is a note with which we close our daily prayers, 'For the Kingdom is Thine, to all eternity; Thou wilt reign in glory, as it is written in Thy Law, The Lord shall reign for ever and ever (Exod. 15: 18). And the Lord shall be King over the whole earth: in that day shall the Lord be One, and his name One (Zech. 14: 9).'[35]

Yes, dear brothers and sisters, in the words of Daniel (2: 39). 'A kingdom shall bear rule over all the earth': not Pan-Germanism, nor Pan-Slavism, not even Western jingoism; but the kingdom that shall bear rule over all the earth is the Kingdom of humanity, the Kingdom of God!

---

* The author signed 'A Memorial against the use of Armed Airships', issued by the 'International Arbitration League', and dated February 1912.

[34] The 'Prayer for Arbitration and World-Peace' offered by Gollancz in March 1911 during a meeting of an international peace organization was included in the second series of his *Sermons and Addresses* (pp. 254–5).

[35] This is the conclusion of the 'Aleinu' prayer, which originated in the 'Sovereignty' (*malkhu-yot*) section of the additional service for Rosh Hashanah, but was later incorporated as the conclusion of all public worship. See Millgram, *Jewish Worship*; Heinemann and Petuchowski, *Literature of the Synagogue*, 63–4.

# CHAPTER TWENTY-ONE

## LEO M. FRANKLIN
# THE LURE OF PEACE

### SUNDAY, 13 OCTOBER 1918

#### BETH EL CONGREGATION, DETROIT

LIKE STEPHEN S. WISE, Leo Franklin was in the middle of a successful rabbinic career in a large metropolitan synagogue during the First World War. Born in 1870, he attended the University of Cincinnati and was ordained by the Hebrew Union College in 1892. Following seven years in Omaha, Nebraska, he became senior rabbi at Detroit's Beth El Congregation, where he remained until his retirement in 1941. In 1903, following the model of Krauskopf, Levy, and others, he instituted the regular Sunday morning service oriented around a major weekly address. Unlike some of these other preachers, he did not have these addresses printed, but the Franklin Archive at Beth El contains the texts of approximately 1,500 of his sermons, a few (from 1899) in his handwriting, the rest typescripts. Franklin received some national exposure because of his friendship with Henry Ford and the break between the two men engendered by the publication of antisemitic material in the *Dearborn Independent*. Recognition by his colleagues was reflected in his service as president of the Central Conference of American Rabbis from 1919 to 1921.

No text of a sermon by Franklin remains from spring 1898, as America moved towards war with Spain, but a handwritten text on the biblical lesson 'Mishpatim', delivered in Omaha on 11 February 1899, and repeated at Beth El on 14 March 1902, recounts a memory of those months in the context of a theme to which he would frequently return, including at the conclusion of the sermon reproduced here: the respective attitudes towards war of Christianity and Judaism.

Here we stand at the end of nineteen centuries of Christian rulership—of 1900 years of the dominion of the religion of love and of mercy, and yet but a few short months ago we saw a Christian world gone mad for the application against a whole nation of that very law of retaliation which the Jew never applied and never meant to apply, but for the authorship of which he was mercilessly tortured and tormented. 'Blood for blood, life for life'[1] was the cry that rang and resounded for weeks and months before the outbreak of our war [in 1902: 'of the Spanish–American war'] throughout this Christian country where the 'prince of peace', the 'loving lamb' has altars in his name at every corner.[2]

Years later, in an Armistice Day sermon delivered on 11 November 1928, he referred to 'the Spanish–American War, which began in the name of humanity—though unfortunately its end was not so noble'.[3]

In his first Sunday morning sermon following the outbreak of the First World War, two weeks after the national day of prayer proclaimed by President Wilson, Franklin showed no inclination towards any American involvement in the fighting, or awareness of any stake in the outcome. Insisting on an American mission to the world, he indicated that a certain aloofness was the best policy:

Though the nations rage and throw themselves as beasts upon each other, let this country, true to her God-given genius for freedom and fraternity, stand as she must stand in this greatest crisis of all history, the calm, the just, the patient, the unselfish, the pitying sponsor of that freedom which in God's own time, through her perhaps, shall be given to all the peoples of the earth.[4]

Franklin was certainly not a pacifist. On the first Hanukah following the outbreak of war, he said:

Sometimes it may be necessary to fight that light shall come. Sometimes it may be necessary to protest with all our might against bigotry and fanaticism and superstition and ignorance and cruelty and all the forms of hate, that eventually the light of love and truth and faith and brotherhood may be reared aloft. Oh, then, if we must fight, let it be the fight against the things that drag men to the level of the brute.[5]

In later wartime sermons, however, he bemoaned the denigration of pacifists that he found rampant in contemporary American society as evidence of the corrupting impact of war even across the ocean.[6]

When America entered the war, Franklin revealed what appeared to be a lack of enthusiasm for the decision, though unambiguously pledging his support, insisting that the battle is 'for justice, for humanity, for freedom':

---

[1] Although this phrase is frequently cited as if it were biblical, it seems to be a composite of Gen 9: 5–6 with Exod 21: 23 and Deut. 19: 21.          [2] 'The Law of Retaliation', 8–9.
[3] 'A War without Armistice', 7.          [4] 'Has Civilization Proved a Failure?', 10.
[5] 'A Warrior's Message of Peace', 5.
[6] 'The Peace Idea in Jewish Literature', 1: 'In these days, when history is being written in blood, the term pacifist has become on the lips of some a title of opprobrium. This, however, is but another evidence of the fact that the prevalence of war's destruction warps the finer sentiments of men and dulls their nobler impulses. For it is only at a time when war, through its very familiarity, has lost its horror and grotesqueness, that men may speak in derision of the lovers of peace.' He made a similar point three weeks later on Memorial Day: 'The Living Dead', 5. Cf. Chatfield, *Pacifism in America*, 4, on the general transformation in the associations with the term 'pacifism' beginning in 1917.

It is too late to argue any longer as to whether this country is justified or is not justified in entering upon this conflict. The time has passed when we can ask as to whether our participation in the war will prolong it or bring it to a more speedy conclusion, and as to whether we should better have served humanity by giving to the world an example of national self-control, by standing aloof and suffering further the indignities to which we have been subject, or by defending our national honor in the same spirit as a man would be called upon to defend his own honor were it dragged into the dust. It is too late for us to discuss these things, even if, now that war has been declared, they may still be regarded as in any sense open to discussion. What seems to me to be the case is that this great people has heard what was spoken to our fathers centuries ago [Hebrew], 'Thou shalt not stand idly by the blood of thy brother' (Lev. 19: 16).

In saying these things to you today, my people, I would not be construed as having changed my deep repugnance to war. I hate war and bloodshed from the depths of my soul. . . . But perhaps there was no other course to follow. Perhaps Almighty God in His great wisdom and justice has sought out this American people, free as no other people on the earth is free, to take up the burden of the free man. We alone can do it. We have nothing to gain from this war except what we shall gain by giving. We want to crush no nation on the earth, but we want to crush unrighteousness and injustice and inhumanity.[7]

By the following Memorial Day, however, his statement about wanting 'to crush no nation on the earth' appears to have been clarified and somewhat modified, with a new emphasis on the need for decisive and uncompromising victory. America's task, he said, is 'not so much to bring the blood-thirsty Teuton to his knees, as it is to wipe out for all time to come the possibility of the spread of that Teutonic autocracy itself'. It is to make it possible for Germany, 'cured of her madness and lifted out of her degradation, humbled in her own sight as she shall be humiliated in the sight of all the world, to sit again in the circle of civilization'. But before that is possible,

America and her Allies must win this war, must win it in no indecisive manner and on no terms of compromise, but must win it in such a way that there shall be no doubt henceforth in the mind of any man or in the consciousness of any people that autocracy is dead beyond the possibility of resurrection, that tyranny is destroyed forever from the earth, and that Prussianism, that foul and filthy thing through which the lowest degradation of the human spirit has expressed itself, shall never lift its hideous head again.[8]

The need for this kind of victory would lie at the core of the sermon reproduced here.

The occasion for the present address was a period of intense diplomatic activity following a note from the German Imperial Chancellor dated 3 October 1918 to President Wilson, requesting a general armistice among all

[7] 'The Free Man's Burden', 5–7.    [8] 'Memorial Day Address', 2–3.

belligerents. This led to negotiations for a restoration of peace, on the basis of
Wilson's message to Congress of 8 January 1918 and his New York address
of 27 September, outlining a plan for a League of Nations. Independently, the
Austro-Hungarians sent a similar note.[9] Wilson replied on 8 October, setting
the evacuation of enemy forces from all Allied territory as a precondition for
any armistice, and seeking unambiguous clarification of whether the Germans
accepted the Fourteen Points of his 8 January message, and whether the
Imperial Chancellor was indeed 'speaking for the constituted authorities of
the Empire who have so far conducted the war'.[10] The British and French generally approved of Wilson's response, many interpreting it as having avoided a
German 'peace trap'. Some, however, criticized it as weakening the Allied position; and there was little public support for an armistice on terms short of an
unconditional German surrender.[11]

The position taken by Franklin in his first Sunday address following the
dramatic exchange of diplomatic correspondence was therefore in the mainstream of American public opinion. His introductory paragraph, after somewhat hyperbolically emphasizing the importance of the historical moment,
unambiguously endorses Wilson's insistence on full German withdrawal from
Allied territory, even if this demand should lead to a continuation of the bloodshed. Despite the popularity of this position, however, Franklin apparently felt
it necessary to justify his apparent lack of enthusiasm for peace in the prevailing circumstances on several grounds.

The body of the sermon begins, therefore, with a powerful evocation of the
devastation wrought by the war. This had become a common topos in Jewish
war preaching, and we can find examples, couched in similar terms, in virtually every generation from the mid-eighteenth century.[12] Franklin begins with
the physical destruction, moves on to the impact on cultural and scientific life,
then focuses on the cost in human suffering. Here there is no assessment of
blame; it is a generic lament over the general losses. Then he turns to the
impact of this war on America, which admittedly had been exempt from many
of the disastrous consequences just described. All this is intended to highlight
the appeal of a peace offer, giving legitimacy to those who intuitively favour
pursuing any opportunity to end the continuing nightmare. This validation of
the more moderate stance communicates the message: 'Those of you who
believe that Wilson should have been more accommodating in order to stop
the fighting as soon as possible: I understand your feelings.'

[9] *New York Times*, 6 Oct. 1918, p. 1; Lowry, *Armistice 1918*, 11–12. On 6 October the *New York Times* reported that Wilson was still waiting for the official text of the German note.
[10] *New York Times*, 9 Oct. 1918, p. 1.      [11] *New York Times*, 10 Oct. 1918, pp. 1, 5, 7.
[12] See M. Saperstein, *'Your Voice Like a Ram's Horn'*, 160, and other examples cited above: pp. 133, 223, 241–2, 273–4, 300, 326.

LEO M. FRANKLIN 379

But then, having made clear his full appreciation of the agony of war and of the natural desire to end it soon, he dismisses that impulse in a manner communicated by his title, 'the lure of peace'. Tough-minded leaders must at this crucial moment resist 'weak emotionalism' and 'the yielding to our softer passions'. The gendered nature of this stance in the preacher's mind becomes explicit in the next sentence: 'It is a time when all the virility, all the strength, all the manhood of our being must come into play.' War, by implication, is an arena for males; not only the fighting, but the decision-making, belongs to them.

A new section of the sermon begins when Franklin responds to the charge that this is not the way a religious leader should be speaking. Here he picks up a theme that he had addressed on many other occasions (as did other Jewish preachers): the disparity between the Christian and the Jewish attitudes towards war. Christians speak of their saviour as the 'Prince of Peace', and cite statements from the gospels about loving their enemies, while denigrating the Old Testament as primitively bellicose; yet Christians have waged brutal wars for centuries. This has led to many Christian thinkers confronting a painful intellectual problem in their efforts to justify war as consistent with Christian pronouncements. Jews, by contrast, have no such problem. Theirs is a more manly tradition; their God is a 'God of armies' who commanded the destruction of biblical enemies; Jews historically have never been tempted to compromise with evil in order to avoid the need of going to war. Thus it is Judaism, not Christianity, that reveals itself as in perfect harmony with America's position today.

We have encountered several sermons delivered during the Civil War period (see Sermons 5, 6, and 8a above by Michelbacher, Morais, and Einhorn respectively) that warned against the seductive temptation of a proffered premature peace that would either entrap the nation into lowering its guard or necessitate a compromise on fundamental principles. The present text presents a preacher in a similar position, claiming that the unwillingness to compromise with evil must trump the natural desire for an early cessation of hostilities. Franklin would feel validated a month later, when the armistice came on uncompromising Allied terms; two months later he insisted that compromise at the peace table would lead to disappointment.[13] Yet he would eventually realize that the vindictive punishment of Germany had led to results he had not anticipated.

---

[13] 'The Doctrine of "Peace on Earth"', 2–3.

# SERMON

====

## [INTRODUCTION]

SINCE the beginning of the world war, there has been no more momentous week than the one just passed. Indeed, without undue exaggeration
it may be said that in some senses it has been the paramount hour of human
history. The plea by our enemies for a temporary cessation of hostilities called
for an answer dictated by the sanest statesmanship and the most far-sighted
wisdom. Upon the character of our response hung the fate of civilization. That
the reply of our President was prompt but not impulsive, statesmanlike but
unambiguous is not surprising. That it cut clear to the heart of the matter at
issue was what might well have been expected. That it leaves no doubt as to
where this American people stands upon the question of a final settlement
with those who have betrayed humanity; that it definitely cuts off all hope that
any may have held for the discussion of terms of peace while Germany and her
Allies occupy an inch of territory that is not rightfully theirs, are causes for
great gratitude on the part of this American people.[14] To have taken this stand
at a time when the whole world is weary of its sorrows, demanded courage of
a high degree and moral heroism such as only the greatest of the nations has
evinced. And yet, it says much for the spirit of the American people that it
stands to a man squarely behind the President in his decision and that its men
and its women are willing to continue their sacrifices of life and of treasure;
yes, that they would have resented as un-American any other attitude than
that which has been taken by our President.

## [BODY OF THE SERMON]

The moral implication of this fact is by no means insignificant. Let us look
matters squarely in the face that we may properly evaluate the spirit of our
people. For four years now, the world has been drenched in blood. Great and

---

[14] As noted above, Wilson's reply stated that 'he would not feel at liberty to propose a cessation
of arms to the Governments with which the Government of the United States is associated
against the Central Powers so long as the armies of those Powers are upon their soil. The good
faith of any discussion would manifestly depend upon the consent of the Central Powers immediately to withdraw their forces everywhere from invaded territory.'

prosperous cities that were the scenes of busy activity less than half a decade ago, are by the dozens—rather perhaps by the hundreds—mere desolate ruins, their crumbling remains silent but eloquent tokens of the devastation of war. Whole countries like Belgium that but a few years ago were the peaceful and pleasant abode of simple, industrious, God-fearing folk have been levelled into howling wildernesses by the ravaging and ruthless destroyer. Temples of religion in which the God of the nations was praised in varied tongues have become the sepulchres of beasts that sought in their protecting walls shelter against the all-defying forces of destruction. Art treasures in which the genius of ages found its expression and whose value was beyond computation have been fuel to the flames. The hand of science has been set back and the quiet of the student's closet has been invaded by the pitiless demon of war. Nothing is as it was. Life has become cheap and millions of men on both sides of the struggle have wetted the soil of Europe with their sacred blood. Ploughshares have been turned into swords and pruning hooks into spears.[15] Woman has been wrested from the sacred protection of the hearthside and driven into industries for which through the ages, men thought she was unfitted. The innocence of childhood has been somehow betrayed, and in vast quarters of the earth little children scarce know how to smile. Every terror that the imagination can conjure up, stalks about the streets of many countries. Nakedness and starvation are not unusual. Bestiality and brutality have driven out the human impulses of men and women. The whole world is in a state of terror.[16]

Even here in America, where for a comparatively short time we have learned the meaning of war, we have been face to face with conditions so gruesome and so terrible as in our nightmares, we had not pictured. All our standards of living and thinking have been upset. Gritting our teeth with grim purpose, we have accepted the conditions which the times lay upon us as the price that we must pay for our part in the saving of humanity from the rapacious beast that would devour it. Almost overnight, we have come to a realizing sense of the worthlessness of money and material goods. By a somewhat slower process but with no

---

[15] Echoing Joel 4: 10, an ironic reversal of the famous verse in Isa. 2: 4.

[16] With this powerful rhetorical passage, compare his words in 'A War without Armistice', delivered on Sunday, 11 Nov. 1928: 'Nobody won the War. Everybody lost. The world is poorer today because it was fought. Mankind was brutalized by it. It idealized the rule of might and set brute force upon a throne. It cut down the flower of many nations. It destroyed beyond repair property, the value of which the human mind cannot conceive. It ravaged the treasures of art that many generations had been required to create and to gather. It set back civilization by a thousand years. It turned the hand of time backward. Worse than all this, however, it hardened the souls of men. It robbed them of their divinity. It made them beasts and brutes' (pp. 1–2).

less certainty and conviction, we have resigned ourselves to the fact that even our children are but instruments in the hand of God through whose sacrifice we must speed the day of making life worth living in the world.

At first, the war seemed distant from us and we looked on with horror indeed but it did not touch us as perforce it did a little later. We waited and we watched the conditions over there, some thought longer than we should. We cried down the plea uttered by earnest men for a greater preparedness.[17] We were entirely sure that no enemy could touch us and no foe could send his ships unto our shores. We were a nation impregnable, we said. But gradually in the face of the tragic events familiar to you all, our thought upon these matters changed and we began to play our part in the great world conflict. As the meaning of it all gradually dawned upon us, divisions ceased and we stood a united nation with but one hope, one prayer, and one purpose; a nation united never again to be separated, in fact or in spirit. Willingly, we gave our treasure to the cause. Willingly, we sent our boys to the front.[18] Proudly, we counted the stars in our service flags and sadly yet proudly, once again, we noted how here and there the star of blue gave way to the more sacred star of gold.[19] And still, we did not wince nor whine, and pray God, this people never shall assume the coward's role so long as the struggle in which we are engaged has not been nobly and wholly won.

And yet, in the face of all these things, our enemy's plea for peace could not have been without its power to lure the weak and the troubled among us. It would be asking too much of human nature that immediate sorrow should not eagerly grasp at a chance of surcease and that many a mother's heart torn and bleeding with anxiety for her boy over there should not have read with a thrill of joy the proffer of peace made by our enemies, and reading, hoped that it might

[17] On the 'preparedness' controversy, see the introduction to Sermon 19 above by Stephen S. Wise.

[18] Cf. Franklin's sermon on 'Student Day', 22 Apr. 1917: 'In a word, we have heard the call to serve . . . All honor to those who are willing to give their youth and their strength when they are called upon, and only disdain and shame for the portion of those craven cowards who slink from the duty that spells danger. Thank God, there are not many such in the rank of our American people, and it shall stand to the enduring credit of our young college men that with unexampled eagerness and enthusiasm they have put themselves at the service of their country in its hour of need' (pp. 1–2).

[19] Referring to the practice, developed in the First World War, of families hanging a banner with a blue star for each child in military service; organizations took up this manner of honouring their members. Joseph Krauskopf spoke on 'Consecration of the Temple Service Flag' (with 'four score of stars in its field of white') at Congregation Keneseth Israel, Philadelphia, on 25 Nov. 1917. For each casualty of the war, a gold star was placed over the blue (<www.usflag.org/service.flag.html>, checked 3 June 2007). On the motif of pride (mixed with sadness) at the loss of Jewish soldiers, see also Sermon 14 above by Adler, p. 293.

be accepted. After all, the mother's heart might be forgiven for hoping for such a consummation. Nor must we judge too harshly those who, wearied of living in a world in which every holy passion seems to have been destroyed would be ready, without too keen an appreciation of all the consequences involved, to end the horror at any cost. Nor yet again must we permit ourselves to brand as traitorous those who, in the first moment that the news of our enemy's plea was printed, began to estimate the tens of thousands—perhaps the millions—of lives of young men that might be spared if cessation of hostilities might have been immediately accomplished.

In dealing with situations such as this, we must not expect too much of human nature. Only in the strongest amongst us does the power of resistance not break down some times. Emotion will now and then have its sway and reason and the better judgment will give way before it. But men and women, this is no time for weak emotionalism or for the yielding to our softer passions. It is a time when all the virility, all the strength, all the manhood of our being must come into play. It is a time when every proposition involving the fate of the nations must be coldly and clearly analyzed with calm judgment and in the light of its bearings upon the future. From what I have already said, you will understand clearly that I am not callous to the abounding suffering and that the mother's heart, full of prayer that her boy may soon return to her from the bloody battlefield, finds no rebuff at my hands.

On the other hand, it would be unworthy of a nation that has risen to the supreme heights of patriotism that we have scaled, were it ready at a time like this to sacrifice the whole future of civilization for what would be at best a temporary rest. To yield now to the pleading of the foe would put the stain of dishonor upon our standards to which in these last times new lustre has been added. To be willing to enter into any sort of a compromise with a nation degraded as no nation in human history has before been degraded, or indeed to stand ready to negotiate with a brutalized people whose national soul has not been chastened, but that is brought to its knees merely through considerations of expediency, or to consent even to a momentary cessation of hostilities with a regime that does not yet understand the iniquity of its philosophy, would be to bring upon our heads not only a well-deserved humiliation at this time, but as well, the disdain and even the hatred of those future generations whose security would be imperiled by our cowardice.

To sum it up in a word: for this great people to veer from its present purpose of utterly destroying a national philosophy which is subversive of the peace of the whole world and which sets at naught the rights of men, which exalts physical strength and puts its trust for supremacy in mere brutality, would be not only unmanly but distinctly un-American. So long as through the voice and arteries of this great people there flows the blood of true Americanism, there shall be no such yielding. We will sacrifice and struggle to the bitter end, that our children and our children's children may be free from the menace that has gripped the modern nations by the throat.

Perhaps there are those who, intense in their Americanism, and deeply resolved as any that we shall not turn from our purpose, are yet surprised that words such as these should be spoken from the pulpit, and in the name of religion. Religion, they say, should teach love and forgiveness and forbearance. Religion, they say, should close its eyes to iniquity and by loving persuasion seek to convert the individual or the nation that sins. Such a position, however, will not be taken by those who understand the spirit of Judaism. Well can I understand that those who have been fed upon the soft sentimentalities of our sister religion might in these times assume such an attitude. Strangely enough, as they who read history must know, a religion in whose name and under whose banner bloody crusades have been carried on through the ages, has been philosophically a teacher of peace. Peace has ever been inscribed upon the banner of the church and the man of Nazareth called by the church 'The Son of God'; nay, the very embodiment of the God-head has been most frequently described as 'The Prince of Peace'.

Moreover, the pulpit of our sister church has never wearied of flinging into the teeth of the Jew the charge that our ethical system was based in a crude and cruel conception of Justice while that of the church was based in a nobler and a gentler conception of love. Today, the church has had to reverse its preachments, and apologetically its expounders are seeking with might and main to justify their attitude toward war which is in contradiction not so much to their practices as to their preachments. Nay, even the greatest of their Bible teachers are by species of mental gymnastics trying to prove that heretofore they were entirely mistaken in believing that love and forgiveness were the highest of virtues.[20]

So far as the Jew is concerned, no such apology and no such explanation is needful. While the Jew has never been a militant people in the ordinary sense of

---

[20] For the challenges posed to Christian thinkers in dealing with the apparently pacifistic and non-violent statements attributed to Jesus, with a critique of pacifist doctrine, see Hoover, *God, Germany, and Britain*, 102–18.

that term, he has never, never, through all the centuries of his existence, sanctioned as an ethical ideal a peace that was based in compromise with evil. His
God is not denominated 'The Prince of Peace'; He is called 'Adonai Zvo-oth'
(The God of Armies), the God who would lead his people unto battle against
those who would defy the principles of justice and humanity. It is in the light of
this fact that one must interpret many of the earlier chapters of Jewish history.[21]

In the name of God, the Jew was commanded to wipe out—root and
branch—the Canaanitish nations whom they were to dispossess.[22] Why, was it
mere blood-thirstiness on the part of the Jew or of his God that drove them on
to battle? No, it was not that. But it was the idea that compromise with those
whose trust was in their brutal strength, could only mean the despair and the
destruction of future generations.[23] In the period of the Kings of Israel, we find
the Jew battling against foes whose ideals were subversive of right living. We
find a Samuel, that stalwart advocate of righteousness, flaying without mercy a
King Saul because he dared to compromise with a King of the Amalekites—
that crafty and cruel nation (1 Sam 1: 7–33). We find a prophet of Israel crying
out in later days, 'Peace, there is no peace for the wicked'.[24]

The Jew, in his ethical system, has recognized throughout, the basic truth
that to compromise with evil is to condone evil. His sentiment is not inaptly
summed up in that suggestive third chapter of the Book of Ecclesiastes wherein
we are told that there is a time to kill as there is a time to heal, that there is a time
for war even as there is a time for peace (Eccles. 3: 3, 8).

[21] Contrast the emphasis on the pacific (though not pacifistic) character of Judaism in Franklin's
'A Warrior's Message of Peace', delivered on 13 Dec. 1914: 'The martial melody has seldom reflected the spirit of the Jews' thinking. Such battles as he has fought have, for the most part, been blood-
less . . . If triumphs he has won, they have been spiritual triumphs and not such as the warrior brings
home from the stripped bodies or the ruined cities of the fallen foe. If fields on which the Jew has
fought have run red with blood, it has usually been the Jew's blood that has reddened them. Never
has he been the aggressor in war . . . In light of these facts, it is not to be marveled at that among
the outstanding heroic figures in the history of the Jew, there are few heroes of the battlefield'
(pp. 1–2). German Christian preachers at this time used Old Testament passages referring to validate the concept of a 'holy' war between nations (Hoover, *God, Germany, and Britain*, 115).
[22] Deut. 7: 1–2. Such passages, which appears to mandate something akin to what we call genocide, were cited by antisemites as proof of the bloodthirsty character of the Jews (e.g. Thomas
Paine in *The Age of Reason* characterized Num. 31: 13–18 as 'too horrid for humanity to read or for
decency to hear', and the book of Joshua as 'military history of rapine and murder . . . savage and
brutal'). See Sermon 2 above by Solomon Hirschel, n. 31. It was indeed unusual for Jews to cite
this passage as proof that no compromise with the enemy was compatible with the divine will.
[23] Cf. the continuation in Deut. 7: 3–5, which describes the danger of seduction to worship
other gods. The formulation 'compromise with those whose trust was in their brutal strength'
seems to apply more to the rhetoric about Germany than to the biblical descriptions of the
Canaanites.        [24] Cf. Isa. 48: 22 and 57: 21; Rashi on Isa. 57: 21; *Leviticus Rabbah* 17: 1.

[PERORATION]

And so I feel, friends, that in bringing these thoughts to you this morning, not only for the purpose of justifying the authorities of this nation for the manly and American stand that they have taken at this crucial time in human history, but also for the purpose of warning those whose emotions might make them weak in their resistance against the lure of peace, that I am bringing to you a message strictly in accord with Jewish sentiment and Jewish ethics. Once more are we grateful in the light of all this, to realize how the things for which our country stands in these tremendous times are the same things for which, through untold centuries, the Jew has stood faithfully and fearlessly. Once again are we grateful that as the battle which this people has been so heroically waging has been in closest consonance with the age-long struggle of the Jew, so shall that righteous peace which in God's own time shall be brought about by the complete vanquishment of the foe of civilization be in harmony with the peace idea of Israel.

Bravely then and proudly, as Americans and Jews, let us continue to put our face against a peace of compromise, buoyed up, should we for a moment hesitate, by the sentiment of the Prophet already quoted, 'En Sholom L'Rshoim' (There can be no peace to the wicked).[25] Amen.

[25] See n. 24 above.

# PART V

# THE SECOND WORLD WAR

# CHAPTER TWENTY-TWO

## ABRAHAM H. FEINBERG
# AMERICA'S HOUR OF DECISION

### 13 SEPTEMBER 1939
### (ROSH HASHANAH)

**TEMPLE BETH EL, ROCKFORD, ILLINOIS**

As in the years 1870, 1914, and 2001, the High Holy Days of 1939 were overshadowed by the outbreak of war. By Rosh Hashanah, much of Poland had already fallen to the German onslaught, while Russian troops had invaded and occupied its eastern sector. Britain and France were gearing up to fight an enemy that appeared if anything more formidable than twenty-five years earlier.

For some American rabbis, the mood was similar to that of September 1914 and September 1870, when, as we have seen, many felt that the outbreak of war among the civilized nations of Europe itself reflected a catastrophic failure of humane values. The opening words of Israel Levinthal's sermon on the first day of Rosh Hashanah reflects a profound sense of gloom:

We find ourselves today in one of the saddest moments in world history, and certainly in Jewish history. The impossible has come to pass. It is only twenty-one years since the close of the last world war. We had imagined that the world had come of age—that it would know better. But no—the world refuses to learn, and the result is that it finds itself once more in the throes of destruction . . . 'The world is hanging on nothingness' (Job 26: 7) . . . It is hanging on a thread; any moment it may fall in ruins. All civilization is threatened with annihilation![1]

Yet there was a significant difference: now a war had been proclaimed against a nation that represented in its ideology and its behaviour a repudiation of all they believed in. This time there could be no question of neutrality; Hitler's belligerent, aggressive, antisemitic Nazi regime had to be defeated. But what was to be America's role in the war?

---

[1] Levinthal, 'Wherefore Is the Earth Destroyed?', 40.

I had long wondered what American rabbis were saying in their September 1939 sermons on this issue: were they calling for the United States to join its former allies in the effort to defeat and destroy Hitler's Germany? The short answer is: they were not. One of the most startling discoveries in my investigation of the material for this book was the consistently anti-interventionist position taken in the American Jewish pulpit at this time. It is not that these rabbis were indifferent to what was happening in Europe. They cared, passionately; many of them had been outspokenly anti-Nazi since the spring of 1933 or before. Some had energetically supported an economic boycott and a boycott of the 1936 Berlin Olympic Games. They detested everything Hitler and his nation represented; they believed that the very survival of the world they recognized was at stake in the outcome of the conflict. Yet I have found no evidence of sermons that drew the conclusion that appears so obvious in retrospect: we must call upon the leaders of our country to do what Britain and France have done, and to stand beside them on the battlefields.

What can explain this reticence, so surprising when we look at this historical moment retrospectively in the light of what we know would later occur? First, there was the legacy of 'the Great War', with its unimaginable toll in human life, leading many to conclude that no evil was as terrible as war itself. Rabbis recalled sermons preached when America had joined the war effort in 1917 in which they had proclaimed the idealistic values of Wilson's oratory about a world safe for democracy, only to discover to their dismay that these ideals bore little relationship to the realities that followed the armistice. War had produced the compromises in American freedoms against which Stephen S. Wise had warned: conscription, censorship, the pressures to conformity of extreme patriotic enthusiasm. The sentiment in American public opinion against repeating the error of engagement in European bloodshed was so strong that President Roosevelt would run for re-election in 1940 on a policy of keeping America out of the war. There was at this time no mass murder of Jews, nor would this begin until the summer of 1941, in the wake of the German invasion of the Soviet Union; the transporting of Jewish populations into death camps would not begin until the spring of 1942. In September 1939, and even in 1940, the condition of central and east European Jewry was not as bad as it had been during the previous war, or in the years that immediately followed it. In short, the case for American intervention seemed far less compelling than it does in the light of the Holocaust that had not yet begun.

High Holy Day sermons, covered by the newspapers of record, provide a fairly consistent picture of what preachers said at this time; though the quotations may not reflect all the nuances of the complete message, they may well be what the listeners remembered. Here is Ira Eisenstein of the Reconstructionist Society for the Advancement of Judaism, asserting that Europe is simply not worth fighting for:

The time is here for those who seek peace to proclaim courageously that our beloved United States must keep itself clear of the intrigues, perfidies, ambitions and plots of the European nations. Why should we involve ourselves in the mess of a continent in which Spain, Austria, Czecho-Slovakia have been betrayed; in which violently anti-Fascist Russia embraces violently anti-Communist Germany; in which ancient wrongs and established feuds are sugar-coated by lofty ideals of freedom and democracy?[2]

Similarly, Benjamin Tintner of Mt Zion Congregation asserted that 'Other peoples may plunge their countries into frightful slaughters. In America we shall guard our peace with care and circumspection, yet with all, with love and with tolerance.' Joseph Lookstein of Kehilath Jeshurun Congregation said, 'As citizens of the world, we are of course profoundly grieved and affected by what seems to lie ahead. Our duty, therefore, is not alone to ourselves, but to all humanity. Our paramount concern and our most earnest prayer in this hour is for peace for our land and for all the world.'[3] Of the essence are prayer and peace; not a call to arms.

Milton Steinberg of the Park Avenue Synagogue emphasized the positive values that must be preserved during 'the horror now being enacted throughout the world':

The efforts to attain a greater measure of truth, to create and interpret the beautiful, to remake our social life into a more equitable pattern are even more essential now than ever, not only because only so can we preserve a reason in action and sanity in mood, but also because it is out of the struggle for the good life that the forces for the reconstruction of man's living will emerge.[4]

This emphasis on preserving humane values for what would follow the war seems perhaps naïve in retrospect—humane values for the world that would emerge from a German victory?—but it was not uncommon. Steinberg's Conservative colleague Israel Levinthal of the Brooklyn Jewish Center used the image of Noah's Ark, safe from the devastating waters of the flood, for America:

The American Jew, like his fellow-citizen of other faiths, is fortunate that he finds himself in an ark of safety, thousands of miles removed from the devastating flood of

---

[2] *New York Times*, 16 Sept. 1939, p. 7.

[3] Ibid. (Tintner and Lookstein). Lookstein's emphasis on prayer and peace is encapsulated most astonishingly in the quotation cited by the *New York Times* from his Kol Nidrei sermon: 'Somewhere in the Vatican a saintly figure, worn through fasting and sleeplessness, stands in reverent prayer for a stricken world. His Eminence the Pope is a symbol of what the world has failed to do and must now do to save itself' (*New York Times*, 23 Sept. 1939, p. 24). The Pope was, of course, Pius XII. For Lookstein's preaching during the war, see his *The Sources of Courage*.

[4] *New York Times*, 15 Sept. 1939, p. 20. In his sermon for the second day of Rosh Hashanah, Steinberg similarly focused on the spiritual quality of life at home: 'The contempt for life which made the war possible, the futilities of culture that does not civilize, the travesties of a morality and religion that are so meaningless as to be suspended—these are the normalities of our existence. It is the duty then of religiously minded Americans to bend their energies to removing from the American society the very manifestations which in violent form are ravaging Europe' (*New York Times*, 16 Sept. 1939, p. 7)

misery and destruction. Ours will be the task, like Noah, to build a new world. We shall have to help in the rebuilding of the old, and, above all, to fashion here in America a new and vital center of Jewish religious and cultural life to carry on the work that has been destroyed in the lands across the sea.[5]

Levinthal's handwritten notes for this sermon provide a more nuanced position:

*We all hope that America will be spared from entering this struggle.* On the other hand, recognize that this is a different war from all previous wars. [not for material benefit, new lands, possessions] This is a war to crush brute force, tyranny, and to preserve democracy. In such a struggle, I fail to see how Americans can say, 'We will shut ourselves up within our ark—don't want to see what is happening—no interest.' In a measure, that same call comes to us, צא מן התבה [Gen. 8: 16], Get Out! We must help in the process of rebuilding. *Not to go to war*, but certainly the President has a keen insight when he asks Revision of the Neutrality Act.[6]

Yet even this recognition that America had a role to play in the European conflict does not place the preacher ahead of the policy of the President.

All of this sets the context for the following sermon, which makes an extended case for American non-intervention despite strong antipathy towards the Nazi regime and the policies that allowed it to flourish.

Abraham H. Feinberg never emerged as a leading figure of the Reform rabbinate, as his life was cut short at age 39. Born in 1907, he was raised in an Orthodox home, but—like many in that generation—decided to study for the Reform rabbinate, attending the University of Cincinnati and the Hebrew Union College, from which he received ordination in 1932. He then served at Temple Beth El in Rockford, Illinois, for ten years, and it was here that he delivered the following sermon. Despite his insistence on this occasion that America should remain out of the fighting, once war was declared against Japan and Germany he supported the war effort and decided to serve as a chaplain; many other rabbis followed the same trajectory.[7] Feinberg, however, was rejected by both the navy and the army for medical reasons.

The sermon for the eve of Rosh Hashanah is divided into two parts that appear to be in tension with each other. The first part is a condemnation of Hitler's Nazi regime and of Hitler as a psychopathic criminal—a John Dillinger on the world stage. Like many other rabbis, the preacher also lashes out against

---

[5] Levinthal, 'As In the Days of Noah' (*New York Times*).

[6] Levinthal, 'As in the Days of Noah' (Israel H. Levinthal Papers), emphasis added. By 12 Apr. 1941, after reviewing the fate of Czechoslovakia, Poland, and Norway, all of which deceived themselves into thinking that they would be safe from German aggression, he wrote in his notes, 'America until recently the same. No room for isolationism' ('Why Has Tragedy Come to the World?').

[7] See e.g. H. Saperstein, 'Must There Be War?' and 'Can Jews Afford to Be Pacifists?', the pacifist sermons of 1936 and 1937, the sentiment against American entry into the war on Rosh Hashanah 1939 ('Unconquered', 69 n. 1), and the decision to enlist as a chaplain ('Farewell', 102).

the self-delusion of European countries that allowed the Nazi regime to survive and flourish despite abundant evidence that Hitler could not be trusted. The second part of the sermon draws a conclusion that seems astonishing today, yet—as we have seen—represents an almost universal consensus among American rabbis at the time: 'impossible as it is to maintain neutrality of opinion, sanity still prescribes neutrality of action'. This second part contains not only an argument to sustain the non-interventionist position, but a rebuke of the failings of American society that need to be corrected. The argument is made without appeal to Jewish sources; the New Year occasion is invoked at the beginning and the end, as the imagery of the final paragraph builds to a rather poignant conclusion.

# SERMON

## [1]

WHEN THE catastrophe of war broke out in 1914, England's Foreign Minister was reported as saying, 'The lights are going out in Europe, everywhere; will they ever be relit in our generation?'[8] As we, Jews, gather on this eve of the Rosh Hashanah, Europe is passing slowly and dreadfully into the valley of the shadows: perturbed, we wonder, how long until the sun of healing will shine again!

Neither sudden nor unexpected has been the explosion, now resounding in the four corners of the earth. As early as 1934, only a year after Hitler seized Power, the Polish Premier, Marshal Piłsudski, saw the inevitable consequences of Nazi re-armament and urged France then, on the ground of treaty-breaking, to wage a preventive war—a war which would have been less of a disaster than a police skirmish and would have, incidentally, crushed Hitlerism.[9] Writers and observers of repute, likewise, presented incontrovertible evidence of the diabolical intentions of the new Nazi regime.

Even more convincing had been the many lying tantrums of the German Fuehrer himself. In a speech of May 21, 1935, he said: 'Germany has neither the wish nor the intention to mix in Austrian internal affairs, or annex, or unite

[8] The most common form of this frequently cited statement by Sir Edward Grey is 'The lights are going out all over Europe; we shall not see them lit again in our lifetime.' It is not easy to document precisely when he said this.

[9] France had been the strongest ally of the new state of Poland since its creation in 1919. When it became clear that Germany was building up its army in violation of the Treaty of Versailles, Piłsudski reportedly proposed to France a joint invasion. There is apparently no documentary evidence of, and no scholarly consensus about, an actual plan for a pre-emptive war against Germany. See Karski, *The Great Powers and Poland*, 184–5; Garlicki, *Józef Piłsudski*, 174–5.

with Austria.'[10] Less than three years later at Berchtesgaden, he told Schuschnigg, 'What is all this nonsense about your independence?'[11]

In a speech delivered in March of 1936, he said, 'Czecho-Slovakia, like Poland, always primarily followed the policy of representing its own national interests. Germany does not desire to attack these states.'[12] In a speech of September 1938, just before the Czecho-Slovak state was destroyed, this promise was solemnly given: 'If this problem (the Sudetan crisis) is solved, there will be no further territorial problems in Europe for Germany.'[13]

Storm signals, therefore, had been hoisted again and again. Reveilles of warning were being sounded hourly. Why, then, did the world of decent men slumber until the strength of morning had passed? Perhaps the statesmanship of Europe was headless and inept! Perhaps Europe's civilized human beings could not conceive the re-enactment of hostility and bloodshed![14] Perhaps they had grown weary of the world's noise and clamor and sought mental repose on the mystic couch of James Hilton's imaginary Shangri-La![15]

Who knows what force or combination of forces dulled the mind of Europe's civilization, that it allowed the vulture in their midst to wax fat and grow mighty in strength! The fact is that that vulture has risen and his out-stretched, flapping wings will obscure for many days to come the light of earthly sanity.[16]

[10] The quotation appears in the newspaper reports of Hitler's Reichstag speech of that date (*New York Times*, 22 May 1935, p. 15).

[11] Hitler 'invited' Kurt von Schuschnigg to a meeting at the Berchtesgaden summer house on 12 Feb. 1938; Schuschnigg was apparently subjected to a private diatribe. Although he left the meeting committed to implementing an agreement he believed was consistent with the earlier German commitments to Austrian independence and arranged for a plebiscite, a German ultimatum, invasion, and Anschluss followed a month later. See Schuschnigg, *The Brutal Takeover*, 180, 188, 192–9. I have not found this precise quotation attributed to Hitler.

[12] Referring to Hitler's Rhineland speech at Karlsruhe, delivered on 12 Mar. 1936, in which he said, 'Germany has neither the intention nor the will to attack France, neither the intention nor the will to attack Czechoslovakia, nor to attack Poland' (*New York Times*, 13 Mar. 1936, p. 14).

[13] Referring to his speech of 26 Sept. at the Sportspalast in Berlin, in which he twice asserted that if the Sudeten territories were ceded, it would be the last German territorial demand in Europe (*New York Times*, 27 Sept. 1938, pp. 1, 17).

[14] A similar statement condemning the European Allies for failure to act against Hitler at an earlier stage was made by Israel Levinthal on this same Rosh Hashanah: 'Britain, France, and their allies bear also a share of responsibility', for they did not make moral issues their primary obligation. 'If they had, they would not have tolerated the rape of Czechoslovakia. If they had, they would have protested against the barbarism of the Nazis all these years!', 'Wherefore Is the Earth Destroyed?', 45–6.

[15] Alluding to Hilton's Utopian novel, *Lost Horizon*, first published in 1933 and made into a film in 1936, in which a group of Europeans whose plane has crashed in the Himalayas are brought to a hidden valley of total tranquillity.

[16] Evoking the metaphor introduced at the beginning of the sermon about the lights going out in Europe.

The fact remains that peace has been pushed beyond the last reach of temporization, that the world is in a state of war, and that men's minds must now become attuned to the harshness of its grim reality.

When a conflagration breaks out, the cause of its origin becomes a matter of constant concern. Sentimental individuals there have been who say that poor Hitler is not altogether to blame. Evil conditions, they say, produced an evil man.[17]

The delusions of kind-hearted people are almost proverbial. The case at hand affords an excellent illustration.

We who would be fair will not understate the poverty of post-war Germany's physical soil or mental climate. We will not minimize either the several harsh provisions of the Treaty at Versailles. We may even grant that Hitler became the illegitimate offspring of Allied callousness and Teutonic chaos. But we who would be fair must also add that an evil man can create intolerable conditions.

John Dillinger, the gangster, was the product also of a corrupt and faulty environment, but when the peace and security of decent citizens became menaced, public sympathy ended and the machinery of the law crushed that malignant influence.[18] If society could not tolerate the crimes of John Dillinger, which, comparatively speaking, were only minor, whence then is derived sympathy for the crimes of Nazi Nihilism?

Condemned before the bar of human decency, repudiated and excoriated even by fellow-countrymen, Adolf Hitler stands convicted as the world's most dangerous criminal—a kidnapper wanted for the kidnapping of Kurt Schuschnigg, an arson-bug wanted for the burning of the Reichstag, a vandal who smeared over Germany's art treasures with concentration camps, a perjurer who violated solemn pledges, a thief who broke down the gates of Austria and Czecho-Slovakia, a murderer who has shattered the lives of innocent Jews, killed the Republic of Germany, death-purged opponents and associates, bombed Polish women and children, and upon whose head lies the guilt for the blood now being shed—German and Allied—in the present European catastrophe.[19]

---

[17] For a survey of various attempts to 'explain' Hitler as a product of circumstances in his environment or of his idiosyncratic psychology, see Rosenbaum, *Explaining Hitler*. Cf. the reference in Sermon 23 below by Jacob Rudin to a tendency in the Christian religious press to empathize with and pray for Hitler; also Solomon Freehof of Pittsburgh, preaching on 13 Apr. 1941: 'There have been people in recent years who have been obsessed by an urgent desire to be fair-minded to the tyrant of Germany' ('Minds Confused', 23).

[18] After a daring escape from an Indiana prison in March 1934, the well-known bank robber was declared 'Public Enemy Number One' by the FBI; he was shot to death in an FBI ambush on 22 July 1934.

[19] The rhetoric in this passage seems a bit excessive, overwhelming the listener with a quick procession of charges that does not allow time for reflection (*Was* Schuschnigg *kidnapped* by

This criminal maniac is now wanted, like a John Dillinger, dead or alive! Let no one be deluded by the casual observations of naïve travelers[20] or with sentimental talk about injustice done to post-war Germany. Even Thomas Mann, Germany's greatest living writer, has declared that this is not the issue now.[21] A seed of sympathy for the cause of Hitlerism may well sprout later into weeds of regret.

## [11]

Faced by the crisis of war abroad and the involvement of Canada here, America's hour of decision is now at hand. Abhoring as all do the Nihilistic terror of Nazism, does it become then our moral duty to make common cause with the forces of democracy against the legions of a snarling autocracy?

Even assuming that Poland, a land of oppressive bigotry, isn't worth saving, that the sincerity of the Chamberlain–Daladier regimes has not yet been proved,[22] the preview of a civilization scarred with the swastika of Nazism affords a spectacle too horrible for contemplation.

Between the banner of democracy and the rag [flag?] of piracy, the moral decision of America will never be in doubt. Yet impossible as it is to maintain neutrality of opinion, sanity still prescribes neutrality of action.[23] There is a heavy burden of pain in our hearts over the tragedy which has befallen Europe, in the realization that the earth still swollen with the bones of a conflict already waged is being cleft asunder hourly to inter the hopes and dreams of this generation's Lost Battalion.[24]

Shall we add the bones of our continent, too? The hatred of war in America has become far too deep-rooted. The American distrust for international

Hitler? Do we know *for sure* that the Nazis set fire to the Reichstag? What does he mean by 'smeared over Germany's art treasures with concentration camps'? Is someone who violates a pledge a *'perjurer'*?). Nevertheless, it may have been an effective, climactic moment, building to the end of the first section of the sermon.

[20] Referring to positive reports about progress made in Hitler's Germany by many visitors, not all of whom were naïve—among them Britain's Lloyd George.

[21] I am not certain to which statement the preacher is referring, but it would fit the sentiments in a passage in Mann's vituperative essay on 'one of the foulest pages in history, this story of the betrayal of the Czechoslovak Republic by European democracy': 'It is a sight unprecedented in history. By a combined policy of non-resistance they have put Germany where she would have been if she had been victorious in 1914; more they cannot do to atone for the blunders and stupidities of the peace. Their souls are free from guilt, they have no more penances to perform; and that may weigh in the position they take up towards future threats and demands' ('This Peace', 183–4).

[22] i.e. the sincerity of Britain and France to fight to the end on behalf of Poland.

[23] Here for the first time, and perhaps going against the grain of almost all that has preceded it, the preacher states his position on America's role in the European conflict.

[24] Six hundred American GIs advancing into the dense Argonne Forest on 2 Oct. 1918 found themselves completely surrounded by enemy forces. Though low on supplies and ammunition, they refused to surrender. Two hundred of them emerged six days later. A popular film called *The Lost Battalion*

intrigue remains still unabated. We Jews, too, know what the meaning of this or any war can be. Even when peace is declared at the end of war, there is for us still not peace: the hysteria in the aftermath of war would gouge out our eyes with its bayonets of prejudice and sear our lungs with its poison-gasses of hate.[25]

But there is still another consideration, one grounded in morality, which renders the call of neutrality imperative. As the iron hand of Mars turns the earth into shambles, as the jaws of brutality open wider and wider, the danger of a pestilence of feverish hatred spreading everywhere and striking down even civilized countries becomes menacingly real. Unless there is a beacon of sanity somewhere, the whole human race may go down shattered by a wild madness. In the days ahead, therefore, there will be need for a place of shelter—far away from the vicinity of aerial warfare or the noise of long-range artillery—where the lamp of civilization may continue to burn with an undiminished flame. Where else on the earth's surface but this American continent can that haven of refuge be found?[26]

Serving the cause of neutrality, America in this way will serve humankind most and civilization best. Let no one imagine that this chosen role of destiny is some slacker's retreat. As custodians of the still, small voice of conscience, our task in America will [be] not less but infinitely greater. Now entrusted with the key to the civilization of tomorrow, our obligation to the earth's still unnumbered generations looms enormously large. On the shoulders of this continent rests a burden of responsibility. We dare not lose our way.

Let no one imagine either that neutrality will not have its dangers. There is danger, first of all, as the toll of sacrifices mounts in a war-torn world, that we shall lose faith in ourselves, faith in the cause for which we have been called. There is danger that we shall lose hope, hope in the possibilities of man and the ultimate triumph of truth and right. But the danger, greatest of all, hinges on the possibility that democracy may collapse here from within, just as it may now explode in Europe from without . . . [*sic*].

was released in 1919. In this passage, the preacher seems to be alluding to the devastating losses rather than the heroism. Jewish soldiers were known to have played a significant role in the Lost Battalion; see Sterba, *Good Americans*, 3, 8, 181. I am grateful to Jonathan Sarna for this reference.

[25] This is a fine example of a lesson being drawn from the aftermath of the First World War and applied to the new situation. Note the use of military metaphors from the earlier war to describe social conflict.

[26] This argument of the need for a 'beacon of sanity', a 'haven of refuge' for humane values, from which civilization can be rebuilt after the war, distinguishes the thinking of the 'moral' non-interventionists from the 'America First' non-interventionists, who argued primarily from a strategic conception of American self-interest and the incapacity of the United States to solve the problems of a traditional Old World power struggle. For an example of the latter, see Oswald Garrison Villard in *Nation* (Sept. 1939): 'the United States cannot settle the future of Europe; only Europe itself can do that' (cited in Jonas, *Isolationism in America*, 235; cf. also 236, 240–1).

Neither the fact of physical geography nor the pious expenditure of shrieks and sighs can give the toxin of immunity against national disintegration and decay. The neutrality of peace, therefore, involves risks fully as serious as the bombardment of war. God only knows what lies ahead for us all in these harrowing times! How we shall fare in the days to come will depend in no small measure on the greater moral resources that this generation can muster. Spiritual fortifications we shall need, even more impregnable than any Maginot line.[27] If in the hour of military combat soldier[s] vow obedience to their high command, can we, the builders of neutrality, give less to the supreme command of conscience?

Dare we allow the greatest enemy of democracy, poverty—which all have perpetuated in selfishness—to break out in 'grapes of wrath!'[28] Dare we indulge still in the luxury of creedal bigotry or racial antagonism? Is this not an hour which calls for a new kind of brotherhood—the brotherhood of Jew and Christian, of negro and white? Is this not an hour to emphasize not the things which divide, but the things which unite, and to unfurl above our heads the banner of our common humanity? And thus bound in vision and purpose, we may move, serenely, hopefully, confidently, from this eve of the New Year through many years, in an America where there will be no black-out of democracy, no black-out of human brotherliness, no 'black-out of peace'.[29]

If our hearts be saddened this night at the turn of European events, let our spirit of faith and hope remain unshaken. The darkness now descending upon the face of the earth is but the twilight sleep of an expectant motherhood,[30] the cry of anguish we now hear represents the travail of the earth ere she give life to a new-born civilization.[31] Even in our day we shall behold the children of that coming civilization standing, as if on a bridge, suspended aloft by great cables spun from the golden strands of peace and liberty, who will look on dictator skulls and concentration-camp debris floating toward the sea. A civilization whose children will look down on godlessness passing by and will then look up and see God.

May this, the beginning of a new year, bring the beginning of a new era.

[27] The supposedly impregnable line of fortifications constructed by France on its border with Germany, which would be bypassed by the Germans in their spring 1940 invasion of France.

[28] Alluding to the 'Battle Hymn of the Republic' and the title of John Steinbeck's great novel, published in 1939. With this sentence the preacher introduces a brief passage of exhortation to social reform.

[29] Echoing Roosevelt's 'Fireside Chat' of 3 Sept. 1939: 'As long as it remains within my power to prevent, there will be no black-out of peace in the United States' (*Rendezvous with Destiny*, 160).

[30] Referring perhaps to the actual darkening during the evening service, but reprising the metaphor of the lights going out in Europe from the sermon's first sentence.

[31] Perhaps an allusion to the traditional Jewish 'birth pangs of the Messiah' metaphor, though without explicit invocation of messianic language.

# CHAPTER TWENTY-THREE

## JACOB PHILIP RUDIN
# GOD IN THE BLACKOUT

### 2 OCTOBER 1940
### (EVE OF ROSH HASHANAH)

**TEMPLE BETH-EL OF GREAT NECK
NEW YORK**

DURING THE MONTHS preceding the High Holy Days of 1940, the war in Europe had taken a terrible toll on the morale of Jews in Britain and the United States. The German blitzkrieg of the spring led to the rapid conquest of Denmark and Norway, and of the Netherlands and Belgium, and the retreat of Allied forces at Dunkirk. Especially shattering was the fall of France in June. By the summer, German armed forces were in control of territory stretching from the Atlantic Ocean to eastern Poland. In August the air offensive against Britain began, with the bombing of London starting on 7 September.

Preaching to a congregation of fellow German refugees in the Overflow Service at Hampstead Synagogue on Rosh Hashanah (held in a separate hall for those people who could not be accommodated in the main sanctuary), Rabbi Ignaz Maybaum tried to articulate their feelings:

> During these days before our Jewish New Year's festival we here in London have night and day had death, devastation and homelessness in front of our eyes. Each of us had to ask, When will my turn come? Will the 'severe decree', as the New Year's Day service has it, spare me and mine? We asked ourselves that question while the German planes roared overhead.

He then continued to cast the role of his congregants in heroic terms, as protagonists in the struggle:

> We here in London are with our wives and our children in the midst of the battlefield. German barbarism has wiped out all distinction between the military and the civilian population. Totalitarian war recognizes no difference between the battlefield and the hinterland. The world views the London battlefield, and the heroism it admires is not only that of the men in uniform. There is also the civilian heroism.[1]

---

[1] Maybaum, *Man and Catastrophe*, 121, 122.

In London, even coming to the synagogue to pray on these holy days entailed a considerable measure of risk.

American rabbis, though showing no more inclination to urge American entry into the war than a year earlier, approached the holy days very much aware of the crisis faced by the British in the face of the Nazi onslaught from the air. 'Grant the men and women of the British Empire the vision which will sustain their morale and strengthen their faith in the force of right rather than in the power of might', prayed Herbert Goldstein of New York's West Side Institutional Synagogue on the sabbath preceding Rosh Hashanah. 'God give victory to the great English-speaking people in its fight for the democratic way of life', said the emeritus rabbi of Congregation Emanu-El in a radio broadcast.[2]

Jacob Philip Rudin was born at Malden, Massachusetts, in 1902. As a Harvard undergraduate, he was deeply affected by hearing Stephen S. Wise on a visit to the campus during his junior year, describing the experience later as a kind of epiphany: 'I heard a man speak as I had never heard a man speak before . . . I knew then and there that I would go to the Jewish Institute of Religion if Dr. Wise would have me.'[3] Upon graduation from Harvard, he entered the third class of the newly established Institute in New York. Founded by Wise, the JIR was officially independent of any of the formal religious movements within Judaism; its commitment to Zionism and to addressing the problems of world Jewry was far stronger than that of the Hebrew Union College in Cincinnati. Following his ordination in 1928, Rudin served for two years as assistant to Wise in the Free Synagogue of New York, a role that provided him with an optimal opportunity to observe and learn from the leadership and preaching of his mentor. In 1930 he went to Temple Beth-El of Great Neck, where the sermon reproduced here was delivered. In June 1942 Rudin volunteered for the chaplaincy and served in the navy in the Pacific theatre throughout the rest of the war. Returning, he remained at his flourishing Great Neck congregation for the rest of his active career, also serving terms as president of the Central Conference of American Rabbis and president of the Synagogue Council of America.

The sermon below reflects an intensifying crisis of faith that we saw emerging in sermons from the First World War, and that would now become a prevalent motif. 'Where is God in this blackout of humanity? How can He permit this savagery to come to pass? How can He allow the destruction of little children, of cities and of homes to go on unchecked?' Rudin asks rhetorically, voicing the questions of his congregants and confessing that he too has wrestled with them. He then, of course, provides an answer, shifting the responsibility from God to human folly and indifference. The 'blackout' experienced in very real terms throughout so many British cities becomes a

---

[2] *New York Times*, 29 Sept. 1940, p. 6.

[3] Rudin, 'Founder's Day Address', 3–4; cf. H. Saperstein, 'A Prince in Israel', 148, incl. n. 1.

metaphor expressing the darkening of the moral landscape, with innocent human beings suffering because of the evil of some and the callousness of others. Throughout the relatively unstructured discourse, the leitmotif of the title frequently recurs: God is indeed present in the blackout, present with the anguished victims, waiting for human beings to learn the lesson of their folly and return to Him. Whether and how the Jewish people in Europe will survive these 'evil days' are questions left unresolved.

# S E R M O N

A RABBI of the older generation said that the war years of '14–'18 were a nightmare for him, when he entered his pulpit week after week in struggle and torment. As he looks back, he says, he does not know how he stood it. I heard his words, not altogether understanding them. It is no harder, I said to myself, to stand in a pulpit in wartime than in peacetime. God's laws are eternal and changeless. War or no war, Jews with conviction know where they stand.[4]

And now we are in another war and in an age of frightfulness and destruction when the imagination is beggared and men's spirits are darkened and their hearts ashamed at the spectacle of bestiality and cruelty and murder.[5] God's laws, although they are indeed eternal and changeless, take on another aspect. They do look different in the glow of incendiary bombs and against the growling, angry background of explosion and fire and death.

Now I know what he meant. No generation of rabbis ever faced a more difficult task than does the one of which I am a part. We see about us a world in disintegration. Jewish life is tortured and hard pressed. Melancholy and despair ride the heavens, glowering birds of prey feeding on the broken hearts of a people well-nigh bereft of hope and faith.

What can we say? What can *I* say? It would be simple to pour forth my own agony, to join my sorrow to your sorrow, to add my questions to yours, the questions that beat like pounding surf against the shore of my inner life and being. I could point up our misfortunes and analyze our tragedy. I could berate and criticize. I could blame and accuse.

[4] The preacher is admitting his earlier naivety to his listeners, leading to his emphasis on the difficulty of the preaching task during times of catastrophe.

[5] It should be noted that at this time the full extent of the devastation was still to come; the invasion of the Soviet Union was nine months in the future, and the mass murder of European Jewry would not begin until the summer of 1941.

But I shall not. I have fought through the tangle of my own fears and doubts and questions. I have hewn some kind of path through the trackless waste of my own darkness and despair.[6] I have found certain answers. In my own searchings I have been helped.

The heavens are not altogether dark for those who lift their eyes unto the hills.[7] Some stars twinkle through and a song can be heard behind the moaning and the cry. I can promise you that during these Holy Days this pulpit will utter no words of despair and hopelessness. Nor will Jews be criticized and attacked and castigated.

I envisage my task on these Holy Days in this dread year as a task of bolstering weakened spirits, of finding comfort and hope and encouragement for the sheep of the flock of Israel. I trust, then, that these pulpit addresses for the Yomim Noraim, the Days of Awe, will bring some help and comfort, that they will offer some degree of inspiration and aid.[8]

And with this idea in mind, I address myself to the central question that flung itself mockingly upon my mind. The question which has been asked me time and time again, the question which I know is in your minds and upon your hearts.

Where is God in this blackout of humanity?[9] How can He permit this savagery to come to pass? How can He allow the destruction of little children, of cities and of homes to go on unchecked?

I asked these questions, too. There is an answer. I said to myself: Now you want miracles to happen! You want man to permit the human spirit to be deprived and degraded across almost a decade of dreadful years. You want a world to sit quietly by while a Hitler is swollen to gigantic and monstrous proportions, infusing his nation with hatred, and poison and falsehood.

You want all this to go along unchecked and unimpeded and then when the floodgates are opened and the world is almost drowned in the rushing torrent of a destruction of its own making, then we turn *for the first time* in our agony and say to God, 'A miracle! Help us! A miracle! Where art Thou, O God, in the blackout?'[10]

---

[6] Note how the preacher has established that, whatever basis for hope comes in the course of the sermon, it is the result of a painfully difficult inner struggle with doubt, fear, and dismay.

[7] Echoing Ps. 121: 1.                [8] The end of the introductory component of the sermon.

[9] The question 'Where is God?' echoes the biblical challenge in Ps. 42: 4 (cf. the quite different use by David Einhorn at n. 81, and the many contemporary examples cited in the Introduction, n. 213). The concrete wartime reality of the blackout as protection against bombers is extended as a metaphor for the human situation in a world war.

[10] The question introduced as a painfully serious challenge a few moments before is here transformed into an ironically foolish question. As is typical of liberal preachers and theologians, Rudin shifts the responsibility for catastrophe from God to the failures of human beings.

There are no miracles. This world *we* have fashioned, not with God, but without God; not through God, but by excluding God; not in God, but despite God. And there are no miracles. We created the Frankenstein that is Hitler and the grotesque monster has turned and would destroy us.

Where is God, then? God is in the blackout. God is in the blood and misery, in the tumbled homes, in the destroyed cities. He is in the air raid shelters. He is in the heavens that rain destruction.[11] We have dragged His purity through the mire and touched His holiness with sin and uncleanness. God is in the war because men refused to fashion peace and to live in brotherhood. Man has made his choice. And out of his own tragedy and infinite pain, he must learn the lesson of placing God in the blackout.

I have found this answer because I see the world always as a spiritual world. I see it moved by laws of morality and of God, even as on a lower level, I see it moved by the laws of nature and of physical science.

I am under no delusion of why there is a war. I *know why!* I am a Jew. The laws of morality and of the spirit were rendered inoperative by mankind against me. I knew it could not stop there.[12] God is God and His law must be fulfilled.

The others, they did not see it. Many *still* do not see it.[13]

One of the greatest Christian preachers this country has ever known has said in a sermon on the war:

This war is not primarily about humanitarianism or democracy. The Nazis, with a cruelty for which history never will forgive them, have persecuted the Jews; but so, too, the Polish Jews have been for years among the most wretched in the world, and the persecution of the Jews could have gone on, as it has gone on for centuries, with no war started about it. This war is not about that. Christianity and democracy are in my faith intimately intertwined, and, of course, our sympathies are with the democracies against the dictatorships. But this war is not primarily about democracy ... This conflict does involve issues that will affect the democratic cause, but at bottom it is a fight for the balance of political power in Europe.[14]

[11] The theological stance reflected here is to make God not the perpetrator of the destruction, or an unconcerned bystander, but one of its victims.

[12] Jewish leaders in the United States protesting against the anti-Jewish policies of the Nazi regime after Hitler's accession to power insisted that not just the Jews but all humane values were endangered by Nazism.

[13] An allusion perhaps to American isolationists who were arguing that the United States was being pushed towards involvement in the European war by Jews who had their own parochial agenda.

[14] Fosdick, 'The Ethical Problems of Neutrality', 432. This sermon was delivered on Armistice Sunday, 12 November 1939, and subsequently republished in a collection of contemporary American speeches that Rudin must have read. This is a strong anti-interventionist sermon, in which the preacher states that 'were the United States to enter the war, I would have to be a conscientious objector' (p. 428) and insists that 'we are under the solemnest obligation to the world to stay out of

Harry Emerson Fosdick is wrong! This war *is* about the Jews![15] It's about those very Polish Jews whose persecution, he says, could have gone on for centuries into the future. This war is about the indifference of the world that let that persecution go on.

This war is about the German Jews who were hounded and torn and crushed into the Nazi mire. This war is about injustice concerning which men kept silent, about unrighteousness that men accepted, about savagery that men said was an internal affair of Germany.

This war is about the repudiation of God's words that men spat upon when they spat upon the Jews and rent to shreds when they tore Jewish flesh.[16] This war is about democracy, about freedom and liberty. It's about all that men hold dear.

And now God's word thunders back upon the ears of mankind.

> For though you wash thee with nitre,
> and take thee much soap,
> yet thine iniquity is marked before Me,
> saith the Lord God. (Jer. 2: 22)

This is now the day of reckoning, the day of carnage and destruction because man is foolish and gross and like the beasts of the field.

Then is this war because of the Jews? No, not because of the Jews. But Jews are the microcosm. They reflect within themselves the larger humanity. It is not because mankind was indifferent to Jews, as Jews, that the war came. It was because mankind was indifferent to mankind. Men thought that one could touch his brother's blood and leave his hands unstained. This war is because men let hate loose in the world and did nothing to stop it. This war will last until hate is purged and the world is clean once more.

But where, you ask, is God for us? Where is He for the Jews who are innocent and the first victims of mankind's madness.

God is in the blackout. God is in the war to save His word and His world; and us, the Jews!

Asiatic and European wars' (p. 433). The sentence immediately preceding the quotation cited by Rudin is 'America cannot thus help the world's humanitarianism and democracy by getting into this war'. It is noteworthy that Rudin does *not* challenge Fosdick on this issue. For a review of Protestant preaching in New York during this period, see Lawrence, *Sundays in New York*, 121–73.

[15] Here Rudin is making a strong particularistic statement that most Jewish spokesmen tried to avoid, at least in public. His point, as he goes on to explain, is not that Jews are the cause of the war, or that the war was being fought to save Jews, but that the war is the result of indifference to fundamental values of human decency, an indifference dramatized by the increasing persecution of Jews in Nazi Germany and in Poland.

[16] By this point, the preacher seems to have moved away from his earlier statement that he would *not* 'berate and criticize . . . blame and accuse'.

I have been reading avidly in the religious press of America for a hint of what men are thinking and praying. I have been amazed at the frequent recurrence of one theme. It runs in this pattern. The war is an evil thing. Hitler certainly deserves the strongest condemnation and merits the scourge of men's anger. But we must not revile him. Rather, we send across the ocean our prayers of love, our prayers that Hitler repent his madness. This is the only truly religious spirit, one that preaches no hate but only pity for the sinner.[17]

God is against that washed-out, colorless, unrealistic tommyrot that passes for the name of religion. God is in the blackout with us! For He has said: 'Surely they are My people ... In all their affliction He was afflicted. And the angel of His presence saved them' (Isa. 63: 8). God's word is a word of courage. By the mouth of his prophet Isaiah, he has spoken: 'No weapon that is formed against thee shall prosper; And every tongue that shall rise against thee in judgment, thou shalt condemn' (Isa. 54: 17). God's word is a word of faith. 'Keep ye justice and do righteousness, For my salvation is near to come, and my favor to be revealed' (Isa. 56: 1).

God is with us who cry out against injustice and oppression. God is with us who know when merely pity is not enough. God is with men whose hearts are not hardened. God is with men whose hearts feel pain and suffering. We know pain and we know suffering. And we know courage and we know faith.

In the blackout God dwells and when the last shot is fired and the last plane downed, God will still be here, waiting, waiting for foolish men to come to Him and to listen to His word.

And Israel? What shall Israel say in this dark hour? Do you seek an easy, comfortable answer? There is none. These are evil days, when men must be giants. Out of every abyss of despair and from every lonely mountain top, Israel's voice of fortitude and of patience, of rock-enduring faith has echoed:

'Even though He slay me, yet will I trust in Him' (Job 13: 15). And Israel on this New Year's Day is not afraid. Israel knows, Israel knows that God, Israel's Redeemer, liveth.[18] Amen.

---

[17] Unlike the passage from Fosdick, this is presented as a paraphrase, not a direct quotation; it is not clear to me whether the position that Christians should 'send across the ocean our prayers of love, our prayers that Hitler repent' can be documented in the religious press. Compare the following passages by a pacifist minister in England, published in January 1940: 'Suppose that the whole people of Britain had been fully and whole-heartedly Christian, the influence of their lives would have been so potent that it might have converted Herr Hitler himself.' 'We may rightly say that some of the actions of Herr Hitler are morally indefensible: but we are not in a position to judge Herr Hitler's soul ... Christians will therefore do their utmost to avoid seeming to judge either the rulers or the people of Germany.' 'We may not like the present rulers of Germany; but we can and should love them.' (All three are in Hartill, 'Christians in War-Time', 9, 12, 16). [18] Echoing Job 19: 25.

# CHAPTER TWENTY-FOUR

## ELIEZER BERKOVITS
# TWO SECOND WORLD
# WAR SERMONS

ELIEZER BERKOVITS, son of a Zionist rabbinic court judge, was born in
1908 near the border between Hungary and Romania. He studied in Press-
burg at the yeshiva of the grandson of the celebrated Hungarian rabbi Moses
Sofer (also known as Hatam Sofer), and then continued rabbinical studies in
Germany with Rabbi David Zvi Hoffman and Rabbi Yehiel Weinberg. After
earning a Ph.D. in philosophy from the University of Berlin, in 1933 he was
appointed rabbi of a Berlin synagogue. Arrested by the Gestapo in 1939, he managed to emigrate to Leeds in England, where he served as a congregational rabbi
during the war.

Following the war, he held rabbinical positions in Australia and in Boston,
Massachusetts. In 1969 he helped found a new Orthodox synagogue in Skokie,
Illinois, and later became chairman of the philosophy department at the
Hebrew Theological College of Chicago. He emigrated to Israel in 1975, and
spent the rest of his life in that country, teaching and writing. At his death in
1992 he was considered one of the most important Jewish theologians of the
second half of the twentieth century.[1]

Berkovits's thought regarding the Second World War and the destruction of
European Jewry by the Nazis is generally associated with such books as *Faith
after the Holocaust* (1973) and *With God in Hell: Judaism in the Ghettos and
Deathcamps* (1979). Unlike such works, the product of leisurely if anguished
contemplation of the significance of events after the fact, the sermons published in *Between Yesterday and Tomorrow* (1945), like those of Berkovits's colleagues, bring us back to the actual historical moments when the future course
of the war was agonizingly unclear. At an intercession sermon delivered on
23 March 1941, Chief Rabbi Joseph Hertz found 'heartening encouragement in

---

[1] Biographical material based on a tribute by Shlomo Riskin, *Jerusalem Post*, international edn,
week ending 3 Oct. 1992.

our fight against godlessness and tyranny . . . The Greeks refused to follow the example of feeble surrender set by other Balkan lands.'[2] A few weeks later, the picture had drastically changed for the worse. A poignant expression of a preacher's mood swing during this period is revealed in the notes made by Israel Levinthal for his sermon on the first day of Passover, 12 April 1941, a few weeks before Berkovits delivered the sermon reproduced below, when the British forces, pledged to defend Greece, had not yet been compelled to abandon the Balkans:

Very difficult to preach. The world is changing every day. You prepare a sermon on hopefulness . . . and before the ink [is] dry, must change. Just a few days ago, our heart filled with new hope. Now suddenly all dark again. Darker than before. New land devastated. As for Jews, another 70,000 in Yugoslavia, another 60,000 in Greece. Life blotted out.[3]

The events of the weeks following the beginning of Passover led to even greater dismay. The king of Greece abandoned the mainland on 23 April, shifting his capital to Crete, and British forces withdrew soon after. On 27 April, Solomon Freehof in Pittsburgh expressed dismay at the events to his Sunday morning congregation: 'There is defeat after defeat for England and victory after victory for the Nazis, and our hope for the achievement of human freedom again is deferred and deferred. The unhindered march of Nazi power brings fear and gloom to our spirits.'[4]

In his speech to Parliament on 9 April 1941, Churchill had described a meeting between senior British governmental officials and the Greek king and prime minister, who—with German forces gathering at the Greek border—pledged that Greece would resist a Nazi invasion even without any foreign support. 'That being so', Churchill continued, 'our duty was clear. We were bound in honour to give them all the aid in our power. If they were resolved to face the might and fury of the Huns, we had no doubts but that we should share their ordeal, and that the soldiers of the British Empire must stand in the line with them.'

Eighteen days later, following the German defeat of Greek and British forces, the removal of the Greek capital to Crete, the loss of a considerable number of British ships, and the evacuation of all British forces from Greece with some 3,000 casualties, Churchill, facing substantial political pressure and conceding that 'great disasters have occurred' and that 'the Greeks have been overwhelmed', again reviewed the events in addressing Parliament:

[2] Hertz, 'Intercession Sermon', 63.
[3] Levinthal, 'Why Has Tragedy Come to the World?' Apparently carried away with the evocation of tragedy, Levinthal actually wrote 'another 60,000,000 [Jews] in Greece'.
[4] Freehof, 'Hearts Bowed Down', 37–8.

In their mortal peril the Greeks turned to us for succour. Strained as were our resources we could not say them nay. By solemn guarantee, given before the war, Great Britain had promised them her help. They declared they would fight for their native soil even if neither of their neighbours made common cause with them and even if we left them to their fate.

But we could not do that. There are rules against that kind of thing and to break those rules would be fatal to the honour of the British Empire, without which we could neither hope nor deserve to win this hard war. Military defeat or miscalculation can be remedied. The fortunes of war are fickle and changing. But an act of shame would deprive us of the respect which we now enjoy throughout the world and thus would sap the vitals of our strength. During the last year we have gained by our bearing and conduct a potent hold upon the sentiments of the people of the United States. Never, never in our long history have we been held in such admiration and regard across the Atlantic Ocean.[5]

Needless to say, there were also tactical and strategic considerations behind the decision to commit British forces to the defence of Greece. Churchill's emphasis on the moral component—the honour at stake in upholding a commitment, the respect gained throughout the world by doing so, the cost in morale of a failure to support an ally—seems to have influenced Berkovits's presentation in the first of the two sermons reproduced below, together with the preacher's structural need to find some positive message even in military disaster.

The sermon undoubtedly follows Churchill's speech of 27 April, and precedes the loss of Crete later in May. It is relatively straightforward; once the historical context is understood, it requires little explication. An introductory section sets out the theme of 'moral strategy' as contrasted with military strategy. This leads to a biblical text—not from the Torah pericope but from Habakkuk's 'The righteous shall live by his faith' (Hab. 2: 4). In the first substantive section, this precept is applied to the apparently disastrous British venture in the Balkans. Here it is a matter of faith not in God, but in the humane values: 'in justice and democracy, in honour and human dignity'. After two decades in which the policies even of the democratic nations showed contempt for these values, the British decision to come to the aid of Greece, made—the listeners are told—for purely idealistic reasons (and thereby paying off with enhanced prestige in America), embodied the commitment that will eventually lead to victory over the forces of evil.

The following section, applied directly to Jews, asserts the importance of faith in more religious terms. Lamenting the loss of faith in the traditional providential understanding of God's rule over nature and human events, he insists on the need for true faith in God—which leads, in this context, not to

[5] Churchill's speech to Parliament, 27 Apr. 1941, <www.ibiblio.org/pha/policy/1941/410427a.html>. According to the report in *Time*, 4 May 1941, when he finished his speech, most of the people of both countries were satisfied with Winston Churchill, if not with the course of the war effort.

increased observance of the traditional commandments, but to 'faith in reason and humanity'; faith that, despite all appearances, Nazi values cannot ultimately triumph. There is no theological or philosophical argumentation here, as there would be in Berkovits's post-war essays; this is a message intended to reassure and inspire, not to convince.

The second sermon was delivered some four months later, at the end of a summer during which the war had dramatically expanded with the German invasion of the Soviet Union. Berkovits uses the occasion of a national day of prayer, commemorating the completion of the second year of the war, to review the events of the recent past and his own homiletical responses to them. Most traumatic was the precipitous surrender of France on 21 June 1940. Berkovits recapitulates at some length the sermon he delivered in London on the sabbath the day after the fall of Paris, drawing on the historical experience of the Jewish people in surviving powerful tyrants of the past to urge hope and faith on his audience. Then came the beginning of the bombing of London, and the fear that Britain might be the next to fall. Berkovits presents this experience much as he did the battle in Greece: as a moral victory, asserting the power of the human spirit over 'steel and iron, high explosive and fire'. His emphasis is not on the valour and skill of the Royal Air Force, but on the courage and faith of 'the common people of this country'. Referring to the monumental struggle on the Eastern Front, the preacher concludes with a series of subjects worthy of the prayers being offered that day. The anguished questions that echo through many American sermons—Where is God in this nightmare? How can God allow such suffering?—seem to be totally absent from this mindset.

24A

# ON A STRATEGY OF FAITH

*After the British Debacle in Greece, Spring 1941*

### 3 MAY 1941

**LEEDS**

━━

I

**I** **WISH TO DWELL** on an important aspect of the strategy of this war. Naturally, not on its military aspect. This is not our business, nor is there place for it in a synagogue.

However, in a struggle like this, which, as it proceeds, reveals itself more and more clearly as a contest between good and evil, there is an aspect of strategy which is just as important as the military one, namely, the moral strategy of the battle.

Let me try to explain what is meant by a moral strategy.

In the last few weeks, this country sustained a number of military and political reverses.[6] People went about with gloomy faces. They were disheartened by the long succession of defeats. Perplexed and bewildered, they listened to every transmission of the wireless, they bought every newspaper they could get hold of, looking for some guidance, hoping for some pleasant surprise, for a voice to tell them that, after all, things were not so bad.

I venture to assert that the reason why their uneasiness was so acute was that they thought in terms of military strategy alone, they thought only of bombers and tanks, of armies and generals, but were unable to judge events by the standard of a moral strategy.

A war between good and evil, however, should mainly be judged in terms of moral strategy.

## II

The prophet Habakkuk expressed the basic principle of moral strategy in one short sentence: 'The righteous shall live by his faith' (Hab. 2: 4). In the context the Prophet in striking language describes that 'bitter and quick nation' (Hab. 1: 6) which marches out over the wide plains of the world, destroying and devouring irresistibly, until it meets with an inglorious end at the end of 'all the remnant of the peoples' (Hab. 2: 8). In that terrible time of trial and suspense, while the 'horsemen' of the enemy 'fly as a vulture that hasteth to devour, while they gather captives as the sand, scoff at kings and princes, deride every stronghold, in that time, the just will live by his faith'.

How one can live by faith alone, confronting all the might of a ruthless adversary, we Jews should know. In the whole record of mankind there is no nobler and more inspiring example of the sustaining and invincible power of faith than the history of the Jewish nation. Our enemies, always many and powerful, disappeared. We, always few and powerless, have survived. They went under, living by their might. We have survived, living by our faith.

---

[6] Characteristically for the sermon genre, there was no need to specify events of which everyone in the congregation was painfully aware. See the Introduction to this sermon, above.

They relied on military strategy and were destroyed; we relied on moral strategy, and were preserved.[7]

Bearing in mind this principle of moral strategy, a strategy based on faith, I was not gloomy, I felt no real uneasiness at the disquieting military and political events of the last few weeks. On the contrary, I noted with a thrill of joy the first signs of a future of hope for mankind. For the following reason:[8]

In this struggle between good and evil one of the most decisive factors will be the rebuilding of faith all over the world. It is the great tragedy of our times that men and nations have lost faith in justice, in freedom, in humanity, in goodness. They do not believe any more that it does pay to be good and humane and just. The Faith of mankind is in ruins. The staggering successes of evil are due to the fact that for many long years so-called democratic statesmen were busy destroying and betraying the faith of mankind.[9] They were stupid enough not to be concerned with moral strategy at all. To re-establish the faith of mankind in justice and democracy, in honour and human dignity, is the first condition for the victory of the just cause. Seen under this aspect, the happenings of the last few weeks mark the beginning of the epoch of justice for which the world is longing.

What happened was something extremely unusual, most uncommon; something the world has not witnessed for a very, very long time indeed.

The newspapers reported: Great Britain sent an army to help a small nation. And then: the army was defeated after having inflicted heavy losses on the enemy.

From the point of view of moral strategy, however, what happened was this: A great Empire, harassed from all sides, fighting for its very existence, struggling with a formidable foe while hampered by the lack of essential military equipment, had thrown overboard all considerations of military prestige and sent help to a forlorn hope in spite of the knowledge that there was no chance of success; and this was done in order to honour a pledge, to keep a given promise; this was done for the sole reason that anything else would have been dishonourable.[10]

[7] The claim that Jewish historical experience validates faith in the ultimate triumph of moral force over military power was commonly used by Jewish preachers at this time; it had been used by Berkovits in a sermon following the fall of Paris the previous June (see the beginning of the next sermon by Berkovits, p. 413).

[8] Having set up a tension in the minds of alert listeners between the prevalent discouragement inspired by the British defeat and his own 'thrill of joy', Berkovits continues to apply his central thesis to the current situation.

[9] A strong condemnation of the policies of the democracies since the end of the First World War. The specific failures are specified in the following sermon.

[10] This formulation echoes Churchill's speech of 27 April, as cited in the introduction to this sermon.

Thus had begun the reconstruction of the betrayed faith of men all over the world.

This is how these weeks will be remembered in the future.

We were witnessing the first important move in the long-neglected moral strategy of the struggle. What we experienced was the first noble effort to blot out the shame of the last two decades, the foolish and sordid haggling of a stupid 'democratic' policy concerning the fulfilment of treaty obligations.[11]

The world will not forget this. The world will gain new courage from this, and new hope. Men and nations will start to learn anew the long forgotten lesson of faithfulness. For the first time, after many years of tragic disappointments during which Machiavellian heresies were current among men and nations, they have seen that a great nation was prepared to lose rather than to betray. In the field of moral strategy this is the first success in the cause of justice. For every deed of decency is a blow against the forces of evil. It encourages humanity. It must bring forth more and mightier deeds of decency all over the world and will gradually build up the invincible power of the just cause.

The time will come when this great country will reap the blessed fruits of this defeat in the cause of faithfulness in the Balkans. The cause of justice cannot be lost by the exercise of justice, but only by the betrayal of it.

## III

In these last weeks of uneasiness, I had often to think of the great change that had taken place in the nature of the Jew. We Jews used to be accustomed to catastrophes, to Jewish and world tragedies. We have seen much, but we seem to have changed much. In former times, in the midst of tragedies, Jews were firm, quiet and steadfast. To-day we are nervous, fidgety and doubting. Our ancestors lived by their faith and were the great masters of moral strategy. We, however, are a generation without real faith.[12] For our ancestors Faith meant the idea of a great pattern of universal and cosmic life, devised by God and carrying a deep, though often hidden, sense. All the happenings around them, all the events of their individual lives or those appertaining to the life of the

---

[11] The precise allusion in this phrase is unclear to me. It could refer to questions about the proper response of the democracies following German violations of provisions of the Treaty of Versailles, but the context suggests that it is more likely to refer to France's treaty obligations (and Britain's moral obligations) to defend Czechoslovakia against Nazi aggression.

[12] This rhetoric, contrasting the simple faithfulness of previous generations (in this case, echoing the text from Habakkuk cited at the beginning of section II) with the faithlessness of the present, is something of a topos in traditional Jewish preaching of many generations.

nation and of mankind, wars, epidemics, natural catastrophes, had their appropriate place in one great Divine scheme. The scheme, as they understood it, may often seem to us naive and simple. Its greatness consisted in the fact that no event was taken at its face-value, but was seen in a certain relation to the whole. A disaster did not count as such, it counted only as the part it had to play in the whole system of a life based upon Faith.[13]

We, however, are a generation without Faith. Because of this we hang on the words of the wireless commentator or the military spokesman; because of this we are sometimes filled with doubt and see no end to this age of darkness.

The reconstruction of life by Faith is among the foremost tasks of our generation. Real faith in God will mean faith in reason and humanity. Faith in God teaches with an iron logic that wrong-doing does not pay in the long run, that it is not the way of life but of destruction and death.

Once there is Faith in us and the nations, the downfall of the forces of evil will be in sight.

Let us build Faith up in the world. Let us learn the logic of Faith and the strategy of Faith, and the world will appear in an entirely new light; even disasters and catastrophes will point to a happier future and a new era of hope for all men and all nations.

## 24B

# TRIUMPH OF THE SPIRIT

### 7 SEPTEMBER 1941
#### (DAY OF INTERCESSION)
#### LEEDS

═══

NOT BY MIGHT, nor by power, but by my spirit—saith the Lord of Hosts' (Zech. 4: 6).

These words seem to me to be the most appropriate for this Day of National Prayer; not only because the present war is more and more developing into a

---

[13] In speaking of the traditional belief in divine providence governing the events of nature and history, Berkovits intentionally omits the central principle of this world-view: that disasters are God's punishments of the Jews for their failures to live up to their obligations under the covenant—a theme that would not fit the context of the sermon, except as applied, a few sentences later, to the enemy. In the following sermon, Berkovits does present the suffering in contemporary Europe as the consequence of sin (though not specifically that of the Jews).

battle between good and evil, a struggle between the spirit and the sword, between immortal moral values and their utter denial by the barbarous forces of darkness;[14] but mainly because, looking back at the second year of the war, we may say to-day that we were witnessing the great miracle of the spirit; the Spirit of God in man triumphant over ruthless barbarous force.

Looking back at the second year of the struggle, we may say that in this country we saw with our own eyes how material might and power were defeated by the spirit and by nothing else but the spirit.

# I

Let us recall for a moment what was the outstanding feature of the past year. In this endeavour my mind travels back, first of all, to that Black Friday last summer[15] when a stunned world learned the news that Paris, the centre of light in Europe, had surrendered to the forces of darkness. The following day, being a Sabbath, I had to preach in a London Synagogue, and among other things, I said something like this to the bewildered congregants:[16]

Do not despair; think for a while of our own Jewish life and be reassured. We 'Asiatic' Jews are the oldest among the nations of Europe. We have a better and longer memory than any of them. And we Jews can say this to-day: We have known most of the great tyrants and tyrannies of the world. We have groaned under their yoke. We saw them all growing mightier and mightier. And yet, here we are to-day to proclaim that never did we see them ultimately triumphant. Here we are to-day to give evidence that as often as we witnessed their rise, we also witnessed their downfall. We knew them terrible and mighty, but there was not one among them whom we Jews have not seen down-trodden and wallowing in the dust.

And I said to them in that London Synagogue: 'Have faith. The very fact that we Jews are still here to-day, even though crouching under the whip of the tyrant, proves that it is not brute power or might that will conquer in the end.'[17]

---

[14] By asserting that the Manichean view of the war has become increasingly pronounced over the past two years, Berkovits seems committed to the conclusion that Stalin's Soviet Union—until a few months earlier, on the sidelines of the war and an occupier of large new territories following its outbreak—is on the side of 'immortal moral values'. See his language about the Russians in the third part of the sermon.

[15] i.e. the summer of 1940, not of 1941. The fall of Paris occurred on Friday, 14 June; the surrender of France the following Friday.

[16] Berkovits published the text of this sermon ('Not By Might . . . : On the Sabbath after the fall of Paris') as the first in his collection *Between Yesterday and Tomorrow* (pp. 9–14).

[17] This appeal to Jewish historical experience as a source of hope in the struggle against Hitler was recapitulated at the beginning of Berkovits's previous sermon. Logically, it must be based on the premise that Hitler's Germany is no worse than the great 'tyrants and tyrannies' of the past

Surely, I said, there will be suffering, for there was sin, sin against the spirit by everybody everywhere.[18] Think of the millions of murdered Chinese, murdered because armament manufacturers all over the world wanted more profit.[19] Think of Abyssinia, left in the lurch by the Great Powers.[20] Think of democratic Spain, left to its fate because reactionaries all over Europe wished the 'gallant Christian gentlemen'[21] to triumph over humanity. Think of Czechoslovakia, betrayed by the so-called democracies.[22]

There was much betrayal of the spirit and because of it there is bound to be much suffering.

But, I said, have faith. Not for a single moment can we Jews doubt the ultimate issue of the battle, for we know that God did not create this world in order that it might be senselessly destroyed.

Yes, even then, at the most critical moment in the modern history of mankind, we Jews had unshakable faith. But we all knew that the hour of trial for these Islands, and with it for us all, was due to come any moment.

And when, just a year ago to-day, on September 7th, on that unforgettable Sabbath afternoon, the sirens sounded in London for the third or fourth or fifth time, we all felt that it had started at least. With the fall of darkness the London sky was glowing red and redder, not towards sunset, but towards the East; the ominous sign of the burning of the London docks.

We knew then that the hour had come and that from now on we would be tested as if by fire.

In the dark winter months that followed, when the bomber was roaming through the skies of Britain, we, let us confess it to-day, often wavered in our faith. We often asked ourselves how long can man endure all this, how long can man of flesh and blood stand up to such incredible trials. One single raid night appeared to last eternities; and this went on night after night, for weeks and months, and still there was no end in sight. A general breakdown of human

which have fallen into history's dustbin while the Jews have survived. Cf. the text in *Between Today and Tomorrow*, 11–12.

[18] An affirmation of the traditional theodicy; cf. the end of the previous sermon.
[19] Referring to armament contracts with Japan that facilitated Japanese aggression against China and atrocities against Chinese civilians.     [20] At the time of the Italian invasion.
[21] A phrase used by British Conservative supporters of General Franco. Berkovits identifies not with the Fascist side supported by the Spanish Church but with the 'atheist' communist revolutionaries.
[22] With this review of the democracies' failures of policy and nerve during the previous years, compare the quotation from Ira Eisenstein (introduction to Sermon 22 above, p. 391) and Sermon 22 itself by Abraham Feinberg. Cf. also the text of this sermon as published by Berkovits, where he condemns 'compromise' as 'the sin of our generation' (*Between Today and Tomorrow*, 13).

endurance seemed a very near possibility and with it everything would have been lost.[23]

But a miracle happened.

It is true, there was death and destruction, there was much suffering and sorrow, but in the midst of the tragedy a miracle was happening. In the midst of suffering the most deadly weapon which the devilish ingenuity of men could invent, the Bomber, had been defeated. And the miracle was that the defeat of the bomber was achieved not by the strategy of brilliant generals, nor by the night-fighters or the A[nti-]A[ircraft] Guns, but by human endurance. Steel and iron, high explosive and fire, had been defeated by human hearts of flesh and blood.

One of the greatest miracles in the history of mankind happened before our own eyes. With our own eyes we could see it: the Spirit of God in the hearts of men, conquering, defeating might and power. This Britain, the common people of this country, have conquered this time in the true Jewish manner, through suffering and by faith.

And this, we feel, will prove to have been the decisive victory in this gigantic struggle between good and evil.

## II

Up to the Battle of Britain Nazi barbarism achieved amazingly cheap victories: not so much by means of its tanks and aeroplanes, but mainly because, where it moved, it found men who were prepared to surrender to the conqueror not only their weapons, but their hearts and their minds as well. Everywhere it was able to find accomplices, but only because, through the many betrayals of the spirit in the last two decades, the faith of men and nations in decency, freedom, and justice had been undermined; because these great ideals of mankind had become empty words; because in a world in which for years the holiest conceptions of mankind had been continually sacrificed on the altar of vested interests the only faith left was the faith in profit and the faith in the tank and the bomber. In such a world of moral decay there was no hope for the future.

But then, the bomber came to Britain. And the common people in these Isles rose to the occasion and through their exertions set an example to the world.[24] Through their readiness to sacrifice everything rather than yield and surrender

---

[23] An honest and poignant evocation of the toll in morale exacted by the continued German bombing of British cities.

[24] Rhetorically, the British response to the German bombing plays the same role in this sermon as the sacrificial British intervention on behalf of the Greeks in the previous one.

to evil, they have restored the dignity of man all over the world. They have begun to rebuild the faith of man and nations in the moral destiny of man. And all over the world people learned anew, and learned eagerly, that love and kindness and unselfishness had not died out among men, for they could point to the new and inspiring comradeship, the freely given mutual aid of the people of Great Britain. And to-day, the eternal watchwords of mankind—freedom, justice, truth, love—shine through the darkness with a new light and give new hope to the nations.

To-day we may look with more confidence into the future because we have more faith in man.

## III

There is reason enough for us to thank God for all this to-day, to be grateful for the miracle.

But let us not forget for one moment that the time for jubilation has not come yet.

The trial is not over yet. We have gained the present breathing-space only because others, millions and millions of our fellow-men in Russia, are suffering all the time for us, just as we have suffered for them.[25] And who knows what turn the storm may take next.

Let us remember the incredible amount of suffering that the second year of the war has spread all over the world.

Let us pay respect to the memory of the many innocent victims of the bomber in this country, of the innumerable victims of tyrannous lust for power in the enslaved countries of Europe and on the gigantic battle-fields in the East.

Let us remember the heartrending sufferings to which our own Jewish nation is being subjected in all the lands that are now being devastated by the hordes of the barbarians. Not even brotherly greetings, no signs of brotherly love, can reach them from us. They are alone in their sorrow. May God be with them. May He protect them.

Let us pray for this unfortunate, bleeding mankind. Let us pray for this Britain, the Britain of that common man in the street who once said to me: Victory, not for Britain, victory for justice.[26]

---

[25] Compare the much more critical evaluation of this 'breathing space' provided by the titanic struggle on the Eastern Front in Sermon 25 below by Eisendrath. Berkovits's formulation that before the German invasion of the Soviet Union the British were suffering for 'their fellow men in Russia' is rather surprising.

[26] This seems to be an incident that the preacher has already shared with his congregation.

Let us pray for the victory of justice, of truth, of humanity and kindness all over the world.

May God Almighty shorten this terrible period of suffering.

May He help us all to that 'new heart' and 'new mind' * that will be needed for the upbuilding of a better and happier life for all men and all nations.

Out of the present world-wide brotherhood of suffering may there rise the brotherhood of peace, the brotherhood of sympathy and understanding among all men and nations, a brotherhood of happiness from which no one is excluded.

* See Ezek. 36: 26.

# CHAPTER TWENTY-FIVE

## MAURICE N. EISENDRATH

# BLACKOUT: HOW LONG, O LORD, HOW LONG?

### *A Sermon for the Evening of the New Year*

## 21 SEPTEMBER 1941

### HOLY BLOSSOM TEMPLE, TORONTO

MAURICE NATHAN EISENDRATH served as President of the Union of American Hebrew Congregations from 1943 until shortly before his death in 1973. Before this, he was a congregational rabbi, briefly in West Virginia and then, for fourteen years beginning in 1943, at the Holy Blossom Temple of Toronto, the flagship congregation of Reform Judaism in Canada.

Born in 1902, Eisendrath grew up under the influence of Rabbi Felix A. Levy of Temple Emanuel on the north side of Chicago, and it may have been this example that made him decide at age 16 to study for the rabbinate. Levy himself, however, was a scholarly type (he earned a doctorate at the University of Chicago studying with the great Egyptologist James H. Breasted) who did not generally preach on currently controversial topics. He was indeed rather critical of the claims of some contemporary Reform rabbis to be the successors of the prophets and the spokesmen of 'prophetic Judaism'.[1] This was, however, precisely the mould of Eisendrath's own rabbinate,[2] and in this he was perhaps influenced by the more charismatic Chicago preacher Emil G. Hirsch. The sermon reproduced below illustrates the fearless and forthright style, with its strong condemnations both of Canadian society and of Jewish behaviour, that would characterize Eisendrath's entire career.

---

[1] On Levy, see Temkin, *His Own Torah*, 15 (Chicago doctorate), 9, 21 (prophetic Judaism). Another disciple of Levy, whose career was perhaps more influenced by Levy's own personal style, was Samuel Dresner (ibid. 15–17).

[2] 'Like many other Reform rabbis of the period, Eisendrath saw himself in the mold of the Hebrew prophets, ever ready to speak his mind publicly for a cause he believed just': Meyer, 'Eisendrath, Maurice N.', 372.

Characteristic of the young liberal rabbis of this generation was a commitment to pacifism. Soon after coming to Toronto, Eisendrath became the
president of the local chapter of the Fellowship of Reconciliation and in 1931
he attended its World Assembly in Holland. His passionate convictions are
expressed in the following passage from a 1931 sermon:

Yes, still through the misled imagination of the masses march the militarists bearing
the mendacious banners, 'for home and fatherland'. But those banners lie. The war system has no right to bear such slogans; the war system is not the defender of any home
or fatherland; the war system is the most flagrant enemy of every fatherland and every
home and some few of us who are not ashamed to call ourselves pacifists would seek to
snatch those banners from the hands which so long and so undeservedly have carried
them and to put them where they belong—in the hands of the peacemakers whom
alone the prophets and Jesus called 'blessed'.[3]

Gradually, with excruciating anguish, Eisendrath (like most but not all of
his colleagues) felt compelled to abandon his pacifist position; the inner tur-
moil was such that, as he wrote some thirty years later, it resulted in 'almost
rendering me impotent to continue to speak from a pulpit from which I had in
the past preached the doctrine. I became embroiled in a crisis of conscience
which has left some scars, certain as yet unresolved conflicts, and some lingering doubts and reservations to this day'.[4]

The following sermon was delivered on the third Rosh Hashanah of the
war. The situation of Canadian rabbis was precariously positioned between
those of American preachers to the south and British preachers to the east.
Canada, as part of the British Commonwealth, had long been part of the war
effort, so the debate over whether or not to enter the war was not an issue, as
it still was for colleagues in the United States. On the other hand, Canada was
not directly affected by the war as was Britain, where one year earlier London
had suffered a sustained air attack unprecedented in its devastation (a situation
that certainly affected the mood in Toronto on the previous Rosh Hashanah,
as the preacher reminds his listeners). Now, although the battles on the recently opened Eastern Front were of almost unimaginable ferocity, to many
Canadians the war seemed distant; life at home seemed almost normal, as it
did to many in the United States. This was precisely the mindset that
Eisendrath set out to censure.

While the power of the sermon is conveyed on the printed page, the text is
certainly not a model of homiletical artistry. The application of a biblical paradigm to the present is reminiscent of the Civil War sermons of Michelbacher

---

[3] Eisendrath, *Can Faith Survive?*, 71; cf. H. Saperstein, 'Must There Be War?' and 'Can Jews
Afford to Be Pacifists?', two pacifist sermons delivered in 1936 and 1937.

[4] Eisendrath, *Can Faith Survive?*, 73; see the entire description of his pacifism and its abandonment, ibid. 71–9.

and Isaacs (Sermons 5 and 7 above). But the structure is difficult to detect, and the preacher provides no verbal clues to the listeners that would help them orient themselves. After twenty minutes of listening, they would have had no way of knowing whether they were close to the end or still near the beginning. In this regard, the contrast with Sermon 26, delivered by Israel Levinthal on the following morning, is striking. In addition, the present text is of inordinate length—more than 7,100 words, which would have taken close to an hour to deliver. That Eisendrath realized this was too long, even for the evening service with its relatively brief liturgy, and edited his text before delivery is indicated by parentheses written by hand in the typescript, bracketing passages that were probably not actually spoken. I have left this material intact, with the parentheses inserted by the preacher after the full text had been written.

Despite its sprawling character, the sermon reveals a preacher proclaiming a strong, militant anti-Nazism combined with a passionate commitment to social justice on the home front, following the brilliant socialist political scientist Harold Laski in arguing that social justice for the poor and the disenfranchised was necessary in order to achieve the optimal war effort.

# SERMON

FOR a number of years now most of us, on this North American continent especially, have been playing at war. To be sure, we have fancied ourselves actually in the fray and have laid the pleasing unction to our souls that we are the dauntless crusaders of freedom; crusaders, however, with words rather than deeds; with banners and bunting and bands rather than with bullets and bombs. While whole populations have huddled in the darkened caverns of the earth, we have hugged our radios to hear the latest commentator's verdict as to how the battle has been going—or have we paid even more heed to the latest stock quotations as our foremost index of the shifting tides of war as the blood of men sends up or down the barometer of our bonds, dependent upon which side spills the largest quantities? We have set aside the proceeds of an occasional golf match or bridge club to the winning of the war and have prided ourselves that we shall thus be enshrined forever as the heroes who have salvaged a dying humanity from the foul clutch of its demonic murderer. A few of our sons have put on the King's uniform—and all honour and glory unto these stalwart and sterling youths—fewer still have crossed the seas to meet the adversary face to face. A bare handful of our number have already made the supreme sacrifice and our hearts bleed tonight for their bereft and be-reaved loved ones. But in the main, the majority among us have but toyed with this grimmest conflict that mankind has ever known. We Jews particularly, enjoying as we do the fat of this treasured land of freedom, have failed even yet to grasp the enormity of the fate which hangs so ominously over the heads of all Jewry, have failed to take literally our enemy's avowed determination to annihilate every last one of us from the face of the earth;[5] and, in consequence, we have not yet risen to the full measure of sacrifice that so crucial an hour demands; demands, not alone out of generosity or gratitude for the precious boon of liberty we have here enjoyed, but demands in sheer self-defense against the most implacable and avaricious foe that has yet assailed us.

For almost a decade now we have poured forth our vilest curses upon the Nazi regime. When the moment struck, however, to send forth our sons and to pour out our means actually to strike these tyrants low, we continued, on the whole, with business as usual, devoting to the herculean challenge of war only the spare hours left over from our habitual foibles and fripperies, fiddling still with our permanent waves and matinees and games while not alone Britain burned, but the whole world has been committed to the flames;[6] piling up profits still—no matter how much we grumble over taxation—while tender, aspiring youths plunge crazily from the skies; confusing our self-centered and personally ambitious scramble for recognition by this military leader or social arbiter, mistaking our rivalry for preferment in this organization or that for the real sacrifices requisite in this desperate battle. Our remoteness from even the foggiest notion of what this struggle really entails has been perhaps best symbolized by those make-believe blackouts such as in this vicinity we put on just a bit over a week ago;[7] those make-believe blackouts, during which for a few swift-fleeting moments, like children in their sham battles of tin soldiers, we fancy that we are enduring something akin to all the horror and terror of those millions of harassed souls across the seas; during which we actually delude ourselves into believing that we are tasting of the bitter cup of this gory carnage.

[5] A strikingly strong formulation of the genocidal intentions of the Nazi regime and the con-sequent potential danger even to Jews in the western hemisphere.

[6] Playing on the allusion to the motif of Nero 'fiddling while Rome burned', and applying it to the obstinate banalities of contemporary Canadian Jewish life.

[7] Blackout exercises, organized by the Air Raid Precautions organization (ARP), were first held in Toronto in May 1941 and apparently repeated periodically thereafter. The 'make-believe black-out' is rhetorically contrasted at the beginning of the next paragraph with the 'genuine blackout', both physical and spiritual, prevailing throughout much of the world.

Not yet has this continent, nor even the whole of Jewry, awakened to the full realization of the genuine blackout that has descended physically over so many lands and spiritually over the entire earth. Else we would not meet tonight in quite so optimistic a mood as that which has seized hold of most of us within the Dominion and which, to an even more alarming degree, has wafted our neighbours across the border into a veritable paradise of fools. Business is booming, stocks are approaching their erstwhile highs. To be sure, the government deprives us of the full measure of our looming profits, but victory, according to not a few, is around the corner and prosperity will soon be ours again. No need for further sacrifices. All this talk of possible invasion or defeat is just so much British propaganda. And so Canada can afford to permit its Enlistment Campaign to go virtually by default,[8] while the United States can be unperturbed by the sinister fact that a recent Congressional measure devised to strengthen its army and buttress its bulwarks was carried by a majority of but a single vote.[9] But let us not cast the first stone at our neighbours to the south. People who live in glass houses dare not indulge in so dangerous a pastime. For so transparent is our own dwelling-place that there is virtually not a single tourist from across the line who is not shocked by the leisurely and lackadaisical war effort of this Dominion, which has not yet risen to the noble example it should set for the United States; particularly mothers and sisters and sweethearts of men who are forced to remain for more than a year in military camps within the non-belligerent United States are staggered by the paradox of a few months compulsory training in a Canada at war. They are amazed when they step into our hotels to find the bright lights blazing and the jazz bands blaring precisely as though we already were celebrating the day of victory. Yes, and even we Jews, who ought to be steeped in mourning over the literal death of a score of once vital and vibrant Jewish centers and the wholesale slaughter of uncounted myriads of their denizens,[10] even we Jews defy the counsel of our leaders and destroy any semblance of communal discipline by persisting in having our

[8] This was the recruitment drive launched on 11 May 1941 with the aim of enlisting 32,000 volunteers as an alternative to conscription. While the quota was actually exceeded, there was a wide public perception that the campaign was a failure: see Granatstein, *Canada's War*, 201–4.

[9] Eisendrath is referring to the Army Service Extension Bill, which extended the original one year of service by an additional eighteen months for draftees, National Guardsmen and reservists. It was passed by the House on 12 Aug. 1941 by a vote of 203 to 202, and was sent to President Roosevelt by the Senate on 14 Aug.

[10] The actual 'wholesale slaughter' had just begun in the summer of 1941 with the *Einsatzkommando* massacres of Jews in territories occupied following the invasion of the Soviet Union; reports of these massacres were not yet known to Jewish leaders at the time of this sermon.

revels: our blatant wedding receptions in public, our lavish exhibitions of wealth and luxury as though life still had no higher purpose even in this desperate hour than sheer self-enjoyment.

(Meanwhile, more men are locked in mortal combat than in any previous chapter in the bloody history of mankind.[11] But that is on a distant eastern frontier, we casually and complacently comment. Our own troops are in the main standing at ease; the nightly devastation of the motherland by Nazi bombers has abated and so we share the hope, so tactlessly uttered aloud by a high official of the British government, that the armies of our enemy and of our newly-acquired ally will speedily annihilate each other;[12] so we remain naively unaware that even in the event of that joyous outcome, the four horsemen of disease and famine and destruction and death may stalk the entire earth.[13]) Just decorate yourself with a sparkling 'V' and convert some uncertain investments into the gilt-edged victory bonds and without a shadow of a doubt we shall have peace in our time.[14]

Such I take it is the temper of this particular Rosh Hashonah hour, so diametrically different from last New Year's Eve when most of us were prepared altogether to abandon hope and perceived not a single glint upon the totally blacked-out horizon.[15] But so mercurial are we that tonight we have sky-

[11] A *New York Times* analysis four weeks before the sermon was delivered (24 Aug. 1941, p. 57) stated that 'The greatest battle in history closed its ninth week. On a front almost a thousand miles long, from Leningrad on the Baltic to Odessa on the Black Sea, perhaps 9,000,000 men were locked in sanguinary struggle.'

[12] This apparently alludes to an accusation made in Britain that Lt-Col. John T. C. Moore-Brabazon, minister of aircraft production and a member of the War Cabinet, believed that the 'Russians and Germans should be allowed to exterminate themselves, thus giving the British continental dominance' (quoting the *New York Times* paraphrase, 3 Sept. 1941, p. 13). Speaking to Parliament a week later, Churchill stated that remarks made by Moore-Brabazon at a private gathering 'might be misconstrued', but that the minister was in full accord with the government policy of providing massive aid to the Soviet armed forces (*New York Times*, 12 Sept. 1941, p. 6).

[13] Alluding to the 'Four Horsemen of the Apocalypse' from Rev. 6: 1–8.

[14] This ironic statement alludes to the 'V for Victory' campaign, popularized by Churchill beginning in the summer of 1940, the 'Buy Victory Bonds' campaign, and the infamous statement of Neville Chamberlain following the Munich Conference of 1938.

[15] The 'totally blacked-out horizon' alludes both to the literal blackouts in England during the German bombings (cf. H. Saperstein, 'The World We Make', 75–6; Rudin, Sermon 23 above), and to the psychological and spiritual blackout caused by the catastrophic reversals in the war during the previous spring and summer. On 3 Nov. 1940 Eisendrath evoked this atmosphere of a month or two previously: 'Then came the full impact and horror of the blitzkrieg which in our blindness we believed would never really descend upon us. Within the space of a single month, the Nazi hordes had seized Denmark and Norway, had all but pulverized the flourishing cities of Holland, forced Belgium into tragic capitulation, and were goose-stepping arrogantly down the Champs Elysées with "la belle France", with beautiful France, crushed and bleeding beneath their mailed and brutal boots. Then, there came those darkest hours in centuries, when the fate of Britain itself, even of all civilization, hung so precariously in the balance' ('Danger Zones—1940').

rocketed to the opposite extreme (and naught but optimism pervades our hearts). Nor would I seek mercilessly and callously to prick this rose-coloured balloon which so many now behold before them, but at the same time I cannot but believe that this still gravely critical hour demands such a solemn word of warning as Jeremiah brought to his equally complacent people in a moment precisely similar to our own.

Some of you may recall the cries of lamentation which rent the air above the streets of Jerusalem when, in accordance with the prophet's dire prediction, the Chaldeans were hammering at the very gates of the Holy City. For many years Jeremiah had dinned into the ears of his unbelieving compatriots the imminence of this savage onslaught. To be sure, they had mocked his prophecy to scorn; but now that the foe was actually laying siege to their beloved home-land, their groans of anguish rose to the very heavens. Likewise to be heard on high were their resolutions to amend their ways, if only God would grant them deliverance. Like a scarlet-tainted sinner upon his death-bed vowing to live a pure and holy life if he will but be restored to health, so this corrupt and wicked generation of Judea solemnly vowed to usher in a new order if only they would be redeemed from this impending doom (brought down upon them by the marauding Chaldean hordes). They even went so far as to offer surety for their change of heart by releasing their slaves; a social and economic and moral revo-lution which Jeremiah had been so long demanding of them and which, as is generally the case, they had stubbornly refused until catastrophe fell upon them. But now they protested that their hearts were purged, and incidentally, since their fortunes would be lost anyway should the enemy succeed in sacking the city, they yielded at long last to Jeremiah's demand[16]—somewhat after the fashion of some of our own latter-day saints who, since the government will take their superfluous income anyway, conclude that they might just as well increase their gifts to charity or to religion.

And, now suddenly as if in answer to their prayers and in response to this tangible demonstration of their repentance the siege was lifted. Of course, they attributed this miraculous salvation to their own intrinsic merit for there were no radio commentators to flash the news that in reality the Chaldean conqueror Nebuchadnezzar had been compelled to abandon the cam-paign against Zion solely because he was being stabbed in the back by the

[16] Jer. 34: 8–10. The passage begins 'Some of you may recall' perhaps because it is the *haftarah* for the weekly lesson 'Mishpatim', or perhaps because Eisendrath has used this chapter from Jeremiah nine months earlier (in a somewhat different historical situation) in his address 'Where Do We Go From Here?'

Egyptians.[17] At all events, Jerusalem abandoned itself to unrestrained joy and became so 'cocksure' of itself and of God's providential care for His chosen people that its men of wealth, the real leaders of the people, then as now, decreed that the recently emancipated bondsmen should be re-enslaved. What could the pathetic figure of a Jeremiah expect in such a triumphant moment other than jeers and jibes when he had the temerity to proclaim: 'Even should ye destroy the whole army of the Chaldeans fighting against you until only the massacred are left, these will rise in their tents, man by man, and burn down the city and destroy you to the uttermost soul among you' (cf. Jer. 37: 10).

Is not history repeating itself? (Does not this perfect analogy out of the past, aptly fit the present moment?) When the bestial Nazi legions went bludgeoning their way across the fields of Flanders and of France, when the fires of Dunkirk blazed as if in sombre warning of the impending conflagration of the entire world, when the battle of Britain raged and its multitudes shuddered in blackened air-raid shelters, was there any sacrifice that most of us would not have offered to stay off this murderous foe (who, if he conquered across the seas, some of us were wise enough to know, would slay us next)? Yes, we too would even free our slaves, our economic slaves; we would steal the enemy's thunder by proclaiming a new order of our own: if only God would get us out of this bloody mess, there would be greater equality between man and man, there would be no exploitation; no prejudice, no bigotry.[18] If only the good Lord—whom we had conveniently forgotten, by the way, through all the years of our prosperity and fortune—would send forth His divine fire and destroy the adversary, we would proclaim His Kingdom of heaven on earth.

And now, like unto the Egyptians striking stealthily from the rear, a new front has distracted the enemy and we are already quite confident of victory. And so we berate once again the clamour of labour for a rightful share in the prosperity which some among us are beginning to enjoy. Our reactionary press rings with denunciation of the toiler to whom in their earlier extremity they

[17] Cf. Jer. 37: 11; and see Bright, *A History of Israel*, 309. The phrase 'stabbed in the back' appears intended to echo the right-wing German explanation for the unanticipated capitulation ending the First World War while no foreign army was on German soil (see the interesting discussion by Schivelbusch, *The Culture of Defeat*, 205–8). The purpose of this allusion is not apparent to me, as the Egyptian attack, by a rival world power, actually occurred, while the German 'stab' was essentially a combination of paranoid fantasy and a cynical attempt to find a scapegoat for the defeat.

[18] In the course of applying the situation from Jeremiah to the present, the preacher introduces a social justice component into the sermon: freeing of the slaves in biblical times is made analogous to ending economic and social oppression. This motif is further given concrete form in the following paragraph.

would have granted all that his heart and shrunken pocketbook demanded. Our bigots become more anti-Semitic and anti-alien than ever as we grow more confident that we can win through without any fundamental changes, without any basic revolution or the mind and heart and soul. A Canadian village can discharge a teacher because she has a 'foreign-sounding' name; more discriminatory signs than ever can burgeon forth on our highways—even in the midst of a so-called crusade against intolerance and totalitarianism.[19] This hour, even more than the hour of deepest blackout last Rosh Hashonah, requires the voice of a Jeremiah sternly to admonish us that unless we far more thoroughly amend our ways than appears as yet to be our inclination and intention, 'Even should we destroy the whole army of the enemies fighting against us until only the massacred be left, these will rise in their tents, man by man',[20] and burn down our whole vaunted civilization; for let me sound the solemn warning that there can be no victory unless and until even the humblest of our brethren is vouchsafed its full enjoyment and is granted his just share therein.

For let no blithe and buoyant optimism blind us to the fact that the vast multitudes of the earth are yet steeped in a deep and impenetrable blackout. Admittedly, certain shafts of light have appeared on the immediate horizon to warrant a happier mood than when we greeted the year 5701, when all hope seemed lost, when we were still staggering under the shattering impact of the unbelievable fall of France, of the jackal-like thrust of Il Duce into the quivering flesh of the languishing Republic, of the devastating bombing of London.[21] But the past year has wrought vast and enheartening changes. Our own strength has increased, the slumbering giant of the United States is beginning—albeit far too slowly—to awaken; we have seized the initiative in the Near East, the Nazi hordes may soon be quagmired in the snowy steppes of Russia, the conquered multitudes are beginning to stir, and finally, our valiant airmen are hammering home in deadly strokes their daily and nightly warning

---

[19] A peak of xenophobia towards immigrant populations was reached in May and June 1940 following the Nazi conquest of most of western Europe; at that time there was indeed a 'wholesale dismissal of immigrants of German or Italian background—or people with German or Italian sounding names in some cases—from their place of employment in many Canadian cities': Dreisziger, 'The Rise of a Bureaucracy for Multiculturalism', 8, and cf. 13 (top). This article analyses subsequent attempts to counter such intolerance, and to foster loyalty in the immigrant groups, in the following years (pp. 8–19). One of the specific tasks of a proposed governmental office to deal with immigrant groups was to 'ensure that people with foreign names were not discriminated against' (p. 18). See also Young, 'Chauvinism and Canadianism', 34–5, esp. on the radio broadcasts on the theme 'Canadians All'—perhaps the 'crusade against intolerance' to which the preacher refers.　　　　　　　　　　　　　　　　　　　[20] Cf. Jer. 37: 10, quoted above.

[21] Again an evocation of the mood of the previous Rosh Hashanah (see n. 15 above).

that the wages of the sin of warmongering is death to the attacker as well as to the attacked—all this does indeed show, as the British Prime Minister phrased it but a few days ago, that though our cause was not so very long ago 'forlorn and even very desperate, we can now confidently exclaim that we are indeed the captains of our fate, the masters of our soul'.[22]

But, being the captains of our fate and the masters of our soul does but place an even greater responsibility upon our own shoulders. We have reached that turn in the road where victory can be ours, if we warrant it, if we toil sufficiently hard, if we shed sufficient tears and sweat and blood to attain it, if we rouse ourselves from our stupor, forgetting our alleged personal safety by virtue of the three thousand miles of ocean which separates us physically from the foe,[23] and transform this Dominion and this continent into the same kind of consecrated phalanx as all during the dreary months of last Fall and Winter faced the enemy across the narrow channel grimly determined never, never, never to live on their knees as slaves of any tyrant, and as even at this moment confronts the selfsame foe, with similar resolution, before the gates of Kiev and Leningrad and Moscow.[24] Victory will not come by decorating ourselves with its first initial,[25] nor by sitting back smugly and permitting the Red and the Brown armies to annihilate each other while we, on this continent particularly, continue to reap in the profits of war. That is what some of our so-called leaders sought to precipitate through all those treasonable days of appeasement and it will lead, now as then, to only more widespread chaos, with revolution and anarchy sweeping the earth; it will lead but to ever deeper blackout.

How long, then, O Lord; how long shall darkness pervade the earth? Once again Jeremiah, so strikingly contemporary a prophet, whose words are so amazingly appropriate for our time, provides the answer. He too had inquired of God, who sent him on his weary mission to predict the doom which could not but descend upon his people, as to how long His divine displeasure would be visited upon that unrighteous generation. In reply, Jeremiah was commis-

[22] The Churchill quotation is taken from his speech to Parliament of 9 Sept. 1941, reporting on his meeting with President Roosevelt on 14 August: 'A year ago our position looked forlorn, and well nigh desperate to all eyes but our own. To-day we may say aloud before an awe-struck world: "We are still masters of our fate. We are still captain of our souls."'
[23] 'Alleged' because in his address of 3 Nov. 1940 Eisendrath challenged the protection afforded by the Atlantic Ocean, asserting that German bases in Norway were only five hours' flight time from Toronto and Montreal for German bombers over the Arctic Circle ('Danger Zones—1940', 9).
[24] The German armies actually took control of Kiev a month earlier on 17 Aug. 1941; the Babi Yar massacre would occur just eight days after the sermon was delivered.
[25] Another allusion to the 'V for Victory' campaign.

sioned to 'root out and to pull down, to destroy and to overthrow, to build and to plant' (Jer. 1:10).

No more radical words have ever been uttered than these; no more revolutionary program has ever been offered than is contained in this charge to Jeremiah, that I feel is the sole hope for righting our way out of the blackout of this sombre and tragic hour. First 'to root out and to pull down': to demolish all the corrupt and flagrant abuses which have characterized, not only our foes but ourselves as well; and only then 'to build and to plant' in altogether virgin soil and on wholly new foundations the more decent society of free men. Only then will we be deserving of deliverance out of the stygian darkness of this day.

Can any one of us dare to suggest that we are as yet deserving of that victory? Have we really been purged of all our selfishness and greed, as individuals and as a nation and empire? Are we prepared to grant complete emancipation, not 'for the duration' but for all time to come to the downtrodden masses of the earth? Are we ready to grant to the representatives of these toiling multitudes their rightful place in government which, while already conceded in Britain, is still denied on this continent?[26] Has our sacrifice of our means and of our sons been such, even in the extremity of the Battle of Britain, to warrant the supposition that when the clouds of war have rolled away we will bring our free-will offerings to the altar of a united humanity? Have there been no reservations whatsoever in even so sacred a document as the pact emanating from that historic conference on the Atlantic between the Prime Minister of Great Britain and the President of the United States,[27] or do we not discern therein certain traces of hedging and of clinging still to that which we have and are determined to hold? Was there not conspicuous by its absence any mention of an erstwhile promise of Zion to Jews; was not this patent silence eloquent testimony to the fact that not yet have we been altogether purged of the craven policy of appeasement; appeasement, in this instance, of the frequently treasonable Arabs, while the Jews of Zion have clamoured to serve the Empire?[28] Has all anti-Jewish

[26] This issue of labour representation in Cabinet will be taken up later in the sermon (see below, p. 432).

[27] The meeting of 14 Aug. 1941, off the coast of Newfoundland, which produced the 'Atlantic Charter' document.

[28] Cf. Eliezer Berkovits's sermon of 16 Aug. 1941, in which he reviews the language of the document pertaining to a long-term goal of national self-determination, wonders whether this includes Jews, and then angrily reaches the conclusion: 'No, we were not meant . . . Somehow, Jews are never meant . . . [N]ot a single responsible word has been uttered on the subject of what is to happen after the war to the millions of homeless, uprooted, and broken Jews in Europe' ('In the Margin of the Atlantic Charter', 58–9). Eisendrath's reference to unfulfilled clamouring by the

prejudice been burned away by the fires of war or has not this most vicious and jaundiced hatred been intensified among vast multitudes who have been only too eager to believe the propagandist and to spread further and wider his noxious doctrines?[29] To my utter amazement and despair, in response to certain comments made in a letter to my cherished friend Dr. James Parkes to the effect that notwithstanding the fact that certain nominal leaders of Canadian Jewry deny the presence of anti-Semitism in a Canada at war, who naively affirm that the task of our Public Relations Committee has been taken over by the Foreign Office of the British Government, still, in my opinion, anti-Semitism has increased rather than decreased in the Dominion since the outbreak of the war; to my utter amazement, in reply to this comment, Dr. Parkes recently informed me that this is likewise true in Great Britain,[30] the one land on earth that has been so singularly free of such bigotry; while in the United States, quite aside from the recent blast of Colonel Lindbergh, even the most casual perusal of its press, to say nothing of more than one blatant outburst in its Congress itself[31]—all this must give us pause and constrain us to question whether we have a right even to pray for Victory until we have rooted out and pulled down, overthrown and destroyed from our own hearts and souls those very lusts and hates which have brought this blackout upon the entire earth.

Jews of Zion to serve the empire alludes to efforts to persuade the British to arm a Jewish Brigade, originally endorsed by Churchill but then put on hold in March 1941 because of opposition by the War Office and the Colonial Office.

[29] 'The propagandist' may be an allusion to Goebbels, or it may be a generic reference.

[30] I am not certain whether the letter from James Parkes has been preserved among the Eisendrath Papers. In a pamphlet published in 1943, Parkes wrote that 'People talk of "the danger of an increase of anti-Semitism in this country"; they question whether there may not be some justification for Hitler's treatment of the Jews. They talk again of "black markets"; whispering campaigns, and gossip, magnify the evil conduct of "the Jews". And the upshot of it all is that men feel less guilty about the murders and torturings going on beyond their sight' (Parkes, 'Jews in Britain', 1). On Jews and the 'black markets', see Sermon 28 by Hertz, below.

[31] The reference is to Lindbergh's infamous speech in Des Moines on 11 Sept. 1941, in which he charged that 'the three most important groups which have been pressing this country toward war are the British, the Jewish and the Roosevelt Administration', and that the 'greatest danger to this country' presented by the Jews 'lies in their large ownership and influence in our motion pictures, our press, our radio, and our government' (*New York Times*, 12 Sept. 1941, p. 2). The speech was widely condemned. See, recently, Wallace, *The American Axis*, 289–95; Sarles, *A Story of America First*, 54–60. The reference to a 'blatant outburst' in Congress may allude to the testimony of Gerald P. Nye, Republican Senator for South Dakota, at a hearing of a subcommittee of the Senate Interstate Commerce Committee on 9 September (two days before Lindbergh's address), in which he charged that the movie industry was feeding 'vicious propaganda' to the American public, intended to lead American into the war; he also charged that the leading producers had an undue concern for Old World quarrels because of their European origins and their financial interest in selling films to Britain (*New York Times*, 10 Sept. 1941, pp. 1, 26).

We are yet a long way from victory even on the battlefield. We are farther still from that victory of the spirit which will assure us that so colossal a sacrifice will not be demanded of us again. To this greater victory we must not alone reconsecrate ourselves upon this sacred New Year's Eve, but we must by our own lives testify to our worthiness to be granted that abiding peace which is in truth God's most precious gift.

I have no fear for the triumph of man's spirit so long as he wills to be free, so long as he cleaves to the way and will of God. I have not been overwhelmed by the military victories of our enemy because I know that these would never have been attained had the way not been prepared by the spiritual conquests that had gone before. Poland would not have fallen had it not been previously rotted from within. France would not have capitulated in but a few brief days had its soul not been depraved and its affections already alienated from its erstwhile zeal for the Republic to the decadent craving for security above and before liberty, fraternity, humanity.[32] Russia too would not be in its present desperate plight had not the first fresh consecration to the workers of the world been betrayed by a tyrannical despot seeking first and foremost the selfish isolation of his own land rather than the rectification of economic wrong throughout the earth.[33] Despite their phenomenal achievements, the Nazi legions have not proved invincible. Their way was paved with the treasonable compromises of men who had lost faith in themselves, but even more seriously, in the democracy which they professed with their lips and betrayed in their lives. Not in violated border-lines and vanquished nations, but in the moral depravity, the spiritual decadence and bankruptcy which made these conquests possible is to be found the deepest blackout of our time.[34]

(Fortunately, however, under the terrifying impact of weeks and months of incessant bombing, Great Britain at least has seemingly been purged of her own vacillation and inner decay and moves ever nearer toward genuine democracy which alone can counter the 'new order' which, however hypocritically, the Nazis hold before the masses of Europe. But, tragic though true it is that

---

[32] This claim that the German victories in Poland and France were facilitated by internal decay in the conquered countries functions to undermine the aura of invincibility of the German Wehrmacht. Eisendrath may be alluding to the spread of virulent antisemitism in Poland in the late 1930s.

[33] Note the positive presentation of the socialist rallying cry of international solidarity among workers juxtaposed with the negative portrayal of Stalin as having betrayed this goal for narrow nationalist interests.

[34] Cf. the formulation by Eliezer Berkovits in a sermon delivered on 7 Sept. 1941 (Sermon 24b above): 'Everywhere [Nazism] was able to find accomplices.'

the same cannot be said of this Dominion, where political leaders and editorial writers pontifically invoke the name of democracy and then savagely denounce every suggested advance toward a larger measure of justice for the multitudes which, in their snobbish heart of hearts, they quite obviously despise. The 'best men' in Canada, the 'best men' who are called upon to direct our Canadian destinies in this crucial hour are exclusively restricted to the most successful so-called wizards in business, banking, manufacturing and finance, while those who actually create the sinews of war with their own hands are disdainfully ignored.[35] Most of these leaders of labour, however, as an outstanding student of Canadian affairs not so long ago commented, are 'perfectly competent to be useful and valuable members of any political cabinet within the country; yet, strangely enough they are avoided as though they were afflicted with some plague'.[36] True enough, their grammar may not be impeccable, but as this satirical writer adds, no one has yet heard of any newly-arisen buccaneer who has had the good luck to uncover a cluster of gold nuggets, or the man who sold to the public sufficient shares in the ownership of a piece of ground on which such nuggets were expected, even if they never came to light, no one has ever heard of such parvenus encountering the slightest difficulty in buying their way into the swankiest social clubs, no matter how atrocious may be their grammar.

It is not thus that we can successfully wage a war for democracy. Nor can we do so by grumbling over rising taxation as those who are best able to afford such taxes usually do. What a travesty on this struggle which is in truth sacred to the youths who are prepared to lay down their very lives for our security that men highly respected in Canadian life, men occupying lofty political posts, should complain, as did one of the most prominent of them all, that 'human nature being the same in war as in peace—instead of helping the war effort, the government is defeating it by stripping us (through the excess profits tax) of the stimulus to toil and run our businesses'.[37] Such men are constrained to conclude, so asserted this widely-acclaimed Canadian leader, that we might just as well take things easier, rest on our oars, for we are only working for taxes anyway. What right has this Dominion to ask its young men to lay down not the 'excess profits' of their years, but their very lives when at the same time it refuses

[35] This apparently alludes to the campaign led by R. J. Manion and the Conservative Party in the spring of 1940 to create a national government of the 'best brains': see Granatstein, *Canada's War*, 84.; id., *The Politics of Survival*, 42–4.  [36] I am unable to identify this reference.
[37] The 'excess profits' tax was imposed by the Canadian government in 1941 in order to generate revenue and discourage profiteering from the war effort; profits beyond a certain percentage above the average from 1936 to 1939 were taxed at 100%, with a promise of a 20% rebate after the war (Granatstein, *Canada's War*, 175).

to bring its Defence of Canada Regulations[38] to bear upon these real saboteurs who I often hear, even in the midst of patriotic rallies, berating the government for its 'socialist tendencies' by taking such mean advantage of the war by depriving its citizens of such large portions of their incomes, by compelling them to drive one car instead of three or four, by reducing the number of their servants, and by robbing them of their happy winter pleasure jaunts in the sunny south. Yet, these are the selfsame factions that are clamouring long and loud for conscription of man power, who insist that all these ne'er-do-wells among the unemployed should be forcefully put into a uniform, but who would be the first to shout red revolution if their accumulated capital should be similarly seized.[39] But how dare we call upon those, who but yesterday were outcast and forsaken, whose home was a park bench and whose food was an obsequiously petitioned cup of coffee and crust of bread, to join up in a consuming and consecrated crusade unless this time,[40] not in words, but in some manner of actual deed, we initiate now that 'revolution of consent', as Harold Laski has it;[41] unless we convince them that this time we are in reality fighting for a genuine democracy which spells out work and bread and dignity and brotherhood for themselves rather than bigger profits for the bosses of yesterday; a democracy in which there shall never be again, any vast armies of forgotten men,[42] of distressed areas, of slums; that this time their sacrifice will convert their country into the fairest home that the sun ever shone upon; that this time we shall not betray

[38] On the Defence of Canada Regulations, which formed the basis for the internment of enemy nationals and naturalized immigrants from enemy countries, see Dreisziger, 'The Rise of a Bureaucracy for Multiculturalism', 2–3.

[39] Conscription was a bitterly contested issue in Canadian politics. At the time of the sermon, the policy of the government was still to rely on volunteer enlistment for overseas service. See Granatstein, *Canada's War*, 201–5, and, more comprehensively, Granatstein and Hitsman, *Broken Promises*.

[40] '*This* time' becomes a rhetorical leitmotif for the rest of this long sentence, contrasting with the previous experience of conscripted soldiers in the First World War, who discovered that many of the slogans used to justify their sacrifice turned out to be unfulfilled.

[41] In his Sunday address of 12 Jan. 1941, in which he discussed Harold Laski's *Where Do We Go From Here?* at length, Eisendrath said: 'it is his contention—and I believe that he is right here too—that we cannot possibly resist successfully this onrushing tide of world revolution—which is what Nazism really is—unless we confront it with, not the promise this time as in 1914–1918, but with the reality of a revolution of our own; a revolution not of barricades or of bloodshed, but a revolution of consent, as he concisely and correctly puts it; a revolution which, without any further delay, will bring to the helm of affairs throughout the democratic world the representatives, not of the classes, but of the masses of men' (Eisendrath, 'Where Do We Go From Here?', 7–8).

[42] Perhaps echoing the popular 1933 song, 'Remember My Forgotten Man', with the chorus, 'Remember my forgotten man, | You put a rifle in his hand; | You sent him far away, | You shouted, 'Hip, hooray!' | But look at him today!'

them; that this time, if we shall release them from the chains which corrode their young lives in factory and in field to fight our battle for us, we are going to permit them, on their return, truly to inherit the earth which they and they more than all others deserve; to inherit all the good things which this abounding land, with its far-spreading wheat fields, its virginal forests, its untapped mineral resources, might offer unto all. Without such a solemn and sacred pledge actually implemented by at least the beginnings of swift and certain progress toward such ends, there can be no consuming crusade for democracy.[43] And because we on this continent, unlike Britain, have not as yet given tangible evidence of this aim, I am not surprised that our war effort lags and that our enlistment campaign becomes a dismal failure. Without such a dynamic democracy, not promised in the future, but initiated now, we shall be destroyed, not by the mechanized monster from without; but by the burrowing termites of dissatisfaction and disaffection within. For, after all, 'in war as in equity, it is vital for those who seek justice to come into court with clean hands'.[44])

And the same is true of Israel. We too will never be shattered by our foes without. Nor do I minimize, in saying this, the unprecedented catastrophe that has overtaken the vast majority of our brethren. Tragically true it is that, with the exception of but a comparative handful of our people who dwell in such God-blessed lands as our own, our multitudes languish amid a blackout such as few of us, pursuing our wonted ways, can even begin to visualize. Not yet have we had sufficient imagination to grasp the grim fact that it is not in mere words, but in indescribable reality that the clock has been set back, for the vastest portion of the House of Israel, to the Middle Ages. For years some of us have used that phrase in our public discourses.[45] We were ever accused, of course, of gross exaggeration. But no smugly complacent Jew, or non-Jew, can any longer argue away those looming walls of concrete which imprison from morning until night and from sunset to sunrise millions upon millions of our brother Jews, crowded into quarters into which none of us would permit our dogs to enter and reduced to rations which would not keep our canaries alive.

[43] Echoing Wilson's phrase, characterizing America's entrance into the First World War on the side of the Allies in 1917.
[44] The legal maxim is 'he who seeks equity must come into court with clean hands'. The application to war would appear to be the preacher's own.
[45] This passage expresses the perception of Nazism as a reactionary movement, based on legislation of the 1930s and initial policies towards Jews in occupied countries as a reinstatement of pre-Emancipation patterns (ghettos, identifying clothing). The radical innovation of Nazi anti-Judaism—annihilation of an entire people—had not yet begun.

But, though my heart is lacerated by such an unspeakable fate which has descended upon millions of human beings, I have no fear for the survival of Israel because of this savage recrudescence of Medieval barbarism. Already reports reach us that there are lights kindled amid that inky blackout, as Jewish culture and—mark you—particularly Jewish religion flourishes in the midst of those harrowing Polish ghettos.[46] Israel will never be physically destroyed. We will no more be bombed and blitzkrieged out of existence by the Luftwaffe of Hitler than by the chariots and horsemen of Pharaoh; we shall no more be starved into abject submission by the blonde beast of Berlin than by the fires and torture of the Inquisition. Of us, as of Britain, the poet might well have chanted: 'Grind us, bind us, burn us in fire, and still ye shall not thus destroy us.'[47] No tyrant has yet been able to extirpate our people. Nor will any foe from without accomplish such annihilation now. For, let it be remembered that, though our numbers have fallen precipitously before; as, for example, when Benjamin of Tudela, some eleven hundred years ago took note during his travels throughout the then known Jewish world that our population had shrivelled from some four million at the time of the Destruction of the Temple by Rome to barely one million scattered and stricken souls in his own time,[48] a fate which even the most dour pessimist dare not to predict for our day; though physically we have and will continue to suffer myriads of casualties, not thus will our proud destiny be brought to its end. But to our generation, as to his own, the prophet Isaiah might well sound his sombre warning: 'M'horsayich oomachareevayich mimech yetseoo', 'Thine enemies and thy destroyers arise out of thine own midst' (Isa. 49: 17).[49] If Israel should die today, the post-mortem of history held over its prostrate body will deliver a verdict not of murder, despite all our massacred multitudes, but of suicide, the wilful and deliberate taking of our centuries-old life with our own hands; because, in these democratic lands, with every opportunity and advantage wherewith to follow,

[46] For a contemporary review of Jewish religious life in the Polish ghettos during the Nazi occupation, see Huberband, *Kiddush Hashem*. The reports known by Eisendrath undoubtedly include the article by Spiesman, 'In the Warsaw Ghetto', 357–66, based on the arrival in the United States of *Gazeta Żydowska*, the sole Jewish newspaper published in occupied Poland.

[47] I cannot identify this reference.

[48] Benjamin of Tudela lived and travelled in the twelfth century, less than 700 years before the preacher. For the population figures of Jews in specific cities, see Benjamin of Tudela, *Itinerary*, 60–135 *passim*. His purpose in recording these figures seems to be rather to emphasize the large number of Jews in the world for his readers, rather than to emphasize the decline from Roman times.

[49] This is not the way the verse is ordinarily translated; it reflects a later homiletical reading (cf. Rashi on Lev. 26: 17, based on *Sifra* ad loc.).

to deepen, to enrich our spiritual heritage, we indifferently permit our glorious heritage to go by default. It is well within the range, not of possibility, but of probability that Judaism on this free western continent may languish and die because of our persistence in becoming *ka-goyim*, like the whole vulgar, despiritualized generation of our day, assimilating ourselves to the very worst, rather than to the best, in our surroundings.[50]

Hardly a single Jew among us but prefaces his every reference to his membership in, or even his most casual relationship to, the historic home of Israel, the synagogue, with the abject apology: 'You know I'm really not religious'—as if his deeds did not speak so much louder than his words to proclaim to all the world that we, the descendants of those who proudly hailed themselves, as the *avde adonoy*, the servants of God, have become instead the slaves of the godless merry-go-round upon which our present civilization is riding madly towards its destruction. We, the people of the spirit, have become spiritually hollowed out. In the words of our Sabbath ritual, 'we exchange our glory for things of naught'.[51] Our worship is largely confined to these Yomim Noroim [Days of Awe], except perhaps for an occasional Sisterhood or Council or B'nai B'rith or special service of one kind or another, which are quite all right in so far as they fulfill the traditional role of the laity in the synagogue, but which become a *Hillul Ha-Shem*, a profanation of God's name and Israel's, when the flock they sporadically draw today, is gone with the wind, or with bogey,[52] or with shopping expeditions tomorrow; when those same good ladies of organizations that purport to be Jewish, that take the name Jewish in fact and in name, can even choose the sacred days of our festivals to absent themselves from the synagogue that they might disport themselves more profitably in some military cantonment or another.[53] Our pursuit of Jewish knowledge which, for adults as well as for children, was once considered *k'neged kulom*,[54] antecedent to all else besides,

---

[50] Apparently echoing the Talmudic statement, 'You have not acted according to their good ways, you have acted according to their perverse ways' (BT *San.* 39*b*). For a stunning homiletical application of this statement, see Saul Levi Morteira in M. Saperstein, *'Your Voice Like a Ram's Horn'*, 54.

[51] Cf. Ps. 106: 20: the sentence is found in the sabbath morning service of *The Union Prayer Book* (newly rev. edn New York: CCAR, 1940), 112.

[52] Apparently a Canadian slang expression that remains unclear to me.

[53] An apparent allusion to something that occurred, perhaps on the previous Passover, with which many of the listeners would have been familiar.

[54] Referring to the rabbinic statement *vetalmud torah keneged kulam*, usually rendered 'and the study of Torah is equal to all of the other deeds that have no limit in the efficacy' (*Pe'ah* i: i, BT *Shab.* 127*a* and parallels).

must now take second, or rather last place to everything else even for our children. Our obedience to the behest to refashion the world nearer to the pattern of God's design[55]—which means in Jewish lore and Hebrew language, *Tsedokah*—justice and not charity[56]—which should actuate us to the daily espousal of acts of righteousness, is exhausted in annual philanthropic campaigns which answer the multitude's piteous plea for equity with alms. The spirit is not in us to give. And yet, it is by that spirit: not by wealth and not by power, but by that spirit[57] alone that Israel has survived.

That is why my apprehension for my people today springs not from the merciless blows of the enemy, heart-breaking though these be, but rather from the fear that of our own free will and accord we will give up the ghost spiritually ourselves. For we Jews in America, in the United States and Canada, are indeed, the *shearis Yisroel*, 'the remnant of Israel' of which we used to read in our Sunday School lessons: the remnant which, when the Temple fell, carried on bravely in the *Mikdosh me'at*, the 'little sanctuary' of the exile;[58] the remnant which, when Jerusalem was pounded into dust by the Romans, arose triumphant in ben Zaccai's tiny school at Jammnia;[59] the remnant which, when Crusaders marched murderously through the continent of Europe, kindled the light of the Golden Age in Spain.[60] We are that remnant now. (Shall we betray the holy privilege which our freedom proffers us? Do we require to have ourselves locked up behind towering ghetto walls; shall we find it necessary to be herded into such restricted quarters, with stern-faced guards vigilantly preventing our exit, before we be awakened to the power which resides within our own tradition, not alone to bring hope and healing to ourselves, but to offer salvation to humanity as a whole?) How long, O Lord, how long shall Israel languish? Until we have rooted out from our own hearts all indifference and apathy to the call of the spirit and the lure of our lofty teaching; until we, whose law-givers enunciated righteousness as the supreme rule of life and whose prophets proclaimed love as the paramount tie that binds all mankind, overthrow and demolish all the injustices and envies of which we ourselves may

---

[55] In Hebrew, *letaken olam bemalkhut shadai*, from the 'Aleinu' prayer of the liturgy.

[56] *Tsedakah*, generally used as the equivalent for 'charity', is etymologically linked with the word for 'justice'. After narrowing the meaning of the rabbinic statement to one word, the preacher presents a broad interpretation of that word.    [57] Echoing Zech. 4: 6.

[58] This familiar term for the synagogue is apparently not in the classical rabbinic texts but appears in later ethical literature.

[59] This transition from Jerusalem to Jammnia (or Yavneh) is recounted in BT *Git.* 56*b*.

[60] Historically, a very problematic statement: the 'Golden Age in Spain' is generally understood to apply to Jewish life from the mid-tenth to the mid-twelfth century under Islamic rule, most of it pre-dating the Crusaders' massacres in the Rhineland.

be guilty, all the false ambitions and spurious cravings of our own hearts; until we really, with a new sense of self-abnegation and sacrifice, [join] to the battle, not of Britain, but of the multitudes of the earth, not merely against an individual Hitler and his hordes, but against all the tyrants and exploiters, the bigots and oppressors throughout the world.

Is that hour nigh? Within our own breasts lies the answer. If the horror and havoc of the past year has had any meaning whatsoever then let us not heave a sigh of relief because the road looks brighter ahead, but let us reconsecrate ourselves to the holy task of building and planting anew upon surer and more lasting foundations. Then will this year, which now is just opening up before us, prove in truth a *shaar ha-shomayim* (Gen. 28: 17), a gate leading into the very kingdom of heaven on earth. Let us remember that when at the beginning the whole universe was *tohu v'vohu* (Gen. 1: 2), 'void and dark', it was the spirit of God alone that brought order out of confusion, cosmos out of chaos, light out of blackout. It is He alone that can perform that creative miracle once more today. Let us cease then our trembling supplication that He hasten to our aid, but seek instead to make certain that we are His light-bearers not unto the privileged few, but unto all the children of men.

(Let us pray that the year 5702 will become just such a year of light and victory, of victory of the spirit as well as of the armies on the field of battle. May it bring to us the consummation of those hopes and prayers which came home to me so vividly on many a quiet evening amid the utter silence of our northern lakes and woods. At the end of not a few calm and tranquil days, far removed from the terror and torture of a world which has been, in truth, too much with us, I stood on the shore of a secluded and sequestered island; far, far from the haunts of men and their evil machinations. The sight that invariably unfolded itself before my eyes was ever such as no artist among men has yet been able to limn. Only the hand of the Supreme Artist could etch so glorious a thing as a northern sunset. It always seemed to my awe-struck vision that in the distant skies a city was ablaze with golden fire. The reflection of it in the placid waters but added to the radiant beauty which human words are all too feeble to describe. But gradually the canvas changed. The gold gave way to the more delicate pastel tints of blue and violet and indigo. Then, suddenly, there appeared from behind a cloud, a great ball of fire so lurid in its brilliancy that the eye was dazzled before it. And there it blazed as though for a few moments it were standing still to proclaim the majesty and power of its Creator. But it was not destined to remain thus for long. Gradually, very gradually, inch by inch, it sank into what seemed to be its tomb beneath the waters, leaving the earth, save for a few moments of soft and lovely afterglow, in total darkness. Many a time, I could not but feel as I watched the dying day, as I feel when I am summoned to the death-bed of some good soul with whose dying gasps the light of the world seems to be extinguished.

But always, as such a mood of momentary depression overtook me, a new and glorious vision arose to dissipate my despair. Just as in the West the sun had set, in the East the silvery moon arose to drive away the darkness; and then the glittering stars appeared to puncture the blackout of the night. And ever and always amid such a changing scene, new hope and faith entered my heart to assure me that even as in the realm of nature, so in the haunts of men God will never forsake altogether His world, nor abandon it to total blackout. The sun goes down, but the gentle moon appears with its precious promise that the sun also rises.[61]

Such is the will of God. But to be realized on earth it must become enshrined in the hearts and souls of men. Such is the lesson we Jews have learned in the annals of our past. Shall we, after so many centuries of heroic struggle and dauntless courage, fail to carry out that will of God in order that out of the darkness there shall come light once more? Triumph shall indeed supplant our present tragedy if we do but become God's co-workers, if with sufficient zeal and sacrifice we carry out His way on earth.) How long, O Lord, how long? Let us cease from this piteous pleading and heed instead the categoric command which comes to us even as it came unto Moses: 'Wherefore criest thou unto *Me*? Speak unto the children of Israel and command them to march forward' (Exod. 14: 15). Forward then, not with overconfidence, but with unflinching courage assured that only as a result of our wrestling heroically with man and God will we, like Jacob, receive the Divine benediction.[62] In the words of an early Nineteenth Century poet,[63] some lines of which our valorous Prime Minister of Britain has been fond of quoting:[64]

> Say not the struggle naught availeth,
> The labour and the wounds are vain,
> The enemy faints not, nor faileth,
> And as things have been, they remain.

[61] Compare this paragraph with Leo M. Franklin, 'Light at the Eventide', 7–8. Since the entire paragraph, along with the preceding paragraph and the following five sentences, were placed within parentheses by the preacher, it is unclear whether or not he included them in his delivery.
[62] Alluding to Gen. 32: 27–9.      [63] Arthur Hugh Clough (1819–61).
[64] Churchill concluded his BBC speech of 27 Apr. 1941 as follows: 'Last time I spoke to you I quoted the lines of Longfellow which President Roosevelt had written out for me in his own hand. I have some other lines which are less well known but which seem apt and appropriate to

If hopes were dupes, fears may be liars;
    It may be, in yon smoke concealed,
Your comrades chase e'en now the fliers,
    And, *but for you*, possess the field.

For while the tired waves, vainly breaking,
    Seem here no painful inch to gain,
Far back, through creeks and inlets making,
    Comes silent, flooding in, the main.

And not by eastern windows only,
    When daylight comes, comes in the light;
In front, the sun climbs slow, how slowly!
    But westward, look! the land is bright.

our fortunes tonight, and I believe they will be so judged wherever the English language is spoken or the flag of freedom flies'—and then recited the last eight lines cited by the preacher (Churchill, *The Grand Alliance*, 236–7; <www.churchill-society-london.org.uk/LngHrdWr.html>).

# CHAPTER TWENTY-SIX

## ISRAEL H. LEVINTHAL
# IS IT DEATH OR REBIRTH OF THE WORLD THAT WE BEHOLD?

### 22 SEPTEMBER 1941
### (ROSH HASHANAH)

**BROOKLYN JEWISH CENTER, NEW YORK**

ISRAEL LEVINTHAL was born in Vilna in 1888. His father, Bernard (1865–1952), a distinguished Orthodox rabbi who emigrated to America with his family in 1891 to assume a rabbinic position at Philadelphia, later helped establish the Union of Orthodox Rabbis of the United States and Canada.[1] As we have seen above (see the introduction to Sermon 13), the young Israel worked as a reporter on Jewish affairs for a Philadelphia periodical and was deeply impressed by the oratorical abilities of the Reform rabbi Joseph Krauskopf. Entering a joint programme with Columbia University (for undergraduate courses) and the Jewish Theological Seminary (for rabbinic courses), despite his father's commitment to the Orthodox Rabbi Isaac Elchanan Theological Seminary, he received his BA from Columbia in 1909 (where he won a silver medal in the university oratorical contest) and was ordained rabbi the following year. He continued his studies, eventually gaining both a law degree from New York University and a doctorate in Hebrew Letters from the seminary.[2]

Following his ordination, Levinthal served in two Brooklyn congregations before becoming in 1919 the first rabbi of the Brooklyn Jewish Center, where he would serve for the rest of his career, during which its membership grew to a peak of close to 2,000 families in 1946. In addition to holding leadership

---

[1] On Bernard Levinthal, see P. Rosen, 'Orthodox Institution Builder', 126–44. I have been unsuccessful in finding sermon texts in the Bernard Levinthal Papers at the Philadelphia Jewish Archives Center, which contain primarily correspondence.

[2] Biographical material based on the Note in the Israel H. Levinthal Papers, and Caplan, 'The Life and Sermons of Rabbi Israel Herbert Levinthal', 1–27; see his sources, p. 2 n. 3.

positions in a variety of Conservative and Zionist organizations, he established a national reputation as one of the outstanding preachers of his time. The books of his published sermons reveal an unusual homiletical artistry and enable the sensitive reader to feel something of the power of the message as it was heard by the congregants. Levinthal himself was aware of his power; the handwritten texts of the sermons in his collected papers contain notations about his perception of their effectiveness, ranging from 'good' to 'most excellent'.[3] These texts were not written out in full; some serve as extensive outlines, while others are no more than a list of phrases. We therefore have in some cases three different versions of the sermon: the handwritten notes, a brief newspaper account with quotations, and the published text.

From the very beginning of the war, Levinthal's sermons reflect a deep anguish. His 1939 Rosh Hashanah sermon was entitled 'Wherefore Is the Earth Destroyed?' and his sermon for the first day of Passover 1941 'Why Has Tragedy Come to the World?' By the following Rosh Hashanah, the mood of gloom had if anything deepened. The sermon reproduced below reflects a dismal moment in the war, with German forces in control of a vast geographical expanse, virtually the entire continent of Europe. Levinthal chose as the structuring element the rabbinic dictum from the Talmud, 'There are three . . . sounds, that resound throughout the whole world, from one end to the other—The sound of . . . the revolution of the sun; the sound of . . . the tumultuous hosts of Rome; and the sound of . . . the soul departing from the body.'[4] Each is briefly explained in its original context and then applied to an aspect of the contemporary reality, culminating with 'the agonizing cry of the millions of souls that have departed on the battle-field or in bomb-stricken lands of Europe—cries that today are heard in every part of the world' and—even more disturbing—the 'Soul of the World' departing, leaving 'a new kind of world, where hate and torture, cruelty and barbarism, shall be the norms of everyday life, where deceit and robbery, violence and falsehood, shall be the mark of the new world order!'

At this point, the message from the aggadah is entirely bleak. Yet listeners would have known that the preacher could not end on this note. There had to be a modulation from the minor to the major key. How would this be done? Levinthal's artistry is revealed in his use of the final element of the aggadic dictum, 'Some say, also the sound of birth'—a sound that is not universally heard or widely acknowledged (as it was not recognized by all the sages in antiquity), but that can be discerned by some.

In our day, too, in the midst of the voices of death and destruction that reverberate throughout the world, there can be heard the *Kol Ledah*, the Voice of birth—a new birth of a chastened, purified humanity, and the birth of a new Jew redeemed through the fires of affliction. That is the meaning of the Battle of Britain, and now also

[3] Caplan, 'Life and Sermons of Rabbi Israel Herbert Levinthal', 14.   [4] BT *Yoma* 20b.

of the war in Russia. From their battle-fields there comes the assuring note: it is not only death that you behold, but through this death there is appearing a new life, a new birth for all the world! America, too, thank God, is determined that for once these *Resha-im*, these forces of darkness and evil, shall be destroyed forever, so that Democracy's triumph may mark a new *Kol Ledah* for all mankind.[5]

This message of hope is reinforced in the peroration with another rabbinic dictum, extremely useful to preachers in the bleakest of times, about Adam's despair when the sun set at the end of his first day on earth, fearing that it would be gone for ever, and his exaltation after the dark night of his soul at seeing the sun rise at dawn.

Needless to say, this sermon reveals a realm of homiletical discourse far removed from that represented by Eisendrath's sermon delivered in Toronto the night before. There are no purple passages or polished periods, no memorable original turns of phrase. Except for the reference to the Battle of Britain and the war in Russia, there is no analysis of the details of the military situation abroad or of the specificity of political machinations. There is no engagement with the behaviour of American Jews in general or of Levinthal's congregants in particular. This is a sermon not of castigation and rebuke but of anguish and solace; the work of a preacher mobilizing the resources of the traditional literature to acknowledge the darkness of the world in his time, and yet to affirm at least the possibility of hope for something new and better.

# SERMON

—

THOUSANDS of years, or aeons—depending on how we reckon—have passed since this world of ours came into being—an event which we recall on this sacred day.[6] But the world is not yet truly fashioned. As a matter of fact, the Biblical description of the universe before creation best portrays the world in which we live today: 'And the earth was unformed and void, and darkness was upon the face of the deep' (Gen. 1: 2).

What is the significance of these cataclysmic events which have shaken our world from its foundations? What is the meaning of this war which has been forced upon the world, and which is dragging nation after nation into its bloody net?[7]

---

[5] Levinthal, *A New World Is Born*, 12; see annotation to this passage at n. 19 below.

[6] Rosh Hashanah is traditionally understood to be the anniversary of the creation of the world. Note the preacher's reference to both the traditional Jewish calendar (the beginning of the year 5702 from the creation) and the modern scientific acceptance of a far greater age for the universe.

[7] A reference to the expansion of the war with the invasion of the Soviet Union the previous June.

There is a passage in the Talmud which I wish to interpret for you because I believe that it offers us in concise and clear fashion a striking analysis of what we behold today. *Shalosh Kolot Holkin Misof Ha-olam V'ad Sofo*. 'There are three voices or sounds, that resound throughout the whole world, from one end to the other: The sound of *Galgal Chamah*, the revolution of the sun; the sound of *Hamonah Shel Romi*, the tumultuous hosts of Rome; and the sound of *Neshamah B'Sha-ah She-yotzoh Min Ha-guf*, the soul departing from the body of man.'*

You have to understand the language of the Rabbis in order to appreciate the full meaning of our text. These men spoke in poetic terms, in mystic language. They, too, faced an era such as ours. The Roman Empire was beginning to take form, and to cast its tentacles about the throats of men. Its serried legions destroyed Palestine, ransacked Jerusalem, burnt the Temple, and carried off the Jews in chains as slaves. But Rome aimed at something more. Palestine was only the beginning, the first target, in its rapacious quest for human plunder. It strove to conquer the earth, to crush beneath the heels of its legions all the peoples of the then known world.[8]

The Rabbis wanted to describe the plight of the world in language which their oppressors would not understand, but which would be perfectly clear to their fellow-Jews. And so they tell of three sounds that reverberate throughout the world. The first is the sound of the 'sun's revolution'. In those days they believed that the sun revolves around the earth. But this notion does not affect their analysis. Ordinarily, when the sun sets upon one part of the earth, it shines on another. But now they beheld a complete *Galgal Chamah*—a universal setting of the sun. It was the sound of a complete blackout for all the world; the voice of a sun disappearing from all humanity. It was not a setting sun for Palestine alone. That was the tragic mistake of the other nations of that day. They thought that Rome's legions aimed at the land of the Jew alone—that they would be safe.[9] The Rabbis had a clearer

---

* BT *Yoma 20b*.

[8] It must be confessed that Levinthal's construction of the historical context for the statement in order to make it parallel to the present—suggesting that Rome was analogous to Nazi Germany—seems somewhat forced. The brutality of the Roman campaign against the Jews in the Land of Israel was a response to two massive rebellions by Jewish forces. The formulation that 'Palestine was only the beginning, the first target, in its rapacious quest for human plunder' seems to be especially intended to create an analogy with the claim that the Jews were only the first target of the Nazi regime. By the late second century, when the rabbinic statement was probably made, the rabbis were living in the era of the Pax Romana, not in the middle of a devastating war. Yet, as we shall see, the statement is used with great homiletical force.

[9] Again, the historical past is moulded to serve the contemporary point, as stated in the following paragraph.

vision, a keener perspective of world events. They knew what was coming—this sound of the setting sun resounded *Misof Ha-olam V'ad Sofo*, from one end of the earth to the other. All humanity was to be engulfed by the spreading darkness.

If you want to know what is happening in the world today, you will find the answer in this Rabbinic description. It is a *Galgal Chamah* that we witness. The sun is setting for the world. It is not only upon the Jew that this darkness has come. Here again, the nations have made the same mistake. The Nazi regime wants only to destroy the Jew, they said. We are safe; the sun will not set upon our lands, upon our peoples! They failed to perceive, what these ancient sages saw so clearly, that such darkness knows no bounds and no limitations—that this darkness must spread *Misof Ha-olam V'ad Sofo*, from one end of the earth to the other. And it has already begun to spread. There is darkness everywhere. There is not a spot in all the world where there is undisturbed, undiminished light and sunshine. It is a blackout of civilization which threatens us.

And the Rabbis continue with their analysis, describing the second sound that can be heard throughout all the world: *Kol Hamonah Shel Romi*, 'the sound of the massed, tramping legions of Rome'. The terrifying force that brought this total eclipse of the sun and that was responsible for the new darkness which fell upon the lives of all nations, is the *Hamonah Shel Romi*—the brutalized armies of Rome, that did not pause after plundering Palestine, but marched on and on, crushing nation after nation.

When Mussolini seized power, he declared that his aim was to restore to Italy the glory of the ancient armies of Rome.[10] Feeble in this respect as he proved himself to be, he found an ally who bettered his instruction and who did succeed in recreating the *Hamonah Shel Romi*, the mighty and ferocious hosts of ancient Rome. The sound of the marching boots of these successors of the *Hamonah Shel Romi* may be heard from nearly one end of the earth to the other. Jews were the first to meet their fierce attacks—but other peoples soon felt their crushing blows, and today no nation is safe, no ocean is a barrier,[11] as these bloodthirsty hosts seek to advance in their march *Misof Ha-olam V'ad Sofo*!

And there is the third sound that may clearly be heard from one earth's end to the other—'the sound of the soul as it departs from the body of man'. The Rabbis, in those tragic days in which they lived, heard not only the anguished cry

[10] On the cult of *Romanità* in Italian Fascism, with its claims of continuity with the imperial Roman state, see Payne, *A History of Fascism*, 217.

[11] A jab at American isolationists who insisted that Nazi Germany could not endanger the United States because of the oceanic barrier.

of the slain and butchered in Palestine and in other lands, of the souls that departed from the bodies of those who fell in battle defending their country and faith, but they heard, too, the sound of the Soul departing from the universe. That was the real aim of conquering Rome. It wanted to crush the World's Soul, it wanted a world without a soul, a world built on force and cruelty alone.[12]

Yea, we, too, hear today the sound of the soul as it departs from the bodies of men. I am not speaking now of the agonizing cry of the millions of souls that have departed on the battle-field or in bomb-stricken lands of Europe—cries that today are heard in every part of the world. It is the Soul of the World that is departing! Herein lies the real danger of the Nazi revolution. Its aim is the destruction of the Soul of Humanity—the breeding of a new kind of world, where hate and torture, cruelty and barbarism, shall be the norms of everyday life, where deceit and robbery, violence and falsehood, shall be the mark of the new world order!

I said at the outset that we are back in the primordial days of *Tohu Vo-vohu*.[13] The Rabbis interpret this Biblical description of the pre-creation period not only in a physical sense, but also in terms of historic truth. 'The darkness that covered the depths (Gen. 1: 2)—*Zu Malkut Harsha'ah*—refers to the wicked kingdom (i.e. Rome). For just as the depths of the earth cannot be measured so, too, there is no measure to the wickedness of this evil power.'\* Surely, these words may equally be said of the evil power that threatens the world today. We Jews have met many a foe before. But no enemy of former days made cruelty the fine art as do the Nazis today. Other nations, too, knew enemies before—the so-called world conquerors of ancient, medieval and modern times. They brought darkness into the lives of men and peoples. But none equalled the ferocity of these *Resha-im*, whose wickedness cannot be measured, who are bringing about the end of Man himself. The brilliant English cartoonist, Low, recently portrayed in graphic lines this great truth. Hitler is pictured holding man in his hand, and challenging God: 'You, God, may have begun man, but I will finish him!'[14]

---

\* *Genesis Rabbah* 2: 5.

[12] Here, too, Roman intentions are presented not from historical sources but from the homiletical need to provide a precursor and model for Nazi Germany.

[13] The Hebrew words from Gen. 1: 2 meaning 'chaos', translated as 'unformed and void' at the beginning of the sermon.

[14] Sir David Low (1891–1963), sometimes characterized as the most influential cartoonist of the twentieth century. See *Low on the War*, and *Years of Wrath*. This is the bleakest moment of the sermon, and it is quite striking that (except for a stylized 'thank God' below) the only reference to God it contains is the caption of a cartoon about Hitler. The evocation of hope that begins with the continuation of the dictum, without explicit reference to God or divine providence, may reflect Levinthal's affinity with Mordecai Kaplan's naturalistic theology.

But the Talmudic comment does not stop here. In describing the voices that resound throughout the world it adds: *V'yesh Omrim*, 'And there are other rabbis who say: *Af Ledah*, there is another voice that is also heard from one end to the other, the sound of birth.' Again, we have here language shrouded in mystery, but of deep significance. It is remarkable that in the midst of the tragedy that came upon their people and upon the world of their day, they could yet hear and distinguish another voice, a still, small voice,[15] but one that resounded throughout the world, the sound of birth! Out of the tragedy they recognized the birth pangs of a new world and a new, revitalized Jew.[16] Not all heard this voice. Even among the sages, while all could recognize the voices of destruction, only some—*Yesh Omrim*, a chosen few—could discern the sound of *Ledah*, of birth, that resounded throughout the earth.[17] Civilization did finally emerge from the clutches of Rome; and the Jew, though driven from hearth and home, arose and was reborn, again to play a noble role upon the stage of history.

In our day, too, in the midst of the voices of death and destruction that reverberate throughout the world, there can be beard the *Kol Ledah*, the voice of birth—a new birth of a chastened, purified humanity, and the birth of a new Jew redeemed through the fires of affliction.[18] That is the meaning of the Battle of Britain, and now also of the war in Russia.* From their battle-fields there comes the assuring note: it is not only death that you behold, but through this death there is appearing a new life, a new birth for all the world! America, too, thank God, is determined that for once these *Resha-im*, these forces of darkness and evil, shall be destroyed forever, so that Democracy's triumph may mark a new *Kol Ledah* for all mankind.[19]

* America's entry into the war, after this sermon was preached, makes this fact even more significant.

[15] Echoing 1 Kgs 19: 12 in the King James translation.
[16] 'Birth pangs' evokes the traditional phrase 'birth pangs of the Messiah' (*hevlei mashiah*), a powerful image of pain necessary to produce redemption, but Levinthal does not refer to a personal messiah here.
[17] *Yesh omerim* means literally 'there are those who say', indicating a statement that did not command a consensus among the sages. Levinthal uses this addition to the talmudic statement to suggest with masterly skill that although the basis for hope cannot yet be detected by everyone, as it is still indistinct, it is none the less real.
[18] This is the first of three uses of the phrase 'new birth' leading up to the 'birth of true freedom' in the final sentence, all echoing the 'new birth of freedom' in Lincoln's Gettysburg Address (see n. 25 below).
[19] Levinthal was probably alluding here to a statement made by President Roosevelt in his 'Fireside Chat' of 11 September, a week and a half before the sermon; see the citation of Roosevelt in H. Saperstein, 'Undying Fires', 88 (a sermon delivered the same day as Levinthal's).

And for us Jews there is also the sound of birth. In the midst of this, our greatest suffering and misery, we must attune our ears to hear the sound of resurrection and new birth. The remarkable spirit that is today displayed by the half million Jews in Eretz Israel is the living proclamation to all the world that the Jew, too, is hearing the *Kol Ledah*![20]

In the midst of the sun's eclipse, and the sound of souls driven from the bodies of men by the tramping hosts of modern Rome,[21] there goes forth from the lips of brave souls and courageous hearts the reassuring message: *Ad Motai Yehei Ha-olam Mitnaheg B'afelah*, 'How long shall the world be led in darkness? *Tavo Ha-orah*, Let there come the light!'*

It is to this faith and voice that we must dedicate ourselves today. When we repeat the words, *Hayom Harat Olam*, 'This day a world came into being',[22] we shall think not only of the world that came into being ages ago, but we shall affirm with all our strength and conviction that this day a new world shall be born,[23] a new world for humanity and a new world for the Jew.

I know that it is not an easy task to hold high this light of faith in the midst of the black night that has come upon the world. I know that many are in despair and feel that the end has come, the end to all men's striving for a better day. To all who see only the dark horizon, I would recall a simple but beautiful tale that the Rabbis in the Talmud tell of Adam, the first human being on earth. When Adam beheld the first sunset and saw the darkness approaching, he became very much frightened and began to weep. *Oi Li*, 'Woe is me,' he sobbed, *Shemah Zu-hi Ha-mitah, V'chozer Ha-olam L'tohu Vo'vohu*, 'This is the end, this must mean Death, the world is returning to void and nothingness!' And so he kept weeping and wailing all through the night until the dawn began to appear. The sun rose again, and the darkness gradually gave way to the oncoming light. Looking at the bright heavens, he joyfully exclaimed, *Kalon Diem*, 'Beautiful day, beautiful world!' †[24]

* *Genesis Rabbah* 2: 4.
† JT *AZ* i: 2 (39c); cf. also R. Hananel on Babli, ibid. 8a, and interesting note of Professor Louis Ginzberg, in *The Legends of the Jews*, v. 116, n. 107.

[20] Cf. H. Saperstein, 'What Have We Jews To Be Thankful For?', 100.
[21] Recapitulating the three parts of the original rabbinic statement.
[22] From the liturgy of Rosh Hashanah (see Arzt, *Justice and Mercy*, 183).
[23] Levinthal took this phrase, 'a new world is born', as the title of the book containing this and other sermons of the period. Note that the duality of the new world expressed at the end of the statement (for humanity, for the Jew) recapitulates a theme that runs throughout the sermon.
[24] Cf. the use of another version of this legend by Chief Rabbi Hertz in his Intercession Day sermon of 1 Jan. 1916 (above, p. 320).

Many who behold the thick darkness that has come upon the world today are crying in the words of Adam of old, 'Woe is us, this must mean the end of it all, this must mean Death—death of all civilization, of all things we hold dear and cherish!' But it is not the end. It is not Death. It is only a black night! The night will pass, the sun will shine again, and out of the horrors and agonies that came with the night will come the dawn of a new day. We, too, like Adam, shall yet joyfully cry out: *Kalon Diem*, 'Beautiful day, beautiful world!'—for it will mark the birth of true freedom and liberty,[25] of lasting peace and joy, for all the children of man!

[25] Picking up the motif from the rabbinic statement ('the sound of birth') and perhaps echoing Lincoln's Gettysburg Address ('a new birth of freedom'); see n. 18 above.

# CHAPTER TWENTY-SEVEN

## FERDINAND M. ISSERMAN
# THE UNITED STATES
# IS AT WAR

### 12 DECEMBER 1941

#### TEMPLE ISRAEL, ST LOUIS

Born in 1898 in Antwerp, Belgium, Ferdinand Isserman emigrated to America with his family in 1906. Like many Reform rabbis of his generation, he completed a combined programme at the University of Cincinnati and the Hebrew Union College. Though exempt from conscription as a rabbinical student, he enlisted in the army in 1918, an experience to which he alluded in his subsequent preaching on war. After ordination, he served as assistant rabbi in Rodef Shalom of Philadelphia, rabbi of Holy Blossom Congregation in Toronto (preceding Eisendrath), and—beginning in 1929—in Temple Israel of St Louis, where he remained until his death in 1971.

In the summer of 1933 Isserman spent a month in Germany, and upon returning in the autumn he preached about his impressions of how Jews were living under the Nazi regime. On 28 October that year, after reporting extensively on the tragic experiences of individuals he had met, he concluded by warning Americans against being deceived by the disinformation circulated by Nazi propagandists:

Americans might believe Hitler's professions of peace and good will, but the people of Czecho-Slovakia, Poland, Holland, Belgium, England and France, who have seen the victims of Hitler's brown-[shirted] soldiers, who have seen the welts on their backs, the bruises on their faces, who have seen them maimed for life, know that Naziism is not the rebirth of a great nation. They know that Naziism is the degradation of a noble people. They know that Hitler is neither a prophet nor a messiah, but a fanatical maniac, who is leading a revolt against civilization, against the humanities, against God.[1]

---

[1] Isserman, 'Personal Experiences with Victims of the Brown Terror', 10. He also published in 1933 a pamphlet based on his impressions with the alarmist yet prescient title, 'Sentenced to Death: The Jews in Nazi Germany'.

Two years later, reporting on a second visit, he concluded that 'the anti-democratic, anti-Christian nationalistic Nazi philosophy is relentlessly being worked out', though—perhaps rather naively—he also claimed that the policies of the regime were creating 'a vast and an increasing opposition'. As for practical advice to Americans and the rest of the civilized world: 'Whoever gives the Nazi regime moral support, whether it be by participating in the [Berlin] Olympic games, or in any other fashion, is strengthening the hands of the barbarians who are in the process of ruining Germany and who may bring chaos upon all of Europe and destroy Western civilization.'[2]

Yet some six months later, on 1 May 1936, convinced that 'another clash between mighty nations is imminent', while drawing lessons from the dismaying aftermath of American involvement in the Great War when 'democracy lost ground after the allied armies were victorious', Isserman strongly opposed from the pulpit the position that the United States must be prepared to defend any nation threatened by fascist aggression. Instead, he supported a policy of proactive neutrality, including legislation to prohibit American businesses from increasing their sales to belligerent nations and American ships from carrying goods to these nations. At present, 'as a result of the war [of 1914–18], I see democracy fighting for its life, militarism enthroned, while another world war looms upon the horizon'. His conclusion was that war itself is the ultimate evil: 'It, therefore, seems that the cause of humanity and of America can best be served by having our country notify the world of its resolution to have nothing to do with the scourge of war.'[3]

This material provides a context for the uncompromising position Isserman adopted when war did break out in Europe. In his sermon delivered on 20 October 1939, the fierce antipathy towards Nazism evidenced in the earlier sermons remains unabated:

Europe today is threatened by a darker foe than some wild and savage conqueror from another continent. It is threatened by a tyrant as ruthless as any that history has ever known who has at his disposal the mechanisms and the technological inventions of modern civilization . . . There is abroad in America a strong propaganda that there is no moral difference between the cause of England and France and the cause of Nazism. True, neither France nor England have been saints, but where is there a nation whose conduct has been perfect? But [Yet] between the causes of France and England and the cause of Nazism today, only he who is morally blind fails to see a vast difference.

---

[2] Isserman, 'My Second Visit to Nazi Germany', 10. On the proposed boycott of the Olympic Games, see also the sermon delivered one week later by Harold Saperstein, 'The Great Olympic Idea'.

[3] Isserman, 'Collective Security, Neutrality or War', 1, 5, 9. He even called for a constitutional amendment removing the power to declare war from the President and Congress and giving it to the people directly through a popular amendment (ibid. 7).

He further attacked some of the isolationist forces in American society, especially Charles A. Lindbergh's argument that America should stay out of the war because it was threatened by no 'yellow peril', no Genghis Khan or Xerxes.[4] This he declared wrong on theological grounds—'The whole idea of the yellow peril is repugnant to any religious person. There is only one God and there is only one humanity'—and on factual grounds:

If by the spirit of Genghis Khan and Xerxes Colonel Lindbergh means the spirit of ruthlessness, the spirit of cruelty, the spirit of tyranny, the spirit of contempt for human life, the spirit of narrow clannishness, then that spirit has been evidenced, not merely in the writings and the speeches, but also in the practice of the Nazi leaders and the Nazi followers.

Yet just like Abraham Feinberg, whose Rosh Hashanah 1939 sermon appears above (Sermon 22), expressing a position that appears to be the consensus of American rabbis at this moment and that he claims reflects the overwhelming consensus of the American public, Isserman draws from these premises a conclusion that was practically identical with Lindbergh's: 'Although Americans may have sympathies and recognize the greater justice of one cause over and against another, nevertheless, Americans should stay out of the war.' The first reason given is very close to that adduced by H. Pereira Mendes regarding the declaration of the War on Spain (Sermon 12 above): consistency. So many other cases of international injustice might be cited to validate American intervention:

In modern civilization, no nation can set itself up as the arbiter of justice or as the policeman of the world. We cannot go to war with peoples whose philosophies challenge our own. There are tyrannies in South America as well as in Europe, though they are not as severe. America would be engaged in perpetual warfare if in every international issue it threw its armed forces on the side of justice.

Then, following a detailed discussion of the nature of American neutrality, in which he continues to oppose allowing American ships to carry arms to any of the belligerent nations, he sets out the second strand of his argument, familiar from Feinberg and many others:

Not merely for our own sake but for the sake of mankind we must not become involved in the European conflict. At the end of this struggle, the world will need one people of sanity, one people whose hands are clean, one people whose energies have not been concentrated on hate and murder and destruction. One people free and self respecting,

---

[4] The reference is to Lindbergh's 'Appeal for Isolation' statement of 15 Sept. 1939: 'These wars in Europe are not wars in which our civilization is defending itself against some Asiatic intruder. There is no Genghis Khan nor Xerxes marching against our Western nations. This is not a question of banding together to defend the white race against foreign invasion. This is simply . . . a quarrel arising from the errors of the last war . . . America has little to gain by taking part in another European war.'

which will be in a position to give council, to bind up wounds, to assuage pain, to bring relief. From civilization, Americans receive a challenge. That challenge is to use these days to protect American democracy, to end American unemployment, to establish social justice, so that at the end of the strife and the conflict, European peoples will gaze to the west and will be cheered and encouraged by the noble example of a free people made up of all the children of Europe which has maintained a just and good civilization. The example of America will inspire and encourage Europeans, perhaps, will teach them the way of their salvation.[5]

His words of reassurance—'There is no force on earth which can impel us into war. There is no armada on air, on sea or on land which can for the present jeopardise our security'—must have seemed painfully ironic when he was compelled to face his congregation at the first sabbath service following the assault on Pearl Harbor of 7 December 1941.

How does a preacher who has taken such a consistently strong anti-war position respond when the nation goes to war following a devastating, unprovoked attack by Japan and an unexpected declaration of war by Hitler? Let us note what is not in the sermon. There is no review of his earlier pronouncements opposing America's involvement in the war and endorsing a position of strict neutrality, of behaviour if not of sympathy. There is no lingering on the devastation and treachery of the Japanese attack, which were by this point, five days later, obvious to every American. There is no appeal to classical Jewish sources. In this his sermon contrasts with that of Israel Levinthal, delivered the same evening, which draws from the weekly Torah pericope 'Vayishlaḥ' the rabbinic interpretation of Esau's duplicity regarding a reconciliation with Jacob—applying it to the Japanese diplomats who feigned cordiality in Washington while their attack on Pearl Harbor was being planned and implemented—and asserts (following the commentaries of Rashi and the Midrash) that the United States would have done better to emulate the model of Jacob, who prepared himself for war while engaged in prayer and diplomacy.[6]

Isserman does, however, derive from the approaching holiday of Hanukah a historical principle that he applies to the present: the distinction between a tyrannical ruler (Antiochus Epiphanes) and the culture that he purportedly represented but actually had betrayed (Hellenism).[7] So, he insists that

---

[5] Isserman, 'We Americans and the War in Europe', 2–3, 9.

[6] Israel H. Levinthal, 'The Hands of Esau'. Levinthal repeated material from this sermon on the first day of the following Rosh Hashanah, in a sermon entitled 'When Thou Goest to War'.

[7] Levinthal, preaching the following morning, also used Hanukah (together with the 150th anniversary of the passing of the Bill of Rights) to argue that Maccabees hated war but hated enslavement even more, and so went to war on behalf of their own Bill of Rights. Strikingly, in this sermon, Levinthal states, 'Thank God we were attacked, for now the Jews cannot be blamed for starting this war' (untitled sermon of 13 Dec. 1941, Levinthal Papers, box 7). I am grateful to my student Alan Dodkowitz for his notes on this sermon.

America's war now is not against the culture of Germany, Italy, or Japan, but against the tyrants who have abandoned that culture; not against the peoples of these countries, but against ruthless dictators from whom these peoples must be liberated. The war must be fought without yielding to the seductions of hatred, especially against Germans, Italians, and Japanese in America. Though acknowledging the difficult military situation at present, the sermon is extremely optimistic about the efficiency of freedom in preparing the materials for war, the potential of the American people to draw together, the economic prosperity that will follow the inevitable victory of the Allies, and America's role to liberate the victims of fascism not only from political but from economic tyranny, through 'the reconstruction and rehabilitation of Europe'. It is a sermon that leaps ahead from a bleak present to a powerful vision of the future.

# S E R M O N

FOR the first time since the war of 1812, the United States has been invaded. After the invasion, which was carried out by Japan, but planned in collaboration with Germany and Italy,[8] war was declared upon us and Congress responded at the request of the President by declaring war in turn upon the three axis powers. That we were assailed by Japan before a formal declaration of war, even as Norway, Poland, Czecho-Slovakia and other states had been assailed by Germany and Italy,[9] is merely another evidence of the decay of international morality and a hint of the ethics that will prevail in the world if the Nazis and their satellites succeed in establishing their much vaunted new order.

By an interesting coincidence, on Sunday evening occurs the anniversary of the Maccabean wars, whose victorious outcome is still celebrated by Jews all over the world in the ceremonies lasting for eight days in connection with the Chanukah festival. The Maccabean war was fought for the same goal for which

[8] Thus, in his 'Fireside Chat' of 9 December, to which the preacher will refer explicitly later in the sermon, President Roosevelt said, 'It is actual collaboration so well calculated that all the continents of the world, and all the oceans, are now considered by the Axis strategists as one gigantic battlefield': Copeland et al. (eds), *The World's Greatest Speeches*, 533.
[9] The analogy between the Pearl Harbor attack without warning and similar, earlier attacks against unsuspecting nations by Germany and Italy was made by Roosevelt in the same 'Fireside Chat'.

the United States is at war at the present time. It was fought for liberty of conscience, for the right of the small nation to worship God in accordance with the dictates of its people. Under the leadership of the old priest Matthias and his valiant sons, the Jews of Judea, though tremendously outnumbered, and though victory seemed hopeless, rose in revolt against a totalitarian ruler and his mighty legions who sought to destroy their religion, their sacred literature, their holy temple.

If the Maccabees had been defeated, Judaism would have disappeared from the face of the earth. The Bible would have been destroyed and the subsequent birth of Christianity would have become impossible. In the war in which we find ourselves engaged, the same issues are at stake for mankind, which were at stake in the Maccabean struggle. If the Nazis win, not merely the allied nations lose, but Judaism and Christianity, the Hebrew–Christian tradition lose. Because if the axis is triumphant, the spiritual, moral and ethical values of life which grew out of the literature of the Bible, the concept of one humanity and one God, the concept of the brotherhood of peoples of all races, the ideal of justice for the weak, the principles of love and mercy as the dominant force in human relationship, will for the time being be wiped off the face of the earth.

The United States is not merely fighting for its national existence. In this struggle, it is the vehicle of the forces of faith and of light and the champion of the hallowed ideals and aspirations of the human race. On the billboard of St. John's Methodist Church, I noticed the sermon theme of my neighbor and colleague, Rev. Dr. John B. Peters. It is 'Christianity is Challenged'. This is his way of stating that the values at stake in the Maccabean struggle are the values that are at stake in the present world war. If the axis wins, moral darkness will brood over the face of the earth. If the United States and her allies win, the dawn of a new and greater justice will brighten the homes and the hearths of men.

At times, it has been erroneously stated that the Maccabean war was a conflict between Hebraism and Hellenism and that the contending armies were merely the puppets through which these two significant cultures were struggling for supremacy and for survival. Today, we know that this is not so. Antiochus Epiphanes was not the champion of the Hellenic values of life. He was not endeavoring to disseminate the culture of Athens or the philosophy of Plato and Aristotle, or the art of Greece in the world. Antiochus Epiphanes was a bastard and illegitimate offshoot of Greek culture. Hellenic culture enriched and influenced the Hebraic tradition. The biblical books of Proverbs and of

Job, the philosophy of Philo and of Saadia and of Maimonides clearly reveal the beneficent influence of Greek culture upon Hebraic history and literature. Hebraism and Hellenism were not at war. Christianity is one of the fruits of the mingling of the culture of Greece and the culture of Judea. Antiochus Epiphanes was a totalitarian tyrant who spoke Greek but whose mind repudiated the noblest in the Greek tradition.[10]

Even so today we must not interpret this war as a struggle on the one hand between the culture of America, Great Britain, China and their allies, and the culture of Germany, Italy, Japan and their allies. Mussolini and Hitler are illegitimate offshoots of German and Italian culture. They are not carrying out the teachings or the traditions of Goethe and of Kant, of Lessing and of Heine, of Garibaldi and of Mazzini. If these great German and Italian spirits were living today they would be either in exile, as is Thomas Mann, or in concentration camps, or the victims of assassins. Therefore, we in America shall be on our guard not to repeat the antics of the previous world war when German literature was condemned, when German books were burned, when German music was outlawed.[11]

Even as we are not at war with the cultural traditions of Germany and of Italy, so we are not at war with the peoples of the axis countries. We are at war with their governments.[12] We are at war with the gangsters and desperados and consciousless [conscienceless] men who by terror and by chicanery, who by fraud and by deceit, who by foul propaganda and unscrupulous demagoguery, by clandestine conspiracy and by cruel conniving, have made themselves the

[10] As a liberal rabbi committed to the values of classical Western civilization, who probably realized that the Jewish Hellenists of the Hasmonean era were in some ways the Reform Jews of their time, Isserman did not want to emphasize the *Kulturkampf* interpretation of the Hanukah story. Furthermore, for the specific homiletical need of the moment, it was more useful to present Antiochus Epiphanes as a tyrant who perverted the best values of his culture, as did Hitler and Mussolini. In this he followed Graetz, who characterized Antiochus as 'a monster, who had a heart of stone, and scorned alike man and law, morality and religion': *History of the Jews*, i. 444.

[11] After America's entry into the war, Beethoven's music was banned in Pittsburgh, and several states passed legislation prohibiting the teaching of German in their schools. German-language books were burned in Oakland, Hooper, and Grand Island (Nebraska), Boulder (Colorado), and elsewhere. See Wiley, 'The Imposition of World War I Era English-Only Policies', esp. 21–9; Luebke, *Bonds of Loyalty*, 248–55. There were efforts to stamp out traces of European identity among immigrants, and vigilante attacks against German-born American citizens: Kennedy, *Over Here*, 67–9.

[12] This distinction was part of the rhetoric of the Allies during the First World War. The rest of this paragraph, and the following one, appear to underestimate considerably the degree of popular support (and even adulation) for Hitler within the German population, which increased significantly between 1933 and 1939, and rose even further with the stunning victories in the first year of the war.

masters of the governmental machinery of those peoples. After having succeeded in that, they first enslaved, cowed and degraded their own peoples so that they became nothing but appendages to the war machine. Then they robbed them of their sons and trained them for a war against the liberties of men, for a war for the conquest of the world.

I am firmly convinced from my own experiences in Germany, from the fact that democracy had to be destroyed before Nazism could triumph, that there are countless thousands, millions among the German people who have not lost their sense of moral values and who groan beneath the lash of their taskmaster, even as do the peoples in conquered lands. Hitler is not Germany. Mussolini is not Italy. And the war party in Japan is not the Japanese people. We in the United States are out to destroy these tyrannical governments, these despotic rulers, these military war-lords, these peddlers of hate, these foes of the Hebrew–Christian tradition, these spokesmen for the evil forces in human life.

We are out to liberate and to emancipate the peoples of these countries from their tyrant masters. One of our war aims must be to free the Germans and the Japanese and the Italian people from the clutches of the gangsters who have befouled their traditions, trampled upon their freedom, denied them their rights and robbed them of their dignity and undermined in them their faith in God. We must, therefore, be very careful that we do not begin to hate all Japanese, all Germans, all Italians. Not only because many of them are innocent of the crimes of their governments, but also because hatred will destroy us spiritually. If not[13] and we yield to hatred and begin to hate Germans, Italians, and Japanese in our midst, who have not been conspiring against our institutions, then psychologically we shall be filled with a burning hate.[14] When the war is over and our foes are gone, we shall do what we did after the last world war, when we began to hate our neighbors and the Ku Klux Klan came into being and for a brief period flourished in American life.

Can we then pursue a war effectively without hate? I believe we can. We can set out on our task with all the calm, with all the resolution of a surgeon who

[13] i.e. if we are not careful to avoid hatred. The continuation of this sentence shifts the object of potential hatred from the people of the Axis countries to Germans, Italians, and Japanese in the United States. I have not been able to determine Isserman's position on the subsequent round-up and deportation of Japanese Americans; my impression is that few rabbis spoke out against it at the time.

[14] A carelessly written sentence which probably would have been changed in the delivery. The following sentence provides an interesting claim, correlating hatred of the enemy produced by American participation in the Great War with the emergence of hate organizations in American society.

seeks to destroy cancer in the body of a human being. To get at the cancer, the surgeon must inflict pain. He must even destroy good tissue. This he does without compunction, unhesitating and decisively. So we Americans must now proceed to cut from the body of humanity the spiritual cancer symbolized by the governments of the axis powers. This we must do resolutely, courageously. This we can do without embroiling our souls in the passions of hate and of vengeance.

At this time too we must resolutely resolve that when victory will be ours, as it must be ours, we shall not seek a peace of vengeance or of retribution, but instead we shall try to establish a peace based on justice and world brotherhood, a peace in which we shall avoid the mistakes of other treaties.[15] A peace in which we shall recognize the need of international institutions to make possible international cooperation, a peace which shall provide to all peoples of the world access to basic raw materials, which shall be built on the rock of justice and on the enduring foundation of having eliminated the causes of war. It must be a peace which will safeguard liberty and freedom not only to all nations, but to all individuals of such nations. In our pursuit of the war, as the President pointed out in his fireside chat, we must not forget the ultimate goals of a nobler peace based on international cooperation.[16]

Our task is a difficult one, and these initial setbacks have served as a warning of [against] smug complacence which might lead us to assume that victory is around the corner.[17] We are arrayed against nations that have been preparing for war for a generation while we have been concerned with peace. While recognizing that, we must not underestimate our own resources, our own power, the caliber of our people and the character of our youth. We are the largest free people in the world and we shall demonstrate that our freedom will make us efficient, that our freedom has not softened us, that our freedom will

[15] Isserman is undoubtedly referring primarily to the Treaty of Versailles. In his earlier sermons, the central lesson drawn from the experience of the First World War was that America should resist being drawn into another world war. With this lesson now moot, Isserman turns to a second lesson about the proper conclusion of the war.

[16] The closest I see in the presidential 'Fireside Chat' of 9 December is the statement, 'The true goal we seek is far above and beyond the ugly field of battle. When we resort to force, as now we must, we are determined that this force shall be directed toward ultimate good as well as against immediate evil. We Americans are not destroyers—we are builders': Copeland et al. (eds), *The World's Greatest Speeches*, 537.

[17] 'These initial setbacks' perhaps echo Roosevelt's 'Fireside Chat' of 9 December: 'So far, the news has been all bad. We have suffered a serious set-back in Hawaii. Our forces in the Philippines, which include the brave people of that Commonwealth, are taking punishment, but are defending themselves vigorously. The reports from Guam and Wake and Midway islands are still confused, but we must be prepared for the announcement that all these three outposts have been seized': Copeland et al. (eds), *The World's Greatest Speeches*, 533.

make us eager and willing to bear burdens and to meet calamity to maintain our liberties. We shall be efficient because we are free, and a free man is the most creative. Thus shall we refute the myth of the inefficiency of democracy.[18]

Our industrial resources, our industrial brains, our industrial capacity are unsurpassed, and we shall multiply them. Our nation will be united. We must call an immediate halt to all feuds in our midst. There must be no labor baiting, and there must be no business baiting. We hope that labor will curb strikes voluntarily, and we hope that business will curb profiteering voluntarily. Every racial group in the American scene must receive the justice which is its due. We must not divide into religious or sectarian groups, nor must we divide into groups of national origins. Whether we were internationalists or isolationists is now to be forgotten. We are Americans all united in a common task.

Our young men when able will go into the armed forces conscious of the dangers that confront them. They will go with heads up and morale high, not complaining of their lot, but cognizant of their privilege to share their blood and to give their lives if need be that liberty may endure. That thus they too might take their places among the heroes and martyrs of Valley Forge and of Gettysburg, of the Argonne and of Pearl Harbor. Those who cannot serve in the armed forces will find other means of serving. They will give of their abilities, if they have them, for the important tasks that will have to be done behind the lines. They will give of their means generously and gladly. We shall not and must not develop another generation of war profiteers. We shall be like one family united in a common purpose and dedicated to a common task.

Nor must we dim our efforts, dampen our enthusiasm or impair our morale by the false speculation that at the end of this war crisis depression is inevitable, and that there must be such an economic dislocation of our life, alongside of [in comparison with] which the last depression will seem like an ant-hill next to a Rocky Mountain peak. On the contrary, I am convinced that after this war, not perdition but paradise awaits us if we can rise morally and spiritually to the opportunities that will abound. We shall expand our industries to produce war machinery. We shall train more workers, and when the war is over, these war industries can be converted by the genius of American engineers and by the skill of American business, by the capacity of American labor, into institutions which can help build up the level of living within our own country.

---

[18] The 'inefficiency of democracy' was an argument that had been raised in the preceding years in favour of the allegedly more efficient planned economy of the Soviet Union. See the discussion by Freehof, 'Minds Confused', 20–2.

We shall produce more steel, and after the war we shall continue to produce steel not for arms, but for homes, to do away with slums, to improve the quality of living for all Americans. But not merely for our own purposes shall we use our expanded industries. Thousands of cities will have to be rebuilt. Scores of countries will need the engineering skill, the craftsmanship and the facilities of America. Destroying the tyrant will be half of our task. Helping rebuild the world, equipping it with the comforts and conveniences which America has produced, will be our second task. If we assume this task and prove to be morally and spiritually big enough for it, then this country will be a happy beehive of people who know they can produce and [that] they are producing for the welfare of all mankind.

We are engaged, therefore, in a war to save for humanity the spiritual values of the Hebrew–Christian tradition. We are out to destroy tyrannical governments and the military monsters they have created. We are out to emancipate the peoples of conquered nations. We are out to free and to liberate the peoples of the axis powers, crushed and groaning beneath the cruelties of their autocratic and despotic rulers. We are out to maintain the liberties for which Americans have suffered and died. We shall guard in this spiritual enterprise from being filled with hate. We are not at war with the culture, the language or the literature of the axis peoples. When the war is over, we shall try to build an international society based on international cooperation and an international conscience. We shall use our expanded industries to promote the needs of peace and to help all mankind attain a higher and a better standard of living. We shall thus first free humanity from political tyranny, and then free humanity from economic tyranny. This is our goal. This is a moral goal. This is a just goal. This goal we shall achieve. Victory will be ours, not merely because we have the manpower, the courage, the will, the resources, but because we are on the side of righteousness, we are on the side of liberty, we are on the side of morality, we are on the side of Jeremiah and of Jesus, we are on the side of God.

Our prayers arise for the President of the United States, who is now the leader of the forces of righteousness. May God keep and preserve him. We pray for the men who are charged with the task of planning for our armed forces and for our industrial program. We pray for the boys in places of danger and their dear ones at home. We pray for the boys who have already fallen and promise them that they have not died in vain. That out of their premature deaths, we are resolved to build a new altar to Almighty God, an altar which shall be the symbol that the Kingdom of peace and justice is at hand.

We pledge our will, our lives, our property to the President of the United States. Let him order and we shall obey. Whatever the next days may bring to us, we shall bear all burdens, all sorrow and all sufferings with the spiritual consciousness that we are bringing an offering to God that His will may be realized on earth and His purpose for the destiny of humanity may be fulfilled.

# CHAPTER TWENTY-EIGHT

## JOSEPH H. HERTZ
# CIVILIAN MORALE

### 2 APRIL 1942
#### (FIRST DAY OF PASSOVER)

#### ST JOHN'S WOOD SYNAGOGUE, LONDON

WITH the rise to power of Hitler and the Nazi regime, Hertz spoke out powerfully from his pulpit about the fate of German Jewry. On the first day of Passover (11 April) 1933 he likened the anti-Jewish policies of the new regime to those of the ancient pharaoh who 'knew not Joseph' and began to oppress the Israelites despite the contributions to Egypt they had made, berating the 'heathen Teutonic nationalism' with its demands that Jews be excluded from German society. This was in response to the one-day boycott of Jewish businesses and the 'Law for the Restoration for the Professional Civil Service' with its 'Aryan Paragraph'. Three months later, speaking at a special service of prayer and intercession, which brought together 'all sections and organizations of the community ... united as one religious brotherhood', at the Royal Albert Hall, his outlook was bleak almost to the point of despair. German Jewry has been

Hurled down from its eminence; facing misery, insult, and degradation; and sinking in deep waters of intolerance and hate. It is battling for very life against a tidal wave of mass hysteria and racial persecution that threatens it with annihilation ... Nothing less than extermination of the Jew would, it seems, satisfy the wilder spirits among the Nazis ... Some of the ringleaders, at any rate, are evidently contemplating a vast St. Bartholomew's Night; and by judicious repetition are accustoming their followers to the thought of such a massacre.[1]

The language seems eerily prophetic of events that were at that time years in the future.

[1] J. Hertz, 'Out of the Depths', 145, 147; for the April 1933 sermon, see 'In Ancient Egypt and Present-Day Germany', 137–44. The allusion to 'St. Bartholomew's Night' (24 February 1572), on which the massacre of French Huguenots by Catholics began in Paris, was hyperbole at the time, as there was no evidence that mass murder of the Jews was contemplated by Nazi leaders in July 1933 when the sermon was delivered.

The outbreak of war summoned the ageing chief rabbi to mobilize his full personal resources to sustain the morale of his people. In addition to his usual holiday sermons and messages, he was frequently called upon to speak at special occasions, all of them sombre; the rhetorical challenge was to balance an articulation of unprecedented tragedy with an expression of invincible faith and hope. On 8 July 1941 he told a gathering at Grosvenor House in London that 'ten Continental nations are now in the grip of the spiritual Black Death called the Nazi terror', and that Hitler's 'declared aim is the total disappearance of the Jew from Europe'. Yet even in so dark a present, Jeremiah's existential hope in the face of Babylonian supremacy points the way : 'It is the eternal glory of God's Englishmen—in Milton's immortal phrase—to be in the forefront of those who are fighting the battle of the Lord against the mighty. With the help of God, the issue of such battle will be the resurrection of all the nations now under the heel of Hitler.'[2] On the day of intercession held on 7 September 1941 (see Sermon 24b above), Hertz delivered a sermon 'From the Ruins of the Great Synagogue, London'. A report in the following issue of the *Jewish Chronicle* stated that 'A temporary platform and reading desk were fixed in the place that originally contained the Ark. The Chief Rabbi delivered his sermon vigorously and forcefully, and his powerful voice could be heard above the droning of the aeroplanes that occasionally passed over.'[3]

By the following Passover, reports of the massacres of Soviet Jews in the wake of the invasion—known to British intelligence in the summer of 1941— had been published in Jewish sources, though they were certainly not yet widely known.[4] The first deportations of Polish Jews from the ghettos in which they were confined to the death camps were taking place, though reports of this would not be publicized in Britain for another two months. The United States had joined the war against the Axis powers, but the military impact of American entry had yet to be felt. There was very little sense that the tide had been turned—although, in a Passover message broadcast over the BBC African Service delivered just four days after the sermon reproduced here, Hertz was already speaking of the 'New World after the War', and insisting that there be no punishment or vengeance against the entire German people.[5]

[2] J. Hertz, 'Palestine Victory Campaign', 194–5. The phrase 'God's Englishmen' is frequently attributed to Milton but rarely identified. It apparently derives from the passage near the end of *Areopagitica* in which Milton asserts that 'God is decreeing to some new and great period in his church, even to the reforming of Reformation itself; what does he then but reveal himself to his servants, and as his manner is, first to his Englishmen'. For Hertz's frequent use of quotations from literature, see the general Introduction above.

[3] J. Hertz, 'The Great Synagogue Will Rise Again', 66–75; quotation from *Jewish Chronicle*, 12 Sept. 1941, p. 66 n. 1.

[4] See e.g. the report of the expulsion of all the Jews from Kiev on 29 Sept. 1941, in *Contemporary Jewish Record*, Dec. 1941, p. 669. This was publicly confirmed by Soviet authorities in January 1942: Gilbert, *Auschwitz and the Allies*, 18–19.     [5] J. Hertz, *Early and Late*, 12.

The sermon below predictably uses motifs from the holiday: the comparison with Pharaoh's oppression of the ancient Israelites, the homiletical application of phrases from the liturgy of the Haggadah ('Next year may we all be free men' to the conquered peoples of Europe, 'Next year in Jerusalem' specifically to the Jewish people). Several themes are perhaps more surprising: the commitment to the integrity of the British empire and, consequently, the insistence on total victory not only in Europe but in the Near and Far East; the reference to failures on the 'civilian front', including Jewish connections with the black market; and the ringing assertion at the sermon's climactic conclusion of Zionist goals, despite their incompatibility with current British policy.

# SERMON

THE tidal wave of ghastly carnage passing over Russian and Polish Jewry is infinitely worse than anything that Pharaoh of old ever was guilty of.[6] The murderers will have the same end; but to-day we can only repeat to the helpless victims of man's inhumanity to man the words of a loyal son of Israel: 'Our brethren in Europe, your faces are ever before us, and especially on the night of Pesach. To the cup of Elijah, the cup of salvation, we now add the cup of suffering and not of wine. And when we open the door and cry שפוך חמתך על הגוים אשר לא ידעוך, "Pour out Thy wrath upon the heathen who know Thee not", we shall be thinking of you, and will recite the words loud enough to drown the throbbing noise of the soaring ambassadors of death overhead.'[7]

So much for Passover and the House of Israel. Though other peoples too—Poland and Yugoslavia, for example—now walk through the valley of the

---

[6] Comparison of contemporary realities with the policies of Pharaoh was a commonplace of Passover preaching: see M. Saperstein, *'Your Voice Like a Ram's Horn'*, 20–1. Reports of the massacres of Jews in Soviet or Soviet-occupied territory were being publicized in the media at this time: see e.g. '50,000 Russians and Ukrainians killed', *The Times*, 28 Mar. 1942, p. 3.

[7] I am unable to identify the source of this quotation. It seems that it may have emanated from a leader of American Jewry, proposing that Jews observing Passover in 1942 place an additional empty cup on the seder table in solidarity with European Jews; if so, this may have been Rabbi Abba Hillel Silver, who concluded a ten-day visit to Britain on behalf of the Keren Hayesod Appeal shortly before Passover with a luncheon attended by the chief rabbi (*Jewish Chronicle*, 27 Mar. 1942, p. 1). The 'cup of suffering' is an extremely common motif of Christian discourse, pertaining to passages such as Matt. 26: 39, although the phrase itself is not in the New Testament.

shadow of death, and we could dwell on their heart-breaking martyrdom, let us now turn to the message of hope for all mankind which Passover proclaims. This day is, moreover, Anglo-Jewry's response to the desire of H.M. the King for a Day of Prayer in order 'to give thanks to Almighty God for past blessings and humbly to pray for strength and guidance in facing the tasks that lie ahead'.[8]

Now, it is evident that if the nation, the community, the individual are to face the tasks that lie ahead, the first requisite is a clear understanding of what is at stake for us in coming months. But the mass of the people in this country have not yet sufficiently grasped the fact that all we have and are—our lives, our faith, our country—all stand in danger of utter and irretrievable destruction, unless *complete* victory is ours. A partial victory would spell disaster to our Cause.[9] Thus, if we lost the Battle of the Far and Near East, that means the end of the British Empire, and its downfall would shake the civilized world to its very foundations. It would mean the definite passing of all those ideals for which that Empire stands in the eyes of men.[10]

The British Empire has not been, and is not to-day, faultless; its rulers do not always know how to distinguish between friends and enemies; and they have often failed to win the love of the peoples under their sway. And yet it is an unchallengeable truth that the British Empire is earth's nearest realization hitherto of might coupled with justice and humanity. If—Heaven forbid—it is succeeded by the New Order announced by the Axis Powers, then—in the

[8] The king 'expressed the desire' that Sunday, 29 March be observed as a national day of prayer (*Jewish Chronicle*, 19 Mar. 1942, p. 1). Because of the nearness to Passover, Chief Rabbi Hertz, in a public letter, proposed that the first day of Passover (Thursday, 2 Apr., when the sermon was being delivered) would serve this purpose for the Jews: *Jewish Chronicle*, 27 Mar. 1942, p. 1.

[9] Here Hertz seems to be saying that victory over Germany and Italy is not enough; 'complete victory' must include the defeat of Japan in the 'Battle of the Far and Near East'. This reflection follows the devastating reversals of the past year, including the fall of Hong Kong and Singapore, which Churchill described on 26 March as 'the scene of the greatest disaster to British arms which our history records' (speech cited at n. 20 below). Cf. the strong repudiations of 'premature peace' in Sermons 5, 6, and 21 above by Michelbacher, Morais, and Franklin respectively.

[10] Like David Woolf Marks and Hermann Adler in Sermons 4 and 14 above, Hertz shows an unwavering (though not entirely uncritical) identification with the British empire. By contrast, on this same first day of Passover, Rabbi Israel Goldstein of Congregation B'nai Jeshurun in New York applied the theme of freedom in his sermon to 'the promise of the long overdue independence of the Indian people' from British rule: *New York Times*, 3 Apr. 1942, p. 18. On British Christian preachers identifying the empire with God's providential plan, see Hoover, *God, Britain, and Hitler*, 101–3.

words of H.M. the King—the lights of freedom, tolerance, and kindliness
would be blotted out for long generations; and, throughout that time, the latest
refinements of Science would be linked with the cruelties of the Stone Age, as
Mr. Churchill put it.[11]

A stalemate of peace would be fatal to us. Even though Britain itself
remained unconquered, the resulting peace would be Carthaginian in its sever-
ity, and would within a few years prove but the prelude to final destruction.
Compared to the fate reserved for Britain by the Nazis, the treatment now
meted out to Poland would be mild. 'Englishmen are the Jews of Western
Europe,' sneered Richard Wagner, the musical anti-Semite who is hailed as a
spiritual ancestor of the Nazi philosophy;[12] and the disappearance of both
Englishman and Jew is the declared aim of Nazi policy.[13] 'We shall win,
or we shall die,' was the Australian Prime Minister's summing-up of the
situation.[14]

We are thus combatants in the most sacred conflict in human history. To
each man and woman throughout the Allied Nations, therefore, comes the
searching question in the Haftorah to-day, הלנו אתה אם לצרינו, 'Art thou for
us, or for our adversaries?' (Josh. 5: 13). Do you by your life advance the cause of
Freedom, or do you by your doings and conduct retard its victory, and dishearten the men and women upholding that sacred cause?

As to readiness to sacrifice life in the Cause of Freedom, there is but one
answer. 'We mothers are called upon to send our children to what often is

[11] The phrase about 'lights of freedom' is taken from the king's message for the day of prayer,
broadcast to the nation on the preceding evening (Saturday night, 28 Mar.); the text is in *The
Times*, 30 Mar. 1942, p. 2. Churchill's statement was made on 26 Mar. 1942, in his address to the
Conservative Party General Council meeting: '[In the current war], the latest refinements of science are linked with the cruelties of the Stone Age' (*The Times*, 27 May 1942, p. 5). In context it
is a description of the present, not a warning about the future.
[12] Cf. Weininger, *Sex and Character*, ch. 13, p. 317: 'I may now touch upon the likeness of the
English to the Jews, a topic discussed at length by Wagner. It cannot be doubted that of the
Germanic races the English are in closest in relations with the Jews.'
[13] Nazi spokesmen did speak of the 'annihilation of England' (e.g. Goebbels, cited in *New York
Times*, 12 Apr. 1941), but, to my knowledge, not of the disappearance of 'the Englishman' in the sense
that they spoke of the annihilation of 'the Jew'. Hertz may have been echoing a statement by
Lord Vansittart, reported in the *Jewish Chronicle* of 20 Mar. 1942: 'The truth was that this nation was
fighting the German nation for its very existence and if it failed it would be literally exterminated'
(p. 6).
[14] Hertz's attribution is incorrect: the statement was made on 26 Mar. 1942, by General Douglas
MacArthur (*Sydney Morning Herald*, 27 Mar. 1942, p. 4; the paper reported that MacArthur's
speech was described afterwards by some present as 'the finest speech in their memory'); also
*The Times*, 27 Mar. 1942, p. 4. The sentence was later used in a poster for US war bonds.

almost certain death!' a young mother said to me during the last War. 'There is, however, one agony'—she continued after a few moments—'that would be even great than that: if the child refused to go to almost certain death at the call of his Country.'[15] Few British mothers, whether Jewish or non-Jewish, suffer that greater agony.

Gratifying as all this is, it must be confessed that there has been in this War a certain failure on the civilian front. Think of the hosts of fifth-columnists and quislings, defeatists and strikers in the Allied countries. In our own land, too, men and women have been sentenced to severe punishments for dealing with the enemy, for spying on his behalf, and for even more treasonable activities.[16] There have also been far too many looting offences. In one area alone, that of Deal, 159 such cases occurred in one year.[17] Remarkably little public attention has been directed to some of these crimes—probably for a most peculiar reason: *because there were next to no Jews among the malefactors*. No Jew among the fifth-columnists and quislings, none among the spies and traitors, and only one or two among the looters! Otherwise, the reaction might have been quite different, as it is in connection with offenders of another class, of the so-called Black Market.

Jews form but a relatively small portion of the 47,000 offenders prosecuted on this head; and yet some enterprising journalists seem to speak of this transgression of the law as an exclusively *Jewish* crime.[18] Even members of Parliament have asked why the Jewish Community does not deal with these

[15] Cf. Sermon 14 above by Adler, pp. 292–3.

[16] In January 1942 Britain had nineteen German spies who agreed to work as double agents to save themselves from prosecution; eight others had been executed under the Treachery Act of 1940. See Weale, *Renegades*, 73, and—on pro-German propagandists during the early part of the war—21–46.

[17] Looting was especially a problem in bombed-out houses. In the first eight weeks of the London Blitz, 390 cases were reported to the police. Deal was a coastal city in the county of Kent, in south-east England, the site of an army base and naval base during the war; this detail was probably chosen because Deal had no Jewish community.

[18] Hertz may have been referring to an article in the *Daily Mail*, cited by the *Jewish Chronicle*, 20 Mar. 1942, p. 10, which discussed alleged efforts by the Jews to control Jewish involvement in the black market: all British Jews, according to the article, 'have been instructed (with the weight of the Rabbis behind the instruction) that whenever a Jew is suspected of dealing in the Black Market, the suspicion must be reported to one of the Trades Advisory Councils'. The same issue reported a lecture by Neville Laski, asserting that 'There has been a wholly disproportionate reporting of offences by the handful of Jewish "scum"', and suggesting that 'The Chief Rabbi and Rabbinate ought to revive the old penalty of *Cherem* [excommunication or social ostracism]' (p. 12). The 'Chief Rabbi's Message' for Passover, published by the *Jewish Chronicle* on the following day, mentions '40,000 malefactors prosecuted for contravention of war-time regulations' (3 Apr. 1942, p. 6).

miscreants.[19] This is ominous. Military and naval disasters of a nature unknown before in British history, following upon political blunders on a colossal scale, rankle in the breast of the nation.[20] It is part of human nature at such times to seek a scapegoat; or, at least, to feel the eventual need of a lightning conductor of the popular discontent. The masses have been made 'Jew-conscious', and demagogues may easily rouse them to blind racial hatred. But racial hatred is a poison which not only embitters but corrodes a people; and, therefore, degrades and weakens the national spirit. Such hatred is worlds asunder from 'the humble prayer for the strength and guidance in facing the tasks that lie ahead' that H.M. the King asked for;[21] and it certainly does not help the triumph of freedom and justice on earth.[22]

A word of caution to some of our own Jews. Let me repeat to them the ancient ethical maxim, 'Be not wicked in thine own esteem.'[23] Self-respect is a cardinal duty, and applies to everyone, both in his individual capacity and as a member of a community. Do not, therefore, look upon yourself or your people

---

[19] Beverley Baxter MP, speaking in the Commons on 3 Mar. 1942, referred to black market offences and continued, 'The Jewish Community, towards which this House has always maintained historical friendship, should exert themselves in this regard. Here are aliens from Europe who have found the best means of activity in making money in these black markets. There are British-born Jewish people in this to far too great an extent. I do not want to go further than that.' In clarifying his statement after challenge, he went on, 'What I said was that the repercussions on the Jews were such that they should be more than careful' (*Jewish Chronicle*, 6 Mar. 1942, p. 5; cf. editorials, 27 Feb., p. 10, and 6 Mar., p. 10). On the black market at this time, see Longmate, *How We Lived Then*, 152–3; the author writes in a note, 'Many Black Market rumours were really veiled anti-Semitism for it was constantly asserted that it was run by Jews. One author, who studied the press reports for three months of 1941–2, claimed that 80 per cent of those convicted had Jewish names.' Unfortunately, no name is provided for this reference.

[20] The 'military disasters' were reviewed in Churchill's speech to the General Council of the Conservative Party on 26 March, cited by the preacher earlier (and see n. 11 above): during the past year, said the Prime Minister, 'we have had an almost unbroken series of military misfortunes. We were driven out of Cyrenaica, and have now only partly re-established ourselves there. We were driven out of Greece and Crete. We have been attacked by a new and most formidable antagonist in the Far-East. Hong-Kong has fallen; the Malay Peninsula and the possessions of the brave Dutch in the East Indies have been overrun. Singapore has been the scene of the greatest disaster to British arms which our history records.' And the litany continues (*The Times*, 27 Mar. 1942, p. 5). The earlier 'political blunders' probably refer to the policy of appeasement towards Nazi Germany in the 1930s.

[21] From the king's proclamation, already cited near the beginning of the sermon.

[22] In his sermon on the holiday of Shavuot, Hertz referred back to this passage from his Passover sermon, noting that, to his surprise, some interpreted his remarks as 'a palliation of Jewish participation in the black market! It is a travesty of the truth. Not only do I unreservedly condemn the violation of a measure framed for the good and safety of the population at a time when our country is fighting for its very existence, but I consider any Jewish participation in unholy dealings to constitute a danger to the honour of every Jew in Britain': 'Pentecost and Commercial Honesty', 22.                                          [23] *Avot* 2: 18.

as hopelessly reprobate. True English men and women never indict a *whole* people or an *entire* community. Is it less reprehensible to do so, when it happens to be your own people and your own community? No one in his senses would hold the Anglican or the Catholic Churches responsible for the looters and traitors who are born Anglicans or born Catholics; why then this alacrity on the part of Jews to condemn both Jews and Judaism because of a few, or even a larger number of, scoundrels? By all means let the Government punish the offenders, not as Jews or Christians, but as *criminals*. Any other policy constitutes a monstrous injustice, and weakens the national effort. Any other policy would make those that follow it unworthy, in the eyes of an all-just God, to witness the fulfilment of the prayer uttered in spirit to-day throughout all the United Nations: לשנה הבאה בני חורין, 'Next year may we all be free men!'

Let our concluding note be another prayerful desire uttered during the Seder.

It is for us to face the fact that even Allied victory may not bring immediate peace to the millions of ruined Jews throughout Europe.[24] Moreover, for years there may be, both in the conquered and conquering lands, upheaval, unrest, the birth-pangs of a new social order. And all this may have its fateful repercussions upon the position of the Jews, especially the homeless Jew. Be it remembered that after the last War, after an Allied victory at that, the *Protocols of Zion* were launched in England, and the Ku Klux Movement started in America. Fervently do we pray that such things do not recur after this Allied victory. However, it is only too probable that hardly any country, and probably no country, will be in a position to absorb any fresh immigrants. All doors, therefore, will be kept shut in the face of the Jewish survivors from the hate and hunger zones of their martyrdom. 'Whither' will for a long time to come be the question tormenting those survivors.

In view of all this, good men and true everywhere demand that at least the doors of Palestine, the one country on earth that can absorb these immigrants, shall be opened to them. The drowning cries of the 759 victims of the *Struma*, fleeing for their lives from a butcher-state like Romania, are still ringing in the ears of all those who are not dead to the call of human Brotherhood.[25] Let there

---

[24] In speaking of millions of surviving European Jews, Hertz shows himself incapable of imagining the enormity of the destruction that was just beginning at this time (except for the massacres already committed in occupied Soviet territory).

[25] *Struma* sank on 24 Feb. 1942, after being forced out to sea from Istanbul: '700 Refugees Drowned', *Jewish Chronicle*, 27 Feb. 1942, p. 1; *Jewish Chronicle*, 6 Mar. 1942, p. 1; 13 Mar. 1942, p. 6.

be no more 'coffin ships' in connection with Eretz Yisroel, the Jewish National Home promised to the Jewish People by Great Britain, and publicly endorsed as such by fifty-five nations.[26] לשנה הבאה בירושלים.[27] Amen.

[26] This sentence also appears in the 'Chief Rabbi's Message' for Passover, published in the *Jewish Chronicle* the following day (3 Apr. 1942, p. 1). Reference is apparently to the League of Nations' grant of the British Mandate on 24 July 1922, stating that 'the Mandatory shall be responsible for placing the country under such political, administrative and economic conditions as will secure the establishment of the Jewish national home'. At that time there were more than fifty members of the League. The term 'coffin ships' was first popularly used to refer to ships carrying Irish immigrants across the Atlantic in the wake of the potato famine.

[27] 'Next year in Jerusalem': this and the Hebrew phrase cited above ('Next year may we all be free men') compose two hopes in the 'Bread of Affliction' paragraph near the beginning of the Passover Haggadah: 'This year, here, next year in Jerusalem; this year we are slaves, next year free men.' Hertz interprets the first hope as applying specifically to the Jewish people, and the second as applying to all human beings under Nazi domination or fighting the Axis powers—'the message of hope for all mankind which Passover proclaims'.

# CHAPTER TWENTY-NINE

## WALTER WURZBURGER
# THE INDIVIDUAL
# IN THE CRISIS

### 9 OCTOBER 1943
### (YOM KIPPUR)

**CONGREGATION CHAI ODOM,
BRIGHTON, MASSACHUSETTS**

DURING the year and a half between Hertz's 1942 Passover sermon and the following address on Yom Kippur 1943, the military situation had improved dramatically for the Allies, with monumental victories at El Alamein and Stalingrad, and an Allied landing in southern Italy five weeks before Wurzburger delivered this sermon. But the situation of Europe's Jews had drastically deteriorated. Some 60 per cent of all the Jewish victims of the Holocaust perished during these months, and while the full dimensions of the catastrophe were not yet public knowledge, reports had been widely circulated placing the number of Jewish victims in the millions. In August and September 1943 the Emergency Committee to Save the Jewish People of Europe placed large newspaper advertisements throughout the United States dramatizing the crisis; on 6 October, just two days before Yom Kippur, 400 Orthodox rabbis gathered in Washington, DC to petition President Roosevelt for American intervention to rescue surviving Jews in Europe.[1] It was against this grim background that Akiba Predmesky delivered the powerful Yom Kippur sermon discussed in the general Introduction.

The sermon below is quite different, in many ways. The preacher, Walter Wurzburger, was at the very beginning of what would be a distinguished rabbinical and academic career. Born in Munich in 1920, he emigrated to the United States in 1938.[2] He received his undergraduate degree and rabbinic

---

[1] For advertisements in the *New York Times* on 14 Sept. and 5 Oct. 1943, see Wyman, *A Race against Death*, tenth and eleventh plates following p. 78.

[2] *The Jewish Week*, 26 Apr. 2002. In a eulogy, his student Shalom Carmy said that Wurzburger had 'walked the streets of Berlin the morning after Kristallnacht' (*Jewish Action*, Spring 2003).

ordination at Yeshiva University, where he became a devoted disciple of Rabbi Joseph Soloveitchik. In the autumn of 1943 he was serving at Congregation Chai Odom in Brighton, Massachusetts, having moved to study for a Ph.D. in philosophy at Harvard. Going on later to hold positions with congregations in Toronto, Canada, and Lawrence, New York, he also taught for many years in the faculty of Yeshiva University, edited *Tradition* magazine, and wrote important books on ethics and Jewish thought.

Like the address by George Silverstone reproduced above (Sermon 15), Wurzburger's sermon features a powerful narrative that had been given considerable exposure in American newspapers: that of ninety-three Polish Jewish girls who had taken their own lives rather than be given over to the lust of German officers. (It is indeed striking that when this story was published in *New York Times*, it occupied more column inches than a report published two months later that two million Jews had been killed.) As with Silverstone's narrative of the Russian Jewish soldier killing an Austrian Jewish soldier, one vivid vignette, even if known to the listeners, can be used to great effect by an accomplished preacher. Several other illustrations—pertaining to the British General Montgomery, the Royal Air Force during the Battle of Britain, and a sign at the entrance to Vineland, New Jersey—provide colour and drama to the discourse.

The central theme of the sermon, however, is expressed by the title. Appropriate to the occasion of Yom Kippur and its liturgy, it focuses on individual responsibility, confession, and atonement (a theme that is totally absent from the Predmesky sermon noted above). The ritual of the high priest in the ancient Temple and the formulations of his confessions, incorporated into a climactic moment of the Yom Kippur liturgy, are applied by the preacher to the present. In time of war, in time of disaster for one's people, the proper response should not be merely to condemn others—whether the Nazis or the Allies—but to accept responsibility for one's own failures to do what might have been done. While this is a very traditional motif, it must have taken some degree of courage for a young rabbi, who had arrived in the United States less than five years earlier and had only recently arrived at his congregation in Boston, to address his auditors in this manner.[3] It is also striking to note that this sermon, by an immigrant rabbi in his early twenties, was selected for publication in the first volume of the Rabbinical Council of America's *Manual of Holiday and Occasional Sermons*.

---

[3] For a similar theme in a Rosh Hashanah 1940 sermon by a far more established rabbi, see Abba Hillel Silver, 'Our Responsibility for Evil'.

# SERMON

—

THE modern preacher has of late assumed the Miltonic task of justifying the ways of G-d to man[4] either because of his anxiety to bring a message of hope to a suffering and toiling humanity, or in order to sell a sugar-coated religion to his congregants. To be sure, nothing is further from the true nature of religion than the passive and apologetic role assigned to it by some of its professional servants. G-d is not on trial. There is no need to rally to his defense.

The fact is that the tendency to defend G-d and religion has increased in intensity in these trying days because of the many questions that the laity asks the spiritual leader to answer. Many of us, for example, have come today to this place of worship in order to receive an answer to the question, 'Where is G-d in this crisis?'[5] We yearn for a message of hope in the face of the tormenting problems that demand a quick solution. A world gone mad with insane ideologies, a universe that is reduced to a vale of tears, the fate of a civilization on its last legs, all these deserve the attention of the pulpiteer, we feel.

Yet let us remember that this is a day of Atonement, when we should be at one with our G-d.[6] Let this be a real day of Atonement, when we face our problems as Individuals. Let us pay attention to our personal relationship to the world and its G-d!

I do not mean to imply that man is a Robinson Crusoe living on an isolated island. But I heartily protest against the attitude that minimizes the importance and the sacredness of the human personality. A modern thinker called religion the opiate of the masses.[7] Yet our so-called scientific philosophy of life[8] proves to be a much stronger opiate. For it enables us to shun all responsibility[9] for the terrible chaos that has engulfed the universe. There is nothing left to the indi-

---

[4] Echoing the opening verses of *Paradise Lost*, bk 1.

[5] Cf. Sermon 23 by Jacob Rudin from three years previously, and the sources cited in the general Introduction, n. 212.

[6] A common homiletical play on words: 'atone' = to be 'at one'.

[7] Cf. Karl Marx, 'Religion is the sigh of the oppressed creature, the heart of a heartless world, and the soul of soulless conditions. It is the opium of the people' (introduction to *A Critique of Hegel's Philosophy of Right*).

[8] It is not clear to me exactly to which philosophy Wurzburger is referring; later in the sermon it is identified as a science that 'maximizes the importance of society and environment and minimizes the significance of the individual'.

[9] Note the triple occurrence of the word 'responsibility/responsible' in this paragraph, and further in the sermon.

vidual but to bewail his bitter lot which placed him in an age that produced a Hitler, a Mussolini and the other henchmen and gangsters. It is very tempting to wash our hands of all responsibility for the debacle of civilization. After all, what is the individual amidst all these powerful forces? Is he not merely a helpless ship tossed about by the political, social and economic waves? The truth of the matter, however, is that religion is no opiate at all. It offers no soothing sedative to calm the individual. It offers no protecting harbor from a stormy sea. Religion stresses the sacredness and the importance of the human personality. There is no alibi, no excuse for our failures, it says. We are responsible for our deeds.[10]

On this Day of Atonement this message is brought home to us with extreme clarity and lucidity. When the Jews lived a normal life in Eretz Yisroel they assembled at this solemn hour, the holiest day of the entire year, at the holiest place, in the Temple of Jerusalem. The eyes of the entire people were focused on the כהן גדול, the High Priest, foremost member of the holiest tribe of the 'Chosen People'. Imagine the awe that gripped the people, when its most saintly son entered the Holy of Holies to ask forgiveness for the sins of the nation. There, facing his G-d, stood the High Priest to give account for all the failures and shortcomings that undermined the structure of all Jewish existence. Who was to blame for the pettiness and the jealousies which have caused untold suffering to the nation? Upon whose shoulders rested the responsibility for the chaos that put man against man, nation against nation? The militaristic Romans? The idolatrous Babylonians? The G-dless Assyrians? The faithless Egyptians? Did the High Priest blame the internal enemies of Israel, the profiteers, the politicians, the criminals? Nay! This is what he said: אנא השם חטאתי עויתי פשעתי לפניך אני וביתי ובני אהרון, 'O Lord I have sinned! I have failed! I am guilty.'* I am responsible for the suffering of man. I caused all the agony, misery and injustice that shakes the structure of our ailing society.

Who utters these terrible words? A traitor to the cause of G-d? A criminal? A social outcast?

Nay, it is the כהן גדול, the High Priest, the chosen representative of the chosen tribe of a chosen people; he who represented the best, the highest, the noblest of Israel realized his responsibility. He began with a process of personal

---

* BT *Yoma* 41b.

[10] Including, presumably, the 'terrible chaos that has engulfed the universe', as mentioned above. For the time being, however, the preacher holds back from supporting this claim, and points to sources for the doctrine of individual responsibility in the Jewish tradition.

cleansing and repentance. Before he spoke of the sins of his people, he thought
of his own. Before he blamed the world, he blamed himself.

Then and only then, had he a right to include others in this terrible
indictment. Did he look for scapegoats?—the legions of Greece? The cohorts
of Rome? The treacherous Sadducees? The rich? The poor?—אנא השם
חטאתי עויתי פשעתי לפניך אני וביתי ובני אהרון, 'O Lord,' he said, 'I have
sinned, I have failed, I and my immediate family, the house of Aaron.' We
sinned, we failed, we are guilty. We brought all this suffering and agony to a
stricken world.

After he blamed himself, he had a right to blame others: אנא השם
חטאו עוו פשעו לפניך עמך בית ישראל, 'O Lord, they have sinned, they have
failed, they are guilty.' Naturally, we must not be shortsighted. Wrongs are
committed by others. There are no two ways about it. Once we make a determined effort to cleanse ourselves from all defilement and contamination, we
have a right to denounce others. Yet, we must never blame others in order to
escape from our own sense of guilt. We must not run away from ourselves.

My friends, how badly have we need of this message today! We are always
ready to denounce and blame others. How much time and energy do we waste in
condemning the Nazis and Fascists! We witness a conflagration of the world that
is unparalleled in history. A civilization goes to pieces, and we seek comfort and
consolation in the thought that ידינו לא שפכו את הדם הזה, 'that our hands did
not spill this blood' (Deut. 21: 8). It is not our fault. We pity ourselves. We lament
our fate and bemoan our misfortune. How deplorable it is to live in an age that
denounces justice, goodness, morality and decency! We throw our hands up in
despair and give up the struggle. We feel that we are merely a pawn in a gigantic
chess game. What can we do in the fare of all the demonic forces of evil?

There comes to my mind the heroism of the 93 girls in the dark ghettos of
Warsaw.[11] They were instructed by the Nazis to beautify themselves with cos-
metics, to put on their best dresses and to prepare for the ordeal of an encounter
with the filthy German officers in their quarters.

[11] The story of the ninety-three girls dates the sermon in 1943, as it is based on a *New York
Times* report of a letter describing the incident, published on 8 Jan. 1943, p. 8; the letter was publicized by the New York rabbi Leo Jung. See the fascinating discussion of this by Baumel and
Schacter, 'The Ninety-Three Bais Yaakov Girls of Cracow'. As the title indicates, the letter states
that the incident occurred in Cracow, but the accompanying explanation from Rabbi Jung placed
it in Warsaw (apparently a clerical error!), which is how it was reported in the newspaper, and in
the sermon. On the reactions to the story in the Jewish community, see ibid. 98–100. Cf. also the
comment by Mendel Piekarz, *Ideological Trends of Hasidism in Poland*, 358.

A terrible struggle went on in the minds of these girls: 'Here we are confronted with a world of brutality, bestiality and tyranny. We witnessed how our fathers were murdered, our mothers violated, our brothers tortured to death, our friends sent to concentration camps. A world has abandoned all that is holy and noble. What is the wrong that is demanded of us in comparison with these crimes, with the blood that cries unto heaven? This is our chance for a life of comfort and security. Why sacrifice ourselves for decency in an already indecent world, for justice in a universe that is full of injustice, for goodness in a criminal social order?'[12]

Thus many of us would have thought, had we been in the place of these 93 girls. But every one of them remained steadfast. They realized their responsibility towards Israel and the world! They preferred death to a life bought by desecration of their souls and their bodies. They recited the וידוי, they confessed their sins and ended their precious lives.[13] They understood that a human being is not merely a piece of chaff tossed to and fro by the wind, the hail and the rain.

My friends! How willing are we to blame the Nazis and Fascists for the chaos that engulfs our civilization! How gladly we accuse England and America for their failure to save the Jews who are being exterminated in war-torn Europe! We hold protest meetings and demand 'action, not pity!'[14]

We are always ready to condemn others. But do we ask ourselves these discomforting questions? Did I send a letter to my Congressman to intervene in behalf of these Jews? Did I join a national Jewish organization that strives to save these doomed people? Did I contribute my money to help those that still can be helped? Did I buy war bonds so that this war may be shortened?

I blame capital, labor, profiteers and racketeers. Did I refuse to patronize the black market? Did I donate my services to a civilian defense unit? I blame the leaders of the Jewish people for the lack of unity among American Jewry, for the deplorable condition of Jewish education. How about myself? Have I done anything to remedy these conditions? Let us all admit, חטאתי עויתי פשעתי לפניך, 'I sinned, I failed, I am guilty.'

---

[12] This is all the preacher's imaginative reconstruction; nothing like it appeared in the letter or the article.

[13] The letter states, 'Today we are together and are learning the *vidui* [liturgical confession upon the deathbed] all day.'

[14] Referring to a large advertisement placed in the *New York Times* of 8 Feb. 1943 (p. 8) by the Committee for a Jewish Army, with the headline ACTION—NOT PITY CAN SAVE MILLIONS NOW. The slogan was used in subsequent campaigns as well. See Wyman, *A Race against Death*, ninth page of plates following p. 87.

Let us now go one step further! After the process of personal cleansing, let us approach our own people. True, the world is shackled by the enslaving chains of Nazi tyranny and oppression. True, international law is violated, prisoners of war are executed. Indeed the world presents a terrible picture which cannot be described in words. But let us not merely deplore conditions and bemoan our fate. We should always keep in mind, what an American poet expressed so beautifully:

> But stay! No age was e'er degenerate
> Unless men held it at too cheap a rate,
> For in our likeness shall we shape our fate. [15]

O yes, it is a degenerate world, a world that kills the innocent and the weak, that desecrates everything that is holy—a world of master-races and of slaves. But we in America have also failed miserably. Do we have to travel to Europe in order to discover racial persecution? Why not go to Detroit with its race riots?[16] Couldn't we have stopped Hitler back in 1933? Of course, we could have, had we not adopted the policy of isolationism and appeasement! And so we behold a world of agony, misery, cruelty, injustice, brutality and tyranny. We are responsible for it. It is our world. No complaints! No excuses! No defense mechanisms! No passing of the buck![17]

חטאתי עויתי פשעתי לפניך אני וביתי ובני אהרון, 'I and my family, we sinned, we failed, we are guilty, we are responsible.'

Once we have taken this bold step, we may venture to blame others, we may say: חטאו עוו פשעו לפניך עמך בית ישראל, 'They sinned, they failed, they are guilty.' Yes, atrocities are committed that are unprecedented in the history of mankind. The Nazis have thrown humanity back into the clutches of savagery, terror, fear and horror. They blot out the spirit of the dignity of man. They eradicate all remembrance of righteousness, justice, decency and humaneness. This indictment, however, does not bring any comfort to us, since it stems from a feeling of self-complacency. For their atrocities are our atrocities, their crimes are our crimes, their murders are our murders. By indicting

---

[15] James Russell Lowell, 'Ode Recited at Harvard Commemoration, July 21, 1865'.

[16] Referring to the riots of 20–1 June 1943, in which nine white people and twenty-five black people were killed (seventeen of the blacks by white policemen). More than 1,800 were arrested for looting and other incidents, the vast majority black. A month later, a race riot broke out in New York.

[17] Note the colloquial language, as contrasted with the highly rhetorical style of the sermon by the preacher's Orthodox colleague Akiba Predmesky, delivered on the same Yom Kippur, and cited above (see Introduction, p. 46).

them, we indict ourselves. Had we abandoned our selfish attitude in the days before Pearl Harbor these brutalities would never have been committed.[18] Each and every one of us is responsible for the debacle of civilization.

Do I not hear a voice from a corner: 'How can you accuse me? I am not a politician. I have no influence. I cannot oppose the powerful political, social and economic forces. I am a helpless individual. Does not science maximize the importance of society and environment and minimize the significance of the individual?'

Friends! Let no one deceive himself! A chain is only as strong as its weakest link. Every individual is a link in a great chain. One of the most interesting and most inspiring stories of the entire war, is the history of the British Eighth Army. Today, it is one of the best striking forces of the United Nations. Yet, we still recall the trying days when the Eighth Army was chased by Rommel through Africa. The Germans stood at the gates of Alexandria. But suddenly the entire picture changed. General Montgomery assumed command and instilled confidence in the hearts of the beaten and shattered legions.[19] Within a few months, he chased Rommel through Libya and Tunisia. Today he leads his victorious legions into the battle against 'Fortress Europe'.[20] What was the secret of General Montgomery's success? He comes from a Puritan and strictly religious family. He knows and appreciates the importance of every individual. At the eve of every campaign he informs his soldiers about all the details of strategy. Every soldier is acquainted with the immediate as well as with the final objective of the campaign. The common soldier no longer feels that he merely is a cog in the wheel, a part of a military machine. He realizes his stake in the battle and is aware of his responsibility. He is no longer the 'forgotten man',[21] the pawn in the hands of the commander. Every soldier is aware that this is his war,

---

[18] A very strong statement, apparently implying that if America had abandoned its isolationist policy and become involved in the war when it began, the Nazis would not have been able to embark on their policy to annihilate European Jewry.

[19] Montgomery assumed command of the Eighth Army on 18 Aug. 1942. The decisive victory of El Alamein, on 23 October, was the first significant victory by an Allied commander over German forces. In a front-page article by its London correspondent on 6 November, the *New York Times* reported that 'Of the British Eighth Army the outstanding fact is that its morale is higher than that of any other army to leave these islands since the war began. The men in it, who have known discouragement time and again, longing for a crack at the Germans, now are getting their heart's desire' (*New York Times*, 6 Nov. 1942, p. 1).

[20] In September 1943 Montgomery was leading British forces in their invasion of mainland Italy.

[21] A phrase made famous by Franklin D. Roosevelt's reference, in his speech in the 1932 presidential campaign, to 'the forgotten man at the bottom of the economic pyramid', here applied to the ordinary soldier as one whose individuality is lost in the huge military mechanism.

his battle, his campaign. This is the secret of the success of the British Eighth Army.[22]

The R.A.F. back in the dark days of the Battle of Britain did not offer any alibis. Britain had suffered defeat after defeat, and the Empire began to crumble. Prime Minister Winston Churchill promised blood, sweat, toil, and tears to his people.[23] The powerful squadrons of the Luftwaffe rained death and destruction upon British civilians. But here was a handful of British pilots who defied all hardship and accepted the almost impossible task. The small and insignificant R.A.F. challenged the powerful might of the Nazi Air Force. Immense was their hardship; herculean their task, yet realizing their responsibility to England and humanity, they overcame all obstacles and saved England and Western civilization. Indeed, as Winston Churchill expressed it so beautifully, 'never have so many owed so much to so few'.[24]

During a recent trip, I came to a small community in New Jersey. At the entrance of the village, I noticed a big poster that read 'America looks at you, Vineland!' I said to myself: 'This is a small and insignificant community. It cannot boast of any important defense industry.[25] How presumptuous on the part of so small a community to say, "America looks at you, Vineland"!'

Suddenly, however, I realized the truth of this statement. We cannot win this war unless every city, every village, every hamlet, every family and every individual hears that voice. 'America looks at you!' Every one of us must realize his responsibility towards his family, his community, his city, his state, his country and his humanity.

Friends, we are now approaching the solemn moment commemorating the עבודת יום הכפורים [the divine service of the Day of Atonement], which once was the most sacred function of the High Priest. He confessed the sins of his

[22] For a recent analysis of Montgomery's unique achievement in lifting the morale of Britain's Eighth Army after a series of defeats, by means of his visits to and conversations with ordinary soldiers, see Hamilton, *The Full Monty*, i. 541–5, 554–6, 561–7, 585–92.

[23] In his address to Parliament on 13 May 1940, following his appointment as Prime Minister. The precise phrase used by Churchill was 'blood, toil, tears, and sweat', but it is generally cited in the form used here, or as 'blood, sweat, and tears': see Safire, *Lend Me Your Ears*, 131.

[24] This was famously said by Churchill in his address to Parliament on 20 Aug. 1940: 'Never in the field of human conflict was so much owed by so many to so few.'

[25] While there was no arms industry there, the website of Kimble Glass, Inc., based in Vineland, reports that 'during World War II, Kimble set up satellite operations to meet the demand for wartime items such as: delousing ampuls, bottles for blood plasma and parts for proximity fuses'. Vineland was also a refuge for German Jewish immigrants in the 1930s, some of whom joined the considerable number of Jewish poultry farmers in the region; see Brandes, *Immigrants to Freedom*, 323–6. I am grateful to Jonathan Sarna for this reference.

people and atoned for his nation. Thus he attained forgiveness and thus he repaired the breaches in the crumbling foundations of the Jewish nation. Let us carry the lesson that the High Priest teaches us well in mind! Let us rededicate ourselves to the eternal fountain of Jewish hope that assures us: כי ביום הזה יכפר עליכם לטהר אתכם מכל חטאותיכם לפני ד' תטהרו (Lev. 16: 30), that G-d will grant us atonement and will cleanse us from all defilement and contamination,[26] and that he will lead us into a future that will be built upon the foundation of harmony and brotherhood, justice and righteousness.

[26] A concluding message that expresses the central theme of Yom Kippur and the central theme of the sermon, but is strikingly different, in its emphasis on the failings of the congregation, from the message in the Predmesky sermon.

# CHAPTER THIRTY

## ROLAND B. GITTELSOHN
# THE BIRTH OF A NEW FREEDOM

### 14 MARCH 1945

#### US MARINE CORPS CEMETERY, IWO JIMA

ROLAND GITTELSOHN, born in 1910 in Cleveland, received a bachelor's degree from Western Reserve University and was ordained at the Hebrew Union College in 1936. Immediately thereafter he began to serve as rabbi of Central Synagogue in Rockville Centre, Long Island. He would remain there until 1953, when he moved to Temple Israel of Boston. For a summary of the rest of Gittelsohn's rabbinic and preaching career, see the introduction to Chapter 31 below.

Like many other rabbis and Christian clergy educated and trained in the 1920s and 1930s, Gittelsohn identified himself during his Long Island years as a pacifist.[1] 'I read avidly every pacifist tome I could find', he later wrote, 'and argued the position with zeal.' In a sermon delivered 'early in World War II, after Hitler's massive initial victories', he said (or 'shouted' as he later reported), 'If we do nothing else, we must stay out of this war . . . I hate Hitler and want desperately to see him defeated, [but] I want us to stay out of the war even if he seems to be winning.'[2] In the following two years of the war, he went through the anguishing transformation of abandoning this strongly held and publicly defended position.[3] In late 1942 he applied for a commission in the navy, and on

---

[1] Cf. the introduction to Sermon 25 above by Eisendrath, including the reference to the similar pattern in the life course of Gittelsohn's Long Island neighbour, colleague, and friend Harold I. Saperstein, trained at the Jewish Institute of Religion.

[2] Gittelsohn, *Here Am I*, 93–4. In this memoir, he refers to the passage as 'my perfervid but foolish words', and writes that he learned from this experience 'to respect those members of congregations who cherish their rabbis' freedom of the pulpit enough to tolerate even such extremist views as I had urged'.

[3] Compare the similar transformation of Harold Saperstein, born in the same year, and rabbi of the congregation in the neighbouring Long Island community of Lynbrook: *Witness from the Pulpit*, 50–61, 68–9, 312–13.

1 July 1943, taking a voluntary leave of absence from his congregation, he began a programme of chaplaincy training. Assigned to the Fifth Marine Division, he participated in the Iwo Jima invasion. Chosen by his commanding officer to deliver the address at the dedication of the American military cemetery on Iwo Jima, he offered to withdraw because of the opposition by other American chaplains to a rabbi preaching at a service primarily for Christians, and instead spoke at an alternative ceremony. The address, which received wide publicity at the time, would become a subject of Sermon 31b below, delivered twenty years later.[4]

Various texts of the sermon are available on the internet, perhaps reflecting abbreviated versions published at the time. It is interesting to compare the full, authentic version with the considerably shorter version on the website of the US Army Chaplain Center and School.[5] The latter version contains some minor editing of language in accordance with contemporary usage, so that, for example, 'negroes and whites' becomes 'Blacks and Whites'. But most strikingly, the Army Chaplain Center text removes some of the sharper sentences, and some that had become more politically problematic, such as the pledge of cooperation with China and Russia, and condemnation (in the penultimate paragraph) of the commitment of big business to trade with militaristic nations during the 1930s. As the complete text is not inordinately long to put on a website, one wonders at the thinking behind the shortening to about half its original length; it is not clear to me whether this was done by the USAChCS or whether it used an already edited text. In the text reproduced below I have indicated with square brackets passages omitted in the shorter version. This full text is consistent with Gittelsohn's own citation of his address twenty years later, at the conclusion of Sermon 31b below.

# SERMON

THIS is perhaps the grimmest, and surely the holiest, task we have faced since D-Day. Before us lie the bodies of comrades and friends.[6] Men who until yesterday or last week laughed with us, joked with us, trained with us.

---

[4] For a fuller account of the circumstances of the sermon's delivery, see Moore, *GI Jews*, 148–53.
[5] *The Army Chaplaincy*, Winter–Spring 2002, 14–17, <www.usachcs.army.mil/TACarchive/ACwinspro2/Gittelsohn.htm>, accessed 10 June 2007. I have used the text printed in 'The Deltan of Phi Sigma Delta' of May 1945, a copy of which was graciously provided to me by Professor Moore (see *GI Jews*, 299 n. 75); this full version is available at <www.ww2gyrene.org/ spotlight4_gittelsohn.htm>, accessed 10 June 2007.
[6] As Moore notes, the battle of Iwo Jima, lasting for thirty-six days, resulted in some 6,000 American deaths, as well as some 17,000 additional casualties. The Fiftieth Marine Division alone suffered 2,265 dead.

Men who were on the same ships with us, and went over the sides with us as we prepared to hit the beaches on this island, men who fought with us and feared with us.

Somewhere in this plot of ground there may lie the man who could have discovered the cure for cancer. Under one of these Christian Crosses, or beneath a Jewish Star of David, there may rest now a man who was destined to be a great prophet—to find the way, perhaps, for all to live in plenty. Now they lie here silently in this sacred soil, and we gather to consecrate this earth in their memory.

[It is not easy to do so. Some of us have buried our closest friends here. We saw these men killed before our very eyes. Any one of us might have died in their places. Indeed, some of us are alive and breathing at this very moment only because men who lie here beneath us had the courage and strength to give their lives for ours.] To speak in memory of such men as these is not easy. Of them, too, can it be said with utter truth: 'The world will little note nor long remember what we say here. It can never forget what they did here.'[7]

[No, our poor power of speech can add nothing to what these men and the other dead of our Division who are not here have already done. All that we even hope to do is follow their example. To show the same selfless courage in peace that they did in war. To swear that by the grace of God and the stubborn strength and power of human will, their sons and ours shall never suffer these pains again.] These men have done their job well. They have paid the ghastly price of freedom. If that freedom be once again lost, as it was after the last war,[8] the unforgivable blame will be ours, not theirs. So it is we, the living, who are here to be dedicated and consecrated.[9]

We dedicate ourselves, first, to live together in peace the way they fought and are buried in this war. Here lie men who loved America because their ancestors generations ago helped in her founding, and other men who loved her with equal passion, because they themselves or their fathers escaped from oppression to her blessed shores. Here lie officers and men, negroes and whites, [rich men and poor men—together.[10] Here are] Protestants, Catholics and Jews—

[7] The preacher assumes these words will be recognized as coming from Lincoln's Gettysburg Address.

[8] This is the first of several references to the aftermath of the First World War, when the ideals that were used to justify and motivate American participation in the war seemed to have been forgotten and abandoned, both in Europe and in the United States.

[9] Continuing to echo Lincoln.

[10] The conventional motif of death as the 'great equalizer' (memorably expressed in e.g. William Cullen Bryant's poem 'Thanatopsis') takes on special resonance because of the egalitarian nature of the military graves and the premises of American ideology—if not of American society.

together. Here no man prefers another because of his faith or despises him because of his color.[11] [Here there are no quotas of how many from each group are admitted or allowed. Among them is no discrimination. No prejudices. No hatred. Theirs is the highest and purest democracy.]

Any man among us, the living, who fails to understand that, will thereby betray those who lie here dead. [Whoever of us lifts up his hand in hate against a brother, or thinks himself superior to those who happen to be in the minority, makes of this ceremony and of the bloody sacrifice it commemorates, an empty, hollow mockery.] To this, then, as our solemn, sacred duty, do we the living now dedicate ourselves—to the rights of Protestants, Catholics and Jews, of white men and negroes alike, to enjoy the democracy for which all of them have here paid the price.

To one thing more do we consecrate ourselves in memory of those who sleep beneath these crosses and stars. [We shall not foolishly suppose, as did the last generation of America's fighting men, that victory on the battlefield will automatically guarantee the triumph of democracy at home.] This war, with all its frightful heartache and suffering, is but the beginning of our generation's struggle for democracy. When the last battle has been won, there will be those at home, as there were last time, who will want us to turn our backs in selfish isolation on the rest of organized humanity, and thus to sabotage the very peace for which we fight. We promise to you who lie here: We will not do that! [We will join hands with Britain, China, Russia in peace, even as we have in war, to build the kind of world for which you died.]

When the last shot has been fired, there will still be those whose eyes are turned backward, not forward, who will be satisfied with those wide extremes of poverty and wealth in which the seeds of another war can be sown. We promise you, our departed comrades: This, too, we will not permit. This war has been fought by the common man[; its fruits of peace must be enjoyed by the common man!]. We promise, by all that is sacred and holy, that your sons, the sons of miners and millers, the sons of farmers and workers, will inherit from your death the right to a living that is decent and secure.

[When the final cross has been placed in the last cemetery, once again there will be those to whom profit is more important than peace, who will insist with the voice of sweet reasonableness and appeasement that it is better to trade with the enemies of mankind than, by crushing them, to lose their

---

[11] The cemetery thus exemplifies the ideal of how American society should indeed be, fleshed out in the following sharp sentences.

profit.[12] To you who sleep here silently, we give our promise: we will not listen! We will not forget that some of you were burnt with oil that came from American wells, that many of you were killed with shells fashioned from American steel. We promise that when once again men seek profit at your expense, we shall remember how you looked when we placed you reverently, lovingly, in the ground.]

Thus do we memorialize those who, having ceased living with us, now live within us. Thus do we consecrate ourselves, the living, to carry on the struggle they began. Too much blood has gone into this soil for us to let it lie barren. Too much pain and heartache have fertilized the earth on which we stand. We here solemnly swear: This shall not be in vain! Out of this, and from the suffering and sorrow of those we mourn, this will come, we promise, the birth of a new freedom for the sons of men everywhere.[13] Amen.

---

[12] A pointed reference perhaps to opponents of the proposed boycott of Nazi Germany in the first years of the Hitler regime, and to the continued trade with Japan despite its aggression in the 1930s.

[13] Echoing, once again, Lincoln's 'new birth of liberty' near the end of his Gettysburg address.

# PART VI

# WARS
## OF THE LATER
# TWENTIETH
# CENTURY

# CHAPTER THIRTY-ONE

## ROLAND B. GITTELSOHN
# TWO VIETNAM WAR
# SERMONS

THE FIRST PART of Gittelsohn's career has been outlined in the introduction to Sermon 30 above. In 1953 he moved from Long Island to Temple Israel of Boston, one of the most prestigious Reform congregations in the United States; there he remained until his retirement in 1977. In addition to his role as a congregational rabbi, he was visible as a leader of Jewish organizations on a national level, including as President of the Central Conference of American Rabbis, 1969–71, and as founding President of the Association of Reform Zionists of America (ARZA), 1977–84. Politically outspoken and actively involved in public affairs, he served on governmental commissions pertaining to the penal system and migratory labour. He wrote widely on Jewish issues and theology, his published works including one collection of sermons, *Fire in My Bones*.

Gittelsohn was one of the first American rabbis of a large urban congregation to condemn from the pulpit the Johnson administration's policy in Vietnam. On the Rosh Hashanah of 1965 on which this sermon was being delivered, the *Boston Globe* quoted Rabbi Joseph S. Shubow's sermon saying that, through the United Nations, 'We [the United States] are exerting our fullest powers to bring an end to hatreds, animosities and bloodshed and to restore faith, confidence and peace among the nations.'[1] There was no *New York Times* report of any High Holy Day sermon from 1965 relating to the war; the first evidence I could find of any such was in an article published on 12 December 1965, reporting that two New York rabbis had called for an end, through negotiations, to the deeper US involvement. They were Louis C. Gerstein, an Orthodox rabbi at the Sephardi Shearith Israel, and Israel Margolies of the Reform Beth Am, the People's Temple. Margolies was

---

[1] *Boston Globe*, evening edn, 27 Sept. 1965, p. 9.

quoted as saying in a sermon, 'Rarely in the history of world affairs has any country indulged in such a colossal act of self-righteous arrogance as did our United States when we decided for the strife-torn people of South Vietnam that they are better off dead than Red.'[2] His preaching against the administration's Vietnam policy received frequent coverage during the following months. In March 1966 he said, 'we have moved steadily, inexorably, and it must be confessed, dishonestly, from the dubious status of "advisers" to total involvement in a war that is no less bloody for being undeclared and that our leading strategists grant cannot be won by force of arms'.[3] By the following September, in the wake of President Johnson's reported concern about opposition from American Jews, a *New York Times* article stated that 'a large number of rabbis have been among the most outspoken of the critics'.[4] On Rosh Hashanah, more rabbis used their pulpits to condemn America's role in South East Asia.[5] Yet even at this time, a year after Gittelsohn's sermon, the Jewish community was sharply divided; and it was not until 4 April 1967 that Martin Luther King Jr delivered his most famous and influential public critique of the war, his 'Declaration of Independence from the War in Vietnam' sermon, at New York's Riverside Church.[6] In this respect, Gittelsohn was a pioneer.

Gittelsohn's characteristic preaching style is well reflected in the two sermons that follow. They are not notable for a florid literary style, purple passages, or rhetorical flourishes; nothing in the sermons would be considered evidence of great 'oratory'. Except perhaps for the opening sentence of the first sermon, there are no melodramatic moments intended to inspire the listeners or move them to tears. The appeal of these sermons is not to the emotions but to the mind. They provide information to buttress the preacher's position: quotations not from Jewish sources but from contemporary experts. The sermons set out an argument point by point, with lucidity and cogency. The recapitulation of points already made helps the listener to recall what has been said and to follow the next step in the exposition. At the end of the sermon, there were certainly listeners who had not been convinced, but every listener would have known exactly where the preacher stood, and alert listeners would have been

[2] *New York Times*, 12 Dec. 1965, p. 6.
[3] *New York Times*, 20 Mar. 1966, p. 35. In June 1966, Harold Saperstein devoted a sermon to articulating his opposition to the administration's policy ('The Dilemma of Vietnam').
[4] *New York Times*, 11 Sept. 1966, p. 4.
[5] *New York Times*, 16 Sept. 1996, p. 10, citing Margolies and Edward Klein. Cf. the title of the sermon delivered by Eugene Lipman of Washington, DC on Rosh Hashanah morning, 1966, 'Vietnam: Can Jewish Values Guide Us?'. The two highest leaders of the Reform movement called for an end to the war in a Yom Kippur statement (*New York Times*, 24 Sept. 1966, p. 3).
[6] The original title was 'Beyond Vietnam'; a slightly revised text was published in *Ramparts*, May 1967, 33–7.

able to summarize the major arguments. One is left with the impression that Gittelsohn must have been a master debater.

Thus the first sermon begins with an introduction justifying the preacher's choice of topic for a sermon on the evening of Rosh Hashanah, despite his initial reservations. The body of the sermon is divisible into component parts. The first tackles the 'two self-imposed myths' of American political discourse: that the central world conflict is between capitalism and communism, and that this division is one between 'good guys' versus 'bad guys'. The rebuttal of the image of America as the 'good guy' entails a review of the more distasteful elements of American involvement in Vietnam since the Second World War. The second section, introduced in the published text by the subheading 'What To Do', presents four concrete action points for American policy, each introduced with 'we must'. The third section turns the spotlight on the individuals in the congregation, on the choices to be made by the 'ethically responsible citizen'. The peroration returns to the starting point of a threat that endangers the continuity of life in the coming year.

The second sermon, delivered some two and a half months later, responds to one particular negative reaction to the first. In his introductory paragraphs, Gittelsohn reviews the response elicited by that sermon, pointing out that it was voluminous, predominantly positive, and almost entirely courteous. He would have ordinarily ignored the one discourteous anonymous letter as unworthy of response, but made an exception because of the 'profound and pervasive issues . . . raised by it'. The full text of the letter follows.

Turning to the substantive issues, Gittelsohn identifies three, either implied or explicit: (1) the subject of Vietnam was not 'spiritual' enough to be appropriate for a Rosh Hashanah sermon; (2) the rabbi is not sufficiently expert to speak publicly about diplomatic or political matters; and (3) public criticism of American policy is unpatriotic. Each of these issues is addressed in turn, with a characteristic recapitulation at the end. Then comes the response to the point that must have infuriated Gittelsohn: the reference at the beginning of the letter to Gittelsohn's Iwo Jima sermon as one of the factors that led to his selection for his present position, and the implication that he had either been insincere on Iwo Jima, using the address 'in order to gain you publicity', or that he had betrayed the ideals of that sermon on Rosh Hashanah by criticizing the American war effort in Vietnam. Gittelsohn ends by reading part of the sermon from 1945, allowing the congregants to 'judge for yourselves', but clearly communicating the message: 'You don't need to remind me about what I said on that day; I know what I said better than you do.'

Both of these sermons are grounded strongly in contemporary discourse of controversy, only minimally in Jewish sources. Were it not for the reference to Rosh Hashanah and its theme of *ḥeshbon hanefesh* (serious 'probing of the soul' or self-scrutiny), it would not be easy to identify from internal evidence that the first sermon was delivered by a rabbi.[7] On Rosh Hashanah, he addressed his listeners as Americans, not as Jews. (This characteristic is shared by not a few of the earlier sermons in this volume.) The second sermon contains a paragraph addressing 'who we are and what destiny demands of us' as Jews—'history's most obstinate and persistent rebels against conformity'—insists that 'in Judaism ethics cannot and must not be isolated from the warp and woof of practical life', and cites several biblical verses and the position of the Central Conference of American Rabbis on 'The Rabbi and the Political Process'. Yet here too, the content is for the most part secular and contemporary. Gittelsohn would have recognized this, insisting nevertheless that the substance of both messages was infused with central Jewish values, and asserting defiantly: 'When my government lies, that's a moral issues. So long as God gives me strength and you give me the privilege of this pulpit, I intend to talk about moral issues, be they pleasant or painful.'

## 31A

# WILL THERE BE A TOMORROW?

### 26 SEPTEMBER 1965
#### (ROSH HASHANAH)

#### TEMPLE ISRAEL, BOSTON

———

THIS COULD BE the last Rosh Hashanah sermon of my life. I commence tonight intentionally with so shocking a statement, not out of any morbid premonition of my own imminent demise, but because mankind in the past few months has been perched more precariously than ever on the raw edge of catastrophe. Unless a dramatic and decisive reversal takes place soon, the year which commences at this moment might well witness the calamitous end of civilization.

Feeling this way, how could I possibly have chosen any other topic for tonight's sermon? This is the season for *cheshbon ha-nefesh*, for the deepest, most pervasive probing of the soul. These are the days when the ethical values

---

[7] Cf. H. Saperstein, 'The Dilemma of Vietnam' (10 June 1966). While the substance is quite similar, Saperstein's sermon is rhetorically grounded by an appeal to the three Hebrew words on the ark of the synagogue, *emet, din, shalom* (truth, justice, peace), presented as the criteria for measuring American policy.

of our faith must be stringently applied not only to our personal lives, but equally to the behavior of societies and nations.[8] When the thought first seized me near the start of the summer that the international situation should be my New Year theme, I tried my best to divert it. I experimented over several weeks with other varieties of inventory, both more personal and more philosophic. But each time, after a few minutes or hours of reflection, I found Vietnam rudely intruding itself again into the spotlight of my consciousness. Finally I surrendered, aware of the fact that unless this problem be solved, there will be no others; unless we find the key to peace for another year, there will be no further opportunity for *cheshbon ha-nefesh* on other terms. You might truthfully say, then, that in this instance my subject chose me, rather than the more customary opposite. Hence this sermon.

Let me plunge at once into its substance. I am fearfully convinced that there will be no tomorrow unless, to begin with, we in the United States emancipate ourselves from two self-imposed myths. The first is the delusion that the world's basic conflict today is between communism and capitalism as systems of political and economic metabolism.

We Americans have been irresponsibly inclined to see every crisis in the world as a communist conspiracy. The instant a revolution breaks out anywhere, we rush to accuse it of being communist-inspired and to insist that it must therefore be suppressed. We forget that there were revolutions in the world—including our own—before the advent of communism and there will be long after its disappearance. The conflict in Vietnam is not fundamentally between communism and capitalism. I am not so naive as to deny that there are communists among the Vietcong or that the communists of North Vietnam and of China will do their best to exploit the struggle to their own advantage. Nor am I so stupid as to pretend there are no differences between the Soviet system and our own. The differences are compellingly real, but they are not at the heart of the events in Vietnam.

The conflict there began as a civil war, directed against the repressive dictatorship of Diem. It has expanded into a war of liberation, aimed at expurgating the last ugly traces of colonialism, including the American kind. Ten centuries or more of history attest to the fact that the people of Vietnam would be almost as violently opposed to intervention against their independence by the Chinese, who are communists, as by our capitalistic selves. The blood being so

[8] A (subsidiary) theme in the Rosh Hashanah liturgy, which emphasizes primarily individual judgement.

copiously shed in Indochina today is not primarily over communism and capitalism.

The courageously prophetic words spoken ten days ago by Senator Fulbright are no less true of Vietnam than of his immediate target—our opportunistic meddling in the Dominican Republic.[9] He said: 'Since just about every revolutionary movement is likely to attract Communist support, at least in the beginning, the approach followed in the Dominican Republic . . . must inevitably make us the enemy of all revolutions and therefore the ally of all the unpopular and corrupt oligarchies of the hemisphere.'[10] His words should effectively warn us against the first monstrous myth of our own making.

## MIRROR OF TRUTH

The second—if you will permit me to put it as a colloquialism—is that the world can be divided into 'good guys' and 'bad guys', with never a doubt, of course, as to where we stand. The record of history in Vietnam portrays us as anything but the unblemished saint we think ourselves to be.

That record—surveyed in the light of truth, not of State and Defense Department propaganda—discloses the following. First: that we poured more than a billion dollars of aid into the French effort to subdue Indochina before France was so ignominiously and disastrously forced out of that area.[11] Second: that after the French capitulation, we took over as heir-presumptive to the throne of colonial power. Third: that we sponsored Ngo Dinh Diem as the puppet ruler of South Vietnam, gave him military support in direct violation of the 1954 Geneva Accord, and encouraged him to subvert the reunification elections promised by the Accord within a period of two years. Fourth: that when Diem's

---

[9] In late April 1965 the President of the Dominican Republic was deposed by a right-wing military junta, which requested American support against leftist rebels. President Johnson responded by sending US military forces; by mid-May there were 14,000 American troops in the country, which was in the midst of a civil war. Both the need to protect the lives of Americans in the Dominican Republic and the concern that rebels might succeed in bringing a communist-sympathizing government to power were communicated to Washington in the period leading to American intervention, but only the first was mentioned by President Johnson in his television announcement on 28 Apr. 1965, shortly after he had briefed leaders of Congress; in his speech to the nation on 2 May, Johnson said that the mission was to 'prevent another Communist state in this hemisphere'. For different assessments of American motivations, see Lowenthal, *The Dominican Intervention*, 132–6.

[10] J. William Fulbright, Chairman of the Senate Foreign Relations Committee, released a scathing criticism of American policy in the Dominican Republic, much of which was given as a speech to the Senate on 15 Sept. 1965; the passage cited by Gittelsohn appears in the *New York Times*, 16 Sept. 1965, p. 16, col. 4.      [11] Following their defeat at Dien Bien Phu in May 1954.

role as our stooge became too apparent to his people, thus destroying his usefulness, we conspired to get rid of him. In case you suspect this last to be only my own surmise, it has been attested by Frederick E. Nolting, Jr., our former Ambassador to South Vietnam.[12] Fifth: that since the murder of Diem we have set up and supported a series of nine successive rulers, not one of whom really represented the South Vietnamese, and have justified our continued presence and the escalation of our power by pointing piously to the invitations of our own proteges.

Our current gigolo, by the way, is Premier Ky, a frank admirer of Hitler. He has publicly praised the German dictator who—and these are Ky's words—'by sheer energy and dynamism, was able to build the unity of Germany . . .' That, if you please, is the symbol in Vietnam of us 'good guys'![13]

A sixth and final item concludes this litany of American complicity in Vietnam. We keep professing that our whole purpose in South Vietnam is to protect and defend the people of that unhappy land. The brutal, ugly fact is that a substantial majority of that people feels nothing but contempt for the Saigon government, which remains in power only because of our presence. In his *New York Times* column of 23 August, James Reston—who is not an extremist, who in general supports American policy in the Far East, who was in South Vietnam at the time—wrote: 'The Saigon Government does not have a popular base among the people; it has seldom had one. Saigon has not been responsive to

[12] I have not found any reference to this in the *New York Times* for 1964 or 1965. In 1954 Diem became Premier and then President of the Republic of Vietnam. A *New York Times* article reviewing his reign nine years later during a coup that ousted him from power stated that 'In recent years, many Americans voiced doubt that Ngo Dinh Diem's anti-Communism was a sufficient asset to offset his weaknesses as an ally of the United States in the fight to stem Communism in Asia' (*New York Times*, 2 Nov. 1963, p. 4). He was reported by the rebels to have committed suicide; Diem supporters claimed that the coup was instigated by the United States and that he had been murdered by the rebels. I have not found the statement by Ambassador Nolting confirming American involvement mentioned by Gittelsohn; on 6 Nov. 1964, Nolting wrote a letter paying tribute to Diem as a 'brave man who died for his country a year ago', which was published in the *New York Times* on 17 Nov. 1964, p. 40.

[13] The military junta headed by Air Marshal Nguyen Cao Ky and General Nguyen Van Thieu came to power on 14 June 1965. I have not found the precise quotation attributed to Premier Ky. In the 4 July issue of the *Sunday Mirror*, a London tabloid, a journalist quoted him as saying, 'People ask me who my heroes are. I have only one—Hitler. I admire Hitler because he pulled his country together when it was in a terrible state in the early thirties.' The *New York Times* of 16 July ran an article headlined 'Premier Ky, in Saigon, Denies That He Called Hitler His Hero', citing him as saying that his incidental reference to Hitler in the interview referred to the idea that 'Vietnam needed above all leadership and a sense of discipline in order to face the criminal aggression of Communism' (p. 3). The sentence, tossed off with a 'by the way', strikes one as a rather flimsy debater's point.

their problems . . . They regard their leaders in Saigon as merely the successors of the French colonial regime . . .'[14]

Let no one suppose that our culpability in Vietnam means the Chinese and the Russians are innocent. But I happen to be addressing Americans, not Russians or Chinese. And I have the strongest kind of conviction that repeatedly identifying the other side's faults while disguising or denying our own, is the road to extinction, not to tomorrow. So it is our record which concerns me now. No one has summarized it with more admirable honesty than Senator Wayne Morse. Listen: 'We have violated the Geneva accords and the UN Charter time and again. We are pursuing neither law nor peace in Southwest Asia. We are not even pursuing freedom. We are maintaining a military dictatorship over the people of South Vietnam, headed by an American puppet to whom we give the orders, and who moves only under our orders.'[15]

That isn't a very palatable or savory confession to make, is it? It doesn't quite square with the diet of pablum-propaganda being fed us by the bulk of our news media. That is why I begin by asserting at some length that there can be no hope, for us or the world, unless we emancipate ourselves from two myths: that the struggle today is only or primarily between communism and capitalism; and that in Vietnam especially, we and our cronies are the 'good guys' opposed to the bad.[16]

## WHAT TO DO?

Very well, then, supposed we succeed in divesting ourselves of these devastating delusions. What follows? What specific concrete steps must we take to move toward peace and make tomorrow possible? Suddenly and summarily to withdraw at this point from Vietnam is clearly not the answer. Then what is? Let me hastily suggest the following as the over-all direction in which we must move.

A:  We must stop bombing North Vietnam. To suppose that serious negotiations can be held while our bombing continues is to defy everything we know about human nature and national pride. The popular impression that we did

---

[14] *New York Times*, 23 Aug. 1965, p. 2, col. 2.

[15] Morse, a Democrat from Oregon, cast one of two dissenting votes (with Ernest Gruening, a Democrat from Alaska) on the Gulf of Tonkin resolution, which authorized President Johnson to commit American military power in defence of any ally in South East Asia without a formal declaration of war. On 10 Aug. 1965 Morse wrote a letter to President Johnson asserting that the President's policy was in violation of the US Constitution and the UN Charter. I have not found the precise quotation cited by the preacher.

[16] Recapitulation of the main points of his argument, signalling to the listeners that one section of the sermon is ending.

once stop the bombing is more mirage than fact. True, we suspended our aerial
attacks last spring, but only for a period of five days, and without any indication
that this was a deliberate item of pacific policy rather than just a breather to
replenish our equipment and supplies.[17] The time has come to end the bombings and to announce that, short of the initiation of such tactics by the Chinese
or the Russians, we do not intend to resume them.

B: We must accept and support the Geneva Accord of 1954 as a reasonable
basis for final settlement in Vietnam. That means, specifically, eventual reunification of the country by free elections, whether they go the way we want them to
or not; it means effective neutralization from either Soviet or American domination, and—at the proper time, in the proper manner—the withdrawal of all
foreign military forces.

C: We must agree to negotiate with all the parties directly involved. That
includes the National Liberation Front of South Vietnam—the military arm of
which is the Vietcong—as well as the governments of Saigon, Hanoi and mainland China. Sooner or later, gracefully or clumsily, whether we like it or not, we
must come to grips with the fact that a fourth of the world's population is under
the control of the Chinese communist government and that peace is a hopeless
illusion until we take the blinders off our own eyes. It makes no more sense for us
to proceed in the Far East as if Red China doesn't exist than it does for the Arab
nations to go about their business in the Near East as if Israel were imaginary.

President Johnson's several offers to negotiate make for impressive rhetoric,
but they are neither constructive nor productive.[18] To repeat over and over
again that we will negotiate only after North Vietnam has ended its aid to the

---

[17] On 19 May 1965, the *New York Times* reported a resumption of bombing raids over North
Vietnam following a six-day pause (which had been urged by Canadian Prime Minister Lester
Pearson and Senator Fulbright). The State Department spokesman said that the administration
was disappointed by the lack of response by North Vietnam; the article suggested that the temporary halt might have been intended for the political purpose of demonstrating that the United
States was not the party preventing a negotiated settlement. Some US military spokesmen had
characterized the pause as not political but 'operational': 'designed to permit military reconnaissance, reassessment of targets, and so on' (*New York Times*, 19 May 1965, pp. 1, 16; 16 May 1965,
editorial, p. E12).
[18] On 6 Apr. 1965 Lyndon Johnson gave an address at Johns Hopkins University that garnered
him headlines and plaudits for offering incentives the President hoped would bring North
Vietnam to the bargaining table: 'We will never be second in the search for such a peaceful settlement in Vietnam. There may be many ways to this kind of peace: in discussion or negotiation
with the governments concerned; in large groups or in small ones; in the reaffirmation of old
agreements or their strengthening with new ones. We have stated this position over and over
again, fifty times and more, to friend and foe alike. And we remain ready, with this purpose, for
unconditional discussions.' Indeed, for much of the next three years Johnson would talk about
negotiations while continuing to escalate the war. See *New York Times*, 8 Apr. 1965, pp. 1, 16.

Vietcong is as idle as for them to promise peace talks only after we have withdrawn. Neither we nor they can make the full achievement of our objectives a precondition for sitting at the conference table. For the other side, that would be abject capitulation, not negotiation.

D: We must try to make Vietnam an incubator for the encouragement of world law. There will be neither peace nor tomorrow if we insist on being both judge and policeman for the whole world. Our only hope for the development of world law is through the infusion of new strength and power into the United Nations. Again contrary to popular impression, we have not fostered such growing strength and power. We have used the UN when it seemed to suit our purposes and have contemptuously by-passed it when we wanted to be sure of having our way. We flaunted it flagrantly in Cuba, in Vietnam, and in the Dominican Republic. The sad, distasteful truth is that we have jeopardized the survival of the UN almost as much as have the Russians.

A glimmer of hope appeared in President Johnson's refusal to intervene unilaterally in the dispute between Pakistan and India on the altogether proper ground that it was within the purview of the UN.[19] If he really means that, if he will apply it to the Dominican Republic and Vietnam and every similar crisis in the future, we may be at long last on our way to peace and hope.

Our very difficult but imperative course of action, then, must include at least the following: an end to the bombing of North Vietnam ... acceptance of the 1954 Geneva Accord, which we were the first to violate ... willingness to negotiate in good faith with all the affected parties ... strengthening of the UN to make it the instrument in Vietnam of world law which will then, step by step, be enlarged to cover our whole planet.[20]

## WHERE WE ENTER

I cannot conscientiously conclude without reference to a question which has undoubtedly been bothering at least some of you for the past twenty-five minutes. What does all this have to do with our personal lives in the new year? I have been speaking, after all, not to the United States Senate or the UN

---

[19] In early September 1965, when war broke out between India and Pakistan over Kashmir, the Johnson administration proclaimed neutrality, refused to become directly involved, froze military aid to both parties, and backed UN efforts to establish a ceasefire (*New York Times*, 3 Sept. 1965, p. 2; 4 Sept. 1965, p. 1; 8 Sept. 1965, p. 1; 10 Sept. 1965, p.1.

[20] Again, a passage of recapitulation of the main points, signalling the end of the second major substantive component of the sermon. The ellipses in this paragraph are in the published original.

General Assembly, but to my friends, the members of my own congregation. What can I expect of them? First and foremost, that they remember and implement the role of responsible citizens in a democracy. In recent weeks there has been some hopeful evidence of improvement in our approach to other nations and the United Nations.[21] There can be no doubt, however, that whatever change for the better has been adumbrated is the direct result of pressure brought to bear by citizens on their government.

The very least every one of us must do, if such wholesome pressure is to be sustained, is to keep himself fully and accurately informed. That means more than just skimming the press or scanning the television newscasts. It means more than reading only the sugar-coated press releases of Washington officials. As citizens in a democracy, we must refuse to be pampered or patronized even by the government we ourselves have elected. We must give careful attention in detail to the views of such men as James Reston and Walter Lippmann and Hans Morgenthau and Wayne Morse; to the unregimented opinions of publications like the *Saturday Review*, the *New Republic*, *Progressive* and the *Nation*. They aren't always right, but neither are they always wrong. Our official government handouts aren't always wrong, but neither are they always right.

The ethically responsible citizen must be alert to acquire the broadest possible spectrum of accurate information and must then act upon it. He must support—both with his money and his effort—the organizations working intensively for peace, among them preeminently the United Nations Association, the United World Federalists, Massachusetts PAX and SANE.[22] He must incessantly bring vigorous pressure to bear on his government wherever he believes it to be needed: writing letters and sending wires to the President, the Secretary of State, our Representative to the UN, our Congressmen and Senators. If you and I really care whether or not there will be a tomorrow, there is much that we can and must do.

Dr. Hudson Hoagland, Director of the Worcester Foundation for Experimental Biology, has written a paragraph which should commend universal attention. It reads as follows:

[21] Referring apparently to the India–Pakistan conflict.
[22] UNA-USA was formed in 1964 by the merger of two similar organizations intended to foster support for the United Nations within the United States. UWF was founded after the Second World War to promote the idea of a world federal government. Massachusetts PAX was a local peace activist organization. The Committee for a SANE Nuclear Policy, founded in 1957, became an early critic of armed intervention in Vietnam. Its 'Emergency Rally' at Madison Square Garden on 8 June 1965 drew some 18,000 participants.

If we were told by the world's astronomers that the earth were on a collision course with a large asteroid, and if the state of physical science were such as to make possible prevention of the collision through a world cooperative effort, there is no doubt that the United States and the Soviet Union would pool their scientific and industrial know-how to save themselves from mutual annihilation.[23]

He then proceeds to underscore the obvious. We are, in fact, on such a collision course. The obstacle which menaces us is not an asteroid, but our own obtuseness in clinging to outworn myths and habits. The calamity, if we continue, will be no less disastrous. Our attempt to avert it must therefore be prodigious.

Will there be a tomorrow? Can we realistically anticipate additional Rosh Hashanah sermons, for me to preach and you to hear? I am not sure whether even God knows the answer. I am positive that He cannot determine it without our help. Amen.

## 31B

# ANSWER TO AN ANONYMOUS LETTER

## 26 NOVEMBER 1965[24]

### TEMPLE ISRAEL, BOSTON

━━

L IKE EVERY PERSON in public life, I have received my share of anonymous correspondence. Usually I ignore it, on the theory that any individual who declines to accept responsibility for his views deserves neither the courtesy nor the dignity of being recognized. Why, then, do I make an

[23] Hudson Hoagland, a professor at Tufts, Boston University, and Harvard, gave a commencement address on 6 June 1965 in which he called for an international law against war (*New York Times*, 7 June 1965, p. 43). He was selected as Humanist of the Year in 1965 in recognition of his work as a physiologist and for his use of science as an instrument for humanitarian advance. In the May–June 1965 issue of the *Humanist* he wrote, 'Our future depends upon an educational system that will teach the young . . . that the most basic human values which are worthy of loyalty and respect are independent of racial, national, political, and religious boundaries.' Gittelsohn's quotation, however, is not in this article, and I have not been able to locate it.

[24] The date is not provided in the book; it comes from Gittelsohn's message in the congregation's monthly bulletin announcing sermon topics for the following weeks, as provided by the Temple Israel archivist (I am grateful to Rabbi Larry J. Halpern for this information).

exception of the anonymous letter which elicits this response?[25] Plainly and simply, because I believe that profound and pervasive issues are raised by it, issues which involve the proper role of a rabbi, the relationship between a rabbi and his congregants, between a rabbi and his conscience. I hope my unidentified correspondent is present tonight. Whether he is or not, however, there are others in our midst who feel as he does and who therefore are entitled to the kind of explanation I now propose to offer.

When I decided to preach on Rosh Hashanah about Vietnam, I was aware of the fact that some of you would take exception to my message. I knew in advance that such a sermon would invite a substantial volume of mail. It did. My only surprise—a very pleasant one, I confess—was to discover that by a margin of about five-to-one these letters supported my position. In view of the well-known truth that most people take to typewriter or pen only in angry opposition, this response speaks most favorably for the social and spiritual maturity of our congregation. All but two of the letters I received—whether in opposition or agreement—were courteous and polite. The anonymous letter, as you will see in a moment, was different.

It contained as an enclosure the lead article in the November *Reader's Digest*, a piece called 'A Hero Comes Home', relating the tragic story of Captain Christopher O'Sullivan's death in Vietnam just before his scheduled return to his wife and two sons. Let me read the letter in its entirety, not even correcting its grammatical errors, lest I be accused of doctoring it to my own advantage.[26] Here it is:

October 31st 1965
One of the chief factors which brought you as a Rabbi to the attention of the world and the Jewish community was the very fine statement you made while you were a United States Chaplain in World War 2. This was printed in newspapers and I am sure was one of the deciding things in choosing you for your present position at Temple Israel.[27]

I am taking the liberty of asking you to read the enclosed article and searching your own heart to see whether your former attitude to war and its results was just a means to an end in order to gain you publicity and 'fame' or Captain Sullivan's idea of the present conflict in Viet Nam and his sacrifice in death for a cause he really believed in.

I am not signing my name to this letter because I believe its sentiment is that of a great many of your Temple members, both friends and detractors.

---

[25] Note the undercutting dismissal of the letter ('any individual who declines to accept responsibility for his views deserves neither the courtesy nor the dignity . . .') and the claim that this case is exceptional because of the profoundly important issues raised.

[26] A two-edged formulation, claiming that his public exposure of the author's uneducated writing style is necessary because of his commitment to total accuracy.

[27] Gittelsohn's Iwo Jima address is printed above as Sermon 30.

Our parents, our teachers and our ministers are supposed to be our examples to live by. When I see the burning of draft cards, the sudden increase in the number of conscientious objectors and statements by young men that they would like to see the Viet Cong lick the United States, I feel that part of this behavior must be attributed to men like you and I feel a little ashamed of you!

The letter ends with an exclamation mark, but without signature.

Before commencing my formal—and I hope restrained—reply, let me assure you that I do not want the Vietcong or anyone else to 'lick the United States', and that I do not approve the empty, vain gesture of burning draft cards. I do admire honest objectors to war on grounds of conscience; even though I haven't entirely agreed with them for many years, I am convinced from personal experience of both kinds that it sometimes requires a higher order of personal courage to be a conscientious objector than to participate in combat. The intent of this somewhat parenthetical paragraph is that I be criticized or credited—as the case may be—for the things I actually believe, not for those created by someone else's fertile imagination.

Very well, then, suppose we turn to the substantive issues. Other letters state explicitly what this one only implies. There are, it appears, three grounds for the discomfort some of you experienced after listening to me on Rosh Hashanah. First, you felt that my theme was not appropriate for the High Holy Days because it wasn't spiritual. Second, you objected that Vietnam isn't the rabbi's public business because he does not qualify as an expert in diplomatic or political matters; his expertise is in the spheres of theology and religion. And third, you resented my criticism of American policy as a threat to your patriotism and love of country. One correspondent admonished me to follow the advice of Stephen Decatur: 'Our country in her intercourse with foreign nations, may she always be in the right; but our country, right or wrong.' Let me deal now with each of these objections in sequence.

Whether or not a sermon on Vietnam—or, for that matter, on any public issue—is spiritual, becomes a matter of semantics. To get anywhere, we must first arrive at a definition of the word spiritual. For me it denotes the transphysical aspect of human experience, anything and everything about man which transcends his physical anatomy as an animal. To be at once more specific, every attitude or action of man which is aimed at the creation or appreciation of truth, of beauty or of moral goodness is spiritual.[28] If, therefore, I seek in a sermon to

[28] This definition reflects Gittelsohn's rationalist, anti-supernaturalist theology, exemplified in (among many other places) his pamphlet 'A Jewish View of God'.

discover and disclose the truth about Vietnam, that immediately qualifies as a spiritual message. If, moreover, I strive to apply the ethical insights of my faith to American foreign policy, that—clearly and unmistakably—is spiritual. The trouble with many of us is that we have grown accustomed to using the word spiritual for things which are vague, amorphous and abstract—and are therefore undisturbing and comfortable. Once we understand the word accurately, the ground is cut out from the first objection to such a sermon.

Up to this point, everything I have said applies to all religious leaders or groups. There is a special emphasis, however, which must be addressed specifically to Jews. We cannot determine what is or is not spiritually appropriate for us as Jews unless first we decide who we are and what destiny demands of us.

We are history's most obstinate and persistent rebels against conformity. We are the descendants of Abraham, who smashed his father's precious idols;[29] of Nathan, who dared point even to the King himself and say: *'You are the man!'* (2 Sam. 12: 7). We are the heirs of Jeremiah, who decried pretenders for shouting 'peace, peace, when there is no peace' (Jer. 6: 14, 8: 11). We spring from the loins of Zechariah, who—in a time no less obsessed with militarism than our own—proclaimed: 'Not by might, and not by power, but by My spirit, saith the Lord' (Zech. 4: 6). We are, in short, a people that has always insisted on applying its moral imperatives to every individual and communal aspect of life. We are that, or we are nothing. And it is, I submit, only in the light of what we really, truly are that we Jews can decide what is spiritual and what belongs in our pulpits.

This brings us to our second objection, that rabbis should refrain from public pronouncement in such areas as political and diplomatic matters, where they are not experts. I am nearly the last person in this congregation to pose as a political or diplomatic specialist, though I don't think I am as ignorant and naive in these fields as some of my critics apparently believe me to be. But I am an expert on ethics. If not, I have no right to wear this robe or occupy this place. And especially in Judaism ethics cannot and must not be isolated from the warp and woof of practical life. The notion that individuals should strive to be righteous in their personal lives but that societies and nations need not, is just about as utterly un-Jewish as anything could be.[30] When you ask whether the rabbi has a right to speak on the ethics of foreign policy, you ask the wrong question. This isn't a matter of right but of obligation—of solemn, ineluctable duty.

[29] A familiar rabbinic legend: see Bialik and Ravnitzky (eds), *The Book of Legends*, 32–3; Ginzberg, *The Legends of the Jews*, i. 195–8, with references in notes.

[30] Compare the discussion of this issue by J. Leonard Levy in Sermon 18 above.

The Central Conference of American Rabbis spoke what should be the last word on this subject. Let me read you a small section of its statement on 'The Rabbi and the Political Process':

We hereby reaffirm the rabbi's right and obligation to exercise political responsibility as a citizen and as a moral teacher ... the rabbi who seeks to affect the character of his congregants must seek to affect the character of the environment in which they live ... Therefore, the rabbi must bring to bear the insights of his faith and experience to aid his congregants to discern the moral dimensions of contemporary problems.[31]

Does anyone here doubt that there are moral dimensions to the conduct of American foreign policy? Then let me share with such doubters the following devastating exchange, published in the *New York Herald–Tribune* of 17 November 1965 under the by-line of David Wise, Washington Bureau Chief. On 24 February of the same year Secretary General U Thant of the United Nations said: 'I have presented certain ideas on my own to some of the principal parties directly involved in the question of Vietnam. I have even presented concrete ideas and proposals ...'. The very next day George Reedy, White House Press Secretary, said: 'The President has received no proposal from U Thant.' At a press conference on 15 November this question was asked: 'Did U Thant in late summer and/or fall of 1964 on one or more occasions advise the US Government that the North Vietnamese government was prepared for talks of some kind?' Answer, by Robert J. McCloskey of the State Department: 'Yes.'[32]

I love my nation. I love it enough to have volunteered for duty as a chaplain when no power other than my own conscience could have compelled me to do so. But my government has lied to me and the world, and that's a moral issue. My government lied to me and the world not only about Hanoi's readiness to negotiate peace, but also in the incident involving the U2 plane shot down over Russia.[33] My government lied about its training of Cuban guerrillas preparing to invade their homeland.[34] My government lied about its attempt to bribe the

[31] Citing the report of the CCAR Committee on Justice and Peace, ratified at the annual convention of 16–20 June 1964, and published in the *Yearbook of the CCAR*, 74 (1965): 85–6.

[32] Eric Sevaraid, *Look*, 16 Nov. 1965; *New York Times*, 16 Nov. 1965, pp. 1, 5; editorial, *New York Times*, 17 Nov. 1965, p. 46.

[33] Francis Gary Powers was shot down over Soviet territory on 1 May 1960. After the incident was announced by Khrushchev on 5 May, Powers was first identified by the Americans as the pilot of a NASA weather observation plane; then the State Department admitted it was an intelligence plane but denied that Washington had authorized a flight across the Soviet border. Eventually, after Powers confessed, the US government admitted that President Eisenhower had authorized the policy of U-2 overflights.

[34] Shortly before this sermon was delivered, Arthur Schlesinger, the former special assistant to President Kennedy, admitted 'lying' to the *New York Times* at the time of the Bay of Pigs

premier of Singapore.[35] Each of these deliberate lies was exposed by the alert conscience of someone who refused to be brainwashed and was only then admitted by officials. When my government lies, that's a moral issue. So long as God gives me strength and you give me the privilege of this pulpit, I intend to talk about moral issues, be they pleasant or painful.

My anonymous correspondent is ashamed of me for the wrong reason. If I ever desist from preaching truth as I see it, from castigating immorality as I understand it, I shall then have deserved shame from him and from all of you.

That leaves us with only the last of the objections to sermons such as mine on Rosh Hashanah, the idea that as a molder of public opinion, I should uphold my nation, right or wrong. Well, I'm afraid that my unidentified pen-pal and I have diametrically different notions on what constitutes true patriotism. What troubles me here most, however, is something else. The claim that one must always support his government, that it is dangerous and subversive to criticize one's government, smacks much more of dictatorship than of democracy. This is the psychology of 'Heil Hitler', not of 'I pledge allegiance'. This was the rationale for millions of Germans to close their eyes and ears and hearts to the painful plight of cremated Jews! No, I don't buy this notion. I won't hold my government always right, any more than I honestly believe that my children or my wife or I myself can always be right. There are times when honest, even trenchant complaint is the most genuine token of love.

Are you aware of what has already begun in American life? We are headed full-speed into a period of neo-McCarthyism. One of the most precious of our democratic privileges—the right to dissent—is being disastrously corroded. Increasingly those who have the honest courage to criticize are being branded as communists. Demonstrations against the war in Vietnam have been countered by the cheapest, shabbiest, most maudlin kind of propaganda: by inciting soldiers to express contempt for all critics; by television screens which show us night after night only the bearded beatniks among the protestors, and only the most handsome and clean-cut of administration defenders. Intelligent criticism is being met not with rational response but with the kind of long TV

invasion by providing an inaccurate 'cover story' about the nature and size of the force that was in Cuba, which diverged from his account in the recently published memoir, *A Thousand Days* (1965): *New York Times*, 25 Nov. 1965, p. 8.

[35] When Singapore split from Malaysia, becoming an independent state on 9 Aug. 1965, its first prime minister was a socialist anti-communist, Lee Kuan Yew. On 31 August, Lee accused the US government of attempting to bribe him in 1960 with $3 million to cover up an abortive CIA operation to purchase information from a Singapore intelligence officer (*Washington Post, Times, Herald*, 1 Sept. 1965, p. 1; *New York Times*, 2 Sept. 1965, p. 1; Lee, *From Third World to First*, 449–51).

sequence I saw Wednesday night, showing a tearful young widow, a tiny infant in her arms, reading the last letter she received from her husband before he was killed in combat.[36]

Letters of protest against policy in Vietnam are now being officially answered by the Internal Security Division of the Justice Department, the division charged with responsibility to prosecute communists and spies. You don't really think that's a simple coincidence, do you?

We who deplore current American policy are accused of letting our soldiers down. Far from it! I wouldn't deliberately let any American in combat down. I know his fear in my own gut.[37] The people who are really betraying him are those who encourage our government to sacrifice his life in vain for a purpose of most dubious morality.

Here, then, is my reply—to my anonymous correspondent and to those who had the decency to sign their communications. I must respectfully reject all three of their premises. I must insist that my theme on Rosh Hashanah was both spiritual and appropriate; that it is precisely my responsibility as a rabbi to subject American policy to the microscope of moral judgment: that he is most patriotic and loyal who most consistently challenges his nation toward truth.[38]

The writer of this letter implies that I have betrayed the ideals of my Iwo Jima sermon. I wonder when he last read it, or if he truly understood it. I am satisfied that my views on Vietnam are in direct fulfillment of the ideals I cherished and the promise I voiced in March of 1945. Listen, will you not?—and judge for yourselves. Perhaps as you do, you will understand why I speak on Vietnam as I have, why anything else would be a gross betrayal of my conscience and my God:

We shall not foolishly suppose, as did the last generation of America's fighting men, that victory on the battlefield will automatically guarantee the triumph of democracy at home. This war, with all its frightful heartache and suffering, is but the beginning of our generation's struggle for democracy . . . We promise you who lie here . . . we will join hands with Britain, China, Russia—in peace, even as we have in war, to build the kind of world for which you died . . .[39]

Thus do we memorialize those who, having ceased living with us, now live within us. Thus do we consecrate ourselves, the living, to carry on the struggle

---

[36] This appears to refer to one of the network 11.00 p.m. news programmes, as none of the feature programmes listed for that evening (Wednesday, 24 Nov. 1965) indicates any Vietnam content.
[37] An allusion to his own experience as a chaplain, which will be introduced explicitly in a few moments.     [38] A characteristic recapitulation of the central points in the three sections.
[39] For the full text, see Sermon 30 above.

they began. Too much blood has gone into this soil for us to let it lie barren. Too much pain and heartache have fertilized the earth on which we stand. We here solemnly swear: this shall not be in vain. Out of this, and from the suffering and sorrow of those who mourn this, will come—we promise—the birth of a new freedom for the sons of men everywhere.

## CHAPTER THIRTY-TWO

## COLIN EIMER
# THE FALKLANDS CRISIS

### FRIDAY EVENING, 14 MAY 1982

#### SOUTHGATE AND DISTRICT REFORM SYNAGOGUE,
#### ENFIELD, LONDON

LIKE the Spanish–American War at the end of the previous century, the Falkland Islands War was of short duration: seventy-four days, from the Argentine invasion beginning on 31 March 1982 until the surrender of the Argentine garrison in Stanley on 13 June. The number of casualties was relatively small: 255 British and 655 Argentine military personnel were killed. From a military perspective, the outcome could not have been very much in doubt. Yet the conflict aroused strong feelings in both countries, especially following dramatic attacks, leading to the destruction first of the Argentine cruiser *General Belgrano* and then, two days later, of the British destroyer *Sheffield*. Colin Eimer, born in 1945 and ordained at London's Leo Baeck College in 1971, was serving in his fifth year as rabbi of a middle-sized Reform congregation in a northern suburb of London. Like many of his colleagues, Eimer felt the need to address issues arising from the war in one of his sabbath sermons.[1]

Several themes emerge from the text, all of which we have encountered in previous sermons. The first is the challenge for the rabbi to find something appropriate to say about the war from the pulpit. Here the sticking point is not so much the anguish and confusion we have noted in sermons inspired by the two world wars, but rather the plenitude of commentary by political and military experts that the modern media have made accessible to the listeners. Should the worship service in the synagogue perhaps be a source of respite from the barrage of news, information, and opinion to which congregants are inevitably exposed in periods of crisis? Apparently, many Jews have come to expect their religious leaders to articulate a response to important events. What

---

[1] I am grateful to Rabbi Eimer for making his own manuscript text available to me, together with a few of his own annotations that I have included below.

can the Jewish preacher add that will not merely recapitulate what others have said, and that will be an authentic 'Jewish' message?

A second theme, which appears in the very first sermon of this anthology and became especially pronounced during the First World War, is the problem of prayer in wartime. What does it mean to invoke God when armies are clashing, knowing that religious leaders of the enemy are also praying for God's help, believing that their cause is right and deserving of divine support? May one legitimately pray for the defeat of the enemy, knowing that this will necessarily entail bloodshed and grief? This problem is introduced by Eimer in the recapitulation of an earlier sermon recounting an incident in which he was asked to offer a prayer at a public occasion with only a few seconds to negotiate the tensions between his own inclinations and the expectations of the members of a borough council.

The central theme of this discourse, however, is the condemnation of the jingoistic sentiments stoked by tabloid journalism. The preacher identifies a 'brutalising process' that tends to dehumanize the enemy and expose every presentation of a viewpoint that diverges from the government position to vituperative attack—as revealed by the firestorm of protest in the media and the House of Commons that followed the statement by a high BBC official that the grief felt by Argentine widows of sailors killed in action was no less painful and tragic than the grief felt by British widows. The preacher takes his stand in defence of this statement, insisting that despite the abhorrent policies of the Argentine government, the enemy soldiers and their loved ones are as fully human as one's own.

This is what the preacher presumably emphasized as the authentically Jewish message in time of war. As we shall see in the following text (Sermon 33), a similar point was made eleven days later, though without explicit reference to contemporary counter-examples, by the chief rabbi, Immanuel Jakobovits, in a lecture on 'The Morality of Warfare' delivered at the Central Synagogue of London: 'First—and this is certainly uniquely characteristic of Judaism—Jewish law insists that we should never gloat over the discomfiture or defeat of our enemies.'[2] This was a point on which the Orthodox chief rabbi and the young Reform rabbi were in full agreement. During the following four months, with the Israeli incursion into Lebanon culminating in massacres at Sabra and Shatila, the humanity of the enemy would become an issue arousing considerable anguish.[3]

[2] Jakobovits, 'The Morality of Warfare', 4; for the continuation of the passage, see Sermon 33 below, p. 521.

[3] This can be seen in the 'circular letter' sent out by Chief Rabbi Jakobovits between Rosh Hashanah and Yom Kippur 1982, containing selections from his Rosh Hashanah sermon, later published in L'Eylah, 2/5 (Spring 5743/1983), pp. 1–6.

As for style, the sermon illustrates a mode of discourse antithetical to the elevated rhetoric that characterized most of the nineteenth- and early twentieth-century sermons. Whether because of the more intimate environment of a smaller congregation or because of changes in taste, we find ideas expressed plainly, without the ornamentation of unusual vocabulary or special literary effects. The formulations may have been polished in the delivery to some extent, but the manuscript gives the impression of serving as a script not for oratory but for conversation; for a religious leader talking directly to his people, not performing in front of them. Nor do we find the highly structured debater's presentation that characterized Gittelsohn's sermons on Vietnam. One senses that the preacher is thinking out loud, and permitting others to listen. Of course, that too may be a rhetorical ploy; but it seems quite genuine.

# SERMON

—

DURING the past weeks, when I have met friends of mine they have often asked me the same question, 'What are you saying in your sermons about the Falklands crisis?' Simon Jenkins of *The Economist* in an article in *The Times* on Monday warned of the danger of soldiers playing at journalists and journalists playing at soldiers. This happens, he says, when the media interview retired admirals who give a political commentary on the crisis, whilst the newspapers, or at least the yellower tabloids, become militaristic. 'Latest Score: Britain 6, Argentina 0', went a headline in the *News of the World*. 'IT'S WAR', went one in the *Sun*, with apparent glee.* This is the danger for journalists, says Jenkins, that they jump on a jingoistic, militaristic bandwagon, and—as is evident in the *News of the World* example—reduce the whole thing to a game.[4]

There is a corresponding danger for religious leaders. Just as professionalism suffers when journalists play at soldiers, so does my professionalism suffer when rabbis become political commentators. So any sermon has to address itself to the crisis in a very particular way. It is impossible to escape the crisis.

---

* Both 'yellow' tabloid newspapers.

[4] Simon Jenkins, 'When Soldiers Play Journalist and Journalists Play at Soldiers', *The Times*, 10 May 1982, p. 8; Jenkins was political editor of *The Economist*. For the *News of the World* headline, see R. Harris, *GOTCHA!*, 48 (the 'six' were 'South Georgia, two airstrips, three warplanes'). Jenkins incorporated some of the material from this article, including the *Sun* headline, into the book he co-authored on the war: see Hastings and Jenkins, *The Battle for the Falklands*, 135.

It is talked about everywhere and all sorts of opinions are being thrown at us. You do not come to the synagogue, I assume, to hear more purely political commentary on the situation. We all come worried and concerned by the crisis. But we also come in a sense to get away from it and in a sense with the hope that somehow, through being here, we might gain some deeper insight into what is going on, what is being said.

Two weeks ago I devoted a bat mitzvah sermon to the crisis, addressing myself to one aspect of it: the way in which each side in every conflict imagines it has God on its side. I related how, as the Chaplain to the Mayor of Enfield,* I say a prayer before each Council meeting. At the last meeting, Clive Goldwater asked me to say something about the Falklands—'Everybody's expecting it,' he said. I was in a quandary. 'What should I say?' Should I ask God, who is, of course, on our side, to pour destruction and ruin on the Argentines? I was only asked literally 30 seconds before going into the meeting so it was all very impromptu and I don't like such prayers. In the end I said something like, 'Our thoughts are with the Task Force. Guard them and protect them so that they all return safely to these shores.' Even that sort of prayer seemed to be right on the edge for me—too close to 'with God on our side'; protect *our* boys but no mention of the Argentines who are also dying.

So if I don't address myself to the crisis too often it is because I do not believe the pulpit should be used for political commentary, but it is, of course, a fine dividing line and not always clear. Political comment may produce interesting sermons, but it won't, I think, produce Jewish statements which speak out of Jewish teaching and Jewish tradition. There is, after all, a difference, a big difference between a statement by a Jew and a Jewish statement.

This week has seen a great deal of controversy over some statements made on Monday's *Panorama*,[†5] which I did not see. The director of the programme said, 'A widow in Portsmouth is no different from a widow in Buenos Aires'.[6]

---

* The mayor of a borough in England—not an elected, political post—usually invites the minister of his/her place of worship to become 'chaplain'. This means, as in this instance, opening Council meetings with a prayer. At that time Clive Goldwater was mayor and, as his rabbi, I became his chaplain.
† A major weekly BBC news programme, usually doing in-depth coverage of one major political/social issue.

5 For a full discussion of this programme and the firestorm of reaction to it, see R. Harris, *GOTCHA!*, 76–91.
6 According to Harris, this statement was made not by the director of *Panorama* but by the managing director of BBC radio, Richard Francis, at the International Press Institute of Madrid; picked up by the British media, it fuelled the attack on the BBC and was savaged by the *Sun*

This created a furore. Demands that he should resign because he is a traitor, or that he should either sack those responsible for the *Panorama* programme or resign himself, and so on.[7]

The war has become a 'matter of principle'. People say, 'You can't let aggression go unchecked, unpunished in the world. If the Argentines succeed, Belize won't be safe, nor will Gibraltar or any other isolated British possession.'[8] Maybe, but the word 'principle' can often hide a multitude of other things, which may in fact have little to do with real 'principles'. Some people say, 'Galtieri is a fascist dictator, Argentina ignores human rights altogether. He needs to be stopped. You can't make an omelette without breaking eggs.'[9] For Jews there is the added complication that Argentina has given sanctuary to ex-Nazis and is a highly antisemitic regime.[10]

There is a brutalising process at work. Calls to suppress unpopular views in the media are just one manifestation of this process. We forget all too easily and quickly that the sailors on the *Belgrano* died just as horribly as those on the *Sheffield*.*[11] A widow in Buenos Aires does grieve just as much as a widow in

---

* The headline in the *Sun* when the *Belgrano* was sunk was 'GOTCHA!'—appalling enough, and even more so in the weeks that followed as it emerged that the *Belgrano* was sailing *away* from the Falklands and was outside the British-declared 'Exclusion Zone'.

(*GOTCHA!*, 83). Francis's statement was cited by Greg Dyke, former director-general of the BBC, in a speech given on 24 Apr. 2003 to the Goldsmiths College Journalism Symposium on the role of the media in the war in Iraq (<www.bbc.co.uk/pressoffice/speeches/stories/dyke_journalism.shtml>, checked 31 July 2006).

[7] This apparently alludes to a meeting of the Tory Media Committee at the House of Commons on 12 May 1982, in which MP Winston Churchill, who strongly attacked the statement by Richard Francis, said that George Howard, chairman of the BBC, 'should have the courage to sack those responsible for *Panorama* or offer his own resignation' (*The Times*, 13 May 1982, p. 1, col. 4; cf. R. Harris, *GOTCHA!*, 84–5.)

[8] This argument combines the 'domino' metaphor familiar from American discourse on South East Asia with an implicit evocation of the (belatedly) defiant stand against Nazi Germany. Cf. Noakes, *War and the British*, 109–10.

[9] General Leopoldo Galtieri, President of Argentina from Dec. 1981. For his human rights abuses, see *Argentina, the Military Juntas and Human Rights*.

[10] The most famous Nazi sheltered by Argentina was, of course, Adolf Eichmann. (Josef Mengele also lived in Argentina for some seven years before moving to other South American countries.) The repressive antisemitism of the contemporary Argentinian regimes had recently been vividly depicted in Timmerman's *Prisoner without a Name*. This legacy complicated the position of British Jews advocating a less militaristic position.

[11] The Argentine cruiser, *General Belgrano*, with its crew of more than 1,100 was torpedoed outside the total exclusion zone on 2 May; it sank quickly, with a loss of 368 dead. For a full account, see Gavshon and Rice, *The Sinking of the Belgrano*; and cf. John Rayner, preaching on the previous Sabbath: 'Was it really necessary to send the Task Force when we did, to sink the *General Belgrano*, to impose the 12-mile limit?' (Rayner, 'Whose Islands?', 4). The British destroyer *Sheffield*, hit by an Exocet missile on 4 May, was abandoned with a loss of 21 killed; it sank on 10 May.

Portsmouth. When we insist too glibly on a 'matter of principle' we have taken a step on the road towards ignoring the human beings who are out there in the South Atlantic on *both* sides of the Exclusion Zone. We have then started to look on them as ciphers, symbols, but not real people. They represent values we don't like and therefore we diminish their nature as human beings.

That is the top of a very dangerous and slippery slope. It is the sort of path that once you have taken one step on it, subsequent ones appear much easier than they did before taking that initial step. For in reducing the human-being-ness of others, we are also inevitably doing the same thing to ourselves. We become more callous, more brutal. I can sense these feelings in myself and don't like them. It is so easy to slip across the border line of our humanity. On one side of the line, being a human being means aspiring to the highest that we humans are capable of. On the other side we say, 'Well, we're only human after all,' as if to say, 'Don't expect too much from us.'

One of the aims of religion in general and prayer in particular is to keep this distinction sharply in focus. It involves a refining of the emotions, elevating ourselves above our baser reactions and feelings—in the case of the Falklands above jingoism, and a couldn't-care-less feeling for the Argentines.

It seems to me that this is one of the dangers we need to guard against through these troubled times.

# CHAPTER THIRTY-THREE

## IMMANUEL JAKOBOVITS
# THE MORALITY OF WARFARE

*United Synagogue Lecture*

### 25 MAY 1982

#### CENTRAL SYNAGOGUE, LONDON

T HE following text is not, strictly speaking, a sermon responding directly to a war situation. It is a transcript 'in slightly revised form' of the inaugural address delivered by the chief rabbi on 25 May 1982 to launch a new series of luncheon lectures sponsored by the United Synagogue at the Central Synagogue in London. The war that began fifty-six days earlier is mentioned explicitly in only a single sentence. None of the specificities of Colin Eimer's text (Sermon 32 above) are to be found here. Yet the lecture is more than a theoretical exercise; the reality of an actual war is discernible both in the choice of the topic for the inaugural lecture and in the nuances of what the speaker says. I have decided to include it because of its survey of themes that provide the background for any wartime sermon drawing on Jewish tradition in response to contemporary circumstances.

Immanuel Jakobovits was born in 1921 into an East Prussian rabbinic family, and moved with them to Berlin when still a child. He arrived in England as a teenager, and completed his higher education at Jews' College and London University. He served as chief rabbi of Ireland for nine years before moving to one of the most prestigious congregations in the United States, New York's Fifth Avenue Synagogue. His influential study *Jewish Medical Ethics*, published during his tenure in New York, established an international reputation. Seven years later, he became chief rabbi of the United Hebrew Congregations of the British Commonwealth; he was knighted in 1981, a year before this lecture was delivered. Chaim Bermant, his biographer, described him as 'liberal when it comes to Zionism, . . . conservative on domestic British issues and resolutely die-hard on religious ones'.[1]

Jakobovits begins his address by justifying his topic in a manner that suggests a reaction to the view that rabbis should 'stick to religion' and stay away from politics.[2] In addition to their primary responsibility to promote the observance and understanding of Jewish law, he insists that 'Rabbis should also be expected to relate the wider moral teachings of Judaism to the contemporary scene.' This is a strong assertion of a point more frequently identified with the progressive movements in Judaism than with an Orthodox chief rabbi,[3] and the continuation of the passage suggests that the propriety of rabbinical statements with 'political overtones' made from the pulpit or lecture stand was under attack and in need of defence. Jakobovits cites as his precedent the literature of the Hebrew prophets, in which concern for the application of moral standards to statecraft and political leadership is a central motif. While most of the lecture is a review of sources, both biblical and rabbinic, that could have been presented at any time, the resonance to the 'contemporary scene' is apparent and occasionally made explicit. 'Alas, Jewish teachings on warfare are all too topical', he says. We are passing through a 'deeply-anxious period'. And then, in a single finely tuned sentence, 'I believe there can be no doubt whatever of the morality of the Falklands action taken by Britain, even if some may question its wisdom.'

The remainder of the lecture contains few surprises. Jewish teachings do not sustain a pacifist repudiation of war under all circumstances; they do not question the right to defend a just cause by war when necessary. Just like an individual, a nation can resort to self-defence, 'whether by pre-emptive strikes or . . . in order to protect its national life'. But this should never be the first recourse; the supreme value of the Jewish tradition is peace. The right of military resort to arms is restricted with reservations and safeguards, pertaining both to the cause and to the conduct of war. There must be no gloating over the defeat of the enemy—a theme we saw explicitly emphasized in Colin Eimer's sermon. The erosion of moral values that often accompanies war is to be robustly resisted.

Allusions are made not just to the Falklands campaign but also to contemporary Israel. In discussing the biblical prohibition of 'scorched earth' tactics in warfare, the 'wanton destruction' of property 'including the demolition of building', Jakobovits notes, 'I will not discuss here the possible relevance to

[1] Bermant, *Lord Jakobovits*, 153.　　　　[2] See the Introduction above, pp. 27–30.
[3] Cf. the Liberal rabbi John Rayner on 8 May: 'Surely, therefore, we must for once give the exposition of Scripture a rest, and take stock of the grave situation our country is facing' (Rayner, 'Whose Islands?', 1).

what happened recently at Yamit', when Israeli buildings were destroyed before the settlement was handed over to the Egyptians. And in distancing himself from the model of the mass suicide at Masada, which followed the final defeat by the Romans of Jewish armed resistance, he concludes: 'This lesson is particularly acute at the present time when the Massada experience, with its all-or-nothing overtones, is held up in certain quarters as exemplifying the supreme ideal of Jewish heroism and defiance.' A month later, the Falklands War had ended and Israel's invasion of Lebanon, following the attempted assassination on 3 June of the Israeli ambassador in London, Shlomo Argov, was under way. Jakobovits said in another public lecture: 'Having experienced, as Britons, the national debate on the morality of the use of armed force in the South Atlantic, the British Jewish community is now facing similar questions in response to the fighting in the Middle East.'[4]

By the following autumn, a few days after the bloodshed at the refugee camps of Sabra and Shatila, he would write a circular letter to rabbis referring to 'the trauma of the Lebanese massacres and their catastrophic aftermath' and describing the approaching Yom Kippur sermons as representing 'a more awesome challenge . . . than ever before'. The last point made in that letter was this: 'If there is any long-term lesson to be learned from the events culminating in the Beirut tragedy, it is that "Not by might nor by power but by My spirit", teaching the futility of might alone, is a pragmatic truism for the Jewish people no less than a religious and moral imperative.'[5] Compared with the delicate balance of values in the lecture below, the emphasis at that agonizing period appears to have swung towards a deep suspicion of war, even when theoretically justifiable.

# SERMON

## [1]

IT IS only right that Rabbis should be expected as their primary function to promote the observance and understanding of Jewish law, for instance, the practice of the Sabbath and kashrut regulations, among members of their congregations. It is equally right that Rabbis should also be expected to relate the wider moral teachings of Judaism to the contemporary scene. If this occa-

[4] *The Times*, 28 June 1982, p. 12. His 'authorized biography' quotes him, without providing a source, as having said or written that he could see 'no greater moral objection to military action for "peace in the Galilee" to protect the lives of tens of thousands of citizens than to such action by Britain to secure the freedom of 1800 islanders 8000 miles away': Bermant, *Lord Jakobovits*, 153.
[5] *L'Eylah*, 2/5 (Spring 5743/1983), p. 3.

sionally means that they have to 'dabble' in politics, or make statements that
have political overtones, to the extent to which such statements are governed
by or impinge on moral considerations, then so be it.

After all, if we were to exclude the political dimension from our Hebrew
Prophets, we would have to expunge from the Books of the Prophets all references to international relations, to statecraft and to political leadership within
the Jewish people. Anyone familiar with our Scriptures will realise at once how
drastically such en exclusion would truncate the teachings and writings of our
Prophets. Judaism being a way of life, a philosophy of life, rather than a mere
cult or a religion that can be confined to the synagogue, the kitchen and the
cemetery, it is only natural that we should from time to time discuss the application of Jewish teachings to present-day concerns.

Alas, Jewish teachings on warfare are all too topical. When 'The Morality of
Warfare' was suggested to me as the theme for my lecture, the subject might
equally well have been 'The Immorality of Warfare'. One could give one talk
on the morality and another on the immorality of warfare. I will try and combine some thoughts on both aspects of Jewish teachings on war and warfare.

We Jews are certainly not pacifists. This statement can be made quite categ-
orically. You only have to have a cursory look at the Bible and biblical history to
be convinced that from time to time and only too frequently we had been
involved in warfare. The very entry of our people into the Promised Land under
Joshua challenged us with a [sic] major and continuous battles. Indeed, in the
biblical record of Jewish history, the periods of peace are relatively exceptional.
On several occasions the Bible goes out of its way to tell us, 'And the land was at
peace for forty years (Judg. 3: 11, 5: 31), or 'For eighty years' (Judg. 3: 30)—and
such interludes between wars were evidently worth recording.

We associate war with God Himself, speaking of Him as 'The Lord, a Man
of war' (Exod. 15: 3). We therefore do not intrinsically see anything incompatible between religion and the fighting of wars. 'The Lord will fight for you, and
you shall hold your peace' (Exod. 14: 14). Whenever the people of Israel were
sent to war, it was 'a priest anointed for war' who conscripted the soldiers for
army service, who encouraged the fighting units and blessed them with 'Shema
Yisrael' as they entered into battle (Deut. 20: 2).

We in the Diaspora should remember only too well the cry of Moses
addressed to the Tribes of Israel whose inheritance was to be on the other side of
the Jordan, and who might have refused to participate with the other Tribes in
the conquest of the Land on the western side of the Jordan: 'Shall your brothers

go to war, and you remain settled here?' (Num. 32: 6). So quite clearly war is affirmed by original, authentic biblical teaching. There can therefore be no truck with pacifism as a philosophy, as an inflexible moral concept in conformity with Judaism.

I may add in a passing reference to the deeply-anxious period through which we are currently passing, I believe there can be no doubt whatever of the morality of the Falklands action taken by Britain, even if some may question its wisdom.[6] What Judaism does not question is the right to defend a just cause even by recourse to war in principle.*

## [ 2 ]

However, as we will look in a moment at the detailed Jewish regulations on war incorporated in our legal code, we will find some major reservations and restrictions in the exercise of this right. Maimonides—the greatest of all the codifiers of Jewish law—covers in his monumental Code the totality of Jewish law, including regulations which lapsed with the Destruction of the Temple and the loss of Jewish national sovereignty, such as the laws on kingship, the priesthood, the sacrificial service, etc. He devotes several chapters of his 'Laws of Kings' dealing with constitutional matters to the regulations on warfare. In the few extracts I propose to give you, you will find three distinct aspects which are emphasised: the moral purpose war must serve to be justified, a judicial ruling required for the declaration of war to establish its justice by a decision of the Supreme Court, and the insistence on exceedingly stringent safeguards to ensure the humane treatment of the enemy—regulations designed to preserve our own humanity, even and especially in times of war.

Here, then, are a few simple regulations taken from the Code of Maimonides, each extract illustrating one of the three principles I have mentioned.

The king may not initiate any battle except 'obligatory war' (*Milchemet Mitzvah*); and which is an obligatory war? War against 'the seven nations' (occupying the Land at the time of Joshua), against Amalek, and to save Israel from the hands of an oppressor

---

* This was of course stated before the Israeli action in the Lebanon. [Author's or editor's comment; the text was published in autumn 1982, *after* the Israeli incursion into Lebanon.]

[6] With this strong support for the morality of the nation's war effort alongside a concession that questions about the practical political consequences of the decision are legitimate, compare Sermon 4 above by David Woolf Marks. Critical questions were raised about government policy on the Falklands crisis by the *Guardian*, the *Daily Mirror*, and the *Financial Times*, though most papers, including *The Times*, strongly supported the government's line, often making parallels with the decision to stand up to aggressive dictatorship in the Second World War: Noakes, *War and the British*, 109–10.

attacking them. After that he may fight an 'optional war', that is, a war fought against other peoples to enlarge Israel's borders or to increase his power and fame.

For an obligatory war, he does not require the sanction of the Beth Din (i.e. the Sanhedrin or Supreme Court), but he may go out on his own at any time and force the people to join him. But he may not take out the people for an optional war except by the verdict of the Court composed of 71 judges (*Hil. Melakhim* 5: 1–2).

In other words, the law distinguishes between two types of war.[7] Wars religiously commanded for the original conquest of the Land or defensive wars fought against an aggressor—these may be prosecuted by the king as the custodian of government and political leadership without further endorsement. But the king must not engage in any other war or conscript an army for it unless its justice is established by the verdict of the supreme custodians of justice, by a ruling of the Supreme Court. Such a decision to go to war must be judicial as well as political.

War must not be waged against anyone in the world until peace has first been offered. This applies both to optional and obligatory wars, as is stated, 'When you draw near to a city to fight against it, then you shall proclaim peace unto it' (Deut. 20: 10). If they make peace and accept the Seven Commandments commanded to the Sons of Noah, then one must not kill a single life, but only impose a tribute on them (*Hil. Melakhim* 6: 1).

   Any war, therefore, had to be preceded by a peace offer, and the peace terms had to include the submission to the basic moral order as defined in the Seven Noahite Laws (against idolatry, murder, adultery and incest, etc.).[8] There was thus a clearly moral objective in any recourse to war.

   And finally the safeguards:

When one lays siege to a city to capture it, one must not encircle it from all four sides but only from three directions, leaving room (for the besieged population) to escape and for anyone who so desires to save his life . . .

One must not cut down fruit trees outside the area nor withhold from the population streams of water so that they dry up, as it is stated, 'And you shall not destroy any trees' (Deut. 20: 19) . . . and this applies not only in a siege, but under any circumstances . . .

   The transgression includes not only trees, but any breakings of utensils, tearing of clothes, destruction of buildings, closing of waterwells, or the wastage of food by destruction (*Hil. Melakhim* 6: 7–10).

---

[7]   The distinction between the two categories of war in Jewish law had become a staple of the American Jewish discourse about the Vietnam War. See e.g. *Judaism and World Peace*; Gendler, 'War and the Jewish Tradition'.
[8]   On the Noahite or Noahide laws, see Novak, *The Image of the Non-Jew in Judaism*.

What is proscribed here is the starvation of a city by siege or a 'scorched earth' policy as a method of warfare. Under these rules, it is forbidden to resort to wanton destruction generally, including the demolition of buildings. I will not discuss here the possible relevance to what happened recently at Yamit.[9] This law of *Bal Tashchit*[10] is a unique Jewish concept: the religious objection to any wastage of resources, or their pollution—in modern parlance. This applies even in war, how much more so in times of peace.

I presented these examples to show the orientation of these laws, designed as they are to ensure that war will not debase us, that especially when we engage in violence we shall not lose our own humanity by inflicting on others forms of brutality and destruction which even war cannot justify.

Obviously, the sanction of war in extreme cases such as defined here is based on the even more fundamental right of self-defence. This right applies not only to a nation, but to individuals as well. The law of self-defence is highly exceptional. Normally one is never permitted to take the law into one's own hands. One cannot exact justice on someone who has done one an injustice. This can only be done by a court of justice, with witnesses and all the requirements of the legal process. The one exception to this rule is the law of self-defence. If you are threatened by a potential aggressor, you are entitled, indeed obliged, to strike him down before he has a chance to kill you. He is still innocent, he has not yet committed a crime, he has not been subjected to any judicial procedure. Nevertheless, in self-defence, you may protect your life at the cost of his. In the words of the Talmud, 'He who comes to kill, anticipate killing him first'.[11]

---

[9] The demolition of Yamit was completed on 23 Apr. 1982, about a month before the address was delivered. There was considerable controversy over whether the buildings of the settlement should be destroyed or turned over to the Egyptians. A front-page *Financial Times* article of 21 April written by a Tel Aviv correspondent reported that 'several former settlers [of Yamit] said they were shocked to learn that even the trees they had planted were being uprooted, but others said they were delighted that the Egyptians would get back nothing but sand'; a front-page *New York Times* article of 24 April stated that 'Many Israelis have expressed concern over the destruction of the town. They would have preferred it to remain intact, even if it were to be inhabited by Egyptians.' The *Financial Times* of the same day reported that 'Criticism of this act of destruction has begun to grow within the country', and cited Amos Elon in *Ha'aretz* of 23 April: 'You destroy a house or up-root a tree so that it will not fall into the hands of an enemy. But here we destroyed an oasis in the desert so that it won't fall into the hands of some one we want to be a friend. It is difficult to imagine such an awful, depressing and degrading end.' Jakobovits would appear to be implying that the Israeli government's decision to destroy the buildings and trees may have entailed a violation of the Torah principle of *bal tashḥit*, cited in the following sentence. Note the preacher's rhetorical technique of raising a question in the minds of the listeners by stating that one will not discuss a particular issue.

[10] 'You shall not destroy', based on the verse (Deut. 20: 19) cited from Maimonides' *Mishneh torah* above.    [11] BT *Ber.* 58a et seq.: *ba laharogkha hashkem lehorgo.*

If possible, disable him. If not, kill the pursuer. This law holds good not only for the victim of a potential aggressor, but for any third party as well. If A pursues B to kill him, then a third party C is entitled to strike down A before he has committed the act, or at least to disable him, if he can thereby save B.[12]

By extension of this law, a nation likewise can resort to self-defence, whether by pre-emptive strikes or by recourse to war in order to protect its national life.[13]

## [3]

Having said all this on the morality of warfare, let me now present the obverse side which is at least equally stressed in Jewish thought and law.

First—and this is certainly uniquely characteristic of Judaism—Jewish law insists that we should never gloat over the discomfiture or defeat of our enemies. The most classic example of this is the most classic war in Jewish history: the original struggle of our people to liberate itself from the bondage of Egypt—the very context in which we declare God to be 'A Man of war' (Exod. 15: 3). As you know, in our celebration of Passover, the original Independence Day which first established us as an independent nation, when we mark the victory not only over a cruel oppressor but over murderers who drowned newly-born Jewish babies in the river, there is in all our songs and victory festivities not a word of rejoicing over the destruction of the enemy. On the contrary, on the first two days of the Festival we recited the full *Hallel*[14] in thanksgiving for our salvation; for the remaining six days we, as it were, lower our flags to half-mast, saying only *Half Hallel* because (in the words of our Sages) God says, 'My creatures are drowning in the Red Sea, and you will sing songs of praise?'[15] The Egyptians were pursuing us, they were mortal enemies; nevertheless, their lives, too, were human and precious. Hence the command: 'You shall not abhor the Egyptian' (Deut. 23: 8). However bitter an enemy, you are never entitled to

[12] This is the law of the 'pursuer'; see Maimonides, *Mishneh torah*, 'Hilkhot rotse'aḥ', 1: 6–8.
[13] This formulation seems to apply more to the Israeli situation than to that of the Falkland Islands.
[14] A selection of psalms incorporated into the liturgy for holidays. 'Half Hallel' omits some of the psalms, and is generally used for the intermediate and final days of Passover and for the New Moon.
[15] BT *Meg.* 10*b*, *San.* 39*b*; see Introduction, above, pp. 3–4. The practice of not saying the complete Hallel on the intermediate days of Passover (while the full Hallel is said on the intermediate days of Sukkot) is explained in association with the death of the Egyptians on the seventh day of Passover and God's rebuke of the angels by former chief rabbi Joseph Hertz in id. (ed.), *The Authorised Daily Prayer Book*, 757.

joy or glee over his downfall. In the words of the Preacher, 'When your enemy falls, do not rejoice' (Prov. 24: 17). For the same reason, when we list the Ten Plagues inflicted on the Egyptians at our Seder tables on Passover, we flick a drop of wine from our cups as a symbol of our sympathy with the ordeal of our oppressor.[16]

Likewise, a medieval Jewish source movingly tells us that the one hundred Shofar sounds at our New Year services correspond to the one hundred groans by the mother of Sisera (cf. Judg. 5: 28) when she saw her son killed in his battle against the Israelites.[17] Sisera was a brutal tyrant, wreaking terror on our people. His death was our salvation. Yet he had a mother, and to this day we hear her cries and recall her grief over the death of her child. Even terrorists have mothers, and we must not be indifferent to their anguish. This is but one of the remarkable features of Judaism in an effort to ensure that even war does not harden us to the point of not caring for the loss and sufferings of our enemies.

## [4]

Moreover, war is never regarded as either a first recourse or a desirable solution to human conflict. It is not only that we must first call out for peace. Anything connected with the ultimate aspirations of our people, with the supreme sanctity of life in Judaism, is incompatible with war. David, King of Israel, first of the Davidic dynasty, conqueror of Jerusalem, yearning to consummate his establishment of Israel's capital and the unification of the Jewish people by building the First Temple there, was told, 'You shall not build a house for My name, for you are a man of war and have shed blood' (1 Chr. 22: 8, 28: 3). The wars he waged certainly belonged to the category of 'obligatory wars'. But however just a war, however worthy and even heroic a battle and its objectives, anyone engaged in it is not fit or qualified to build a Temple unto God. For the Temple is a symbol of peace.

For the same reason, it was forbidden to build the altar with 'hewn stones', that is, cut with metal implements. By objects from which swords are made being

---

[16] This explanation for the practice of flicking a drop of wine with the recitation of each of the ten plagues is also a modern homiletical and probably apologetical innovation. See Nahum Glatzer's note in *The Passover Haggadah*, 41, attributing the explanation to Samson Raphael Hirsch and Eduard Baneth.

[17] The association between Sisera's mother and the sounding of the shofar was made on technical linguistic grounds in BT *RH* 33b; a later tradition connected the one hundred sounds of the shofar with the one hundred groans of Sisera's mother not as she saw her son killed but as she waited in vain for him to return from battle (Tosafot BT *RH* 33b, beginning *shi'ur teru'ah*; cf. Ginzberg, *The Legends of the Jews*, vi. 199 n. 89.).

lifted upon it, it is profaned (Exod. 20: 22). As the Ibn Ezra remarks on this passage, the Hebrew language uses *Cherev* for 'sword' because it 'destroys' (*Charav*: hence *Churban*).[18] War can never be constructive; it is a synonym for destruction.

The Temple and particularly the altar are meant to promote peace, an ideal attainable only through some *sacrifice* and mutual concession. Therefore, any link between war and worship, however remote, disqualifies the Temple and the altar from serving their purpose.

Peace is the supreme Jewish ideal far transcending the horror of war and its destructiveness. In the vision of the Prophets, the central and ultimate focus of all our Messianic hopes lies in universal peace, when 'they shall beat their swords into ploughshares, and their spears into pruning-hooks; nation shall not lift up sword against nation, neither shall they learn war any more' (Isa. 2: 4). In the Jewish view, the whole vision of the eventual moral order presupposes as a prime-condition the elimination of war. There can be no perfect world, no redemption of man, without the destruction of war itself as the first and ultimate prerequisite.

When we speak of peace, *Shalom*, it is not just the absence of war. It is not just a purely negative virtue. The very word *Shalom* derives from *Shalem* which means 'perfection'. There is a positive ideal in peace. Every major prayer in our liturgy concludes with a plea for peace. With it we end the Grace-After-Meals, the *Amidah* and the *Kaddish*. Symbolically, when we recite this passage in public worship, we walk back three steps.[19] You cannot have peace without going back and surrendering something. There must be conciliation through some sacrifice, as already indicated by the association of the altar with peace. Pacification must require a readiness to give up some claim or even a right conflicting with someone else's.[20]

## [5]

Two historical references may be pertinent here. In Jewish history, there have been conflicting schools of thought on the circumstances under which wars

[18] Ibn Ezra on Exod. 20: 22.

[19] On the practice of taking three steps backwards at the end of the Amidah prayer, based on the statement in BT *Yoma* 53*b*, see M. Saperstein, *Decoding the Rabbis*, 141–2, with references at 257 n. 79. The homiletical interpretation of the reason given by the preacher may be his own; a more common explanation (of Sa'adiah Gaon) is that it is done 'just as slaves step backwards when they leave the royal chamber'.

[20] One wonders whether the resonance of this statement implied a willingness to compromise with Argentina over the status of the Falkland Islands, or an endorsement of territorial compromise in the Israeli political stance towards the Palestinians.

should be engaged in or continued to avert supreme national perils. The classic illustration is the argument between Rabbi Yochanan ben Zakkai and the contemporary Zealots on the battle against the Romans at the time of the Destruction of the Temple in 70 CE. Whilst the Zealots held that the war should be fought to the finish, however hopeless the prospects of throwing back the Roman legions to preserve Jewish national independence, the greatest Sage of the period secretly negotiated terms with the Romans, agreeing to a political and military surrender in exchange for permission to establish the Academy of Yavneh.[21] And by this fateful decision, for which there is probably no parallel in the whole of Jewish history, he assured the continuity of Jewish life. As a result of that decision, we are here to tell the story. But the conflict was there. Rabbi Yochanan held that war is to be prosecuted only so long as some realistic hopes of victory still exist. The opposition, on the other hand, embracing large numbers of Jews at the time, said no; we are not prepared to live under foreign domination and would rather fight to the bitter end.

This conflict eventually found the most dramatic expression at Massada. This is the only incidence [sic] in Jewish history when a Jewish religious sect decided by a pact among themselves that, rather than live under foreign subjection in humiliation, they would die with dignity by their own hands.[22] While some scholars have lately justified this action in the light of Jewish teachings,[23] I believe with many others that it was an entirely exceptional episode in complete conflict with the Jewish tradition. The absence of any reference in the Talmud to this epic itself indicates that the defenders of Massada, heroic as their stand may have been, were not regarded as having acted in conformity with Jewish teachings, and that their example was not held up as an ideal to be followed. After all, the authors of the Talmud witnessed the event, which must have made an enormously traumatic impact at the time; yet they suppressed any mention of it, no doubt because of their disinclination to give any sanction to this mass suicide in preference to coming to terms with Roman rule.

[21] See BT *Git.* 57*b*. Even according to the narrative, this was not exactly a case of 'negotiation' with the Roman commander.

[22] The claim about the uniqueness of the mass suicide at Masada overlooks the incidents of mass suicide during the Rhineland attacks by Crusaders in the spring of 1096, in which the alternative to be avoided was not 'foreign subjection' but forced conversion to Christianity. For later legal discussion about this and other medieval examples of 'active martyrdom', see Gross, *Struggling with Tradition.*

[23] The preacher may well be alluding here to Shlomo Goren, chief chaplain of the Israeli army during the Six Day War, who wrote two Hebrew articles in the 1960s maintaining that the mass suicide of Masada was legally justifiable; see the review of the debate by Zerubavel, *Recovered Roots*, 202–7.

Martyrdom was certainly affirmed when the alternative to death was apostasy, the conversion to another faith, but not as an alternative to national freedom and independence. In the authentic Jewish tradition, therefore, neither national death in war nor voluntary self-destruction was justified as an escape from life without freedom.

This lesson is particularly acute at the present time when the Massada experience, with its all-or-nothing overtones, is held up in certain quarters as exemplifying the supreme ideal of Jewish heroism and defiance.[24]

## [6]

Let me conclude with some wider reflections on the morality of warfare. I was always fond of telling young couples whose marriage I was due to solemnize of a regulation which sheds a particularly revealing light on the relations between morality and warfare in Jewish thought. Among the biblical rules of conscription, exemption from army service is granted to betrothed and newly-wed men (Deut. 20: 7, 24: 5). The express reason given for this exemption is that the newly-married man 'shall be free for his house one year, and he shall rejoice his wife whom he has taken' (Deut. 24: 5). To rejoice one's wife is regarded as a full-time occupation, especially during the first year of marriage which often either makes or breaks the marriage.

This duty is considered as a national and not just personal obligation. By consolidating your marriage, this law teaches, you perform a greater service to your nation, to the survival of your people, by having a stable home than by joining the army and defending the people in military battle. The ultimate security of our people lies in our homes. Had we relied merely on military strength and victories, we would have been extinct long ago. Hence, in the choice to be made here between home and army, priority was to be given to the home. By staying home for the first year 'to rejoice your wife' you render a more essential service to the nation than by joining its defenders in the trenches. In the moral scale of values, then, even in terms of Jewish security, happy homes come before powerful armies. Jewish homes are our principal fortifications, our first line of national defence.

Not unrelated to this is another moral dimension of warfare, as taught with remarkable insight by our Sages in a striking comment on the very

---

[24] The preacher's criticism appears to be levelled not just at extremist expressions of Jewish nationalism but at something more fundamental in Zionist ideology. On the role of Masada in the Israeli collective consciousness, see Zerubavel, *Recovered Roots*.

Portion-of-the-Law (*Ki Thetze*) which opens with the law on 'going out to war'. They stressed the teaching implied in the sequence of this and the following laws of the Torah.

The first of these laws deals with the treatment of a non-Jewish captive woman (Deut. 21: 10–14). War is liable to relax moral standards, to cheapen life and to arouse passions. In such times there is a special need to be on guard against taking moral liberties and the erosion of moral values.

Immediately following is the law on two wives, 'the one beloved and the other hated' (Deut. 21: 15–17). War leads first to the depreciation of the moral currency through sexual laxity, and then in turn to broken homes through hatred between husband and wife. Right next comes the law on 'the rebellious son, who does not listen to the voice of his father or the voice of his mother' (Deut. 21: 18–21). Broken or unhappy marriages lead to delinquency. And this is finally followed by the law on the capital criminal, and how after his execution even his body must be treated with dignity, since its disgrace would be an affront to man created in the Divine Image (Deut. 21: 22–3).[25]

Thus the cycle is complete: from the violence of war to immorality, to unhappy marriages, to juvenile delinquency, to the violence of capital crime—all to be redeemed by the reminder that all men are created in God's image and therefore infinitely precious. We are to recognise that if we find ourselves now afflicted with rising crime rates, this is not unconnected with the instability of international affairs, with wars past and present continuing to undermine the moral fabric of society. The price of war is not just human life laid down in the just defence of values in which we believe. It is also paid in the cheapening of moral values in which we believe. In the face of this danger, Jewish law sets out all the restrictions to be observed, with the prime objective of always reaching out for peace as the overriding ideal.

For ultimately we are to use our strength and power not to achieve victory in war, but to secure peace, as it is written, 'The Lord will give *strength* unto His people; the Lord will bless His people with *peace*' (Ps. 29: 11).

---

[25] This passage is based on connections made in such rabbinic texts as *Deuteronomy Rabbah* 6: 4, *Midrash tanḥuma*, 'Vayetse' 1, and Rashi on Deut. 21: 11.

# PART VII

## RESPONSES TO 9/11

# CHAPTER THIRTY-FOUR

# THREE SERMONS
# RESPONDING TO
# THE EVENTS OF
# 11 SEPTEMBER 2001

T HE FIRST regular preaching occasions after the terrorist attacks against
New York and Washington of Tuesday, 11 September 2001 came on the
following sabbath and then on Rosh Hashanah, which began the following
Monday night. This timing presented a classic challenge for the preacher. Most
rabbis already had Rosh Hashanah sermons prepared by 11 September: should
they change them in order to articulate their response to the events before a large
congregation? By the first time their congregations gathered after those events, a
great deal had already been written and said, and people were soaking up every
new piece of information and every new slant from the pundits and experts
interviewed on the non-stop news coverage. What new insight could a rabbi
add? What Jewish texts were relevant to the atrocity? Should the message
emphasize the need to recognize the power of evil and to mobilize our strength
to defeat it, or the need to re-examine how national policy and behaviour might
have motivated educated and sophisticated young men to become suicide
bombers,[1] or the need to restrain the natural impulse towards vengeance? No
matter how uncertain the rabbis may have felt, no matter how emotionally and
intellectually paralysed by shock and outrage, it was clear that they could not
avoid addressing the subject from the pulpit.

Fortunately, there is abundant material readily available to document the
response to 9/11 from the Jewish pulpit. In the United States a website was
established to solicit, preserve, and make accessible the texts of these sermons,

---

[1] Rabbis who chose to respond in this prophetic mode of self-criticism and rebuke, especially
if they lived in the New York or Washington areas, ran the risk of increasing the anguish of congregants who had lost members of their immediate families in the World Trade Center or the
Pentagon.

given the name 'Torah from Terror: The Rabbinic Response to 9/11'.[2] In Britain a fine review of sermons preached on the High Holy Days by Liberal, Reform, and Masorti UK rabbis, containing both full sermon texts and a thematic overview with short passages from other sermons, was published in the journal *European Judaism* the following spring.[3] In contrast to the paucity of records for the nineteenth-century wars, here we have an abundance of raw material for the historian or student of religion, waiting to be mined and processed.

Any selection from this wealth of textual data is bound to be subjective. The first sermon reproduced here, by Elias Lieberman of Cape Cod, came to my attention on Sunday morning, 16 September, when I heard a selection incorporated into a National Public Radio news programme. Although concentrating on something else at the time, I thought I heard a very striking statement of dissent from the response voiced by the President, and this was confirmed to me the following day in an e-mail from Rabbi Lieberman. It will be highlighted below. Lieberman, ordained in 1984 by the Hebrew Union College–Jewish Institute of Religion, adopts a conversational and personal style. Two Jewish sources are used. Job's silence when confronted with a display of the whirlwind's power appears in the introduction, which is based on a rhetorical topos of the reasons why the preacher wanted to remain silent, yet ultimately feels impelled to speak. And the injunction to 'choose life', from the Torah lesson of that sabbath, serves as the central theme in the body of the sermon, emphasizing the importance of choices to be made in response to evil. Though it is not the major thrust of the message, there is a strong element of criticism against those who would blame Israel and American support for Israel for arousing hatred, against those who would scapegoat Arab Americans, and against President Bush's setting the 'war against terrorism' as the highest American priority.

I came to the sermon by Alexandra Wright, a British Liberal rabbi ordained at the Leo Baeck College, from the material in *European Judaism*; her writing impressed me as reflecting an impressive homiletical gift. The sermon published below was her second Rosh Hashanah sermon to address the events of 9/11. The previous evening, she had poignantly articulated the difficulty of preparing something to say and, more important, of retaining a belief in the power of hope and faith in the face of the dramatic evidence of evil. Much of that sermon is a response to the Oxford professor and public intellectual Richard Dawkins, who had attacked religion as the source of unending danger, writing in the *Guardian*, 'To fill a world with religion, or religions of the

[2]  <www.torahfromterror.com>, accessed 27 Nov. 2006.
[3]  Magonet, 'A Survey of New Year Sermons', followed by the texts of sermons by eight rabbis.

Abrahamic kind, is like littering the streets with loaded guns. Do not be surprised if they are used.'[4] In the Rosh Hashanah morning sermon before us, which Rabbi Wright was kind enough to provide to me, the theme is no longer a defence of religion against an intellectual assault, but rather the challenge to replace the natural emotional response of fury seeking vengeance with a more tempered, constructive reassertion of justice. Jewish sources pointing in both directions are explored, but the heart of the sermon is a reading of the story of Hagar, the traditional lesson for the first morning of Rosh Hashanah, as a model for the capacity to endure life-threatening injustice and then, surviving, continue to build a new life.

As this book opens with sermons from the two leading Orthodox synagogues of London, it seemed fitting to me to conclude it with a sermon from the leading Orthodox synagogue of America's capital. My third subjective choice, then, is a sermon by Barry Freundel, who was ordained in 1976 at Yeshiva University and has served for some years as rabbi of the Orthodox Kesher Israel Congregation in Georgetown, where I have heard him preach many times. His sermon for the sabbath following 9/11, accessible on the synagogue website,[5] addresses directly one particular aspect of the events of that day—not the attack on the Pentagon or the attempted attacks on the Capitol or White House, both in the immediate vicinity of the synagogue, but rather the visual image of New York's twin towers disintegrating into towers of smoke. This phrase becomes a leitmotif of the sermon, which artistically weaves together various passages from the full range of classical Jewish sources to elucidate different aspects of the visual image that had become so intensely haunting to people throughout the world: towers of smoke representing destruction, and associated with different memories of destruction in the Jewish past, but also, in a different usage, representing the desire for justice and redemption. No policy is articulated here; the preacher mines the rich resources of Jewish literature to set forth stark alternatives, and a faith that destruction will not prevail.

Because the precipitating events are still so fresh in the mind, this material requires far less extensive annotation than the sermons responding to earlier wars.

---

[4] Quoted by Wright in 'After Judgement: Freedom', 65–6, from the *Guardian* of 15 Sept. 2001.
[5] <www.kesher.org/study/drashot/r_twin_smoke.html>, checked 11 June 2007.

3 4 A

## ELIAS LIEBERMAN
# A SERMON
### FRIDAY NIGHT
### 14 SEPTEMBER 2001
#### FALMOUTH JEWISH CONGREGATION,
#### CAPE COD, MASSACHUSETTS

———

A SK ME, on any given day, if I enjoy the work I do as a rabbi and my answer will be an emphatic 'yes'. I am blessed in a great many ways in the work I do. I am privileged to share moments of intense joy and profound sorrow with members of this community and the larger community as well; I am given opportunities to teach, and learn from, members of this community; I am afforded the privilege of putting forth for your consideration my views on a wide range of issues, not all of which are popular but all of which, I believe, touch our lives as Jews; I have what I deem a sacred responsibility to help the Jewish community of which I am a part see its world through Jewish eyes, informed by Jewish values which are filtered through our perspective as Reform Jews.

But there are also times, friends, when I think I'd rather be driving a truck, or selling guitars, or doing anything other than what I've been called upon to do this week. Thankfully, I have not been called upon to counsel anyone whose loved ones were claimed by this terror. I am only beginning to hear of tangential connections: in my own family, my niece's fiancé lost a brother-in-law in the World Trade Center collapse. I have been spared that firsthand encounter with the searing pain, the devastation, the anger, and confusion attendant upon this heretofore unbelievable experience.

So what am I complaining about? What makes my rabbinic duties feel burdensome this week? It is simply, friends, the responsibility of needing to stand here in front of you and speak words which make sense.[6] Friends, I read the same papers you do; I listen to National Public Radio just as religiously; I have

---

[6] A concise articulation of the preacher's burden when faced with the need to represent the wisdom of a tradition in the face of events that seem incomprehensible. Cf. the beginning of Sermon 23 above by Jacob Rudin.

gone glassy-eyed in front of the television screen this week; my computer has brought me countless e-mails . . . and yet I feel no closer to understanding than I did in those first horrible hours when the news reports sounded like a bad Hollywood script.

In the Book of Job, when that man whose life has been turned inside-out and utterly destroyed ultimately confronts God and questions God's justice, he hears not a defense of God's actions, not a logical explanation of why God put Job through such a horrifying test. Instead God rails at him saying, in essence, 'Just who do you think you are to question Me? Did you create this world? Are you the power behind its natural phenomena?'[7] Poor Job, in response, says: 'I clap my hand to my mouth' (Job 40: 4).

That is what I wanted to do this week. Sit with my hand clapped over my mouth in silence . . . just listening . . . not trying to offer words of meaning or explanations . . . just sitting in silence hoping, somehow, to hear the voice of God.[8]

But I could not remain in silence.[9] I have a wife to whom I needed to express my love; I have children who needed and deserved explanations appropriate to their respective abilities to comprehend this tragedy.

And I have a job, don't I? I needed to respond to, and represent our community. And so I took part in interfaith observances on Wednesday evening, at the John Wesley United Methodist Church and again, early this evening, at the Veterans Memorial in Falmouth. And I knew that I would need to share words with you this evening, as I will again on Erev Rosh Hashana, about what has happened to all of us. And this is when I felt the burden, and felt myself inadequate to the task of finding meaning that I might reflect back to you.

But, for better or for worse, I am rarely at a loss for words. So let me share with you some of the thoughts, feelings, and concerns I have been experiencing since Tuesday.

Everyone has used the word 'numb' to describe their emotional life this week. One congregant offered what struck me as a perfect metaphor: she said she felt as if she were walking under water.

[7] A summary of God's speech from the whirlwind, Job 38–9.
[8] The ellipses here and elsewhere in this sermon are in the preacher's original text and do not indicate omissions.
[9] Whether consciously or not, the preacher reflects here a convention of traditional Jewish preaching going back at least to the fifteenth century, in which the preacher presents reasons why he should remain silent, and then explains why he cannot do so. See M. Saperstein, *Jewish Preaching*, index, s.v. ' "reasons" for silence and preaching'.

The full impact of this disaster hit me yesterday morning. I was sitting at my breakfast table, reading the paper. I began to read an account of some of the last-minute phone calls to loved ones which were made by doomed passengers on the hijacked jets. A wave of grief washed over me and I found myself sobbing uncontrollably. The pain of families ripped apart, the awareness of imminent death, the courage manifest in the most horrifying of situations, brought it all painfully home to me.

Let me share with you some of my reactions, in no particular order:

With this act of carnage, many of us have a deeper appreciation of the suffering our Israeli sisters and brothers have been enduring for decades at the hands of terrorists, many of whom have been motivated by the same blind fury directed at us on Tuesday. We are beginning to hear, and will hear more of, blame leveled at Israel or at the United States' policy of standing behind Israel. Let us hope it becomes increasingly and abundantly clear that those who would deny Israel its right to exist would also deny our right to exist safely and securely in the freedom with which we are blessed.

The ever-widening ripples of pain are unimaginable. We can barely bring ourselves to look at the photos of the victims, to read of their lives which, of course, were exactly like ours in so many ways. Most of the time we shield ourselves with the belief that we lead charmed lives; that we wouldn't board a doomed airliner; that somehow our business appointment in New York wouldn't be at the World Trade Center. But Tuesday's events ripped mercilessly through our ability to defend ourselves from the reality that the coin of life always has two sides; that a chance decision can mean the difference between life and death, whether that death comes at the hands of someone intent on unspeakable evil or it comes in the form of a shark attack during a summer vacation.

Friends, we cannot defend ourselves against life itself nor, in our calmer and more reflective moments, would we wish to do so. Life always brings us a mixture of good and evil, rapture and terror, uplift to exalted heights and plunges into the abyss. Above all else, we need to maintain the perspective which Judaism affords us: we recognize that God is the source of life and death, joy and sorrow, the source of the valor and self-sacrifice which led firefighters, police and emergency workers into the heart of the maelstrom.

And what of evil? Does God stand behind twisted minds and bitter hearts who scheme the destruction of thousands of innocent lives? This is not a time for a theology lesson. Each of us carries within us some understanding of God that may, or may not, withstand the crucible of doubt, pain, and anger into which we have been plunged. My own understanding of God is rooted in that which is, ultimately, unknowable: God as the source of all. And evil? What do I do with the question of the motivation behind this terror?

Ironically, this week's Torah portion provides me an answer. In 'Nitzavim' Moses speaks to the Israelites who, like us, are poised on the threshold of a new world, totally different from what they have known before. With words we will hear again at Yom Kippur,[10] God says: 'See, I set before you this day life and death, the blessing and the curse. Therefore, choose life—that you and your children may live—by loving Adonai your God, heeding God's commands, and holding fast to God' (Deut. 30: 19–20).

It is always about choice. Those who planned the hijackings, those who opted for suicide and mass murder to make a point, chose evil. And we, friends, are confronted with choices every moment of our lives in which we have the opportunity to choose goodness. By speaking out forcefully against the scapegoating and violence being directed at Arab-Americans and at others whom angry and ignorant Americans assume to be of Arab descent because they look different. We Jews have far-too-often borne the brunt of mob violence and ill-conceived calls for vengeance to sit idly while our neighbors bleed.[11]

We can choose life by examining closely the nature of the juggernaut which is propelling our nation toward a 'war' against an unnamed enemy. That President Bush has expressed a determination to make the 'war against terrorism' the central focus of his presidency says more to me about his inadequacies as a leader than it does about any real potential to end a scourge which is incredibly complex in nature.[12] I am a proud American but I do not feel pride when flags are flown as symbols of vengeance rather than as cherished symbols of the very freedoms our rush to 'war' may curtail.

---

[10] Reflecting the Reform movement's liturgical choice to substitute verses from the weekly lesson 'Nitsavim' (Deut. 29: 9–30: 20) for the traditional Yom Kippur Torah reading (Lev. 16).

[11] Echoing Lev. 19: 16.

[12] This is the original text of the sentence as delivered on Friday night, and as played the following Sunday morning on National Public Radio. When the text of the sermon was placed on the synagogue website, the sentence was modified to read, 'That our country's leaders have expressed a determination to make the "war against terrorism" their central focus for the foreseeable future says more to me about our sense of helplessness than it does about any real potential to end a scourge which is incredibly complex in nature' (<www.falmouthjewish.org/archive.asp?AID=88>, checked 11 June 2007). The original text was confirmed to me in an e-mail from Rabbi Lieberman sent on 17 Sept. 2001. President Bush used the phrase 'war against terrorism' in his speech to the nation on 11 Sept. 2001: 'America and our friends and allies join with all those who want peace and security in the world. And we stand together to win the war against terrorism.'

We can choose life when we contribute to relief funds such as the one the Union of American Hebrew Congregations has established to provide some measure of support to the families of victims; when we donate blood; when we extend to one another the fundamental decency and compassion each of us deserves every day; when we take the time to analyze carefully the proposed solutions to the threat of terror which we are already hearing and which we will continue to hear for months and years to come.

We can choose life when we strengthen the bonds which form our community. Is anyone surprised at the numbers of people here tonight? We instinctively seek each other out for comfort, solace, a friendly face, a hug ... all of which are life-affirming choices, all of which are important reasons why we choose to support a congregation. We need each other, never more than at the present moment, if not to make sense of what has happened, then to find a way to move forward despite what has happened to us and to our world.

And isn't that the final and ultimate truth to emerge from the ashes? That to live our lives otherwise is to grant a victory to evil and to render meaningless the lives cut short. We have a duty to the dead and we have a duty to the living ... to live our lives fully, even in the shadow of loss. As Jews we know no other way.

## 34B

## ALEXANDRA WRIGHT

# NEW YORK: 11 SEPTEMBER, 2001

### 18 SEPTEMBER 2001
#### (ROSH HASHANAH)

#### RADLETT AND BUSHEY REFORM SYNAGOGUE, ENGLAND

━━

DEAR FRIENDS: as always I want to begin by welcoming each one of you to this service to celebrate Rosh Hashanah. I don't want to hear the apologies at the end of the service, I am sorry I don't come more often, it is just very good to see all of you here and to know that a week after the horrendous atrocities in New York, in Washington and in Pennsylvania, we can come together to mark the beginning of a new spiritual year, we can support each other and extend companionship and sympathy to our American friends in the community, and to those of us with family and friends in the United States, and particularly to those who have heard no news about friends and family since last Tuesday.

I had intended to speak about the concept of change this morning. Hebrew, as always neat, clever and economical, has one root—which means both 'year' (*shanah*) and 'change' (*shinuy*). I wanted to say quite simply how the New Year is an opportunity for change, and how our community at thirty years old has in some instances, become a little set in its ways, often resistant to change and innovation. But last week, as the events of Tuesday unfolded—first the snippet of news I heard on the radio at two o'clock that a plane had crashed into the World Trade Centre, and then at 2.15 that a second plane had with a technical preciseness that defies imagination, been steered into the second tower—it became clear that the interests of our own community, however important, were not going to be able to address the questions and reactions that have arisen over the past week.[13]

Perhaps it is enough to say, that we are all, to some extent, changed at this Rosh Hashanah. That this tragically unexpected and shattering event has altered us for ever. That we have been slowed down in our daily routines, that as we have watched images replaying on the television, read articles and testimonies from bewildered and distraught survivors, we have looked at our own lives in a different light and thought to ourselves, if this can happen just a little way across the water, then it could happen to us. Nothing sharpens the human focus more clearly, than the contemplation of our own vulnerability and the transient fragility of our own lives.

The sickening fear that refused to dissipate, the disbelief and unutterable shock of seeing those elegantly poised silver towers, knifed by the steel of two airliners, buckle slowly, almost gracefully, crumbling, shattering into a million pieces amidst a plume of lethal dust and smoke, held back for a little while any contemplation of the global implications of this attack.

But by the following morning, a voice of anger, outrage and retribution had been discovered. America would avenge the deaths of its thousands. Retaliation would be its bitter-sweet comfort and solace in its hour of loss. It

[13] Wright uses here a rhetorical topos—I had intended to speak about *x*, but the events compel me to speak about *y*—though leaving just a hint of the original, more intra-mural, message for the congregations to ponder.

was an understandable response. An eye for an eye, a tooth for a tooth, a life
for a life (cf. Exod. 21: 23–4). We wanted to scourge the guilty, to feel no mercy
for those at the heart of such an operation. It was an instinctive attempt at
self-preservation at a time of intense vulnerability and profound fear.

But, as Coleridge has written—and this could quite easily refer to the murderers motivated by religious fanaticism and passion as to those thrashing
about for a retaliatory response—the greater the passion, the more diminished
one's insight; and the more insecure one's belief in human safety or happiness,
the more one is induced into an 'uneasy state of feeling, an involuntary sense
of fear from which nature has no means of rescuing herself but by anger.
Experience informs us that the first defence of weak minds is to recriminate.'[14]

One might argue—mistakenly—that vindication is a noble and even God-
given response to enmity and violence. Did we not read just last Shabbat in
our Haftarah the words of the sixth century prophet of consolation, Deutero-
Isaiah: *Ani medaber biTsedakah, rav lehoshi'ah*, 'I [God] am the One proclaiming vindication, mighty to save' (Isa. 63: 1)? And does not the Psalmist in his
desire to punish the murderers of innocent women and fatherless children,
invoke, not once, but twice, *El nekamot Adonai, el nekamot hofi'a*—'The God
of vengeance, the Eternal One, the God of vengeance, appear! to shine forth
and judge the earth, giving to the proud what they deserve, repaying evil-doers
for their iniquity' (Ps. 94: 1–2). Even Jeremiah, in the aftermath of the destruction of the Temple and Jerusalem, stands back to await God's retribution on
his own people, who through their vile deeds have brought such shame and
tragedy upon Israel.[15] And in Moses' final Song to the Israelites before his
death, the lawgiver ascribes to God the exclusive prerogative of vengeance: *Li
nakam veshilem*—a phrase which has been translated as 'vengeance is Mine,
and recompense' (Deut. 32: 35) and which gave rise to a perception about
Judaism as a religion of vengeance, in the Greek Bible based on Paul's quotation of that verse, 'Vengeance is mine, I will repay, says the Lord' (Rom. 12: 19).

Put together with the *lex talionis*, the law of retaliation—'an eye for an eye'—
that is found not only once but three times in the Hebrew Bible,[16] one could be
forgiven for concluding that Judaism exacts physical retribution for acts of terror or violence perpetrated against human beings. But the fact is, that this law

---

[14] Coleridge, *Biographia Literaria*, beginning of ch. 2.
[15] The preacher has informed me in a personal communication that she was thinking of ch. 44,
in which the prophet justifies the destruction that God has brought upon Jerusalem and warns
those who have fled to Egypt that dire punishment awaits them.
[16] Exod. 21: 24; Lev. 24: 20; Deut. 19: 21.

was never interpreted literally, but was always understood to mean that a perpetrator had to pay financial compensation to the person who was harmed. The precise point about this law was that it restricted the penalty exacted in proportion to the wrong that was done, so that individuals could not be overcompensated or take vengeance out of proportion to the wrong done to them. The death penalty was viewed with such anathema by the rabbis that when the Sanhedrin, the highest court in the land, pronounced a death sentence, it was enough to make people call 'You murderers' after the judges.[17]

Nor was it simply that more sophisticated interpreters of the law had taken the *lex talionis* to mean pecuniary compensation. The Holiness Code enshrined a prohibition against vengeance in the Book of Leviticus in the words: *Lo tikom velo titor et benei amekha*, 'You shall not take vengeance, nor shall you bear a grudge against the children of your people.' And in this very same verse, we read *Ve'ahavta leRe'akha kamokha*, 'You shall love your neighbour as yourself, I am the Eternal' (Lev. 19: 18). And the Book of Proverbs counselled the aggrieved: *Al tomar ka'asher asah li, ken e'eseh lo*, 'Do not say, As he has done to me, so will I do to him' (Prov. 24: 29). The author must have recognised that vengeance is an emotional, unguided and inappropriate response to suffering:

> Wise warriors are mightier than strong ones,
> and those who have knowledge than those who have strength
> for by wise guidance you can wage your war,
> and in abundance of counsellors there is victory. (Prov. 24: 5–6)

If vengeance is the outcome of anger and outrage, of impassioned, unvented despair; if it is not the appropriate response to the events of last week, how can one move beyond this inevitable and instinctive reaction to find a measured and morally defensible and just response [to] the atrocities in the United States? How do you acquire the vision to move from a sense of wanting to kick out in blind anger and grief, to a position of foresight and justice?

The answer lies partly, I think, in the Torah reading we heard this morning. Hagar, the Egyptian maidservant of Sarah, bears Abraham a son. When Sarah perceives that a close affinity exists between Ishmael and the younger Isaac, she instructs Abraham to send away Hagar with Ishmael. 'No son of that slave shall share the inheritance with my son, not with Isaac' (Gen. 21: 10), she announces to her husband. Hagar and Ishmael are accompanied by Abraham into the wilderness of Beersheva. When the skin of water is finished,

---

[17] Apparently referring to *Mak.* 1: 10.

she leaves the child under one of the bushes, moving herself away so that she need not watch the boy die. In fact the Hebrew in this poignant narrative tells us that Hagar did not simply sit the child down under his bush, but that she 'threw' him down on to the ground: *Vatashlekh et haYeled tachat achad ha-sichim* (Gen. 21: 15). It is an act of neglect and abandonment, a gesture of utter despair and perhaps even of anger. She takes out her anger against Sarah, against Abraham, against life, on her own son, for she lacks the foresight to see what effect her actions will have on him. It is only after her weeping and the contemplation of her own and her child's inevitable death without food and water, that she hears the voice of the angel calling to her and sees what she could not see before, the well of water that assuages her thirst and allows her to continue her journey (Gen. 21: 17–19).

'We need', said one newspaper commentator last week, 'to do the right things, the intelligent things, the things that we are not bitterly regretting in ten years' time.'* And in a letter to the *Independent*, Dr Philip Schofield of University College, London wrote: 'This of all times is a time to be humble, not militant; to try to end the cycle of violence, not escalate it still further; and to hold out the hand of reconciliation . . .'.†

The model of Hagar may not sound a particularly powerful one, but it is, I think, a helpful one. For to begin with, Hagar cannot move back into the rigid, illiberal and intolerant environment of her mistress. She must continue her journey in a different direction, holding on to the voice of God speaking to her in the wilderness, and the vision of an oasis that will continually nourish her. And so it must be for us. We must recognise the enormity of the danger that fanatical religionists present to our world, with their psychotic and perverted view of the value of human life and death. But we cannot abandon our vision of religion as an irreplaceable redemptive force in human history. A liberal and tolerant expression of religion should allow us to move beyond vengeance, beyond the raw anger and desire for retribution. It should offer us vision and foresight, the desire, at least, to understand, both the moral imperative to bring to justice those who have perpetrated this evil and the determination to extend hands of friendship and possibilities of dialogue . . . particularly with British Muslims in this country.

There is part of me that knows with regret that even a tragedy of this magnitude will not change our lives utterly, completely. For a few days we have slowed ourselves down, we have reflected, we have been truly shocked and

---

* David Aaronovitch, *The Independent*, 14 Sept. 2001.      † 14 Sept. 2001.

shaken to our very core, sickened by the knowledge that so many lie incarcerated in that twisted mass of steel and stone. This year as we usher in the New Year, sombrely and with a huge sense of sadness and grief which we share with bereaved families in America, and indeed all over the world, we pray that a tiny part of us will hold on to our altered consciousness, not for one week, nor for ten days, but for all time. The vision that emerged from Hagar's distress and despair about her own personal world, allowed her to conceive of a future and a hope for herself and her son.

Let us not forget the responsibility we have for future generations who will inherit the world after we have gone. And let us pray, as we cast the burden of our prayers upon God: may the enmity and hatred that exists in our world be lessened, may we preserve our moral courage by pursuing a pathway of justice and truth. And may we preserve our faith and hope that the world can still be redeemed and find peace. Amen.

## 34C

### BARRY FREUNDEL

# TWIN TOWERS OF SMOKE

## 15 SEPTEMBER 2001
### (SHABBAT PARSHAT NITZAVIM 5761)

#### KESHER ISRAEL CONGREGATION, WASHINGTON, DC

——

TUESDAY NIGHT after *Ma'ariv*, many of us gathered to recite *Tehillim* and other appropriate prayers. I said that evening that we were in a time of *Aninut*. That is the period defined in halachah as the time between the death of a close relative and burial. During that period, the shock is so new and so great that the focus is only on getting through the next minute, the next hour, the next day, trying to make the arrangements necessary to get to the burial. The consolations, and the questions of moving forward, are simply irrelevant. It is what is described in halachah as מתו מוטל לפניו, 'his dead lies before him',[18] and there is nothing else except that reality. For many people—for example, those we see on our television screens carrying pictures of loved ones, searching desperately to find them—that period continues and may continue

---

[18] BT *Ber.* 17*b*; Maimonides, *Mishneh torah*, 'Hilkhot avel', 4: 6.

for many months. For others of us, we have begun to move past the period of *Aninut* ever so slowly, and I would like, today, to help in that process in some small measure.

One of the ways that I deal with difficult times, times that are so overwhelming that I cannot grasp their magnitude, is to latch on to a symbol [visual image] of the events and to search out that symbol [image] in our sources and in our tradition. That is what I propose to do this morning. As I was watching the scene in New York, from approximately half an hour after the second plane crashed into the World Trade Center, an image was seared into my mind. It became even stronger after the two buildings collapsed. Interestingly, the image finds echo in our tradition, not from this time of year. It is not from Rosh Hashana or Yom Kippur or Succot, it is rather from halfway around the year, from Pesach. Somehow, that seemed appropriate. The world turned upside-down this week and grasping for an image from half a year away just seems like the right thing to do given the circumstances in which we are living.

The image appears in a verse from [the prophet] Yoel that we recite in the Haggadah.[19] The verse reads: ונתתי מופתים בשמים ובארץ, 'I, G-d, will place unbelievable signs in the sky and on earth, דם, blood, ואש, and fire, ותימרות עשן, and towers of smoke' (Joel 3: 3). Of these three symbols, the one that stood out most for me was the last—the *tower of smoke*. That is the symbol which I have been dealing with in trying to get a hold of the enormity of what has occurred. In fact, if you go back and look at the original text in Yoel, the prophet also continues with the tower of smoke image. השמש יהפך לחשך, 'The sun will be turned to darkness' (and you will remember that Tuesday was a very sunny day, suddenly overshadowed by the tower of smoke), והירח לדם, 'and the moon will turn blood red' (Joel 3: 4). Surprisingly, I saw some pictures on network television that showed what one could see of the moon through the smoke, and there clearly was a reddish tinge to it.

As I thought about the image of the tower of smoke, I came to realize how often in our history a tower of smoke has marked life-changing tragedies. On investigating those moments in history, I discovered that there is at least some consolation in how often Rabbinic discussions surrounding those events parallel the emotions we all felt this week.

The first event that I thought of turns out, actually, not to be the earliest. We will get back to the earliest event a little later. Nonetheless, the first event

[19] See Glatzer (ed.), *The Passover Haggadah*, 39.

that I thought of was the destruction of the first Temple. It, too, went up in fire and in a tower of smoke. There is a remarkable Midrash in *Pesikta Rabbati* that I want to share with you.[20] It sounds remarkably like something I heard on television over and over again this past week.

Reads the Midrash: ירמיהו הנביא יצא מענתות לבוא לירושלים, 'Jeremiah the prophet', who lived in a suburb of Jerusalem called Anatot, was making his morning commute. He was out on I-95 in Virginia or the West Side Highway in New York riding on his donkey, and he 'was traveling from Anatot to Jerusalem' to go about his day's prophecy, or perhaps, since he was a *kohen*, his day's work at the Temple. נטל עיניו וראה עשן בית המקדש עולה, 'He raised his eyes, and he saw the tower of smoke rising from the just destroyed Temple.' אמר בלבו, 'He said in his heart', שמא חזרה ישראל בתשובה להקריב קרבנות, 'Perhaps the smoke reflects the fact that the Jews have repented and therefore, that they have offered many sacrifices.' Like so many people, seeing the smoke for the first time, there was *denial*. It cannot be what it appears to be. It cannot be that what I am hearing on the radio or seeing on television and being told by the commentators has occurred. It cannot be. It must be something else.

And the Midrash continues, עמד בחומה, 'He stood up on the walls,' and he saw that the Temple had collapsed, and that there were rows upon rows of fallen stones; then he turned to G-d and he cried out, פתיתני ה' ואיפת (Jer. 20:7). In this context, I understand that verse to mean, 'G-d, You seduced me, and I allowed myself to be seduced.'[21] I understand that cry today to mean that even though he was the prophet of doom and the prophet of destruction, even though he kept telling the Jews that the Temple would be destroyed, he always believed that they would listen to him, that they would repent and that somehow, it would never happen. It could never happen. He was like so many people this week, who turned wherever they turned, and said, 'We were seduced. We were fooled. Yes, there were warnings. Yes, there were articles that said this kind of thing could happen, but we never believed, we couldn't believe, that it would happen here, and yet, it did.'

A second tower of smoke in our history is the destruction of the second Temple. Rabban Yochanan ben Zakkai is famous for having escaped from Jerusalem during the final siege and making his way to Vespasian, the Roman

[20] Ch. 26, 6; see *Pesikta rabati*, 536.
[21] In the new translation by the Jewish Publication Society, 'You enticed me, O Lord, and I was enticed'; the preacher's version emphasizes the weakness in the prophet (and, by implication, in the preacher and his listeners) in the initial denial of the inconceivably harsh reality represented by the 'tower of smoke'.

general. There he ingratiated himself to Vespasian who would soon become emperor, and who asked Rabban Yochanan ben Zakkai what boon he would want. Rabban Yochanan ben Zakkai at that moment made the fateful decision to give up on Jerusalem, to decide that it was lost, and, in his famous request, chose 'Yavneh and her sages.'[22] The Midrash in *Avot D'Rabbi Natan* tells us some more detail. Having given up on Jerusalem, knowing it would be destroyed, here is what happened.

Says the Midrash, באותה שעה נלכדה ירושלים, 'At that moment, Jerusalem was captured,' ורבן יוחנן בן זכאי היה יושב, 'and Rabban Yochanan ben Zakkai was sitting', presumably in Yavneh, ומצפה וחרד, 'he was hoping and he was trembling.'[23] That was the mood and the sense that so many of us had this past week. Once we assimilated exactly what had occurred, once we knew that the World Trade Center and part of the Pentagon were lost, we sat and hoped against hope that the immensity of the tragedy would not be what everything told us it was going to be. We hoped and we also trembled in fear. Eventually, says the Midrash, the news of the fire and the smoke that had destroyed the Temple came to Rabban Yochanan ben Zakkai, קרע בגדיו וקרעו תלמידיו בגדיהם—'he tore his clothes, and along with him, his students tore their clothes'.[24] The moment had come to mourn, as the moment is coming for us to mourn.

That brings me to a third tower of smoke. It is the one that either we or our parents or our grandparents lived through. It is the tower of smoke that rose over the crematoria that gave the name 'Holocaust' to the events of the middle of the past century. Despite the terrible images and memories evoked by that era, there is some consolation in that tower of smoke because we know that we or people close to us have shown the ability to live through a catastrophe marked by such a tower, and to go on to rebuild.

But I am not yet up to talking about consolation. There is another point to be made here. The perpetrators of the events this past week are ideological brothers to the Nazis. Both groups believe that their system, that who they are, is so far superior to others that in pursuit of their goals, they can turn human beings into fodder, into victims, to accomplish their dreams of global superiority. We thought that we had ended such fantasies of superiority after the Second World War, or perhaps after the fall of Communism in Eastern Europe. The

---

[22] BT *Git.* 56b.  [23] *Avot derabi natan* 4: 5.

[24] Mourning (*avelut*) is a stage following the initial stage of *aninut* mentioned at the beginning of the sermon.

columns of smoke rising in New York and at the Pentagon tell us that we were kidding ourselves. The fight against that unspeakable evil continues.

That brings me to the earliest tower, the true first tower of smoke—the one that I had forgotten initially, but that needs to be mentioned here. It is the tower of smoke that once rose from a place known as *Gei Ben Hinnom*. *Gei Ben Hinnom* is a valley. If you stand on the southern wall of the city of Jerusalem (not of the Temple Mount) and look down, you are looking into *Gei Ben Hinnom*. I assume we all will recognize that the name of this valley is related to the name *Gei Hinnom*, which is the Jewish term for 'Hell': 'Gehenna'. How did *Gei Hinnom*, this pleasant valley, become the place that gave its name to 'Hell'? It originates from a tower of smoke that came from people offering what the Bible calls the ultimate abomination: human sacrifice (Jer. 7: 30–4; 32: 35; 2 Chr. 26: 3). Now that raises a question for me that I share with you. If we have named 'Hell' after a place where people sacrificed their children in the name of their deity, what is the place worse than 'Hell' that we will name after people who sacrifice their children to their deity and in doing so, take thousands of innocents along with them? I would truly like to know, what is the place worse than 'Hell' that will carry that name for all eternity?

One last point about the tower of smoke from Yoel. During the medieval period, Jewish thinkers, like many people in the world, were trying to make sense of the universe as they knew it, in light of Greek thought and Greek science. The understanding of physics in those days was that the world was composed of four elements: earth, air, water and fire. There is a discussion in that literature about how to fit smoke into this schematic of the four elements. There are a number of sources that speak of smoke as *Hafradat ha-yesodot*, as a sign that the elements are separating and breaking apart.[25] But one can legitimately translate that phrase as *separation of the foundations*. Just as the foundations on which the twin towers and the Pentagon stood, separated and collapsed in whole or in part, the foundations on which our world has been built, have separated and come apart. There really will be a new world order for us to live in. The paradigms by which people lived, the understandings that people have had, the policies on what to do with hijackers aboard a flight, all of those things have been radically changed, because there has been *hafradat*

[25] This Hebrew phrase often refers to the differentiation of the four fundamental elements from the primal matter (*hule*) or of the elements of the human body at death. It is associated with the phrase 'towers of smoke' in Joel 3: 3 and applied to the first plague in Egypt by a mystical commentary on the Haggadah, *Yad mitsrayim*. I am grateful to Rabbi Freundel for this reference.

*ha-yesodot*, a falling apart of the foundations. And all of those things are represented historically in Jewish literature by the tower of smoke that we saw this week and that stands before my eyes, whether they are open or closed, whether I am watching television or not.

But I do not stop here. The phrase, תימרות עשן, towers of smoke, that appears in Yoel appears but one other time in TaNaCH [the Bible]. [In other words,] there are twin towers of smoke in the Bible. The second one appears in *Shir Ha-Shirim*, and there it is a very different image. מי זאת עולה מן המדבר —King Solomon asks the question, 'Who is this that rises up out of the desolation of the desert', כתימרות עשן, 'like a tower of smoke', מקוטרת מור ולבונה מכל אבקת רוכל, 'spreading its aroma of myrrh and frankincense, with all of the fine spices of the apothecary' (S. of S. 3: 6). As opposed to Yoel, where the tower of smoke was associated with blood and fire, obviously, this is meant to be some type of positive image associated with the tower of smoke.

Here I want to explain a bit about the history of a Midrash. I will start by quoting that Midrash in the way one can find it in Rabbenu Bachaya.[26] For Rabbenu Bachaya, it evokes images best known to us from *Raiders of the Lost Ark*. Says Rabbenu Bachaya, כל הנסים שנעשו לישראל, 'All of the miracles that were done for Israel', היו נעשים בארון, 'they were all done through the Ark'—the Ark of the Torah—'where the Divine Presence resides.' Bachaya then continues (and here I present only the translation),

as it says, 'the Ark of the Covenant of the Lord was traveling before them' (Num. 10: 33), and it was killing the snakes and the scorpions, and it was killing all of the enemies of Israel. Said Rabbi Elazar ben Pedat in the name of Rabbi Yose ben Zimra, two sparks emerged from between the two staves of the Ark. Those sparks killed the snakes and the scorpions and they burned the thorns. *The smoke rose* and spread all over the world, and the world was sweetened by the smell of this smoke. The nations of the world responded and said, 'Who is this rising up out of the desert? It is a tower of smoke spreading its sweet scent of myrrh and frankincense, and all of the spices of the apothecary' (S. of S. 3: 6).

Obviously, this is a source that speaks to our desire for justice, to the removal of evil from this world and to the glorious consequences that will come on that day. That would seem to be something about which all decent people could agree. However, in *Shir HaShirim Rabbah* (3: 8), this Midrash is carried a step further and is said to represent a clash of values. Some of the nations of the world, says the Midrash, understood this manifestation coming

[26] Bachaya or Bahya ben Asher, an early fourteenth-century biblical commentator and author of ethical literature. The quotation is from his commentary on Exod. 25: 10.

from the desert to mean that G-d was the fire and G-d was the smoke. The truth, of course, is that the power of justice came from the Ark, from the Torah in the Ark and from the presence of G-d in the Ark.[27] The Midrash is a reminder that for many in the world, including those who perpetrated this act and even for some who oppose them, physical power is the be-all and end-all. For Jews, it is the power of G-d, the power of the ideas and values of Torah that are the controlling principles in all areas of life. Those were the true sources of power that created the sweet aroma according to the Midrash, not the raw power of fire and destruction.

In the months ahead, we are going to be sorely tested in terms of those values, and we must remember that at the base of this tower of smoke from Shir Ha-Shirim (S. of S. 3: 6) it is those values which created the tower and which need to lead us.

So here you have it. Within TaNaCH, we are presented with twin towers as we had twin towers before Tuesday, and as we have them no longer. These are twin towers of smoke. There is the tower of Yoel with its fire, its blood, its destruction and its symbolic representation of many of the tragedies of Jewish history. On the other hand, there is the tower of smoke mentioned in Shir Ha-Shirim. That is a very different tower. It is a tower of justice, a tower of Jewish values, a tower of Torah. It is that second tower that will eventually dissipate the first and bring us what we seek so desperately this week.

I am going to end with one last remarkable source that with a few small word changes, really expresses all of our hopes and all of our emotions this day. A little bit of background to the source needs to come first. I am sure you all know that in the early years of the last century, America was considered the great *midbar*—the great spiritual desert—and that there was real concern on the part of the Rabbinic authorities in Europe when anyone contemplated going to America, because they were afraid that the immigrant would be lost to Judaism.[28] Rabbi Meir Simcha HaCohen of Dvinsk, the *Meshekh ḥokhmah*,[29] writes the following words in that regard:

---

[27] As stated in the text of the *midrash* cited by Bahya. The text of the *midrash* in Song of Songs Rabbah does not mention the divine presence (Shekhinah) in the ark. The conflict, then, is between the nations that view the ark as a source of magical destructive power, and the ark as representing the presence of God and Torah in the world.

[28] For a review of negative attitudes towards America expressed by European Orthodox rabbis, including immigrants, with their pessimistic prognosis for the survival of Torah-true Judaism in the new environment, see Caplan, *Orthodoxy in the New World*, 222–53.

[29] Following the traditional pattern of referring to a scholar by the name of his best-known book: *Meshekh ḥokhmah*, a commentary on the Pentateuch.

This is true even of Jews in the Diaspora, that even though they are forced to flee to America, (the great desert) nonetheless, they will not be scattered, and they will not be lost. Instead, in all places that they reach, they join with one another, they become communities and groups working together for the sake of Torah and service with many acts of charity and good deeds. Therefore, there is fulfilled in them, 'Who is this who rises from the desert? It is a tower of smoke spreading its sweet scent of myrrh and frankincense, and all of the spices of the apothecary' (S. of S. 3: 6).[30]

With slight changes, those words could be written about America today. I will provide that paraphrase as follows. Here in America, in New York and Washington, there are patches of ground that have become sites of searing desolation, veritable deserts, in the sense of places where life has become impossible, where only wreckage and ruin can be found. But America will not scatter, America will not shatter, America will not be lost. Wherever Americans are, we will come together, we will join one another and we will become communities working in service, doing great acts of charity, doing marvelous and heroic good deeds. In us, then, as proud citizens of this country, will be fulfilled the verse, 'Who is this rising up from the desert as a tower of smoke? It is a tower of smoke spreading its sweet scent of myrrh and frankincense, and all of the spices of the apothecary.'

Rabbi Meir Simcha of Dvinsk concludes as follows: 'And this teaches us about G-d's Divine and Personal Providence.' It is that Divine and Personal Providence that we pray for this day, and that we hope and trust we will find during the days, months, and years ahead. May it appear in the tower of smoke of Shir Ha-Shirim that will rise to overcome the symbolism of the tower of smoke in Yoel, and the terrible searing image of the tower of smoke that we have lived with since last Tuesday. May G-d grant all of us strength and blessing.

Shabbat Shalom to you all.

---

[30] Meir Simhah Hakohen, *Meshekh ḥokhmah* on Lev. 19: 18, 1: 347*b*–348*a*. The author compares the Jews in their various exiles to the smoke arising from the pile of wood in the Temple which, according to the Talmud (BT *Yoma* 21*a*), could not be diverted from its place even by all the winds of the world.

# Source Acknowledgements

—

The author would like to thank the following for permission to use and reproduce material for this volume: the Jewish Theological Seminary of America, for digitized versions of Sermons 1 by Isaac Luria and 2 by Solomon Hirschel; the American Jewish Historical Society, for permission to publish Sermon 3 by Gershom Mendes Seixas; the University of North Carolina Library, for the digitized version of Sermon 5 by Maximilan Michelbacher; Andover–Harvard Theological Library, for access to the pamphlet containing Sermon 8a by David Einhorn; the University of Pennsylvania Library for reproductions of newspaper articles containing Sermons 6 and 11 by Sabato Morais; the Rabbi Leo M. Franklin Archives, for permission to publish Sermon 21 by Leo M. Franklin; the Hertz Trustees, for permission to publish Sermons 17 and 28 by Joseph H. Hertz; the American Jewish Archives, for permission to publish Sermons 22 by Abraham H. Feinberg, 25 by Maurice N. Eisendrath, and 27 by Ferdinand M. Isserman; Bloch Publishing Company, for permission to publish Sermons 23 by Jacob Philip Rudin and 31b by Roland B. Gittelsohn; the Berkovits Institute at the Shalem Center for permission to publish Sermon 24 by Eliezer Berkovits; the National Archives of the UK, for permission to publish the General Fast Proclamation of 14 September 1803; the Rabbinical Council of America, for permission to publish Sermon 29 by Walter Wurzburger; Temple Israel (Boston) Archives, for permission to publish sermon 31a by Roland B. Gittelsohn; the London School of Jewish Studies (formerly Jews' College), for permission to publish Sermon 33 by Immanuel Jakobovits; Rabbis Colin Eimer, Elias Lieberman, Alexandra Wright, and Barry Freundel for permission to publish their own addresses (Sermons 32 and 34 a–c).

Every effort has been made to trace copyright holders and to obtain their permission for the use of copyright material. The author apologizes for any errors or omissions in the above list and would be grateful to be notified of any corrections that should be incorporated in future reprints or editions of this book.

# Bibliography

―

### Newspapers

*American Hebrew* (New York)
*Boston Globe*
*Chicago Tribune*
*Christian Conservator* (Dayton, Ohio)
*Contemporary Jewish Record* (New York)
*Evening Telegraph* (Philadelphia)
*Gentleman's Magazine* (London)
*Israelite* [1854–74], *American Israelite* [beginning 1874] (Cincinnati)
*Jewish Chronicle, Jewish Chronicle and Hebrew Observer* (London)
*Jewish Exponent* (Philadelphia)
*Jewish Messenger* (New York)
*Jewish South* (Richmond, Virginia)
*Jewish Week* (New York)
*Jewish World* (London)
*New York Evening Post*
*New York Spectator*
*New York Sunday Herald*
*The New York Times*
*The Occident and American Jewish Advocate* (Philadelphia)
*Philadelphia Jewish Record*
*Public Ledger* (Philadelphia)
*Reform Advocate* (Chicago)
*Richmond Dispatch*
*Richmond Examiner*
*The Times* (London)

### Archival Collections

Maurice N. Eisendrath Papers, American Jewish Archives, Cincinnati
Abraham Feinberg Papers, American Jewish Archives, Cincinnati
Leo M. Franklin Archives, Beth-El Congregation, Bloomfield Hills, Michigan
Myer S. Isaacs Collection, American Jewish Historical Society, New York
Ferdinand Isserman Papers, American Jewish Archives, Cincinnati
Joseph Krauskopf Papers, Keneseth Israel Archives, Philadelphia

Israel H. Levinthal Papers, The Joseph and Miriam Ratner Center for the
Study of Conservative Judaism Archives, Jewish Theological Seminary of America,
New York

Jacques Judah Lyons Collection, American Jewish Historical Society, New York

Sabato Morais Ledger, University of Pennsylvania Library

Sabato Morais Papers, University of Pennsylvania Library

John D. Rayner Papers, Leo Baeck College Library, London

Papers of the Seixas Family, American Jewish Historical Society, New York

Abba Hillel Silver Papers, Western Reserve Historical Society, Cleveland

British National Archives, Kew

Temple Israel of Boston Archives, Boston

West London Synagogue of British Jews Archives, London

## *Individual Sermons*

Sermons are listed by preacher *in order of date of delivery.*
An asterisk (*) indicates that the sermon is published in full in the present volume.
Full details of the collections in which these sermons were published are given below
on the first reference only; subsequent references are by short title.

ABRAHAMS, ISRAEL, 'The Proclamation of the Jewish State', 16 May 1948, in
*Living Waters: Collection of Sermons, Addresses and Prayers* (Cape Town: Cape
Town Hebrew Congregation, 1968), 341–70.

—— 'Israel's Victory', 19 June 1967, in *Living Waters*, 370–4.

ADLER, HERMANN, 'On *Rishus* in Germany and Russia', 28 May 1881, *Jewish
Chronicle*, 3 June 1881, p. 12.

—— 'A Pilgrimage to Zion', June (*Koraḥ*) 1885, in *The Jewish Pulpit* (London: 'Jewish
Chronicle', 1886), sermon no. 3.

—— 'The Death of Cardinal Manning', 9 Jan. 1892, *Jewish Chronicle*, 15 Jan. 1892,
pp. 12–13.

—— 'The Sinners in Zion', 10 Oct. 1894, in id., *Anglo-Jewish Memories and Other
Sermons* (London: George Routledge & Sons, 1909), 168–76.

—— 'Religious versus Political Zionism', 12 Nov. 1898, *Jewish Chronicle*, 25 Nov. 1898,
pp. 13–14.

—— 'The Dreyfus Judgement', 14 Sept. 1899, *Jewish Chronicle*, 22 Sept. 1899, pp. 12–13.

* —— 'Judaism and War', 4 Nov. 1899, in id., *Anglo-Jewish Memories and Other
Sermons*, 106–16.

—— 'The Queen and the War', 6 Jan. 1900, *Jewish Chronicle*, 12 Jan. 1900, p. 22.

—— 'The Late Queen', 2 Feb. 1901, in id., *Anglo-Jewish Memories and Other Sermons*,
117–25.

—— 'Address at the Unveiling of the Memorial to the Jewish Soldiers Who Fell in the South African War', 19 Mar. 1905, in id., *Anglo-Jewish Memories and Other Sermons*, 141–7.

—— 'The Russo-Jewish Martyrs', 19 Nov. 1905, in id., *Anglo-Jewish Memories and Other Sermons*, 148–56.

ADLER, NATHAN, 'Solomon's Judgement: A Picture of Israel, A Sermon Delivered at the Great Synagogue', 31 Dec. 1853 (London: Wertheimer, 1854).

—— 'Sermon on the Franco-Prussian War', 20 Aug. 1870, *Jewish Chronicle*, 26 Aug. 1870, p. 8.

* ARTOM, BENJAMIN, 'The War', 17 Sept. 1870, in id., *Sermons Preached in Several Synagogues* (London: Trübner & Co., 1873), 144–58.

AZEVEDO, MOSES COHEN DE, 'On the Revolt of the American Colonies', 13 Dec. 1776 (London: W. Gilbert, 1777).

BEECHER, HENRY WARD, 'Against the Mexican War', 27 Apr. 1848, Beecher Papers, Yale University Library.

—— 'Modes and Duties of Emancipation', 28 Nov. 1861, in id., *Patriotic Addresses in America and England from 1850 to 1885* (New York: Fords, Howard & Hulbert, 1887), 322–41.

—— 'The Success of American Democracy', 13 Apr. 1862, in id., *Patriotic Addresses in America and England*, 342–58.

—— 'Our Good Progress and Prospects', 27 Nov. 1862, in id., *Freedom and War: Discourses on Topics Suggested by the Times* (Boston: Ticknor & Fields, 1863), 368–94.

—— 'Fast-Day Sermon', 30 Apr. 1863, *New York Times*, 1 May 1863, p. 2.

—— 'Thanksgiving Day Sermon', 26 Nov. 1863, *New York Times*, 27 Nov. 1863, p. 2.

* BERKOVITS, ELIEZER, 'On a Strategy of Faith: After the British Debacle in Greece', [3] May 1941, in id., *Between Yesterday and Tomorrow* (Oxford: East and West Library, 1945), 30–4.

* —— 'Triumph of the Spirit', 7 Sept. 1941, in id., *Between Yesterday and Tomorrow*, 51–5.

—— 'God's Precious Son', 23 Sept. 1941, in id., *Between Yesterday and Tomorrow*, 84–8.

—— 'In the Margin of the Atlantic Charter', 16 Aug. 1941, in id., *Between Yesterday and Tomorrow*, 56–61.

BERKOWITZ, HENRY, 'Why I Am Not a Zionist', 17 Dec. 1898, *Jewish Exponent*, 23 Dec. 1898; repub. in *Yearbook of the Central Conference of American Rabbis*, 8 (1899), 167–74.

—— 'The Great Delusion', 20 Sept. 1914, *Jewish Exponent*, 25 Sept. 1914, p. 3.

BOSNIAK, JACOB, 'The Distinction of the Jew', 14 Sept. 1939, in id., *Interpreting Jewish Life: Sermons and Addresses* (New York: Bloch, 1944), 48–55.

BRANDON, DAVID, 'Discourse Delivered at the Spanish and Portuguese Jews' Synagogue', 21 Mar. 1832 (London: J. Wertheimer, 1832).

BRODIE, ISRAEL, 'Tribute to the Late President John Fitzgerald Kennedy', 30 Nov. 1963 (London: Office of the Chief Rabbi, 1963).

BULL, NICHOLAS, 'A Thanksgiving Sermon, for the Victory of Trafalgar', 5 Dec. 1805 (London: Rivington, 1805).

CARIGAL, HAIM ISAAC, 'The Salvation of Israel', 28 May 1773, pub. with foreword as *Rabbi Carigal Preaches in Newport* (Cincinnati: American Jewish Archives, 1966).

CHARLES, JAMES, 'The Lord's Voice to Britain from the Far East', 7 Oct. 1857 (Edinburgh: Paton & Ritchie, 1857).

COHEN, FRANCIS L., 'Our Duty at this Crisis', 14 Oct. 1899, *Jewish Chronicle*, 20 Oct. 1899, pp. 11–12.

COHN, ELKAN, 'Abraham Lincoln', 15 Apr. 1865, *Daily Alta California*, 16 Apr. 1865, in Emanuel Hertz (ed.), *Abraham Lincoln: The Tribute of the Synagogue* (New York: Bloch, 1927), 138–9.

COLOGNA, ABRAHAM DE, 'Discours prononcé . . . à l'occasion des actions de grâces rendues à l'Éternel, pour la grande victoire remportée par l'armée française au camp de Lützen', 23 May 1813 (Paris: L. P. Sétier, 1813).

CROWE, W. S., 'Prayer and War', 24 Apr. 1898, *New York Times*, 25 Apr. 1898, p. 10.

DIXON, THOMAS, JR, 'The Battle Cry of Freedom', in id., *Dixon's Sermons: Delivered in the Grand Opera House, New York, 1898–1899* (New York: F. L. Bussey, 1899), 1–6.

DREYFUSS, JACQUES HENRI, 'Patrie', 21 Sept. 1914, in *Sermons de guerre* (Paris: Librairie Durlacher, 1921), 33–44.

* EIMER, COLIN, 'The Falklands Crisis', 14 May 1982, preacher's personal collection.

* EINHORN, DAVID, 'Sermon Delivered on Thanksgiving Day', 26 Nov. 1863 (Philadelphia: Stein & Jones, 1863).

* —— 'War With Amalek!', 19 Mar. 1864 (Philadelphia: Stein & Jones, 1864), in Michael Warner (ed.), *American Sermons: The Pilgrims to Martin Luther King Jr.* (New York: Literary Classics of the United States, 1999), 665–73.

—— 'Predigt, am 19ten März 1864, als am Sabbath P. Sachor, im Tempel der Knesseth Israel Gemeinde dahier gehalten, zum Besten der Sanitary Fair' (Philadelphia: Stein & Jones, 1864).

—— 'Der Rettengel mitten in der Zerstörung', 4 July 1864, in Kaufmann Kohler (ed.), *David Einhorn Memorial Volume* (New York: Bloch, 1911), 129–39.

EISENDRATH, MAURICE N., 'A New Basis for Religion', 22 Sept. 1930, in *A Set of Holiday Sermons 5691/1930* (Cincinnati: The Tract Commission, 1930), 5–14.

—— 'Danger Zones—1940', 3 Nov. 1940, *Holy Blossom Pulpit*, 10/1 (Toronto: Holy Blossom Temple, 1940).

—— 'Where Do We Go From Here?', 12 Jan. 1941, *Holy Blossom Pulpit*, 10/5 (Toronto: Holy Blossom Temple, 1941).

* —— 'Blackout: How Lord, O Lord, How Long?', 21 Sept. 1941, American Jewish Archives, MS collection 167, box 1, folder 4.

EISENSTEIN, IRA, 'Rosh Hashanah Sermon', 15 Sept. 1939, *New York Times*, 16 Sept. 1939, p. 7.

ELLIOTT, STEPHEN, 'Samson's Riddle', 27 Mar. 1863 (Macon, Ga: Boykin, 1863), <docsouth.unc.edu/imls/samson/samson.html>.

ENELOW, HYMAN G., 'Armistice Day: How Observe It?', 11 Nov. 1923, American Jewish Archives, MS collection 11, box 26, folder 1.

FAUNCE, WILLIAM HERBERT PERRY, 'God in the Nation's Life', 24 Apr. 1898, *New York Times*, 25 Apr. 1898, p. 10.

* FEINBERG, ABRAHAM, 'America's Hour of Decision', 19 Sept. 1939, American Jewish Archives, MS collection 85, box 1, folder 1.

FLEISCHER, CHARLES, 'War', 13 Mar. 1898, *Boston Globe*, 14 Mar. 1898, p. 7; repr. *Reform Advocate*, 19 Mar. 1898, p. 81.

FOSDICK, HARRY EMERSON, 'The Ethical Problems of Neutrality', 12 Nov. 1939, in Albert Craig Baird (ed.), *Representative American Speeches: 1939–1940* (vol. xiv, no. 1, of *The Reference Shelf*) (New York: H. W. Wilson Co., 1940), 427–37.

FRÄNCKEL, DAVID, 'Dankpredigt über den grossen und herrlichen Sieg', 10 Dec. 1757 (Berlin: Friedrich Bernstiel, 1757); pub. in Eng. as 'Thanksgiving Sermon for the Important and Astonishing Victory [of Leuthen]' (Boston: Green & Russell, 1758).

FRANKLIN, LEO M., 'The Law of Retaliation', 11 Feb. 1899, Leo M. Franklin Archives, no. 629.

—— 'Has Civilization Proved a Failure?', 18 Oct. 1914, Leo M. Franklin Archives, no. 115.

—— 'A Warrior's Message of Peace', 13 Dec. 1914, Leo M. Franklin Archives, no. 597.

—— 'The Peace Idea in Jewish Literature', 7 May 1916, Leo M. Franklin Archives, no. 598.

—— 'The Living Dead', 28 May 1916, Leo M. Franklin Archives, no. 175.

—— 'The Free Man's Burden', 8 Apr. 1917, Leo M. Franklin Archives, no. 234.

—— 'Student Day', 22 Apr. 1917, Leo M. Franklin Archives, no. 679.

—— 'Memorial Day Address', 30 May 1918, Leo M. Franklin Archives, no. 502.

* —— 'The Lure of Peace', 13 Oct. 1918, Leo M. Franklin Archives, no. 606.

—— 'The Doctrine of "Peace on Earth"', 22 Dec. 1918, Leo M. Franklin Archives, no. 603.

—— 'The Armistice Anniversary: Its Moral Significance', 9 Nov. 1919, Leo M. Franklin Archives, no. 30.

—— 'A War without Armistice', 11 Nov. 1928, Leo M. Franklin Archives, no. 981.

FRANKLIN, LEO M., 'Light at the Eventide: A New Year's Sermon Delivered at Temple Beth El, Detroit, Michigan on the Eve of Rosh Hashono 5699, Sunday, Sept. 25, 1938' (Detroit: Temple Beth El, 1938).

—— 'Every Man's Problem', 2 Oct. 1940, Leo M. Franklin Archives, no. 1476.

FREEHOF, SOLOMON, 'Judaism and the War', 2 July 1918, *American Israelite*, 1 Aug. 1918, p. 1.

—— 'Minds Confused', 13 Apr. 1941, in *Living in Crisis: Rodef Shalom Pulpit*, new ser., 7/1–3 (Pittsburgh: Rodef Shalom Congregation, 1941) 3–15.

—— 'Hearts Bowed Down', 27 Apr. 1941, in *Living in Crisis*, 31–41.

—— 'Our Martyred President', 24 Nov. 1963, in *President John F. Kennedy: In Memoriam* (Pittsburgh: Rodef Shalom Congregation, 1963).

FREUDENTHAL, MAX, 'Predigt bei der Trauerfeier für die Opfer der russischen Juden-Verfolgungen', 17 Dec. 1905 (Danzig: D. Becker, 1906).

* FREUNDEL, BARRY, 'Shabbat Morning Sermon', 15 Sept. 2001, preacher's personal collection, <www.kesher.org/study/drashot/r_twin_smoke.html>.

GASTER, MOSES, 'A Sound of Battle', 11 Nov. 1899, *Jewish Chronicle*, 17 Nov. 1899, p. 12.

GEIGER, ABRAHAM, 'On the Admission of Jews to Citizenship: Delivered in Breslau to Commemorate the Royal Edict of Mar. 11, 1812', 7 Mar. 1840, in Max Wiener, *Abraham Geiger and Liberal Judaism: The Challenge of the Nineteenth Century* (Philadelphia: Jewish Publication Society, 1962), 249–53.

—— 'On the Occasion of the Fiftieth Anniversary of the Battle of Leipzig', 18 Oct. 1863, in Wiener, *Abraham Geiger and Liberal Judaism*, 253–7.

* GITTELSOHN, ROLAND B., 'The Birth of a New Freedom', 14 Mar. 1945, in *The Deltan of Phi Sigma Delta*, May 1945; abbrev. version pub. in *The Army Chaplaincy*, Winter–Spring 2002, 14–17, <www.usachcs.army.mil/TACarchive/ACwinspro2/Gittlesohn.htm>, accessed 11 Jan. 2007.

* —— 'Will There Be a Tomorrow?', 26 Sept. 1965, printed pamphlet, Archival Collection, Temple Israel of Boston.

* —— 'Answer to an Anonymous Letter', 26 Nov. 1965, in id., *Fire in My Bones: Essays on Judaism in a Time of Crisis* (New York: Bloch, 1969), 1–9.

GLADDEN, WASHINGTON, 'The Church and Peace', 6 Jan. 1915, in *The Great War: Six Sermons* (Columbus, Ohio: McClelland, 1915), 50–8.

GOLLANCZ, HERMANN, 'Archbishop Tait', 2 Sept. 1882, in id., *Sermons and Addresses* (New York: Bloch, 1909), 313–14.

—— 'The Sabbath', 2 Mar. 1895, in id., *Sermons and Addresses*, 75–80.

—— 'Which Is the True Sabbath?', 13 Nov. 1895, in id., *Sermons and Addresses*, 81–7.

—— 'The Prayer *Av ha-Rahamim* in the Light of the Current Events in Russia', undated [spring 1903], in id., *Sermons and Addresses*, 318–21.

—— 'Kischineff!!', 6 July 1903, in id., *Sermons and Addresses*, 322–8.

—— 'The Russian Crisis', 11 Nov. 1905, in id., *Sermons and Addresses*, 304–11.

—— 'The War and the Jews of Eastern Europe', 23 Sept. 1915, in id., *Sermons and Addresses, Second Series* (London: Chapman & Hall, 1916), 241.

—— ' "Noblesse Oblige"—The Motto for Nations as Well as for Individuals', 9 Sept. 1916, in H. Gollancz, *Fifty Years After: Sermons and Addresses, Third Series* (London: Humphrey Milford/Oxford University Press, 1924), 87–93.

—— 'Agony Cry of a Brother', 27 Jan. 1917, in id., *Fifty Years After*, 97–101.

* —— 'Nationalism within Bounds', 7 Sept. 1918, in id., *Fifty Years After*, 78–86.

GORKY, A., 'Thanksgiving Day Sermon', 26 Nov. 1863, *New York Times*, 27 Nov. 1863, p. 3.

GREEN, A. L., 'The Cry for Help from Gibraltar', 12 Nov. 1859, *Jewish Chronicle and Hebrew Observer*, 18 Nov. 1859, p. 5.

GROSSMAN, RUDOLPH, 'Patriotic Address', 22 May 1898, *New York Times*, 23 May 1898, p. 7.

GUTHEIM, JAMES KOPPEL, 'Thanksgiving Day Sermon', 29 Nov. 1860, American Jewish Archives, MS collection 224, box 1.

—— 'Inaugural Sermon' (Second Part), 21 Nov. 1868, in *The Temple Pulpit* (New York: Jewish Times, 1872), 22–37.

—— 'Sermon Delivered at the Consecration of the Temple Shaare Emeth, at St. Louis', 27 Aug. 1869, in *The Temple Pulpit*, 37–50.

—— 'Address Delivered at the Laying of the Corner-Stone of Temple Sinai of New Orleans', 19 Nov. 1871, in *The Temple Pulpit*, 51–62.

—— 'Sermon Delivered at the Dedication of the Temple Ahawath Chesed of New York', 19 Apr. 1879, in *The Temple Pulpit*, 63–76.

HALPERN, ABRAHAM E., 'The Birth of a Nation', 4 Oct. 1948, in Bernard S. Raskas (ed.), *A Son of Faith: From the Sermons of Abraham E. Halpern, 1891–1962* (New York: Bloch, 1962), 228–33.

HARRIS, ISIDORE, 'Jewish Patriotism', 12 Sept. 1914, *Jewish Chronicle*, 18 Sept. 1914, p. 27.

HARRIS, MAURICE H., 'Rosh Hashanah Sermon', 21 Sept. 1914, *New York Times*, 22 Sept. 1914, p. 5.

HARRISON, LEON, 'What Would Lincoln Do in the White House Now?', 27 Mar. 1914, in Emanuel Hertz (ed.), *Abraham Lincoln: The Tribute of the Synagogue* (New York: Bloch, 1927), 452–6.

HELLER, MAX, 'The War with Spain', 6 May 1898, *Israelite*, 19 May 1898, p. 5.

HENRY, H. A. 'The Perpetuity of the Law', 4 June 1862, *Occident*, 20/6 (Sept. 1862).

HEPWORTH, GEORGE H., 'War and Civilization', 25 Sept. 1970, *New York Times*, 26 Sept. 1870, p. 5.

HERTZ, JOSEPH H., 'Installation Sermon', 14 Apr. 1913, in id., *Sermons, Addresses and Studies*, 3 vols (London: Soncino Press, 1938), i. 1–14.

HERTZ, JOSEPH H., 'The "Strange Fire" of Schism', 26 Apr. 1914, in id., *Sermons, Addresses and Studies*, i. 305–11.

\* —— 'Through Darkness and Death unto Light', 1 Jan. 1916, in id., *Sermons, Addresses and Studies*, i. 25–9.

—— 'The Eternal City of the Eternal People', 15 Dec. 1917, in id., *Sermons, Addresses and Studies*, i. 213–19.

—— 'Our Polish Brethren', 26 June 1919, in id., *Sermons, Addresses and Studies*, i. 43–9.

—— 'In Ancient Egypt and Present-Day Germany', 11 Apr. 1933, in id., *Sermons, Addresses and Studies*, i. 137–44.

—— 'Out of the Depths I Cry Unto Thee', 9 July 1933, in id., *Sermons, Addresses and Studies*, i. 145–52.

—— 'A Moral Challenge to British Jewry', 6 Apr. 1934, in id., *Sermons, Addresses and Studies*, i. 153–9.

—— 'Baron Edmond de Rothschild', 13 Dec. 1934, in id., *Sermons, Addresses and Studies*, i. 129–30, 132.

—— 'Intercession Sermon', 23 Mar. 1941, in id., *Early and Late: Addresses, Messages, and Papers* (Hindhead, Surrey: Soncino Press, 1943), 61–5.

—— 'Palestine Victory Campaign, July 8, 1941', in id., *Early and Late*, 194–6.

—— 'The Great Synagogue Will Rise Again', 7 Sept. 1941, in id., *Early and Late*, 66–75.

—— 'The Meaning of Pesach', 10 Apr. 1941, in id., *Early and Late*, 1–4.

\* —— 'Civilian Morale', 2 Apr. 1942, in id., *Early and Late*, 14–18.

—— 'Pentecost and Commercial Honesty', 22 May 1942, in id., *Early and Late*, 19–24.

—— 'England, Awake', 13 Dec. 1942, in id., *Early and Late*, 80–5.

—— 'The "Battle of Warsaw"', 22 May 1944 (London: Office of the Chief Rabbi, 1944).

HERZOG, DAVID, 'Das Gelöbnis der Treue', 4 Aug. 1914, in id., *Kriegspredigten* (Frankfurt am Main: J. Kauffmann, 1915), 14–18.

HIRSCH, EMIL G. 'The Crossing of the Jordan', 5 Sept. 1880, in *The American Jewish Pulpit* (Cincinnati: Bloch & Co., 1881), 139–53.

—— 'The Ancient Anti-Semite and his Modern Successors', undated, in *Sermons by American Rabbis* (Chicago: Central Conference of American Rabbis, 1896), 122–46.

—— 'Men of Light and Leading', 21 Feb. 1898, selection in *Reform Advocate*, 26 Feb. 1898, p. 32; full text in *Reform Advocate*, 12 Mar. 1898, pp. 63–6.

—— 'The Responsibility for the Russian Massacres', 3 Dec. 1905 (Chicago: Bloch & Newman, 1905).

HIRSCH, SAMUEL, 'Peace Sermon', 14 May 1871, *Philadelphia Inquirer*, 15 May 1871, p. 2.

* HIRSCHEL, SOLOMON, 'A Sermon Preached at the Great Synagogue, Duke's Place . . . Trafalgar', 5 Dec. 1805 (London: T. Malden, 1805).

HIRSCHOWITZ, ABRAHAM E., 'Jewish Patriotism and its Martyrs', 28 Jan. 1899 (New York: A. Sheinkopf, 1899).

HORSLEY, SAMUEL, 'The Watchers and the Holy Ones', 5 Dec. 1805 (London: n.p., 1806).

HYAMSON, MOSES, 'In Memoriam: Queen Victoria', 2 Feb. 1901, in id., *The Oral Law and Other Sermons* (London: David Nutt, 1910), 161–7.

ILLOWY, BERNARD, 'Fast-Day Sermon', 4 Jan. 1861, <www.jewish-history.com/ Illoway/sermon.html>, checked 8 Aug. 2006.

ISAACS, D. M., 'Funeral Oration, delivered on the occasion of the burial of his most gracious Majesty, King William the Fourth', 8 July 1837 (Liverpool: n.p., 1837).

ISAACS, SAMUEL MYER, 'The Corner Stone', undated [early summer 1846], *Occident and American Jewish Advocate*, Aug. 1846, <www.jewish-history.com/ Occident/volume4/aug1846/cornerstone.html>, checked 8 Aug. 2006.

—— 'Fast-Day Sermon', 26 Sept. 1861, *Jewish Messenger*, 4 Oct. 1861, p. 51.

* —— 'Sermon for the National Fast-Day', 30 Apr. 1863, *Jewish Messenger*, 8 May 1863, pp. 152–3.

ISSERMAN, FERDINAND M., 'Personal Experiences with Victims of the Brown Terror—Nazi Atrocities: Anti-German Propaganda or Shocking Truth?', 27 Oct. 1933, Isserman Papers, American Jewish Archives, MS collection 6, box 13, folder 5.

—— 'My Second Visit to Nazi Germany', 25 Oct. 1935, Isserman Papers, American Jewish Archives, MS collection 6, box 14, folder 2.

—— 'Collective Security, Neutrality or War: Which Will America Choose?', 1 May 1936, Isserman Papers, American Jewish Archives, MS collection 6, box 14, folder 4.

—— 'We Americans and the War in Europe', 20 Oct. 1939, Isserman Papers, American Jewish Archives, MS collection 6, box 15, folder 5.

* —— 'The United States Is at War', 12 Dec. 1941, Isserman Papers, American Jewish Archives, MS collection 6, box 15, folder 5.

JACOBSON, MOSES, 'Der beste deutsche Mann', June 1888, in id., *Reden über des Staates Führer, Dinge und Fragen* (Breslau: Wilhelm Jacobsohn, 1901), 51–8.

JAKOBOVITS, IMMANUEL, 'Israel's Bar Mitzvah', 28 Apr. 1961, in I. Jakobovits, *Journal of a Rabbi* (London: W. H. Allen, 1967), 118–24.

* JAKOBOVITS, IMMANUEL, 'The Morality of Warfare', 25 May 1982, *L'Eylah*, 2/4 (Autumn 5743/1982), 1–7.

JASTROW, MARCUS, 'Thanksgiving Day Sermon', 26 Nov. 1868 (Philadelphia: R. Stein, 1868).

JASTROW, MARCUS, 'Peace Sermon', 13 May 1871, *Philadelphia Inquirer*, 15 May 1871, p. 2.

JELLINEK, ADOLF, '5631!: Neujahr 1870', 26 Sept. 1870, in id., *Zeitstimmen*, ii (Vienna: Herzfeld and Bauer, 1871), 31–40.

JOSEPH, MORRIS, 'Judaism and Christianity', undated, in *The Ideal in Judaism, and Other Sermons; Preached During 1890–91–92* (London: David Nutt, 1893), 31–9.

—— 'War', 28 Oct. 1899, *Jewish Chronicle*, 3 Nov. 1899, p. 22.

—— 'The War and the Future', undated [Aug. 1914?], in id., *The Spirit of Judaism: Sermons Preached Chiefly at the West London Synagogue* (London: Routledge, 1930), 207–13.

—— 'The War and Our Responsibility', 17 Oct. 1914, *Jewish Chronicle*, 23 Oct. 1914, pp. 22–3.

* —— 'Christmas and War', 25 Dec. 1915, in id., *The Spirit of Judaism*, 214–19.

—— 'The War and Religion', undated [autumn 1917], in id., *The Spirit of Judaism*, 199–206.

—— 'Peace and Good Will', 21 Dec. [1918], in id., *The Spirit of Judaism*, 220–5.

JUNG, LEO, 'God in the Crisis', 1940, in id., *Crumbs and Character: Sermons, Addresses and Essays* (New York: Night and Day Press, 1942), 25–31.

KAHN, ZADOC, 'Allocution prononcée à l'occasion du départ des Séminaristes israélites pour l'armée', Nov. 1892, in id., *Religion et Patrie: Deux allocutions prononcées à la Synagogue de la Rue de la Victoire* (Paris: Librairies-Imprimeries Réunies, 1892), 19–30.

KALLOCH, I. S., 'Thanksgiving Day Sermon', 26 Nov. 1863, *New York Times*, 27 Nov. 1863, p. 2.

KELL, EDMUND, 'What Patriotism, Justice, and Christianity Demand for India', 11 Oct. 1857 (London: Whitfield, 1857).

KELSON, BENJAMIN, 'Ten Plagues of Today', 19 Apr. 1930, in *A Set of Holiday Sermons 5691–1930* (Cincinnati: The Tract Commission, 1930, 70–7).

KINGSBURGY, WILLIAM, 'Victory Mourning', 5 Dec. 1805, *Gentleman's Magazine*, Feb. 1806, p. 151.

KOCHIN, ELIHU WOLF, 'Sermon on Sabbath *Naḥamu*' (Heb.), 12 Aug. 1916, in *Aderet eliyahu* [Elijah's Mantle], 3 vols (Pittsburgh: A. W. Kochin, 1917–1933), i. 3–21.

KOHLER, KAUFMANN, 'Are Sunday Lectures Treason to Judaism?', 8 Jan. 1888, in Samuel S. Cohon (ed.), *A Living Faith* (Cincinnati: HUC Press, 1948), 19–30.

—— 'God's Ultimatum to Spain', 23 Apr. 1898, *New York Sunday Herald*, 24 Apr. 1898, p. 7; fuller text in *American Hebrew*, 29 Apr. 1898, p. 771.

KRAUSKOPF, JOSEPH, 'The People without a Country', 3 Jan. 1897, *Sunday Lectures*, ser. 10, 1896–7 (Philadelphia: S. W. Goodwin, 1897).

—— 'Condemned Unheard—The Dreyfus Case', 6 Feb. 1898, *Sunday Lectures*, ser. 11, 1897–8 (Philadelphia: Oscar Klonower, 1898).

—— 'The Martyr-Race', 20 Feb. 1898, *Sunday Lectures*, ser. 11, 1897–8.

—— 'Beating Plowshares into Swords', 20 Mar. 1898, *Sunday Lectures*, ser. 11, 1897–8.

\* —— 'A Time of War, and a Time of Peace', 1 May 1898, *Sunday Lectures*, ser. 11, 1897–8; preacher's manuscript in Keneseth Israel Archives.

—— 'Rosh Hashanah Evening Sermon', 20 Sept. 1914, *Jewish Exponent*, 25 Sept. 1914, p. 3.

—— 'To the Front', 14 Nov. 1915, *Sunday Discourses*, ser. 29, 1915–16 (Philadelphia: Oscar Klonower, 1916).

—— 'To Prepare or Not to Prepare?', 9 Jan. 1916, *Sunday Discourses*, ser. 29, 1915–16.

—— 'Has God Forsaken Man?', 25 Sept. 1917, *Sunday Discourses*, ser. 31, 1917–18 (Philadelphia: Oscar Klonower, 1918).

—— 'Hands that Toil and Hearts that Feel', 23 Dec. 1917, *Sunday Discourses*, ser. 31, 1917–18.

—— 'Had Gadya (Retribution)', 28 Mar. 1918, *Sunday Discourses*, ser. 31, 1917–18.

—— 'The Ukrainian Pogroms', 17 Dec. 1919, *Sunday Discourses*, ser. 32, 1919–20 (Philadelphia: Oscar Klonower, 1920).

LEESER, ISAAC, 'The Sorrows of Israel', 24 July 1840, in *Discourses on the Jewish Religion*, 10 vols (Philadelphia: Sherman, 1866–8), iii. 153–71.

—— 'Address on the Persecution of the Jews in the East', 27 Aug. 1840, in *Discourses on the Jewish Religion*, iii. 347–64.

—— 'Pres. W. H. Harrison', 9 Apr. 1841, in *Discourses on the Jewish Religion*, iv. 30–45.

—— 'The Strength of our Religion', 26 Jan. 1849, in *Discourses on the Jewish Religion*, viii. 84–99.

—— 'The Plague', 3 Aug. 1849, in *Discourses on the Jewish Religion*, viii. 188–203.

—— 'God our Atonement', 1 Mar. 1850, in *Discourses on the Jewish Religion*, viii. 341–54.

—— 'The Israelites' Thanksgiving', 29 Nov. 1860, in *Discourses on the Jewish Religion*, ix. 148–63.

—— 'Mr Lincoln's Death', 15 Apr. 1865, in *Discourses on the Jewish Religion*, x. 235–42; also in Emanuel Hertz (ed.), *Abraham Lincoln: The Tribute of the Synagogue* (New York: Bloch, 1927), 133–7.

LEVI, GERSON B., 'A Challenge to Society of Days of Depression', 7 Dec. 1930, in id., *The Thanksgiving of the Spirit and Other Sermons* (Chicago: Argus Book Shop, 1938), 94–104.

LEVIN, HIRSCHEL, 'Fast-Day Sermon on *Beha'alotekha*', undated [late spring 1757 or 1758], in Marc Saperstein, *Jewish Preaching, 1200–1800* (New Haven: Yale University Press, 1989), 350–8.

LEVIN, MORITZ, 'Kaiser Wilhelm: Ein Messias unserer Zeit. Rede bei dem Trauer-Gottesdienst der juedischen Reform-Gemeinde zu Berlin', 18 Mar. 1888 (Berlin: Rosenthal & Co., 1888).

LEVINTHAL, ISRAEL HERBERT, 'Wherefore Is the Earth Destroyed?', 14 Sept. 1939, in id., *A New World Is Born: Sermons and Addresses* (New York: Funk & Wagnalls, 1943), 40–7.

—— 'As in the Days of Noah', 15 Sept. 1939, *New York Times*, 16 Sept. 1949, p. 7; Israel H. Levinthal Papers, box 6.

—— 'Why Has Tragedy Come to the World?', 12 Apr. 1941, Israel H. Levinthal Papers, box 7.

\* —— 'Is It Death or Rebirth of the World that We Behold?', 22 Sept. 1941, in id., *A New World Is Born*, 7–14.

—— 'Where Is God?', 1 Oct. 1941, Israel H. Levinthal Papers, box 7.

—— 'The Hands of Esau', 12 Dec. 1941, Israel H. Levinthal Papers, box 7.

—— 'When Thou Goest to War', 11 Sept. 1942, Israel H. Levinthal Papers, box 7.

—— 'The Miracle and the Message of Israel's Triumph', 14 June 1967, in *The Message of Israel: Sermons, Addresses, Memoirs* (New York: Lex Printing, 1973), 75–82.

LEVY, J. LEONARD, 'Which Sabbath Ought We Observe?', 27 Feb. 1898, in *Sunday Lectures*, ser. 11, 1897–8 (Philadelphia: Oscar Klonower, 1898).

—— 'The Altar at the Hearth', 24 Apr. 1898, *Sunday Lectures*, ser. 11, 1897–8.

—— 'When Dreams Come True', 1 Nov. 1914, in *The Reform Pulpit: Sunday Lectures before Rodef Shalom Congregation*, ser. 14 (Pittsburgh: B. Calloman, 1915), no. 1.

—— 'The War against War', 15 Nov. 1914, in *The Reform Pulpit*, ser. 14, no. 3.

—— 'The War against War, II', 22 Nov. 1914, in *The Reform Pulpit*, ser. 14, no. 4.

—— 'The War against War, III', 6 Dec. 1914, in *The Reform Pulpit*, ser. 14, no. 6.

—— 'The Fruits of War', 5 Dec. 1915, in *The Reform Pulpit*, ser. 15, no. 5.

—— 'The Butterfly', 3 Dec. 1916, in Solomon B. Freehof and Vigdor W. Kavalar (eds), *J. Leonard Levy: Prophetic Voice* (Pittsburgh: Rodef Shalom Congregation, 1970), 195–208.

—— 'The Making of Munitions', 24 Dec. 1916, in *The Reform Pulpit*, ser. 16 (Pittsburgh: B. Calloman, 1917), no. 9.

\* —— 'A Time for War, and a Time for Peace', 8 Apr. 1917, in *The Reform Pulpit*, ser. 16, no. 21.

LEVY, M. B., 'Fast-Day Sermon', 26 Apr. 1854, *Jewish Chronicle*, 12 May 1854, p. 273.

\* LIEBERMAN, ELIAS, 'Friday Evening Sermon', 14 Sept. 2001, preacher's personal collection; segment excerpted on National Public Radio's *Weekend Edition—Sunday*, 16 Sept. 2001.

LIGHTFOOT, JOSEPH BARBER, 'Balaam and Balak', 4 May 1873, in *Sermons Preached in St Paul's Cathedral* (London: Macmillan and Co., 1891), 1–15.

LILIENTHAL, MAX, 'The Prejudice against the Jews', Aug. 1870, *Israelite*, 26 Aug. 1870, pp. 9–10

LIPMAN, EUGENE, 'Racial Justice: A Pledge of Conscience', 27 Sept. 1963, in *Yamim Nora'im: Sinai Sermons* (Washington, DC: Temple Sinai, 1987), 21–7.

—— 'Vietnam: Can Jewish Values Guide Us?', 15 Sept. 1966, in *Yamim Nora'im*, 34–9.

—— 'Black Power Slogans', 24 Sept. 1966, in *Yamim Nora'im*, 40–4.

LOOKSTEIN, JOSEPH, 'Rosh Hashanah Sermon', 15 Sept. 1939, *New York Times*, 16 Sept. 1939, p. 7.

—— 'Kol Nidre Sermon', 22 Sept. 1939, *New York Times*, 23 Sept. 1939, p. 24.

* LURIA, ISAAC, 'A Penitential Sermon Preached in the Spanish and Portuguese Jews' Synagogue', 3 Oct. 1803 (London: William Lane, 1803).

LYNCH, P. N., 'The Vatican Council and the Italian Occupation of Rome', 25 Sept. 1870, *New York Times*, 26 Sept. 1870, p. 5.

LYONS, JACQUES JUDAH, 'Sermon on the Occasion of the Death of President Harrison', 14 May 1841, American Jewish Historical Society Archives, P-16, box 6, folder 341.

MARKS, DAVID WOOLF, 'Sermon on the Sabbath Nahamoo', 24 July 1842[?], *Occident and American Jewish Advocate*, Nov. 1843, <www.jewish-history. com/Occident/volume1/nov1843/marks.html>.

—— 'On the Day of Thanksgiving for the Abundant Harvest', 16 Oct. 1847, in id., *Sermons Preached on Various Occasions*, i (London: Groombridge, 1851), sermon 9, pp. 119–31.

—— 'Fast-Day Sermon', 26 Apr. 1854, *Jewish Chronicle*, 12 May 1854, p. 273.

* —— 'God Protects our Fatherland', 7 Oct. 1857, in id., *Sermons Preached on Various Occasions*, 2nd ser. (London: Trübner & Co., 1885), 155–65.

—— 'Sermon by Rev. Professor Marks', 19 Nov. 1859, *Jewish Chronicle and Hebrew Observer*, 25 Nov. 1859, p. 7.

MAYER, JACOB, 'The Discipline of Nations under the Government of Supreme Wisdom', Sept. 1870, *Israelite*, 7 Oct. 1870, pp. 8–9.

* MENDES, H. PEREIRA, 'The Plague of Inconsistency' (selections), 23 Apr. 1898, *New York Herald*, 24 Apr. 1898, sec. 3, p. 4.

* MICHELBACHER, MAXIMILIAN, 'A Sermon Delivered on the Day of Prayer', 27 Mar. 1863 (Richmond, Va: MacFarlane & Fergusson, 1863).

MONTEFIORE, CLAUDE G., 'One God, One Worship', Feb. 1896, *Jewish Chronicle*, 14 Feb. 1896, pp. 19–20.

MORAIS, SABATO, 'A Sermon delivered on Thanksgiving Day (November 25, 1852) Before the Congregation Mikvé Israel, at their Synagogue in Cherry Street, by the Rev. S. Morais, Reader of the Congregation' (Philadelphia: Judaica Americana Collection of Jewish Theological Seminary of America Library, 5613 [1852]).

—— 'Address Delivered by the Rev. S. Morais, Minister of the Congregation Mikveh Israel, Philadelphia, on the National "Fast-Day"', 26 Sept. 1861, *Jewish Messenger*, 4 Oct. 1861, p. 63; Sabato Morais Ledger, 39.

* —— 'Sermon for the National Fast-Day', 30 Apr. 1863, *Philadelphia Inquirer*, 2 May 1863; *Jewish Messenger*, 15 May 1863, p. 165; Sabato Morais Ledger, 23.

MORAIS, SABATO, 'Independence Day Sermon', 4 July 1863, *Jewish Messenger*, 10 July 1863; Sabato Morais Ledger, 22.

—— 'Thanksgiving Day Sermon', 26 Nov. 1863, *Philadelphia Inquirer*, 27 Nov. 1863, p. 8.

—— 'Thanksgiving Day Sermon', 24 Nov. 1864, *Philadelphia Inquirer*, 25 Nov. 1864; Sabato Morais Ledger, 23.

—— 'Thanksgiving Day Sermon', 28 Nov. 1867, *Philadelphia Inquirer*, 29 Nov. 1867; Sabato Morais Ledger, 35.

—— 'Thanksgiving Day Sermon, 26 Nov. 1868, *Philadelphia Inquirer*, 27 Nov. 1868; Sabato Morais Ledger, 36.

* —— 'Thanksgiving Day Sermon', 24 Nov. 1870, *Philadelphia Inquirer*, 25 Nov. 1870, pp. 2–3; Sabato Morais Ledger, 44.

—— 'On the Ill Treatment of the Chinese in the Far West', 26 Nov. 1885, Morais Papers, University of Pennsylvania Library, box 13, FF 24.

—— 'Eulogy for Emperor Frederick III', 16 June 1888, *Public Ledger—Philadelphia*, 18 June 1888; Sabato Morais Ledger, 391.

NEWMAN, LOUIS I., 'We Are All Semites Spiritually: The Message of Pope Pius XI', 25 Feb. 1939, in id., *Sermons and Addresses*, ii (New York: Bloch, 1941), n.p.

—— 'Why Hast Thou Forsaken Me?', 12 Oct. 1940, in id., *Sermons and Addresses*, ii, n.p.

—— 'Our American Citizenship and the New Jewish State', 7 Nov. 1947, in *Sermons and Addresses*, vi: *Becoming a New Person* (New York: Bloch, 1950), n.p.

NIETO [NETTO], ISAAC, 'Sermon Preached in the Jews Synagogue', 6 Feb. 1756 (London: Richard Reily, 1756).

PARKER, THEODORE, 'A Sermon of War', 7 June 1846, in Michael Warner (ed.), *American Sermons* (New York: Library of America, 1999), 600–29.

POLACK, J., 'Sermon at Special Service on Behalf of Russian Jews', 19 June 1881, *Jewish Chronicle*, 24 June 1881, p. 8.

POLISH, DAVID, '"Why Do the Nations Rage?"—"How Can Jacob Stand?"', 17 Sept. 1982, in id., *Abraham's Gamble: Selected Sermons for Our Times* (Evanston, Ill.: n.p., 1988), 169–73.

PREDMESKY, AKIBA, 'The Ark of G-d Has Been Taken', in Bernard L. Berzon (ed.), *Manual of Holiday and Occasional Sermons* (New York: Rabbinical Council Press, 1943), 51–60.

RAINSFORD, WILLIAM S., 'Who Is My Neighbor?', 1 May 1898, *New York Times*, 2 May 1898, p. 12.

RAPHALL, MORRIS JACOB, 'The Bible View of Slavery', 4 Jan. 1861 (New York: Rudd & Carleton, 1861); repr. in Morris U. Schappes (ed.), *A Documentary History of the Jews in the United States, 1654–1875* (New York: Citadel Press, 1971), 405–18.

—— 'Fast-Day Sermon', 26 Sept. 1861, *Jewish Messenger*, 4 Oct. 1861, p. 51.

—— 'Fast-Day Sermon', 30 Apr. 1863, selected passages in *New York Times*, 1 May 1863, p. 2, and *Jewish Messenger*, 8 May 1863, p. 154.

RAYNER, JOHN D., 'Morality and Expediency in International Conduct (with Reference to the Middle East Crisis', 2 Nov. 1956, Rayner Papers, sermon no. 130.

—— 'John F. Kennedy', 22 Nov. 1963, in id., *A Jewish Understanding of the World* (Oxford: Berghahn Books, 1998), 102–3.

—— 'Whose Islands? A Sermon about the Falklands Crisis', 8 May 1982, Rayner Papers, sermon no. 779.

REICHERT, IRVING, 'How Can We Find Happiness in the New Year?', 2 Oct. 1940, in id., *Judaism and the American Jew: Selected Sermons and Addresses* (San Francisco: Grabhorn, 1953), 225–30.

—— 'Where Is thy God?', 11 Oct. 1940, in id., *Judaism and the American Jew*, 83–92.

RICE, ABRAHAM, 'The Messiah', 19 Mar. 1842, *Occident and American Jewish Advocate*, Sept. 1843, <www.jewish-history.com/Occident/volume1/sept1843/ messiah.html>.

ROBERTS, WILLIAM, 'Thanksgiving Day Sermon', 26 Nov. 1863, *New York Times*, 27 Nov. 1863, p. 2.

ROTHSCHILD, JACOB M., 'The Greater Sin', 13 Oct. 1948, in Melissa Fay Greene, *The Temple Bombing* (Reading, Mass.: Addison-Wesley, 1996), 173–4.

* RUDIN, JACOB PHILIP, 'God in the Blackout—1940', 2 Oct. 1940, in id., *Very Truly Yours: A Creative Harvest of Forty Years in the Pulpit* (New York: Bloch, 1971), 234–40.

—— 'Founder's Day Address', 12 Mar. 1954 (New York: Hebrew Union College–Jewish Institute of Religion, 1954).

—— 'The March on Washington', 18 Sept. 1963, in id., *Very Truly Yours*, 250–8.

SAPERSTEIN, HAROLD I., 'The Great Olympic Idea', 1 Nov. 1935, in id., *Witness from the Pulpit: Topical Sermons, 1933–1980* (Lanham, Md.: Lexington Books, 2000), 44–9.

—— 'Must There Be War?', 11 Nov. 1936, in id., *Witness from the Pulpit*, 50–5.

—— 'Can Jews Afford to Be Pacifists?', [Dec. 1937], in id., *Witness from the Pulpit*, 56–61.

—— 'Unconquered', 14 Sept. 1939, in id., *Witness from the Pulpit*, 68–74.

—— 'The World We Make', 2 Oct. 1940, in id., *Witness from the Pulpit*, 75–6.

—— 'Undying Fires', 22 Sept. 1941, in id., *Witness from the Pulpit*, 83–9.

—— 'The Mount of Sacrifice', 11 Sept. 1942, in id., *Witness from the Pulpit*, 94–5.

—— 'What Have We Jews To Be Thankful For?', 27 Nov. 1942, in id., *Witness from the Pulpit*, 96–101.

—— 'Farewell', 20 June 1943, in id., *Witness from the Pulpit*, 102–5.

—— 'Israel and Us', 21 May 1948, in id., *Witness from the Pulpit*, 141–6.

SAPERSTEIN, HAROLD I., 'A Prince in Israel', 22 Apr. 1949, in id., *Witness from the Pulpit*, 147–53.

—— 'Jewish Life behind the Iron Curtain', 11 Sept. 1959, in id., *Witness from the Pulpit*, 200–5.

—— 'The American Dream, in Color', 6 Sept. 1963, in id., *Witness from the Pulpit*, 218–25.

—— 'Martyr for the American Dream', 22 Nov. 1963, in id., *Witness from the Pulpit*, 226–9.

—— 'The Dilemma of Vietnam', 10 June 1966, in id., *Witness from the Pulpit*, 252–8.

—— 'A Great Miracle Happened There', 8 Sept. 1967, in id., *Witness from the Pulpit*, 259–66.

—— 'The Ordeal of Soviet Jewry', 29 Dec. 1970, in id., *Witness from the Pulpit*, 279–84.

SCHILLER-SZINESSY, S. M., 'Confirmation: a Genuine Jewish Institution', 24 May 1852 (Manchester: Cave & Sever Printers, 1852).

—— 'Fast-Day Sermon', 7 Oct. 1857, *Jewish Chronicle and Hebrew Observer*, 16 Oct. 1857, p. 1181.

SEIXAS, GERSHOM MENDES, 'A Religious Discourse: Thanksgiving Day Sermon', 26 Nov. 1789 (New York: Archibald M'Lean, 1789; repr. Jewish Historical Society of New York, 1977).

—— 'Discourse Delivered in the Synagogue in New York', 9 May 1798 (New York: Naphtali Judah, 1798).

* —— 'Fast-Day Sermon', 2 Feb. 1814, Papers of the Seixas Family, P-60, box 2, folder 2.

SILVER, ABBA HILLEL, 'The Battle Hymn of America', 28 Oct. 1917, Abba Hillel Silver Papers, container no. 51, folder 15.

—— 'Is God in this War?', 6 Jan. 1918, Abba Hillel Silver Papers, container no. 51, folder 24.

—— 'Pope Pius XI', 19 Feb. 1939, in *A Word in its Season*, Selected Sermons, Addresses, and Writings of Abba Hillel Silver, ii, ed. Herbert Weiner (New York: World Publishing, 1972), 359–65.

—— 'Our Responsibility for Evil', 3 Oct. 1940, in *Therefore Choose Life*, Selected Sermons, Addresses, and Writings of Abba Hillel Silver, i, ed. Herbert Weiner (New York: World Publishing, 1967), 60–6.

SILVERMAN, JOSEPH, 'My Country Right or Wrong', 1 May 1898, *New York Times*, 2 May 1898, p. 12.

* SILVERSTONE, GEORGE (GEDALIAH), 'On the Terrible War of 5765' (Heb.), 25 Oct. 1914, in *Peninim Yeqarim* [Precious Pearls], 2 vols (Washington, DC: n.p., 1915), i. 6–8.

SINGER, SIMEON, 'Answer Him Not', 1 Feb. 1896, *Jewish Chronicle*, 7 Feb. 1896, p. 14.

—— 'Sermon on Genesis 14: 14', 14 Oct. 1899, *Jewish Chronicle*, 20 Oct. 1899, p. 11.

—— 'The War', 6 Jan. 1900, *Jewish Chronicle*, 12 Jan. 1900, p. 23.

—— 'Sweated Industries', 26 May 1906, in *The Literary Remains of the Rev. Simeon Singer: Sermons*, ed. Israel Abrahams, i (London: Routledge & Sons, 1908), 209–15.

SINZHEIM, DAVID, *Sermon prononcé dans la grande synagogue à Strasbourg, le 2 Brumaire an 14, pour célébrer les glorieuses victoires de sa Majesté l'Empéreur des Français, Roi d'Italie*, 24 Oct. 1805 (Strasbourg: n.p., 1805).

SIVITZ, MOSES SIMON, 'Sermon for *Shabbat Hagadol*' (Heb.), [2?] Apr. 1898, in *Beit paga* (Jerusalem: Salamon, 1904), 108–14.

—— 'Eulogy for Those Who Have Fallen in the War' (Heb.), Feb. 1917, in *Mateh aharon* (Jerusalem: Solomon, 1914–?), 244–6.

SLOAN, J. R. W., 'Fast-Day Sermon', 30 Apr. 1863, *New York Times*, 1 May 1863, p. 2.

SOLA, DAVID AARON DE, 'Consolation of Jerusalem', 27 July 1833 (London: John Wertheimer, 1833).

—— 'Sermon Delivered at the Spanish and Portuguese Jews' Synagogue', 24 Mar. 1847 (London: Meldola, Cohn & Co., 1847); *Occident and American Jewish Advocate*, Mar. 1848.

SPURGEON, CHARLES HADDON, 'India's Ills and England's Sorrows', 6 Sept. 1857, in *The New Park Street Pulpit: Sermons Preached and Revised by the Rev. C. H. Spurgeon*, 7 vols (London: Passmore & Alabaster, 1856–64), iii. 341–8.

—— 'Fast-Day Sermon', 7 Oct. 1857, in *The New Park Street Pulpit*, iii. 373–88.

—— 'Think Well and Do Well', 23 Oct. 1870, in *Metropolitan Tabernacle Pulpit: Sermons Preached and Revised by the Rev. C. H. Spurgeon*, 55 vols (London: Passmore & Alabaster, 1856–1916), xvi. 577–88.

STEIN, LEOPOLD, 'Der Kampf des Lebens', 25 Sept. 1870, in *Der Kampf des Lebens: Ein Cyclus von Festpredigten, in Beziehung zu dem grossen Völkerkampfe der Gegenwart . . . (5631–1870) im israelitischen Betsaale Westend-Union zu Frankfurt a. M.* (Mannheim: Schneider, 1871), 3–10.

STEINBERG, MILTON, 'Rosh Hashanah Sermon, First Day', 14 Sept. 1939, *New York Times*, 15 Sept. 1939, p. 20.

—— 'Rosh Hashanah Sermon, Second Day', 15 Sept. 1939, *New York Times*, 16 Sept. 1939, p. 7.

SZOLD, BENJAMIN, 'The Sabbath', 15 Dec. 1888 (Baltimore: Schneidereith & Sons, 1889).

TAUBENHAUS, GODFREY, 'Nation Shall Not Lift Up Sword Against Nation', 27 Mar. 1898, *Brooklyn Eagle*, 28 Mar. 1898, p. 7.

—— 'The Last Words of President McKinley', 19 Sept. 1901, *Brooklyn Eagle*, 20 Sept. 1901, p. 14.

TINTNER, BENJAMIN, 'Rosh Hashanah Sermon', 15 Sept. 1939, *New York Times*, 16 Sept. 1939, p. 7.

TOWNSEND, JOHN, 'The Goodness of God to Israel, and also to Great Britain', 19 Oct. 1803 (London: Matthew, Byfield, & Hawkesworth, 1803).

TUCKER, JOEL W., 'God's Providence in War', 16 May 1862 (Fayetteville, NC: Presbyterian Office, 1862), <docsouth.unc.edu/tucker/tucker.html>, checked 9 Aug. 2006.

WASSERZUG, D., 'Sermon for the First Day of Shavu'ot', 19 May 1915, *Jewish Chronicle*, 28 May 1915, p. 16.

WEISS, JOHN, 'Northern Strengths and Weaknesses: An Address on Occasion of the National Fast', 30 Apr. 1863 (Boston: Walker Wise, 1863).

WELLBELOVED, CHARLES, 'A Sermon preached on . . . the day of national humiliation, to a Congregation of Protestant-Dissenters in St. Saviourgate, York', 19 Oct. 1803 (York: T. Wilson, 1803).

WENIG, MARGARET MOERS, 'God Is a Woman, and She Is Growing Older', 29 Sept. 1990, in E. Lee Hancock (ed.), *The Book of Women's Sermons* (New York: Riverhead Books, 1999), 255–61.

WISE, ISAAC MAYER, 'Funeral Address', 19 Apr. 1865, in Emanuel Hertz (ed.), *Abraham Lincoln: The Tribute of the Synagogue* (New York: Bloch, 1927), 92–9.

* —— 'The Fall of the Second French Empire', 9 Sept. 1870, *Israelite*, 16 Sept. 1870, p. 8.

WISE, STEPHEN S., 'Shall the Pulpit Be Free?', Jan. 1907, in *Free Synagogue Pulpit: Sermons and Addresses*, i (New York, Bloch, 1908), 27–48.

—— 'The Social Message of the Hebrew Prophets', Feb. 1910, in *Free Synagogue Pulpit*, ii (New York: Bloch, 1910), 25–42.

—— 'Must We Have a Larger Army and Navy?', 13 Dec. 1914, in *Free Synagogue Pulpit*, iii (New York: Bloch, 1915), 1–22.

—— 'The Case of Leo Frank: A Last Appeal', May 1915, in *Free Synagogue Pulpit*, iii. 79–96.

—— 'Peace-Preparedness versus War-Preparedness', undated [autumn 1916], in *Free Synagogue Pulpit*, iii. 176–80.

—— 'The World-War for Humanity', 8 Apr. 1917, in *Free Synagogue Pulpit*, iv (New York: Bloch, 1917), 101–20.

* —— 'Can We Win the War without Losing America?', 20 May 1917, in *Free Synagogue Pulpit*, iv. 121–36.

—— 'What Are We Fighting For?', May/June 1917, in *Free Synagogue Pulpit*, iv. 151–78.

WRIGHT, ALEXANDRA, 'After Judgement: Freedom', 17 Sept. 2001, *European Judaism* 35/1 (Spring 2002), 65–7.

* —— 'New York: 11th September 2001', 18 Sept. 2001, preacher's personal collection.

* WURZBURGER, WALTER, 'The Individual in the Crisis', 9 Oct. 1943, in Bernard L. Berzon (ed.), *Manual of Holiday and Occasional Sermons* (New York: Rabbinical Council Press, 1943), 61–70.

## Secondary Literature and Collections of Sermons

ABRAHAMS, ISRAEL, 'Artom's Sermons', in id., *By-Paths in Jewish Bookland* (Philadelphia: Jewish Publication Society, 1920), 297–302.

ABRAHAMS, ISRAEL, *Living Waters: Collection of Sermons, Addresses and Prayers* (Cape Town: Cape Town Hebrew Congregation, 1968).

ABRAMS, JEANNE, 'Remembering the *Maine*: The Jewish Attitude toward the Spanish–American War as Reflected in the *American Israelite*', *American Jewish History*, 76 (1987), 439–55.

ABRAMS, M. H. (ed.), *The Norton Anthology of English Literature*, 2 vols (New York: W. W. Norton, 1962).

ABRAMS, RAY H., *Preachers Present Arms: A Study of the War-Time Attitudes and Activities of the Churches and Clergy in the United States, 1914–1918* (Philadelphia: Round Table Press, 1933).

ABRAVANEL, ISAAC, *Perush al nevi'im rishonim* [Commentary on the Early Prophets] (Jerusalem: Torah Veda'at, 1956).

ADLER, CYRUS, *The Voice of America on Kishineff* (Philadelphia: Jewish Publication Society, 1904).

ADLER, HERMANN, *Anglo-Jewish Memories and Other Sermons* (London: George Routledge & Sons, 1909).

—— *Naftulei Elohim* [God's Struggles]: *A Course of Sermons on the Biblical Passages Adduced by Christian Theologians in Support of the Dogmas of their Faith* (London: Trübner & Co., 1869).

ALDERMAN, GEOFFREY, *The Jewish Community in British Politics* (Oxford: Clarendon Press, 1983).

—— *Modern British Jewry* (Oxford: Clarendon Press, 1992).

ALLISON, JIM, 'In God We Trust', <members.tripod.com/~candst/motto.htm>, checked 1 June 2006.

—— 'The NRA (National Reform Association) and the Christian Amendment', <members.tripod.com/~candst/nra.htm>, checked 1 June 2006.

ALTMANN, ALEXANDER, 'The New Style of Preaching in Nineteenth-Century German Jewry', in id. (ed.), *Studies in Nineteenth-Century Jewish Intellectual History* (Cambridge, Mass.: Harvard University Press, 1964), 65–116.

*The American Jewish Pulpit: A Collection of Sermons by the Most Eminent American Rabbis* (Cincinnati: Bloch & Co., 1881).

ANGEL, MARC D., 'Mendes, Henry Pereira', in *American National Biography*, 24 vols (New York: Oxford University Press, 1999), xv. 300–1.

—— 'Seixas, Gershom Mendes', in *American National Biography*, 24 vols (New York: Oxford University Press, 1999), xix. 9–10.

AN-SKY, S., *The Enemy at his Pleasure: A Journey through the Jewish Pale of Settlement during World War I*, ed. Joachim Neugroschel (New York: Henry Holt, 2003).

*Argentina, the Military Juntas and Human Rights: Report of the Trial of the Former Junta Members, 1985* (London: Amnesty International Publications, 1987).

ARZT, MAX, *Justice and Mercy: Commentary on the Liturgy of the New Year and Day of Atonement* (New York: Holt, Rinehart & Winston, 1963).

ATTIE, JEANIE, *Patriotic Toil: Northern Women and the American Civil War* (Ithaca, NY: Cornell University Press, 1998).

AUERBACH, JEFFREY A., *The Great Exhibition of 1851: A Nation on Display* (New Haven: Yale University Press, 1999).

AYER, I. WINSLOW, *The Great Northwestern Conspiracy* (Chicago: Rounds & James, 1865).

BABCOCK, LOUIS L., *The War of 1812 on the Niagara Frontier* (Buffalo, NY: Buffalo Historical Society, 1927).

BAGULEY, DAVID, *Napoleon III and his Regime: An Extravaganza* (Baton Rouge: Louisiana State University Press, 2000).

BANG, J. P., *Hurrah and Halleluyah: The Teachings of Germany's Poets, Prophets, Professors and Preachers* (New York: George H. Doran Co., 1917).

BARKER, E., H. W. C. DAVIS, C. R. L. FLETCHER, ARTHUR HASSALL, L. G. WICKHAM LEGG, and F. MORGAN, *Why We Are at War: Great Britain's Case*, 2nd rev. edn (Oxford: Clarendon Press, 1914).

BARNETT, ARTHUR, *The Western Synagogue through Two Centuries* (London: Vallentine Mitchell, 1961).

BARON, SALO W., 'The Revolution of 1848 and Jewish Scholarship', *Proceedings of the American Academy for Jewish Research*, 20 (1951), 83–100.

BAUMAN, MARK K., and BERKLEY KALIN (eds), *The Quiet Voices: Southern Rabbis and Black Civil Rights, 1880s to 1990s* (Tuscaloosa: University of Alabama Press, 1997).

BAUMEL, JUDITH TYDOR, and JACOB J. SCHACTER, 'The Ninety-three Bais Yaakov Girls of Cracow: History or Typology?', in Jacob J. Schacter (ed.), *Reverence, Righteousness, Rahmanut* (Northvale, NJ: J. Aronson, 1992), 93–130.

BEATTY, WILLIAM, *The Death of Lord Nelson* (London, 1807; repr. Birmingham: War Library, 1894).

BEIFELD, MARTIN P., 'The Americanization of Reform Judaism: Joseph Krauskopf—A Case Study', in Murray Friedman (ed.), *When Philadelphia Was the Capital of Jewish America* (Philadelphia: Balch Institute Press, 1993), 156–72.

BENDLEBURY, ALYSON, *Portraying 'The Jew' in First World War Britain* (London: Vallentine Mitchell, 2006).

BENJAMIN OF TUDELA, *The Itinerary of Benjamin of Tudela: Travels in the Middle Ages* (Malibu, Calif.: Joseph Simon, 1983).

BENNETT, GEOFFREY, *The Battle of Trafalgar* (London: B. T. Batsford, 1977).

—— *Nelson the Commander* (London: B. T. Batsford, 1972).

BERENDS, KURT, ' "Wholesome Reading Purifies and Elevates the Man": The Religious Military Press in the Confederacy', in Randall M. Miller, Harry S. South, and Charles Reagan Wilson (eds), *Religion and the American Civil War* (New York: Oxford University Press, 1998), 131–66.

BERGER, DORREN, *The Jewish Victorian: Genealogical Information from the Jewish Newspapers, 1871–1880* (Witney: Robert Boyd, 1999).

BERKOVITS, ELIEZER, *Between Yesterday and Tomorrow* (Oxford: East and West Library, 1945).

BERMAN, MYRON, *Richmond's Jewry, 1769–1976* (Charlottesville: University Press of Virginia, 1979).

BERMANT, CHAIM, *Lord Jakobovits: The Authorised Biography of the Chief Rabbi* (London: Weidenfeld & Nicolson, 1990).

BERNHARDI, FRIEDERICH VON, *Germany and the Next War* (New York: Charles A. Aron, 1912).

BERNSTEIN, IVER, *The New York City Draft Riots* (New York: Oxford University Press, 1990).

BERTON, PIERRE, *Flames across the Border: 1813–1814* (Toronto: McClelland & Stewart, 1981).

BIALIK, HAYIM NACHMAN, and YEHOSHUA HANA RAVNITZKY (eds), *The Book of Legends, Sefer Ha-Aggadah: Legends from the Talmud and Midrash* (New York: Schocken, 1992).

BILLINGTON, MARY FRANCES, *The Red Cross in War: Woman's Part in the Relief of Suffering* (London: Hodder & Stoughton, 1914).

BIRNBAUM, PIERRE, *Prier pour l'État: Les Juifs, l'alliance royale et la démocratie* (Paris: Calmann-Lévy, 2005).

BLEICH, JUDITH, 'Military Service: Ambivalence and Contradiction', in Joel B. Wolowelsky (ed.), *War, Peace and the Jewish Tradition* (New York: Yeshiva University Press, 2007), 415–76.

BLONDHEIM, MENACHEM, 'Cultural Instruments of Communication in Transition: From the Traditional Sermon to the Jewish Press' (Heb.), *Kesher*, 21 (1997), 63–79.

—— 'Divine Comedy: The Jewish Orthodox Sermon in America, 1881–1939', in Werner Sollors (ed.), *Multilingual America: Transnationalism, Ethnicity, and the Languages of American Literature* (New York: New York University Press, 1998), 191–214.

BLOOD, WILLIAM W., *Apostle of Reason: A Biography of Joseph Krauskopf* (Philadelphia: Dorrance & Co., 1973).

BLUMBERG, ARNOLD, *A Carefully Planned Accident: The Italian War of 1859* (Selinsgrove, Penn.: Susquehanna University Press, 1990).

BLUMBERG, JANICE ROTHSCHILD, 'Rabbi Alphabet Browne: The Atlanta Years', *Southern Jewish History*, 5 (2002), 1–67.

Bos, William, and Clyde Faries, 'The Social Gospel', in DeWitte Holland (ed.), *Preaching in American History: Selected Issues in the American Pulpit, 1630–1967* (Nashville: Abingdon Press, 1969), 223–38.

Bosco, Ronald A. (ed.), *The Puritan Sermon in America, 1630–1750*, 3 vols; i: *Sermons for Days of Fast, Prayer, and Humiliation, and Execution Sermons*; ii—iii, *Connecticut and Massachusetts Election Sermons* (Delmar, NY: Scholars' Facsimiles and Reprints, 1978).

Bosniak, Jacob, *Interpreting Jewish Life: Sermons and Addresses* (New York: Bloch, 1944).

Boyer, Paul, *When Time Shall Be No More: Prophecy Belief in Modern American Culture* (Cambridge, Mass.: Harvard University Press, 1992).

Brandes, Joseph, *Immigrants to Freedom: Jewish Communities in Rural New Jersey since 1882* (Philadelphia: University of Pennsylvania Press, 1971).

Braude, Benjamin, 'The Sons of Noah and the Construction of Ethnic and Geographical Identities in the Medieval and Early Modern Periods', *William and Mary Quarterly*, 54 (1997), 103–42.

Bright, John, *A History of Israel* (Philadelphia: Westminster Press, 1959).

Brown, Malcolm, *The Christmas Truce* (New York: Hippocrene Books, 1984).

Bury, J. H., *The Idea of Progress* (London: Macmillan, 1920).

Calderhead, William L., 'Philadelphia in Crisis: June–July, 1863', *Pennsylvania History*, 28 (1961), 142–55.

Callahan, Allen, 'Remembering Nehemiah: a Note on Biblical Theology', in Yvonne Chireau and Nathaniel Deutsch (eds), *Black Zion* (New York: Oxford University Press, 2000), 153–67.

Caplan, Kimmy, 'The Concerns of an Immigrant Rabbi: the Life and Sermons of Rabbi Moshe Shimon Sivitz', *Polin*, 11 (1998), 192–215.

—— 'The Life and Sermons of Rabbi Israel Herbert Levinthal', *American Jewish History*, 87 (1999), 1–27.

—— *Orthodoxy in the New World: Immigrant Rabbis and Preaching in America (1881–1924)* [Ortodoksiyah ba'olam heḥadash: rabanim vedarshanim ba'amerikah (1881–1924)] (Jerusalem: Merkaz Zalman Shazar, 2002).

Cassell, Curtis, 'David Woolf Marks: Father of Anglo-Jewish Reform', unpublished typescript, West London Synagogue of British Jews Archives.

Cesarani, David, 'An Alien Concept? The Continuity of Anti-Alienism in British Society before 1940', in David Cesarani and Tony Kushner (eds), *The Internment of Aliens in Britain* (London: Frank Cass, 1993), 25–52.

Channing, William Ellery, *Discourses, Reviews, and Miscellanies* (Boston: Gray & Bower, 1830).

—— *Discourses on War* (Boston: Ginn & Co., 1903).

CHATFIELD, CHARLES, *Pacifism in America, 1914–1941* (Knoxville: University of Tennessee Press, 1971).

CHESEBROUGH, DAVID B. (ed.), *'God Ordained this War': Sermons on the Sectional Conflict, 1830–1865* (Columbia: University of South Carolina Press, 1991).

CHURCHILL, WINSTON, *The Grand Alliance* (Boston: Houghton Mifflin, 1950).

CLAR, REVA, and WILLIAM M. KRAMER, 'The Girl Rabbi of the Golden West', *Western States Jewish History*, 18 (1986), 99–111, 223–36, 336–51.

CLIFFORD, JOHN G., *Citizen Soldiers: The Plattsburg Training Camp Movement, 1913–1920* (Lexington: University Press of Kentucky, 1972).

COHEN, BERNARD N., 'Early German Preaching in America', *Historia Judaica*, 15 (1953), 86–134.

COHEN, GERSON, 'Esau as Symbol in Early Medieval Thought', in id., *Studies in the Variety of Rabbinic Cultures* (Philadelphia: Jewish Publication Society, 1991), 243–69.

COHEN, JUDAH M., *Through the Sands of Time: A History of the Jewish Community of St Thomas, US Virgin Islands* (Hanover: University Press of New England, 2004).

COHEN, NAOMI, *Jews in Christian America: The Pursuit of Religious Equality* (New York: Oxford University Press, 1992).

COHEN, PHILIP, 'The Problem of Paganism and its Solution in the Theology of David Einhorn', in Leonard H. Ehrlich, Shmuel Bolozky, Robert A. Rothstein, Murray Schwartz, Jay R. Berkovitz, and James E. Young (eds), *Textures and Meanings: Thirty Years of Judaic Studies at the University of Massachusetts Amherst*, 311–20, <www-unix.oit.umass.edu/~accodev3/judaic/articles/22-D5-PCohen.pdf>, accessed 12 Dec. 2006.

COHEN, STUART, *English Zionists and British Jews* (Princeton: Princeton University Press, 1982).

COHON, SAMUEL S. (ed.) *A Living Faith* (Cincinnati: HUC Press, 1948).

*Collected Diplomatic Documents Relating to the Outbreak of the European War* (London: Harrison & Sons, 1915).

COOPER, SANDI E., *Patriotic Pacifism: Waging War in Europe, 1815–1914* (New York: Oxford University Press, 1991).

COPELAND, LEWIS, LAURENCE W. LAMM, and STEVEN J. McKENNA (eds), *The World's Greatest Speeches* (Mineola, NY: Dover Publishing, 1999).

CORRÉ, ALAN D., 'Sabato Morais and Social Justice in Philadelphia, 1858–1897', in id. (ed.), *The Quest for Social Justice*, ii (Milwaukee: Golda Meir Library, 1992), 19–35.

CORRY, JOHN H., *1898: Prelude to a Century* (New York: J. A. Corry, 1998).

COWETT, MARK, *Birmingham's Rabbi: Morris Newfield and Alabama, 1895–1940* (University: University of Alabama Press, 1986).

—— 'Rabbi Morris Newfield and the Social Gospel: Theology and Societal Reform in the South', *American Jewish Archives*, 34 (1982), 52–74.

CUNNINGHAM, MICHELE, *Mexico and the Foreign Policy of Napoleon III* (Basingstoke, NH: Palgrave, 2001).

CURRAN, THOMAS F., *Soldiers of Peace: Civil War Pacifism and the Post-War Radical Peace Movement* (New York: Fordham University Press, 2003).

DAVEY, ARTHUR, *The British Pro-Boers, 1877–1902* (Cape Town: Tafelberg, 1978).

DAVIDSON, DAVID, *Sabbath or Sunday?* (Cincinnati: Bloch, 1889).

DAVIDSON, EDWARD H., and WILLIAM J. SCHEICK, *Paine, Scripture, and Authority: The Age of Reason as Religious and Political Ideal* (Bethlehem, Pa.: Lehigh University Press, 1994).

DAVIS, RICHARD, *The English Rothschilds* (London: Collins, 1983).

DAWSON, WILLIAM HARBUTT, *Social Insurance in Germany, 1883–1911* (London: T. Fisher Unwin, 1912).

DIMENT, GALYA, and YURI SLEZKINE, *Between Heaven and Hell: The Myth of Siberia in Russian Culture* (New York: St Martin's Press, 1993).

DINABURG (DINUR), BEN-ZION, 'From the Archive of Peretz Smolenskin' (Heb.), *Kirjath Sepher*, 1 (1924–5), 77–84.

DINER, HASIA, *The Jews of the United States, 1654–2000* (Berkeley: University of California Press, 2004).

—— *A Time for Gathering: The Second Migration, 1820–1880* (Baltimore: Johns Hopkins University Press, 1992).

DINNERSTEIN, LEONARD, *Antisemitism in America* (New York: Oxford University Press, 1994).

DONNE, JOHN, *Donne's Sermons: Selected Passages*, ed. Logan Pearsall Smith (Oxford: Clarendon Press, 1964).

DREISZIGER, N. F., 'The Rise of a Bureaucracy for Multiculturalism: The Origins of the Nationalities Branch, 1939–1941', in Norman Hillmer, Bohdan Kordan, and Lubomyr Luciuk (eds), *On Guard for Thee: War, Ethnicity, and the Canadian State, 1939–1945* (Ottawa: Canadian Committee for the History of the Second World War, 1988), 1–29.

DREYFUSS, JACQUES HENRI, *Sermons de guerre* (Paris: Librairie Durlacher, 1921).

DUBNOW, SIMON, *History of the Jews in Russia and Poland*, 3 vols (Philadelphia: Jewish Publication Society, 1916–20).

DUSINBERRE, WILLIAM, *Civil War Issues in Philadelphia, 1856–1865* (Philadelphia: University of Pennsylvania Press, 1965).

ECHARD, WILLIAM E., *Napoleon III and the Concert of Europe* (Baton Rouge: Louisiana State University Press, 1983).

EDGERTON, ROBERT, *'Remember the Maine, To Hell With Spain'* (Lewiston, NY: Edwin Mellen, 2004).

EDWARDS, O. C., Jr, *A History of Preaching* (Nashville: Abingdon Press, 2004).

EINHORN, DAVID, *Ausgewählte Predigten und Reden*, ed. Kaufmann Kohler (New York: E. Steiger, 1880).

EISENDRATH, MAURICE N., *Can Faith Survive?* (New York: McGraw-Hill, 1964).

ELLIS, MARK, *Race, War and Surveillance: African Americans and the United States Government during World War I* (Bloomington: Indiana University Press, 2001).

ELON, AMOS, *The Israelis: Founders and Sons* (New York: Bantam Books, 1971).

—— *The Pity of It All: A History of Jews in Germany, 1743–1933* (New York: Metropolitan Books, 2002).

EMMANUEL, ISAAC, *History of the Jews in Netherlands Antilles*, 2 vols (Cincinnati: American Jewish Archives, 1970).

ENDELMAN, TODD M., *The Jews of Britain, 1656–2000* (Berkeley: University of California Press, 2002).

—— *The Jews of Georgian England, 1714–1830: Tradition and Change in a Liberal Society* (Philadelphia: Jewish Publication Society, 1979).

—— *Radical Assimilation in English Jewish History, 1656–1945* (Bloomington: Indiana University Press), 1990.

ERICSON, DAVID F., *The Debate over Slavery: Antislavery and Proslavery Liberalism in Antebellum America* (New York: New York University Press, 2000).

EVERETT, EDWARD, *Address of the Hon. Edward Everett, at the Consecration of the National Cemetery at Gettysburg* (Boston: Little Brown & Co., 1864).

EZEKIEL, HERBERT T., and GASTON LICHTENSTEIN, *The History of the Jews of Richmond from 1769 to 1917* (Richmond, Va: Herbert T. Ezekiel Publisher, 1917).

FARWELL, BYRON, *The Great Boer War* (London: A. Lane, 1977).

*Fast-Day Sermons, or The Pulpit on the State of the Country* (New York: Rudd & Carleton, 1861)

FELDMAN, ABRAHAM J., 'Rabbi Joseph Krauskopf: A Biographical Sketch', in *American Jewish Year Book 5685 (1924–25)* (Philadelphia: Jewish Publication Society, 1924), 420–47.

FELDMAN, DAVID, *Englishmen and Jews: Social Relations and Political Culture, 1840–1914* (New Haven: Yale University Press, 1994).

FINE, ISAAC, 'Baltimore Jews during the Civil War', *American Jewish Historical Quarterly*, 51 (1961–2), 67–96.

FINESTEIN, I., *Anglo-Jewry in Changing Times: Studies in Diversity, 1840–1914* (London: Vallentine Mitchell, 1999).

FINKELSTEIN, LUDWIK, 'History of the Rabbinical School of Warsaw from its Establishment in 1826 to its Closure in 1863', Ph.D. diss., Leo Baeck College, London, 2005.

FISCH, HAROLD, *The Zionist Revolution: A New Perspective* (New York: St Martin's Press, 1978).

FRANKEL, JONATHAN, *The Damascus Affair: 'Ritual Murder', Politics, and the Jews in 1840* (Cambridge: Cambridge University Press, 1997).

FREDERICKSON, GEORGE M., 'The Coming of the Lord', in Randall M. Miller, Harry S. South, and Charles Reagan Wilson (eds), *Religion and the Civil War* (New York: Oxford University Press, 1998), 110–30.

FREEHOF, SOLOMON B., and VIGDOR W. KAVALER (eds), *J. Leonard Levy: Prophetic Voice* (Pittsburgh: Rodef Shalom Congregation, 1970).

FREMANTLE, A. F., *England in the Nineteenth Century*, 2 vols (Millwood, NY: Kraus Reprint Co., 1978).

FREUDENTHAL, GAD, 'Ein symbolischer Anfang der Berliner Haskala: Veitel Ephraim, David Fränckel, Aron Gumpertz und die patriotische Feier in der Synagoge am 28. Dezember 1745', *Judaica*, 61 (2005), 193–251.

FRIEDENBERG, ROBERT, *'Hear O Israel': The History of American Jewish Preaching, 1654–1970* (Tuscaloosa: University of Alabama Press, 1989).

GAINER, BERNARD, *The Alien Invasion: The Origins of the Aliens Act of 1905* (New York: Crane, Russak, 1972).

GALLMAN, J. MATTHEW, *Mastering Wartime: A Social History of Philadelphia during the Civil War* (Cambridge: Cambridge University Press, 1990).

GARLICKI, ANDRZEJ, *Józef Piłsudski, 1867–1935* (Brookfield, Vt.: Ashgate, 1995).

GARRARD, JOHN A., *The English and Immigration: A Comparative Study of the Jewish Influx, 1880–1910* (New York: Oxford University Press, 1971).

GARTNER, LLOYD P., *The Jewish Immigrant in England 1870–1914* (London: Vallentine Mitchell, 2001).

GASTER, MOSES, *History of the Ancient Synagogue of the Spanish and Portuguese Jews: The Cathedral Synagogue of the Jews in England, Situate in Bevis Marks* (London: n.p., 1901).

GATRELL, VIC, *City of Laughter: Sex and Satire in Eighteenth-Century London* (London: Atlantic Books, 2006).

GAVSHON, ARTHUR, and DESMOND RICE, *The Sinking of the Belgrano* (London: Secker & Warburg, 1984).

GAZLEY, JOHN GEROW, *American Opinion of German Unification, 1848–1871* (New York: Columbia University Press, 1926).

GEIGER, ABRAHAM, *Abraham Geigers Nachgelassene Schriften*, ed. Ludwig Geiger, 5 vols (Berlin: Louis Gerschel, 1875–8).

GENDLER, EVERETT E., 'War and the Jewish Tradition', in Menachem Marc Kellner (ed.), *Contemporary Jewish Ethics* (New York: Sanhedrin Press, 1978), 189–210.

GHOSE, S. N., *Dante Gabriel Rossetti and Contemporary Criticism (1849–1882)* (Philadelphia: Richard West, 1977).

GIESBERG, JUDITH ANN, *Civil War Sisterhood: The US Sanitary Commission and Women's Politics in Transition* (Boston: Northeastern University Press, 2000).

GILBERT, MARTIN, *Auschwitz and the Allies* (London: Michael Joseph, 1981).

GILMAN, SANDER, *Jewish Self-Hatred: Anti-Semitism and the Hidden Languages of the Jews* (Baltimore: Johns Hopkins University Press, 1986).

GINZBERG, LOUIS, *The Legends of the Jews*, 7 vols (Philadelphia: Jewish Publication Society, 1913).

GITTELSOHN, ROLAND B., *Here Am I—Harnessed to Hope* (New York: Vantage Press, 1988).

—— 'A Jewish View of God' (Washington: B'nai B'rith Youth Organization, 1965).

GLADDEN, WASHINGTON, *The Great War: Six Sermons* (Columbus, Ohio: McClelland, 1915).

GLATZER, NAHUM N. (ed.), *The Passover Haggadah* (New York: Schocken, 1969).

GOLDENBERG, DAVID M., *The Curse of Ham: Race and Slavery in Early Judaism, Christianity, and Islam* (Princeton: Princeton University Press, 2003).

GOLDSCHMIDT-LEHMANN, RUTH P., 'Hermann Adler: A Bibliography of his Published Works', *Folklore Research Center Studies*, 5 (1975), 101–50.

GOLDSTEIN, ISRAEL, *A Century of Judaism in New York* (New York: Congregation B'nai Jeshurun, 1930).

GOLLANCZ, HERMANN, *Fifty Years After: Sermons and Addresses (Third Series)* (London: Humphrey Milford/Oxford University Press, 1924).

—— *Sermons and Addresses* (New York: Bloch, 1909).

—— *Sermons and Addresses: Second Series* (London: Chapman & Hall, 1916).

GORKY, MAXIM ANDREYEV, and FYODOR SOLOGUB (eds), *The Shield* (New York: Alfred A. Knopf, 1917).

GOSLING, FRANCIS G., *Before Freud: Neurasthenia and the American Medical Community, 1870–1910* (Urbana: University of Illinois Press, 1987).

GOTTHEIL, GUSTAV, *Moses versus Slavery: Being Two Discourses on the Slave Question* (Manchester: Heywood, 1861).

GRAETZ, HEINRICH, *History of the Jews*, 6 vols (Philadelphia: Jewish Publication Society, 1891).

GRANATSTEIN, J. L., *Canada's War: The Politics of the Mackenzie King Government, 1939–1945* (Toronto: University of Toronto Press, 1990).

—— *The Politics of Survival: The Conservative Party of Canada, 1939–1945* (Toronto: University of Toronto Press, 1967).

—— and J. M. HITSMAN, *Broken Promises: A History of Conscription in Canada* (Toronto: Oxford University Press, 1977).

GREEN, A. A., *Sermons*, ed. Henrietta Adler (London: Martin Hopkinson, 1935).

GREENBERG, GERSHON, 'The Significance of America in David Einhorn's Conception of History', *American Jewish Historical Quarterly*, 63/2 (1973), 160–84.

GREENE, MELISSA FAY, *The Temple Bombing* (Reading, Mass.: Addison-Wesley, 1996).

GREENSTEIN, HOWARD R., *Turning Point: Zionism and Reform Judaism* (Chico, Calif.: Scholars Press, 1981).

GROSS, AVI, *Struggling with Tradition: Reservations about Active Martyrdom in the Middle Ages* (Leiden: Brill, 2004).

GULLACE, NICOLETTA F., *'The Blood of our Sons': Men, Women, and the Renegotiation of British Citizenship during the Great War* (New York: Palgrave Macmillan, 2002).

GUTHEIM, JAMES KOPPEL, *The Temple Pulpit* (New York: Jewish Times, 1872).

GUTTMANN, ALEXANDER, *The Struggle over Reform in Rabbinic Literature* (New York: World Union for Progressive Judaism, 1977).

HAGY, JAMES WILLIAM, *This Happy Land: The Jews of Colonial and Antebellum Charleston* (Tuscaloosa: University of Alabama Press, 1993).

HAKOHEN, MORDECAI BEN HILLEL, *Olami* [My World], 5 vols (Jerusalem: Defus Hapo'alim, 1926–9).

HALSTED, MURAT, *Our Country in War and Relations with All Nations: A History of War Times, and American Heroes on Land and Sea* (n.p.: United Subscription Book Publishers of America, 1898).

—— *The Story of Cuba* (Akron: Werner, 1898).

HAMILTON, NIGEL, *The Full Monty*, vol. i (London: Penguin Press, 2001).

HANDY, ROBERT T. (ed.), *The Social Gospel in America, 1870–1920* (New York: Oxford University Press, 1966).

HANHA, H. J., 'Religion and Nationality in the Mid-Victorian Army', in M. R. D. Foot (ed.), *War and Society* (New York: Harper & Row, 1973), 159–81.

HARRIS, ROBERT, *GOTCHA! The Media, the Government and the Falklands Crisis* (London: Faber & Faber, 1983).

HARRISON, LEON, *The Religion of a Modern Liberal*, ed. Abram Sachar (New York: Bloch, 1931).

HARTILL, PERCY, 'Christians in War-Time' (Lichfield: Lomax's Successors, 1940).

HASTINGS, MAX, and SIMON JENKINS, *The Battle for the Falklands* (New York: Norton, 1983).

HEINEMANN, JOSEPH, *Aggadah and its Development* [Agadot vetoledoteihen] (Jerusalem: Keter, 1974).

—— and JAKOB PETUCHOWSKI, *Literature of the Synagogue* (New York: Behrman House, 1975).

HELLER, JAMES G., *Isaac M. Wise: His Life, Work, and Thought* (New York: UAHC, 1965).

HENDRICKSON, KENNETH E., *Making Saints: Religion and the Public Image of the British Army, 1809–1885* (Madison, NJ: Fairleigh Dickinson University Press, 1998).

HERTZ, EMANUEL (ed.), *Abraham Lincoln: The Tribute of the Synagogue* (New York: Bloch, 1927).

HERTZ, JOSEPH H., *Early and Late: Addresses, Messages, and Papers* (Hindhead, Surrey: Soncino Press, 1943).

—— *The New Paths: Whither Do They Lead? Three Sermons by the Chief Rabbi* (London: Oxford University Press, 1926).

—— *Sermons, Addresses and Studies*, 3 vols (London: Soncino Press, 1938).

—— (ed.), *The Authorised Daily Prayer Book*, rev. edn (New York: Bloch, 1963).

—— (ed.), *The Pentateuch and Haftorahs*, 2nd edn (London: Soncino Press, 1994).

HERZOG, DAVID, *Kriegspredigten* (Frankfurt am Main: J. Kauffmann, 1915).

HIBBERT, CHRISTOPHER, *The Great Mutiny: India 1857* (New York: Viking, 1978).

HIRSCH, DAVID EINHORN, 'The Biography of Rabbi Emil G. Hirsch', in *The Jewish Preacher: Rabbi Emil G. Hirsch* (Naples, Fla.: Collage Books, 2003), 409–512.

HOBHOUSE, HERMIONE, *The Crystal Palace and the Great Exhibition: Art, Science, and Productive Industry* (London: Athlone Press, 2002).

HOLLAND, DeWITTE (ed.), *Preaching in American History: Selected Issues in the American Pulpit, 1630–1967* (Nashville: Abingdon Press, 1969).

—— (ed.), *Sermons in American History: Selected Issues in the American Pulpit, 1630–1967* (Nashville: Abingdon Press, 1971).

HOOVER, ARLIE J., *God, Britain, and Hitler in World War II: The View of the British Clergy, 1939–1945* (Westport, Conn.: Praeger, 1999).

—— *God, Germany, and Britain in the Great War: A Study in Clerical Nationalism* (New York: Praeger, 1989).

—— *The Gospel of Nationalism: German Patriotic Preaching from Napoleon to Versailles* (Stuttgart: Franz Steiner, 1986).

HOWARTH, DAVID, *Trafalgar: The Nelson Touch* (London: Collins, 1969).

HUBERBAND, SHIMON, *Kiddush Hashem: Jewish Religious and Cultural Life during the Holocaust* (New York: Yeshiva University Press, 1987).

HÜHNER, LEON, 'Jews in the War of 1812', *Publications of the American Jewish Historical Society*, 26 (1918), 184–5.

—— 'The Patriot Jewish Minister of the American Revolution', *Jewish Comment*, 10 Jan. 1902, pp. 1–5.

HYAMSON, ALBERT M., *The Sephardim of England: A History of the Spanish and Portuguese Jewish Community, 1492–1951* (London: Methuen, 1951).

HYDER, CLYDE KENNETH (ed.), *Swinburne Replies* (Syracuse: Syracuse University Press, 1966).

IDZERDA, STANLEY J., *Lafayette: Hero of Two Worlds* (Hanover, NH: University Press of New England, 1989).

INGERSOLL, ROBERT G., 'Spain and the Spaniard', in *The Works of Robert G. Ingersoll*, 12 vols (New York: Ingersoll League, 1929), xii. 267–72; <www.infidels.org/library/historical/robert_ingersoll/spain_and_spaniard.html>.

ISSERMAN, FERDINAND M., 'Sentenced to Death: The Jews in Nazi Germany' (St Louis: The Modern View Publishing Co., 1933).

JACOB, ALEX M., 'Aaron Levy Green, 1821–1883', *Transactions of the Jewish Historical Society of England*, 25 (1977), 87–106.

JACOB, WALTER, ' "Prophetic Judaism": The History of a Term', *Journal of Reform Judaism*, 26 (1979), 33–46.

JACOBSON, MOSES, *Reden über des Staates Führer, Dinge und Fragen (Bischlomah schel malkhuth)* (Dresden: Wilhelm Jacobsohn, 1901).

JAHER, FREDERIC COPLE, *A Scapegoat in the New Wilderness: The Origins and Rise of Anti-Semitism in America* (Cambridge, Mass.: Harvard University Press, 1994).

JAKOBOVITS, IMMANUEL, *The Attitude to Zionism of Britain's Chief Rabbis as Reflected in their Writings* (London: Jewish Historical Society of England, 1982).

—— *'If Only My People . . .': Zionism in my Life* (London: Weidenfeld & Nicolson, 1984).

—— *The Timely and the Timeless: Jews, Judaism and Society in a Storm-Tossed Decade* (London: Vallentine Mitchell, 1977).

*The Jewish Pulpit: Annual Volume* (London: *Jewish Chronicle*, 1886).

*The Jews in the Eastern War Zone* (New York: American Jewish Committee, 1916).

JICK, LEON, *The Americanization of the Synagogue, 1820–1870* (Hanover, NH: University Press of New England for Brandeis University Press, 1976).

JONAS, MANFRED, *Isolationism in America, 1935–1945* (Ithaca, NY: Cornell University Press, 1966).

JONES, HOWARD, *Crucible of Power: A History of American Foreign Relations to 1913* (Wilmington, Del.: SR Books, 2002).

JOSEPH, MORRIS, *Judaism as Creed and Life* (London: Macmillan, 1903).

—— *The Message of Judaism* (London: Routledge, 1907).

—— *The Spirit of Judaism: Sermons Preached Chiefly at the West London Synagogue* (London: Routledge, 1930).

*Judaism and World Peace: Focus Viet Nam* (New York: Synagogue Council of America, 1966).

KAGANOFF, NATHAN M., 'The Traditional Jewish Sermon in the United States from its Beginnings to the First World War', Ph.D. diss., American University, Washington, DC, 1961.

KAHN, ZADOC, *Sermons et allocutions: Première série* (Paris: Joseph Baer, 1875).

KARSKI, JAN, *The Great Powers and Poland, 1919–1935* (Lanham, Md.: University Press of America, 1985).

KATZ, DAVID S., *The Jews in the History of England, 1485–1850* (Oxford: Clarendon Press, 1994).

KELLENBACH, KATERINA VON, ' "God Does Not Oppress Any Human Being": The Life and Thought of Rabbi Regina Jonas', in *Leo Baeck Institute Yearbook*, 39 (1994), 213–25.

KELLNER, ABRAHAM A. (ed.), *Sunset at Mid-Day: A Tribute to the Late John Fitzgerald Kennedy* (New York: K'das Publishing Co., 1994).

KENNAN, GEORGE, *Siberia and the Exile System* (London: Osgood, 1891; repr. New York: Praeger, 1970).

KENNEDY, DAVID M., *Over Here: The First World War and American Society* (New York: Oxford University Press, 1980).

KERSHEN, ANNE J., and JONATHAN A. ROMAIN, *Tradition and Change: A History of Reform Judaism in Britain, 1840–1995* (London: Vallentine Mitchell, 1995).

KERTZER, DAVID, *The Kidnapping of Edgardo Mortara* (New York: Vintage, 1998).

—— *Prisoner of the Vatican: The Popes' Secret Plot to Capture Rome from the New Italian State* (Boston: Houghton Mifflin, 2004).

KESSNER, THOMAS, 'Gershom Mendes Seixas: His Religious "Calling", Outlook and Competence', *American Jewish Historical Quarterly*, 58 (1969), 445–71.

KIRON, ARTHUR, ' "Dust and Ashes": The Funeral and Forgetting of Sabato Morais', *American Jewish History*, 84/3 (1996), 155–88.

—— 'Golden Ages, Promised Lands: The Victorian Rabbinic Humanism of Sabato Morais', Ph.D. diss., Columbia University, New York, 1999.

—— 'Livornese Traces in American Jewish History: Sabato Morais and Elia Benamosegh', in *Atti del convegno internazionale di studi nel centenario della morte di Elia Benamozegh* (Milan: De Pas Editrice, 2002), 45–67.

KLEMENT, FRANK L., *The Limits of Dissent: Clement L. Vallandigham and the Civil War* (New York: Fordham University Press, 1998).

—— *Lincoln's Critics: The Copperheads of the North* (Shippensburg, Pa.: White Mane, 1999).

KOBER, ADOLF, 'Jewish Preaching and Preachers', *Historica Judaica*, 7 (1945), 103–34.

KOHLER, KAUFMANN (ed.), *David Einhorn Memorial Volume* (New York: Bloch, 1911).

KOHLER, MAX J., 'Phases in the History of Religious Liberty in America with Particular Reference to the Jews, II', *Publications of the American Jewish Historical Society*, 13 (1905), 7–36.

KORN, BERTRAM, *American Jewry and the Civil War* (Philadelphia: Jewish Publication Society, 2001).

—— 'Isaac Mayer Wise on the Civil War', *Hebrew Union College Annual*, 20 (1947), 635–58.

KORN, BERTRAM, 'Jewish Welfare Activities for the Military in the Spanish-American War', in id., *Eventful Years and Experiences: Studies in Nineteenth-Century American Jewish History* (Cincinnati: American Jewish Archives, 1954), 214–37.

KRAUSKOPF, JOSEPH, *A Rabbi's Impressions of the Oberammergau Passion Play* (Philadelphia: Raynor, 1901).

KRAUT, BENNY, 'Judaism Triumphant: Isaac Mayer Wise on Unitarianism and Liberal Christianity', *Association for Jewish Studies Review*, 7–8 (1982–3), 179–230.

KUZMACK, LINDA, *Woman's Cause: The Jewish Woman's Movement in England and the United States, 1881–1933* (Columbus: Ohio State University Press, 1990).

LACHOFF, IRWIN, 'Rabbi Bernard Illowy: Counter Reformer', *Southern Jewish History*, 5 (2002), 43–67.

LAFOURCADE, GEORGES, *Swinburne: A Literary Biography* (New York: William Morris, 1932).

LAITY, PAUL, *The British Peace Movement, 1870–1914* (Oxford: Clarendon Press, 2001).

LASKI, HAROLD, *Where Do We Go From Here?* (New York: Viking, 1940).

LAWRENCE, WILLIAM B., *Sundays in New York: Pulpit Theology at the Crest of the Protestant Mainstream, 1930–1955* (Lanham, Md.: Scarecrow Press, 1996).

LE MAY, G. H. L., *British Supremacy in South Africa, 1899–1907* (Oxford: Clarendon Press, 1965).

LEACH, JACK FRANKLIN, *Conscription in the United States: Historical Background* (Rutland, Vt.: Charles E. Tuttle, 1952).

LEE, KUAN YEW, *From Third World to First: The Singapore Story, 1965–2000* (New York: HarperCollins, 2000).

LEESER, ISAAC, 'The Demands of the Times', *Occident*, Oct. 1844, <www.jewish-history.com/Occident/volume2/oct1844/demands.html>, accessed 5 Aug. 2006.

—— *Discourses on the Jewish Religion*, 10 vols (Philadelphia: Sherman, 1866–8).

LEVINE, EPHRAIM, 'Memoir', in Isidore Epstein (ed.), *Joseph Herman Hertz, 1872–1946: In Memoriam* (London: Soncino Press, 1947), 1–32.

LEVINE, HILLEL, ' "Should Napoleon Be Victorious": Politics and Spirituality in Early Modern Jewish Messianism', in Rachel Elior (ed.), *The Sabbatian Movement and its Aftermath*, 2 vols (Jerusalem: Hebrew University, 2001), ii. 5–83.

LEVINTHAL, ISRAEL H., *The Message of Israel: Sermons, Addresses, Memoirs* (New York: Lex Printing Co., 1973).

—— *A New World Is Born: Sermons and Addresses* (New York: Funk & Wagnalls, 1943).

LINCOLN, ABRAHAM, *The Collected Works of Abraham Lincoln*, ed. Roy P. Basler, 9 vols (New Brunswick: Rutgers University Press, 1953–5).

LINDBERGH, CHARLES A., 'Appeal for Isolation: Let Us Look to Our Own Defense', *Vital Speeches of the Day*, 5 (1 Oct. 1939), 751–2.

LINDNER, ERIK, *Patriotismus deutscher Juden von der napoleonische Ära bis zum Kaiserreich* (Frankfurt am Main: Peter Lang, 1997).

LITMAN, SIMON, *Ray Frank Litman: A Memoir* (New York: American Jewish Historical Association, 1957).

*Living Words: Best High Holy Day Sermons, 5759, 5760, 5761, 5762* (New York: Sh'ma, 1999–2002).

LONGMATE, NORMAN, *How We Lived Then* (London: Hutchinson, 1971).

LOOKSTEIN, JOSEPH, *The Sources of Courage: War Time Sermons* (New York: Bloch, 1943).

LOVEGROVE, DERYCK, 'English Dissent and the European Conflict', in W. J. Sheils (ed.), *The Church and War* (Oxford: Blackwell, 1983), 263–76.

LOW, DAVID, *Low on the War: A Cartoon Commentary of the Years 1939–41* (New York: Simon & Schuster, 1941).

—— *Years of Wrath: A Cartoon History, 1931–1945* (New York: Simon & Schuster, 1946).

LOWENTHAL, ABRAHAM, *The Dominican Intervention* (Cambridge, Mass.: Harvard University Press, 1972).

LOWRY, BULLITT, *Armistice 1918* (Kent, Ohio: Kent State University Press, 1996).

LUEBKE, F. C., *Bonds of Loyalty: German-Americans and World War I* (DeKalb: Northern Illinois University Press, 1974).

MCALLISTER, DAVID, *The National Reform Movement: Its History and Principles. A Manual of Christian Civil Government* (Allegheny: Christian Statesman Co., 1898).

MCCLURE, S. S., *Obstacles to Peace* (Boston: Houghton Mifflin, 1917).

MCPHERSON, JAMES, *Ordeal by Fire: The Civil War and Reconstruction*, 3rd edn (Boston: McGraw-Hill, 2001).

MAGONET, JONATHAN, 'A Survey of New Year Sermons', *European Judaism*, 35/1 (Spring 2002), 4–29.

MAHLER, RAPHAEL, 'American Jewry and the Idea of Return to Zion in the Period of the American Revolution' (Heb.), *Zion*, 15 (1950), 106–34.

MALONE, BOBBIE, *Rabbi Max Heller: Reformer, Zionist, Southerner, 1860–1929* (Tuscaloosa: University of Alabama Press, 1997).

MAN, ALBON P. Jr., 'The Church and the New York Draft Riots of 1863', *Records of the American Catholic Historical Society of Philadelphia*, 62/1 (Mar. 1951), 33–50.

MANN, THOMAS, 'This Peace' (New York: Knopf, 1938); repr. in id., *Order of the Day: Political Essays and Speeches of Two Decades* (New York: Knopf, 1942), 167–85.

MARCUS, JACOB RADER, *The Colonial American Jew*, 2 vols (Detroit: Wayne State University Press, 1970).

—— 'The Handsome Young Priest in the Black Gown', *Hebrew Union College Annual*, 40–1 (1969–70), 409–67.

MARKOVITZ, EUGENE, 'Henry Pereira Mendes: Architect of the Union of Orthodox Jewish Congregations of America', *American Jewish Historical Quarterly*, 55 (1966), 364–84.

—— 'Henry Pereira Mendes: Builder of Traditional Judaism in America', Ph.D. diss., Revel Graduate School of Yeshiva University, New York, 1961.

MARKS, DAVID WOOLF, *Lectures and Sermons Preached on Various Occasions at the West London Synagogue of British Jews* (London: The Synagogue, 1884).

—— *Sermons Preached on Various Occasions at the West London Synagogue of British Jews*, i (London: R. Groombridge & Sons, 1851).

—— *Sermons Preached on Various Occasions at the West London Synagogue of British Jews*, ii (London: Trübner & Co., 1885).

—— *Torah Or, 'The Law Is Light': A Course of Four Lectures on the Sufficiency of the Law of Moses as the Guide of Israel* (London: Wertheimer, 1854).

MARRUS, MICHAEL, *The Politics of Assimilation: The French Jewish Community at the Time of the Dreyfus Affair* (Oxford: Clarendon Press, 1971).

MASLIANSKY, ZEVI HIRSCH, *Sermons*, ed. Abraham J. Feldman (New York: Hebrew Publishing Co., 1926).

MAURICE, FREDERICK, *History of the War in South Africa, 1899–1902* (London: Hurst & Blackett, 1906–7).

MAY, ERNEST R., *Imperial Democracy: The Emergence of America as a Great Power* (Chicago: Imprint Publications, 1991).

MAYBAUM, IGNAZ, *Man and Catastrophe: Sermons Preached at the Refugees' Services of the United Synagogue, London* (London: Allenson & Co., 1941).

MAZABOW, GERALD, *To Reach for the Moon: The South African Rabbinate of Rabbi Dr L. I. Rabinowitz* (Johannesburg: privately pub., 1999).

MAZEH, JACOB, *Zikhronot* [Memoirs], 4 vols (Tel Aviv: Yalkut, 1936).

MEDOFF, RAPHAEL, *Militant Zionism in America: The Rise and Impact of the Jabotinsky Movement in the United States, 1926–1948* (Tuscaloosa: University of Alabama Press, 2002).

MEIR SIMHAH HAKOHEN OF DVINSK, *Meshekh ḥokhmah*, 2 vols (Jerusalem(?): n.p., 2002).

MENDES, ABRAHAM P., *Sermons* (London: John Chapman, 1855).

MENDES-FLOHR, PAUL, 'The *Kriegserlebnis* and Jewish Consciousness', in Wolfgang Benz, Arnold Paucker, and Peter Pulzer (eds), *Jews in the Weimar Republic* (Tübingen: Mohr Siebeck, 1998), 225–37.

—— and YEHUDA REINHARZ, *The Jew in the Modern World*, 2nd edn (Oxford: Oxford University Press, 1995).

METCALF, THOMAS R., *The Aftermath of Revolt: India, 1857–1870* (Princeton: Princeton University Press, 1964).

MEVORAKH, BARUKH (ed.), *Napoleon and his Era* [Napoleon utekufato] (Jerusalem: Mosad Bialik, 1968).

MEYER, MICHAEL A., 'Eisendrath, Maurice N.', in *American National Biography*, 24 vols (New York: Oxford University Press, 1999), vii. 371–2.

—— ' "How Awesome Is This Place!": The Reconceptualization of the Synagogue in Nineteenth-Century Germany', in id., *Judaism within Modernity: Essays on Jewish History and Religion* (Detroit: Wayne State University Press, 2001), 223–38.

—— *Response to Modernity: A History of the Reform Movement in Judaism* (New York: Oxford University Press, 1988).

MIELZINER, ELLA, *Moses Mielziner, 1829–1903: A Biography with a Bibliography of his Writings* (New York: n.p., 1931).

MILLGRAM, ABRAHAM, *Jewish Worship* (Philadelphia: Jewish Publication Society, 1971).

MINDEL, NISSAN, *Rabbi Schneur Zalman* (Brooklyn: Kehot Publication Society, 1969).

*Minutes of the Common Council of the City of New York, 1784–1831*, 19 vols (New York: City of New York, 1917).

MONTAGU, LILY, *Sermons, Addresses, Letters, Prayers*, ed. Ellen M. Umansky (New York: E. Mellen Press, 1985).

MOORE, DEBORAH DASH, *GI Jews: How World War II Changed a Generation* (Cambridge, Mass.: Belknap Press, 2002).

MORAIS, HENRY SAMUEL, *Eminent Israelites of the Nineteenth Century* (Philadelphia: E. Stern, 1880).

—— *The Jews of Philadelphia: The History from the Earliest Settlements to the Present Time* (Philadelphia: Levytype, 1894).

MORRIS, R. J., *Cholera 1832: The Social Response to an Epidemic* (London: Croom Helm, 1976).

MOSES, ISAAC S., 'On the Height: Five Sermons delivered on New Year's Eve and Morning, September 21st and 22nd; on the Eve, Morning, and Evening of the Day of Atonement, October 1st and 2nd, 1892' (Chicago: Chas. H. Kerr & Co., 1892).

MOSSE, GEORGE, *Toward the Final Solution: A History of European Racism* (Madison: University of Wisconsin Press, 1985).

MOTLEY, JOHN LOTHROP, *The Rise of the Dutch Republic: A History*, 3 vols (New York: Harper, 1858).

NADELL, PAMELA, 'Morais, Sabato', in *American National Biography*, 24 vols (New York: Oxford University Press, 1999), xv. 794–5.

—— *Women Who Would Be Rabbis: A History of Women's Ordination, 1889–1985* (Boston: Beacon Press, 1998).

NELSON, DANIEL, *Unemployment Insurance: The American Experience, 1915–1935* (Madison: University of Wisconsin Press, 1969).

NEVINS, ALLAN, *The War for the Union*, 4 vols (New York: Charles Scribner's Sons, 1959).

NISSENBAUM, ISAAC, *Festive Occasions: Selected Sermons* [Mo'adim: derashot nivḥarim leḥagim ulemo'adim], ed. Isarel Shapira (Jerusalem: Reuven Mass, 1980).

NOAKES, LUCY, *War and the British: Gender, Memory and National Identity* (London: I. B. Tauris, 1998).

NOLL, MARK A., 'The Bible and Slavery', in Randall M. Miller, Harry S. South, and Charles Reagan Wilson (eds), *Religion and the American Civil War* (New York: Oxford University Press, 1998), 43–73.

NOVAK, DAVID, *The Image of the Non-Jew in Judaism: An Historical and Constructive Study of the Noahide Laws* (Lampeter, Wales: E. Mellen Press, 1983).

O'CONNELL, ROBERT, *Of Arms and Men: A History of War, Weapons and Aggression* (New York: Oxford University Press, 1989).

OLITZKY, KERRY M., 'The Sunday-Sabbath Movement in American Reform Judaism: Strategy or Evolution?', *American Jewish Archives*, 34 (1982), 75–88.

—— 'Sundays at Chicago Sinai Congregation: Paradigm for a Movement', *American Jewish History*, 74 (1985), 356–68.

PAINE, THOMAS, *The Age of Reason* (Secaucus, NJ: Citadel Press, 1974; 1st pub. 1794–5).

PAKENHAM, THOMAS, *The Boer War* (New York: Random House, 1994).

PANAYI, PANIKOS, *The Enemy in our Midst: Germans in Britain during the First World War* (Providence, RI: Berg, 1991).

PARKES, JAMES WILLIAM, 'Jews in Britain' (London: Council of Christians and Jews, 1943).

PATAI, RAPHAEL, *The Jews of Hungary: History, Culture, Psychology* (Detroit: Wayne State University Press, 1966).

PAYNE, STANLEY G., *A History of Fascism, 1914–1945* (Madison: University of Wisconsin Press, 1995).

PÉREZ, LOUIS A., Jr, *Intervention, Revolution, and Politics in Cuba, 1913–1921* (Pittsburgh: University of Pittsburgh Press, 1978).

*Pesikta Rabbati: Discourses for Feasts, Fasts, and Special Sabbaths*, trans. William G. Braude, 2 vols (New Haven: Yale University Press, 1968).

PHILIPPSON, LUDWIG, *Die Rhetorik und jüdische Homiletik* (Leipzig: Th. Grieben, 1890).

PHILIPSON, DAVID, *The Reform Movement in Judaism* (New York: Macmillan, 1931).

PHILLIPS, N. TAYLOR, 'Rev. Gershom Mendez Seixas', in *American Jewish Year Book, 5665* (1904–5), 40–51.

PHILLIPS, OLGA SOMECH, and HYMAN A. SIMONS, *The History of the Bayswater Synagogue: 1863–1963* (London: Harmac Press, 1963).

PICCIOTTO, JAMES, *Sketches of Anglo-Jewish History*, rev. edn (London: Soncino Press, 1956; 1st pub. 1875).

PIECHOWSKI, PAUL, *Die Kriegspredigt von 1870/71* (Leipzig: Scholl, 1916).

PIEKARZ, MENDEL, *Ideological Trends of Hasidism in Poland during the Interwar Period and the Holocaust* [Ḥasidut polin: megamot ra'ayoniyot bein shetei hamilḥamot uvigezerot 700–705 ('Hasho'ah')] (Jerusalem: Mosad Bialik, 1990).

PIKE, G. HOLDEN, *The Life and Work of Charles Hadden Spurgeon*, new edn, 2 vols (Edinburgh: Banner of Truth Trust, 1991).

PLAUT, W. GUNTHER, *The Growth of Reform Judaism* (New York: World Union for Progressive Judaism, 1965).

—— *The Rise of Reform Judaism* (New York: World Union for Progressive Judaism, 1964).

POCOCK, TOM, *The Terror before Trafalgar: Nelson, Napoleon and the Secret War* (New York: W. W. Norton, 2002).

POLISH, DAVID, *Abraham's Gamble: Selected Sermons for Our Times* (Evanston, Ill.: n.p., 1988).

—— *Renew our Days: The Zionist Issue in Reform Judaism* (Jerusalem: World Zionist Organization, 1976).

POOL, DAVID DE SOLA, 'Gershom Mendes Seixas' Letters, 1813–1815, to his Daughter Sarah (Seixas) Kursheedt and Son-in-Law Israel Baer Kursheedt', *American Jewish Historical Society*, 35 (1939), 189–205.

—— *Portraits Etched in Stone: Early Jewish Settlers, 1682–1831* (New York: Columbia University Press, 1952).

—— and POOL, TAMAR DE SOLA, *An Old Faith in the New World: Portrait of Shearith Israel, 1654–1954* (New York: Columbia University Press, 1955).

POTTER, BERNARD, *The Refugee Question in Mid-Victorian Politics* (Cambridge: Cambridge University Press, 1979).

PROCTER, BEN, *William Randolph Hearst: The Early Years, 1863–1910* (New York: Oxford University Press, 1998).

RABINOWITZ, LOUIS I., *Light and Salvation: Sermons for the High Holy Days* (New York: Bloch, 1965).

—— *Out of the Depths: Sermons for Sabbaths and Festivals* (Johannesburg: Eagle Press, 1951).

—— *Sparks from the Anvil: Sermons for Sabbaths, Holy Days and Festivals* (New York: Bloch, 1955).

RAWLS, WALTER H., *Wake Up America: World War I and the American Poster* (New York: Abbeville Press, 1988).

RAYMOND, DORA NEILL, *British Policy and Opinion during the Franco-Prussian War* (New York: Columbia University Press, 1921).

RICHMOND, MARY E., 'To the Volunteers of 1915', in *The Long View: Papers and Addresses by Mary E. Richmond* (New York: Russell Sage Foundation, 1930).

ROCKAWAY, ROBERT A., *The Jews of Detroit* (Detroit: Wayne University Press, 1986).

ROOSEVELT, F. D., *Rendezvous with Destiny: Addresses and Opinions of Franklin Delano Roosevelt*, ed. J. B. S. Hardman (New York: Dryden Press, 1944).

ROSE, PAUL LAWRENCE, *German Question, Jewish Question* (Princeton: Princeton University Press, 1990).

ROSEN, PHILIP, 'Dr. Solomon Solis-Cohen and the Philadelphia Group', in Murray Friedman (ed.), *When Philadelphia Was the Capital of Jewish America* (Philadelphia: Balch Institute Press, 1993), 106–25.

—— 'Orthodox Institution Builder: Rabbi Bernard Lewis Levinthal', in Murray Friedman (ed.), *When Philadelphia Was the Capital of Jewish America* (Philadelphia: Balch Institute Press, 1993), 126–44.

ROSEN, ROBERT N., *The Jewish Confederates* (Columbia: University of South Carolina Press, 2000).

ROSENBAUM, RON, *Explaining Hitler: The Search for the Origins of his Evil* (New York: Random House, 1998).

ROTH, CECIL, *Anglo-Jewish Letters, 1158–1917* (London: Soncino Press, 1938).

—— *Bayswater Synagogue, 1863–1938: Origin and History* (London: United Synagogue, 1939).

—— *The Great Synagogue, London, 1690–1940* (London: E. Goldston, 1950).

—— *The Jews in the Renaissance* (Philadelphia: Jewish Publication Society, 1959).

—— *Magna Bibliotheca Anglo-Judaica: A Bibliographical Guide to Anglo-Jewish History* (London: Jewish Historical Society of England, 1937).

RUDERMAN, DAVID, *Jewish Enlightenment in an English Key: Anglo-Jewry's Construction of Modern Jewish Thought* (Princeton: Princeton University Press, 2000).

RUDIN, JACOB, *Very Truly Yours: A Creative Harvest of Forty Years in the Pulpit* (New York: Bloch, 1971).

SACHS, MICHAEL, *Predigten: aus dessen schriftlichem Nachlass herausgegeben*, ed. David Rosin (Berlin: Goeschel, 1866).

SAFIRE, WILLIAM, *Lend Me Your Ears: Great Speeches in History* (New York: W. W. Norton, 1992).

SALOMON, GOTTHOLD, *Twelve Sermons Delivered in the New Temple of the Israelites at Hamburgh*, trans. Anna Maria Goldsmid (London: John Murray, 1839).

SALOMON, H. P., 'Joseph Jesurun Pinto (1729–1782), a Dutch Hazan in Colonial New York', *Studia Rosenthaliana*, 13 (1979), 18–29.

SANDMEYER, ELMER, *The Anti-Chinese Movement in California* (Urbana: University of Illinois Press, 1939).

SANDOZ, ELLIS (ed.), *Political Sermons of the American Founding Era*, 2 vols (Indianapolis: Liberty Fund, 1998).

SAPERSTEIN, HAROLD I., *Witness from the Pulpit: Topical Sermons, 1933–1980* (Lanham, Md.: Lexington Books, 2000).

SAPERSTEIN, MARC, *Decoding the Rabbis: A Thirteenth-Century Commentary on the Aggadah* (Cambridge, Mass.: Harvard University Press, 1980).

—— *Exile in Amsterdam: Saul Levi Morteira's Sermons to a Congregation of 'New Jews'* (Cincinnati: Hebrew Union College Press, 2005).

—— *Jewish Preaching, 1200–1800* (New Haven: Yale University Press, 1989).

—— 'The Method of Doubts: The Problematizing of Scripture in the Late Middle Ages', in J. D. McAuliffe, B. D. Walfish, and J. W. Goering (eds), *With Reverence for the Word* (New York: Oxford University Press, 2003), 133–56.

—— 'Sermons in Modern Judaism', in Jacob Neusner, Alan J. Avery-Peck, and William Scott Green (eds), *The Encyclopaedia of Judaism*, vol. v, suppl. 2 (Leiden: E. J. Brill, 2004), 2265–83.

—— '*Your Voice Like a Ram's Horn': Themes and Texts in Traditional Jewish Preaching* (Cincinnati: Hebrew Union College Press, 1996).

—— and EPHRAIM KANARFOGEL, 'A Byzantine Manuscript of Sermons' (Heb.), *Pe'amim*, 78 (1999), 164–74.

SARAH, ELIZABETH, 'Rabbiner Regina Jonas 1902–1944', in Sybil Sheridan (ed.), *Hear our Voice: Women in the British Rabbinate* (Columbia: University of South Carolina Press, 1998), 2–8.

SARLES, RUTH, *A Story of America First* (Westport, Conn.: Praeger, 2003).

SARNA, JONATHAN, *American Judaism: A History* (New Haven: Yale University Press, 2004).

—— 'Jewish Prayers for the US Government: A Study in the Liturgy of Politics and the Politics of Liturgy', in Karen Halttunen and Lewis Perry (eds), *Moral Problems in American Life: New Perspectives on Cultural History* (Ithaca: Cornell University Press, 1998), 201–21.

—— and DAVID DALIN, *Religion and State in the American Jewish Experience* (Notre Dame: Notre Dame University Press, 1997).

SAROLEA, CHARLES, *German Problems and Personalities* (London: Chatto & Windus, 1917).

SAVAGE, MINOT J., *The Messiah Pulpit*, 10 vols (Boston: G. H. Ellis, 1897–1906).

—— *Unity Pulpit*, 17 vols (Boston: G. H. Ellis, 1879–96).

SCHAPPES, MORRIS U., 'Anti-Semitism and Reaction, 1795–1800', *Publications of the American Jewish Historical Society*, 38 (1948–9), 109–37.

—— *A Documentary History of the Jews in the United States, 1654–1875* (New York: Citadel Press, 1971).

SCHECHTER, RONALD, *Obstinate Hebrews: Representations of Jews in France, 1715–1815* (Berkeley: University of California Press, 2003).

SCHECHTER, SOLOMON, *Seminary Addresses and Other Papers* (New York: Burning Bush Press, 1959).

—— *Some Aspects of Rabbinic Theology* (New York: Schocken, 1961).

SCHEICK, WILLIAM J., *Paine, Scripture, and Authority:* The Age of Reason *as Religious and Political Idea* (Bethlehem: Lehigh University Press, 1994).

SCHISCHA, ABRAHAM, 'Hermann Adler, Yeshivah Bahur, Prague 1860–1862', in John M. Shaftesley (ed.), *Remember the Days: Essays on Anglo-Jewish History Presented to Cecil Roth* (London: Jewish Historical Society of England, 1966), 241–77.

SCHIVELBUSCH, WOLFGANG, *The Culture of Defeat: On National Trauma, Mourning and Recovery* (New York: Henry Holt, 2003).

SCHNITZER, SHIRA, ' "No Conflict of Principle": The Patriotic Rhetoric of Anglo-Jewish Sermons during the Boer War', *Journal of Modern Jewish Studies*, 3 (2004), 289–305.

SCHORSCH, JONATHAN, *Jews and Blacks in the Early Modern World* (Cambridge: Cambridge University Press, 2004).

SCHUSCHNIGG, KURT, *The Brutal Takeover: The Austrian Ex-Chancellor's Account of the Anschluss of Austria by Hitler* (London: Weidenfeld & Nicolson, 1971).

SCHWEINBURG, S., and S. EIBENSCHUETZ, 'Une confiscation des livres hébreux à Prague', *Revue des études juives*, 29 (1894), 266–71.

SCULT, MEL, *Millennial Expectations and Jewish Liberties: A Study of the Efforts to Convert the Jews in Britain up to the Mid-Nineteenth Century* (Leiden: Brill, 1978).

SEITTER, JOHN REID, 'Union City: Philadelphia and the Battle of Gettysburg', *Gettysburg Magazine*, no. 21 (1999), 5–13.

SEMMEL, STUART, *Napoleon and the British* (New Haven: Yale University Press, 2004).

*Sermons by American Rabbis* (Chicago: Central Conference of American Rabbis, 1896).

*Sermons Preached in St Paul's Cathedral* (London: Macmillan & Co., 1891).

SHANE, A. L., 'The Dreyfus Affair': Could It Have Happened in England?', *Jewish Historical Studies*, 30 (1989), 135–48.

SHAPIRO, ROBERT D., *A Reform Rabbi in the Progressive Era: The Early Career of Stephen S. Wise* (New York: Garland Publishing, 1988).

SHAZAR, ZALMAN, *Morning Stars* (Philadelphia, Jewish Publication Society, 1967).

SHERMAN, MOSHE D., 'Isaacs, Samuel Myer', in *American National Biography*, 24 vols (New York: Oxford University Press, 1999), xi. 700–1.

SHULIM, JOSEPH, 'Napoleon I as the Jewish Messiah: Some Contemporary Conceptions in Virginia', *Jewish Social Studies*, 7 (1945), 275–80.

SIGEL, LISA Z., *Governing Pleasures: Pornography and Social Change in England, 1815–1914* (New Brunswick: Rutgers University Press, 2002).

SILVER, DANIEL JEREMY, 'What We Said about Lebanon', *Journal of Reform Judaism*, 30/2 (Spring 1983), 20–37.

SILVERSTONE, GEORGE (GEDALIAH), 'Sermon against Reform' (Heb.), in *Imrei yosher* [Straight Speaking] (St Louis: n.p., 1925), 5–7.

SIMON, E. YECHIEL, 'Samuel Myer Isaacs: A 19th-Century Jewish Ministry in New York City', Ph.D. diss, Revel Graduate School of Yeshiva University, New York, 1974.

SIMONS, HYMAN A., *Forty Years a Chief Rabbi: The Life and Times of Solomon Hirschel* (London: Robson Books, 1980).

SINGER, SIMEON, *The Literary Remains of the Rev. Simeon Singer*, 3 vols, ed. Israel Abrahams (London: George Routledge & Sons, 1908).

SINGERMAN, ROBERT, *Judaica Americana: A Bibliography of Publications to 1900*, 2 vols (Westport, Conn.: Greenwood Press, 1990).

SISMONDI, J.-C.-L. SIMONDE DE, *The History of the Italian Republics: Being a View of the Rise, Progress and Fall of Italian Freedom* (Philadelphia: Carey & Lea, 1832; new edn, New York: Harper, 1864).

SIVITZ, MOSES SIMON, *Beit paga* (Jerusalem: Salamon, 1904).

—— *Mateh aharon* (Jerusalem: Solomon, 1914–?).

SMITH, JOSEPH, *The Spanish–American War: Conflict in the Caribbean and the Pacific, 1895–1902* (New York: Longman, 1994).

SOKOLOW, JAYME A., 'Revolution and Reform: The Antebellum Jewish Abolitionists', *Journal of Ethnic Studies*, 9 (1991), 27–41.

SOLA, AARON DE, *Biography of David Aaron de Sola* (Philadelphia: n.p., 1864).

SOLIS-COHEN, SOLOMON, 'An Unholy War', *American Hebrew*, 13 May 1898, p. 40.

SOLOMON, CLARA, *The Civil War Diary of Clara Solomon*, ed. Elliott Ashkenazi (Baton Rouge: Louisiana State University Press, 1995).

SORKIN, DAVID, 'Preacher, Teacher, Publicist: Joseph Wolf', in Frances Malino and David Sorkin (eds), *From East and West: Jews in a Changing Europe, 1750–1870* (Oxford: Basil Blackwell, 1990), 107–25.

SOUTHEY, ROBERT, *The Life of Nelson* (London: Hutchinson & Co., 1903; 1st pub. 1813).

SPIES, S. B., *Methods of Barbarism? Roberts and Kitchener and Civilians in the Boer Republics, January 1900–May 2002* (Cape Town: Human & Rousseau, 1977).

SPIESMAN, LEIB, 'In the Warsaw Ghetto', *Contemporary Jewish Record*, Aug. 1941, pp. 357–66.

SPURGEON, CHARLES HADDEN, *Autobiography: The Early Years: 1834–1859*, rev. edn (London: Banner of Truth Trust, 1962).

SPURGEON, CHARLES HADDEN, *The Metropolitan Pulpit*, 55 vols (London: Passmore & Alabaster, 1856–1916).

STANLEY, BRIAN, 'Christian Responses to the Indian Mutiny of 1857', in W. J. Sheils (ed.), *The Church and War* (Oxford: Blackwell, 1983), 277–89.

STANLEY, GEORGE F. G., *The War of 1812: Land Operations* (Toronto: Macmillan of Canada, 1983).

STAUB, MICHAEL E., *Torn at the Roots: The Crisis of Jewish Liberalism in Postwar America* (New York: Columbia University Press, 2002).

STEIN, LEOPOLD, *Der Kampf des Lebens: Ein Cyclus von Festpredigten, in Beziehung zu dem grossen Völkerkampfe der Gegenwart ... (5631–1870) im israelitischen Betsaale Westend-Union zu Frankfurt a. M.* (Mannheim: Schneider, 1871).

STERBA, CHRISTOPHER M., *Good Americans: Italian and Jewish Immigrants during the First World War* (New York: Oxford University Press, 2003).

STERN, FRITZ, *Gold and Iron: Bismarck, Bleichröder, and the Building of the German Empire* (New York: Vintage Books, 1979).

STERN, NORTON B., 'When the Franco-Prussian War Came to Los Angeles', *Western States Jewish Historical Quarterly*, 1 (1977), 68–73.

STEWART, CHARLES, 'Civil War Preaching', in DeWitte Holland (ed.), *Preaching in American History* (Nashville: Abingdon Press, 1971), 184–205.

STONE, GEOFFREY R., *Perilous Times: Free Speech in Wartime from the Sedition Act of 1798 to the War on Terrorism* (New York: W. W. Norton, 2004).

STOUT, HARRY S., *The New England Soul: Preaching and Religious Culture in Colonial England* (New York: Oxford University Press, 1986).

—— and CHRISTOPHER GRASSO, 'Civil War, Religion, and Communications: The Case of Richmond', in Randall M. Miller, Harry S. South, and Charles Reagan Wilson (eds), *Religion and the American Civil War* (New York: Oxford University Press, 1998), 313–59.

STREGE, MERLE D., 'An Uncertain Voice for Peace', in Theron D. Schlabach and Richard T. Hughes (eds), *Proclaim Peace: Christian Pacifism from Unexpected Quarters* (Urbana: University of Illinois Press, 1997), 115–27.

SUSSMAN, LANCE J., *Isaac Leeser and the Making of American Judaism* (Detroit: Wayne State University Press, 1995).

SWANBERG, W. A., *Citizen Hearst: A Biography of William Randolph Hearst* (New York: Scribner, 1961).

SZAJKOWSKI, ZOSA, 'Judaica-Napoleonica', *Studies in Bibliography and Booklore*, 2 (June 1956), 971–1016.

TARSHISH, ALLAN, 'The Charleston Organ Case', *American Jewish Historical Quarterly*, 54 (1965), 411–49.

TAYLOR, A. J. P., *The Trouble Makers: Dissent Over Foreign Policy, 1792–1939* (Bloomington: Indiana University Press, 1958).

TEMKIN, SEFTON D., *His Own Torah: Selected Papers and Sermons of Felix A. Levy* (New York: Jonathan David, 1969).

—— *Isaac Mayer Wise: Shaping American Judaism* (Oxford: Littman Library of Jewish Civilization/Oxford University Press, 1992).

—— 'Isaac Mayer Wise and the Civil War', in *Critical Studies in American Jewish History*, 3 vols (Cincinnati: American Jewish Archives, 1971), ii. 154–74.

TEPLITZ, SAUL I. (ed.), 'Best Jewish Sermons' series (New York: Jonathan David, 1956–74)

—— *The Rabbis Speak: A Quarter Century of Sermons for the High Holy Days from the New York Board of Rabbis* (New York: New York Board of Rabbis, 1986).

TIMMERMAN, JACOBO, *Prisoner without a Name, Cell without a Number* (New York: Knopf, 1981).

TRASK, DAVID F., *The War with Spain in 1898* (New York: Macmillan, 1981).

TREVOR-ROPER, HUGH, 'The Fast Sermons of the Long Parliament', in id., *Religion, the Reformation and Social Change, and other Essays*, 3rd rev. edn (London: Secker & Warburg, 1984), 294–342.

TSANOFF, RADOSLAV, *Civilization and Progress* (Lexington: University of Kentucky Press, 1971).

UMANSKY, ELLEN M., *Lily Montagu and the Advancement of Liberal Judaism: From Vision to Vocation* (New York: E. Mellen Press, 1983).

UROFSKY, MELVIN I., *A Voice that Spoke for Justice: The Life and Times of Stephen S. Wise* (Albany: State University of New York Press, 1982).

VALLANDIGHAM, CLEMENT L., *Speeches, Arguments, Addresses, and Letters* (New York: J. Walter, 1864).

VIOTTI, ANDREA, *Garibaldi: The Revolutionary and his Men* (Poole, Dorset: Blandford Press, 1979).

VOLTAIRE, *Correspondence*, ed. Theodore Besterman, 107 vols (Geneva: Institut et Musée Voltaire, 1953–65).

VOSS, CARL HERMANN, *Rabbi and Minister* (Cleveland: World Publishing Co., 1964).

—— (ed.), *Stephen S. Wise: Servant of the People* (Philadelphia: Jewish Publication Society, 1970).

VUCINICH, WAYNE S., *The Ottoman Empire: Its Record and Legacy* (Princeton: D. Van Nostrand Co., 1965).

WAGENKNECHT, EDWARD, *Ambassadors of Christ: Seven American Preachers* (New York: Oxford University Press, 1972).

WAGNER, MARGARET, GARRY GALLAGHER, and PAUL FINKELMAN (eds), *Library of Congress Civil War Desk Reference* (New York: Simon & Schuster, 2002).

WAGNER, RICHARD, *Judaism in Music and Other Essays* (Lincoln: University of Nebraska Press, 1995).

WALDER, DAVID, *Nelson* (London: Hamish Hamilton, 1978).

WALLACE, MAX, *The American Axis: Henry Ford, Charles Lindbergh, and the Rise of the Third Reich* (New York: St Martin's Press, 2003).

WALLETT, BART, 'Religious Oratory and the Improvement of Congregants: Dutch Jewish Preaching in the First Half of the Nineteenth Century', *Studia Rosenthaliana*, 34/2 (2000), 168–92.

WARD, ANDREW, *Our Bodies Are Scattered: The Cawnpore Massacres and the Indian Mutiny of 1857* (New York: Henry Holt, 1996).

WARNER, MICHAEL (ed.), *American Sermons: The Pilgrims to Martin Luther King Jr.* (New York: Library of America, 1999).

WAWRO, GEOFFREY, *The Franco-Prussian War: The German Conquest of France in 1870–1871* (Cambridge: Cambridge University Press, 2003).

WEALE, ADRIAN, *Renegades: Hitler's Englishmen* (London: Pimlico, 2002).

WEIGLEY, RUSSELL, *The American Way of War: A History of United States Military Strategy and Policy* (Bloomington: Indiana University Pres, 1977).

WEILL, JULIEN, *Zadoc Kahn (1839–1905)* (Paris: F. Alcan, 1912).

WEINER, MAX, *Abraham Geiger and Liberal Judaism: The Challenge of the Nineteenth Century* (Philadelphia: Jewish Publication Society, 1962).

WEININGER, OTTO, *Sex and Character* (New York: Howard Fertig, 2003).

WHEELER, HAROLD F. B., and ALEXANDER M. BROADLEY, *Napoleon and the Invasion of England: The Story of the Great Terror*, 2 vols (London: J. Lane, 1908).

WHITEMAN, MAXWELL, 'Western Impact on East European Jews: A Philadelphia Fragment', in Randall M. Miller and Thomas D. Marzik (eds), *Immigrants and Religion in Urban America* (Philadelphia: Temple University Press, 1977), 231–55.

WIENER, MAX, *Abraham Geiger and Liberal Judaism: The Challenge of the Nineteenth Century* (Philadelphia: Jewish Publication Society, 1962)

WILCOCK, EVELYN, *Pacifism and the Jews* (Lansdown, Glos.: Hawthorne Press, 1988).

WILEY, TERRENCE G., 'The Imposition of World War I Era English-Only Policies and the Fate of Germans in North America', in Thomas Ricento and Barbara Burnaby (eds), *Language and Politics in the United States*, (Mahwah, NJ: L. Erlbaum, 1998), 11–41.

WISE, STEPHEN S., *Challenging Years: The Autobiography of Stephen Wise* (New York: Putnam's Sons, 1949).

—— *Free Synagogue Pulpit: Sermons and Addresses*, 4 vols (New York, Bloch, 1908–17).

WODZIŃSKI, MARCIN, *Haskalah and Hasidism in the Kingdom of Poland: A History of Conflict* (Oxford: Littman Library of Jewish Civilization, 2005).

WOLF, EDWIN II, and MAXWELL WHITEMAN, *The History of the Jews of Philadelphia from Colonial Times to the Age of Jackson* (Philadelphia: Jewish Publication Society, 1957).

WOLF, JOSEPH, *Sechs deutsche Reden, gehalten in der Synagoge zu Dessau* (Dessau: M. Philippsohn, 1813).

WOLFFE, JOHN, 'Responding to National Grief: Memorial Sermons on the Famous in Britain 1800–1914', *Mortality*, 1/3 (1996), 283–96.

WOOD, ALAN, 'Russia's "Wild East": Exile, Vagrancy, and Crime in Nineteenth-Century Siberia', in id. (ed.), *History of Siberia* (London: Routledge, 1991), 117–39.

WOODHAM SMITH, CECIL, *The Reason Why* (New York: McGraw-Hill, 1954).

WYMAN, DAVID S., *A Race against Death: Peter Bergson, America, and the Holocaust* (New York: New Press, 2002).

YOUNG, WILLIAM R., 'Chauvinism and Canadianism: Canadian Ethnic Groups and the Failure of Wartime Information', in Norman Hillmer, Bohdan Kordan, and Lubomyr Luciuk (eds), *On Guard for Thee: War, Ethnicity, and the Canadian State, 1939–1945* (Ottawa: Canadian Committee for the History of the Second World War, 1988), 31–51.

ZERUBAVEL, YAEL, *Recovered Roots: Collective Memory and the Making of Israeli National Tradition* (Chicago: Chicago University Press, 1995).

ZIMMERMAN, MOSHE, *Wilhelm Marr: The Patriarch of Antisemitism* (New York: Oxford University Press, 1986).

# Index of Passages Cited

---

# General Index

## A

Abraham (biblical) 503
Abrahams, Israel 236
Abyssinia 415
Adams, John 7, 111
Adath Israel (Boston) 268
  *see also* Temple Israel (Boston)
Adler, Hermann 284–95
  and Benjamin Artom marriage 235
  biography of 284–5
  Boer War sermon by 14, 237
  on Dreyfus trial 22–3, 38 n., 285–6
  literary quotations by 22–3, 25
  on missionary arguments 37
  on pogroms of 1881: 40, 285
  on pogroms of 1905: 42 n., 285
  as preacher 285–6
  on scepticism regarding prayer 292
  on 'Sinners in Zion' 55–6
  on Zionism 48–9
Adler, Marcus Baer 284
Adler, Nathan 20, 32–3, 284
aggadah 3–4
  cited by Joseph H. Hertz 318–19
  used by Israel Levinthal 442, 444–9
Ahad Ha'am 49
Albert, Prince of Wales 141, 235, 237
Alderman, Geoffrey 287
Alexander, Levi 94 n.
Alexander III (tsar) 8
Alliance Israélite Universelle 152
Almosnino, Moses 106 n.
Alsheikh, Moses 2 n.
Altmann, Alexander 64 n.
Alva, duke of 270, 281
Amalek 197–8, 210–21, 518
  as conscience enslavement 214–19
  in First World War 198 n.
  and Napoleon III 256
  as race enslavement 211–14
  and Spanish–American War 265
  as spirit enslavement 219–21
  as type 211
America:
  anti-interventionism in 390, 404 n., 452

  as being on God's side 460
  call to unite in 459
  as Christian nation 215
  and communism 493
  Declaration of Independence of 270
  God's blessing of 187–8, 253–4
  hatred for war in 397
  as haven 190, 254
  inconsistency of 264
  Independence Day 11
  Jewish status in 331–2
  Jews of, as remnant 437
  lies by government of 504–5
  mission of 196, 208, 209 n., 257, 376
  myths of 493–6
  Negroes in 350, 361
  and neutrality 397
  and propagation of peace 269, 273
  as refuge for humane values 397
  religious intolerance in 198
  role of, Sabato Morais on 174, 257
  segregation in 268
  as source of peace 258
  as spiritual desert 547–8
  unique history of 187
  uprising of 276–7
  *see also* civil rights (US); Civil War (US)
American Civil Liberties Union 359 n.
*American Hebrew* 263, 268, 302, 304–5
American Jewish Archives 16, 144 n.
American Jewish Historical Society 16
American Peace Centenary Committee
  338 n.
American Union Against Militarism 348–9,
  359
Amsterdam 25–6
*aninut* (intense grief) 541–2
An-Sky, S. 303, 307 n.
Antiochus Epiphanes 455–6
antisemitism 38, 366
  in Britain 430, 468 n.
  in Canada 427, 430
  in United States 430
Arab Americans 535
arbitration 262, 265, 273, 374

Lightning Source UK Ltd.
Milton Keynes UK
UKOW030500111212

203474UK00002B/7/P